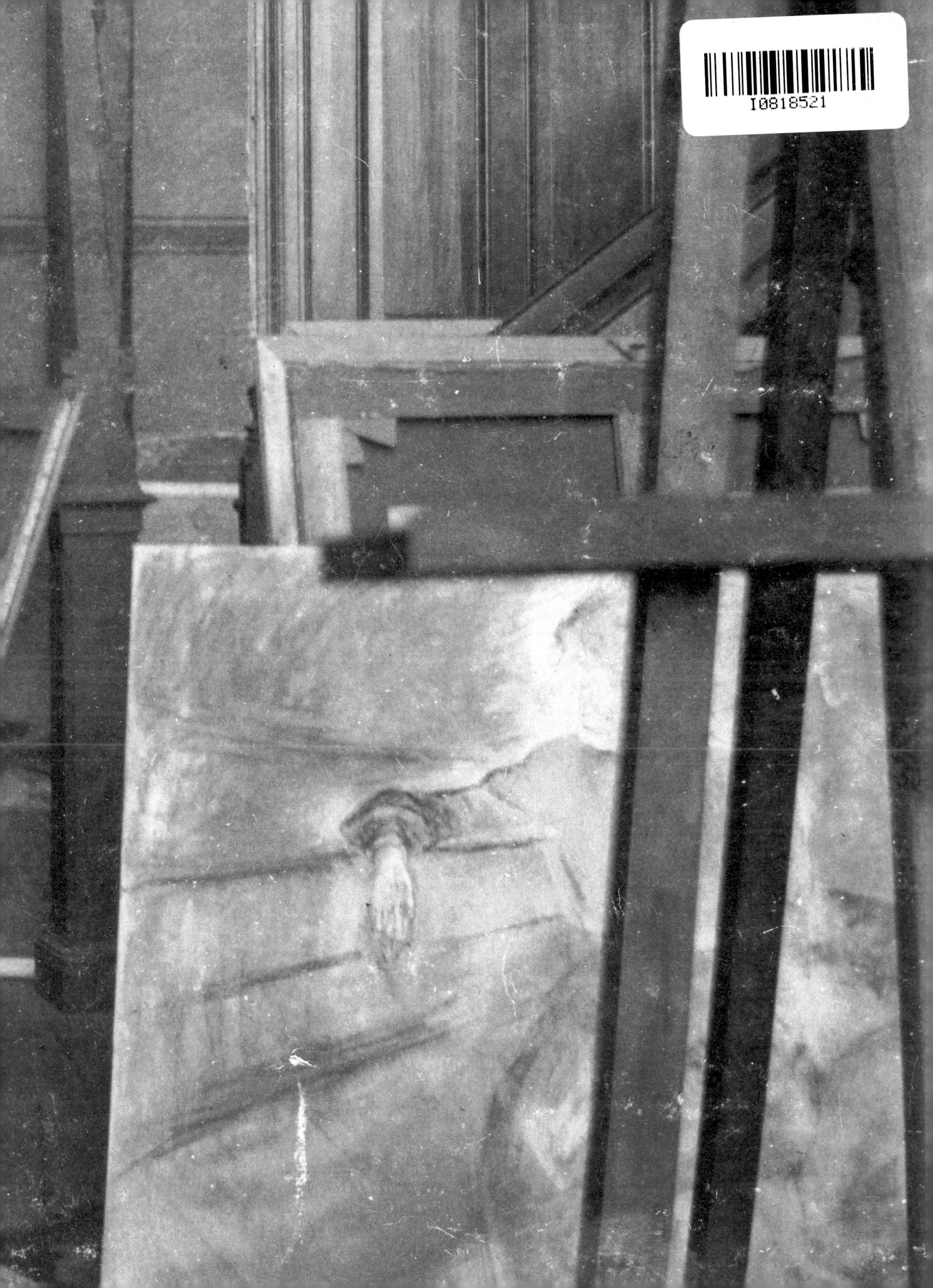

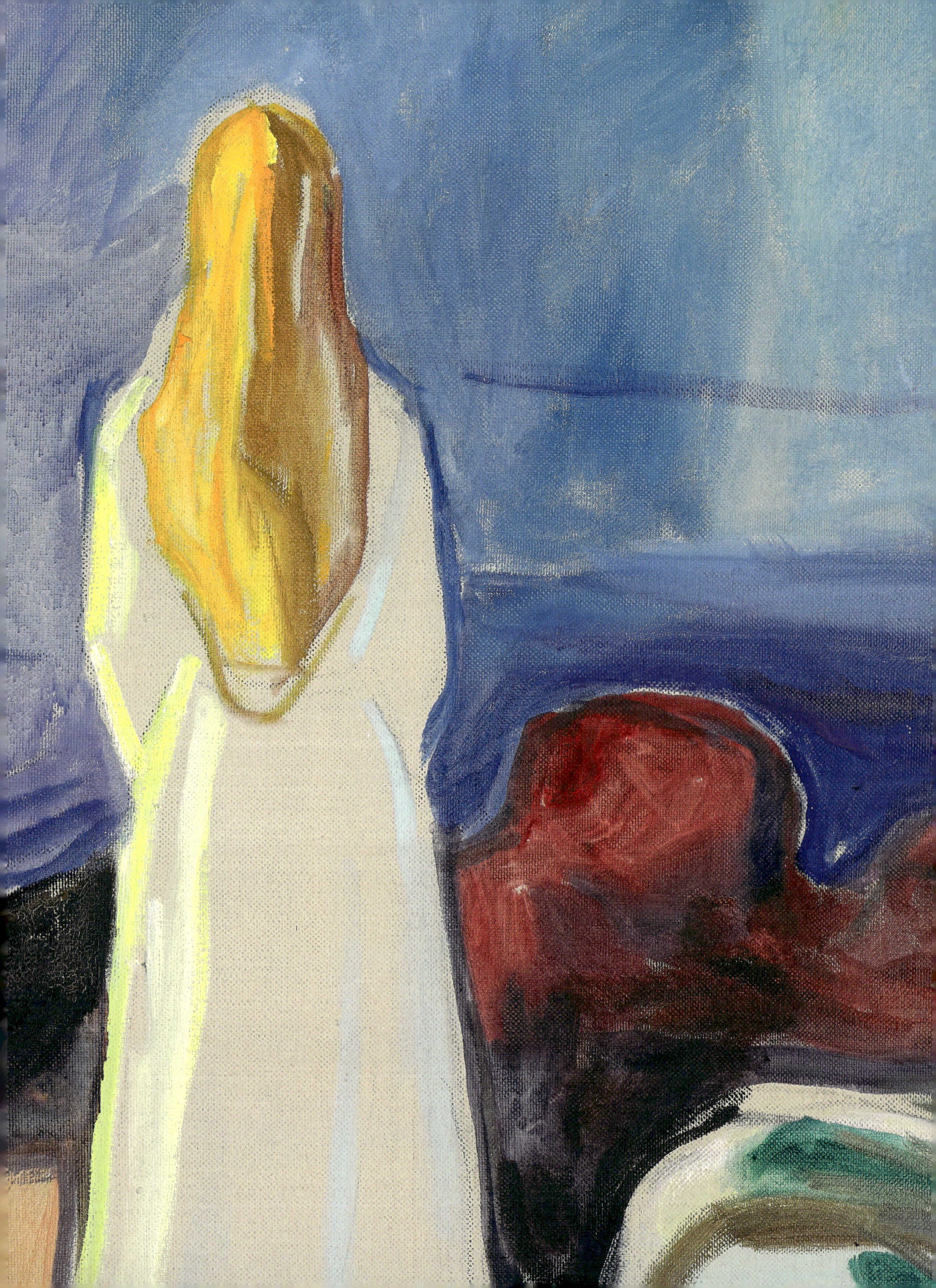

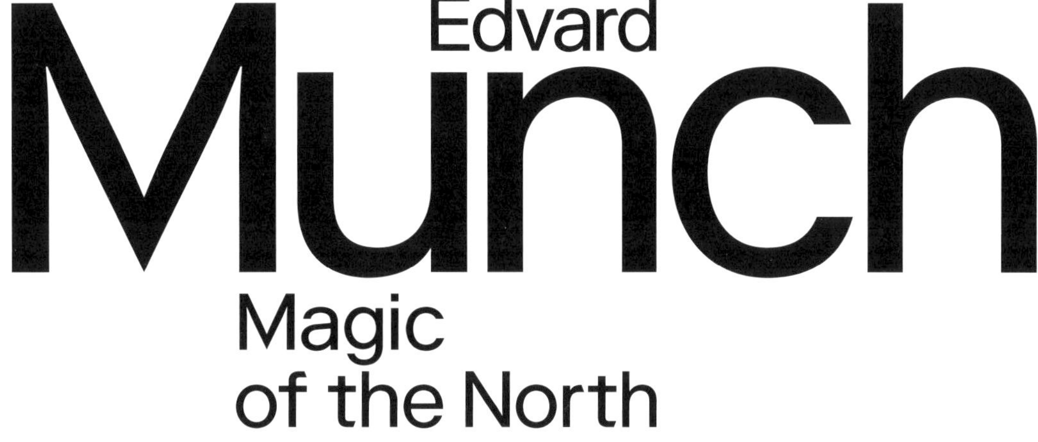

Edited by
Thomas Köhler
Stefanie Heckmann
Janina Nentwig

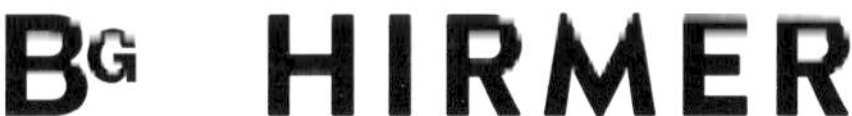

Edvard Munch
Magic of the North

In partnership with

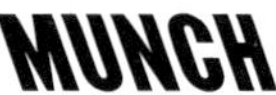

With decisive support from

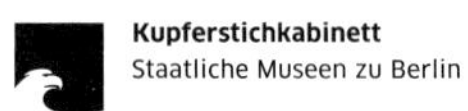

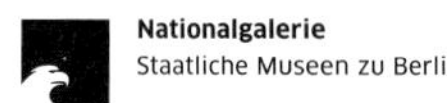

This exhibition enjoys the joint patronage of
Frank-Walter Steinmeier, President of the Federal Republic of Germany,
and His Majesty King Harald V of Norway.

The exhibition and catalogue are supported by

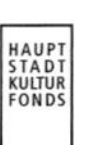
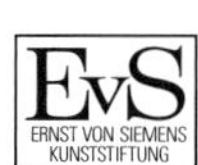
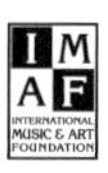
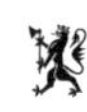
Norwegian Embassy
Berlin

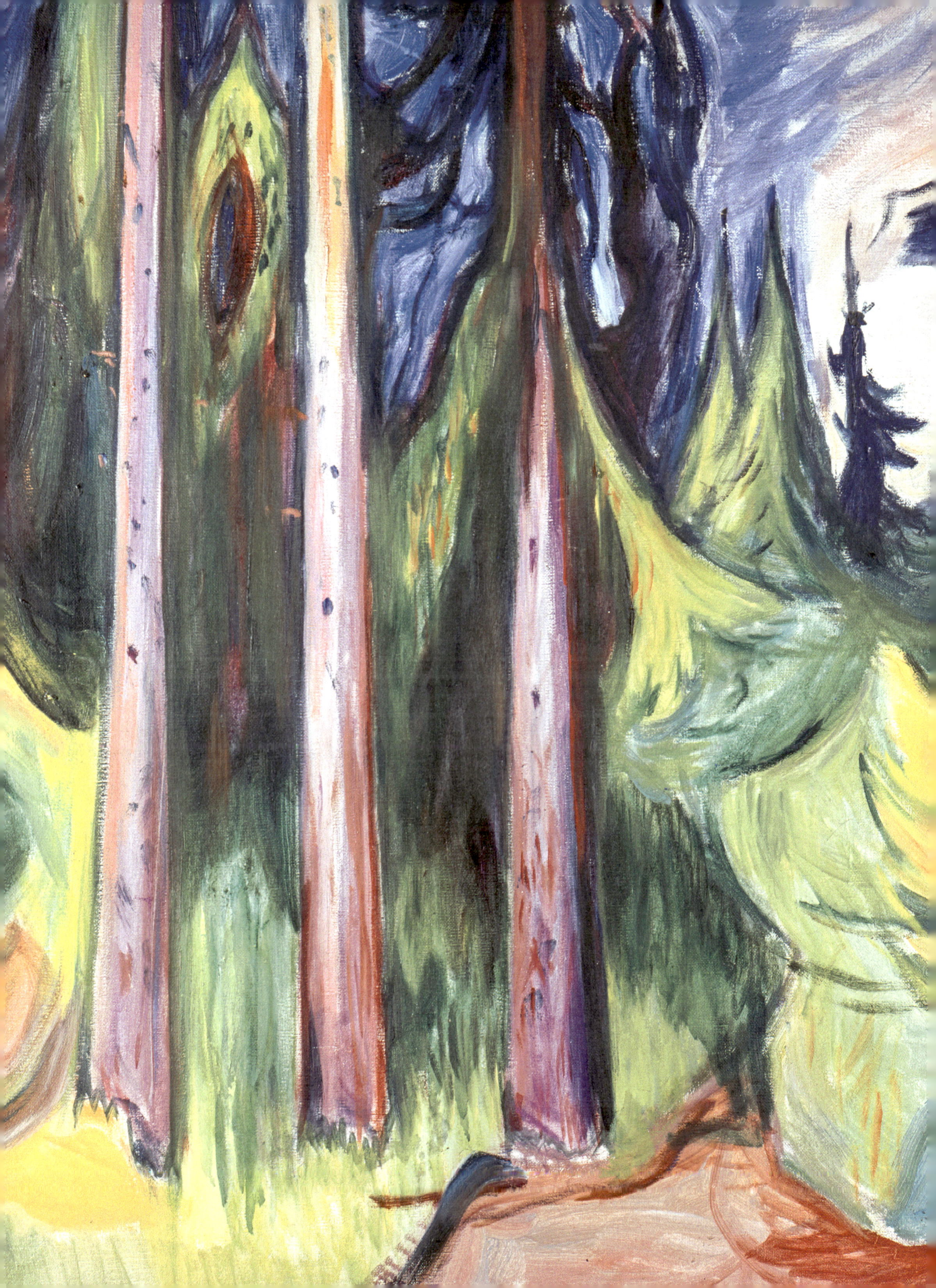

Essays

Biography

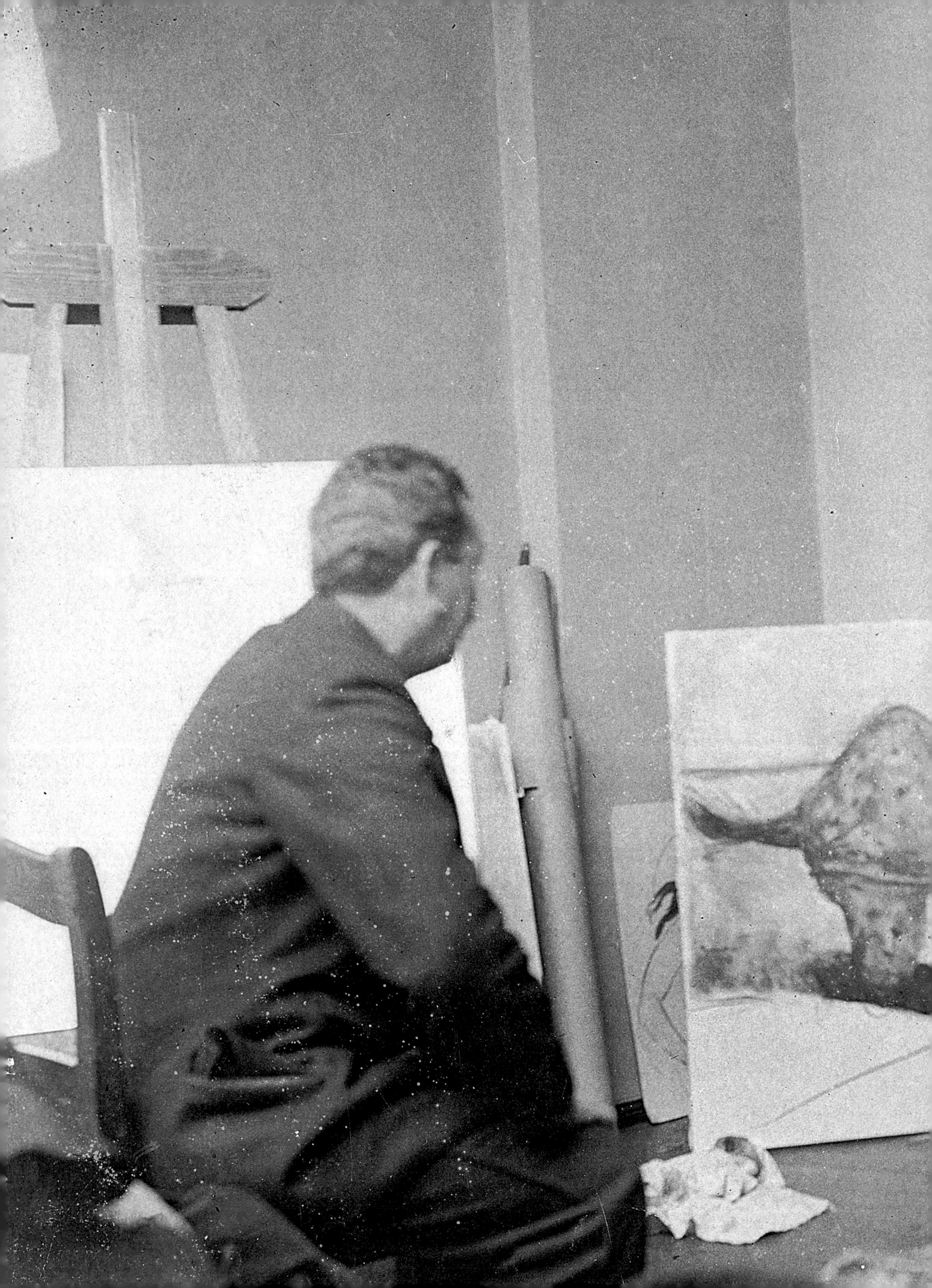

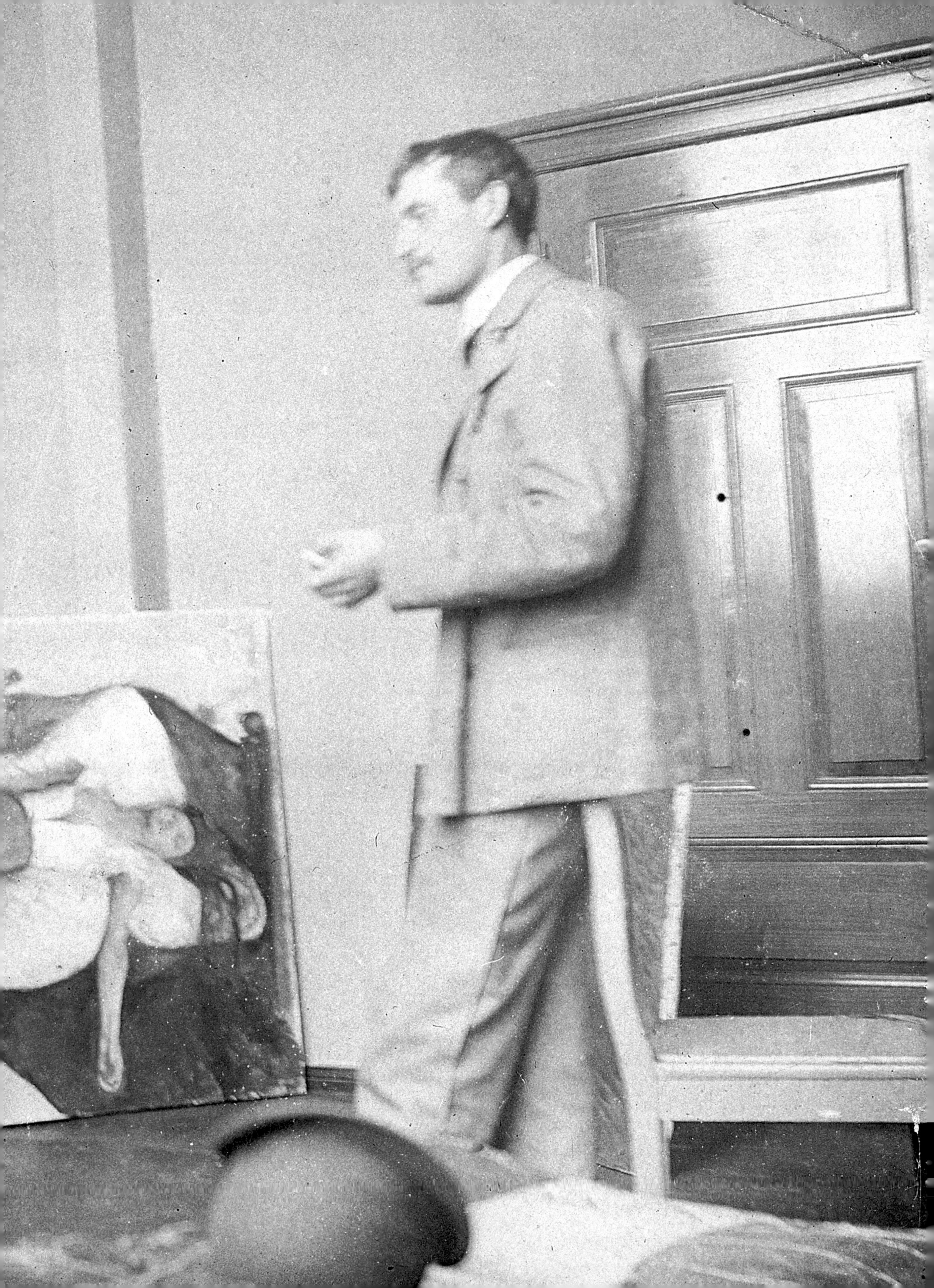

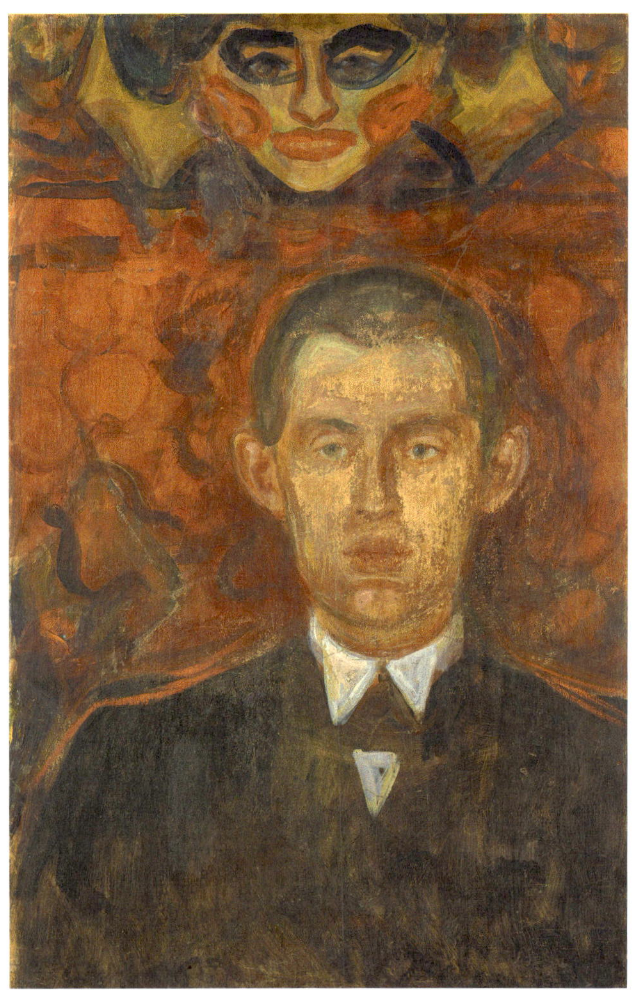

Edvard Munch
Self-Portrait under the Mask of a Woman — 1893
Munchmuseet — Oslo

Foreword and Acknowledgments

Edvard Munch's importance for the evolution of modernism in Berlin has been studied and analyzed repeatedly by art historians. No exhibition yet, however, has examined the artist's special relationship to Berlin, the reception of his art in the capital of the empire, and the development of an aesthetic practice of his own.

Between 1892 and 1908, Edvard Munch lived in Berlin repeatedly for increasingly long periods, usually spending the spring and summer months in Norway. In studios and hotel rooms in Berlin, he produced an extensive oeuvre. Munch left behind around 1,800 paintings, but it is difficult to determine how many of them were produced in Berlin because he changed places so often. The situation is similar with his printmaking—a medium that Munch adopted in Berlin. Just under 750 different motifs are known. It would scarcely be possible to count all of the copies. At least 10,000 copies were made in Germany alone during Munch's lifetime, nearly all of them in Berlin.[1] In 1892, Munch accepted an invitation from the Verein Berliner Künstler (Association of Berlin Artists), which the exhibition committee had apparently approved "unanimously" at the recommendation of a fellow Norwegian artist, Adelsteen Normann. The latter had seen a Munch exhibition in Kristiania, present-day Oslo, and was enthusiastic about his colleague's painting. He informed Munch about the committee's decision in a brief letter. Munch, who had previously been represented by three paintings in the *Münchener Jahresausstellung von Kunstwerken aller Nationen im Königlichen Glaspalaste* (Munich Annual Exhibition of Artworks of All Nations in the Royal Glass Palace), presumably made essentially the same selection for Berlin that he had made for his exhibition in Kristiania. This invitation represented a great honor for the young artist, since he would reach a larger audience than he had in Munich and Oslo.[2] The exhibition was scheduled to last two weeks, from November 5 to 19, 1892, in the hall of honor of the rotunda on the ground floor of the Architektenhaus (Architects' House) at Wilhelmstrasse 92/93, where the association organized its special exhibitions. The sensation that the presentation of the paintings in conservative Berlin caused was enormous. The influential circles around Anton von Werner, the director of the Königliche akademische Hochschule für die bildenden Künste (Royal Academic University of Fine Arts) and chairman of the Verein Berliner Künstler, initiated a wave of criticism.[3] Adolf Rosenberg, an art historian and art critic who was himself a decided supporter of von Werner's regressive view of art, wrote a devastating review in the newspaper *Berliner Tageblatt* and at the same time insinuated that even fellow artists had taken sides against the Norwegian painter. Rosenberg wrote:

"The works of the painter Munch that, as reviewed yesterday, currently 'decorate' the exhibition of the Künstlerverein have roused pure outrage in the ranks of artists, and twenty-three respected painters and sculptors—including Eschke, Streckfuss, Hundrieser, Moser, Spangenberg, Douzette—already proposed closing the rotunda with the works of the painter Munch from Christiania, specifically 'out of great respect for art and honest artistic effort and for the certainly justified desire to protect the Verein Berliner Künstler from such unworthy enterprises.'"[4]

Several members of the Verein Berliner Künstler did indeed submit a proposal for the immediate closure of the Munch exhibition, and Anton von Werner called for a vote on the matter at a meeting of the members convened on November 12. The proposal was approved with 120 versus 105 votes, and on the morning of the following Sunday the paintings were removed from the rotunda. Despite these negative reactions, Munch remained faithful to Berlin for many years. He understood how important that site of production and exhibition was for him. From 1892 to 1933, Edvard Munch had around sixty exhibitions in Berlin, including at least fifteen solo presentations. It is difficult to determine an exact number of group and solo exhibitions, since catalogues were not published for all of the presentations or have not been preserved. There are many documents of his artistic work in the holdings of Berlin museums. We have been able to bring a large number of them together for our exhibition in order to retell the story of this chapter of the history of art in Berlin. This has been a great feat for the Berlinische Galerie, in both financial and organizational terms.

I would therefore like to thank the exhibition team most sincerely. Stefanie Heckmann, who has been head of the Department of Fine Art since 2014, was responsible for curating this extremely carefully prepared exhibition at our institution. She was crucially supported by Janina Nentwig, whose scholarly research and knowledge have been invaluable to the exhibition. Pauline Behrmann supported the planning and organization of the exhibition as a trainee curator. Rebecca Kruppert provided important assistance during the initial research.

Without the collegial support of Munchmuseet in Oslo, this exhibition at the Berlinische Galerie would not have been possible. I therefore thank first its director Tone Hansen, who took over the project from her predecessor Stein Olav Henrichsen and very constructively supported it. In many conversations in Berlin and Oslo, the museum's head of programming, Lars Toft-Eriksen, paved the way for the loans. Kasper Teglgaard Koch as Acting Head of the Department of Exhibition and Collection and Mathis Junker Gran and Cecilie Krokeide as project managers were important partners in realizing the exhibition. I thank all of them very much for their professional collaboration.

The exhibition on the modern art scene in Berlin that is planned at Munchmuseet in 2026, with many loans from the Berlinische Galerie, is being curated by Kari Brandtzæg. I would like to take this opportunity to already thank her for her work.

This is the first cooperation between the Berlinische Galerie and the Museum Barberini in Potsdam. I am very grateful to its director, Ortrud Westheider, for her willingness to join us in spreading the word about the exhibitions, and I look forward to the extensive supporting program.

The authors of the catalogue have brought together valuable new insights into Edvard Munch's time in Berlin. I thank them for the time they have invested in meticulously researching and writing their texts.

The visual communication of the exhibition and the graphic design of the catalogue have been the responsibility Gregor Schreiter, and, as always, he has found highly aesthetic solutions for all of the printed matter. The spaces of the Berlinische Galerie can be experienced anew on the occasion of this show thanks to the exhibition architect, David Saik, who always designs strongly individual sequences of space and color for our exhibitions.

We are profoundly indebted to all of the lenders who entrusted us with works from their holdings. The selection of works was very specific, and that persuaded the lenders to support our project. Nearly all of our loan requests were granted. Many thanks for your faith in us.

Our colleagues from the Staatliche Museen zu Berlin (National Museums in Berlin) were decidedly generous and supported us with crucial loans. At the Kupferstichkabinett (Museum of Prints and Drawings), they were its director, Dagmar Korbacher, and the curator Andreas Schalhorn, who also wrote an essay for the catalogue. At the Neue Nationalgalerie and Alte Nationalgalerie (New and Old National Galleries), they were Joachim Jäger, Dieter Scholz, and Ralph Gleis, all of whom supported our project with extraordinary goodwill.

At the Berlinische Galerie, Birgitta Müller-Brandeck as Director of Administration, Susanne Teuber as head of Finance and Controlling, Ulrike Andres as head of the Department of Communication and Education, Wolfgang Heigl as head of the Technical Department, and Andreas Piel as head of Conservation helped to make this project a marvelous reality. The associated teams from these departments were motivated and in good spirits and also made a crucial contribution to its success!

The Hauptstadtkulturfonds (Capital Cultural Fund) supporting exhibitions with large audiences, the International Music and Art Foundation (IMAF) in Lucerne, the Ernst von Siemens Kunststiftung (Ernst von Siemens Art Foundation), and, last but not least, the Förderverein der Berlinischen Galerie (Friends of the Berlinische Galerie) made this exhibition possible with their significant financial support. We extend our most sincere thanks to all those who provided funding.

The Embassy of the Kingdom of Norway in Berlin deserves very special thanks. Its staff provided us with contacts, stood by us with words and deeds, and, finally, financed the exhibition's supporting program. We are very grateful for their straightforward assistance.

This exhibition enjoys the joint patronage of Frank-Walter Steinmeier, President of the Federal Republic of Germany, and His Majesty King Harald V of Norway, which pleases us extraordinarily.

Thomas Köhler
Director

(1) See the catalogues raisonnés of Munch's graphic works and of his paintings, Woll 2001 and 2009, as well as Woll 1994, p. 46.
(2) Heller 1993.
(3) Anton von Werner's positions and their significance for cultural policy have been researched in detail in Sabine Meister's dissertation: Meister 2006, pp. 51–52.
(4) Rosenberg 1892a.

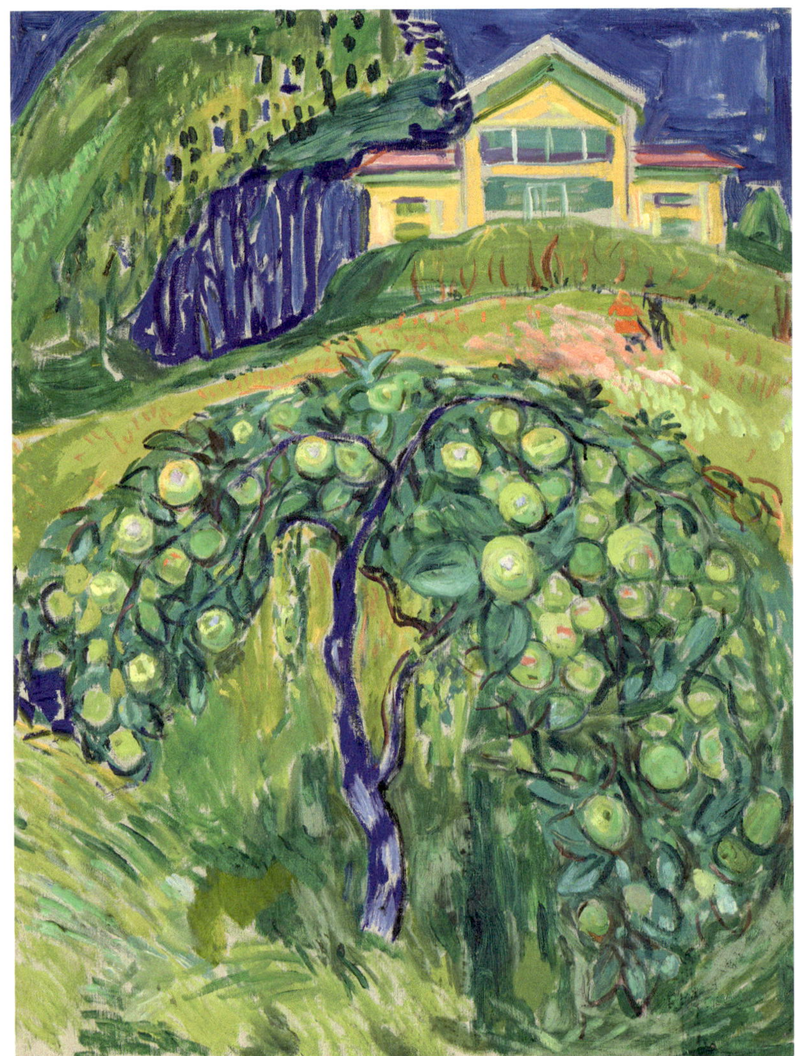

Edvard Munch
Apple Tree in the Garden — 1932–42
Munchmuseet — Oslo

Edvard Munch
Magic of the North

Stefanie Heckmann

In 1927, Berlin's Nationalgalerie (National Gallery) showed what was then the largest ever exhibition by the Norwegian painter Edvard Munch (1863–1944).[1] Munch, who was sixty-three at the time, was said to be exceedingly enthusiastic about it, according to the Oslo daily newspaper *Tidens Tegn*.[2] At the time, the artist was living in seclusion on his property Ekely, a villa and former nursery with hundreds of apple trees, near Oslo. Figure p.16 He had been in Berlin during the installation of his exhibition but then continued on to Rome and escaped the hubbub of the opening.[3] It was the largest exhibition yet for a solo artist in the modern department of the Nationalgalerie. People poured through the three floors that had been cleared for Munch's work in the former crown prince's palace, the Kronprinzenpalais, on the boulevard Unter den Linden, the "gallery of the living." They could admire around 250 works from all the artist's creative phases. Director Ludwig Justi praised him in the exhibition catalogue: "Munch stands in the front rank of living artists; his art is a convincing expression of the emotion and sense of form of our time."[4] He had had "no less influence, but probably a more enduring one, than Cézanne and Van Gogh" on the younger generation in Germany—a reference

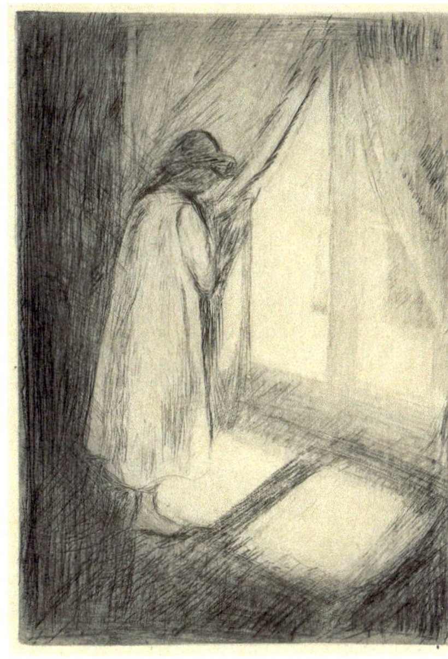

Edvard Munch
The Girl at the Window — 1894
Staatliche Museen zu Berlin
Kupferstichkabinett

to Expressionism. The press referred to Munch's often-discussed "almost instinctively confident ability to render in painting and graphic work the depths of the soul in the human themes and mystically oppressive moods in the landscapes."[5] Many reviews emphasized the specifically Northern quality of his art. It was said to be Munch's great historical achievement "to have designed for the soul of the Nordic human being a language of its own."[6] His name stood for "the specifically Nordic sense of the world that had emerged in revolt already in the 1890s."[7]

Munch's emotionally condensed, intensely colorful visual worlds represented a "magic of the North" that was entirely a matter of course in Berlin in the 1920s,[8] even though the Arcadia of the North was increasingly instrumentalized after World War I for an aggressive myth of Germania.[9] Hardly anyone writing in the press about the triumphant retrospective at the Nationalgalerie failed to allude to Munch's spectacular first appearance in Berlin in the late nineteenth century.

The "Affaire Munch" (Munch Affair), as the contemporaneous press ironically referred to the scandal around his exhibition at the Verein Berliner Künstler (Association of Berlin Artists),[10] was the beginning of modernism in the city and of the painter's international career.[11] Munch's works were so avant-garde and foreign for Berlin in 1892 that they struck the art world like a meteorite and tore it asunder. The conflict between the conservatives and the moderns, which also played out in the press, made his name famous far beyond Berlin.[12] Munch moved to the city on the Spree River, which offered him great opportunities. Until the beginning of 1908, he lived there repeatedly for extended periods with interruptions. He was a member of the Berlin Secession, the Deutscher Künstlerbund (Association of German Artists), and later also the Preussische Akademie der Künste (Prussian Academy of Arts).[13] Although Munch's works could be seen in many international shows in his day, Berlin remained one of the most important places in Europe for him, with around sixty exhibitions between 1892 and 1933, including many solo shows.[14] He found here progressive intellectuals, artists, gallerists,[15] and collectors who appreciated and supported his work. He learned printing techniques in close collaboration with leading Berlin printing houses and began taking photographs.[16] In 1895, the art historian Julius Meier-Graefe published a first portfolio of etchings accompanied by a text.[17] Figures [illegible] Just under fifteen years later, Curt Glaser, who was responsible for the modern department of the Kupferstichkabinett (Museum of Prints and Drawings) in Berlin, began to assemble an extensive collection of Munch's graphic work.[18] In Berlin in 1893, moreover, the Norwegian artist presented his paintings as a coherent series for the first time. He expanded this idea, which came to be essential for his work, in a Berlin Secession exhibition in 1902 to what he would later call his *Frieze of Life*,[19] which he then tried out in many exhibitions internationally. Until 1933, Munch was taken for granted as part of Berlin modernism, even though he had returned to Norway in 1909. His presence in the city's art scene also changed the idea of the North. It was now associated with Munch's works rather than with romantic or naturalistic landscape paintings of fjords.

After the National Socialists took power in 1933, Munch's position was ambiguous for that very reason. He was instrumentalized as a Nordic, Germanic artist, but also defamed early on as "degenerate." Ten years after his triumph at the Nationalgalerie, for example, eighty-three of his works were confiscated from public collections as part of the "Entartete Kunst" (Degenerate Art) action.[20] After Norway was occupied by German troops on April 9, 1940, the seventy-six-year-old wrote his will and bequeathed all of his works, including his literary remains, to the city of Oslo. He hoped this would provide a place for his *Frieze of Life* and make his works available to a large public.[21]

The "Munch Affair"

"The best of Germany, the whole of creative literature, fell for the magic of the North around the turn of the century. Scandinavia meant to that generation what Russia meant to yesterday's and what the Far East perhaps already means to today's: new territory for the soul, a primal source of unsuspected problems," the writer Stefan Zweig recalled in 1925.[22] And Munch's friend the writer Max Dauthendey wrote the following as a representative of his generation: "For everything Nordic exercised a strong attraction on me. Those nearly uninhabited countries seemed to have a purer and more virtuous air, a stronger, more ruthless spirit, tied to sharper self-knowledge .... And every new book that came over the German border from the North then had the breath of an enlivening sea breeze."[23] The contrasting influences that shaped the idea of the North ranged from interests in the Old Nordic to romantic or naturalist landscapes in paintings and fantasies about Vikings, to the boom triggered by current Scandinavian literature in German publishing houses and in the public,[24] or the success of the modern, sociocritical dramas of the Norwegian Henrik Ibsen and the Swede August Strindberg via the Verein Freie Bühne (Free Stage Association) in Berlin.[25] From 1889 to 1914, William II traveled annually to the fjords in his yacht *Hohenzollern* and boosted the still young tourism industry there.[26] Figure p.19A Inspired by Old Norse myths, the emperor was enthusiastic about an antimodern, nationalistically tinged utopia of a "North," a cradle of Germanic culture with unspoiled landscapes and people, without taking into account the political and social realities of these countries.[27] This sort of dream world offered an alternative to rapidly advancing industrialization in Germany's strictly organized, modern state, with the rather sober metropolis of Berlin at its center.

Sympathies for everything Scandinavian offered an occasion to invite Munch, who at the time was largely unknown, to a solo exhibition at the Verein Berliner Künstler in November 1892.[28] He had been proposed by a compatriot living in Berlin, the painter Adelsteen Normann.[29] Normann

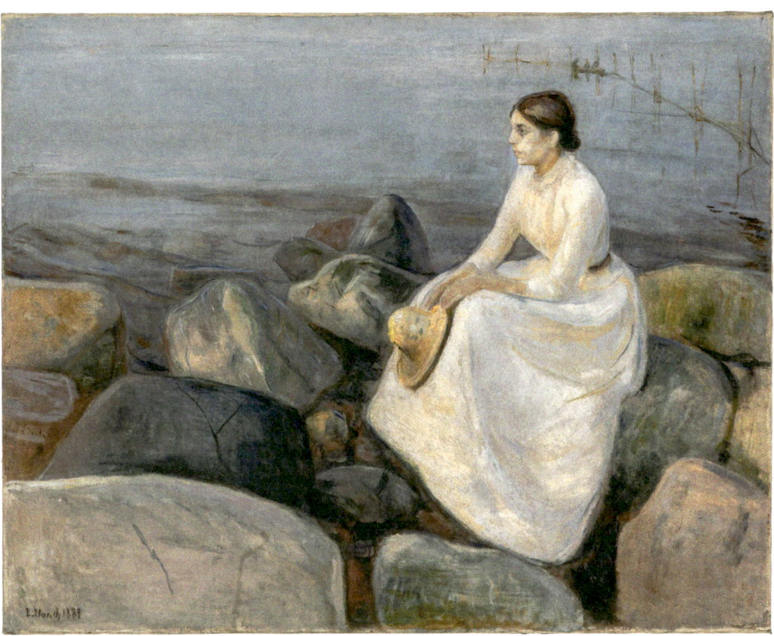

(B)
Edvard Munch
Summer Night (Inger on the Beach) — 1889
Kode — Bergen

(A)
Adelsteen Normann
Imperial Yacht "Hohenzollern" — 1910
Norsk Maritimt Museum — Oslo

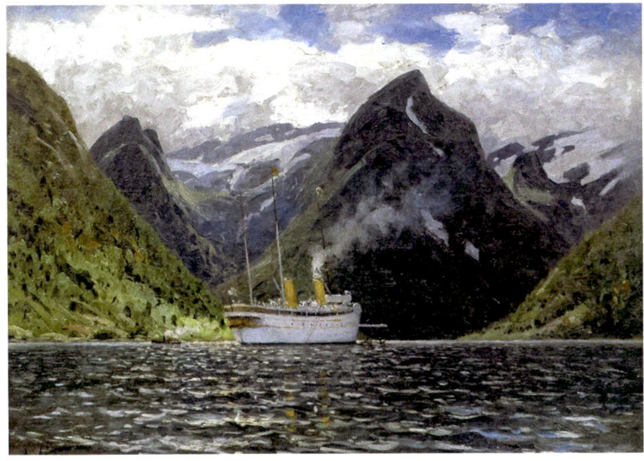

was specialized in popular fjord landscapes that sold very well—to William II, among others. Figure pp.48–49 In the summer of 1892, he had seen a Munch exhibition in Kristiania (now Oslo) while passing through. The exhibition committee of the Verein Berliner Künstler had a number of young members and an interest in bringing international artists to the city. Munch may have been invited in order to present modern approaches other than that of influential French art. The fifty-five paintings in the show, which opened on November 5, 1892, were described as a "series of imaginative designs in an Ibsen-like atmosphere."[30] Some of the members had already seen works by Munch in Munich at the *Jahresausstellung von Kunstwerken aller Nationen* (Annual Exhibition of Artworks of All Nations) in 1891.[31] Figure p.19B The Norwegian section, including Munch, had attracted great attention there. The Berlin art scene in the early 1890s was, by contrast, still not very progressive. It was dominated by a taste for art that focused on prestige and tradition, which was encouraged by the emperor and the influential artist Anton von Werner, who was the chairman of the Verein Berliner Künstler.[32]

The radicalness of Munch's painting challenged and polarized his contemporaries. Many members of the association and of the public were shocked by the paintings, which they perceived as raw, sketchlike, and unfinished, among other things.[33] His works violated romantic ideas of the North and of art in general and triggered a scandal.[34] Established members of the association were outraged and proposed a motion that the show be closed immediately. A special general assembly was held on November 12, called on short notice just a week after the exhibition opening. There was hot debate, in which violating the rules of hospitality also played a large role, and the conservative circles of the artists prevailed over the progressives by a small margin. Not long after it had opened, the show had to be taken down again.[35] Munch, who was not even thirty at the time, enjoyed the unexpected publicity. Figure p.20A He wrote home: "That is, by the way, the best that can happen / I cannot get better advertising."[36] He promptly moved to the city on the Spree, where he lived and worked repeatedly for increasingly long periods during his years of travel from 1892 to 1908 before returning to reside in Norway in 1909.

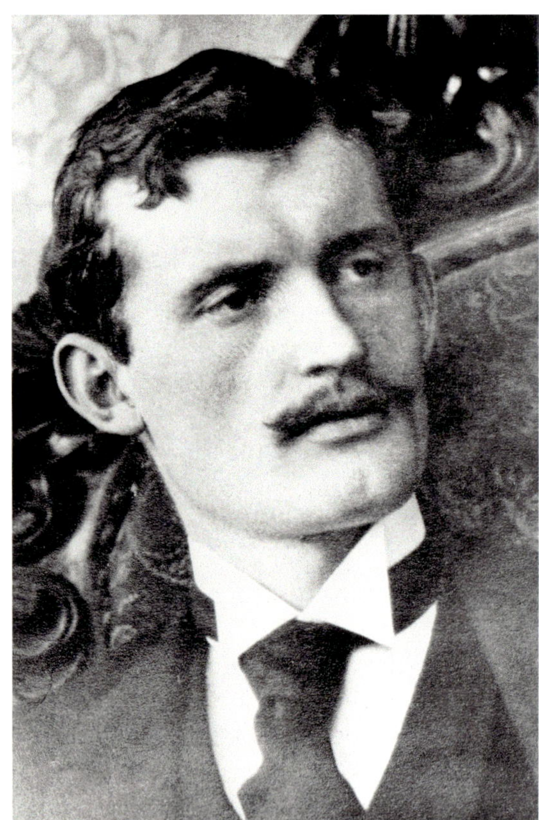

(A)
Edvard Munch — 1892
Munchmuseet — Oslo

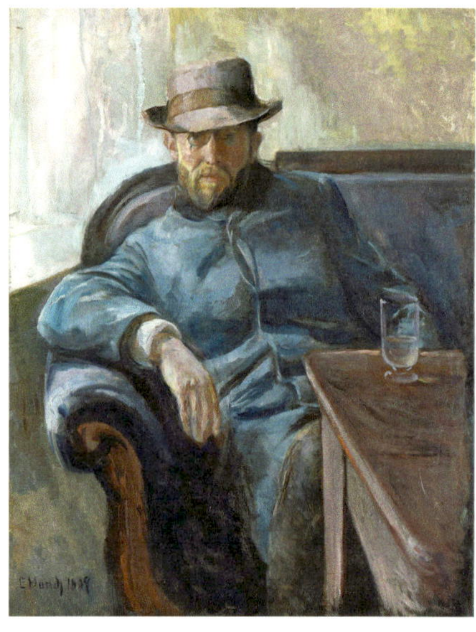

(B)
Edvard Munch
Hans Jæger — 1889
Nasjonalmuseet — Oslo

While Berlin was looking yearningly to the north at the end of the nineteenth century, the modern capital of the German Reich conversely held great appeal for Nordic countries. Scandinavian authors such as Strindberg and Ola Hansson, whose works were sharply criticized and even censored in their own countries, found in Berlin niches and opportunities to publish and audiences for their plays, above all thanks to the Verein Freie Bühne. For example, Ibsen's drama *Ghosts*, which was published in 1881, was subject to censorship in Scandinavia, France, Britain, and Germany and could only be performed in private productions at small, independent theaters.[37] Berlin offered visual artists exhibition opportunities. Georg Brandes, an influential Danish literary critic, who faced hostility in Copenhagen for his Jewish origins, lived in Berlin from 1877 to 1883. In his book *Berlin som tysk rigshovedstad* (Berlin as the Capital of the German Empire), which was published in Copenhagen in 1885 but not translated into German in full until 1989 as *Berlin als Reichshauptstadt*, he promoted, among other things, cultural exchange between Scandinavia and Germany.[38] Brandes wrote of the "world city Berlin": "The attraction of the social life ... is just as great as in Paris and London."[39] In the past ten years, Berlin had transformed "from the Prussian capital to that of the German Reich":[40] Brandes saw the "spiritual and political life of the Scandinavian countries" as "necessarily always deeply influenced by German conditions."[41] Adolf Paul, a German-Swedish-Finnish writer who was part of the close circle around Strindberg in Berlin around the turn of the century, summed up Berlin's significance for "Nordic art" and Munch, looking back on the occasion of the artist's large retrospective in 1927: "Berlin as a springboard — Berlin as a hub from which paths lead everywhere — as a burning mirror whose radiation has an infinite range — this Berlin in which work mania is in the air, and the tempo of development does not stop — this Berlin cannot be sidestepped."[42] Paul continued: "Artists all swear by Paris, and they may be right. But they need — their art needs — a shot of Berlin to thrive properly. One proof of this is the large exhibition of works by Munch that we can see in Berlin now. Of Munch who learned in Paris but became in Berlin!"[43]

Zum schwarzen Ferkel

Berlin did indeed play a central role in Munch's development. Especially in his early years there, he met figures from literature, art, and science who were also aware of the upheavals and contradictions of the era.[44] In Europe at the end of the nineteenth century, modernization and rationalization processes were encroaching on nearly every sphere of life. Young intellectuals and artists were stoking social uncertainty with antibourgeois protests and revolutionary ideas.[45] Even before he went to Berlin, Munch had come into contact with the ideas of the bohemia there via the charismatic, radically sociocritical author Hans Jæger in Kristiania (Oslo from 1925). Figure p.20B Jæger's provocative novel *Fra Kristiania-Bohêmen* (From Kristiania's Bohemia) had been published there in 1885.[46] He had also written "Bohêmens ni bud" (Nine Bohemian Commandments), the first of which is: "Thou shalt write thine own life."[47] This motto would become an important reference point for Munch's work. Berlin's intellectual circles, with recourse to Friedrich Nietzsche, focused on the concept of heroic, creative individuals who liberate themselves from religious, moral, and social constraints and create their own reality.[48] They shared interests in psychology, psychopathology, occultism, issues of subjectivity, new philosophical ideas—above all Nietzsche—and current movements in literature and art apart from the naturalism they despised, such as French and Belgian Symbolism.[49] In exchanges with friends and acquaintances, Munch's artistic stance became more precise, and he found inspiration and support. The meeting place of the young international bohemia in Berlin was Gustav Türke's wine store and tasting room on Unter den Linden, at the corner of Neue Wilhelmstrasse.[50] Under the name Zum schwarzen Ferkel (The Black Piglet) the wine bar became legendary. Strindberg had coined its name, after having mistaken, in the dark, a wine bag hanging over the door for a piglet.[51]

The circle around Munch, which met in Berlin from around November 1892 until September or October 1894—and not just at Zum schwarzen Ferkel—was not a fixed group. The various people who were closely or even loosely connected to it traveled frequently. Munch, too, was often on the road during his early Berlin years and lived in the city only weeks or months at a time, with interruptions. There he met primarily with modern authors and artists from Sweden, Norway, Denmark, and Finland. On January 20, 1893, he wrote to his sister Inger: "We Scandinavians—[August] Strindberg, Gunnar Heiberg, [Holger] Drachmann, and I, as well as a certain [Adolf] Paul—are almost always together and meet in a small wine bar."[52] The Swedish poet Ola Hansson and his wife, the writer Laura Marholm, helped Strindberg get settled in Friedrichshagen, near Berlin, when his private and professional living situation in Sweden had grown difficult.[53] Figure p.140 Through his works, Strindberg had a strong influence on Munch, but the time they shared in Berlin was only around half a year, from November 1892 to April 1893. They met again in Paris later. The Finnish artist Axel Gallén, with whom Munch exhibited at the Galerie Ugo Barroccio in Berlin in 1895, also spent just a few months in total in Berlin.[54] Figures pp.45A+263

Munch naturally also cultivated contacts to figures from a wide variety of spheres of intellectual life who were living in Berlin: patrons such as Harry Graf Kessler and Walther Rathenau, who had him portray them and purchased his works; artists such as Walter Leistikow; art critics such as Julius

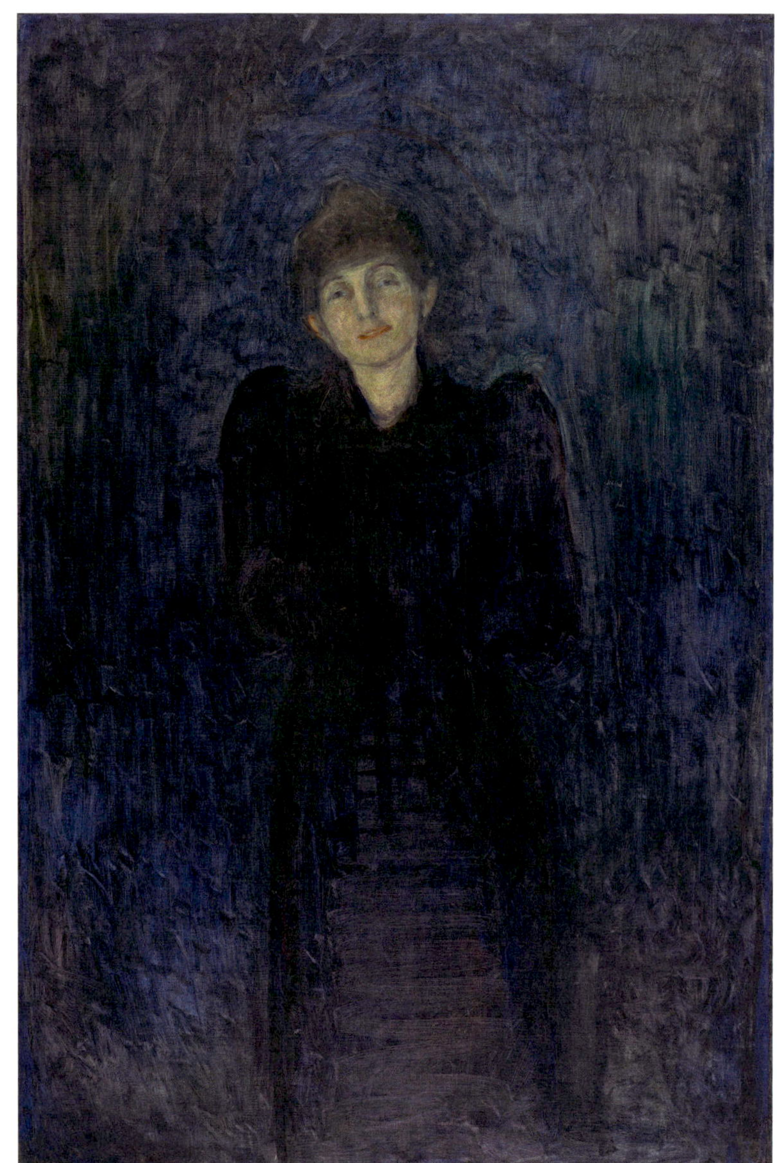

Edvard Munch
Dagny Juel Przybyszewska — 1893
Munchmuseet — Oslo

Meier-Graefe, Franz Servaes, and Willy Pastor; writers such as Richard Dehmel; and physicians such as Gustav Asch and Carl Ludwig Schleich. Figures pp.114, 135, 123 + 219 The Polish writer Stanisław Przybyszewski, who published in both Polish and German and had begun medical studies with a focus on neurology, and the Norwegian writer Dagny Juel were particularly important.[55] Figures pp.22 + 138 With her charisma, which Munch captured in a portrait, she was the sparkling center of the crowd at Zum schwarzen Ferkel. Juel had come to Berlin to continue her piano studies. Later she began to write short dramas and poetry.[56] She married Przybyszewski; like Strindberg, both belonged to Berlin's bohemia.

Much has been written about evenings and nights at the wine bar. Not only Munch but also Strindberg, Paul, Przybyszewski, and Meier-Graefe memorialized Zum schwarzen Ferkel, but above all themselves, in their writings. Many of the men projected their erotic and misogynistic fantasies on Dagny Juel, which later Munch scholars often misinterpreted as facts. Juel was desired, feared, and slandered as a femme fatale but also idealized as an angel, Madonna, and muse—very much in keeping with the era's stereotypical image of women.[57] Many of these stories have repeatedly been associated with Munch. His own image of women was, however, clearly more complex than writers on the Ferkel circle have suggested, thereby reinforcing the view of Munch as a misogynist and loner. The art historian Patricia G. Berman has persuasively proposed seeing Munch more neutrally as a chronicler of the crisis

Edvard Munch
Stanisław Przybyszewski — 1895
Munchmuseet — Oslo

in the relationship between the sexes.[58] Even leaving aside the legends that have formed around Zum schwarzen Ferkel, it must be said that the wine bar was a place of exhilaration and a sounding board, which came to represent a historical crossing of paths, and not just for Munch. Freed of bourgeois constraints, spurred on by alcohol, music, and dance, in the bar they could live out emotions, moods, and rivalries; share and discuss progressive ideas and views; or simply remain quiet, as Przybyszewski described it in his memoirs: "Somewhere in a corner, the great visionary Edvard Munch was brooding over a glass of whiskey."[59]

Specimens of the Soul

It was above all Przybyszewski who controlled the later reception with the first publication on Munch in Berlin in 1894.[60] Figure p.23 In a book of just under a hundred pages with four contributions about Munch's work, *Das Werk des Edvard Munch: Vier Beiträge von Stanisław Przybyszewski, Dr. Franz Servaes, Willy Pastor, Julius Meier-Graefe*, he collected a text of his own and one each by the critics.[61] Przybyszewski had recently published, after being expelled from the department of medicine in Berlin,[62] his book *Zur Psychologie des Individuums* (On the Psychology of the Individual), volume 1, on two *Rauschkünstler* (artists of ecstasy): the Franco-Polish composer Frédéric Chopin[63] and the philosopher Friedrich Nietzsche.[64] In 1893, the first of his "explosive 'rhapsodies'" appeared:[65] *Totenmesse* (Requiem Mass), an obsessive literary text that eliminated the taboos on neurological ailments, states of ecstasy, and sexuality and celebrated them as consciousness-expanding, forward-looking, creative potential.[66] Przybyszewski applied similar premises to Chopin, Nietzsche, and Munch. He wrote that Munch was the first "to have attempted to depict the finest and most subtle movements of the soul ... His pictures are tantamount to painted specimens of the soul, fixed at the moment when all the voices of rationality have fallen silent, when all mental activity has ceased. They are specimens of the soul-as-animal, the reasonless soul captured as it writhes, as it swirls up tempestuously, as it sinks into states of gloomy semi-existence, as it screams in paroxysms of pain, as it howls with hunger."[67] Munch paints "hauntedness and existential angst; he paints the chaos of the fevered mind and the presentient dread of the abyss."[68] The depiction of the tortured soul that screams isolation, anxiety, and pain is, of course, inspired by what is now his best-known motif: *The Scream*, of which Munch made several paintings and prints.[69] Figures pp. 225B + 261 Przybyszewski had seen the work under the title *Despair* in Munch's exhibition in Berlin in 1893, where it was the conclusion of the first series of paintings: *Study for a Series "Love."*[70] He interpreted Munch's works as "manifestations of a naked individuality, products of a somnambulic, transcendental consciousness commonly dubbed 'the unconscious.'"[71] The concept of the unconscious was of great importance for the Ferkel circle, whose members read Nietzsche intensely; Nietzsche was of course intent on exploring the unconscious and formulated the aphoristic, often-cited sentence: "All expansion of our knowledge results from making the unconscious conscious."[72] Przybyszewski advocated a similar view and saw a psychologically unstable constitution not as a limitation but rather as a gift that could be made productive for art. He put in concrete terms something that would shape Munch's later reception: "And that is precisely what is great and forward-looking about Munch that everything deep and dark, everything for which language has not yet found sounds, and that is expressed only as a dark, foreboding compulsion, is dressed up in color in his work and thus enters consciousness."[73]

Less a Painter of the Senses than a Painter of the Inside

Outside of Zum schwarzen Ferkel, Naturalism and Impressionism were the most important movements in Berlin in the late nineteenth century. In Paris, Vienna, and Brussels, by contrast, Symbolism and Art Nouveau were already increasingly important alternative movements. Whereas Impressionism concentrated its interest on the visual perception of the human being and of nature, as they appeared at a given moment and under the existing external conditions, Symbolism turned the gaze inward. The soul was discovered as a new organ of reception, and its sensations became an important theme of modern art. The Danish author Emanuel Goldstein, a close friend of Munch's, whom he had met in Paris in the autumn of 1889, distinguished in an essay of 1892 between the concepts of Impressionism and Symbolism: "No longer shall plastic images of conventional reality be reproduced, but rather a plastic image of the reality alive in one's mind ... The poet shall produce his reality himself."[74]

Symbolism was not much appreciated in Berlin initially. The art critic Hans Rosenhagen noted in 1902 that Berlin artists had been under the leadership of Adolf Menzel, Max Liebermann, and Anton von Werner for nearly fifty years. That was in part based "on a certain sober sense of the people for whom reality is the only standard."[75] In contrast to Paris or Brussels, the city on the Spree had only a few Symbolists who were exhibiting regularly around the turn of the century. In addition to Munch, they included above all Ludwig von Hofmann and Max Klinger, as well as the Swiss artists Arnold Böcklin and Ferdinand Hodler, all of whom remained much closer to the tradition than Munch and pursued other goals than he did. Figures pp. 46B + 25

Munch's distanced stance on Naturalism and Impressionism is immediately evident in many of his notes on art: "To copy Nature—We could not surpass Nature anyway—better then to depict Emotions—one's own—"[76] In retrospect, he categorized his own work as follows: "I began as an impressionist but during the intense emotional and existential upheavals of the Bohemian period Impressionism no longer provided me with enough expression[.] I had to find a style to express what moved my mind—"[77] The art critic

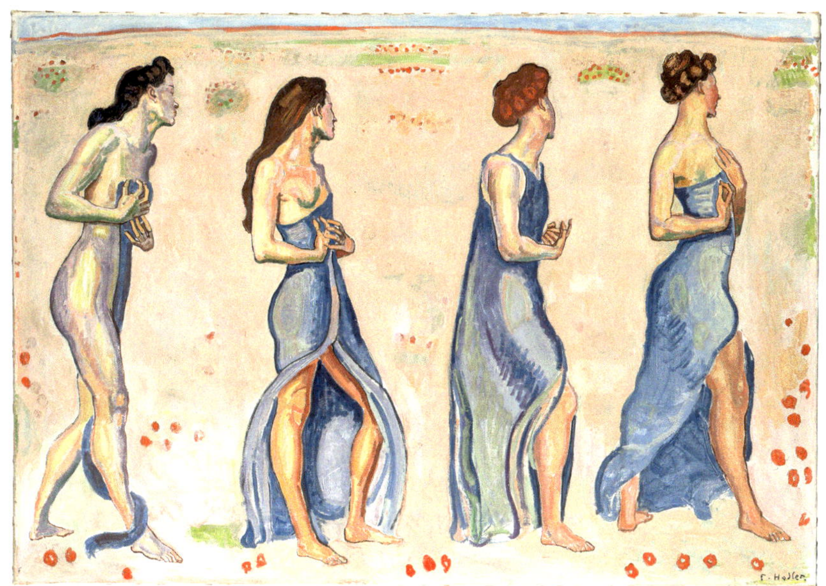

Ferdinand Hodler
Emotion — ca. 1909
Stiftung für Kunst, Kultur und Geschichte — Winterthur

Servaes characterized Munch in 1894 in the first publication on the artist: "He is less a painter of the senses than a painter of the inside, less a naturalist than a visionary Impressionist. A phenomenology of the soul in images — that appears to be the goal of his artistic work."[78]

In the years 1892 to 1908, when he was closely tied to Berlin, Munch uncompromisingly refined the form and content of his works. That is true for both painting and the graphic arts — etching, lithography, and the woodcut — whose techniques he acquired in Berlin in a very brief span from 1894 onward and handled with great virtuosity.[79] His friend the lawyer and judge Gustav Schiefler of Hamburg, who collected graphic art and later prepared a catalogue raisonné of Munch's graphic work, described in his diary his first encounter with these sheets in 1902: "It is the strongest and I can surely say most thrilling impression I have ever gotten from works of contemporary art."[80] Figure p.26A Curt Glaser, who, as noted above, purchased many graphic works by Munch for the modern department of the Kupferstichkabinett in Berlin and had published a monograph on him in 1917,[81] summed it up in 1922: "Munch represents in the most recent history of graphic art the central personality to a much greater degree than any artist of the earlier nineteenth century had been in his era. All of the threads come together in his hand. All graphic techniques — not just the woodcut — gain through him previously unsuspected expressive possibilities. New content creates a new vessel for itself."[82]

Until the second decade of the twentieth century, when Expressionism was becoming established, there was no one in Berlin's art scene who thought and worked in a radically modern way comparable to Munch's, even though works of the international avant-garde were shown at the Secession exhibitions from 1900 onward. The fifty-five works in his first show in 1892 had already proven him to be an avant-garde artist.[83] They had included many of his latest works in which he had broken with Scandinavian Impressionism and Naturalism and set off on new paths. One can see him grappling with French Impressionism and Neo-Impressionism,[84] but also with Symbolism, which as we have seen was little known in Berlin at this time. With support from state stipends in 1889 and 1891, for several months in both cases, Munch had spent time in Paris and Nice,[85] and even in the unstable years between 1892 and 1909 he stayed in the French capital a number of times, sometimes for extended periods.[86] Figure p.26B Among other times, in 1896 he went from Kristiania by way of Berlin to what was still the most important European center for art. His exhibitions in Paris were not very successful; he studied the avant-garde, including Paul Gauguin's paintings and prints, the Nabis artists' group, and Van Gogh;

(A)
Edvard Munch
Portrait of Gustaf Schiefler — 1908
Ateneum — Helsinki

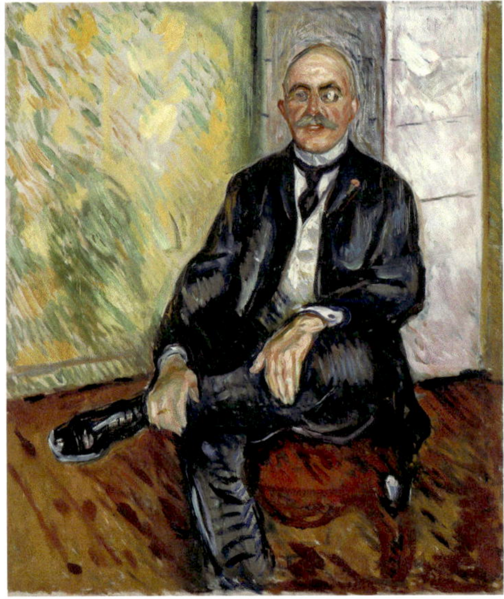

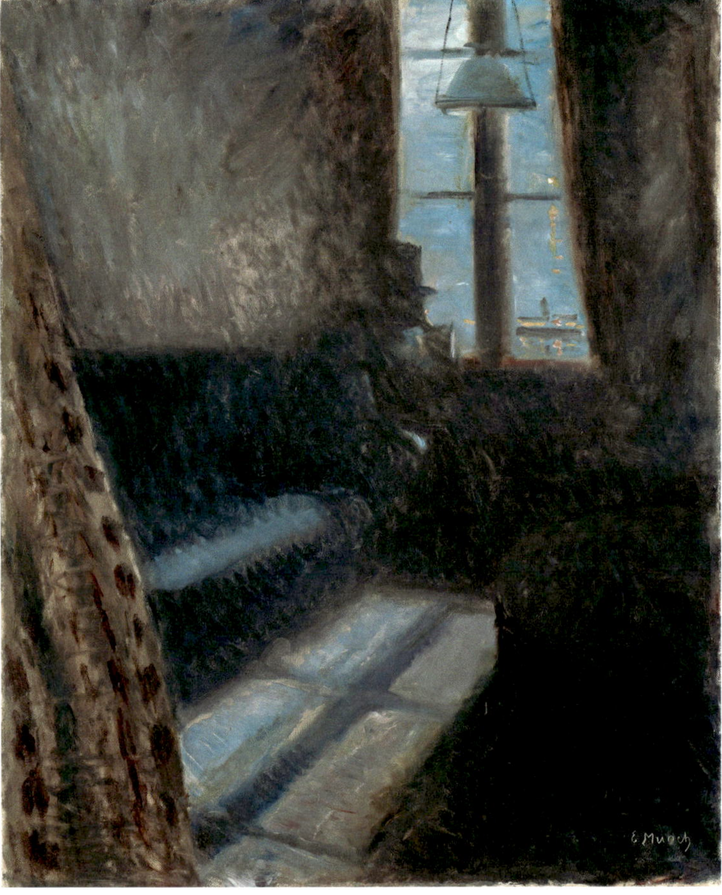

(B)
Edvard Munch
Night in Saint-Cloud — 1890
Nasjonalmuseet — Oslo

he made contacts and found inspiration.[87] Berlin was still stuck in Naturalism and Impressionism at the time, so it was hardly the place from which to expect inspiration and the great breakthrough. There was a lack of understanding of his "painting of the future."[88] The response of the public and the critics in Paris to Munch was also restrained, albeit for other reasons. The city was one of the large centers of Symbolism, but Munch's works were too unconventional, too somber, and too expressive for the French art scene.[89] Beginning in 1901, Munch undertook a new effort to make his mark in Berlin, although Paris continued to be a destination at first. He revived old contacts and made new ones, including to Albert Kollmann,[90] a businessman and collector who supported Munch from 1901 with the distribution of his graphic work and by providing contacts to other supporters. Figures pp.125A + 141 Munch wrote the following to Kollmann in 1904: "By the way, I have little hope in Berlin — I have to try everything to get as much money as possible so I can do a large exhibition in Paris — I have many enemies in Berlin, I think — even among the painters."[91] With his works on the "modern life of the soul,"[92] his graphic art, and his portraits, in which he assimilated European influences, Munch increasingly became part of Berlin modernism with his big appearance in the Secession exhibition of 1902.

Eye — Brain and Heart

But how can Munch's works, which in Berlin from 1900 onward increasingly represented the "magic of the North," be characterized stylistically? How did his contemporaries come to discover the soul in his works? And wherein lay the modernity of his years working in Berlin? In many of his works — the later decorations of the auditorium for the University of Kristiania excepted — Munch dispensed with the mythological and literary references that were certainly common in Symbolism. He was interested in the elemental emotional states that constitute every human life, and he framed them in overarching themes such as love, anxiety, and death. Munch's motifs in works such as *The Kiss*, *Despair*, *The Scream*, *Vampire*, and *Melancholy* can be understood immediately without any prior knowledge; his works are connected by a basic tone of melancholy.

Munch concentrated on simply constructed scenes whose effects are nevertheless contradictory and complex.[93] Figure p.28 Many of his figures look clumsy, almost stiff. They are distinguished by little action, radiate vulnerability, and are one with the space that surrounds them. Often it seems as if they were pausing alone or in pairs—sometimes shocked—as if the space or nature were filling them with fear. The natural or interior spaces are usually more intensely colored than the pale faces. Munch drastically reduces the representational. He combines elements from nature, figures, things, light, and shadow into large, often curved forms that develop lives of their own. He subordinated details to the effects of color and form. Munch drew on the entire spectrum of painting.[94] He worked with fluid watercolors, placed rhythmic brushstrokes against curved lines, applied the paint thick with a palette knife, scratched surfaces, drew over the oil painting in colored chalks, left the raw canvas exposed, or added impasto accents. He often worked with primary colors, placing them next to each other without the paintings ever appearing motley.[95] Layers of paint float into one another like puddles of oil on water. In his day, one also spoke of the "tapestry-like beauty" of the color harmonies, which refers to his accentuating the plane rather than the pictorial space.[96] Something Edvard Munch wrote to the ophthalmologist and art collector Max Linde in Lübeck on March 15, 1903, just after an exhibition in Paris, is enlightening in this context: "In my view, contemporary art in Paris goes a little in the direction of the trivial—and sweet, which could also be seen already in the Neo-Impressionists—one mostly sees small, pleasant contrasts of color, but not the big lines."[97]

Nothing of the like could be said of Munch's powerfully colorful painting. It is therefore no coincidence that his art was appreciated more and grasped more precisely from the 1910s onward, after Expressionism had gained acceptance internationally and in Berlin as well. Karl Scheffler, who was rather critical of that movement, wrote dismissively in 1914: "but now when Impressionism is supposed to be 'overcome' from all sides, when there is loud and ever-louder talk of it being the task of painting to depict the experiences of the soul, he [Munch] is pulled out of his Nordic isolation, placed in the bright light of contemporary trends, and praised as a long unrecognized prophet."[98] Although it is intended critically, his description captures important aspects: "Munch's distinctiveness emerges victoriously only from the totality of works. Only in this totality is his personality complete; the individual work is usually dominated by the approximate and the spirit of the sketch.... Munch must really always stop with the first outline, because otherwise he would imperil his expressive power. He renders almost everything in underpainting, glazes .... He is an improviser who manages the compelling form for his mental, optical impressions only in the first draft."[99] The myth of the first draft in relation to Munch's paintings endured stubbornly. Looking at the works from this period from close up makes it clear how Munch constructed them in refined and complex ways. The impression of the sketch-like, the spontaneous, and open is carefully worked out, and the artist intended it to be in tension with the subject matter. Early on, Servaes also pointed to Munch's sensitivity with regard to the portraits with which he had great success in Berlin: "A painter like Munch whose every fiber is rooted in the

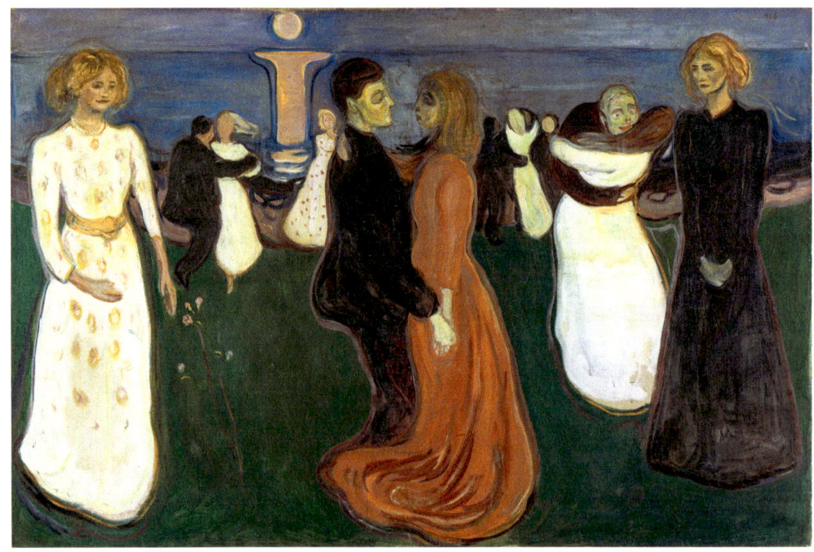

Edvard Munch
The Dance of Life — 1899–1900
Nasjonalmuseet — Oslo

psychological, and who cannot even render a landscape except by making its soul his own, must necessarily be a subtle portraitist."[100]

Just how much the experience of a situation, of a landscape, is influenced by one's own mood was already an important theme for Romanticism.[101] Heinrich von Kleist in Germany anticipated this when he wrote in 1807: "For the real work of art is not that which is offered to the senses, but which the mind, aroused by the senses, thinks to itself within."[102] Munch, who called himself a Romantic,[103] formulated it in a note: "In an intense state of mind, a landscape will make a certain impression on one—by depicting this landscape one will arrive at an image of one's own mood—it is this mood that is the main thing—Nature is merely the means—"[104] In another note on art and nature, Munch observed: "Art is the opposite of Nature—(in a Way at least). A Work of Art comes from the Inner soul of a Human Being—Art is the Picture's [Form]—manifested through Human Nerves—Eye—Brain and Heart."[105] Another of his notes shows just how demanding Munch found this process of empathizing with himself and with the other, whether landscape, motif, or persona: "To depict intense Emotions only through working Directly from Nature—or Nature seen in an intense emotional state is extremely Nerve-wracking work—"[106]

Breathing and Feeling, Suffering and Loving

It is not just Munch's distinctiveness that first emerges from the totality of the works, as Scheffler expressed it. The latter also offers an ongoing narrative on Munch's great theme: the "modern life of the soul."[107] His major work, which later became known under the title *The Frieze of Life*, is based on this idea. The artist regarded the frieze as the essence of his creative activity and worked on the project for the rest of his life.[108]

Munch first presented six paintings under the joint title *Study for a Series "Love"* in a larger solo exhibition at Unter den Linden 19 in Berlin in 1893–94 and then added several works each time in subsequent exhibitions.[109] The idea was that the paintings, independent of and yet at the same time related to one another, would shed light on and explain one another.[110] "Currently, I am working on studies for a series of paintings," he wrote in an undated letter from the early 1890s that he sent from the Hotel Hippodrom in Berlin-Charlottenburg to his friend the Danish painter Johan Rohde in Copenhagen: "These [paintings] that were now rather difficult to understand—will

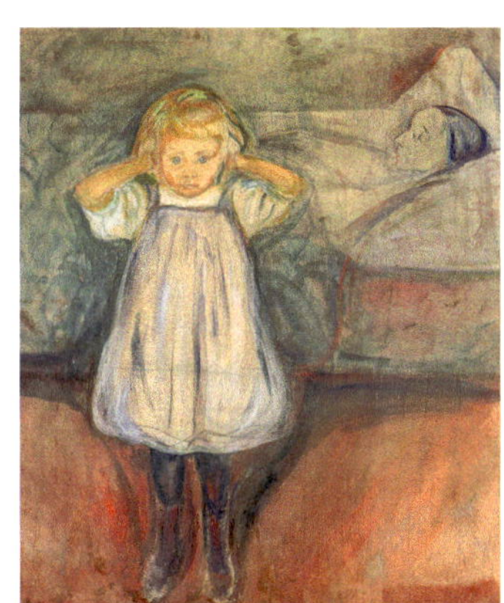

(A)
Edvard Munch
Death and the Child — 1899
Kunsthalle Bremen
Der Kunstverein in Bremen

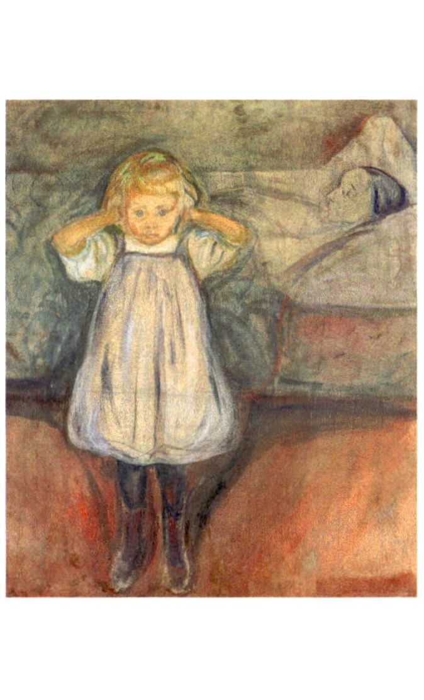

(B)
Edvard Munch
Portrait of Dr. Linde — 1904
Kulturstiftung
Sachsen-Anhalt
Kunstmuseum Moritzburg
Halle an der Saale

be, I believe, more easily understood when they all come together—it will be about love and death."[111] Looking back later, he wrote about the process: "I arranged them together and felt that some of the pictures were connected to each other in content—When they were positioned together there immediately arose a resonance between them and they became totally different than when [displayed] individually. It became a symphony."[112] *The Frieze of Life*, of which Munch would produce a number of variations in the coming years, does not follow any fixed dramaturgy. There are no climaxes as in a film, no tension that compellingly drives the events forward. All of the paintings are given similar weight; there is no strict temporal sequence or fixed order. Every individual painting corresponds to one compressed scene, a paused, expanded moment.

Munch later downplayed the importance of Berlin for the genesis of *The Frieze of Life*. It was wrong to assert, as many had, he wrote in 1926, "that this occurred under Strindberg's and German influence—during my stay in Berlin in 1893–94. My ideas had already ripened at this time."[113] It is correct, in any case, that Munch had already developed his themes under the influence of Hans Jæger and of the bohemia in Kristiania before coming to Berlin.[114] And doubtlessly he had already observed in earlier exhibitions how the paintings reacted to one another when shown together. In 1889, he had noted first ideas that helped prepare the way for the later *Frieze of Life*: "I would make a number of such paintings. No longer would interiors, people who read and women who knit, be painted. There should be living people who breathe and feel, suffer and love."[115] He had, however, exhibited the first series of paintings in Berlin and tried out their effect on the public there.

Not quite a decade later, in April 1902, also in Berlin in the Secession exhibition, Munch expanded this idea into *Darstellung einer Reihe von Lebensbildern* (Depiction of a Series of Images of Life).[116] Kollmann, who was supporting Munch in the preparations for the presentation of the frieze, described its themes: "Life—love—jealousy—madness—anxiety—death."[117] It is noteworthy that for Munch the cycle of life begins with puberty and the dramas of love. He leaves childhood out. Depictions of infants and children are rare, except in traumatic situations of death or illness or in his portraits. Figure p.29A In the variation of 1902, the frieze comprised twenty-two works and was presented on all four walls of the sculpture hall of the Secession, beneath a white fabric frame. Each of the series that Munch exhibited in variations between 1893 and 1927 comprised works from different creative phases that differed considerably from one another in size and painting style. In Berlin in 1902, Munch was hoping that his big appearance at the Secession would provide a breakthrough after failing to achieve the success he had sought in Paris.[118] This extensive presentation in frieze form thus underscored the internal coherence of Munch's work of the past decade. For the public in Berlin, which was not very familiar with Symbolism, it was, however, too early to appreciate and evaluate what was unique and forward-looking about Munch's position. The art critic Hans Rosenhagen expressed regret in the art journal *Die Kunst für Alle*: "They [the visitors] do not recognize that the uniting of brutal Nordic lust in color, inspiration from Manet, and a penchant for dreaminess has produced something quite unique."[119]

In 1904—in Berlin—Munch painted the so-called *Linde Frieze* for the ophthalmologist and art collector Max Linde in Lübeck.[120] Figures pp.29B + 74–85 It was conceived as an interrelated decoration for the children's room. When arranging the paintings for a test with Linde, Munch himself found that although they worked well together, they were too powerful and heavy for the small room with white Empire furniture, as he wrote to Kollmann: "but full of fervor and colors."[121] After the commissioner had rejected the frieze, which he found too frivolous for a children's room, the series was exhibited in Leonhard Boldt's studio in Berlin in 1905–6.[122] In 1906–7, Munch produced stage designs for Max Reinhardt's Kammerspiele (Chamber Theater) in Berlin, the more intimate supplemental stage of the Deutsches Theater (German Theater), which Reinhardt had taken over in 1905.[123] Reinhardt regularly hired visual artists for stage sets and costume designs: not only Munch but also Emil Orlik and Lovis Corinth.[124] Munch was entrusted with coming up with ideas for the stage set for Ibsen's drama *Ghosts* for the opening of the Kammerspiele in 1906, which was already part of standard modern repertoire.[125] The artist was also commissioned to decorate a banquet hall on the first floor—the so-called *Reinhardt Frieze*.[126] Figures pp.86–99 + 238 It is Munch's only frieze in which the horizon line runs continuously at the same height, and figures and trees establish the rhythm of the beach landscape like bar lines. In 1913, he celebrated a great success at the Berlin Secession with studies for his monumental work decorating the auditorium of the university in Kristiania. Figure p.31A These works received almost unanimously positive reviews in the Berlin press.[127] Munch distinguished between *The Frieze of Life* and the large-format frieze for the auditorium: "The Frieze of Life represents the individual's sorrows and joys seen at close range—the University decorations represent the great enduring forces."[128] Figure p.31B

These commissioned works for a specified place are distinguished by the greater coherence of content, style, and form of the series. This raises the question of what a permanent installation of Munch's *Frieze of Life* would have looked like if Munch had painted it again in a consistent form for an architecture of its own, as suggested in drawings.[129] Decorating large wall surfaces was an idea in his head early on.[130] From the time Munch returned to settle in Norway in 1909, he pursued the plan to present *The Frieze of Life* in a permanent display at one location. This large project was one of the reasons he found it so difficult to sell paintings.[131] In 1918, Munch said of *The Frieze of Life*: "The paintings are, certainly, for the most part observations—documentations—sketches—rough drafts—themes. That is their strength .... The room to be decorated was more than anything a pipe dream.—"[132]

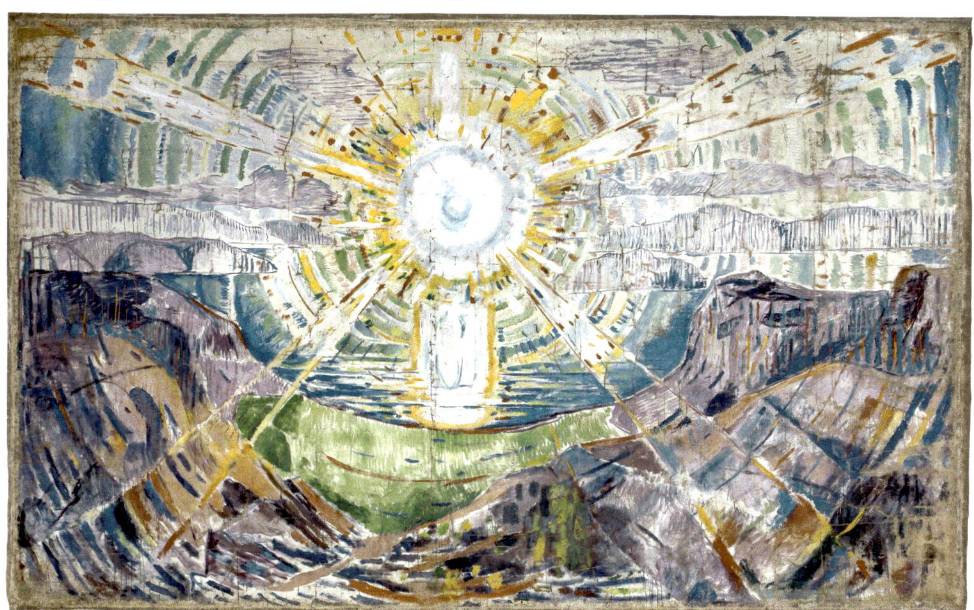

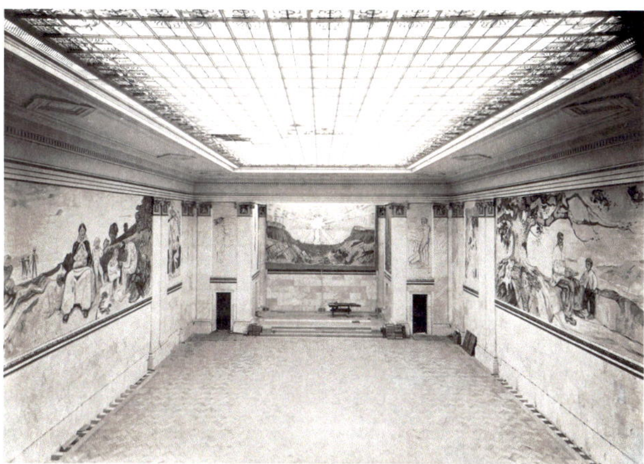

(A)
Edvard Munch
The Sun — 1912–13
Munchmuseet — Oslo

(B)
O. Væring
Test hanging of Munch's works
in the auditorium, University of Oslo — 1911
Munchmuseet — Oslo

Triumph and Tragedy

Munch's influence on the next generation, the Expressionists, was widely thematized in Berlin from 1910 onward.[133] Figures p.33A+B A review of the *Schwarz-Weissausstellung der Berliner Sezession* (Black and White Exhibition of the Berlin Secession) in 1909 was one example: "And next to them a new youth is making its way upward, a group of strangely related spirits who gather around Munch and include such talents as Nolde, Heckel, Kirchner, Pechstein, Matthes, Schocken, Schmidt-Rottluff, Paul Klee, R. Sterl, and others."[134] There had, however, been only few direct contacts between Munch and the Brücke artists before he returned to Norway in 1909.[135] Ernst Ludwig Kirchner, who was a member of the artists' association founded in Dresden in 1905, moved with his colleagues Karl Schmidt-Rottluff and Erich Heckel to Berlin, where Max Pechstein had been living since 1908.[136] From 1906 to 1909, Munch is said not to have reacted to offers to exhibit with them.[137] In Berlin, conflicts between the representatives of Expressionism and established artists ultimately led to the founding of the Neue Secession in 1910. Alongside Herwarth Walden's Galerie Der Sturm, its exhibitions became the most important venue for the Expressionist avant-garde. In his *Erster deutscher Herbstsalon* (First German Autumn Salon) in 1913, Walden offered a survey of the recent avant-garde painting from Europe of a size not seen previously. Munch had declined to participate in the exhibition.[138] He presented instead his designs for the auditorium at the Berlin Secession in order to help them gain acceptance in Kristiania. The Sonderbund exhibition in Cologne the previous year had offered a broad overview of international modernism, especially Expressionist currents. Munch had a room of his own, as did Paul Cézanne, Vincent van Gogh, and Paul Gauguin, and was now considered "one of the pillars of modern painting."[139] The Expressionist painter August Macke, who was about twenty-five years younger than Munch and had participated in the exhibition, wrote him: "We 'young ones' are making you a figurehead."[140]

The paradigm shift in Berlin represented a turning point in the evaluation of Munch's position. Against the backdrop of Expressionism, he became a classic.[141] That went hand in hand with classifying his style as "Nordic-Germanic" and the increasingly ideological monopolization of him as a Germanic artist. Ludwig Justi, who took over as director of the Nationalgalerie in Berlin in 1909, championed Expressionism, and shared the "desire for a stronger assessment of the spiritual."[142] After the end of World War I and the abdication of Emperor William II, Justi took over the former crown prince's palace and opened the "Modern Department of the National-Galerie" there. He built it up into an ambitious venue for contemporary art and showed above all Expressionist and Post-Expressionist artists. Justi observed in his memoirs that this new view of form "had been introduced by two great Germanic masters, Van Gogh and Munch, already in 1890."[143] It was therefore only logical that he organized, together with Glaser who was in the meantime the director of the Staatliche Kunstbibliothek (State Art Library), an extensive solo exhibition for Munch in the Kronprinzenpalais in 1927.[144] It became a milestone for Munch. Thanks to this exhibition, his name stood in Berlin and Germany for "the specifically Nordic world feeling,"[145] and he was taken for granted as part of German art history. In his exhibitions and projects, Munch had been concentrating on Norway for some time.[146] In 1920, Julius Meier-Graefe published his ambitious, revised edition of *Entwicklungsgeschichte der Modernen Kunst* (the first edition had been translated as *Modern Art, Being a Contribution to a New System of Aesthetics*), clearly assessing Munch's position in more detail than he had in the first edition of 1904. In the chapter "Der Norden" (The North), he presents Munch's art as the icy opposite pole to Vincent van Gogh's feverish, ecstatic South. For Meier-Graefe, "the North" is neither a geographic region nor an ur-Germanic mythical dream. Inspired by the psychological content of Munch's paintings, he understood it primarily metaphorically as a psychic landscape of extremes, characterized by, among other things, the cold, isolation, and silence: "Norway was insignificant compared to this North. A supra-Nordic artist constructed the image from his intuition. A new spiritual human being entered art."[147]

From 1933 onward, under the National Socialist dictatorship, art in Germany was forced into the service of the state. In March of that year, Joseph Goebbels took over the newly founded Ministry for Propaganda and Popular Education.[148] Many modern artists lost their posts, were prohibited from teaching, and had few opportunities to exhibit. There were, however, still possibilities at first. The National Socialist leadership had not yet settled on whether to judge Expressionism to be "German art," as long as the artists were not of Jewish origin or of oppositional politics. That applied to Munch's work as well, who had been received as a Nordic-Germanic artist since his first exhibition in Berlin and had generally been considered a proto-Expressionist artist since 1910. At the same time, however, his works were slandered as "degenerate" already in the early defamatory exhibitions of 1933.[149]

In December 1933, Goebbels sent a congratulatory telegram to Oslo on the occasion of Munch's seventieth birthday—eloquent testimony that Germany's future orientation in cultural policy had not yet been clearly decided. Goebbels used the official telegram, which was reprinted in various

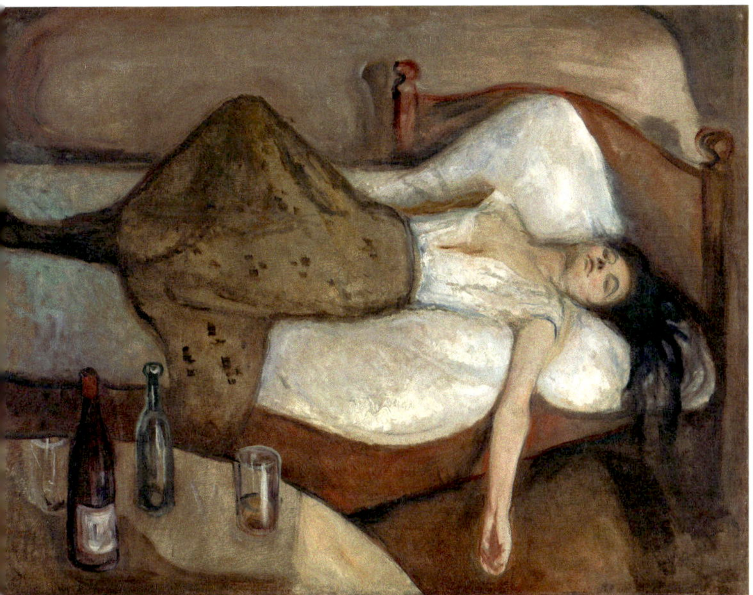

(A)
Edvard Munch
The Day After — 1894
Nasjonalmuseet — Oslo

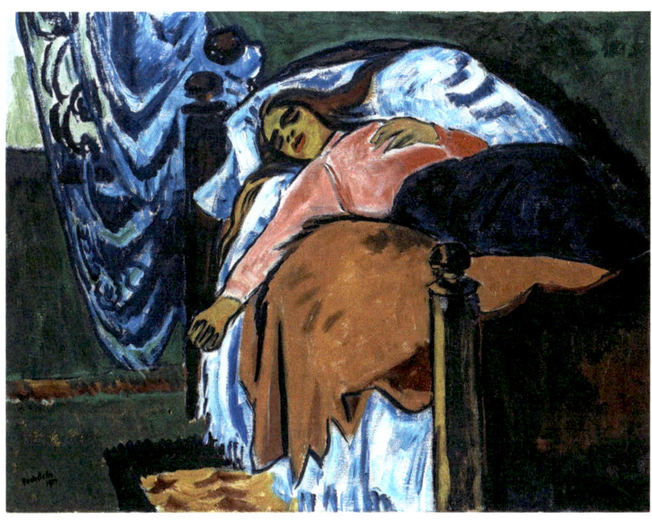

(B)
Max Pechstein
Woman Resting — 1911
Private collection

newspapers, to go out on a limb and adopt a position in support of Munch and Expressionism.[150] Munch's works had "sprouted from Nordic-Germanic soil," as Goebbels began his congratulations. The artist wrestled with "grasping nature in its truth and capturing it while ruthlessly dismissing everything academic and formal in the painting. As a powerful, independent spirit—heir to Nordic nature—he liberates himself of any naturalism and has recourse to the eternal principles of racially pure art making." In 1933, "ruthlessly dismissing everything academic and formal" and turning away from "any naturalism" could just as easily have been used as arguments to declare Munch's works "degenerate." The painter Max Liebermann, who had made a crucial contribution to the shaping of modernism in Berlin for nearly half a century, found himself directly affected by the repressions of National Socialist cultural policy after 1933 because of his Jewish origins. In a letter to the English painter Sir William Rothenstein, director of the Royal College of Art in London, he wrote bitterly on August 10, 1932, shortly before the National Socialists took power: "In Germany, Impressionism is now ostracized as French, and the fashionable word is 'Aufnorden' [Northernize]. Everything is supposed to be as blond as Van Gogh and Munch, the Scandinavian, even though both the Dutchman and the Norwegian had every bit they had from France. But the swastika is everywhere."[151] On June 30, 1937, when the "Führer's decree" to confiscate works of art from German museums for the planned *Entartete Kunst* (Degenerate Art) exhibition was issued, the decision against Expressionism had been made.[152] Eighty-three works by Munch were among those confiscated. Because the stance on the artist was ambiguous, several of these works were successfully reclaimed by museums, including, for example, the painting *Dr. Linde's Sons* (1903) in Lübeck, which had been confiscated, and *Self-Portrait after Influenza* (1919).[153] Figures 34A+B, 158–59 When Norway was occupied by German troops on April 9, 1940, Munch, who was living in isolation entirely for his art, feared that he would be forced out of Ekely and his works would be confiscated or even

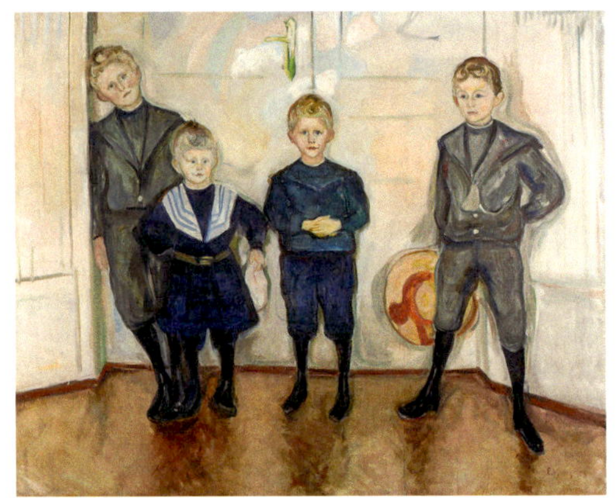

(A)
Edvard Munch
Dr. Linde's Sons — 1903
Die Lübecker Museen, Museum Behnhaus
Drägerhaus — Lübeck

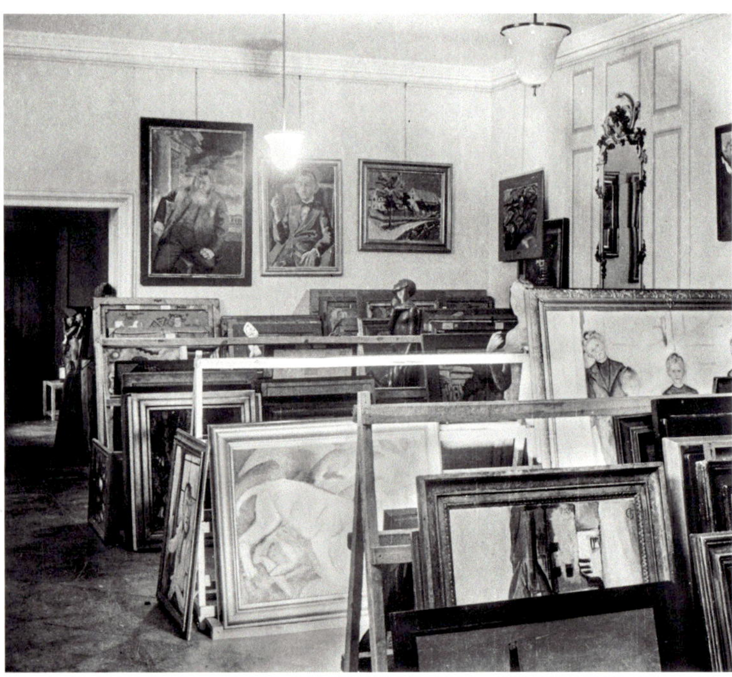

(B)
Depot room for confiscated "degenerate art" in Schloss Schönhausen, Berlin
(on the right: Edvard Munch's *Dr. Linde's Sons*) — 1937
bpk Bildagentur

destroyed.[154] He commented on the confiscation of his works from German museums to his friend the journalist Christian Gierløff: "I have been thrown out of Germany for the second time ... I can be pleased that I was so unwilling to sell. In Germany and here, people were crawling on their knees in order to purchase them. With great sadness I sold my paintings, all of which have been so important for my continued work."[155]

The way Munch explored and depicted the human psyche and internal and interpersonal conflicts completely contradicted the National Socialist ideology of the "healthy master race" and of a pedantic, academic idea of art based on beauty, purity, and strength. Munch's themes, his sensitive approach, and not least his unmistakable modern visual language, which drew from many international sources, could not be reconciled with the cultural politics of the National Socialist state, however much Goebbels might have used the concept of "Nordic" in his telegram in 1933 as a way of locating Munch within his own racist ideology.[156] Munch's art offers no promise, no solution, no way out of the human drama other than the path pointed to by avant-garde painting: vibrant spaces of color that are removed from time and prefigure abstraction.

Today, we appreciate Munch as one of the important representatives of European modernism. His art points beyond his time, and the uninterrupted topicality of his themes and his painting still influences numerous artists internationally. At the same time, Munch's works have offered us a new perspective on the North. We see it with his eyes, connect it to his light, colors, and the melancholy so characteristic of his works. Munch's own artistic credo is modest by comparison: "In my art I have endeavoured to explain life to myself and sought to gain clarity about my fate. I have also thought that it might contribute to others attaining clarity about their fates."[157]

(1) See the essay by Dieter Scholz in the present catalogue; Clarke 2013; Brauner 1994.

(2) *Tidens Tegn*, March 8, 1927, quoted in Næss 2015, p. 474, source given on p. 579.

(3) Næss 2015, pp. 473–75.

(4) For this and the following quotations, see Justi, [introduction], in Berlin 1927, p. 8.

(5) Schulz-Albrecht 1927, p. 502.

(6) Kuhn 1927, p. 144.

(7) Schulz-Albrecht 1927, p. 502.

(8) Zweig 1925, p. 256.

(9) On Munch's reception in Germany until 1944 as a "Nordic artist," see, among others, März 1994, pp. 131–39. Julia Zernack argues that the enthusiasm of the Wilhelmine era was distinct from the German view of the North in the 1920s and 1930s. See Julia Zernack, "Nordenschwärmerei und Germanenbegeisterung im Kaiserreich," in Berlin 1997–98, pp. 71–78, esp. p. 71.

(10) Wolff 1892.

(11) See the essay by Sabine Meister in the present catalogue.

(12) On the "Affaire Munch" as reflected in contemporaneous reviews, see Krisch 1997.

(13) On Munch's membership in the Berlin Secession from 1904 to 1913, see Matelowski 2017, p. 573. On his membership in the Deutscher Künstlerbund, see Moormann-Schulz 2017, pp. 336 and 394. Munch is in all three available lists of members: 1906, 1929, and 1935–36. In 1923, Munch was named a member of the Preussische Akademie der Künste; see Max Liebermann to Edvard Munch, March 10, 1923, and Edvard Munch to Max Liebermann, April 17, 1923, in Braun 2011–21, vol. 7, 1922–26, letter no. 136, p. 143, and letter no. 143, p. 149.

(14) The precise number cannot be determined; see also the list of exhibitions in the present catalogue.

(15) See the essay by Christina Feilchenfeldt in the present catalogue.

(16) On Munch's graphic work, see the essay by Andreas Schalhorn in the present catalogue. On Munch as a photographer, see, for example, Holt 2013; Paris, Frankfurt am Main, and London 2011–12; Eggum 1989.

(17) On this, see Kneher 1994, pp. 78–80.

(18) On Curt Glaser, see the essays by Andreas Schalhorn and Dieter Scholz in the present catalogue, as well as Basel 2022; Woll 1994; Berlin 2003–4; Clarke 2016.

(19) See the essay by Janina Nentwig in the present catalogue.

(20) These works can be researched in the inventory of the "Entartete Kunst" confiscation action: Forschungsstelle "Entartete Kunst," Kunsthistorisches Institut der Freien Universität Berlin, http://emuseum.campus.fu-berlin.de/eMuseumPlus.

(21) Næss 2015, p. 526.

(22) Zweig 1925, p. 256; cf. Schneede 1994a, p. 13; Marx 1988, p. 165.

(23) Max Dauthendey, *Sieben Meere nahmen mich auf: Ein Lebensbild mit Dokumenten aus dem Nachlass und 19 Abbildungen*, ed. Hermann Gerstner (Munich, 1987), p. 83.

(24) Fritz Paul, "Deutschland: Skandinaviens Tor zur Weltliteratur," in Berlin 1997–98, pp. 193–202.

(25) On the founding and function of the Verein Freie Bühne in 1889, see Norbert Jaron, Renate Möhrmann, and Hedwig Müller, eds., *Berlin: Theater der Jahrhundertwende; Bühnengeschichte der Reichshauptstadt im Spiegel der Kritik, 1889–1914* (Tübingen, 1986), pp. 20–26, including the introductions and excerpts from press reviews of performances of plays by Ibsen and Strindberg in the early 1890s. On Ibsen's *A Doll's House* at the Residenztheater in Berlin, November 21, 1880, see Brandes 1885, pp. 357–63.

(26) Birgit Grimm, "Wilhelm II. und Norwegen," in Berlin 1997–98, pp. 100–112.

(27) Industrialization and modernization were progressing locally and regionally in the Scandinavian countries as well. But poverty, rapidly growing populations, a lack of prospects for the future, and political restrictions led to many people emigrating from Scandinavia from the mid-nineteenth century until well into the twentieth century, to North America in particular. See Zernack, "Nordenschwärmerei und Germanenbegeisterung im Kaiserreich," in Berlin 1997–98, p. 71. Grimm, "Wilhelm II. und Norwegen," in Berlin 1997–98.

(28) The literature on this is very extensive. A selection: Krisch 1997, pp. 17–28; Schneede 1994a, pp. 12–19; Kneher 1994, pp. 9–22; Heller 1993; Marx 1988; Meister 2006, pp. 265–71; Næss 2015, pp. 129–34. See also the essay by Sabine Meister in the present catalogue.

(29) Adelsteen Normann to Edvard Munch, September 24, 1892, Munchmuseet, Oslo, MM K 789 (this document and all of the archival materials in Munchmuseet that follow are accessible at emunch.no).

(30) *Staatsbürger-Zeitung*, no. 523 (November 8, 1892): p. 9; Rosenberg 1892b, p. 75, quotes in his review the announcement of Munch's exhibition in 1892 as an "Ibsenian mood."

(31) Springer 1893a, p. 102; Krisch 1997, p. 21; Heller 1993, p. 102; Moormann-Schulz 2017, pp. 38–39.

(32) Shortly before this, also in 1892, eleven artists interested in new stylistic movements, including Max Liebermann and Walter Leistikow, came together to form the artists' group Vereinigung der XI (Association of the XI). On this, see Meister 2006; on Anton von Werner, see Berlin 1993.

(33) This reproach runs like a thread through Munch's reception during his lifetime. On early reviews of the exhibition in 1892, which were likewise critical, see: Krisch 1997, pp. 59–79. For a characterization of Munch's painting style, see Mørstad 2007.

(34) On the question of the extent to which contemporaneous reviews of the exhibition adopted stereotypes of Munch as a "Nordländer," see Krisch 1997, pp. 146–65.

(35) Krisch 1997, pp. 18–19.

(36) Edvard Munch to his aunt Karen Bjølstad, November 12, 1892, Munchmuseet, Oslo, MM N 785.

(37) Cummings 2001, pp. 113–14; on the Freie Bühne, see note 25.

(38) On Brandes, see Erik M. Christensen, "Nachwort: Ein Europäer in Berlin," in Brandes 1885, pp. 599–619; Uwe Englert, "Der 'Moderne Durchbruch,'" in Berlin 1997–98, pp. 209–12.

(39) Brandes 1885, pp. 410–19, esp. p. 412.

(40) Brandes 1885, p. 412.

(41) Brandes 1885, "Slutningsord af en tale," pp. 553–54, esp. p. 553.

(42) Paul 1927.

(43) Paul 1927.

(44) See, most recently, Herfried Münkler, *Marx, Wagner, Nietzsche: Welt im Umbruch* (Berlin, 2021).

(45) Christine Magerski, *Gelebte Ambivalenz: Die Bohème als Prototyp der Moderne* (Wiesbaden, 2015).

(46) See Erik Glossmann, "Ein rasendes Verlangen nach mehr: Zu Hans Jaegers Roman 'Kristiania-Bohème'" (afterword), in Hans Jaeger, *Kristiania-Bohème*, [based on the German edition of 1902, translator unidentified] (Munich, 2006), pp. 481–98; Næss 2015, pp. 67–84.

(47) Quoted in Glossmann 2006 (see note 46), p. 488.

(48) On Nietzsche here and below, see Jochen Schmidt, *Geschichte des Genie-Gedankens in der deutschen Literatur, Philosophie und Politik*, vol. 2 (Darmstadt, 1985), pp. 129–68. See also Münkler 2021 (see note 44).

(49) See the essay by Lars Toft-Eriksen in the present catalogue; Klim 1992; Głuchowska 2009; Paszkiewicz 1996.

(50) Also spelled "Türcke" in relevant literature, such as in Bruns 1998, p. 406.

(51) Much has been written about Zum schwarzen Ferkel in the secondary literature on Munch. See, with numerous references to people and primary and secondary sources, Bruns 1998; Lathe 1972; Schneede 1994a; Kneher 1994, pp. 30–31 and 47–52; Norseng 1991, pp. 4–16; Lathe 1983, pp. 192–96; Głuchowska 2009; Eggum 1996; Klim 1992, pp. 55–73; Marx 1988; Brandt 2019; Næss 2015, pp. 135–41.

(52) Edvard Munch to his sister Inger Munch, January 20, 1893, quoted in German in Munich, Hamburg, and Berlin 1994–95, p. 63. See also Larsson 1996, p. 170.

(53) On Strindberg in Berlin, see Olof Lagercrantz, *August Strindberg*, trans. Anselm Hollo (1979; repr., New York, 1984), pp. 231–40; Lathe 1983; Larsson 1996, pp. 161–78. On the history of the performance of Strindberg's plays in Berlin around the turn of the century, see the index in Jaron, Möhrmann, and Müller 1986 (see note 25), as well as the literature on Zum schwarzen Ferkel (see note 51).

(54) In 1907, Axel Gallén officially adopted a Finnish version of his name: Akseli Gallen-Kallela. See Paris 2011, p. 19. On the artist's relationship to Berlin, see Espoo 2014. On the exhibition at the Galerie Ugo Barroccio, see Kneher 1994, pp. 65–76.

(55) For a detailed account of Przybyszewski, see Klim 1992. Facts and myths are closely interwoven in the literature on Juel. For a critique of the sources, see Norseng 1991; Brandt 2019; cf. the productive approach in Berman 1997. On the collaboration of Juel and Przybyszewski, see Brodal 1996. It is not certain whether Munch and Juel had already met in Norway; see Norseng 1991, p. 9.

(56) Juel's collected writings have been published in German translation: Juel 2019; the afterword is worth reading: Brandt 2019, pp. 96–167.

(57) On Juel, see, for example, Norseng 1991; Brandt 2019; Lathe 1983; Berman 1997; Brodal 1996.

(58) Berman 1997, p. 13: "Munch emerged not so much as the reactionary priest of the femme fatale as a chronicler of gender crises."

(59) Przybyszewski 1926, p. 167.

(60) Przybyszewski 1894a. Przybyszewski first published his text in February 1894 under the title "Psychischer Naturalismus," *Die neue deutsche Rundschau (Freie Bühne)* 5 (1894): pp. 150–56. See also Lathe 1979: "Edvard Munch and the Concept of 'Psychic Naturalism.'"

(61) For a brief annotated summary and assessment of the four texts, see Kneher 1994, pp. 40–47.

(62) Przybyszewski 1926, p. 82.

(63) Przybyszewski played piano. His performances of Chopin at Zum schwarzen Ferkel were unforgettable for many, including Munch. Munch, "Mein Freund Przybyszewski: Eine Erinnerung des berühmten Künstlers," *Pologne Littéraire* 27 (1928): p. 2.

(64) Klim 1992, p. 41. For a bibliography of Przybyszewski's writings, see Klim 1992, pp. 335–39; Stanislaus [*sic*] Przybyszewski, *Zur Psychologie des Individuums I: Chopin und Nietzsche* (Berlin, 1892).

(65) Przybyszewski 1926, p. 180.

(66) Klim 1992, pp. 67–73. Stanislaw [*sic*] Przybyszewski, *Totenmesse* (Berlin, 1893). On *Totenmesse* and more, see Głuchowska 2009, pp. 79–82.

(67) Przybyszewski 1894b, pp. 16–17, published in English as Stanisław Przybyszewski, "The Work of Edvard Munch" (1894), in Nielsen 2015, p. 85.

(68) Przybyszewski 1894b, pp. 26–27, quoted in English from Przybyszewski 1894/2015 (see note 67), p. 90.

(69) On the genesis of *The Scream*, see the entries in the catalogue raisonné of paintings: Woll 2009, Woll 264, 332, 333, 363, and 364; as well as, for example, Eggum 1996, esp. pp. 71–72. On Munch and Przybyszewski, see Głuchowska 2009, esp. pp. 98–101.

(70) Przybyszewski addresses the painting later in his text "The Work of Edvard Munch": Przybyszewski 1894b, pp. 21–24, quoted in English from Przybyszewski 1894/2015 (see note 67), p. 87.

(71) Przybyszewski 1894b, p. 12, quoted in English from Przybyszewski 1894/2015 (see note 67), p. 83.

(72) Friedrich Wilhelm Nietzsche, *Werke, 1844–1900*, pt. 2, vol. 9, *Nachgelassene Werke aus den Jahren 1869–1872*, 3rd ed. (Stuttgart, 1921), p. 122; on this, see Rainer Danziger, "Zur Geschichte des Begriffs 'Das Unbewusste' bis zu Sigmund Freuds Arbeit von 1915," in Marianne Scheinost-Reimann, Sabine Schlüter, and Elisabeth Skale, *Vom Unbewussten, I–III*, Sigmund-Freud-Vorlesungen 8, ed. Wiener Psychoanalytische Akademie (Vienna, 2014), p. 28.

(73) Przybyszewski 1894a, foreword, pp. 3–7, esp. pp. 4–5. Pzybyszewski had made similar remarks about Chopin; see Przybyszewski 1892 (see note 64), p. 27: "And precisely for these secondary emotions, for everything that works its way up from the depths of the unconscious, ... for everything ineffable, vanishing, frightening, and joyful, for which we could offer no reason, for which language has no words, for which the most insightful explanation is merely a clever parlor trick: we can express it in music."

(74) Emanuel Goldstein, quoted in Heller 1984, p. 67.

(75) Rosenhagen 1902, pp. 436 and 439.

(76) Edvard Munch, sketchbook, 1908, Munchmuseet, Oslo MM T 2800, p. 35. English translation by Francesca M. Nichols.

(77) Edvard Munch, note, 1927–33, Munchmuseet, Oslo, MM N 122, fol. 1r. English translation by Francesca M. Nichols.

(78) Servaes 1894, pp. 43–44.

(79) See Woll 1994 and the essay by Andreas Schalhorn in the present catalogue.

(80) Gustav Schiefler, diary, October 11, 1902, in Munch and Schiefler 1987 and 1990, p. 1:37.

(81) Glaser 1917.

(82) Glaser 1922, pp. 517–18.

(83) Kneher 1994, pp. 9–12.

(84) Heller 1984, pp. 65–67.

(85) Eggum 1991–92a; Rapetti 1991–92a.

(86) On the chronologies of Munch in Paris, see Paris 2022–23, pp. 14–21; Paris, Oslo, and Frankfurt am Main 1991–92, pp. 366–83.

(87) Eggum 1991–92b.

(88) Edvard Munch, *The Violet Journal*, sketchbook, MM T 2760, fol. 15v. English translation by Francesca M. Nichols.

(89) Rapetti 1991–92b; Eggum 1991–92b. On Munch and Paris, see also Heller 1984, pp. 50–73 and 158–64; Paris 2022–23.

(90) On Munch meeting Kollmann, see, for example, Næss 2015, pp. 234–35; Eggum 1982, p. 6.

(91) Edvard Munch to Albert Kollmann, August 19, 1904, Munchmuseet, Oslo, MM N 3178.

(92) In 1904, Munch exhibited eighteen paintings in Kristiania under the title *Frieze: Motifs from the Modern Life of the Soul*. On the exhibition, see Kneher 1994, pp. 199–202.

(93) I am grateful to Axel Eichhorst for suggestions, ideas, and inspiration on Munch's method.

(94) On his painting style, see Topalova-Casadiego 2009; Ohlsen 2013; Mørstad 2007; Magnaguagno 1987; Schütz 1987; Thurmann-Moe 1987.

(95) Munch's contemporaries were already emphasizing this; see Rosenhagen 1902, p. 458.

(96) "But his problematic sensorium is always accompanied by a powerful decorative sense. The color harmonies, taken for themselves, are of a unique, tapestry-like beauty." Scheffler 1902, p. 426.

(97) Edvard Munch to Max Linde, March 16, 1903, according to emunch.no, in the Stadtbibliothek der Hansestadt Lübeck, PN 138, quoted in Eggum 1991–92c, p. 296. It is also quoted, with different wording and date, in Eggum 1982, p. 14.

(98) Scheffler 1914, p. 415.

(99) Scheffler 1914, p. 416.
(100) Servaes 1894, p. 54.
(101) On the influences of French Romanticism, see the essay by Lars Toft-Eriksen in the present catalogue.
(102) Heinrich von Kleist, in Châlons sur Marne, to Marie von Kleist, June 1807, in Heinrich von Kleist, *An Abyss Deep Enough: Letters of Heinrich von Kleist, with a Selection of Essays and Anecdotes*, ed. and trans. Philip B. Miller (New York, 1982), pp. 170–71, esp. p. 171.
(103) Edvard Munch, "I have been compared to Toulouse-Lautrec, but that is totally wrong, because I am a Romantic." Quoted in Næss 2015, p. 444.
(104) Edvard Munch, note, 1890–92, Munchmuseet, Oslo, MM N 29, pp. 1–2. English translation by Francesca M. Nichols.
(105) Edvard Munch, sketchbook, 1908, Munchmuseet, Oslo, MM T 2785, p. 122. English translation by Francesca M. Nichols.
(106) Edvard Munch, sketchbook, 1908, Munchmuseet, Oslo, MM T 2785, p. 124. English translation by Francesca M. Nichols.
(107) Berman 1997, p. 14. On the concept of the "modern life of the soul," see note 92.
(108) The literature on this is very extensive. A selection: Schneede 1994b; Kneher 1994, pp. 150–58; Eggum 1996; Guleng 2013; and the essay by Janina Nentwig in the present catalogue.
(109) List of exhibitions in Kneher 1994, p. 32. It is followed by a categorization and discussion of reviews of the exhibition.
(110) Berman 1997, p. 14.
(111) Edvard Munch to Johan Rohde, undated letter, quoted in German in Munich, Hamburg, and Berlin 1994–95, p. 63.
(112) Edvard Munch, note, 1930–34, Munchmuseet, Oslo, MM N 46, fol. 3r. English translation by Francesca M. Nichols.
(113) Edvard Munch to Rudolf Broby-Johansen, December 11, 1926, Munchmuseet, Oslo, MM N 2173.
(114) For lists of works in and reviews of the first exhibitions in Berlin, see Kneher 1994, pp. 9–40.
(115) Edvard Munch, "Saint Cloud Manifesto," 1889, in Munch, *Livsfrisens tilblivelse* (Oslo, [1928]), Munchmuseet, Oslo, MM UT 13, English translation from Heller 1984, p. 64. On the "Saint Cloud Manifesto," see the excerpts of the unpublished journal that Munch kept in France, edited and annotated by Sissel Bjørnstad and Arne Eggum, in Paris, Oslo, and Frankfurt am Main 1991–92, pp. 341–64.
(116) On Munch's restart in Berlin from 1901 onward, his presentation at the Berlin Secession in 1902 (including a list of the works exhibited), and his *Frieze of Life*, see Kneher 1994, pp. 147–58, and the essay by Janina Nentwig in the present catalogue.
(117) Albert Kollmann to Max Linde, March 27, 1902, private collection, quoted in Schneede 1994b, p. 23.
(118) On Munch and Paris, see Rapetti 1991–92b; Eggum 1991–92b; Heller 1984, pp. 50–73 and 158–64; Paris 2022–23.
(119) Rosenhagen 1902, p. 458.
(120) Eggum 1982.
(121) Edvard Munch to Albert Kollmann, December 9, 1904, quoted in Eggum 1982, p. 34.
(122) Christiane Zeiller, "'... More or Less My Antipode': The Influence of Edvard Munch on Max Beckmann's Early Work," trans. Steven Lindberg, in *Max Beckmann and Berlin*, ed. Thomas Köhler and Stefanie Heckmann, exh. cat. Berlinische Galerie (Berlin, 2015), pp. 46–54, esp. p. 48.
(123) On Reinhardt's role at the Deutsches Theater and the Kammerspiele, see Jaron, Möhrmann, and Müller 1986 (see note 25), pp. 64–72.
(124) Jaron, Möhrmann, and Müller 1986 (see note 25), pp. 68–69. On the collaboration of Munch and Reinhardt, see also Cummings 2001.
(125) See Cummings 2001, pp. 117–18.
(126) Bernau 2005, pp. 65–77. Bernau documents, among other things, that the room was not bean-shaped, as scholars had long assumed. See also Lampe 2012; Cummings 2001; and the essay by Pauline Behrmann in the present catalogue.
(127) Berlin 1913, pp. 35–36; Munch exhibited eleven studies. Studies for this cycle will be included in a forthcoming exhibition at the Barberini Museum, *Edvard Munch: Trembling Earth*, in Potsdam, 2023–24.
(128) Edvard Munch, "Livsfrisen," *Tidens Tegn*, October 15, 1918. English translation by Francesca M. Nichols. On the decoration of the auditorium, see, most recently, Berman 2022.
(129) For example, see Schneede 1994b.
(130) Eggum 1991–92b, p. 218; Julius Meier-Graefe, "Edvard Munch," *Dekorative Kunst* 4 (1899): p. 133.
(131) Brauner 1994, pp. 129–30.
(132) Edvard Munch, "Kritiken over Livsfrisen," *Tidens Tegn*, October 29, 1918. English translation by Francesca M. Nichols.
(133) See New York 2016.
(134) "[Kunstausstellungen: Schwarz-Weiss]," *Kunst und Künstler* 7, no. 4 (1909): pp. 185–86, esp. p. 186.
(135) Heller 2016, pp. 39–44; Eggum 1994.
(136) On Expressionism in Berlin, see *Liebermanns Gegner: Die Neue Secession in Berlin und der Expressionismus*, exh. cat. Stiftung Brandenburger Tor, Max Liebermann Haus, Berlin, and Stiftung Schleswig-Holsteinische Landesmuseen Schloss Gottorf, Schleswig (Cologne, 2011).
(137) Heller 2016, p. 42.
(138) Heller 2016, p. 45.
(139) Glaser 1922, p. 23; Schneede 1994c. For an overview of the works shown by Munch, see Munich, Hamburg, and Berlin 1994–95, pp. 270–71; *Mission Moderne: Die Jahrhundertschau des Sonderbundes*, ed. Barbara Schaefer, exh. cat. Wallraf-Richartz-Museum and Fondation Corboud, Cologne (Cologne, 2021); Stern 1912.
(140) August Macke to Edvard Munch, March 29, 1913, quoted in Schneede 1994c, p. 101.
(141) Clarke 2013, pp. 173–76; Clarke 2016, p. 201; Heller 2016, p. 43; Cernuschi 2001; Eggum 1994; Hansen 1994.
(142) Justi 2000, p. 1:451.
(143) Justi 2000, p. 1:441.
(144) See the essay by Dieter Scholz in the present catalogue.
(145) Schulz-Albrecht 1927, p. 502.
(146) On this, see, for example, Clarke 2013; Heller 2016.
(147) Julius Meier-Graefe, *Entwicklungsgeschichte der modernen Kunst*, 2nd rev. and exp. ed., 3 vols. (Munich, 1920), p. 3:646.

(148) "Die Reichskulturkammer," *LeMO—Lebendiges Museum Online*, www.dhm.de/lemo/kapitel/ns-regime/kunst-und-kultur/reichskultur kammer.html; Stefanie Heckmann and Hans Ottomeyer, eds., *Kassandra: Visionen des Unheils 1914–1945*, exh. cat. Deutsches Historisches Museum, Berlin (Dresden, 2008).

(149) On the exhibition *Kulturbolschewistische Bilder* (Cultural Bolshevist Paintings), Mannheim, Städtische Kunsthalle, April 4 to June 5, 1933, see Zuschlag 1995, pp. 58–69. See also Gerner 1988.

(150) März (1994, pp. 133–34) cites the telegram in full. It was reprinted, for example, in *Deutsche Allgemeine Zeitung* (December 12, 1933) and the Oslo daily newspaper *Tidens Tegn*. For details on the background and the ideological monopolization of Munch as a Nordic artist, see März 1994; Gerner 1988, p. 340.

(151) Max Liebermann to William Rothenstein, August 10, 1932, in Braun 2011–21, vol. 8, 1927–35, letter no. 615, pp. 487–88.

(152) On the background of the "Entartete Kunst" action, see www.geschkult.fu-berlin.de/e/db_entart_kunst/geschichte/beschlagnahme/index.html; Zuschlag 1995.

(153) The Munch works that were removed can be researched in the inventory of the confiscations of "Entartete Kunst," Forschungsstelle "Entartete Kunst," Kunsthistorisches Institut der Freien Universität Berlin, http://emuseum.campus.fu-berlin.de/eMuseumPlus. On this theme, see März 1994; Gerner 1988.

(154) März 1994, p. 135.

(155) Edvard Munch to Christian Gierløff, undated letter, quoted in Gerner 1988, p. 347, n. 85; Gerner suspects that the letter dates from 1937.

(156) On the irreconcilability of Expressionism and National Socialist ideology, see Cernuschi 2001, pp. 163–65.

(157) Edvard Munch, note, 1933–40, Munchmuseet, Oslo, MM N 62. English translation by Francesca M. Nichols.

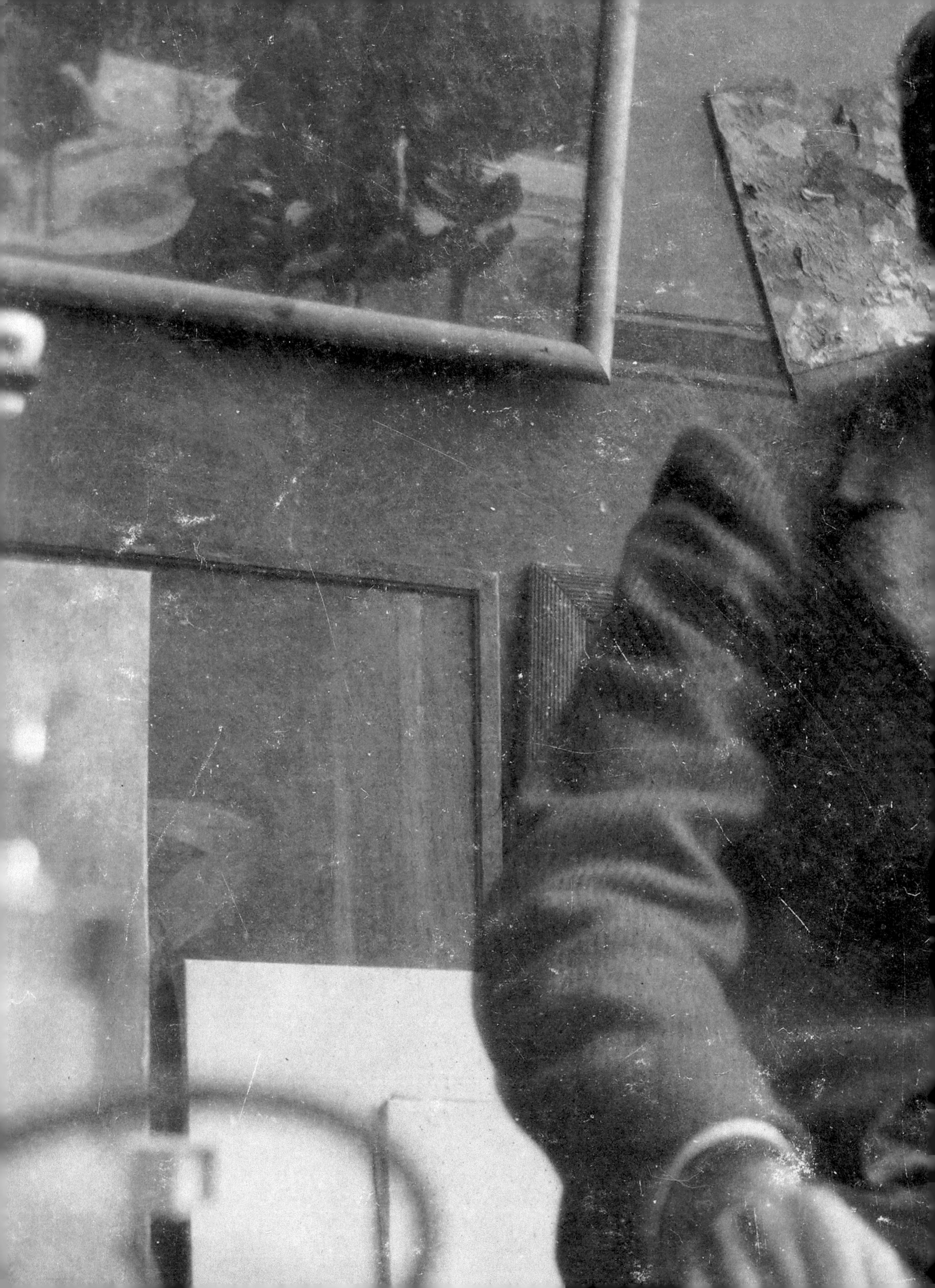

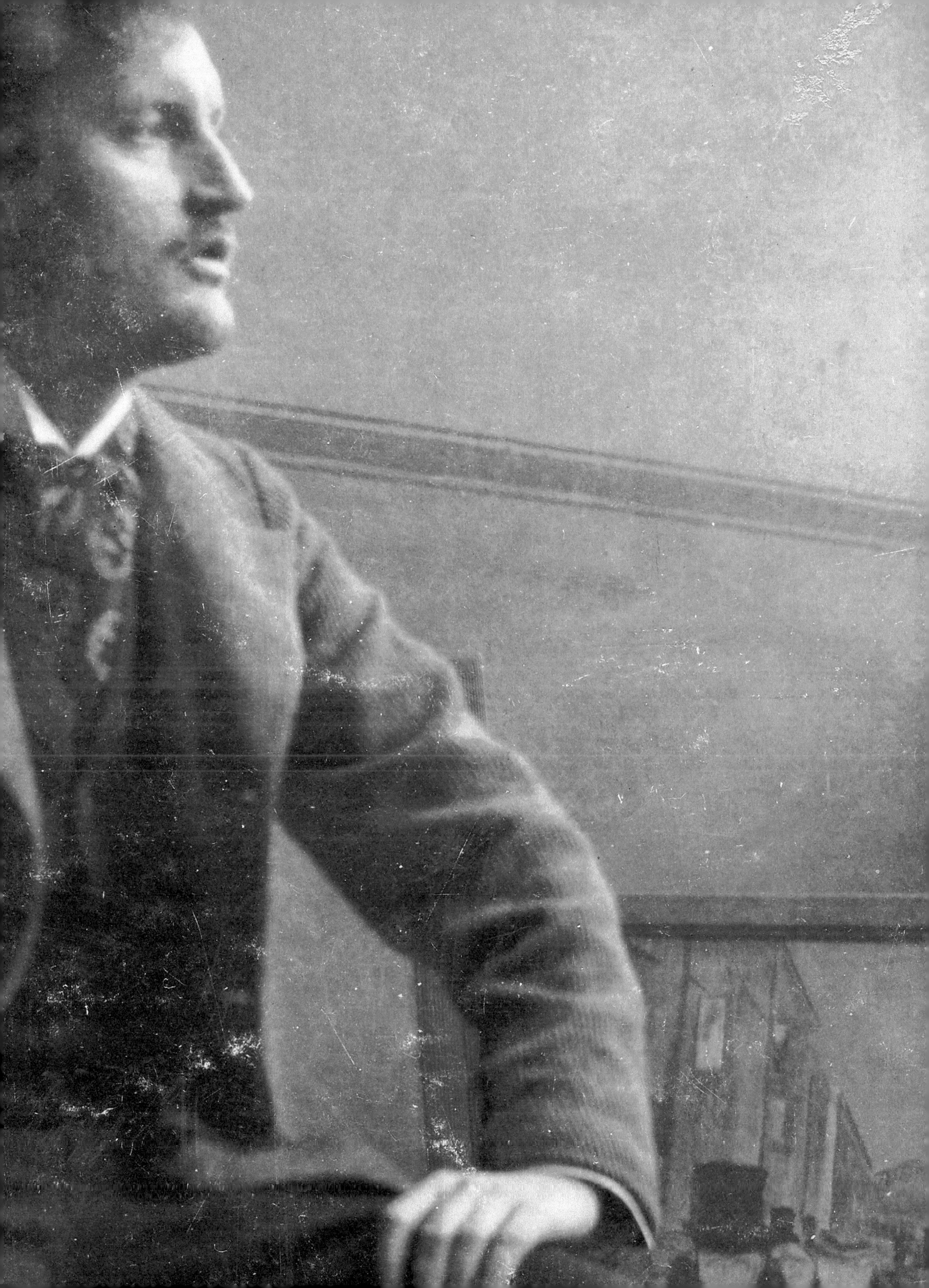

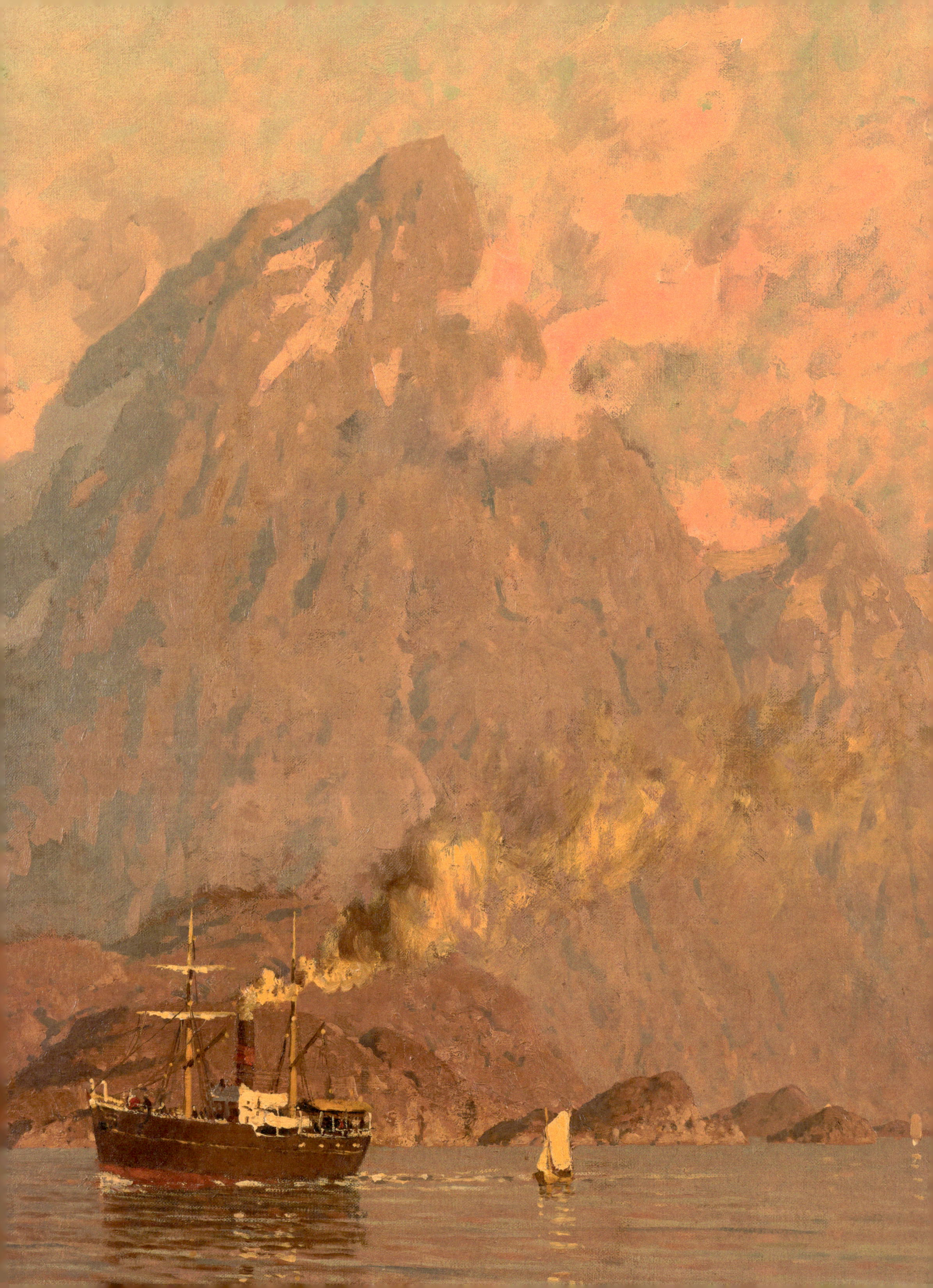

The Dream of the North and the "Munch Affair"

Enthusiasm for everything Nordic seized Berlin, the capital of the German Reich, like a fever toward the end of the nineteenth century. It had a wide-ranging effect, and not just on intellectual circles, which were interested in Scandinavian landscape painting and literature, such as the modern, naturalistic social drama of Henrik Ibsen. From 1889 to 1914, Emperor William II set off annually with his yacht *Hohenzollern* on a "journey to the North."

This fascination was one reason that the largely unknown Norwegian artist Edvard Munch was invited to present a solo exhibition at the Verein Berliner Künstler (Association of Berlin Artists) in 1892. The young painter had been proposed by his compatriot Adelsteen Normann, who divided his time between Berlin and Norway and whose popular fjord landscapes were also greatly appreciated by the emperor.

The radicalness of Munch's painting challenged the art scene. Whereas younger members of the association were mostly open to Munch's art, many of the older ones and the majority of the public were shocked by the paintings exhibited, which were criticized as raw, sketchy, and unfinished. The show was closed just a week after its opening. The "Affaire Munch" (Munch Affair), as the contemporaneous press ironically referred to the scandal around his exhibition, was the beginning of modernism in Berlin and of the painter's international career. Munch used the publicity and moved to the city on the Spree River, where he lived and worked repeatedly, with interruptions, until 1908.

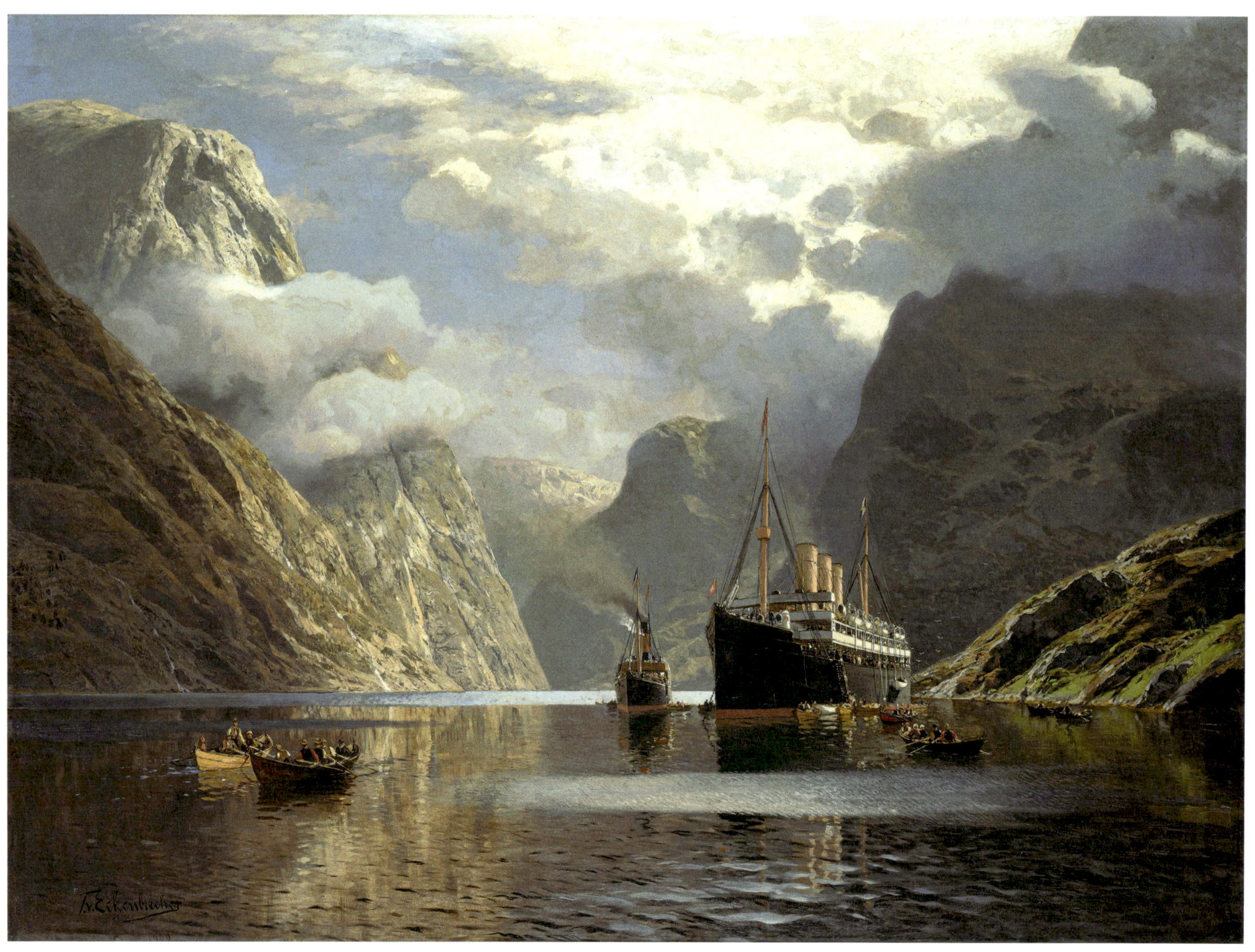

Themistokles von Eckenbrecher
The "Auguste Victoria" in the Nærøyfjord — 1900
Staatliche Schlösser, Gärten und Kunstsammlungen
Mecklenburg-Vorpommern — Schwerin

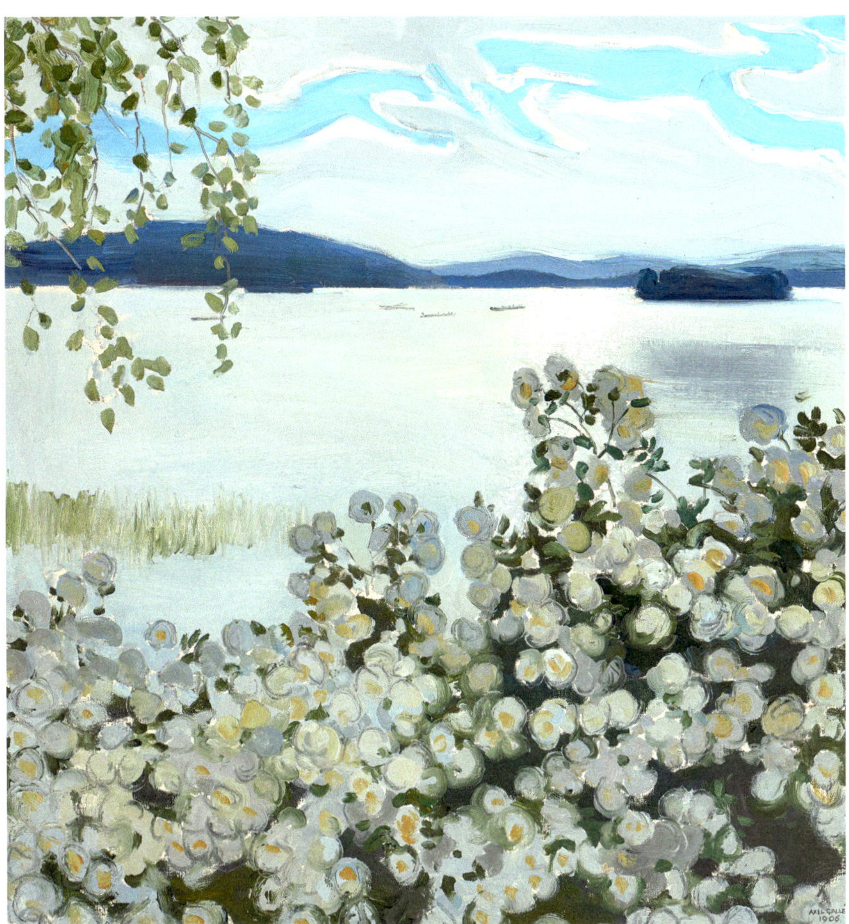

⟨A⟩
Axel Gallén
White Roses — 1906
Private collection,
northern Germany

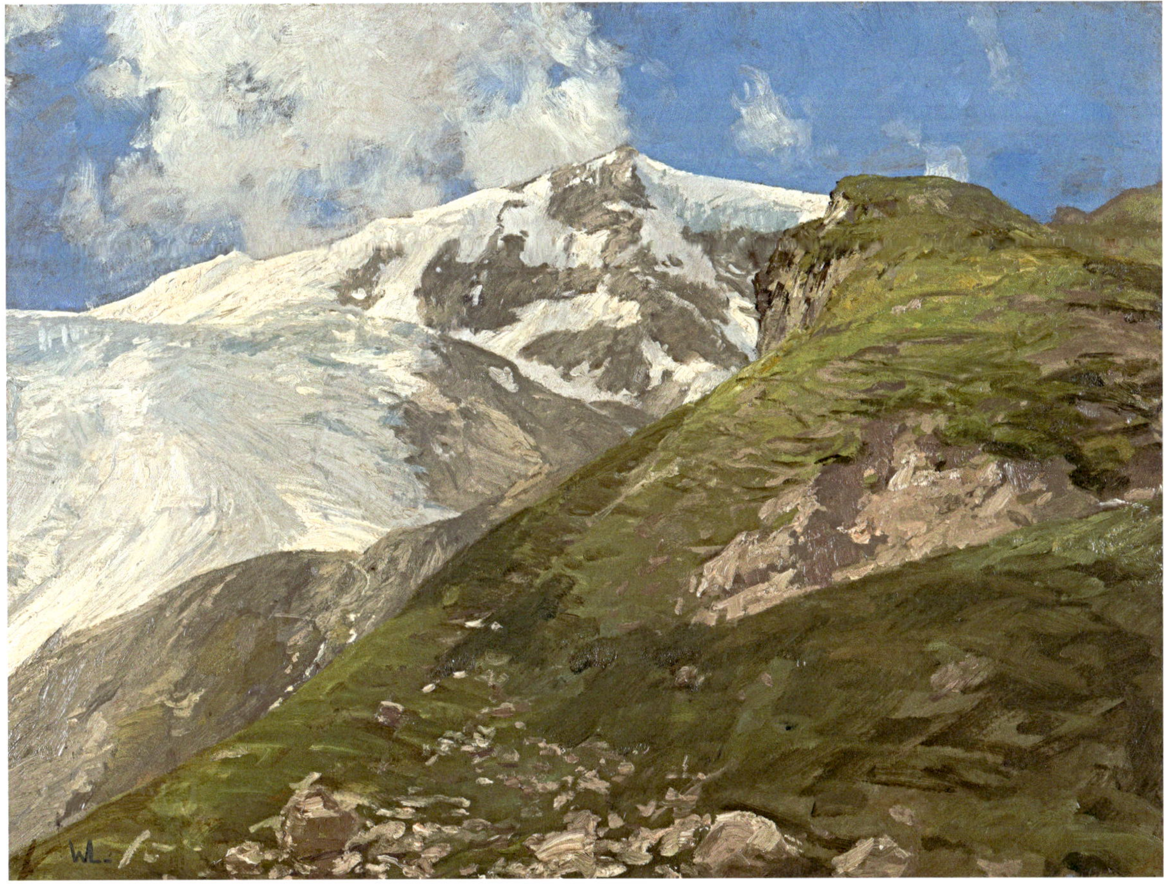

⟨B⟩
Walter Leistikow
Fjord Landscape ca. 1897
Berlinische Galerie

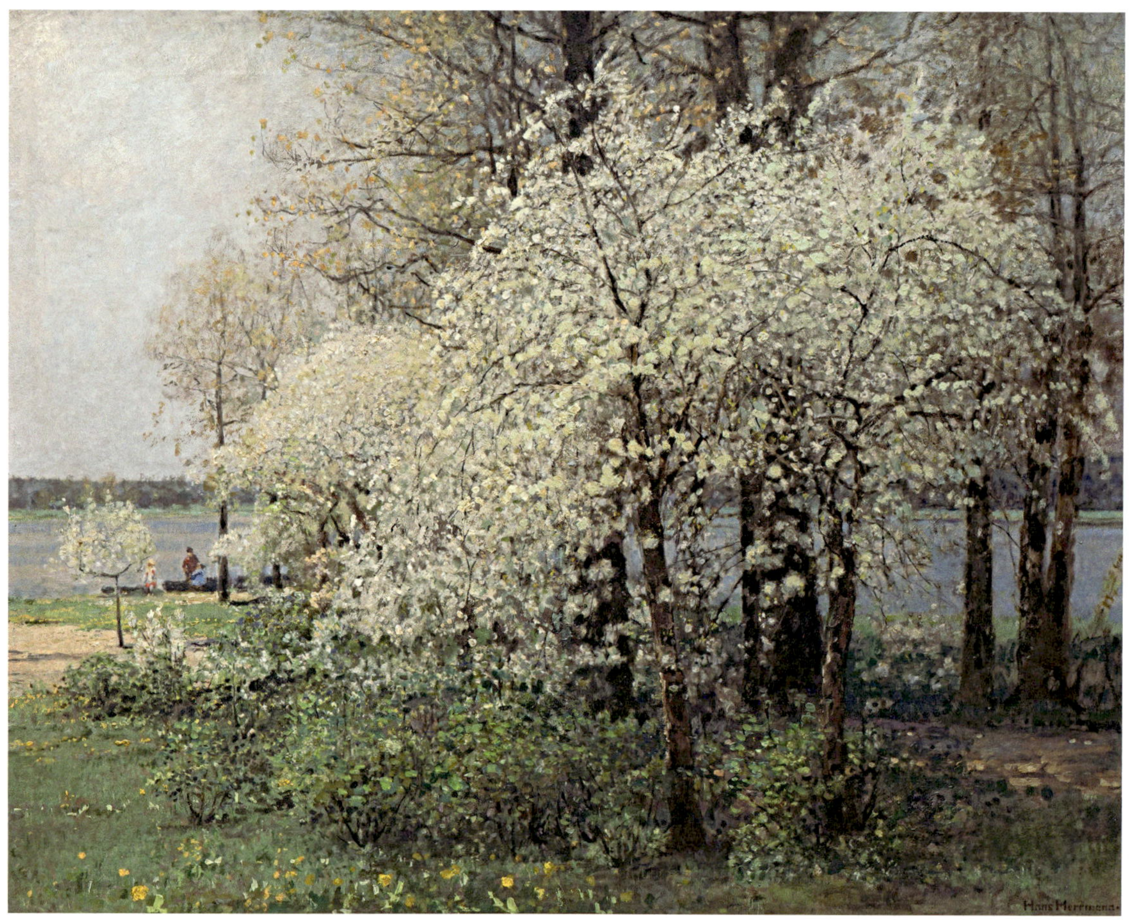

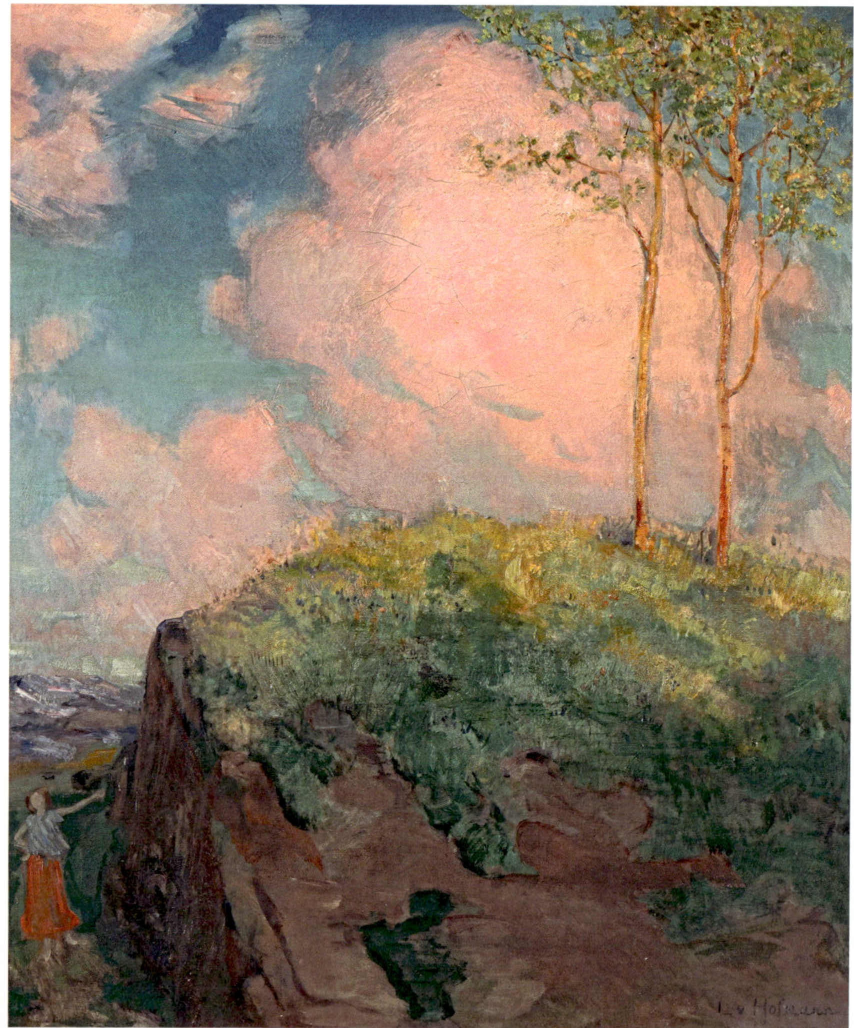

(A)
Hans Hermann
Blossoming Trees — 1894
Berlinische Galerie

(B)
Ludwig von Hofmann
The Pink Cloud — ca. 1903
Berlinische Galerie

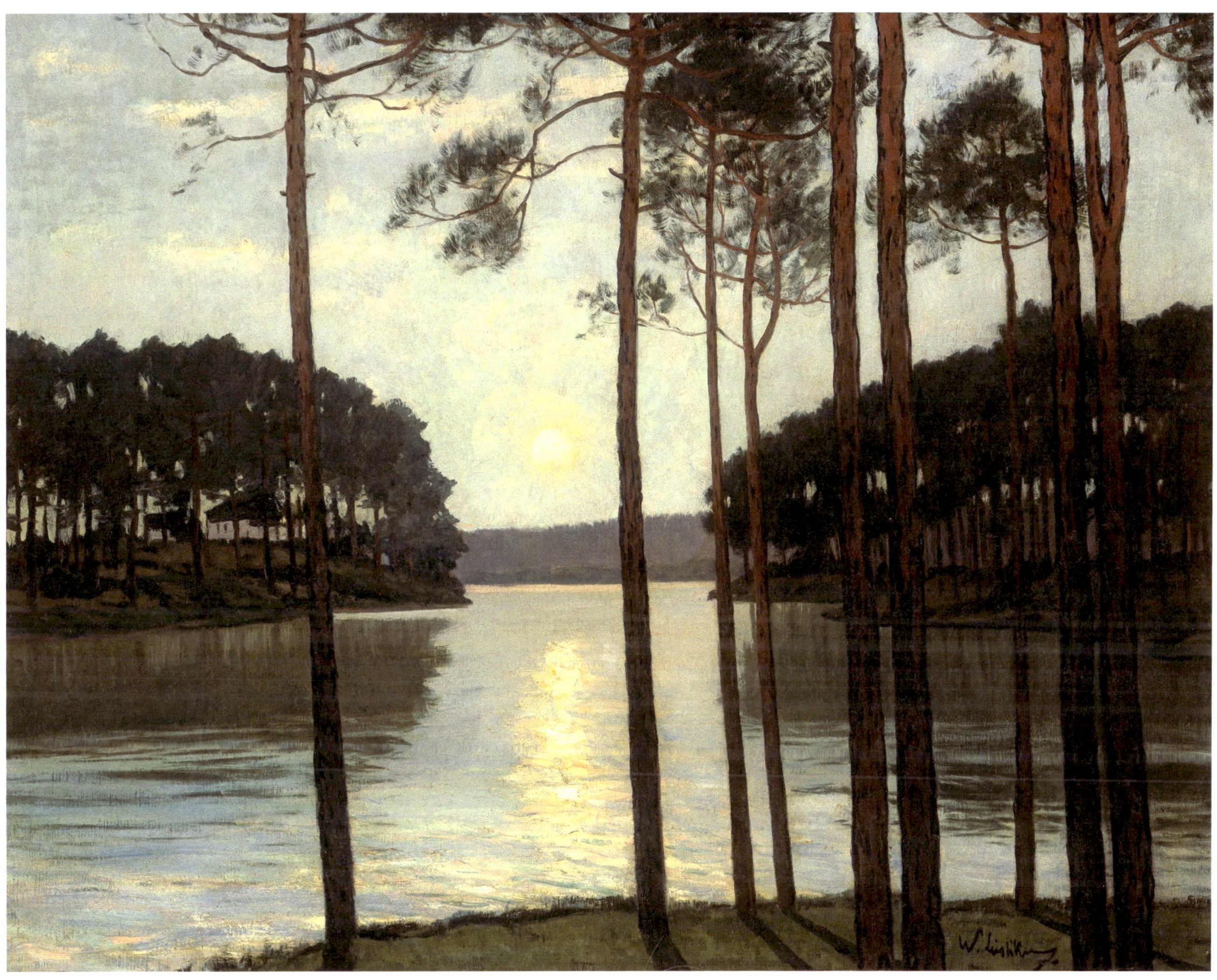

Walter Leistikow
Evening at Schlachtensee — ca. 1895
Stiftung Stadtmuseum — Berlin

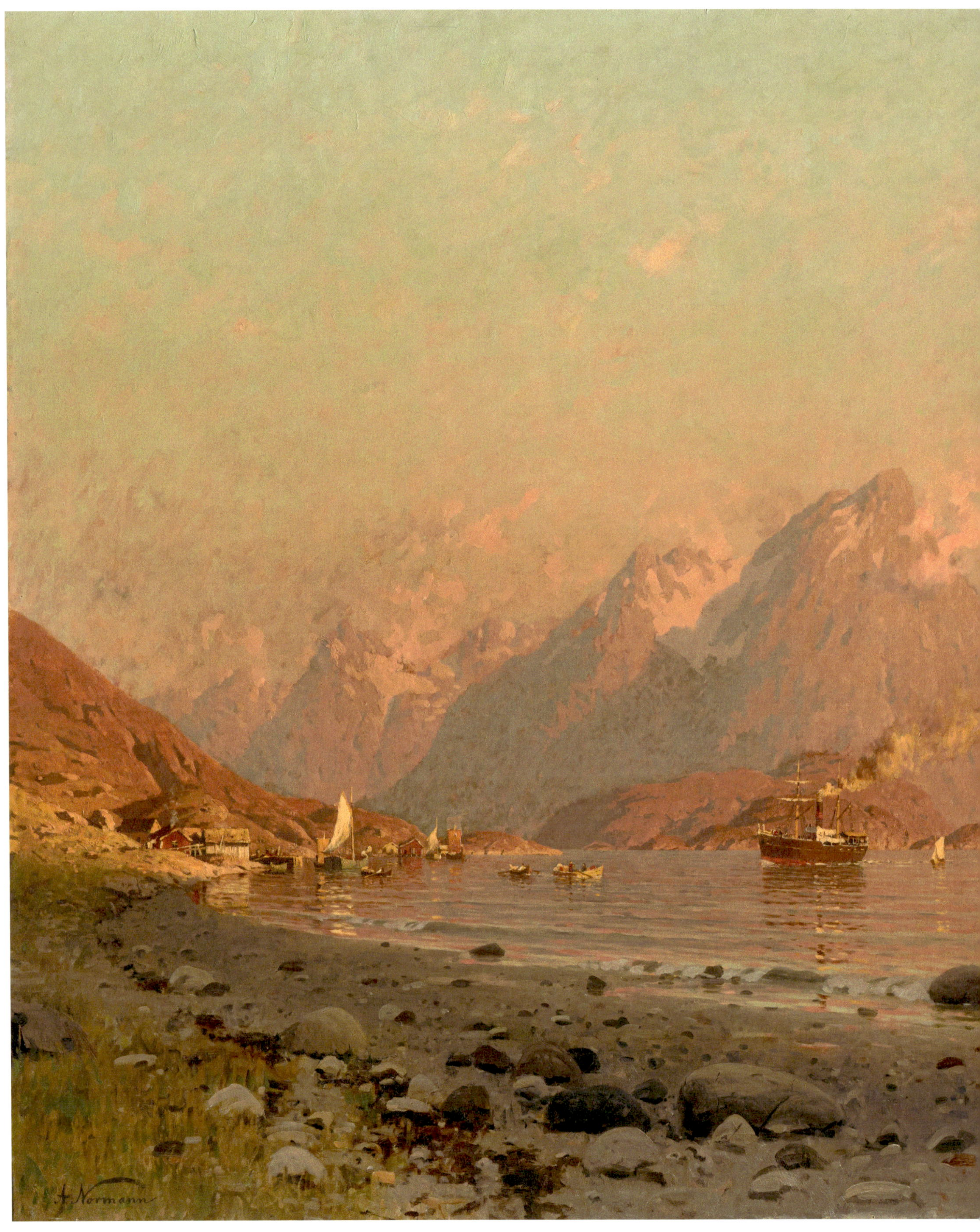
A. Normann

Adelsteen Normann
Summer Evening in the Lofoten — before 1891
Staatliche Museen zu Berlin
Nationalgalerie

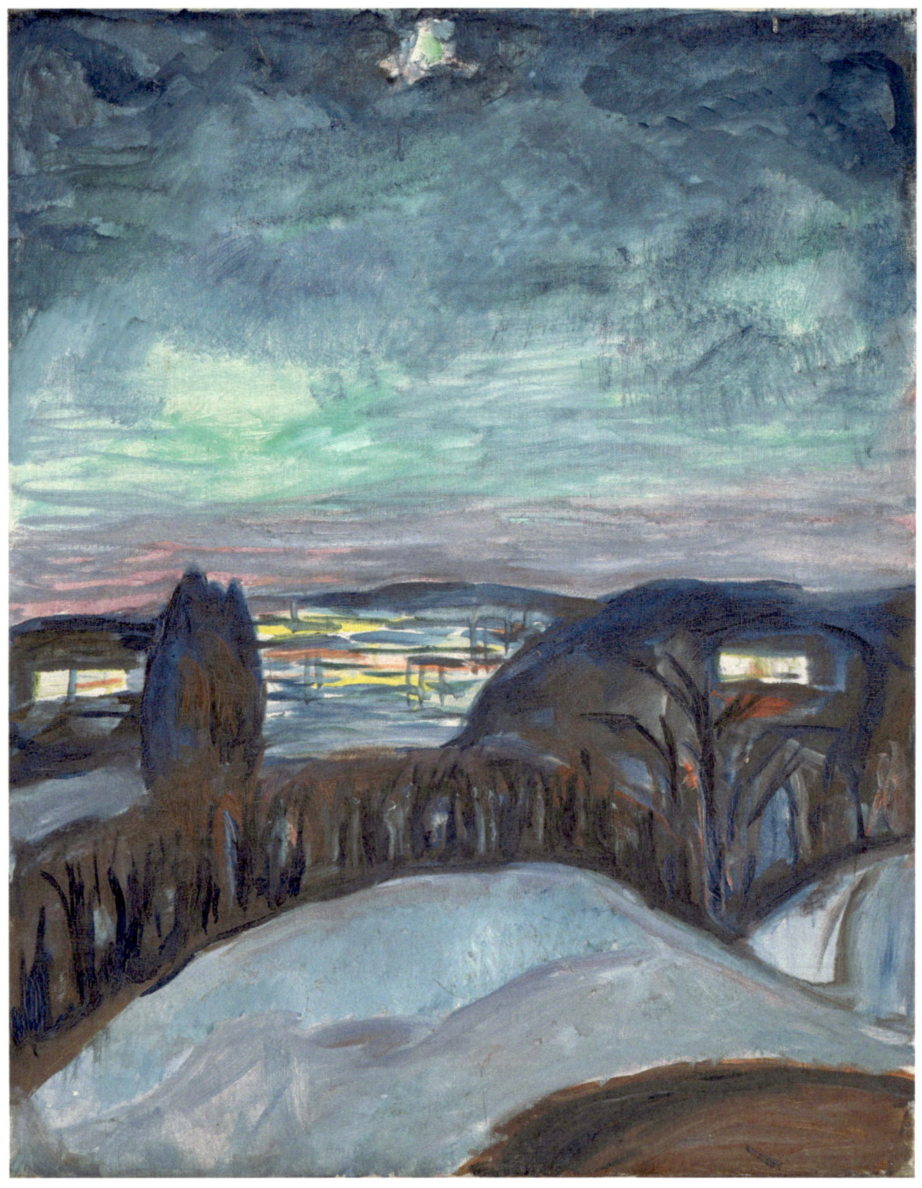

Edvard Munch
Starry Night — 1922–24
Munchmuseet — Oslo

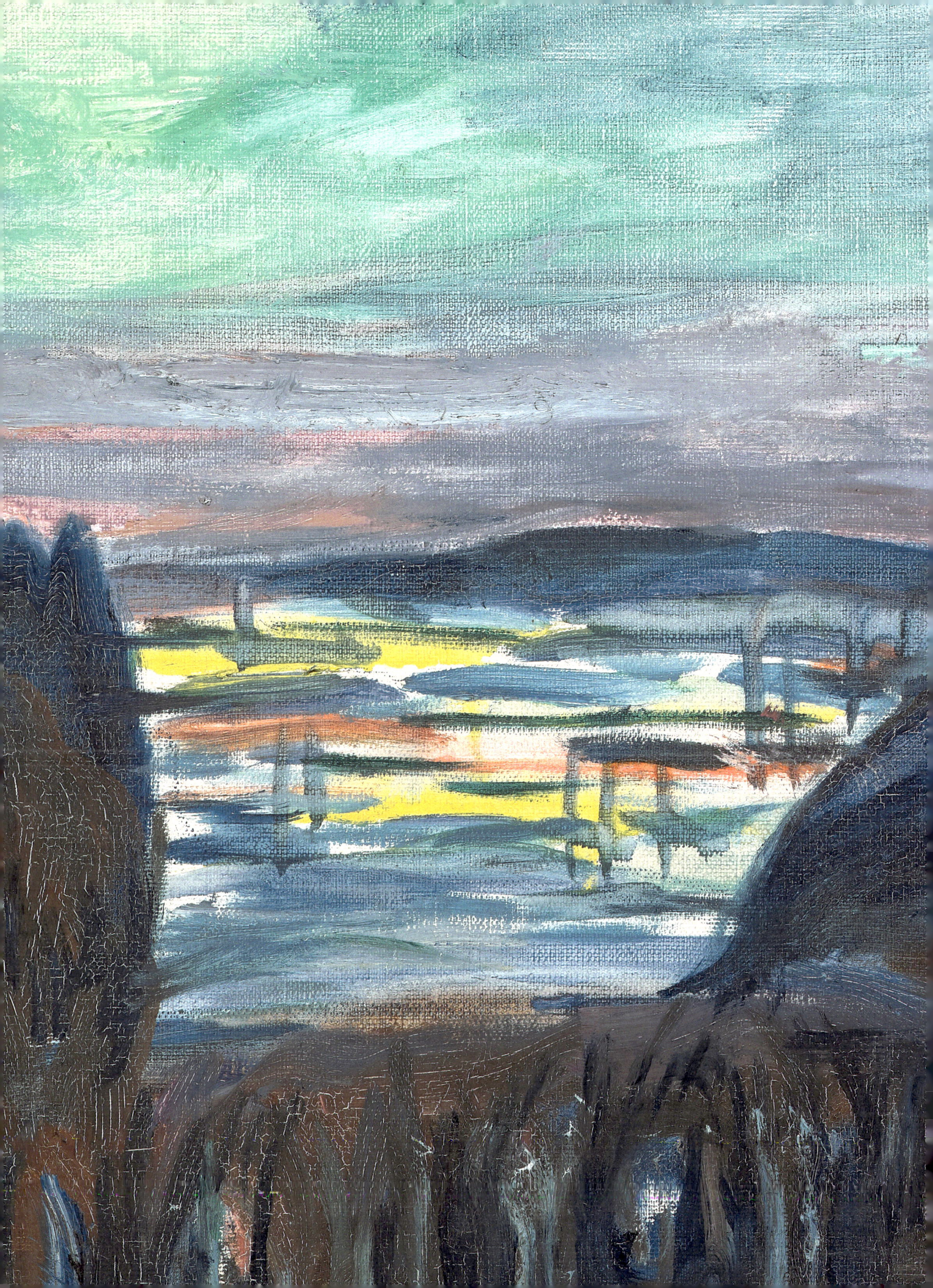

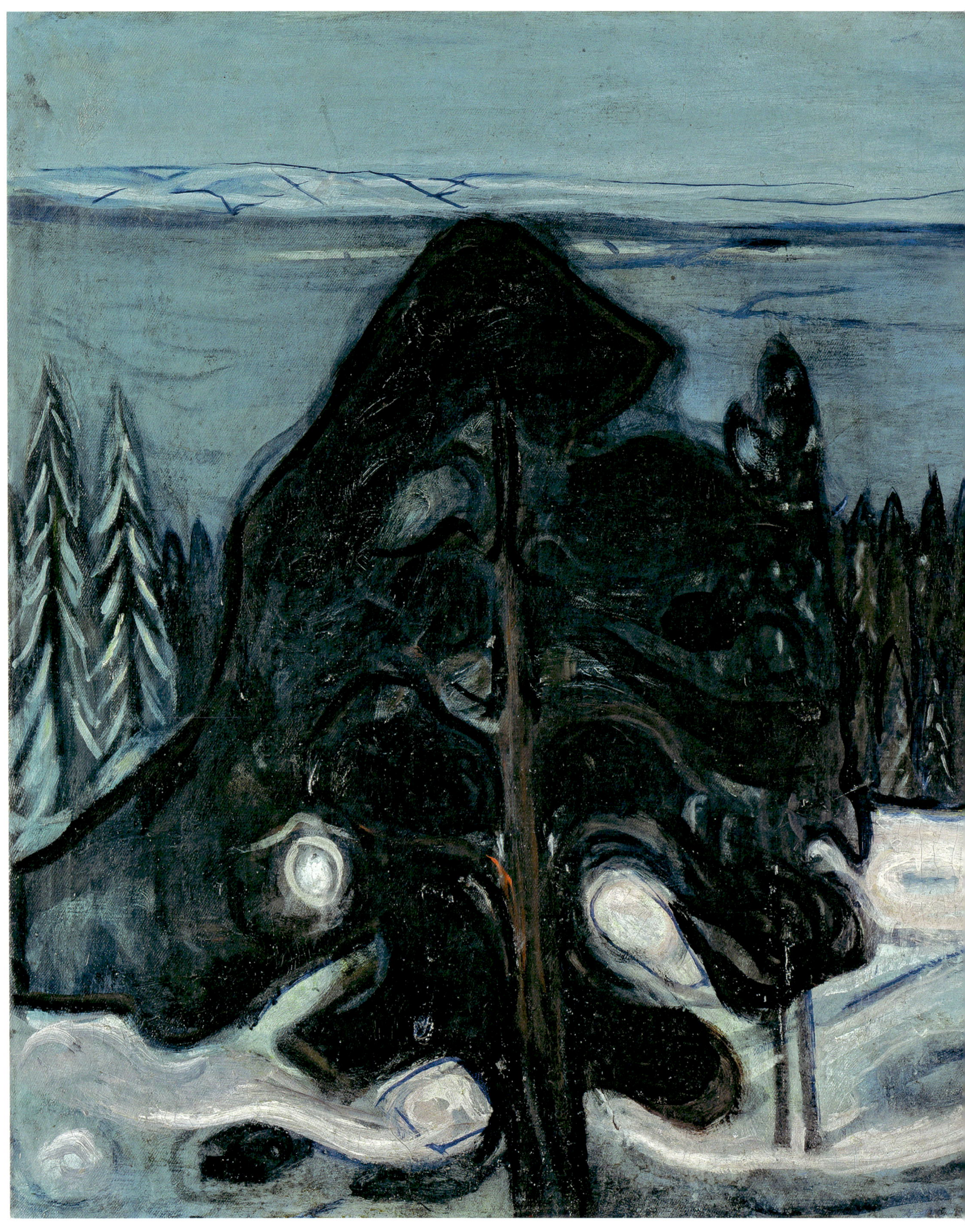

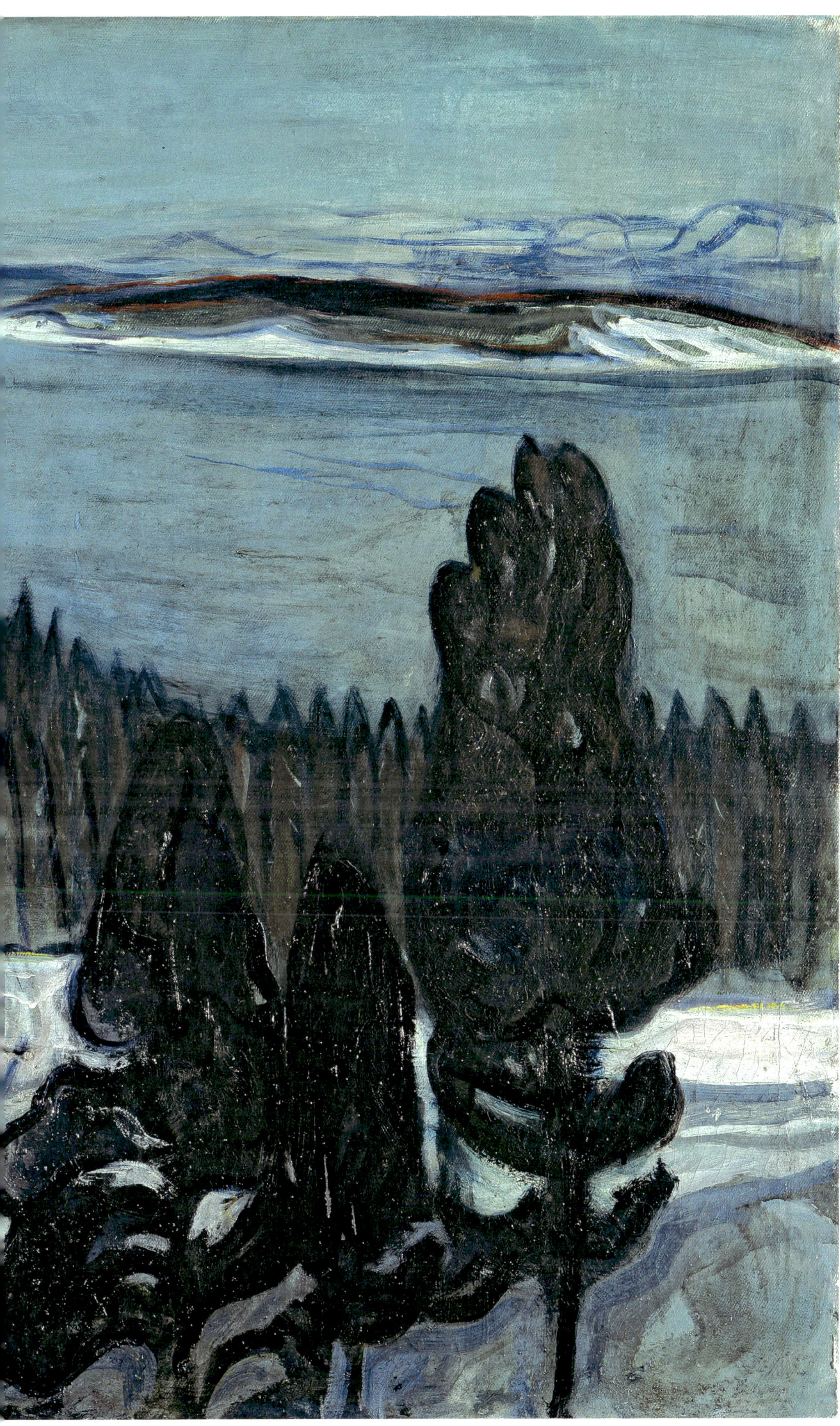

Edvard Munch
Winter Night — ca. 1900
Kunsthaus Zürich

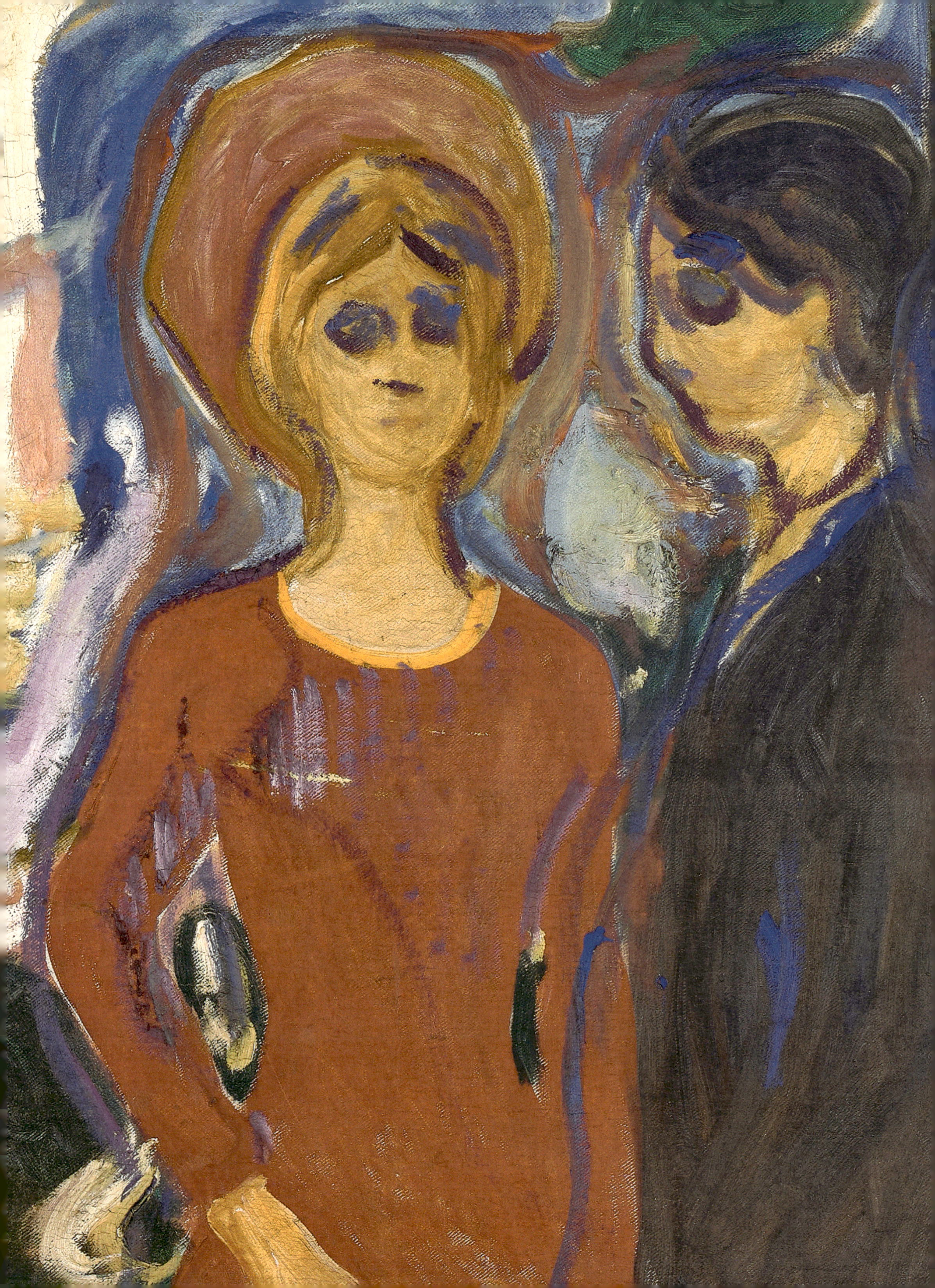

Breathing and Feeling, Suffering and Loving

The Frieze of Life

Edvard Munch was ahead of the art of his time. He was interested in psychology, in the elemental emotional states that constitute life and that he saw as the connection between people. His avant-garde paintings on the themes of love, anxiety, and death met with a lack of understanding and resistance from the public in his early years. In Berlin, Munch began to experiment with presenting his works as series. He himself had noted early on: "There should be living people who breathe and feel, suffer and love." As an open narrative on a "modern life of the soul," Munch wanted to bring his works closer to his audience.

The Frieze of Life, as the artist later called this project, became Munch's magnum opus and remained a work in progress until his death, varied again and again with different versions of his central motifs. In 1902, the artist exhibited his most extensive version, with twenty-two paintings, in the sculpture hall of the Berlin Secession. But this "depiction of a series of images of life" did not result in the great breakthrough for which he had been hoping. He continued to pursue the concept of a decorative frieze in other contexts: in 1904, working primarily in Berlin, he created the so-called *Linde Frieze* for the Lübeck art collector Max Linde. After the client rejected the frieze, it was exhibited in Berlin in 1905–6 in the studio of the artist Leonhard Boldt. In 1906–7, Munch painted what came to be known as the *Reinhardt Frieze* for a banquet hall at the Kammerspiele (Chamber Theater).

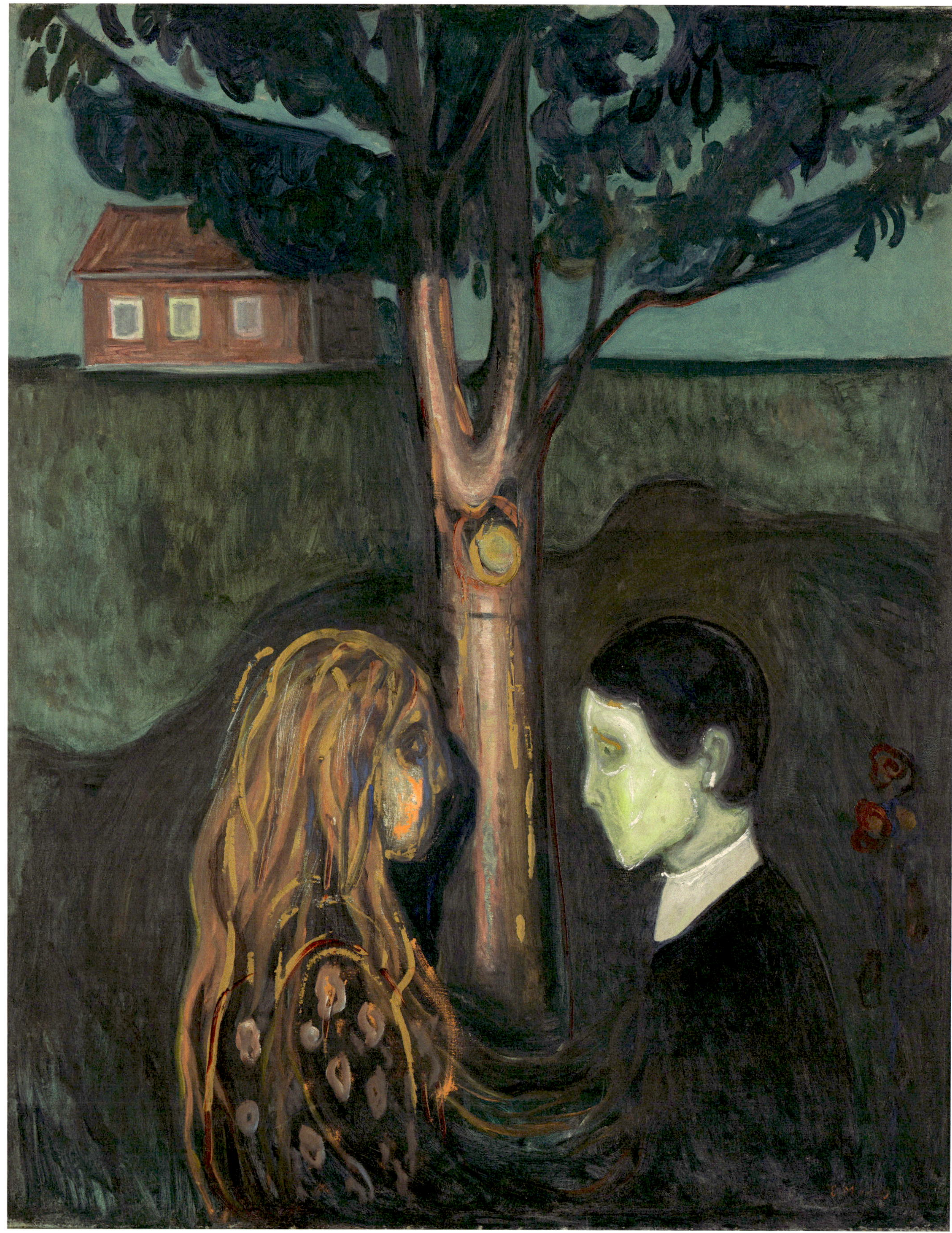

Edvard Munch
Eye in Eye — 1899–1900
Munchmuseet — Oslo

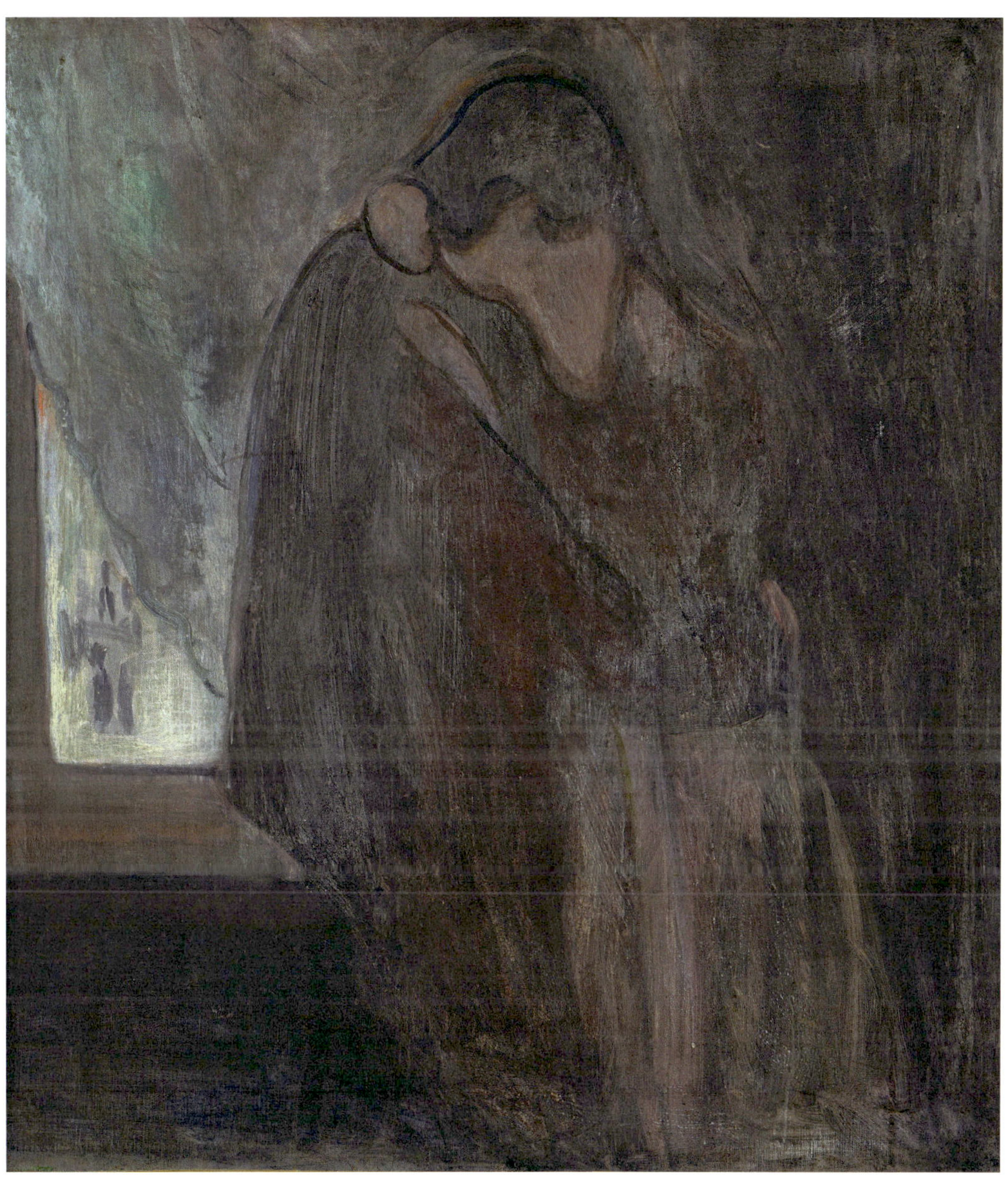

Edvard Munch
The Kiss — 1897
Munchmuseet — Oslo

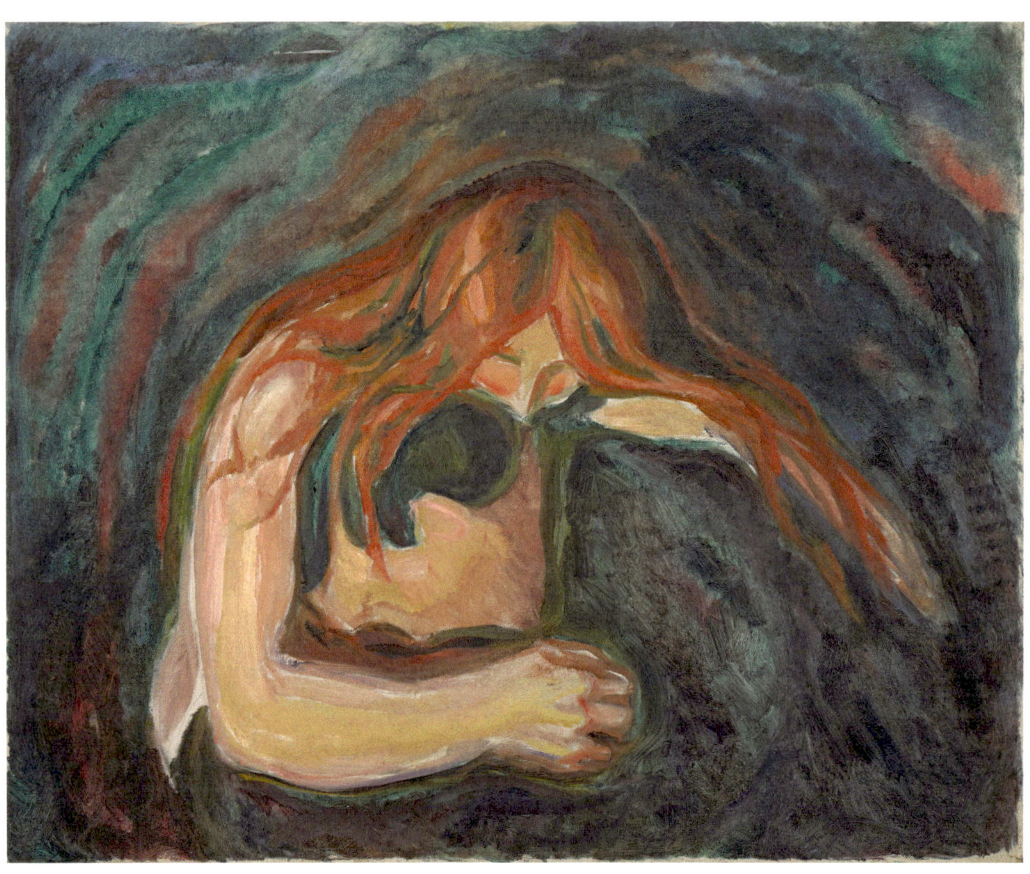

Edvard Munch
Vampire — 1916–18
Munchmuseet — Oslo

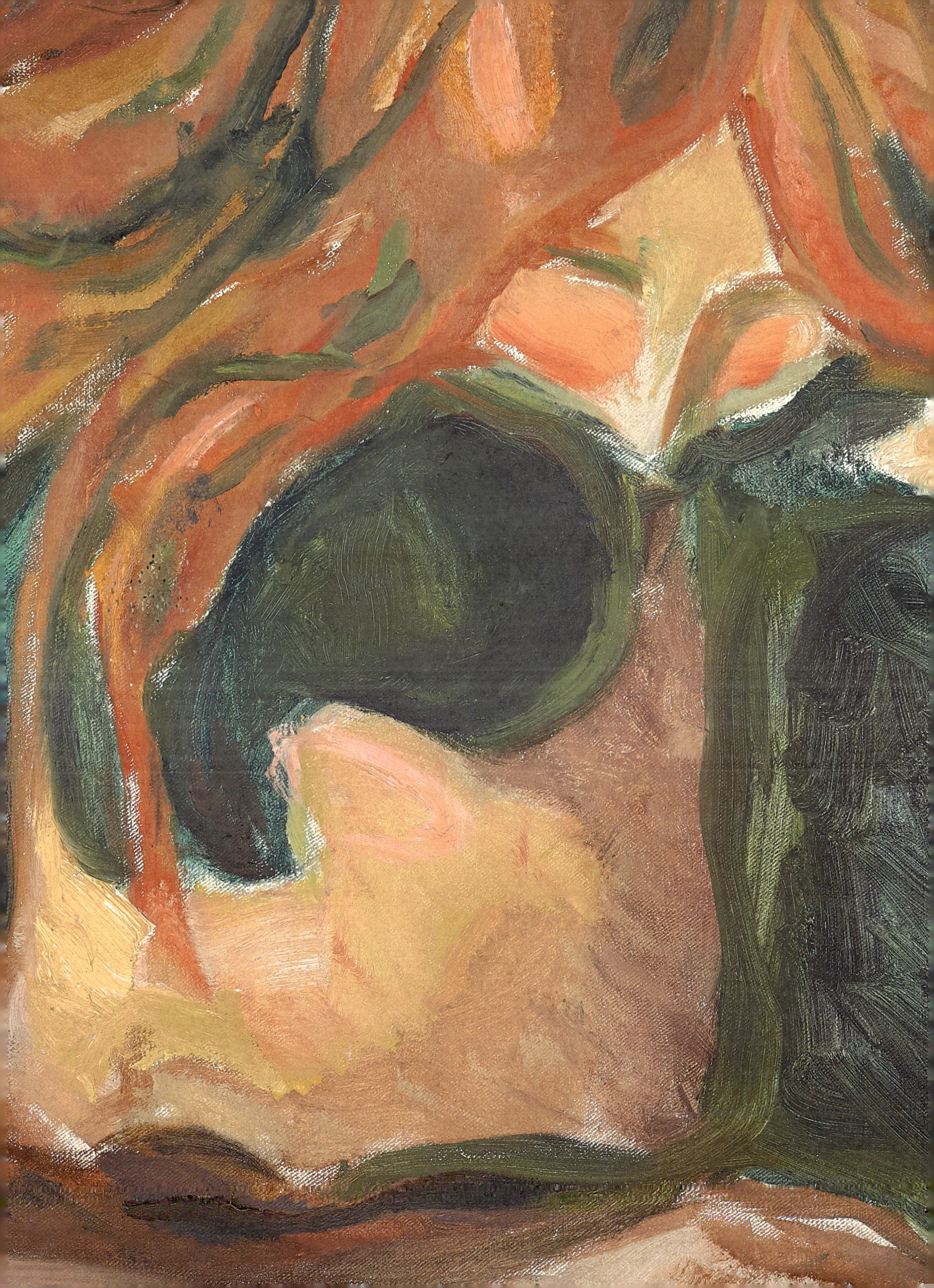

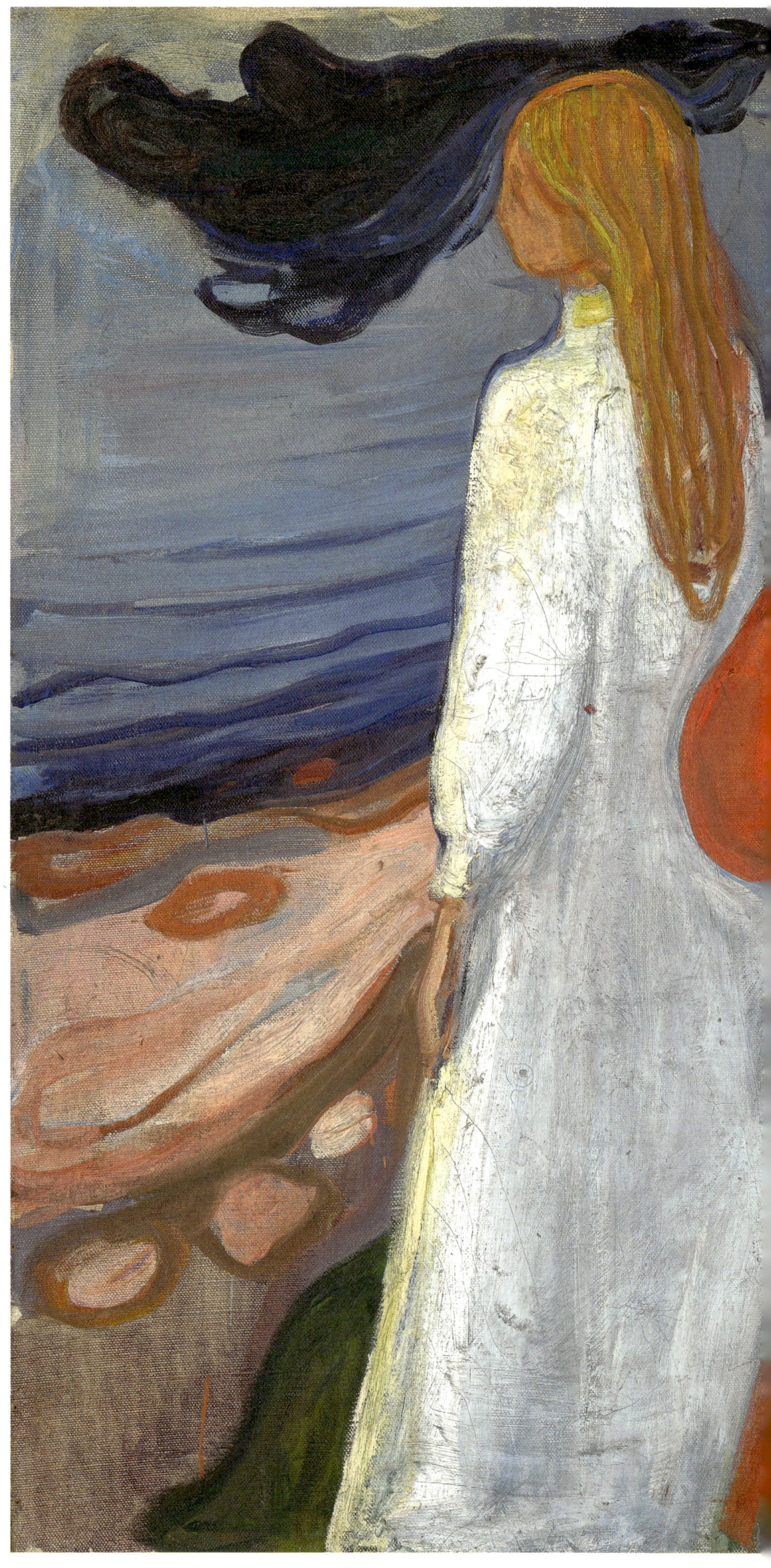

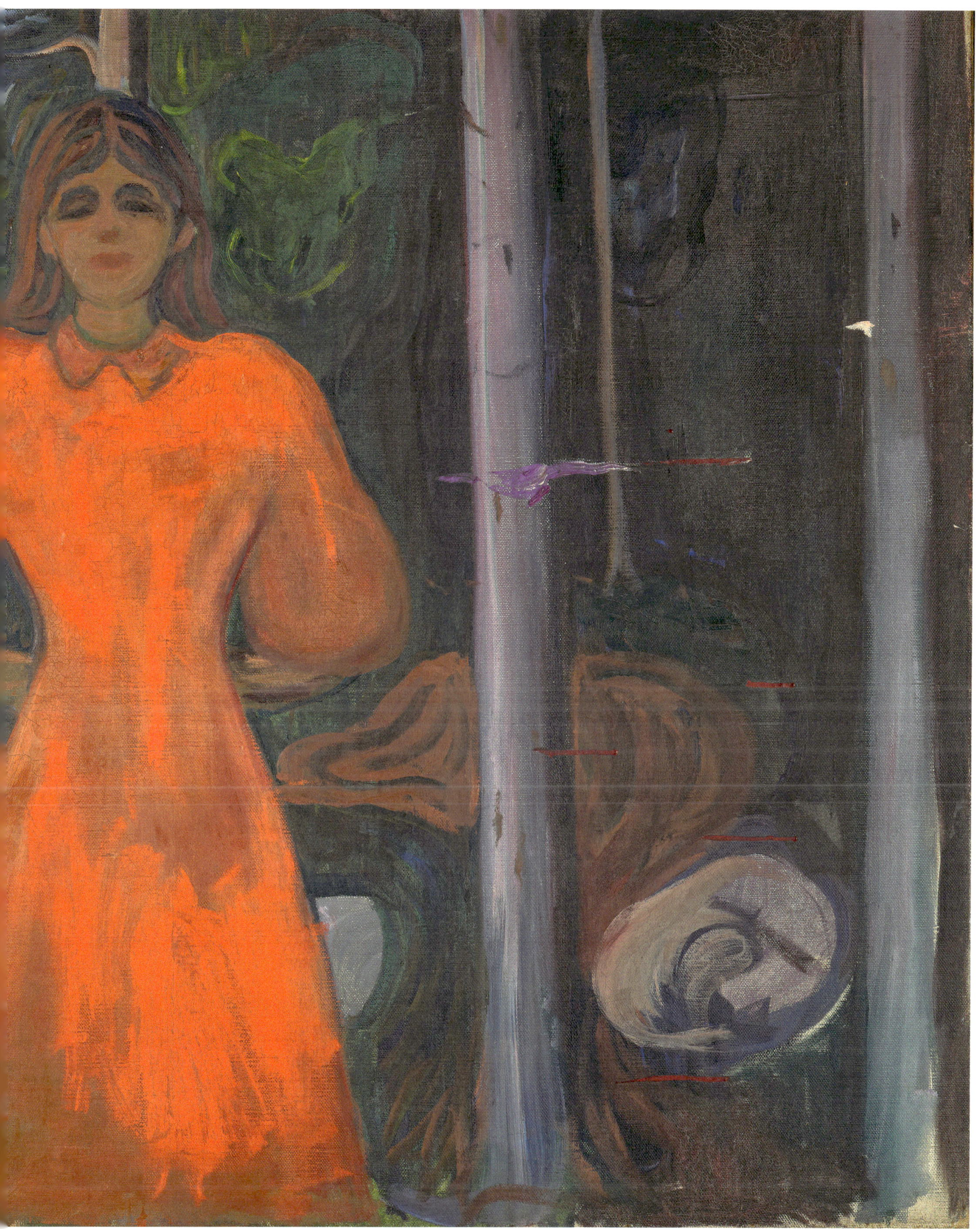

Edvard Munch
Red and White — 1899–1900
Munchmuseet — Oslo

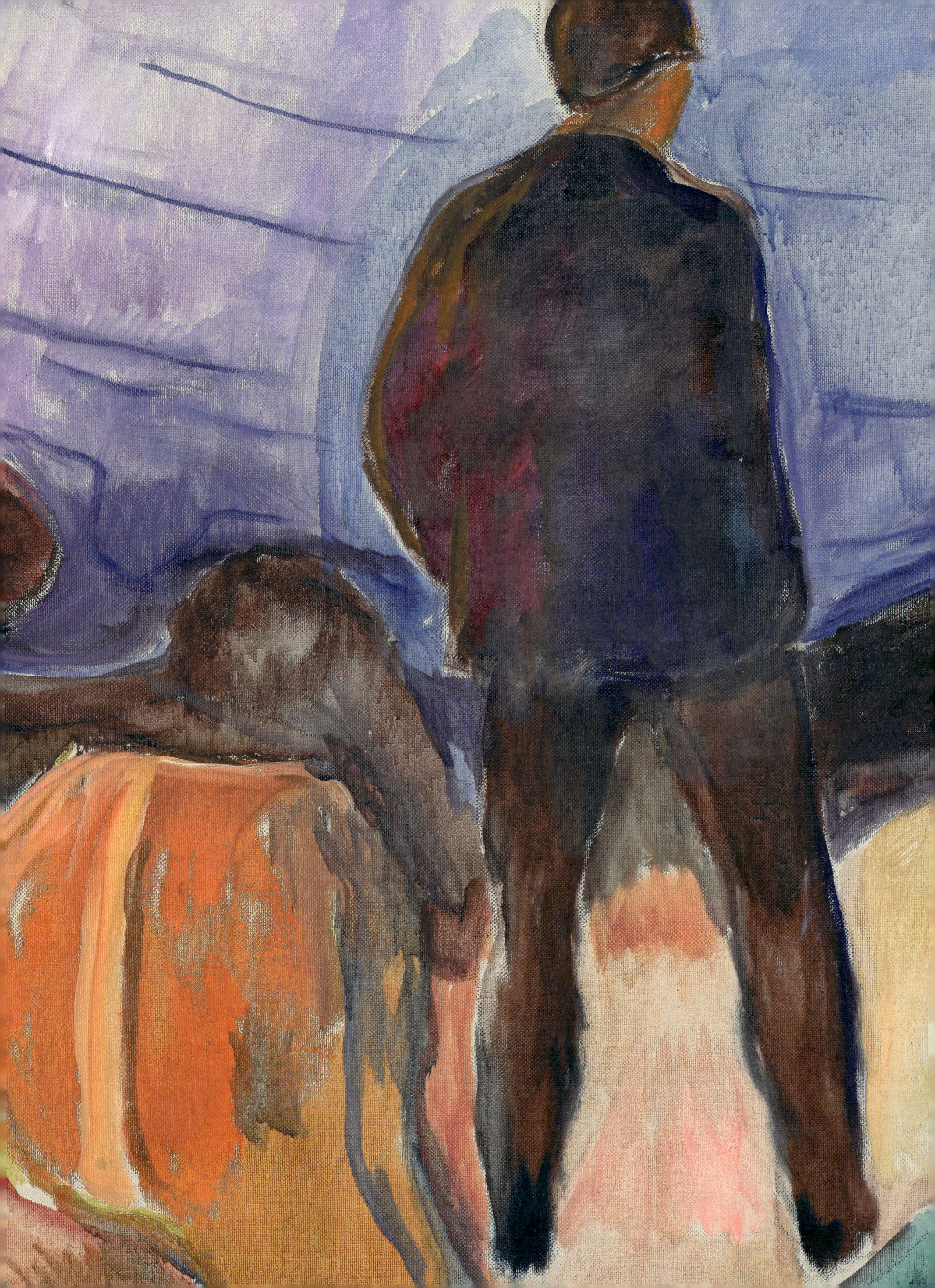

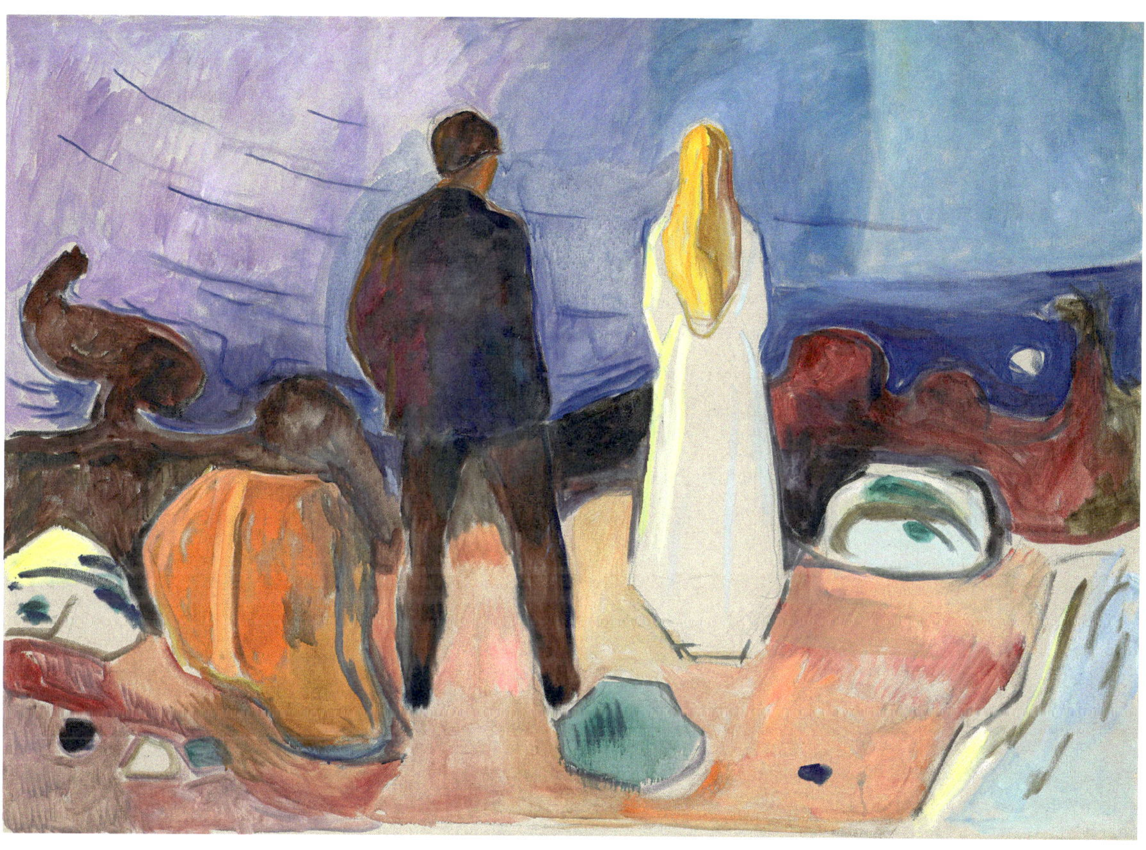

Edvard Munch
Two Human Beings (The Lonely Ones) — ca. 1935
Munchmuseet — Oslo

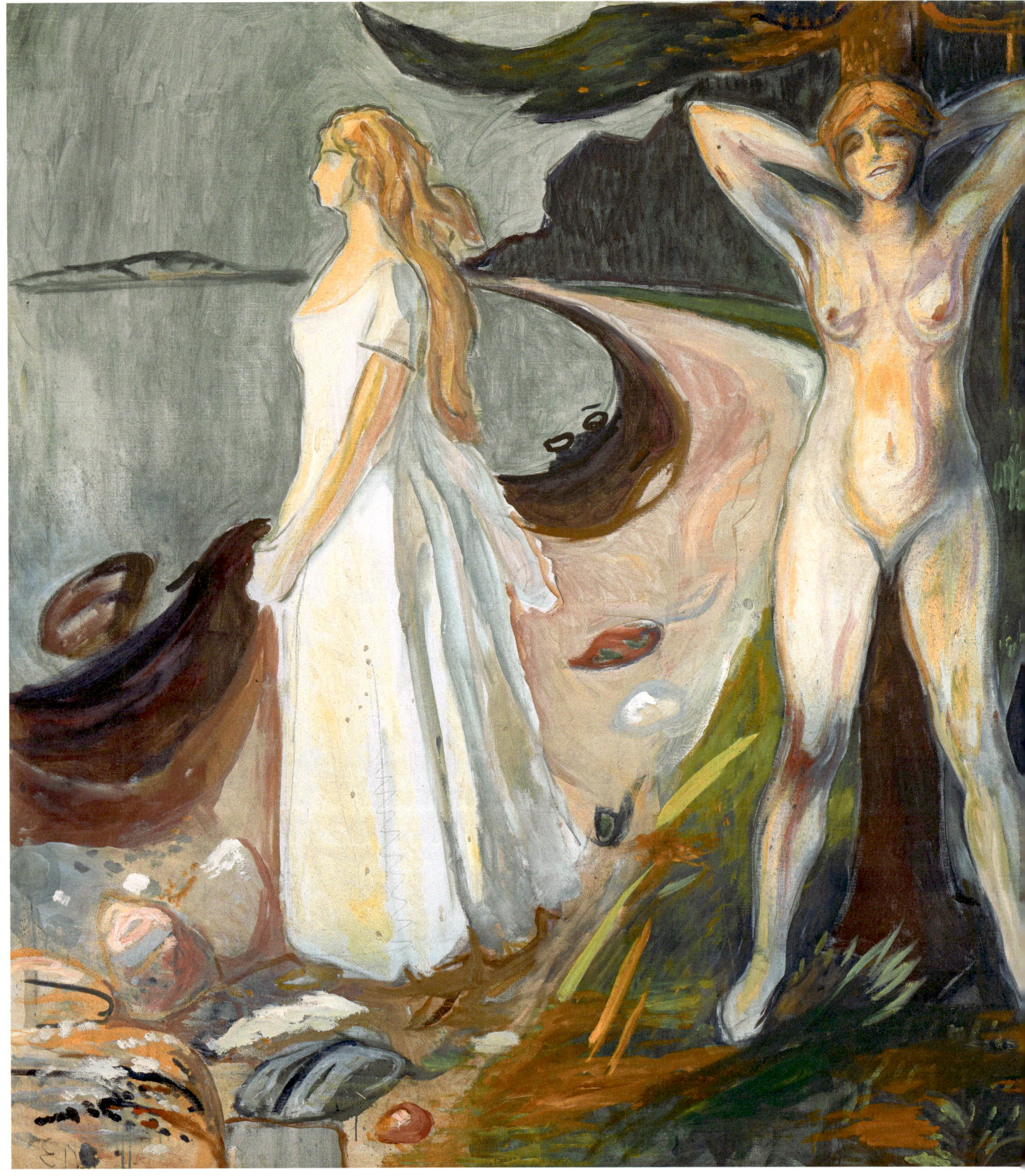

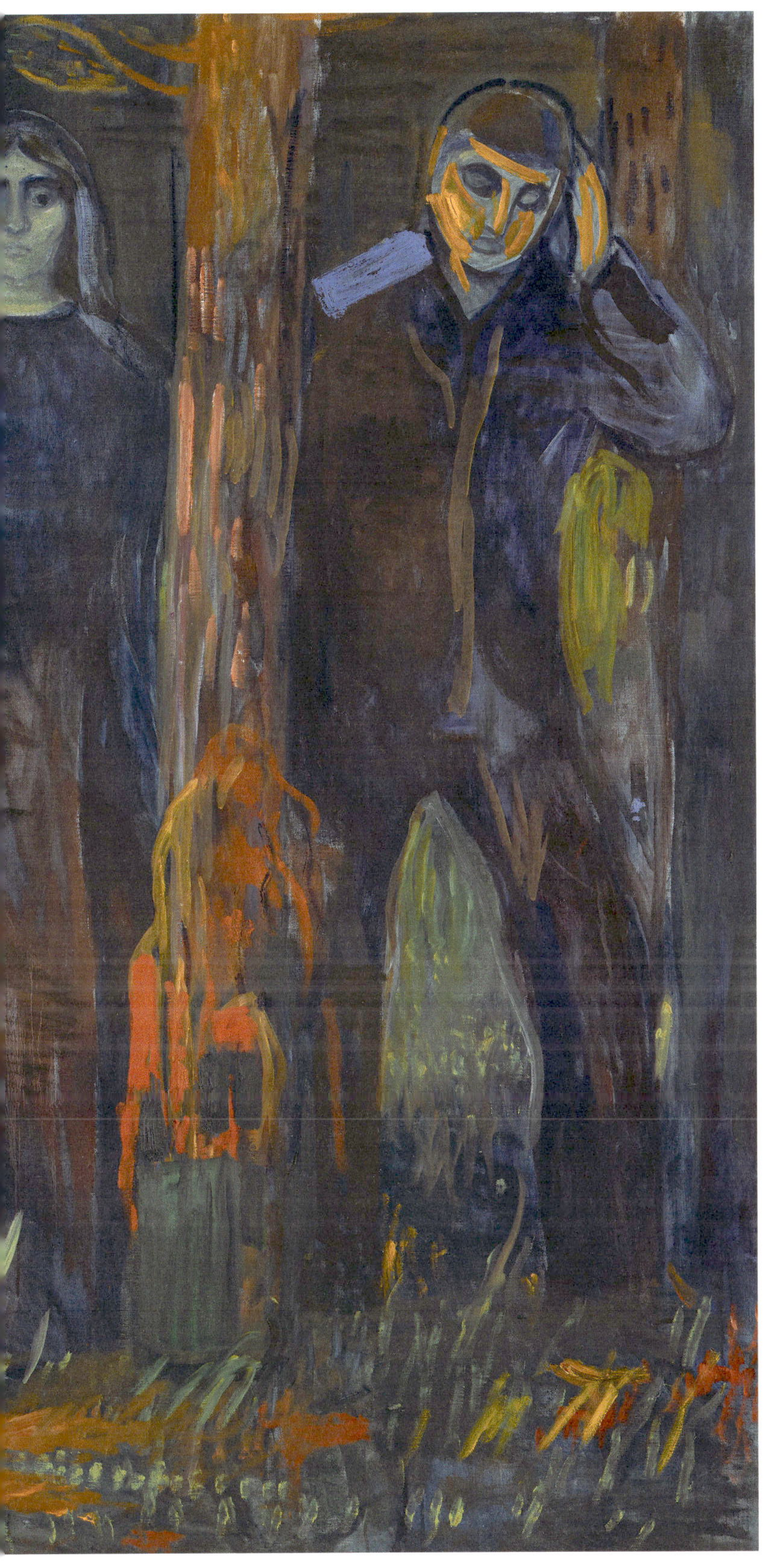

Edvard Munch
Woman — 1925
Munchmuseet — Oslo

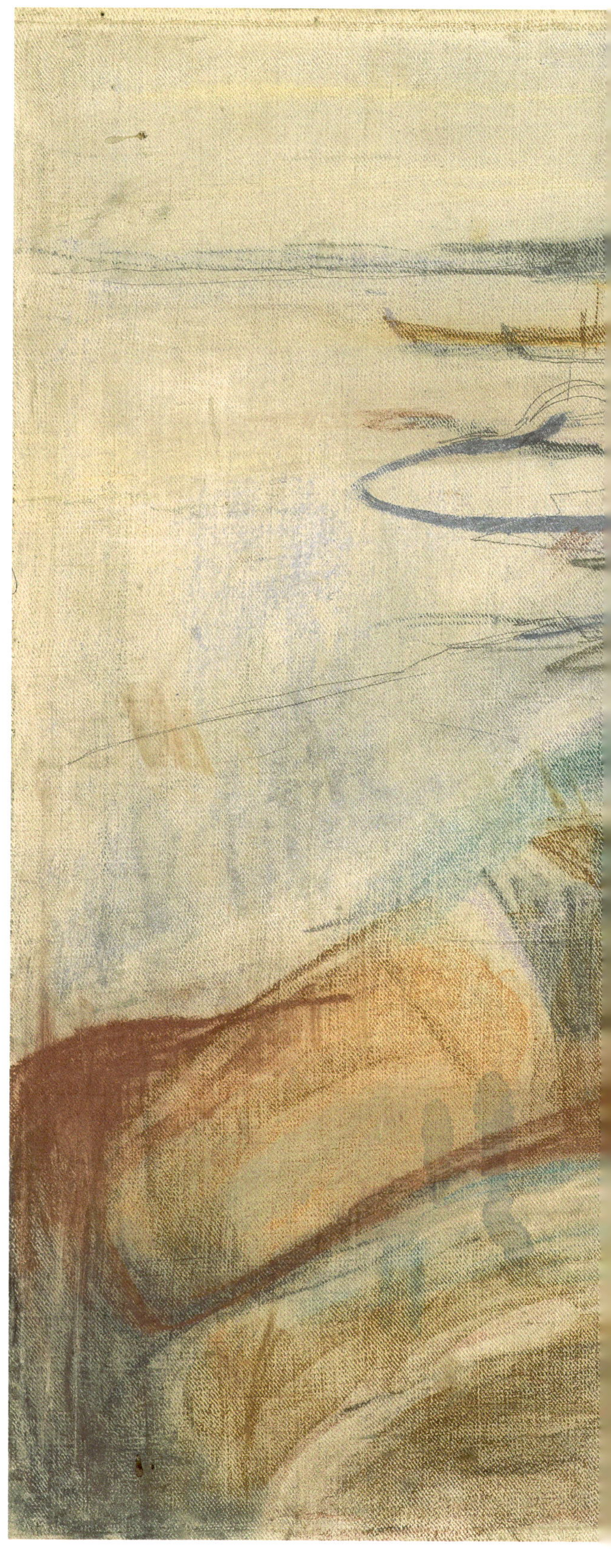

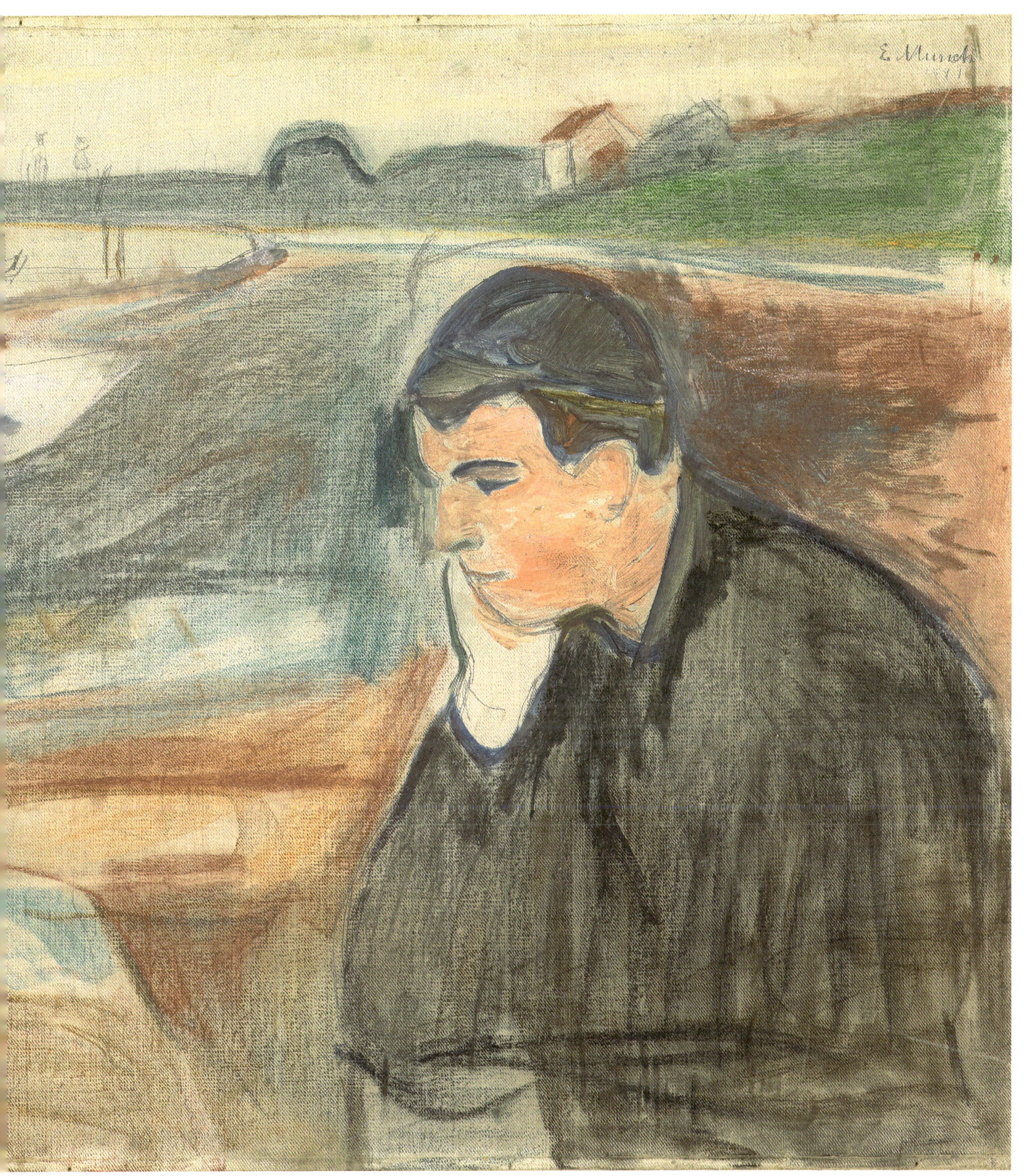

Edvard Munch
Melancholy (Evening) — 1891
Munchmuseet — Oslo

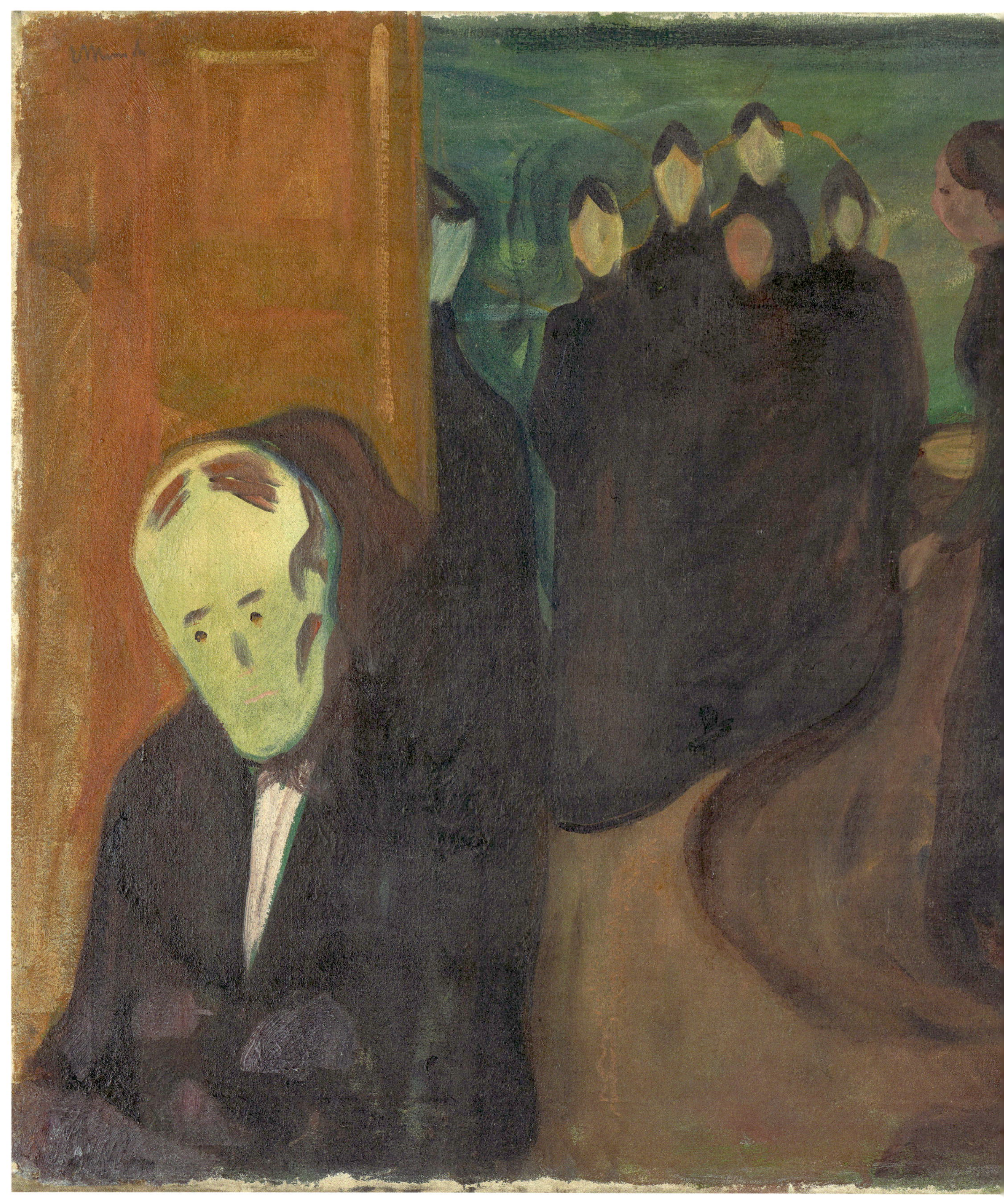

Edvard Munch
Sanatorium — 1902–3
Munchmuseet — Oslo

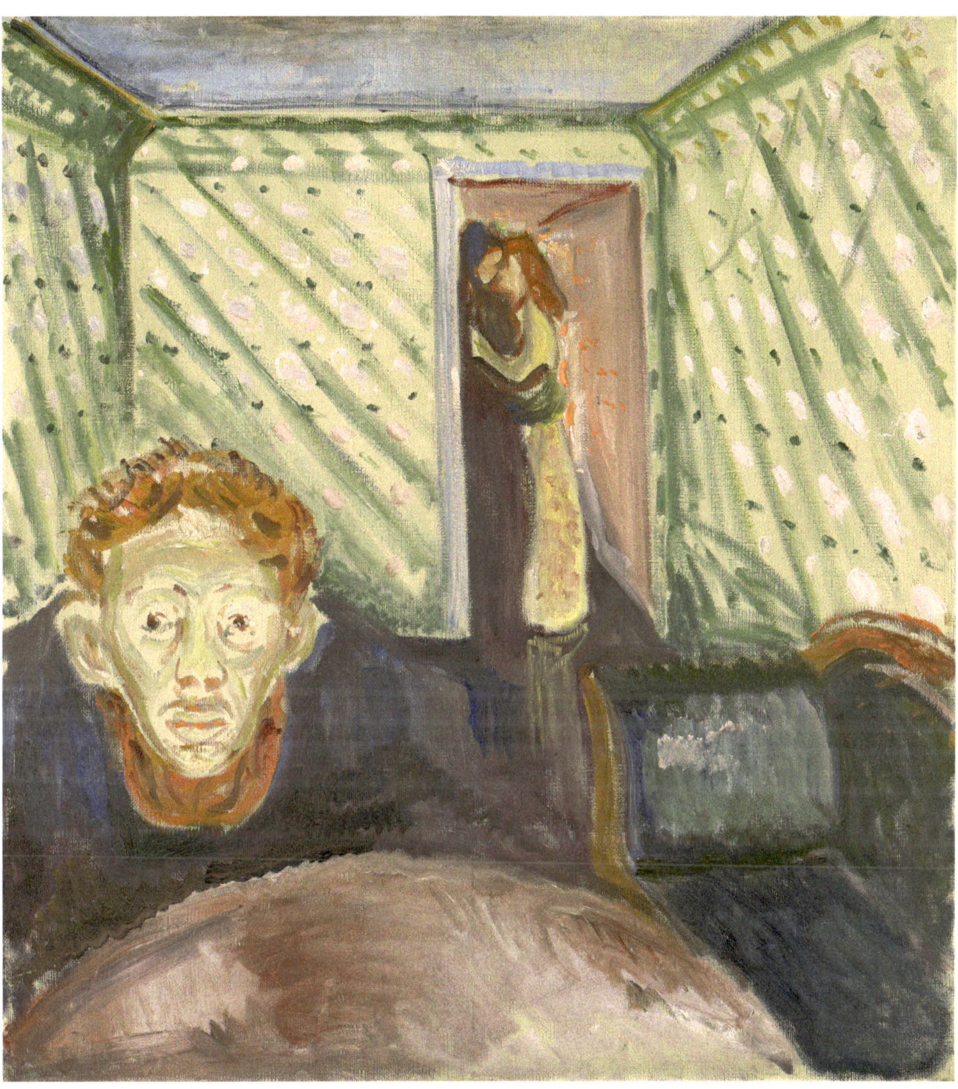

Edvard Munch
Jealousy — 1907
Munchmuseet — Oslo

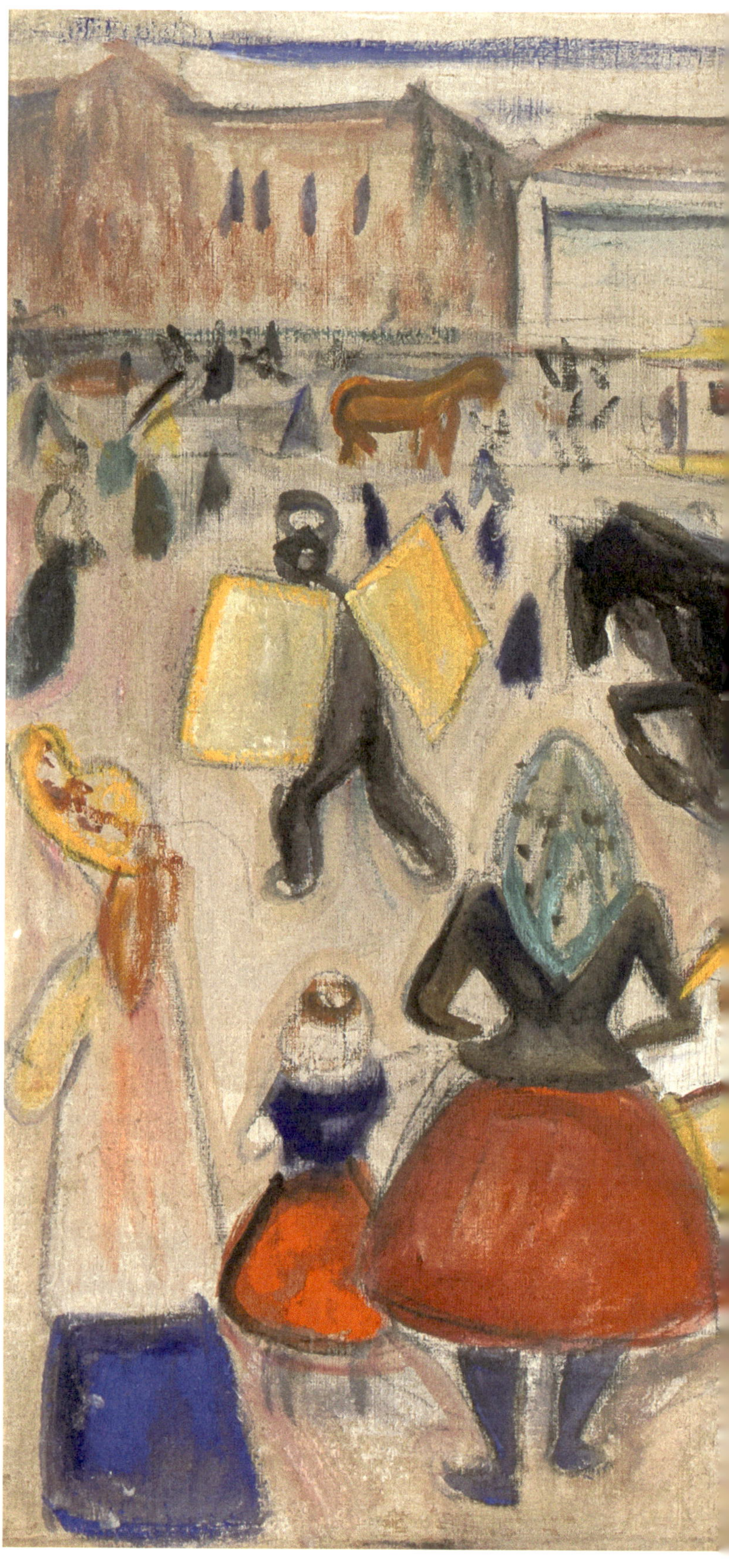

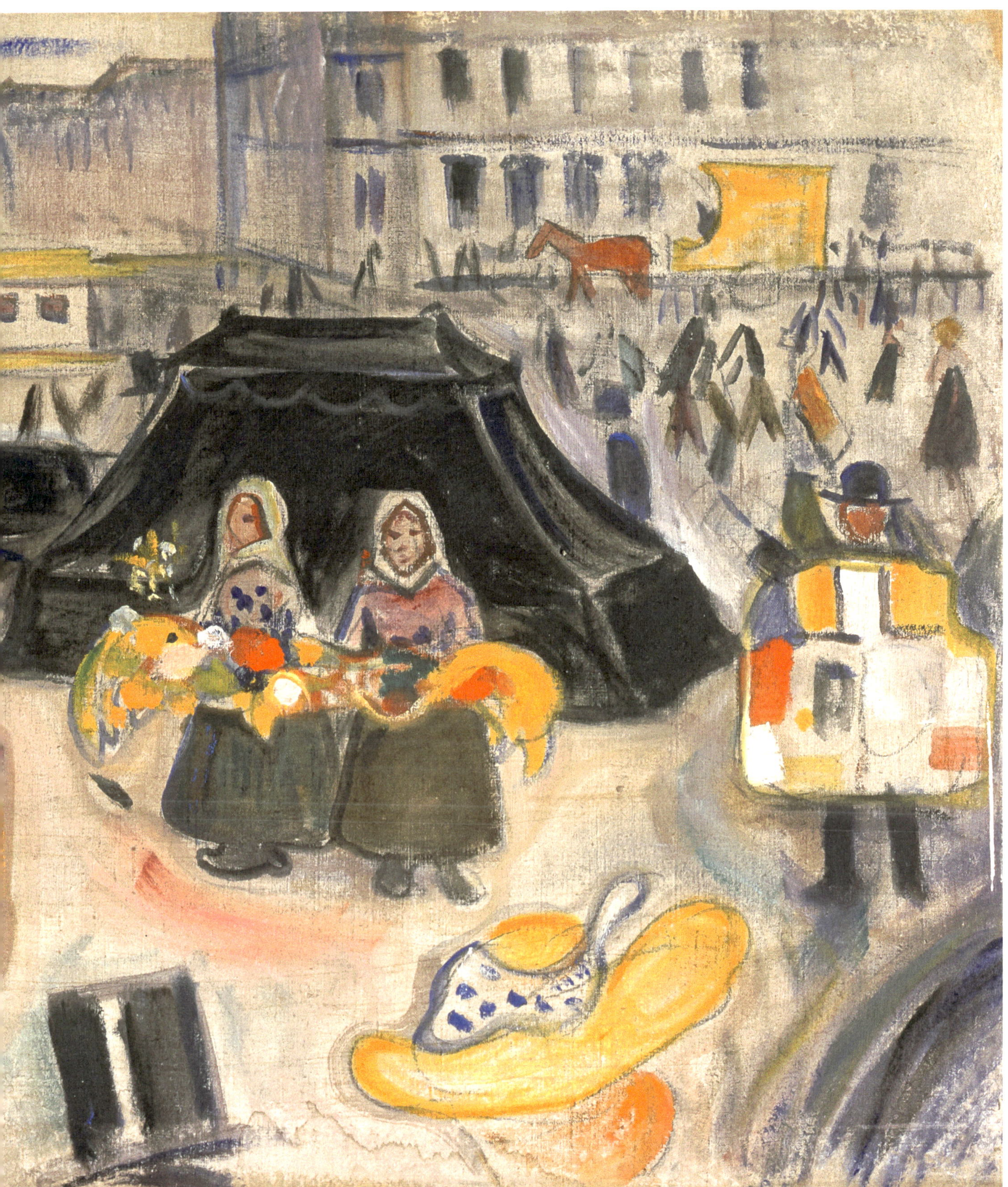

Edvard Munch
The Hearse on Potsdamer Platz — 1902
Munchmuseet — Oslo

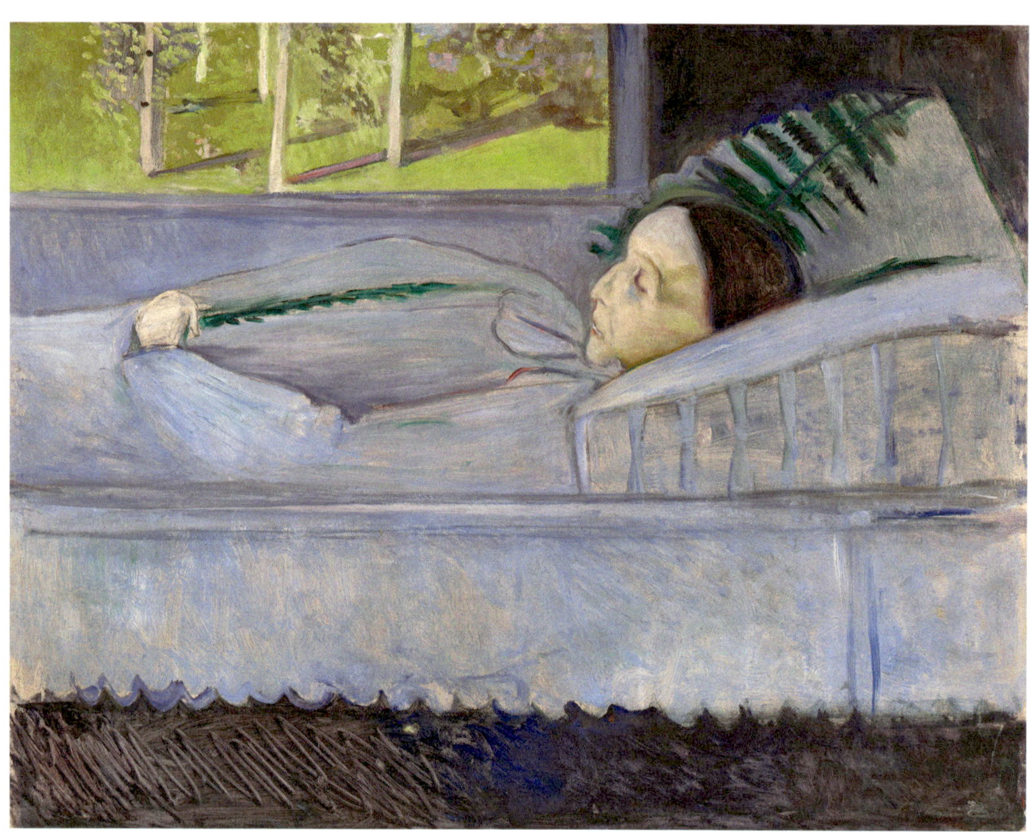

Edvard Munch
Death and Spring — 1893
Munchmuseet — Oslo

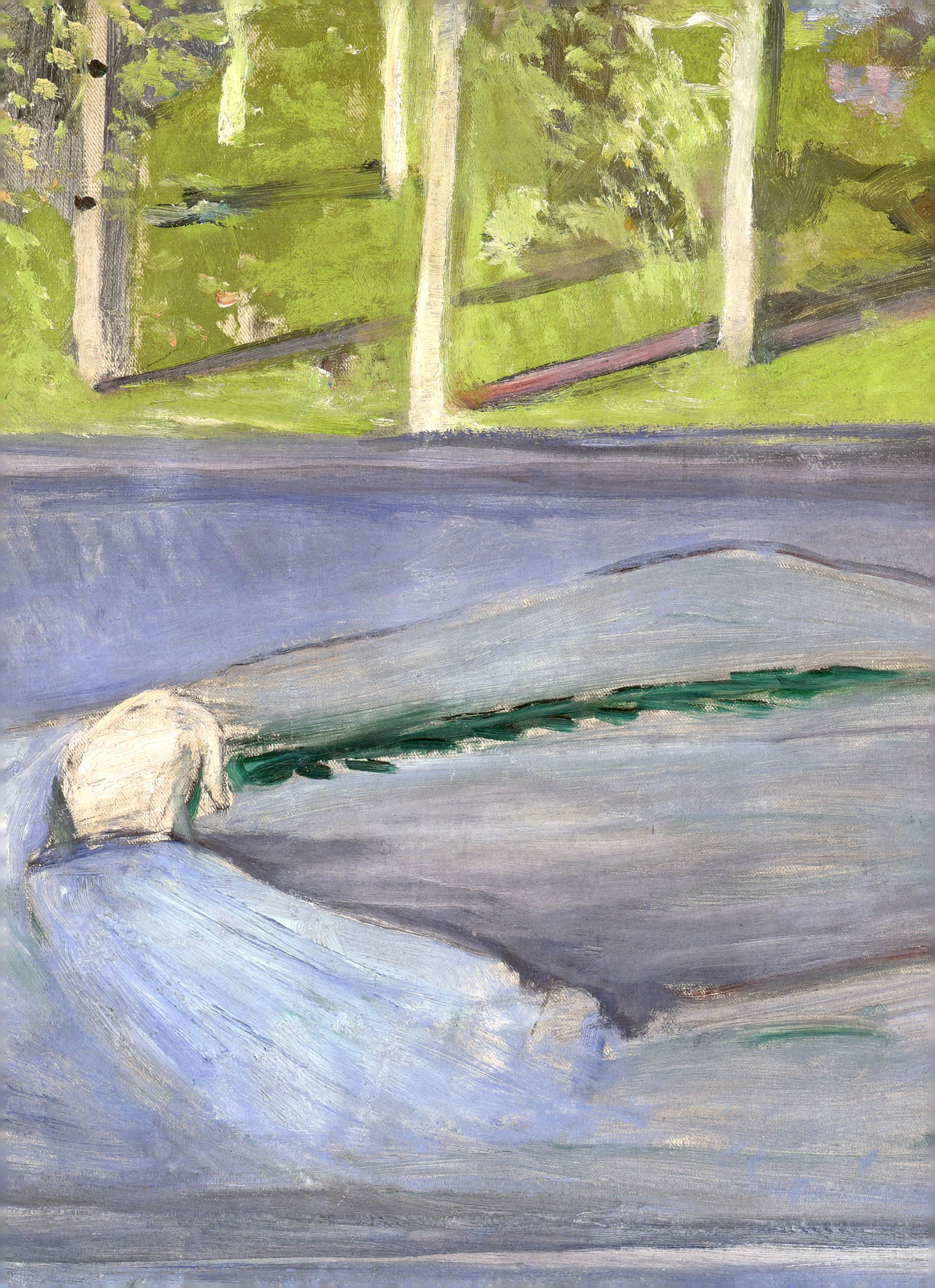

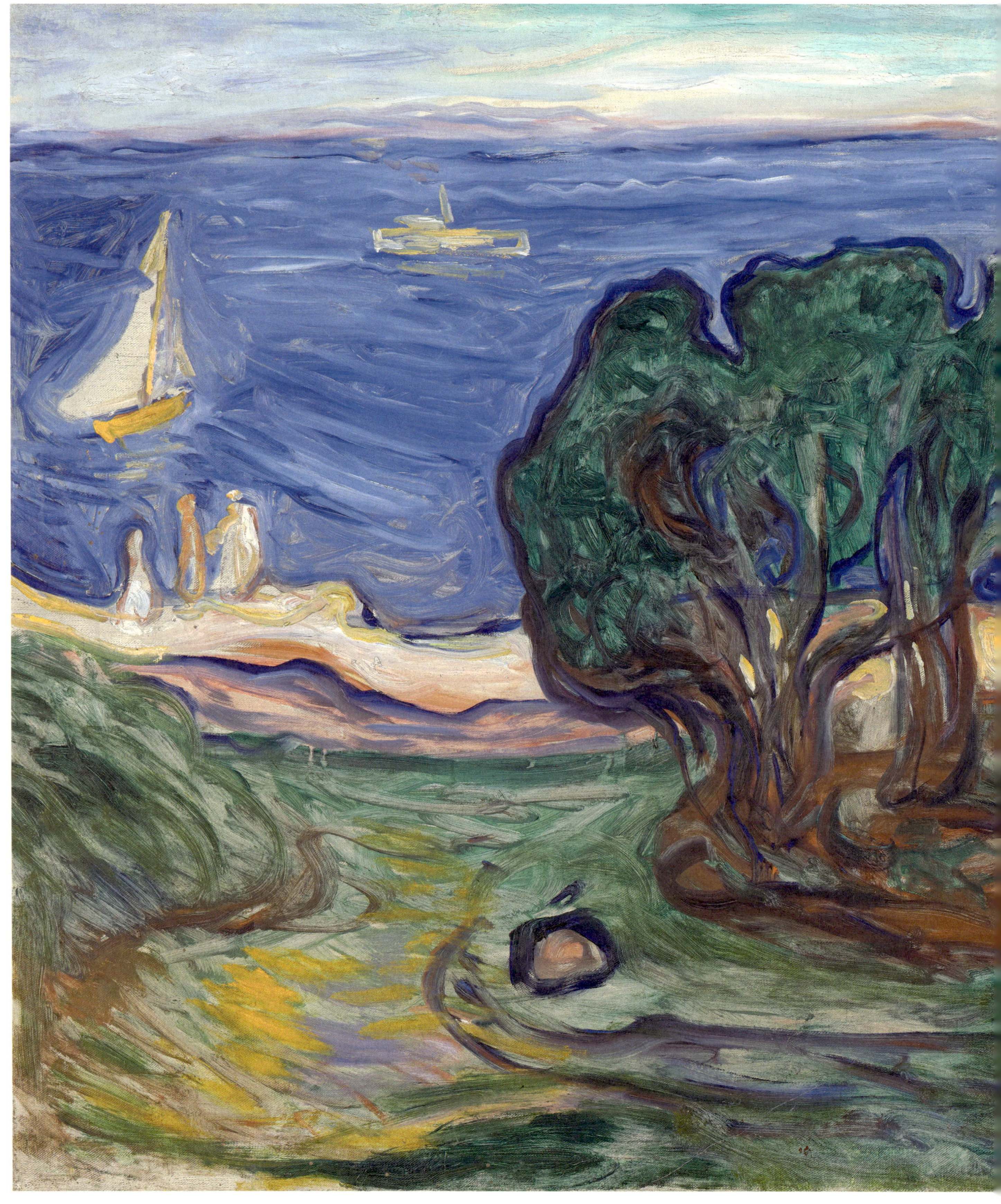

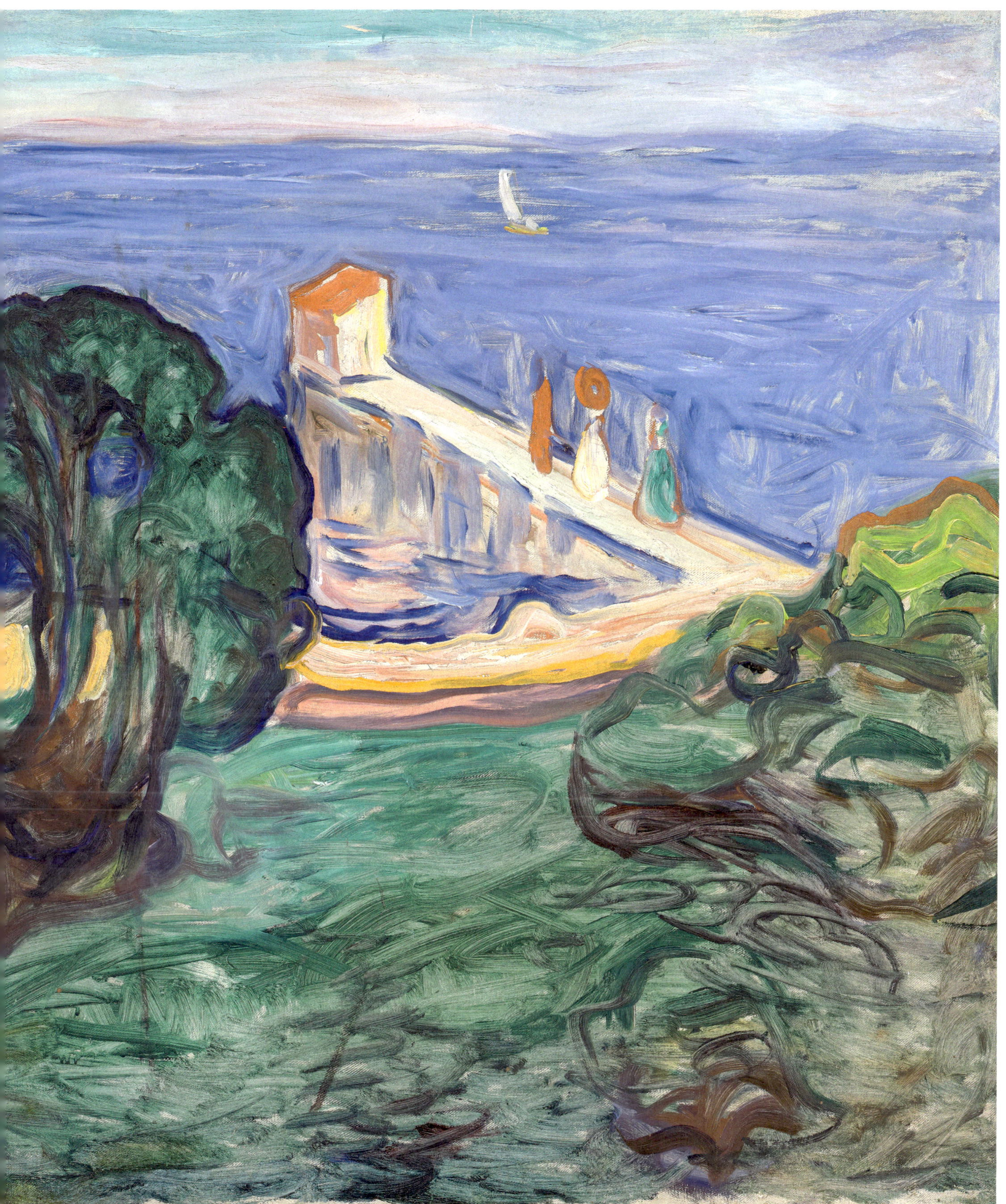

Edvard Munch
Trees by the Beach (The Linde Frieze) — 1904
Munchmuseet — Oslo

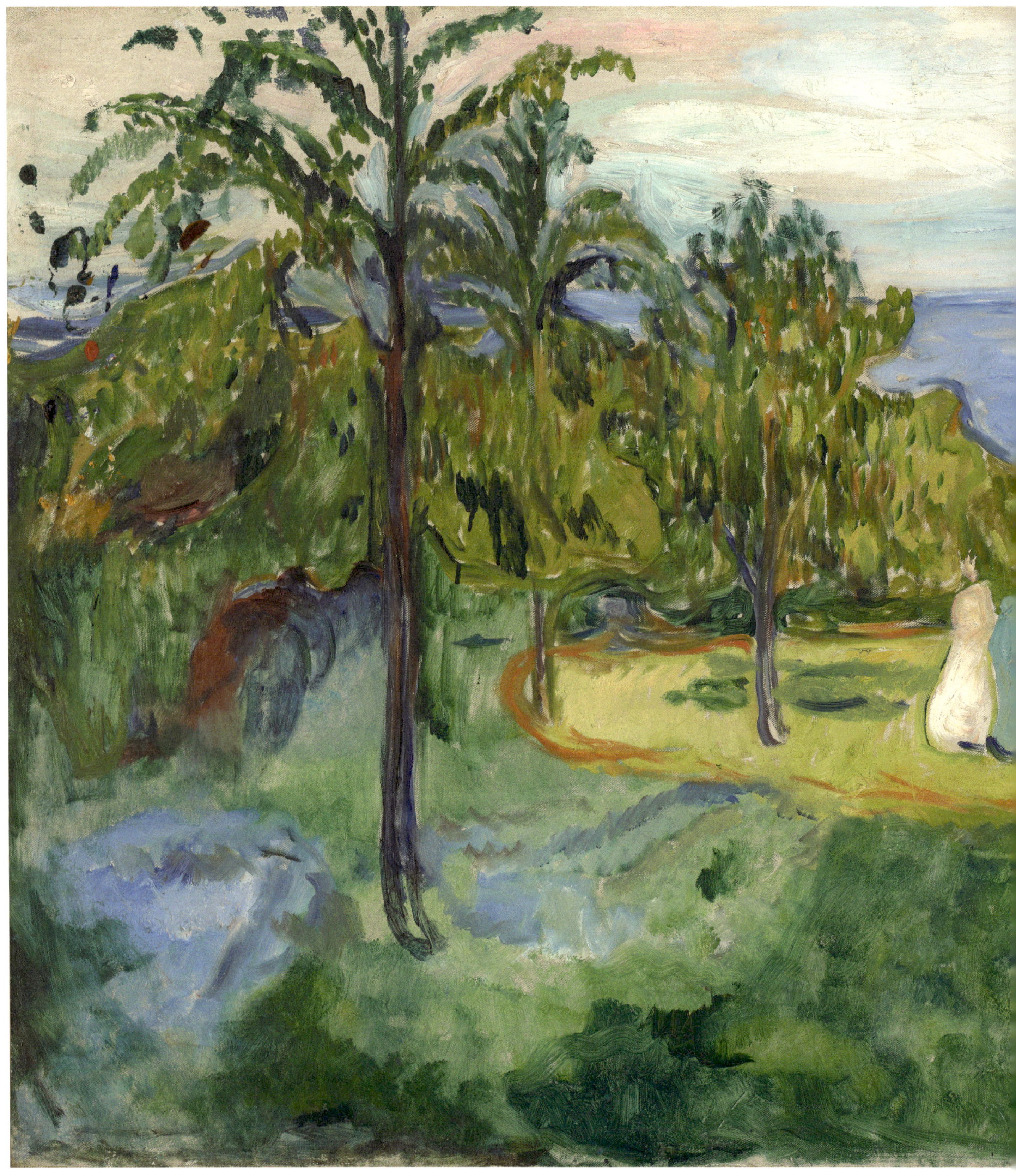

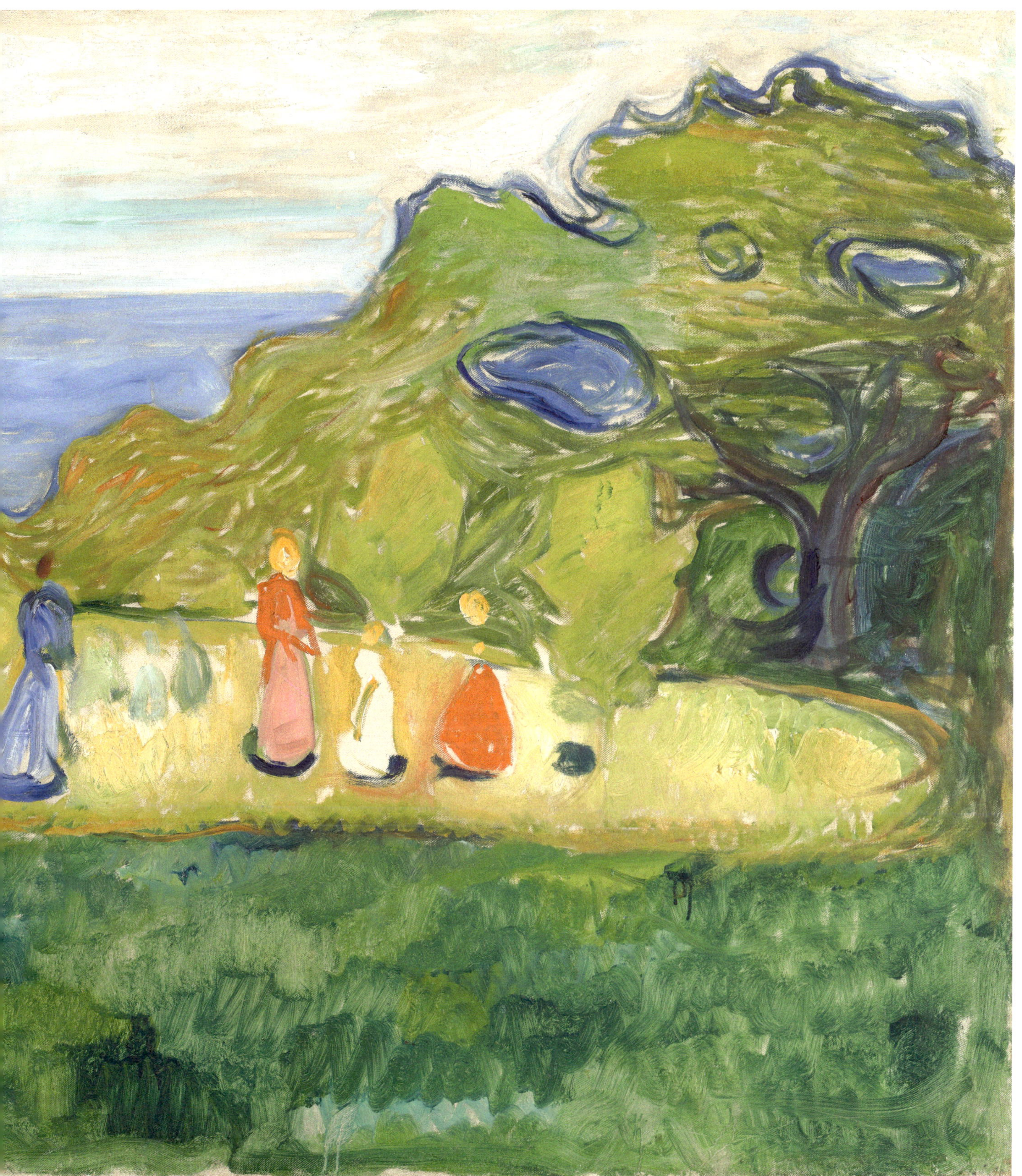

Edvard Munch
Summer in the Park (The Linde Frieze) — 1904
Munchmuseet — Oslo

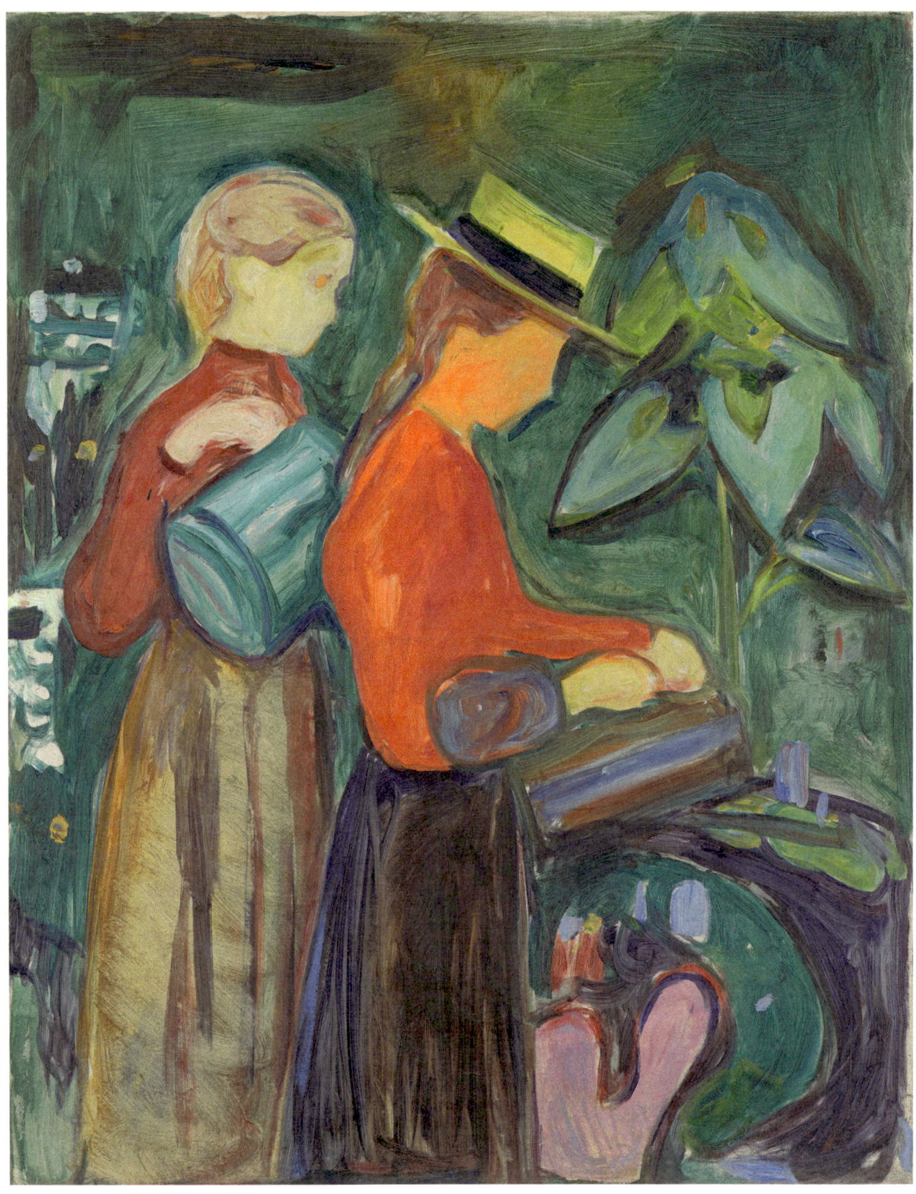

Edvard Munch
Girls Watering Flowers (The Linde Frieze) — 1904
Munchmuseet — Oslo

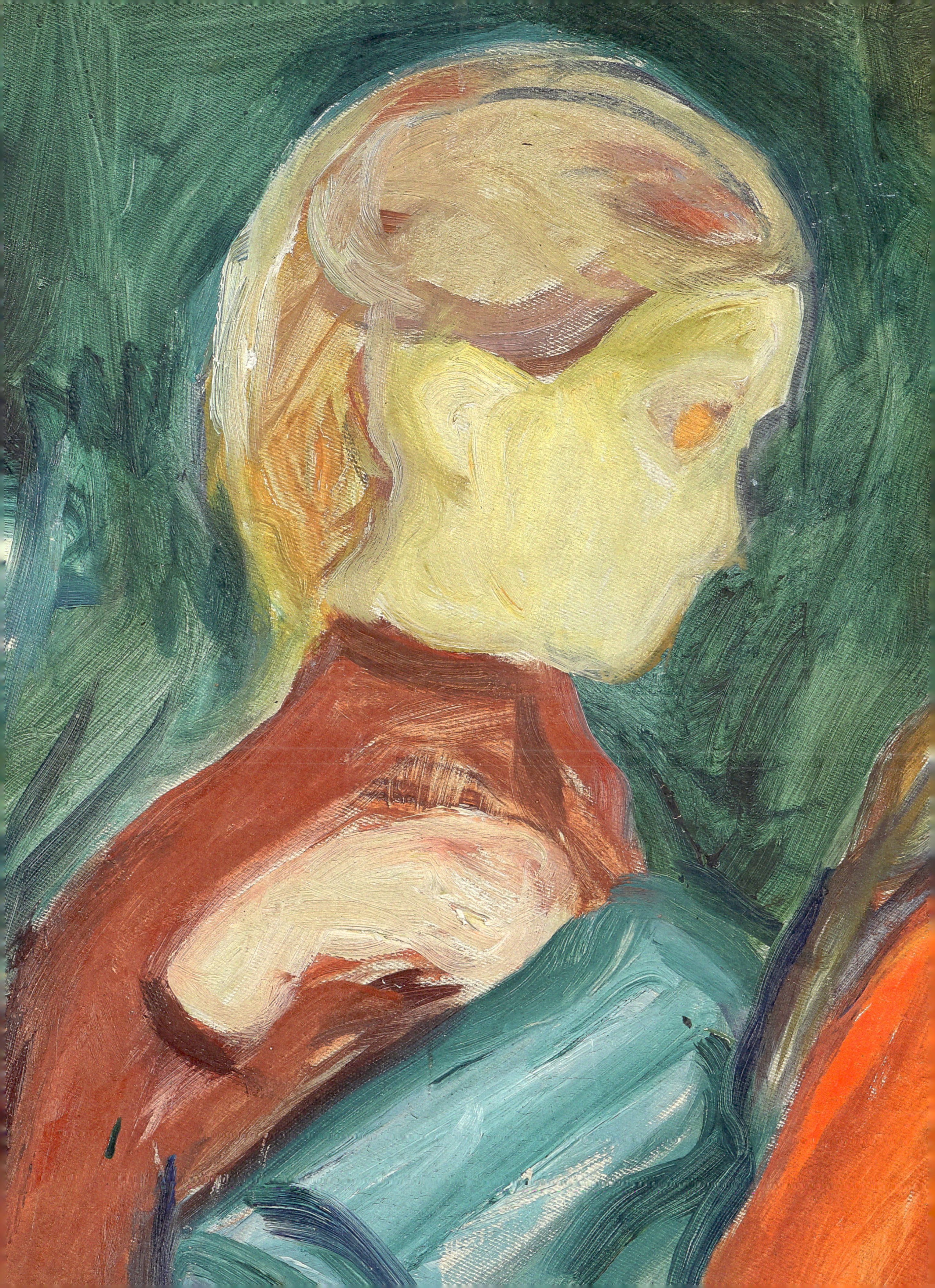

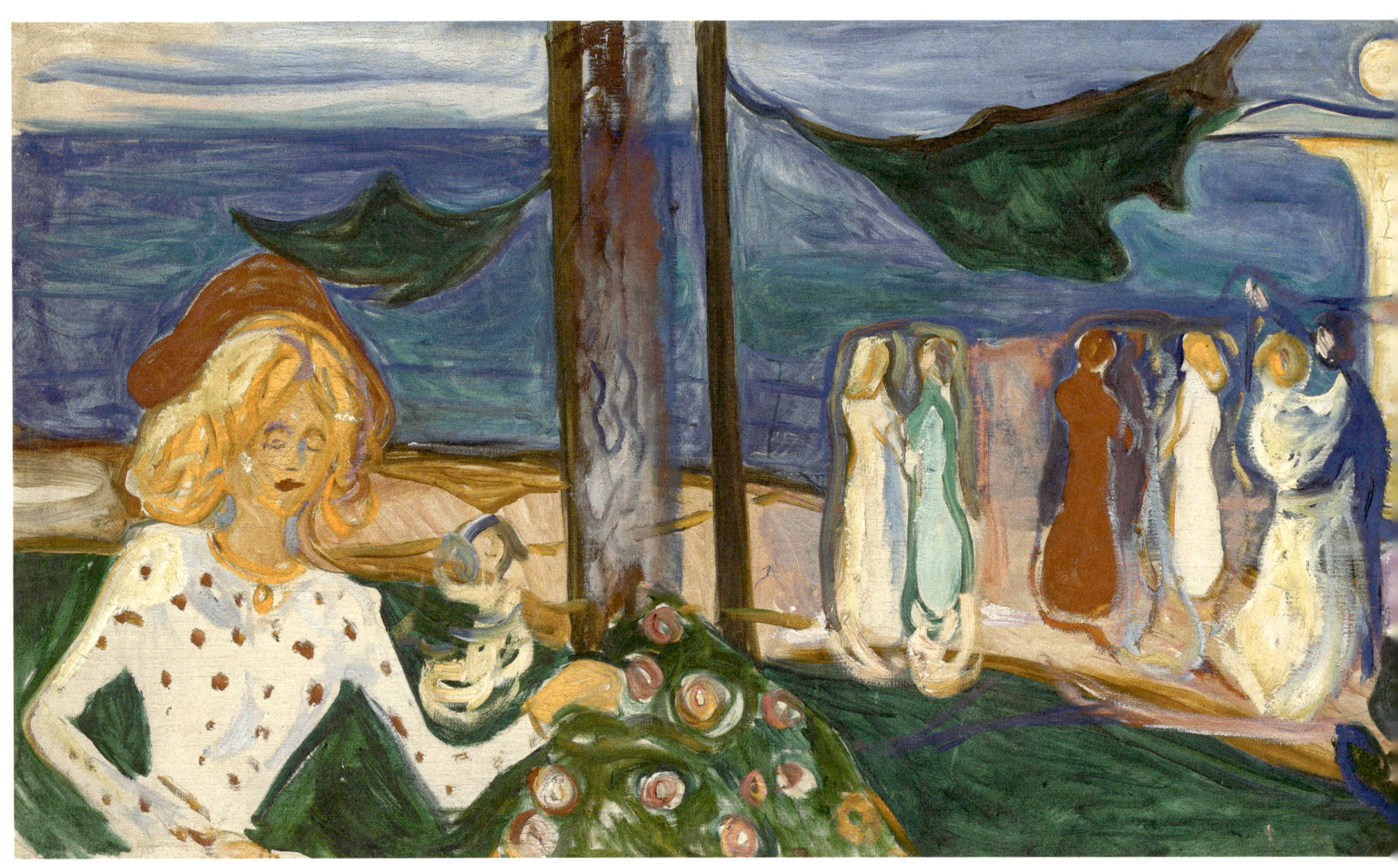

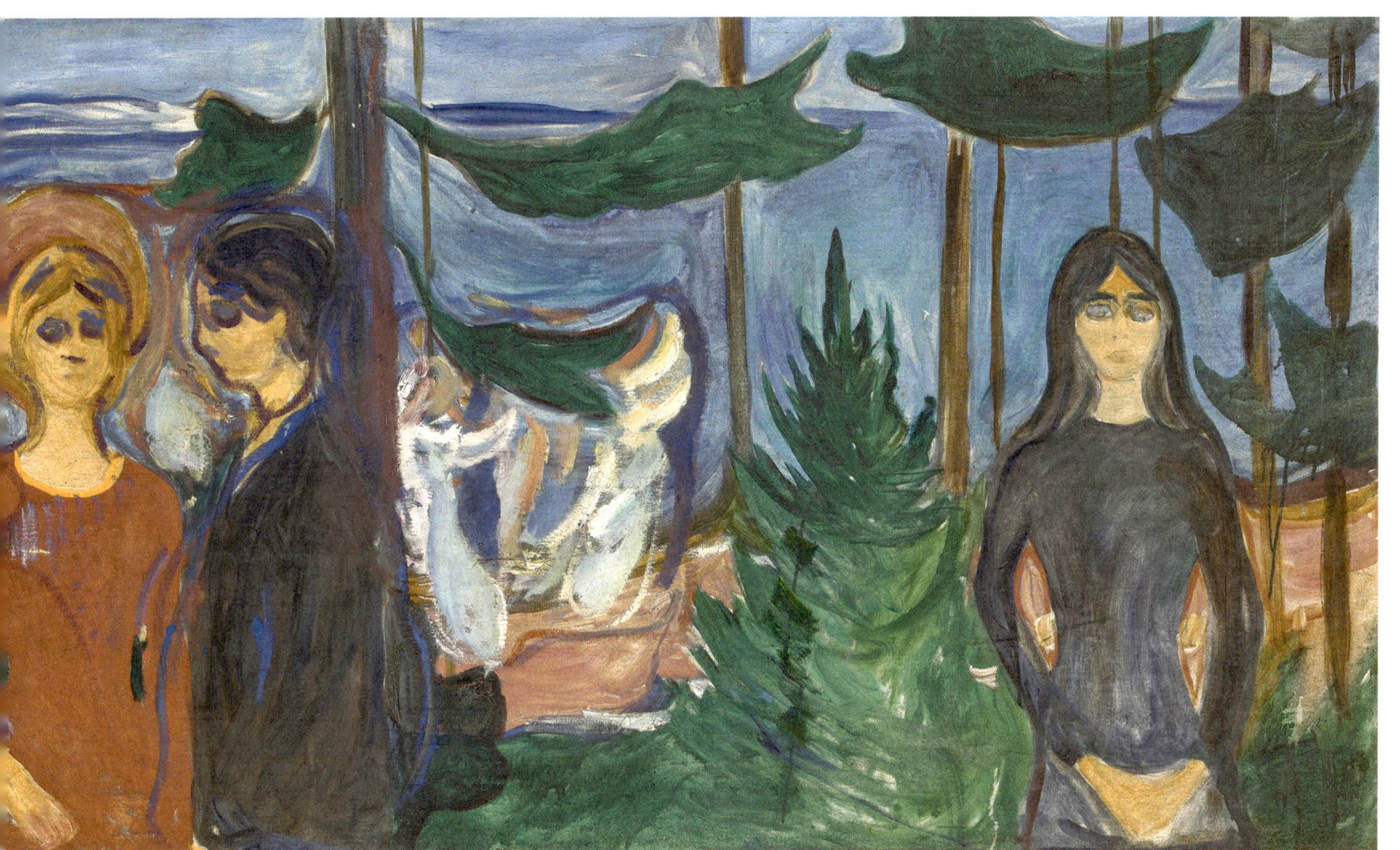

Edvard Munch
Dance on the Beach (The Linde Frieze) — 1904
Munchmuseet — Oslo

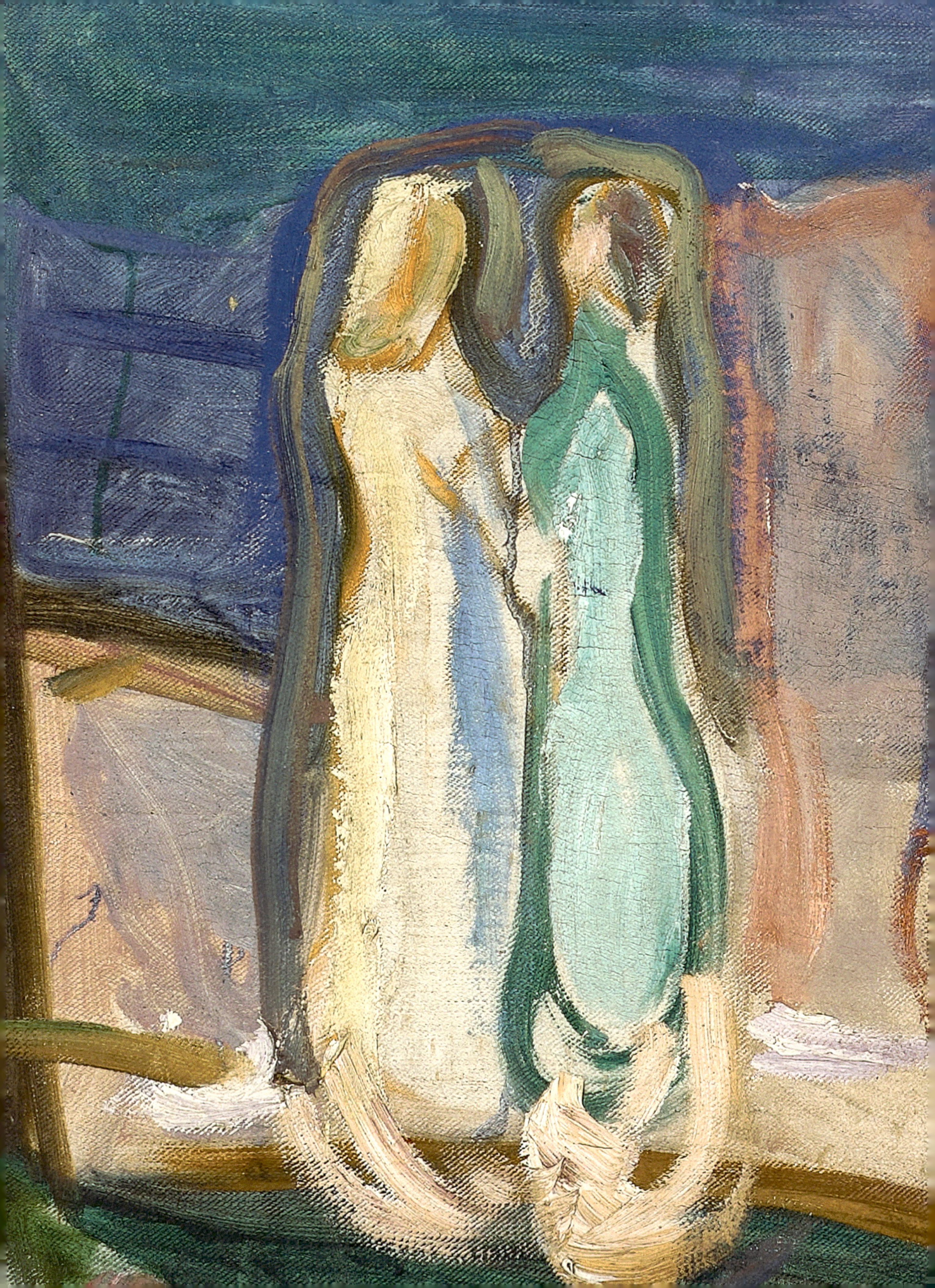

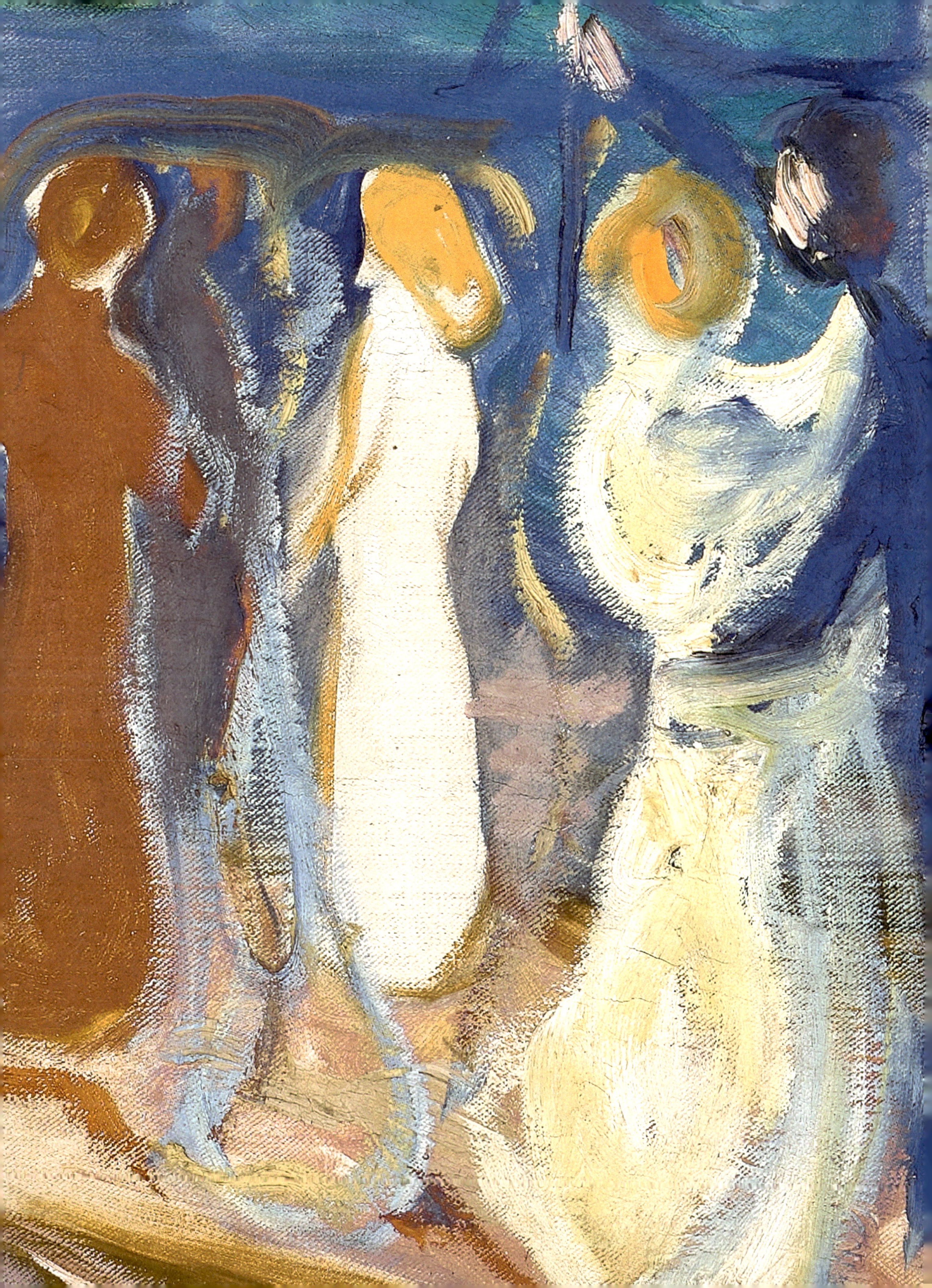

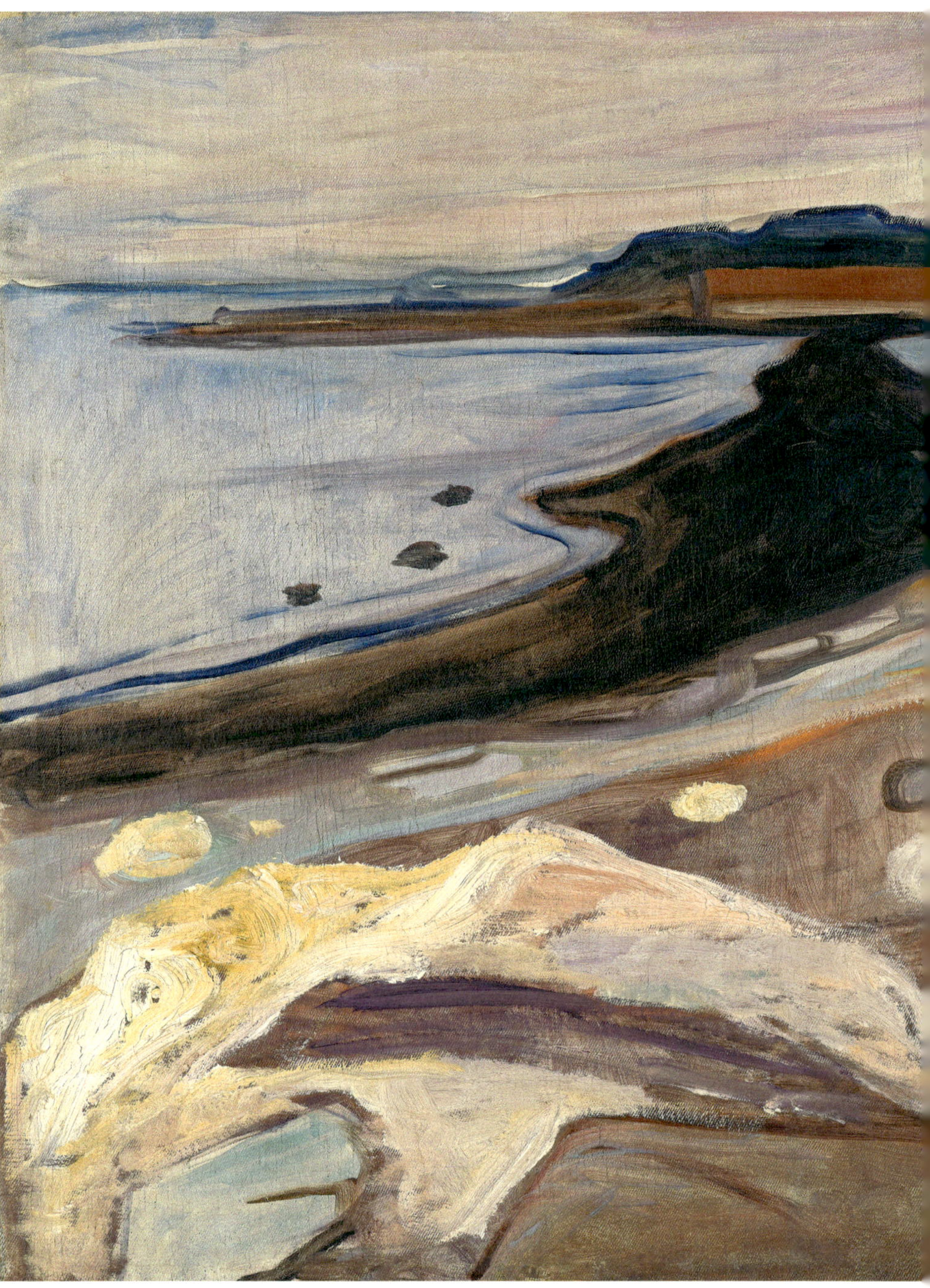

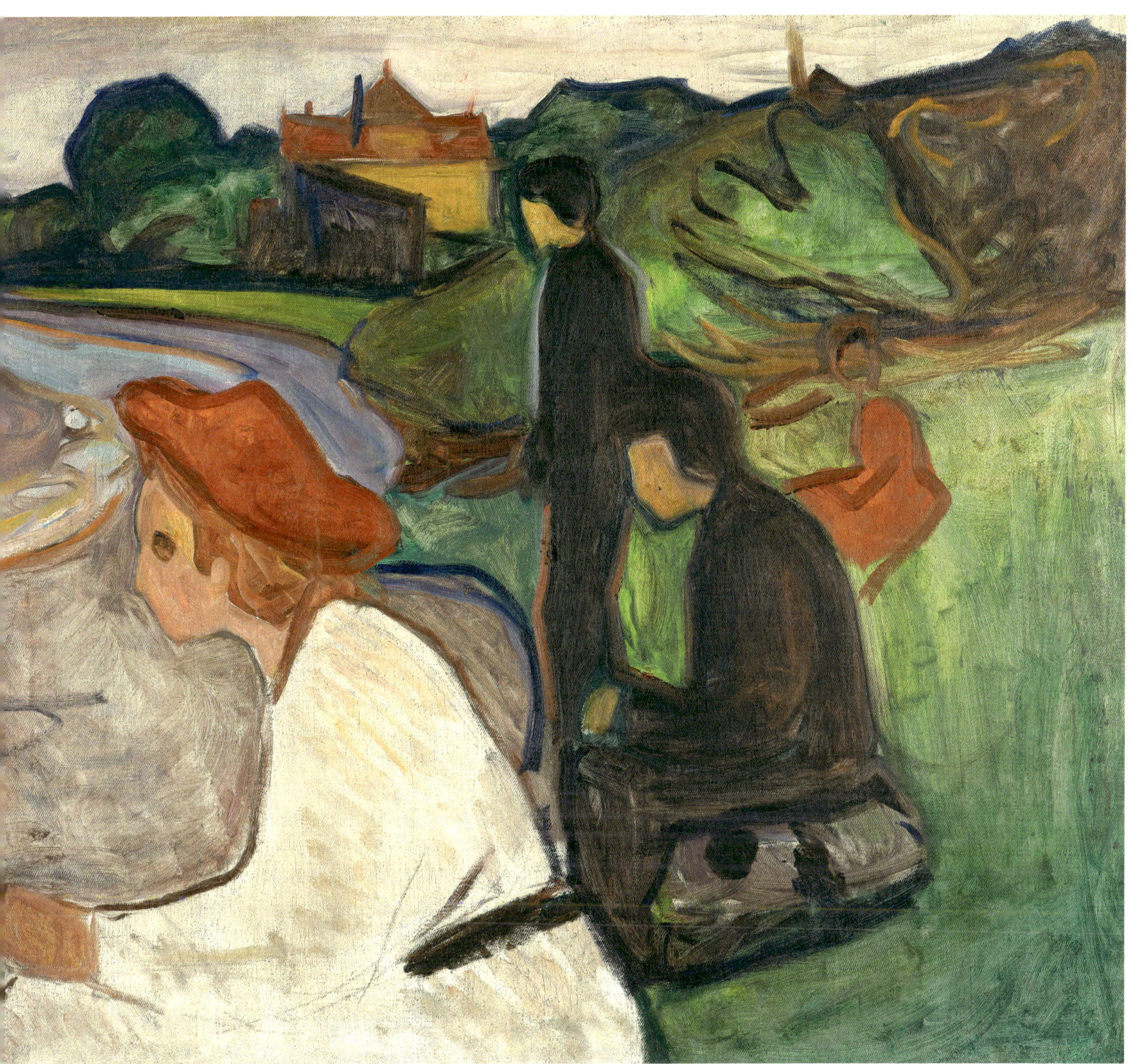

Edvard Munch
Young People on the Beach (The Linde Frieze) — 1904
Munchmuseet — Oslo

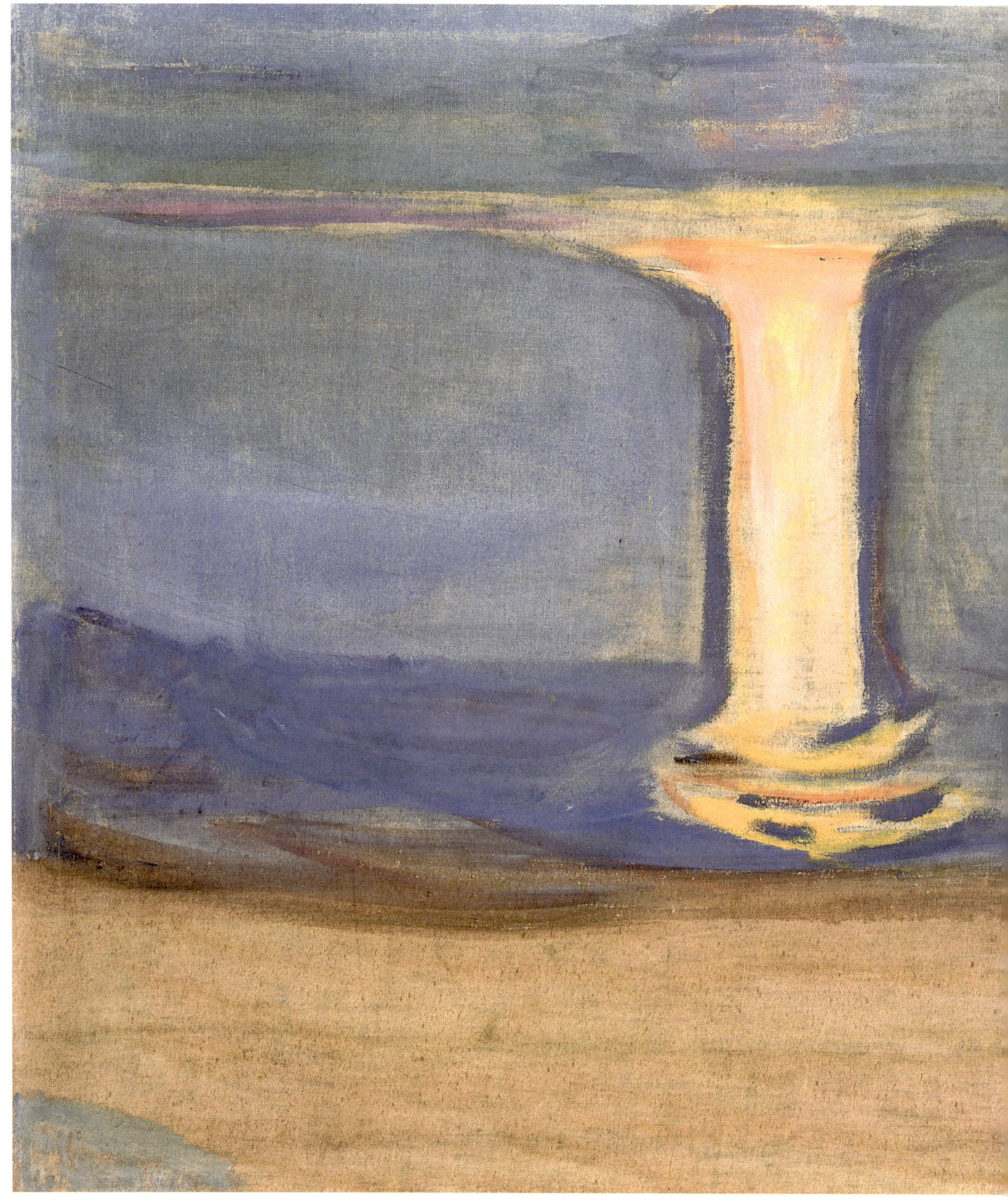

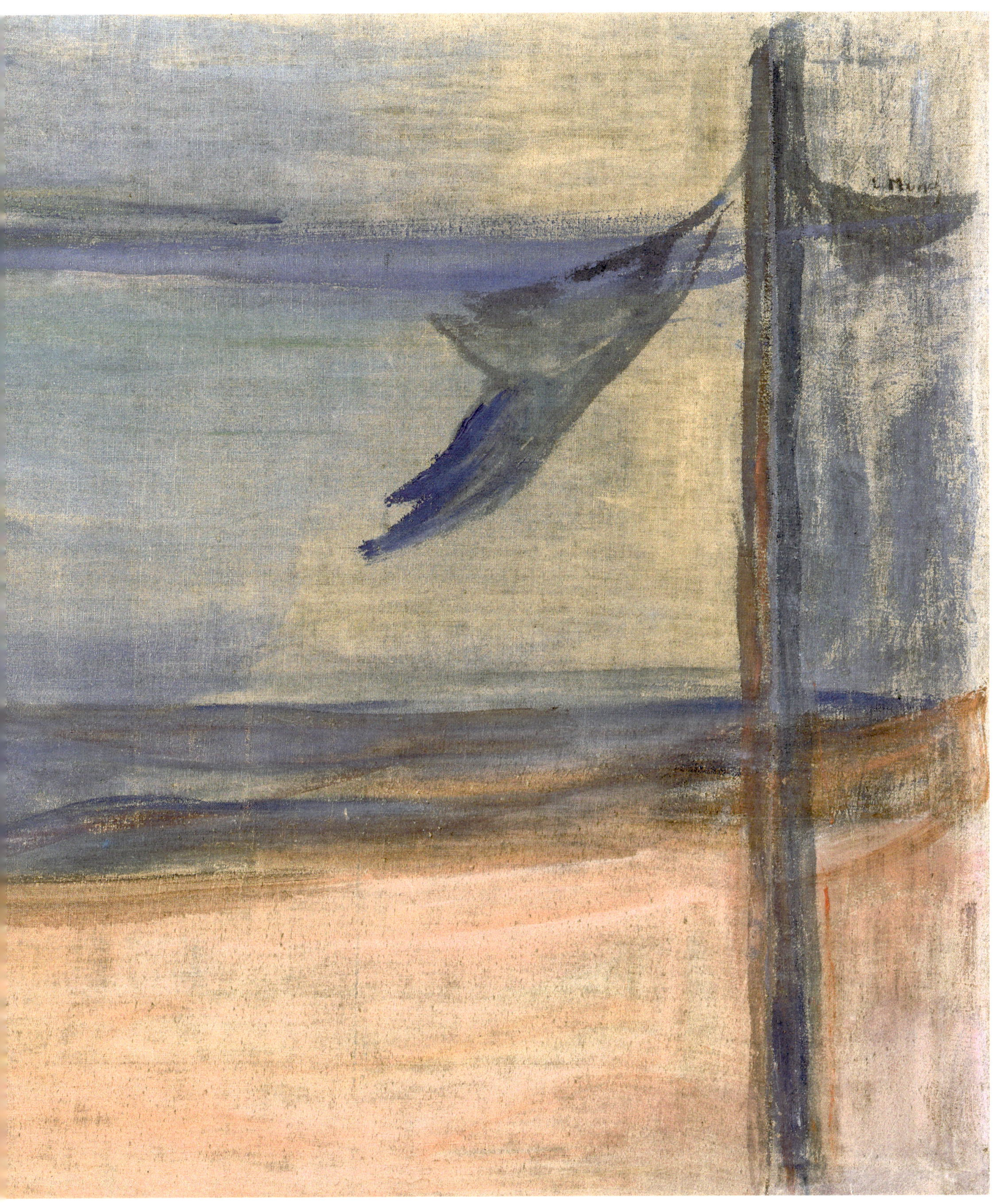

Edvard Munch
Moonlight on the Sea
(The Reinhardt Frieze) — 1906–7
Staatliche Museen zu Berlin
Nationalgalerie

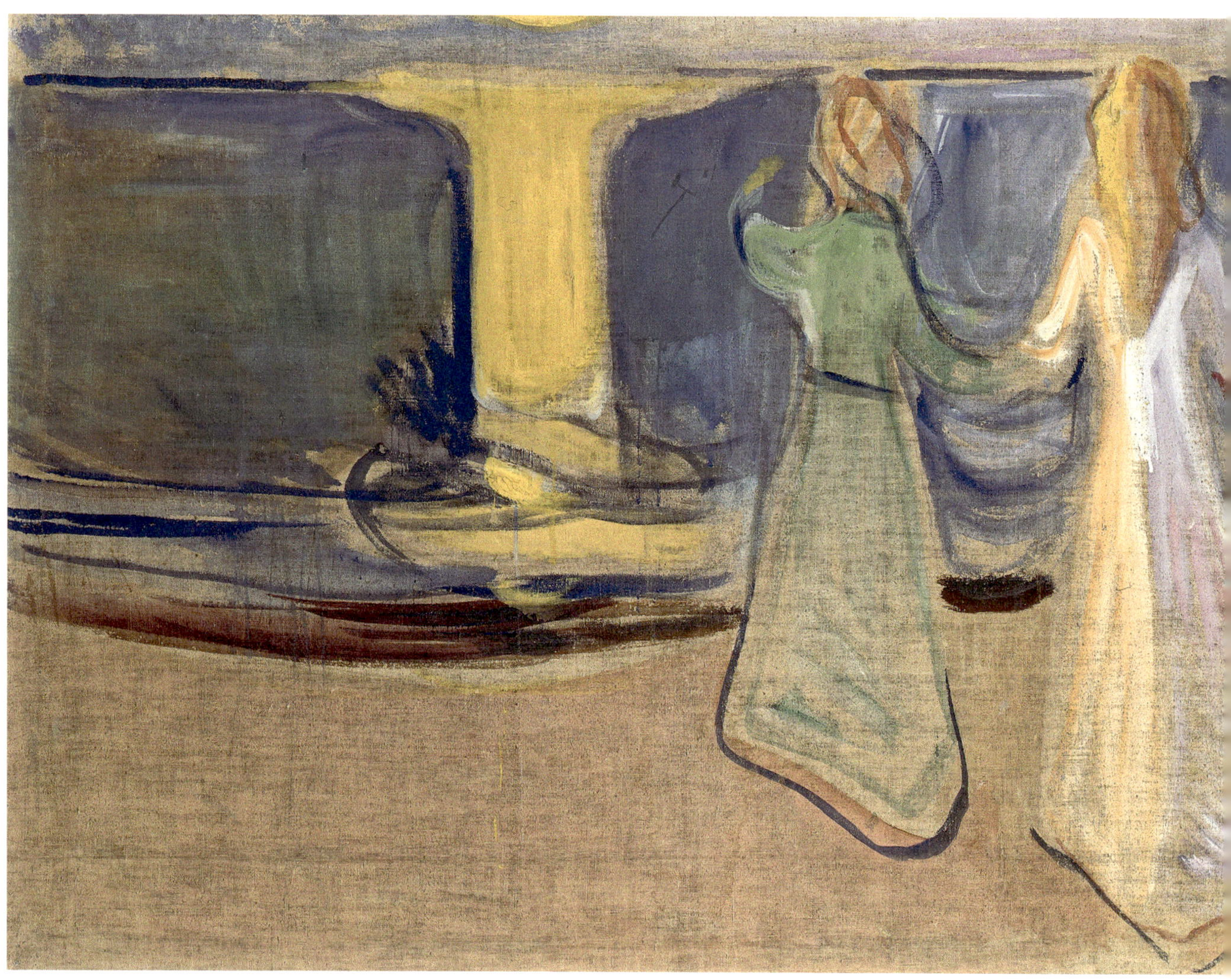

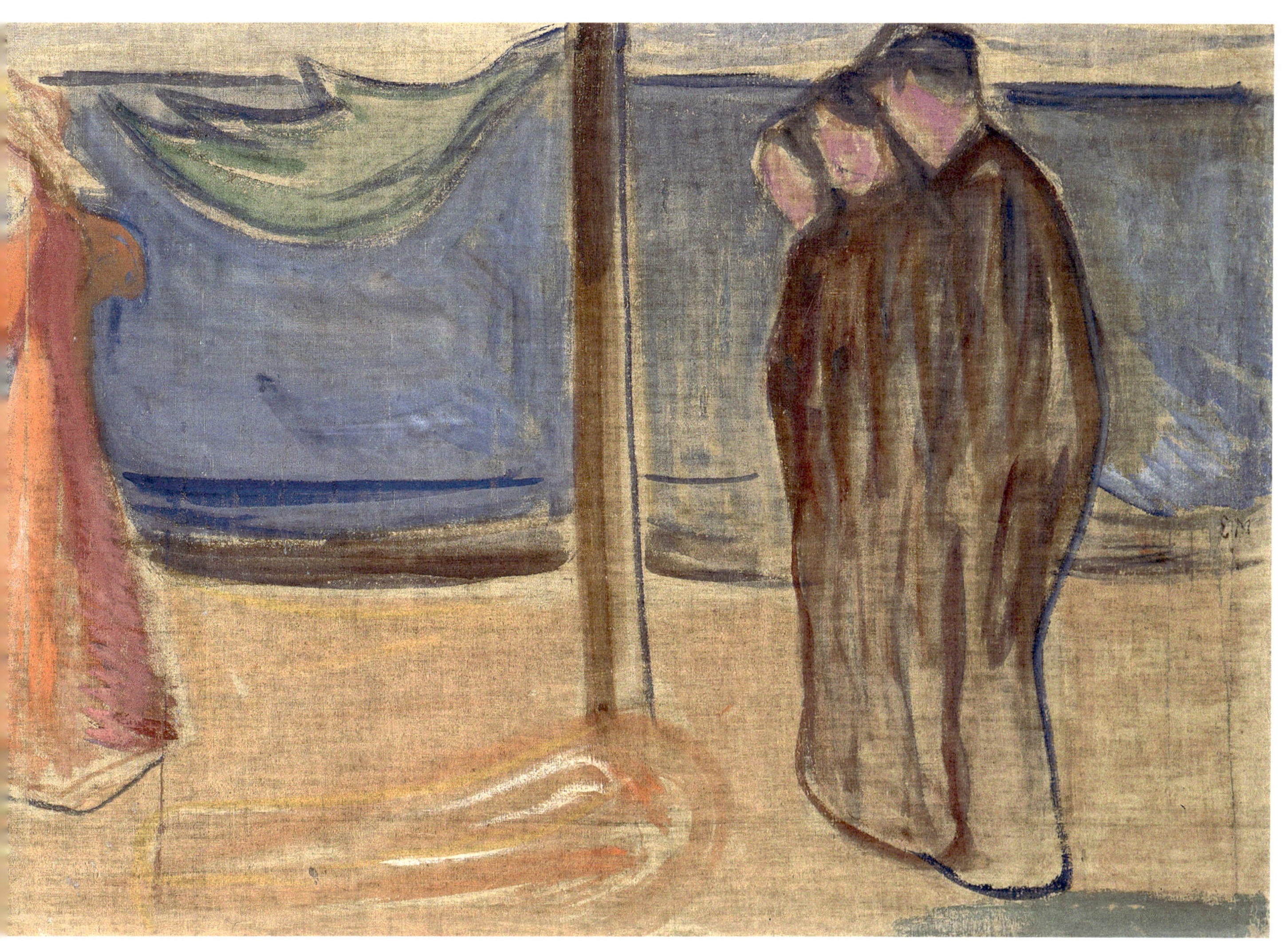

Edvard Munch
Desire (The Reinhardt Frieze) — 1906–7
Staatliche Museen zu Berlin
Nationalgalerie

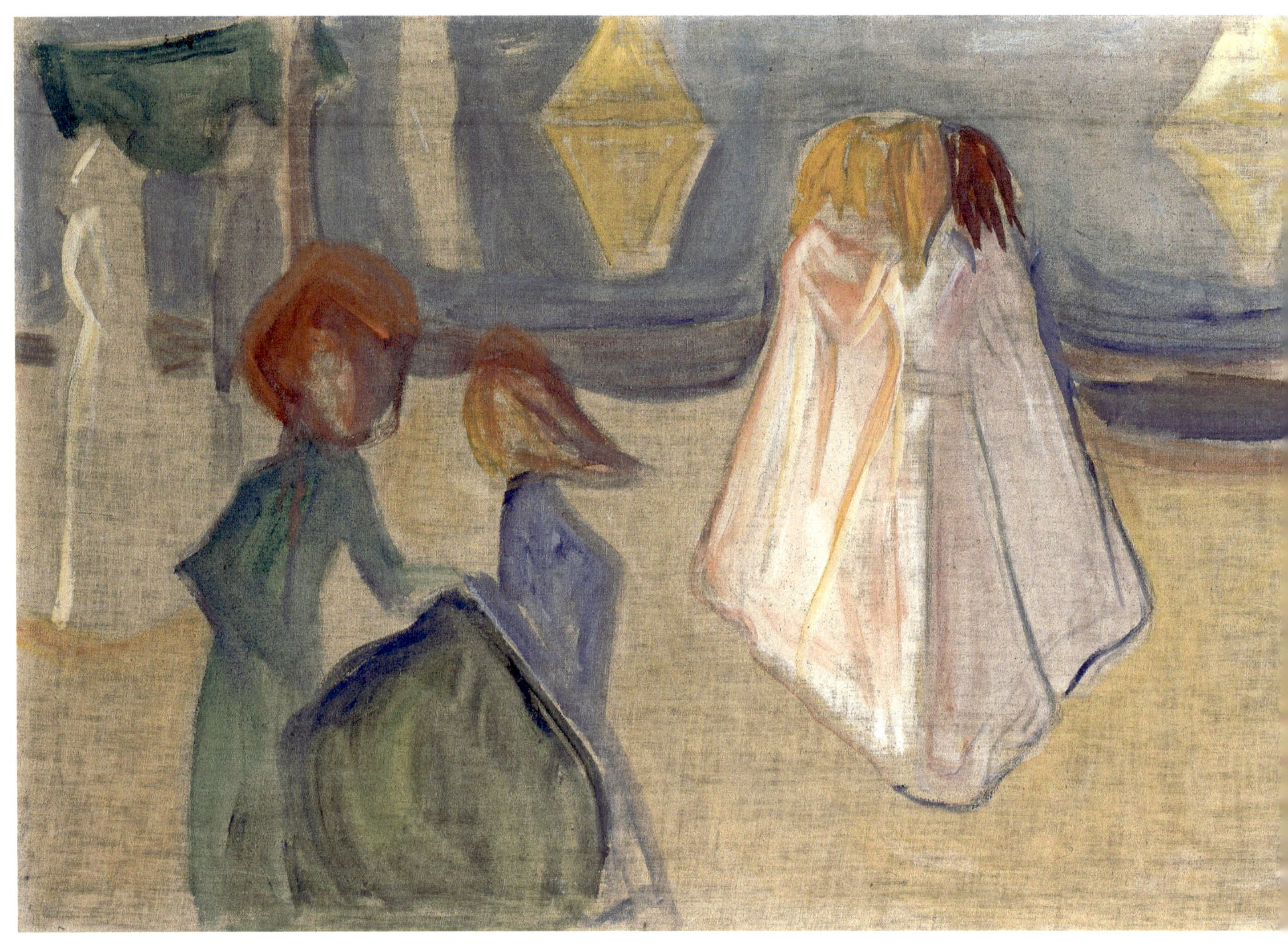

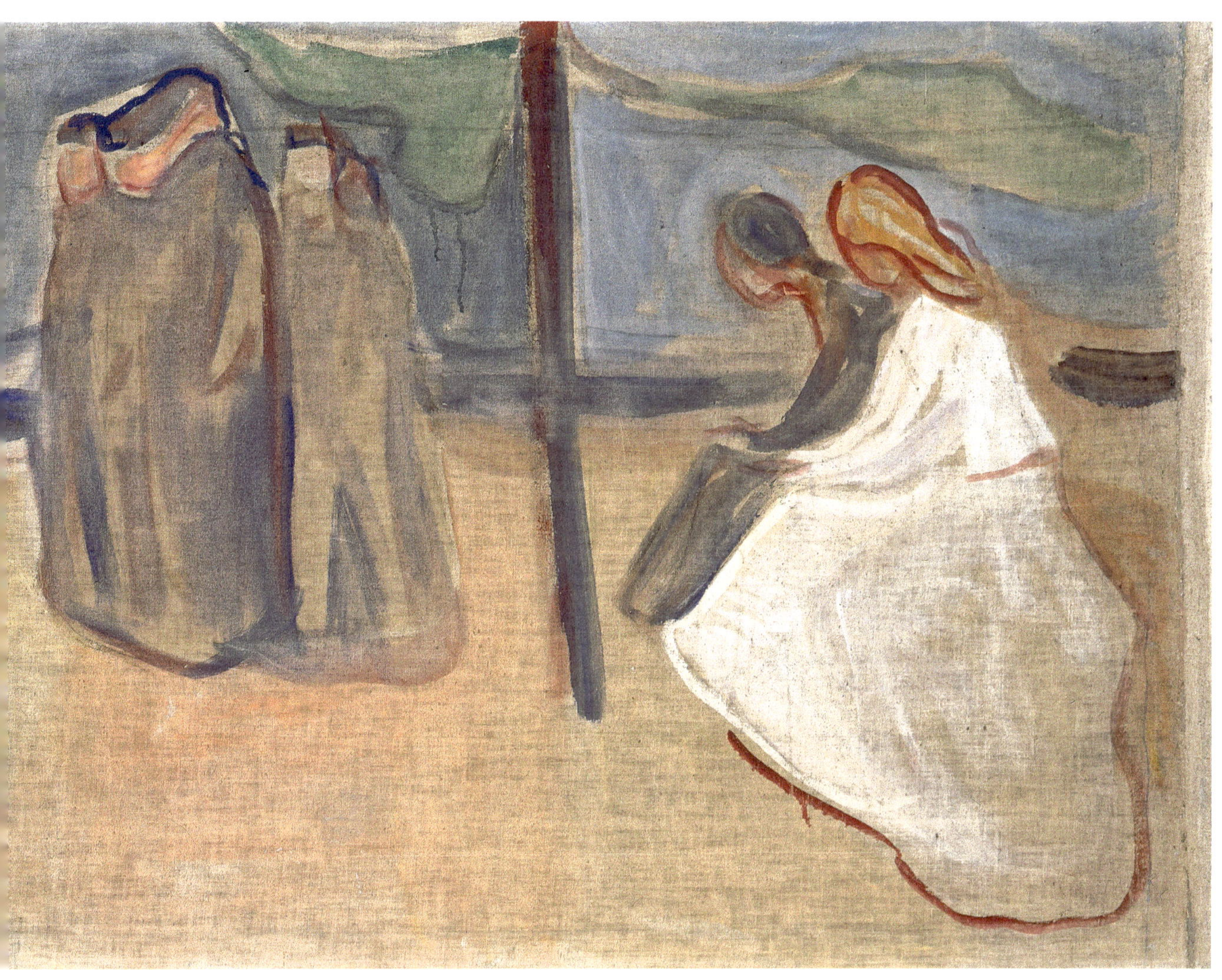

Edvard Munch
Summer Night (The Reinhardt Frieze) — 1906–7
Staatliche Museen zu Berlin
Nationalgalerie

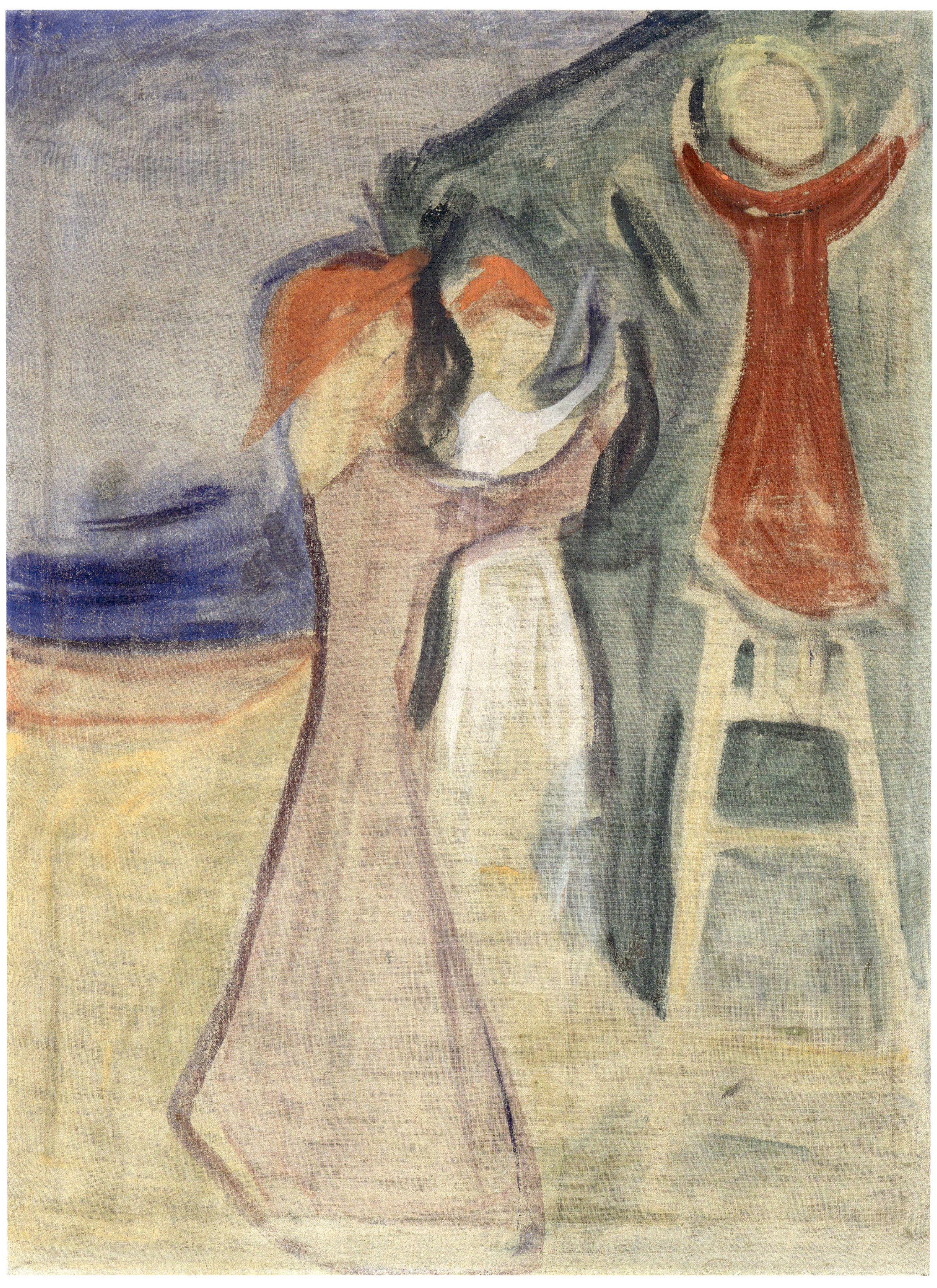

Edvard Munch
Young Women Picking Fruit
(The Reinhardt Frieze) — 1906–7
Staatliche Museen zu Berlin, Nationalgalerie

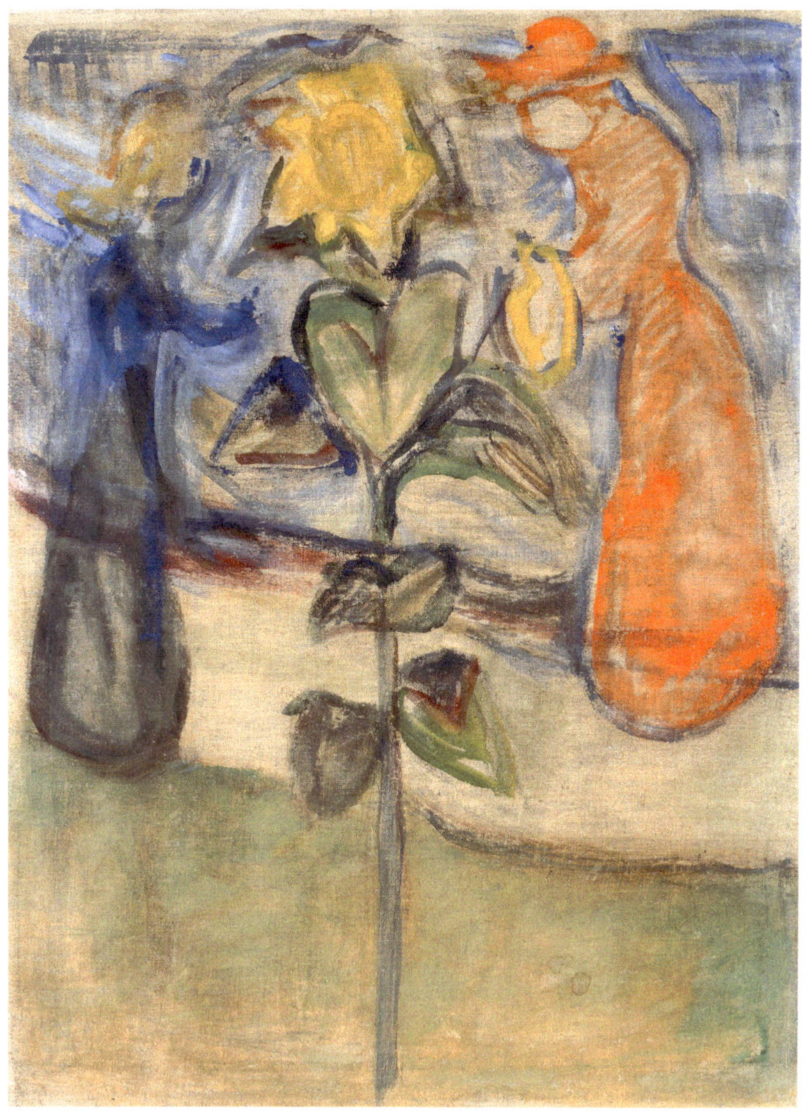

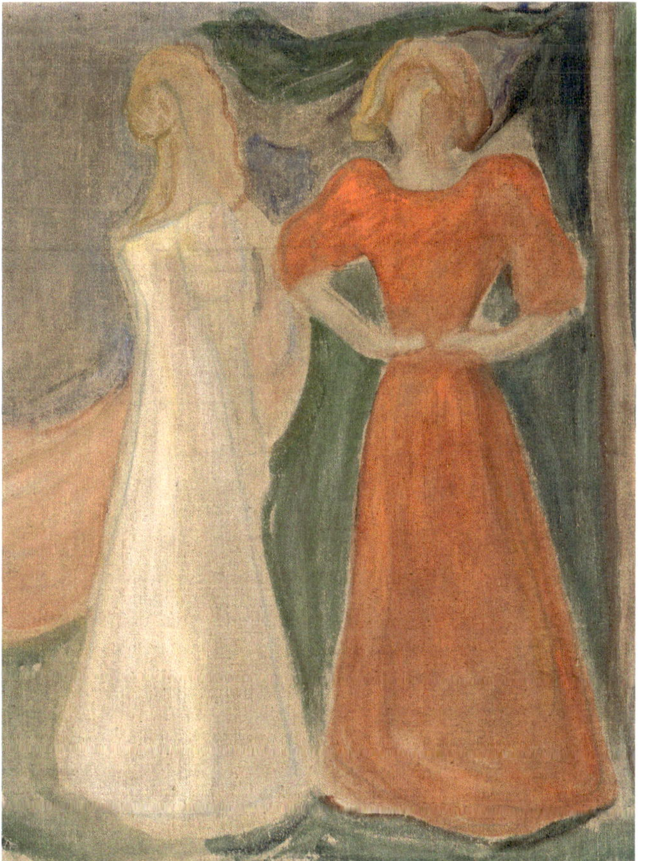

(A)
Edvard Munch
Sun Flower
(*The Reinhardt Frieze*) — 1906–7
Staatliche Museen zu Berlin
Nationalgalerie

(B)
Edvard Munch
Two Young Women in Red and White
(*The Reinhardt Frieze*) — 1906–7
Staatliche Museen zu Berlin
Nationalgalerie

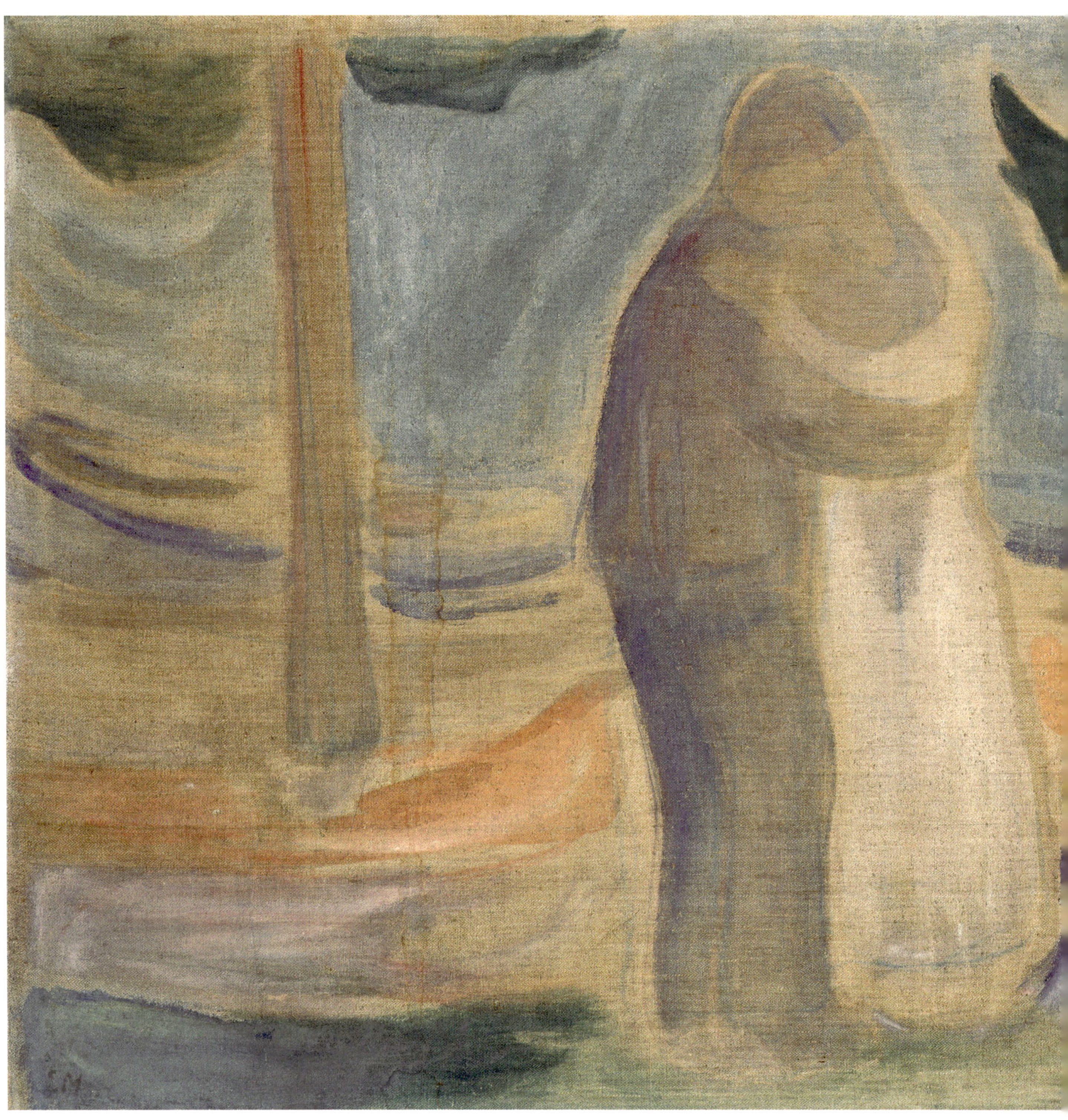

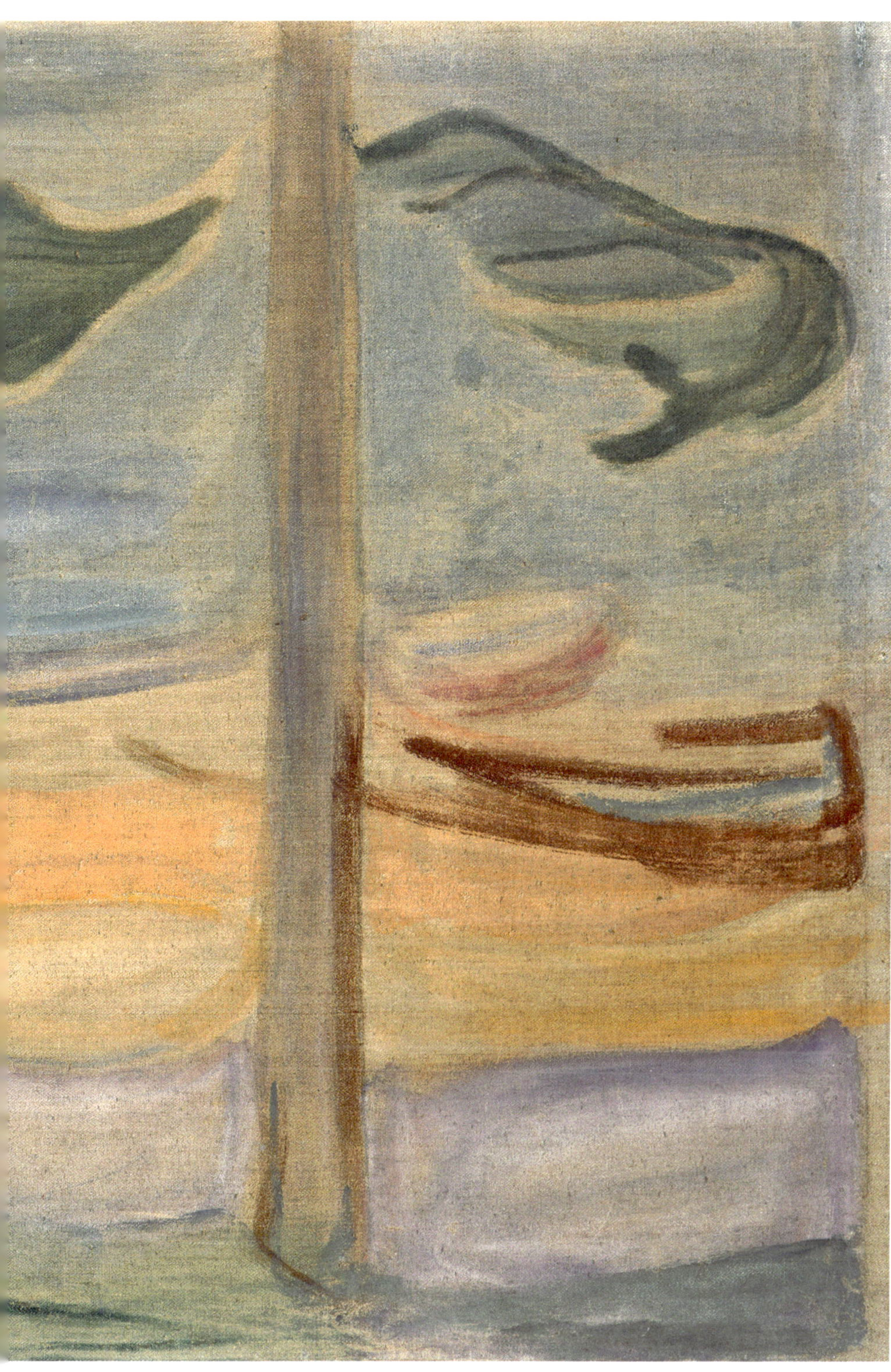

Edvard Munch
Kiss on the Beach (The Reinhardt Frieze) — 1906–7
Staatliche Museen zu Berlin
Nationalgalerie

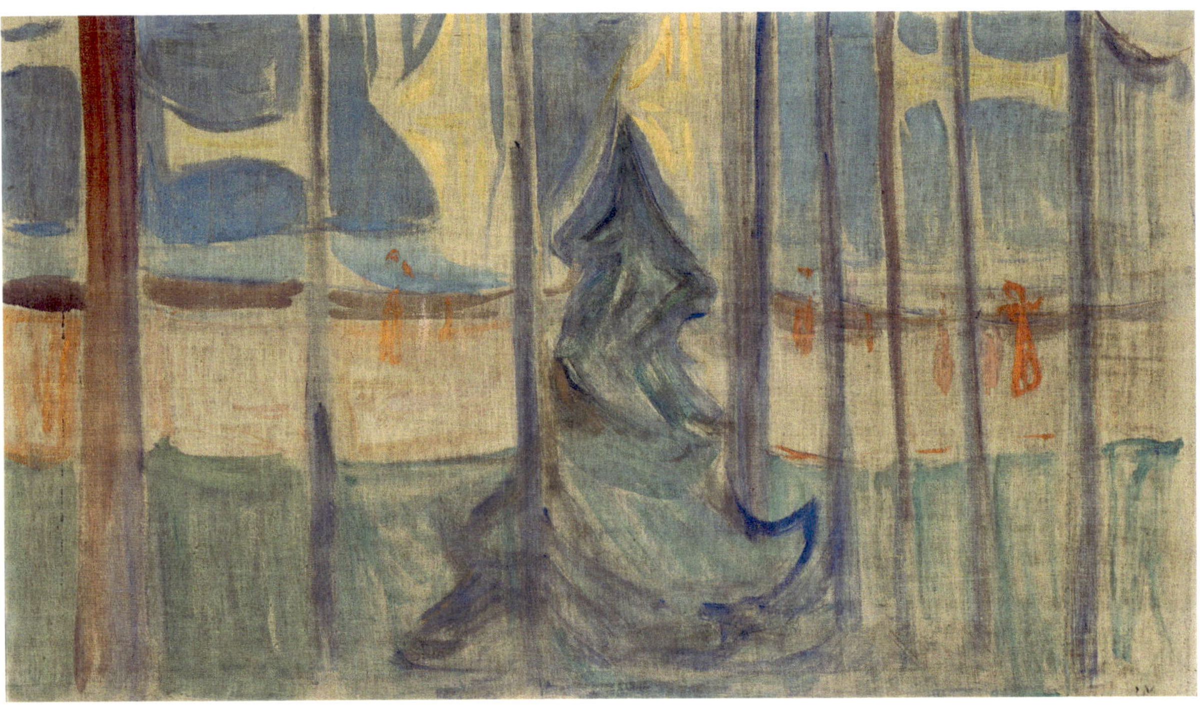

Edvard Munch
Trees by the Sea (The Reinhardt Frieze) — 1906–7
Staatliche Museen zu Berlin
Nationalgalerie

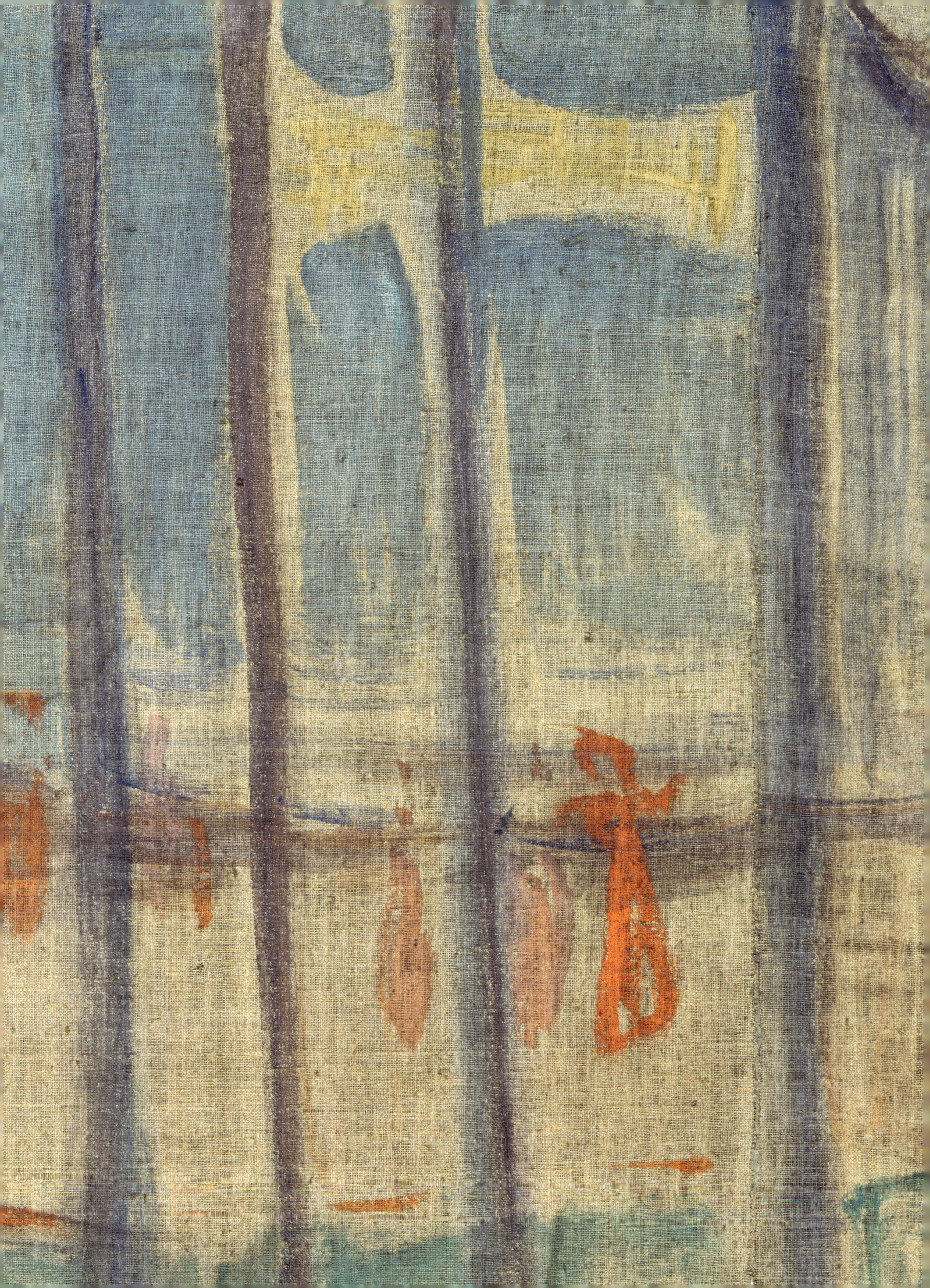

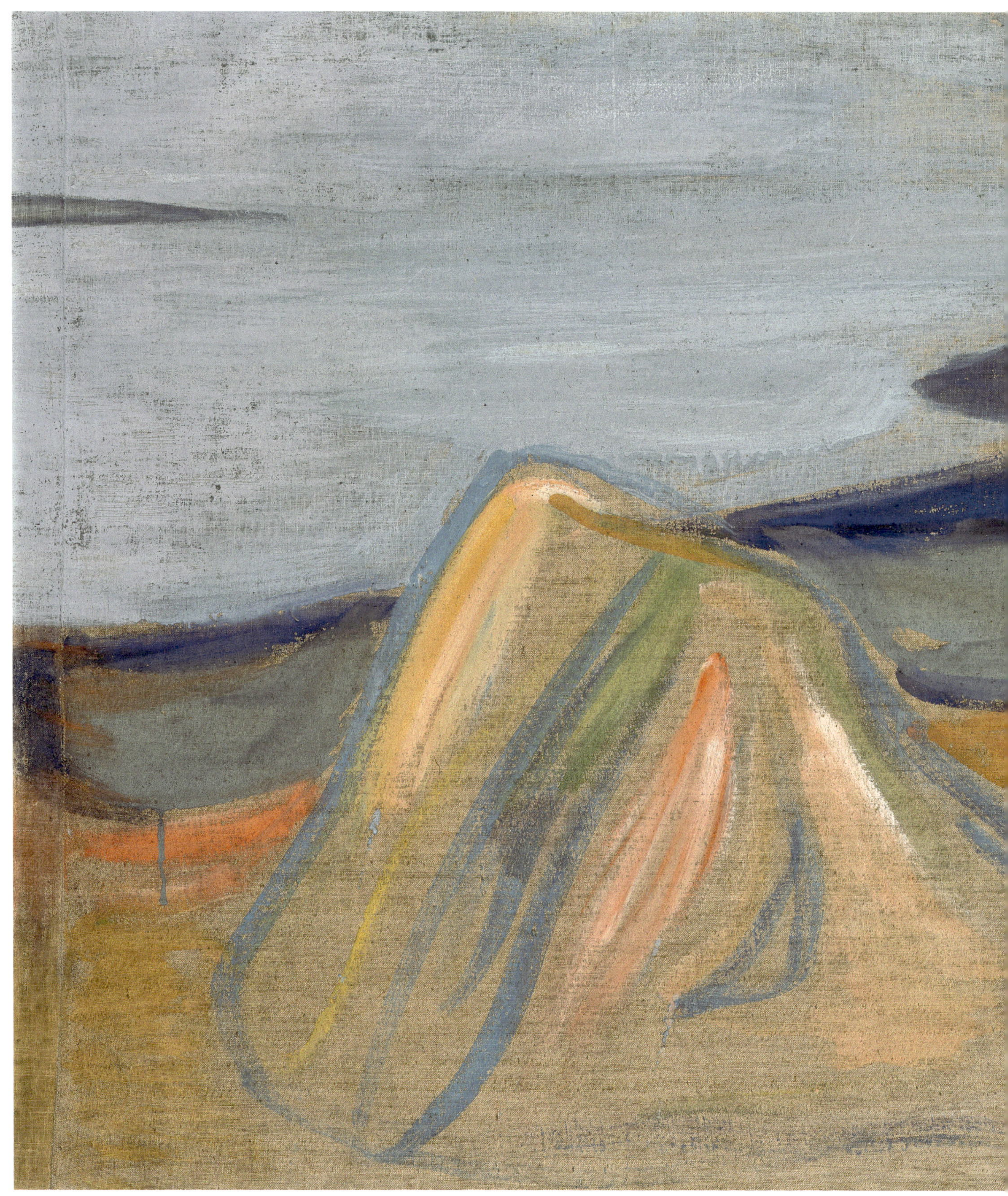

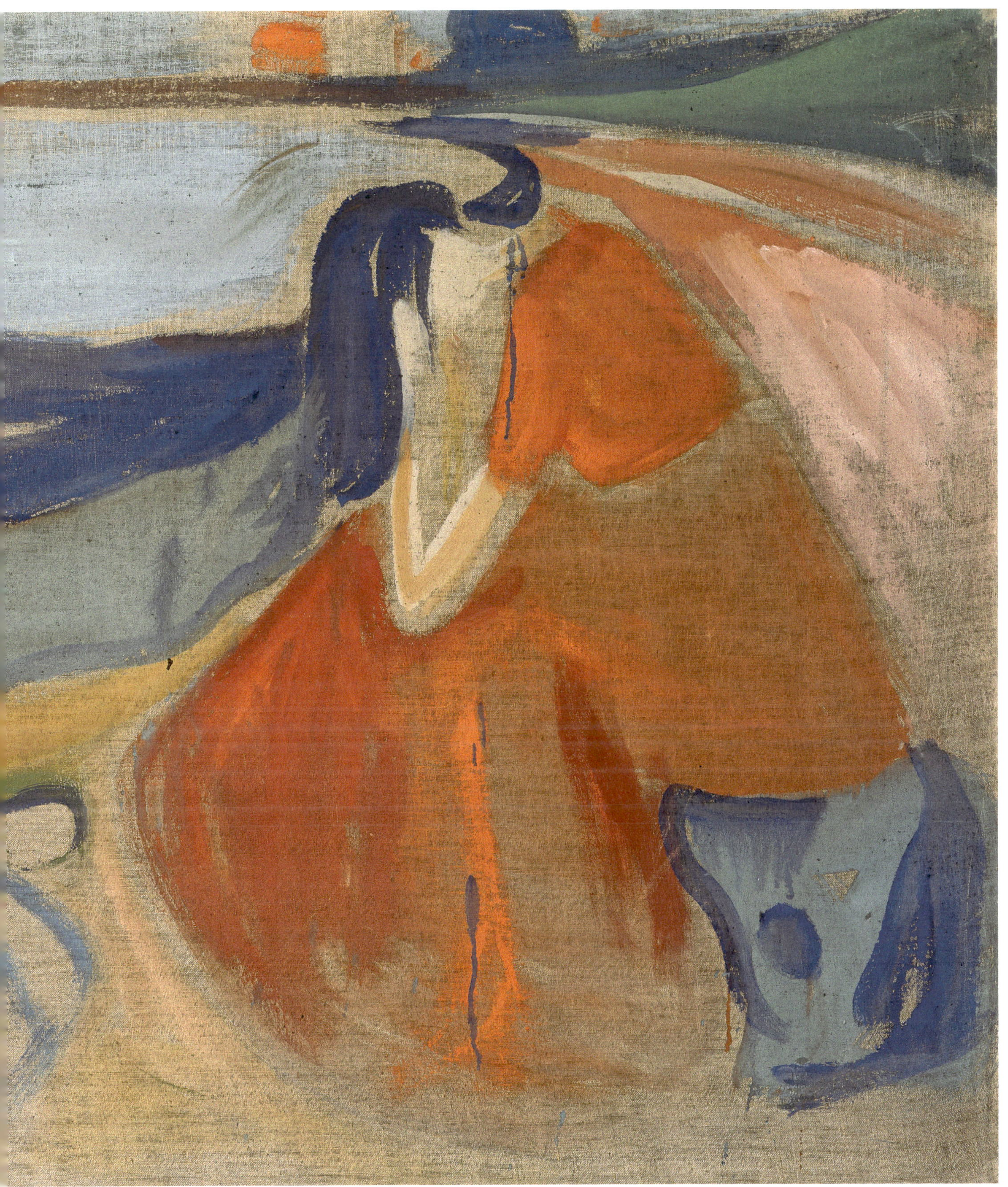

Edvard Munch
Melancholy (The Reinhardt Frieze) — 1906–7
Staatliche Museen zu Berlin
Nationalgalerie

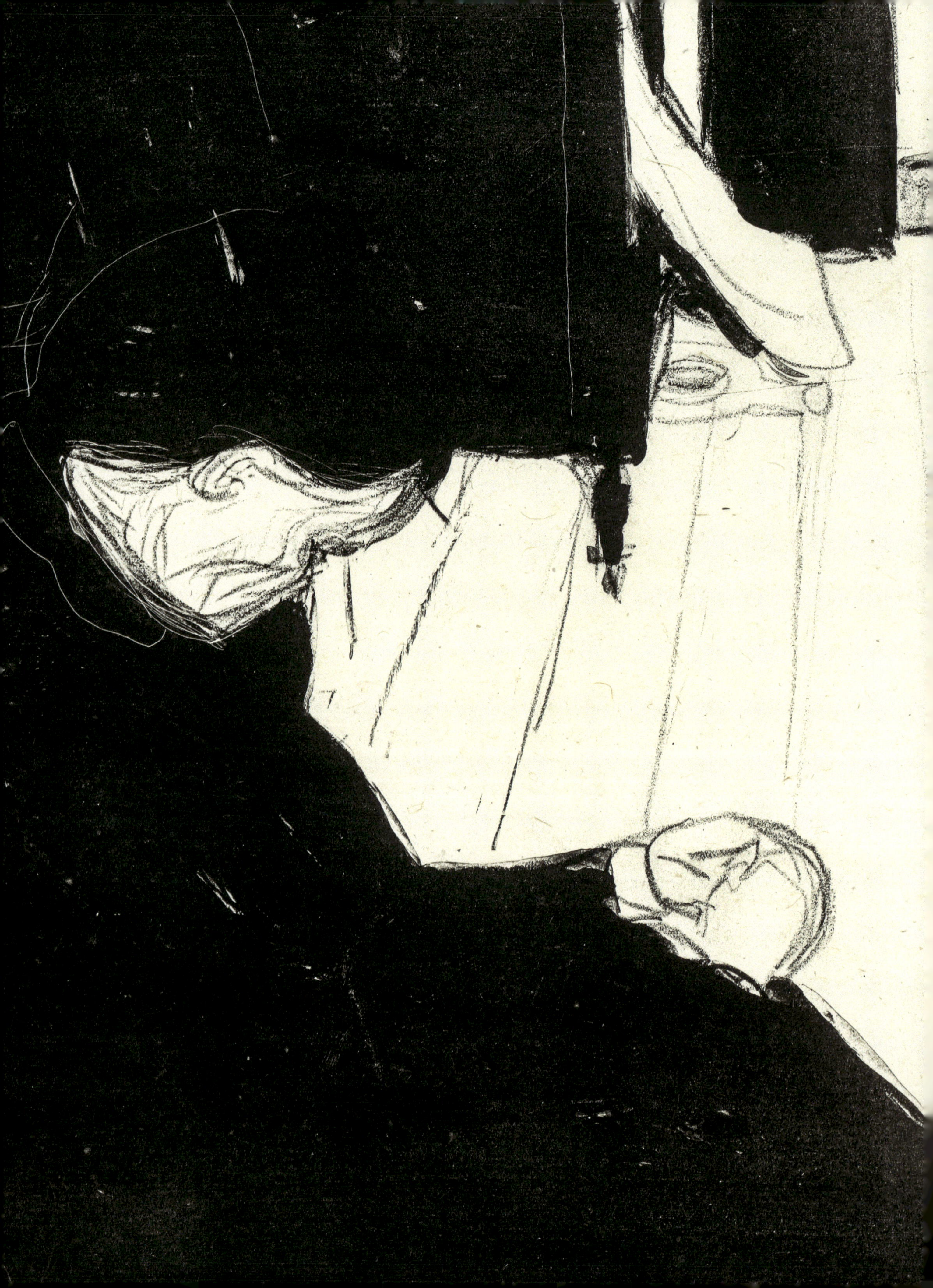

Experimental and Virtuosic

In Berlin in 1894, Edvard Munch discovered printmaking as an artistic technique. Professional and highly specialized printing houses assisted him. In the briefest span, the artist taught himself etching and lithography, and later in Paris the woodcut as well. Very soon thereafter, he was executing all three with the greatest virtuosity. Just one year later, the art historian Julius Meier-Graefe published a first portfolio of etchings in Berlin, though he sold hardly any of them. The judge and graphic arts specialist Gustav Schiefler of Hamburg, who was a close friend of Munch's, described his first encounter with Munch's prints in his diary in 1902: "It is the strongest and I can surely say most thrilling impression I have ever gotten from works of contemporary art."

Also in Berlin, Munch took up photography in 1902 and proved to be similarly experimental here as he was in his paintings and prints. He employed unusual perspectives and supposed technical mistakes such as blurriness from long exposure times—effects that correspond to his strategies in painting and printmaking. Most of the photographs show his private surroundings, including self-portraits in his studio at Lützowstrasse 82. But Munch also used a camera to document his exhibitions.

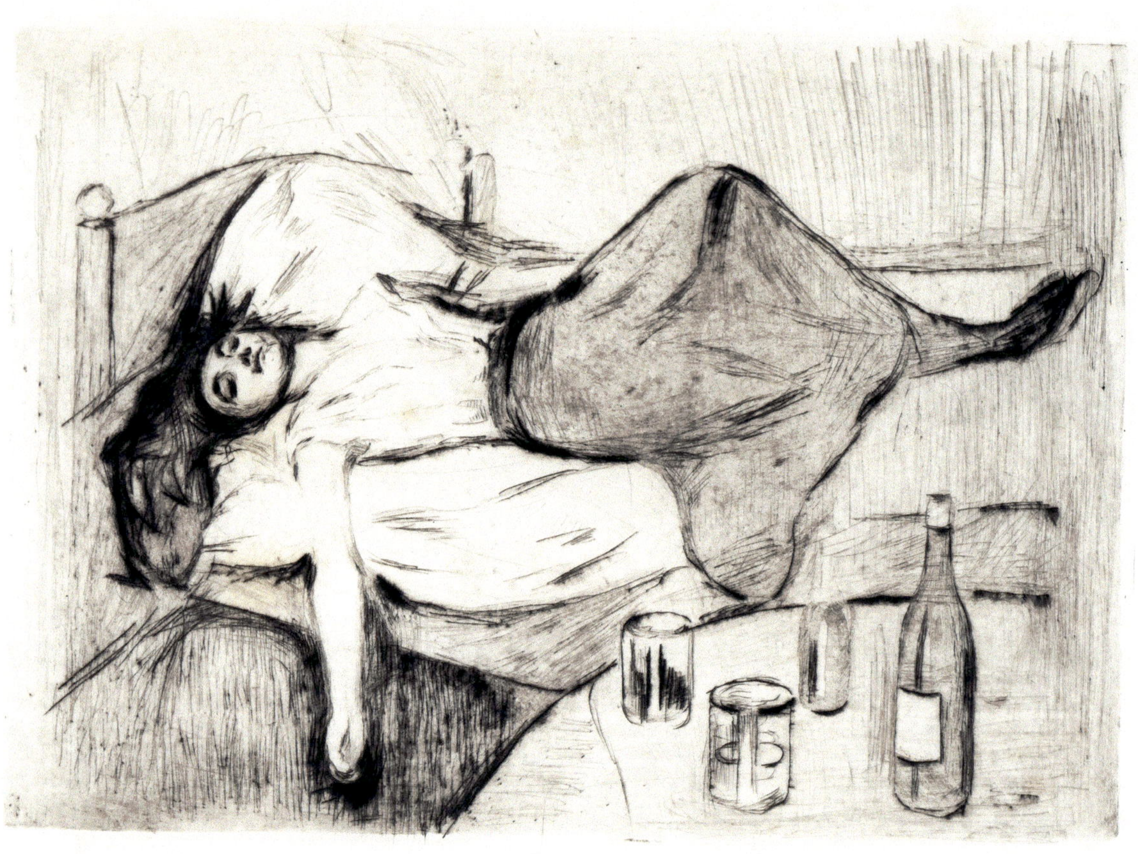

Edvard Munch
The Day After — 1894
Staatliche Museen zu Berlin
Kupferstichkabinett

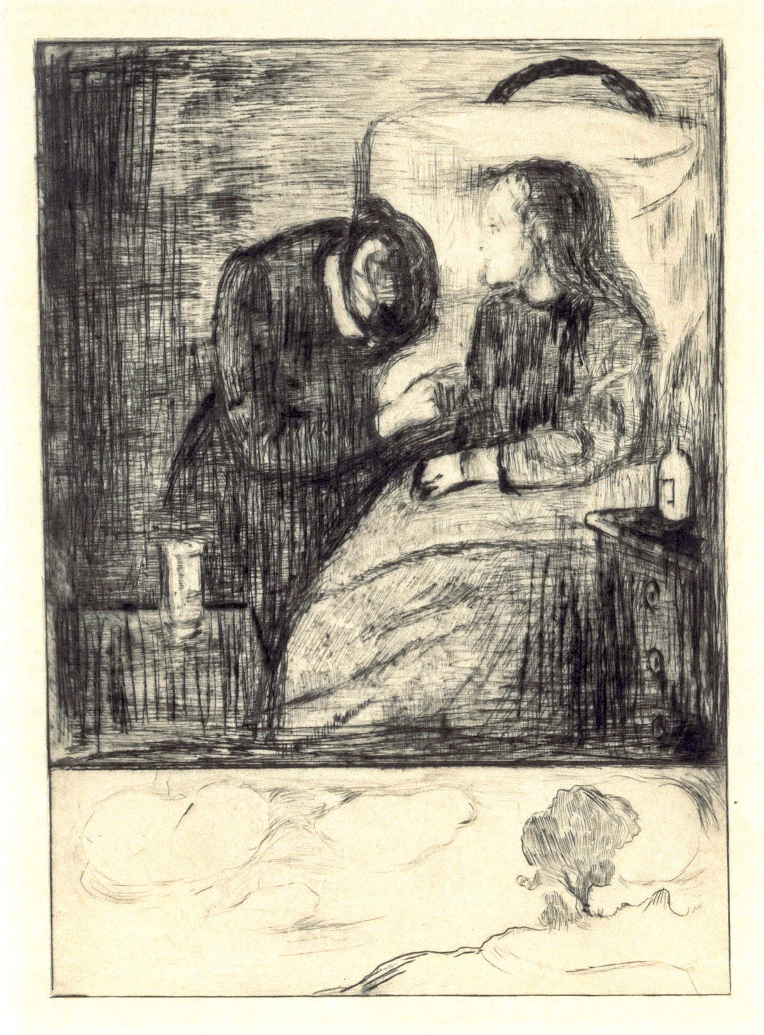

(A)
Edvard Munch
The Sick Child I — 1894
Staatliche Museen zu Berlin
Kupferstichkabinett

(B)
Edvard Munch
Two Human Beings
(The Lonely Ones) — 1894
Staatliche Museen zu Berlin
Kupferstichkabinett

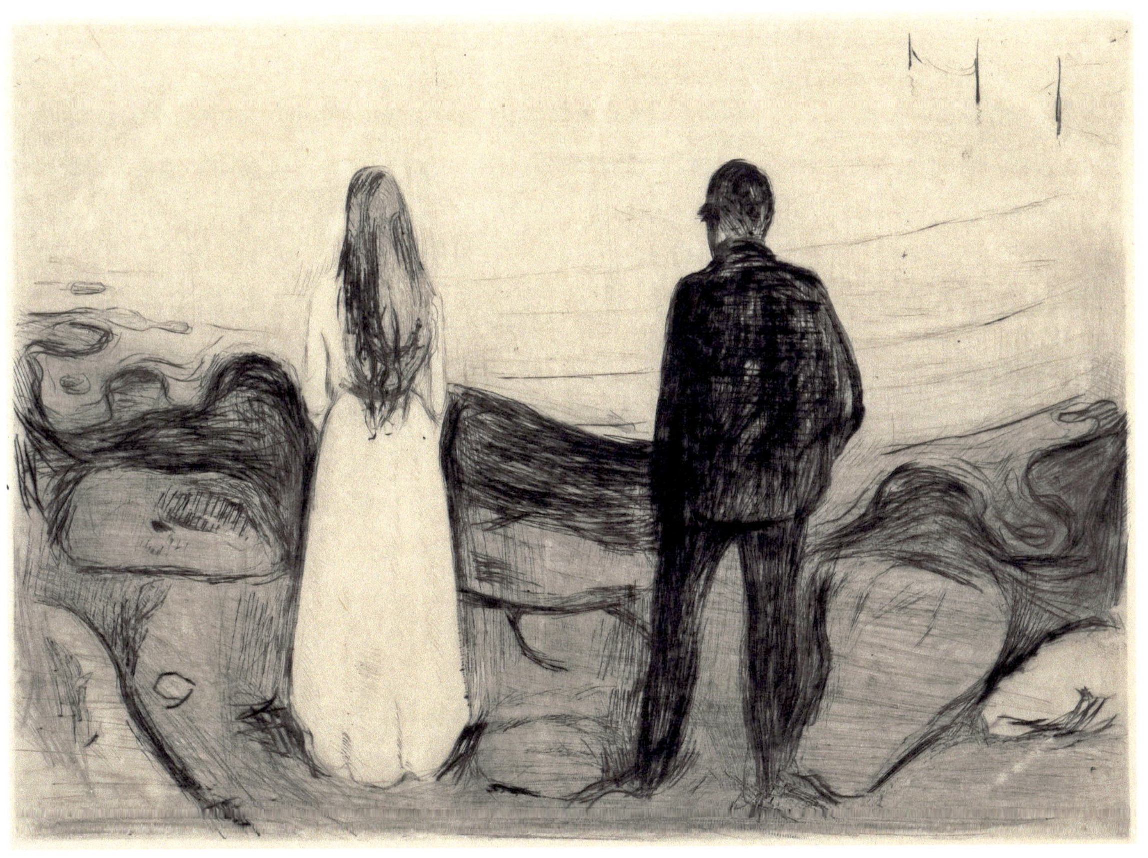

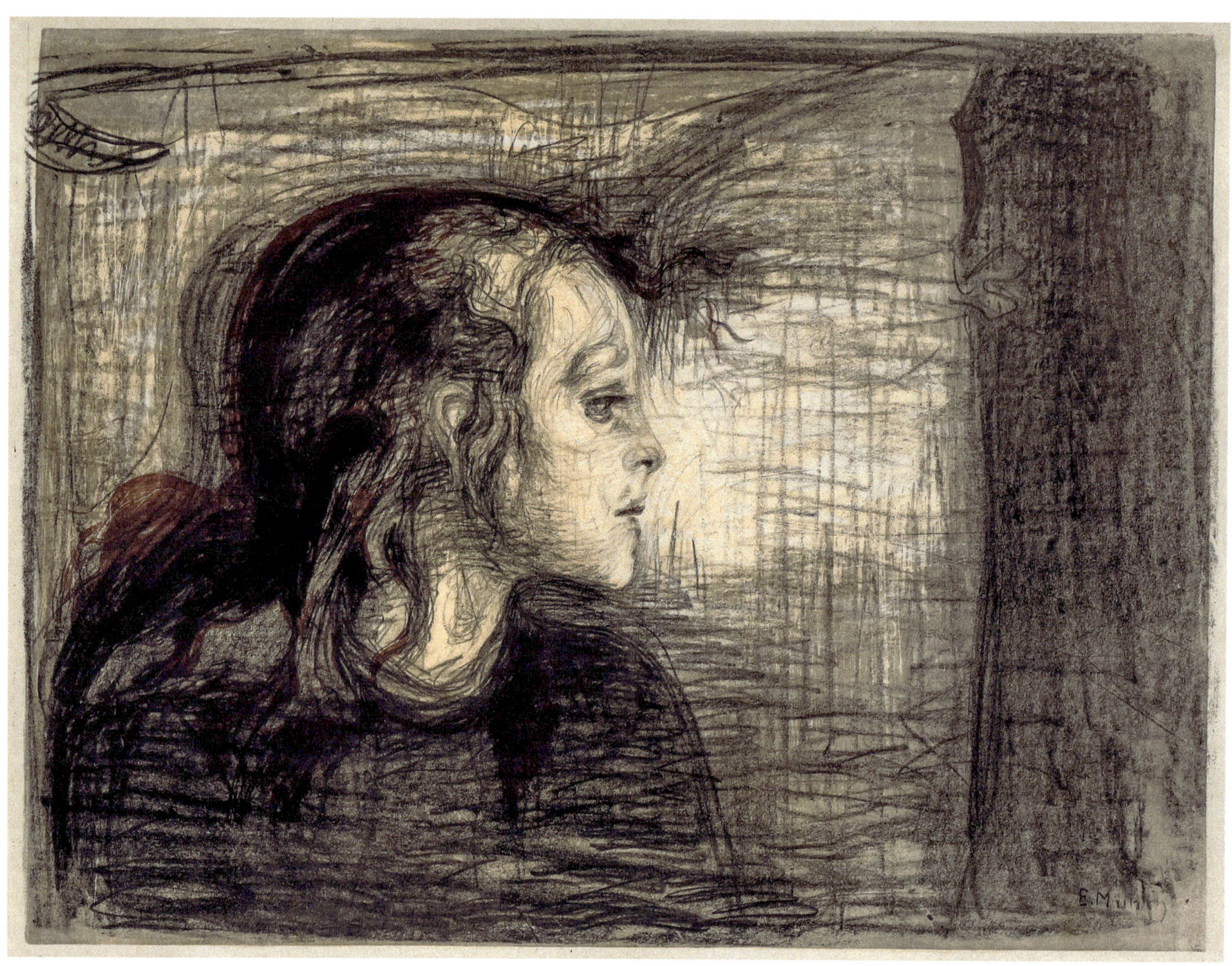

Edvard Munch
The Sick Child I — 1896
Staatliche Museen zu Berlin
Kupferstichkabinett

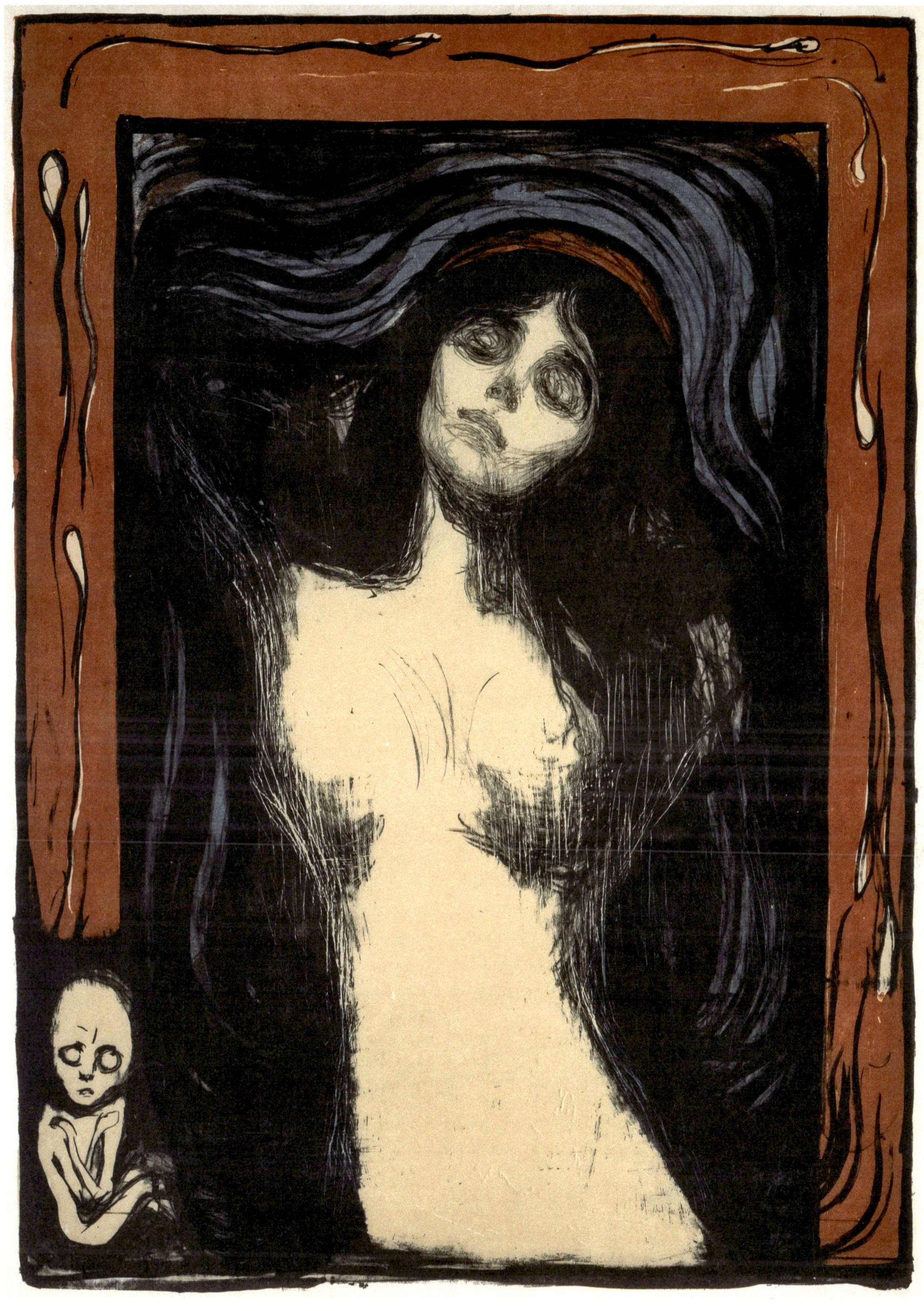

Edvard Munch
Madonna (Woman Making Love) — 1895/1902
Staatliche Museen zu Berlin
Kupferstichkabinett

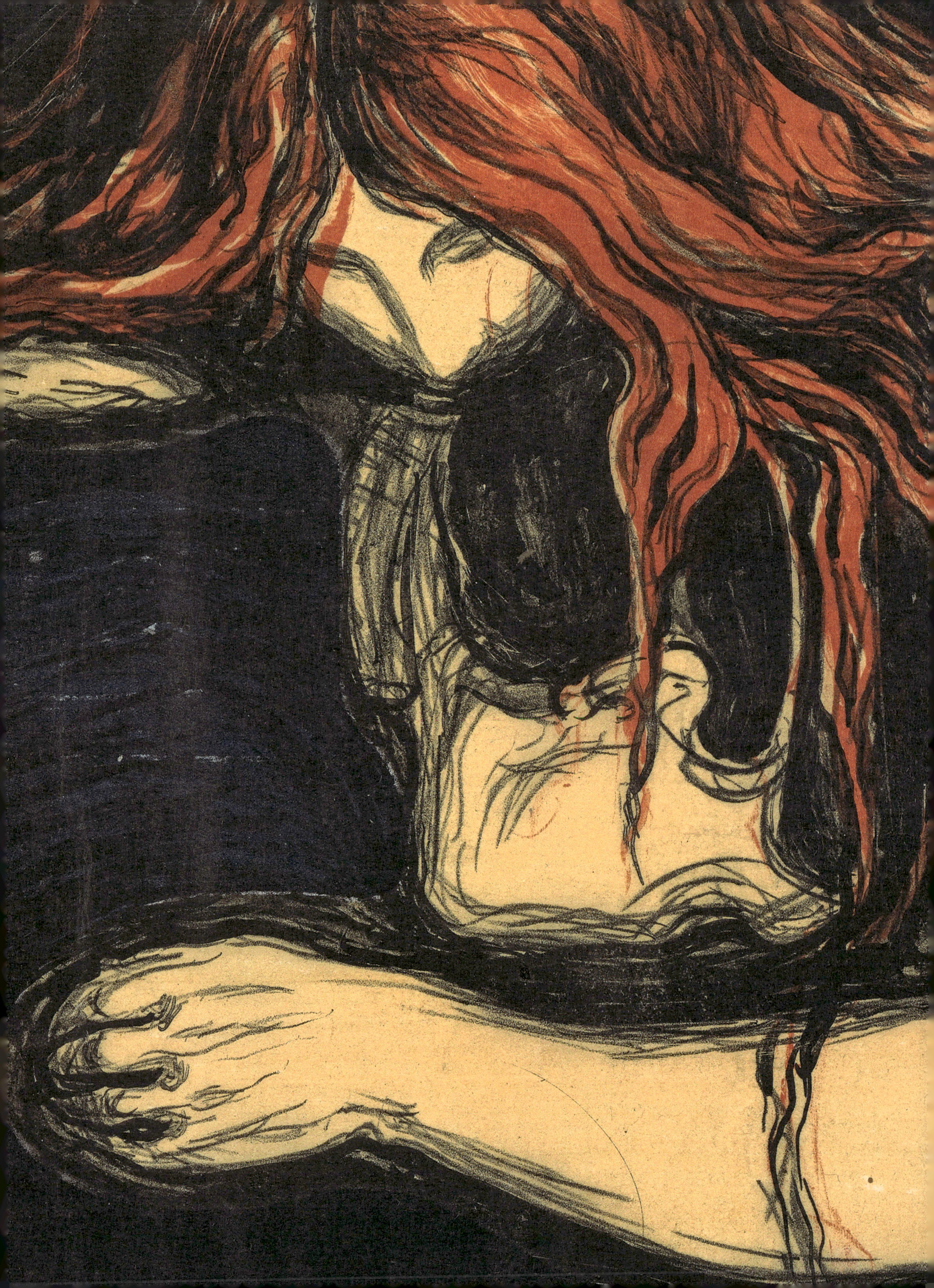

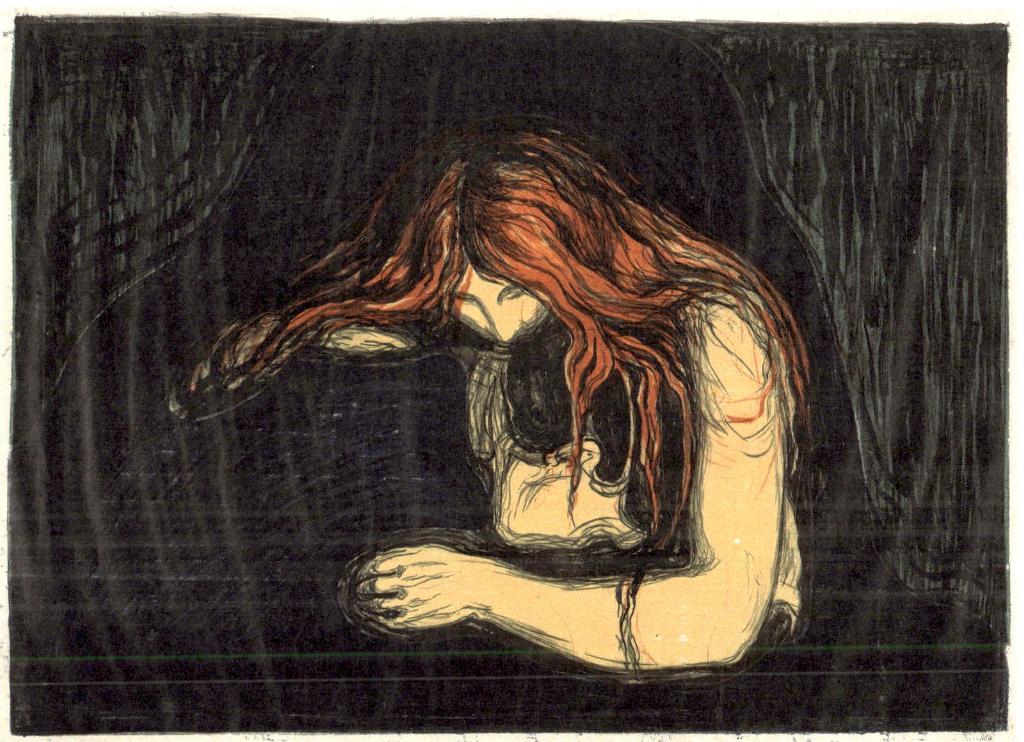

Edvard Munch
Vampire II — 1902
Munchmuseet — Oslo

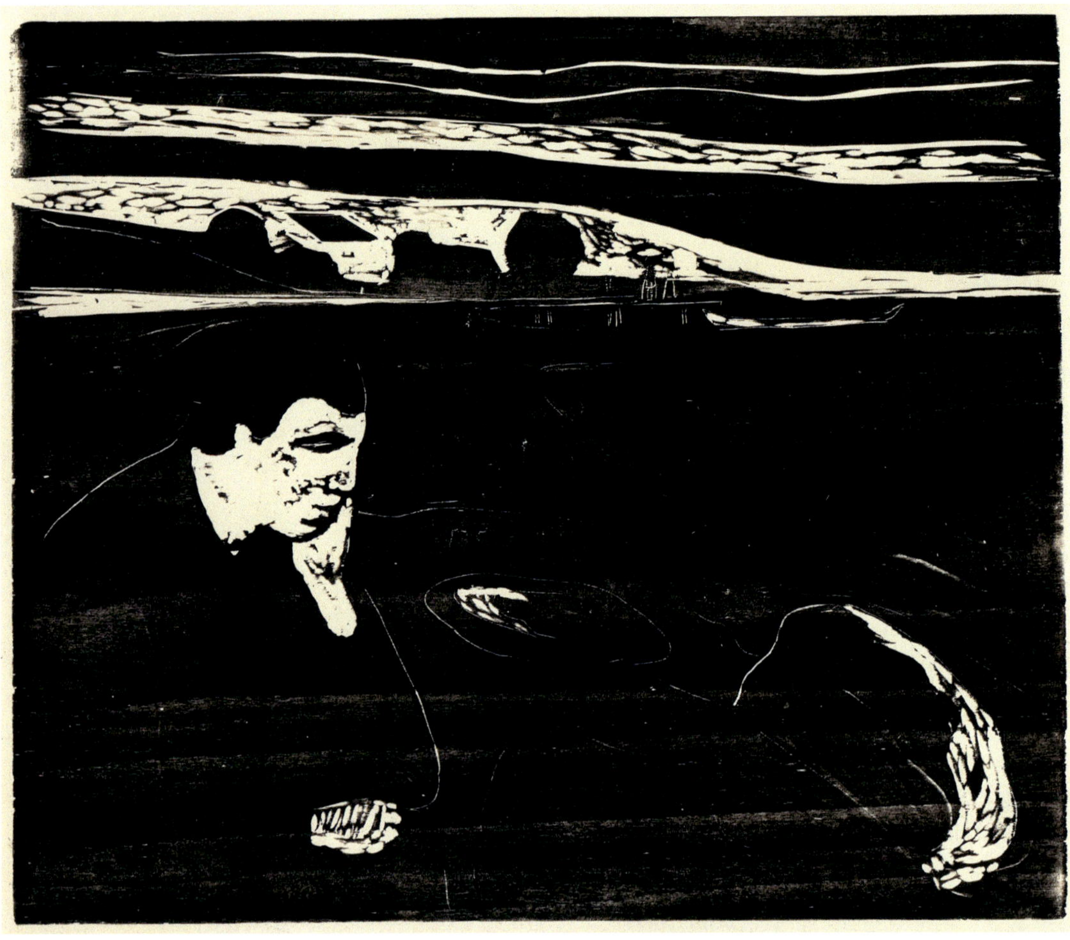

(A)
Edvard Munch
Evening. Melancholy I (By the Shore) — 1896
Staatliche Museen zu Berlin
Kupferstichkabinett

(B)
Edvard Munch
Angst (Feeling of Anxiety) — 1896
Staatliche Museen zu Berlin
Kupferstichkabinett

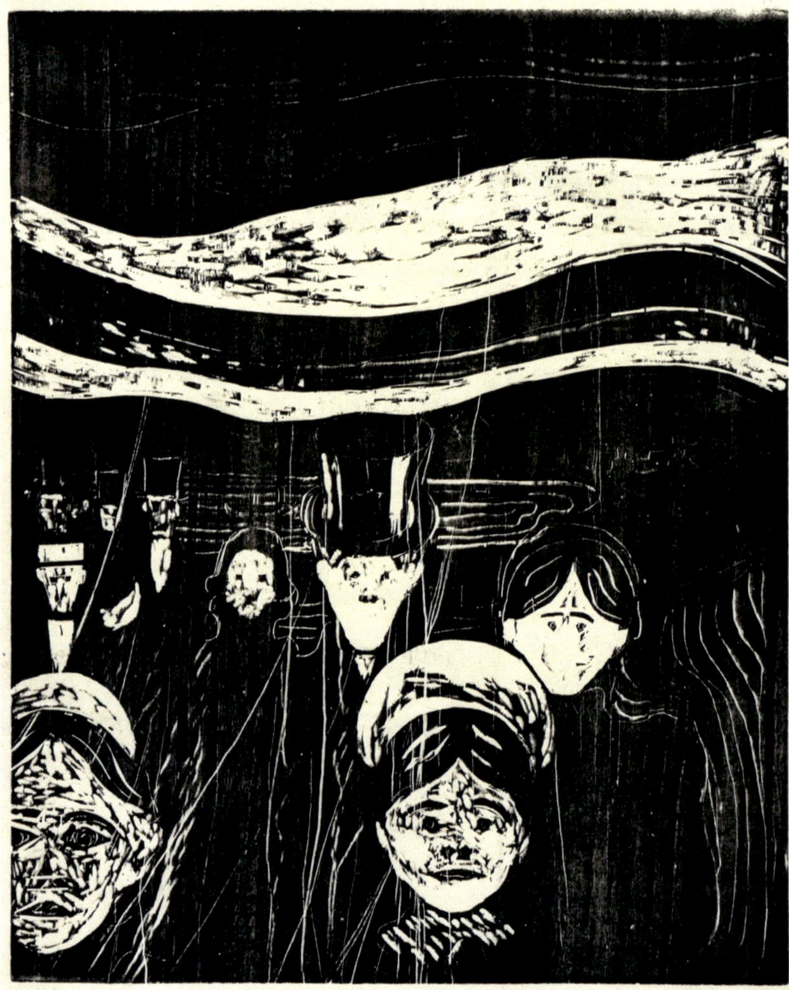

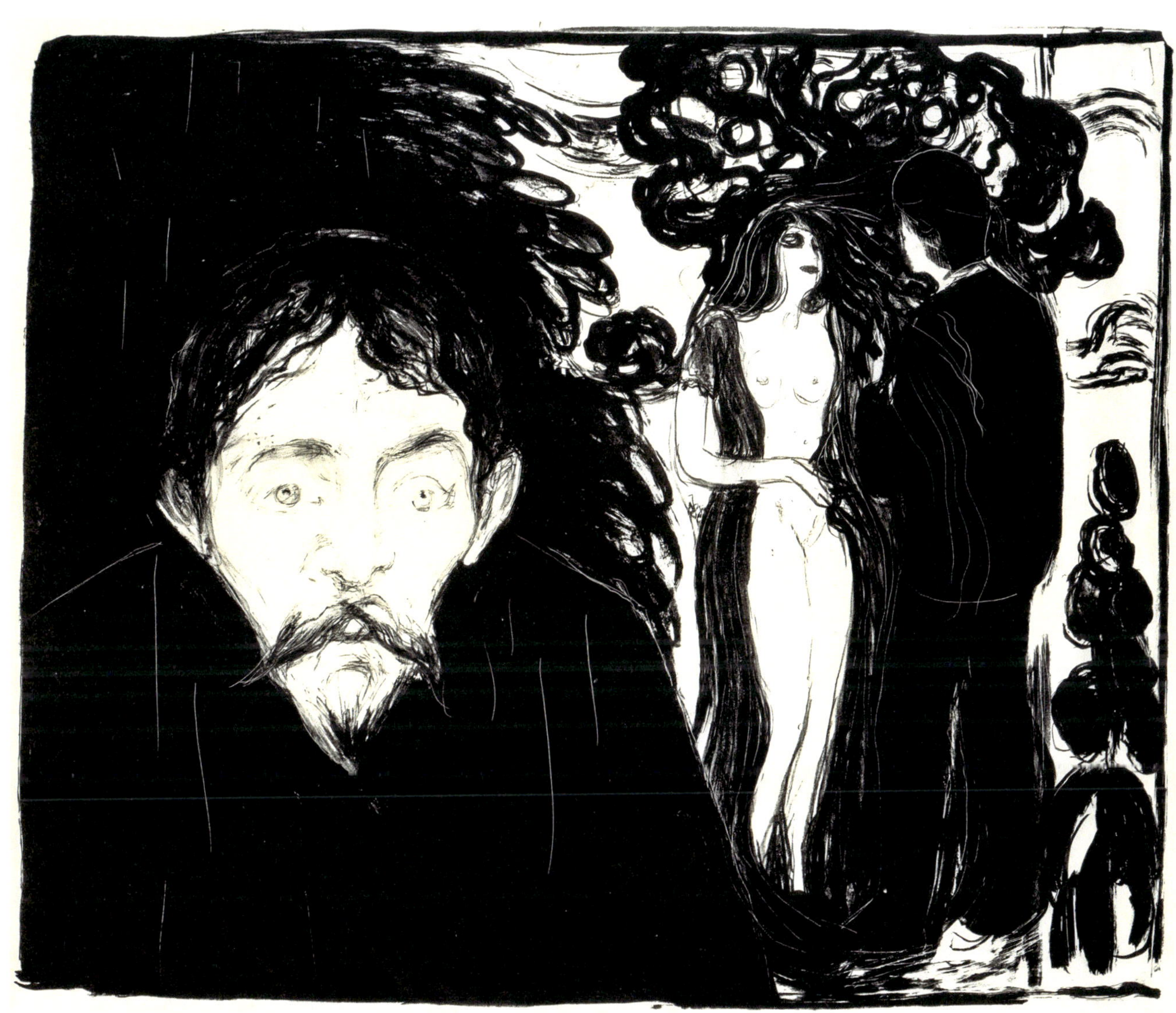

Edvard Munch
Jealousy II — 1896
Staatliche Museen zu Berlin
Kupferstichkabinett

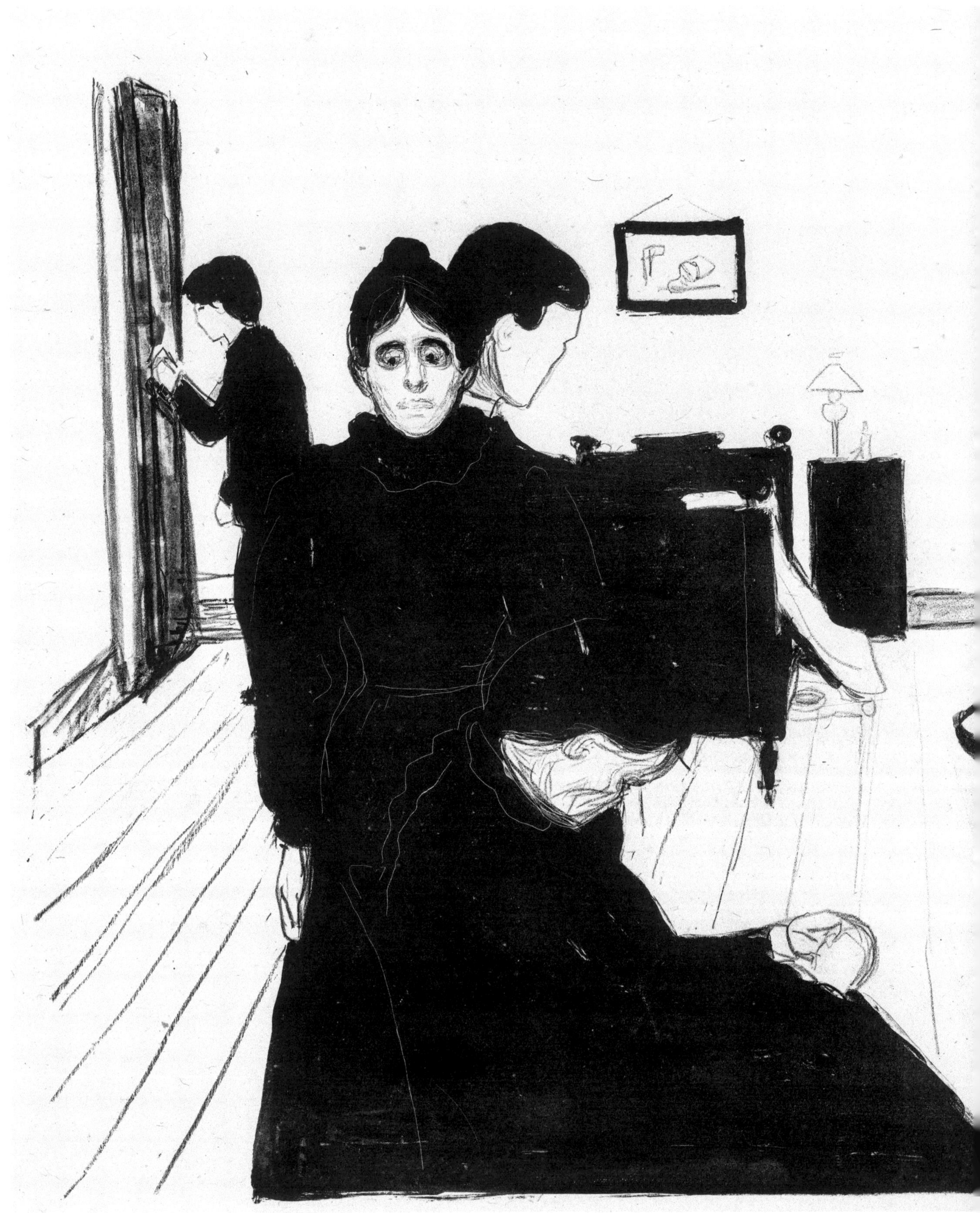

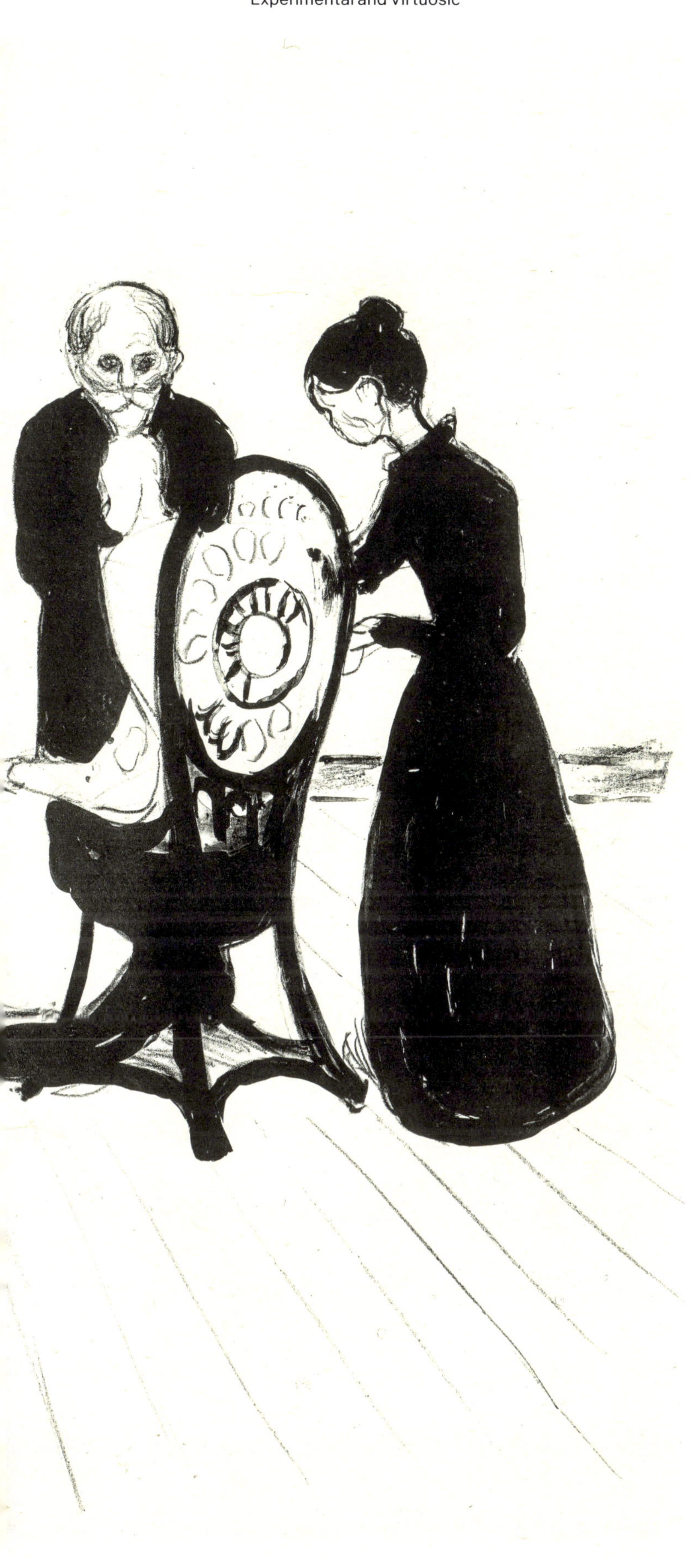

Edvard Munch
Death in the Sickroom — 1896
Staatliche Museen zu Berlin
Kupferstichkabinett

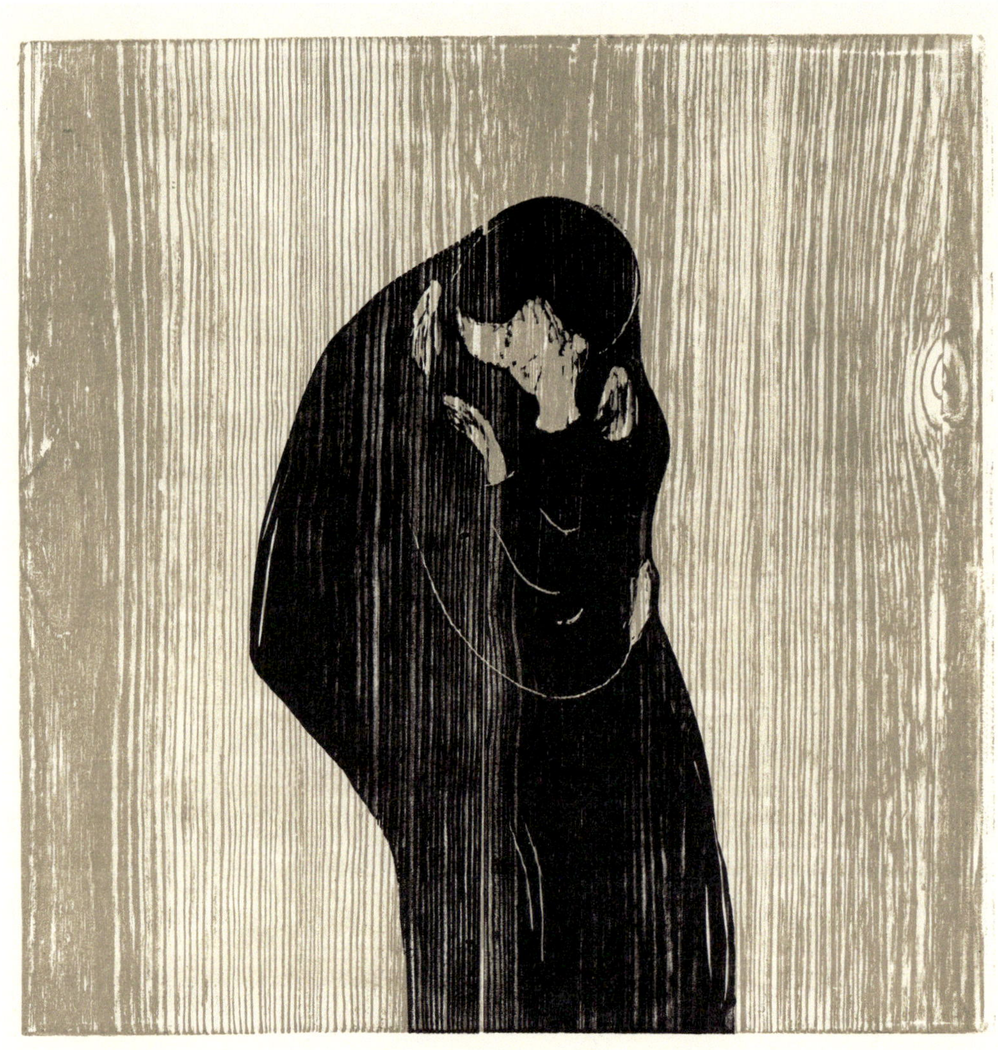

Edvard Munch
The Kiss IV — 1902
Munchmuseet — Oslo

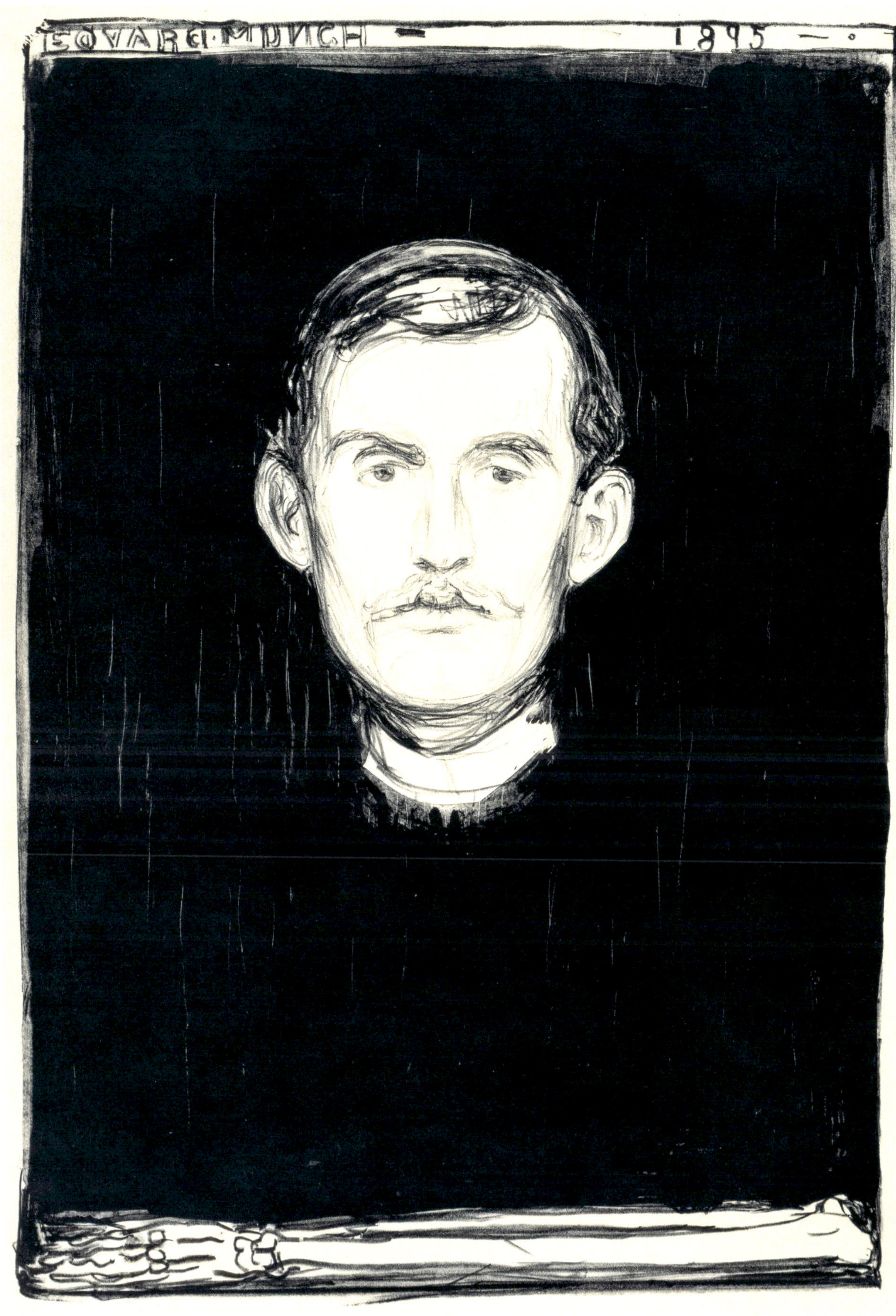

Edvard Munch
Self-Portrait (with Skeleton Arm) — 1895
Staatliche Museen zu Berlin
Kupferstichkabinett

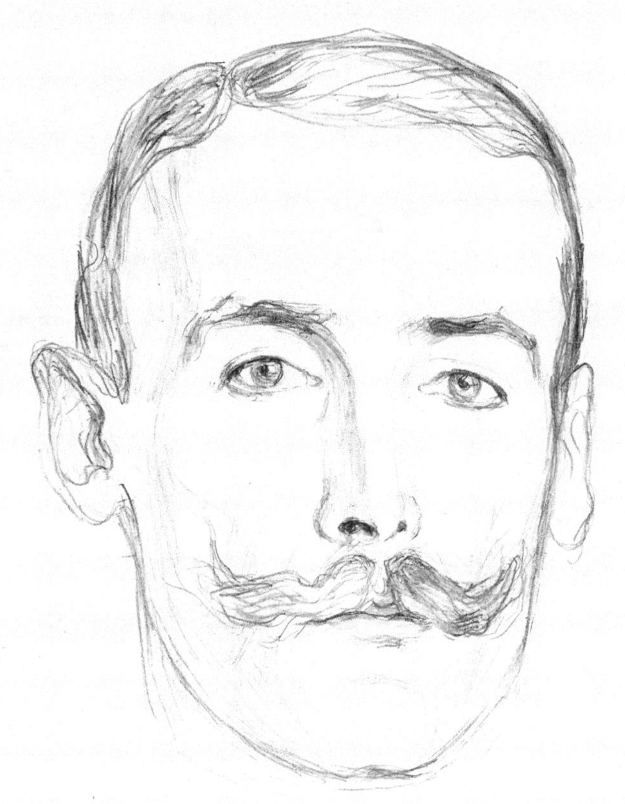

Edvard Munch
Harry Graf Kessler II — 1895
Staatliche Museen zu Berlin
Kupferstichkabinett

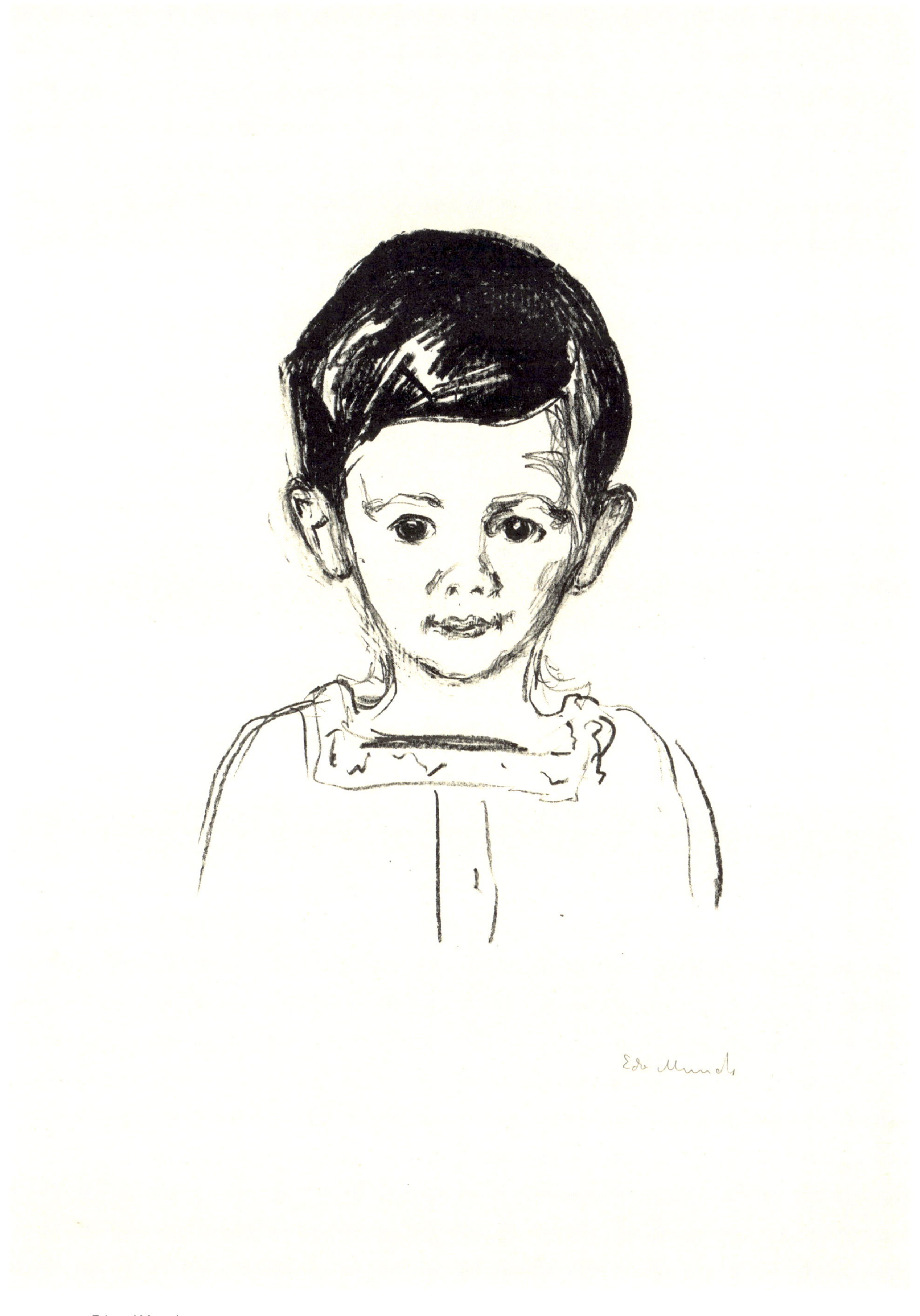

Edvard Munch
Andreas Schwarz — 1906 [1907?]
Staatliche Museen zu Berlin
Kupferstichkabinett

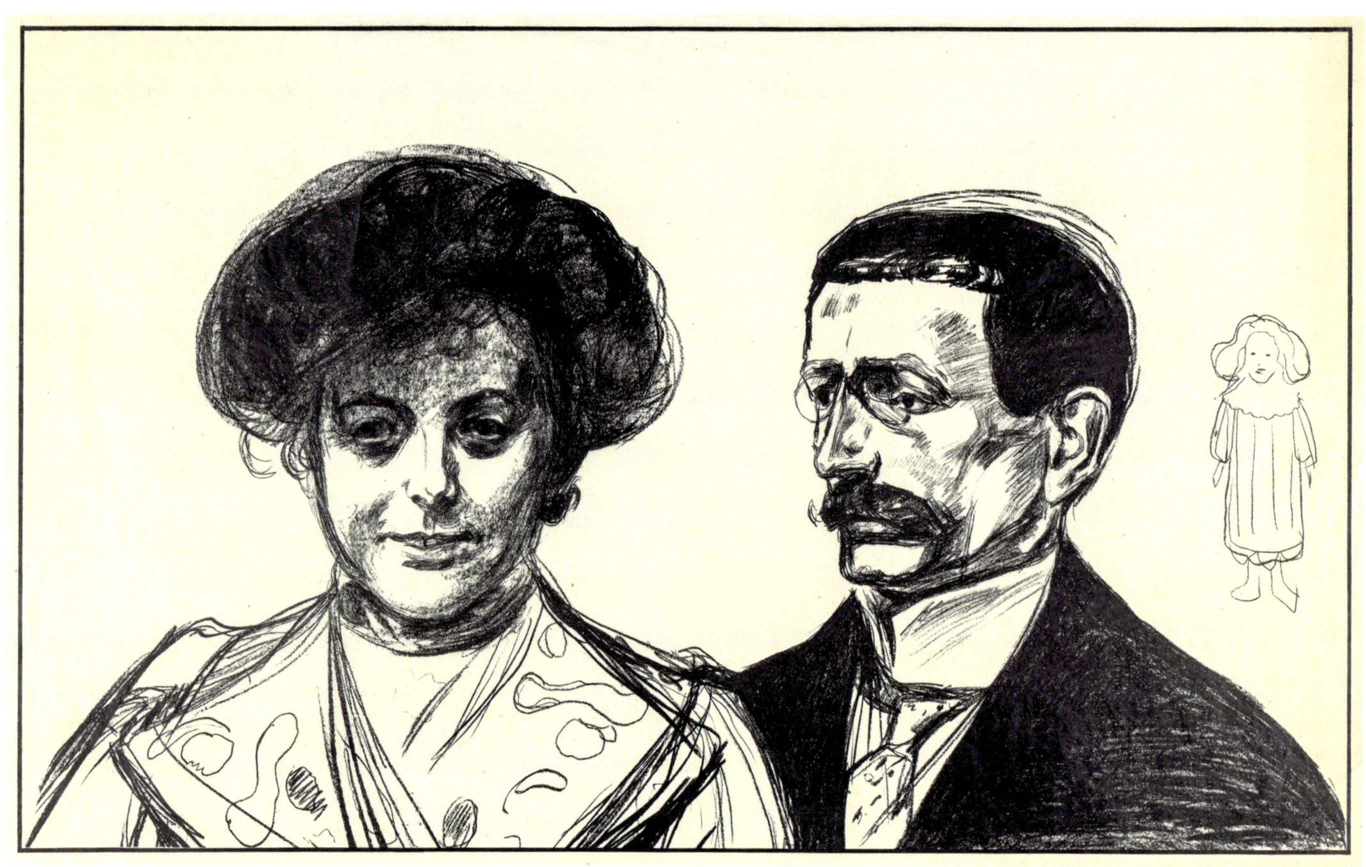

Edvard Munch
Anna and Walter Leistikow — 1902
Munchmuseet — Oslo

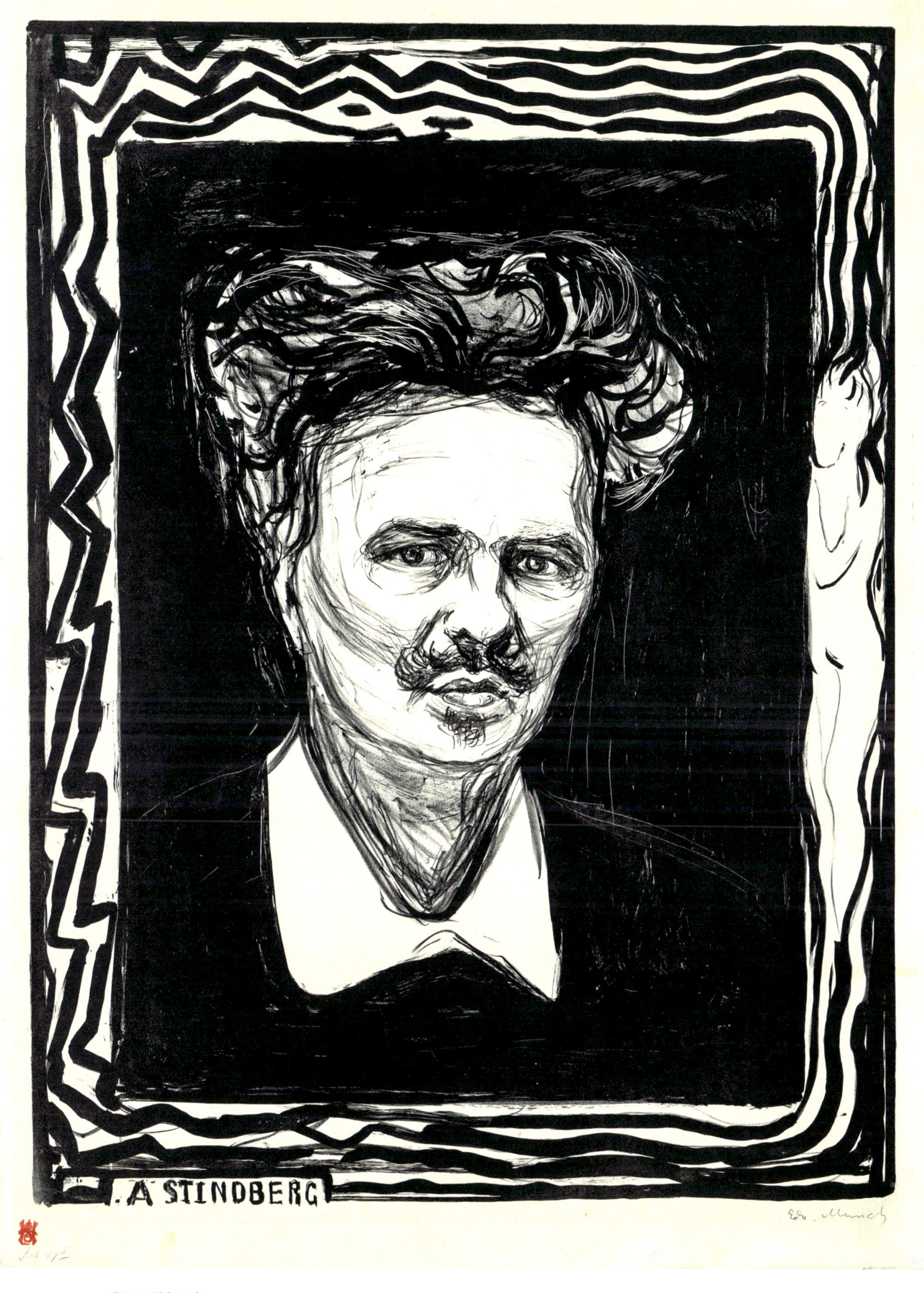

Edvard Munch
August Strindberg — 1896
Staatliche Museen zu Berlin
Kupferstichkabinett

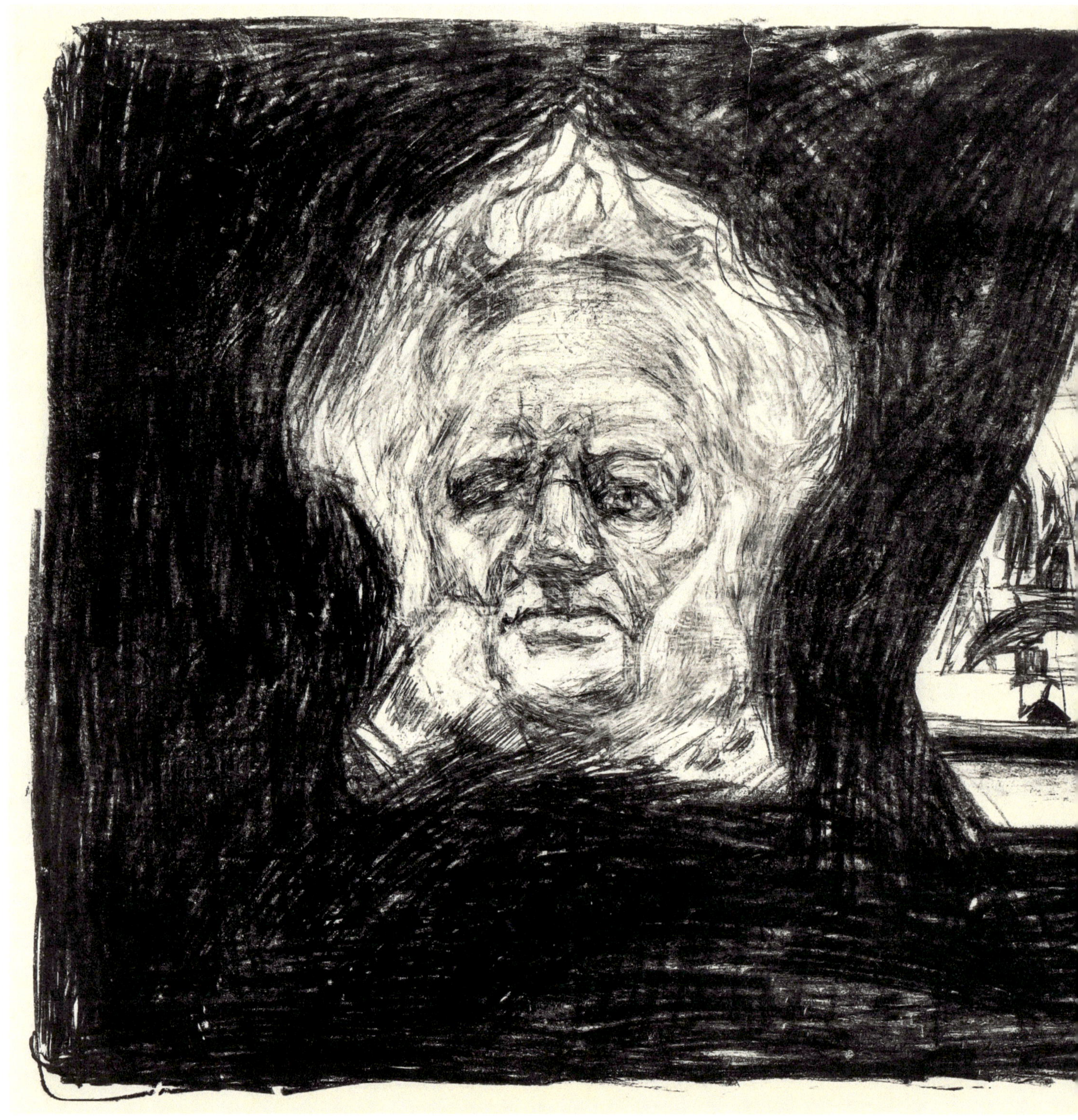

Edvard Munch
Henrik Ibsen at the Grand Café — 1902
Staatliche Museen zu Berlin
Kupferstichkabinett

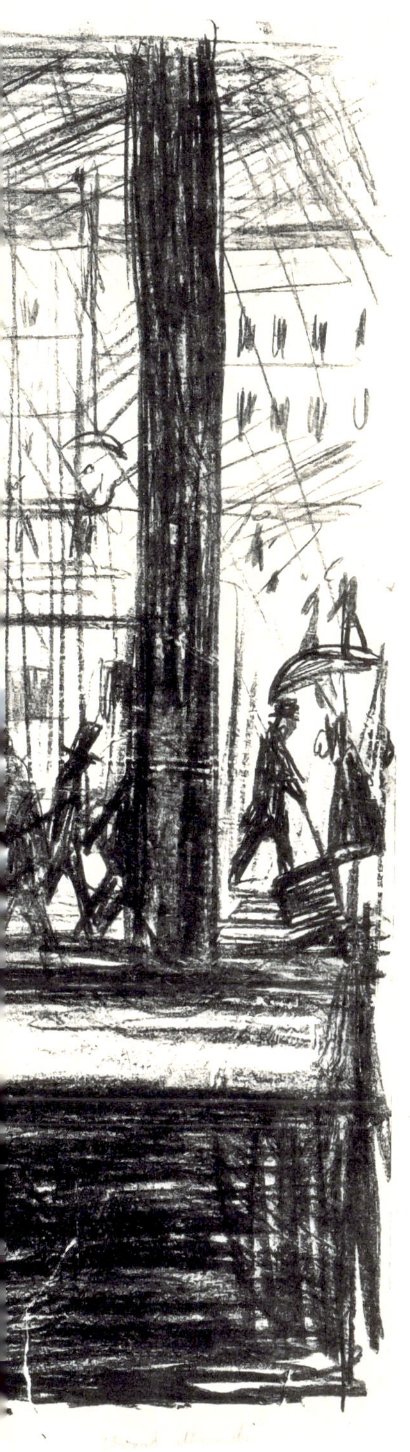

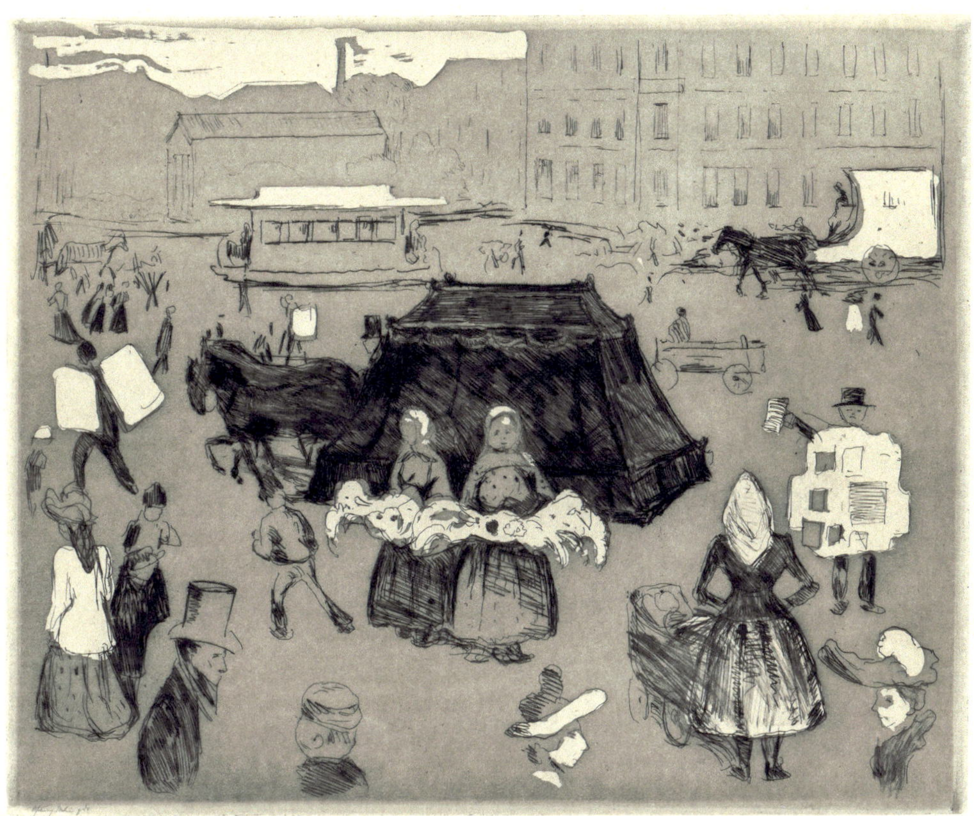

Edvard Munch
The Hearse. Potsdamer Platz — 1902
Staatliche Museen zu Berlin
Kupferstichkabinett

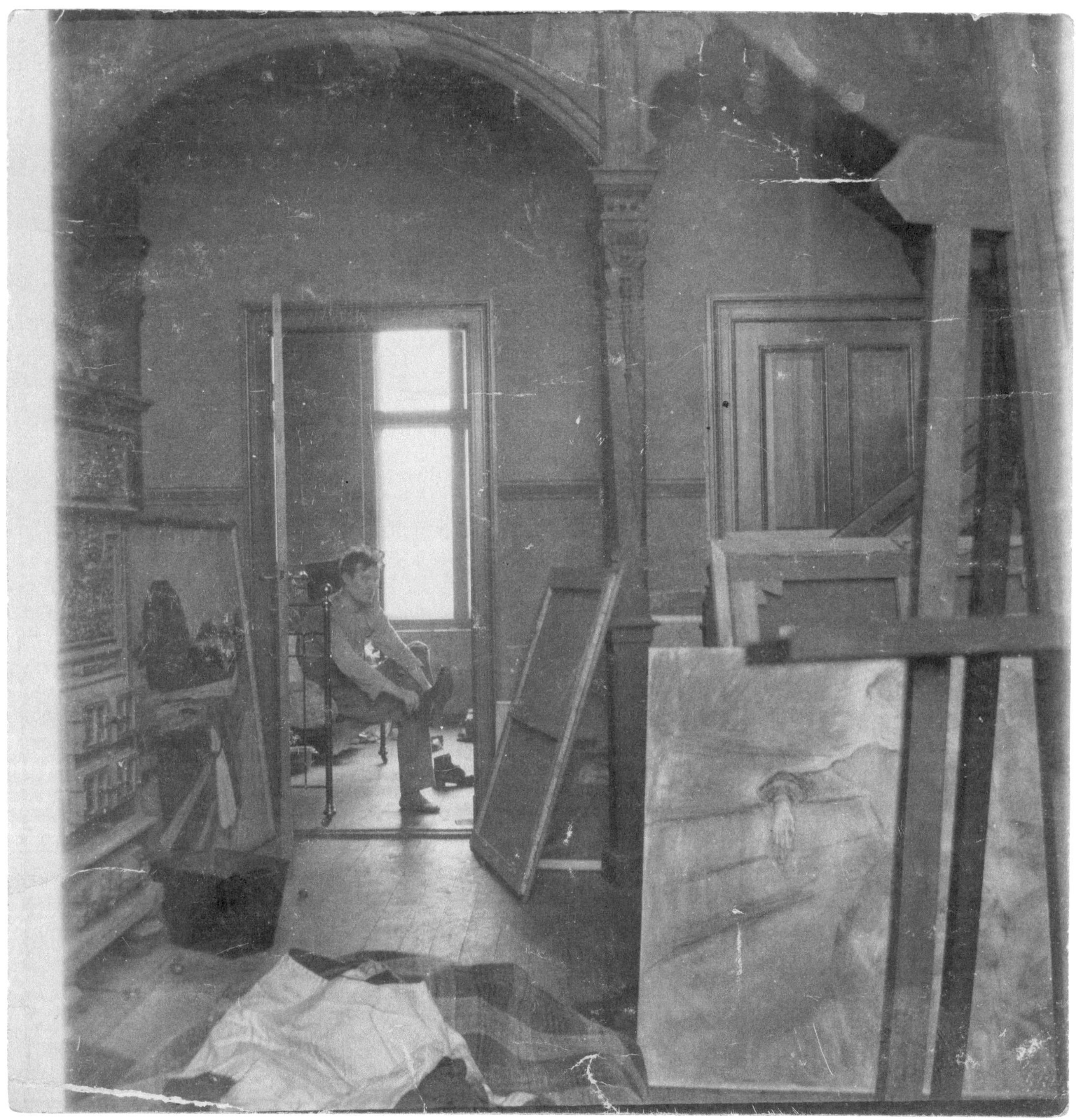

Edvard Munch
Self-Portrait in His Studio
Lützowstrasse 82, Berlin — 1902
Munchmuseet — Oslo

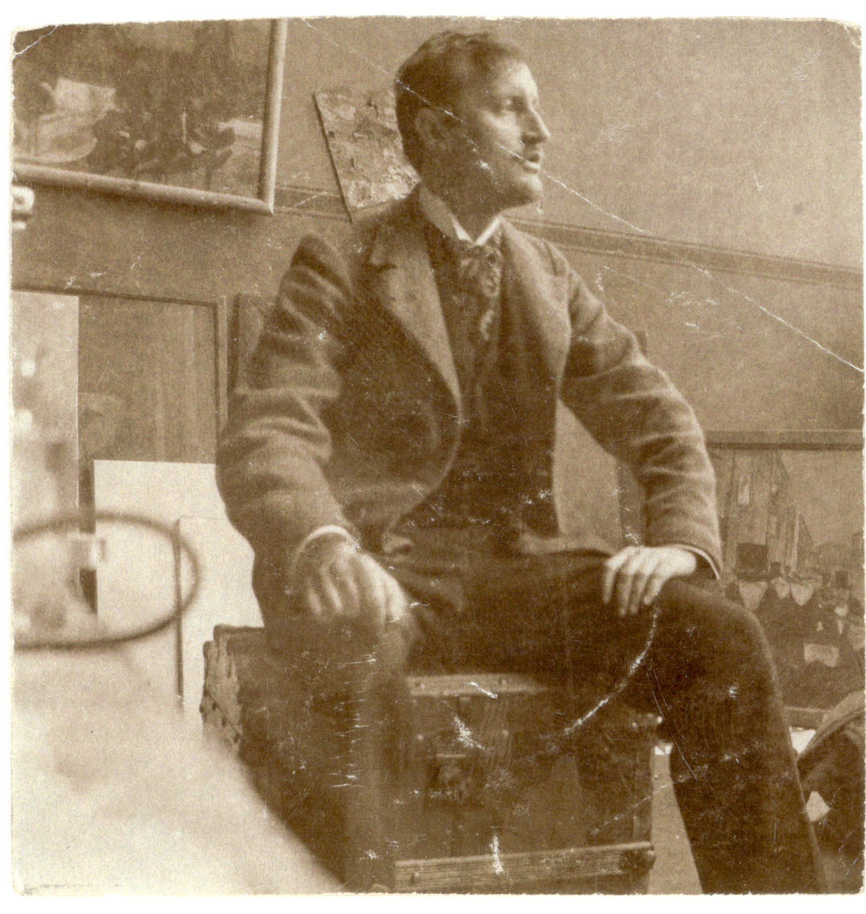

(A + B)
Edvard Munch
Self-Portrait on a Valise in His Studio
Lützowstrasse 82, Berlin — 1902
Munchmuseet — Oslo

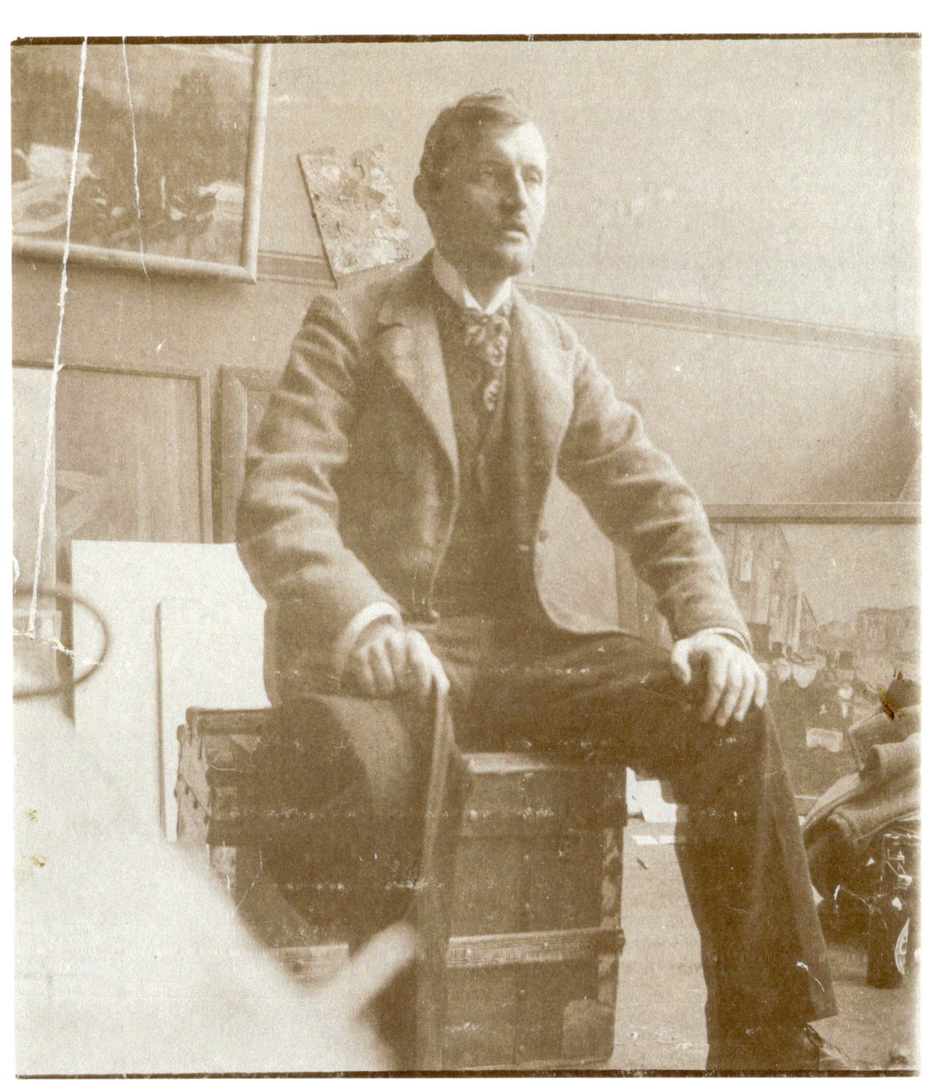

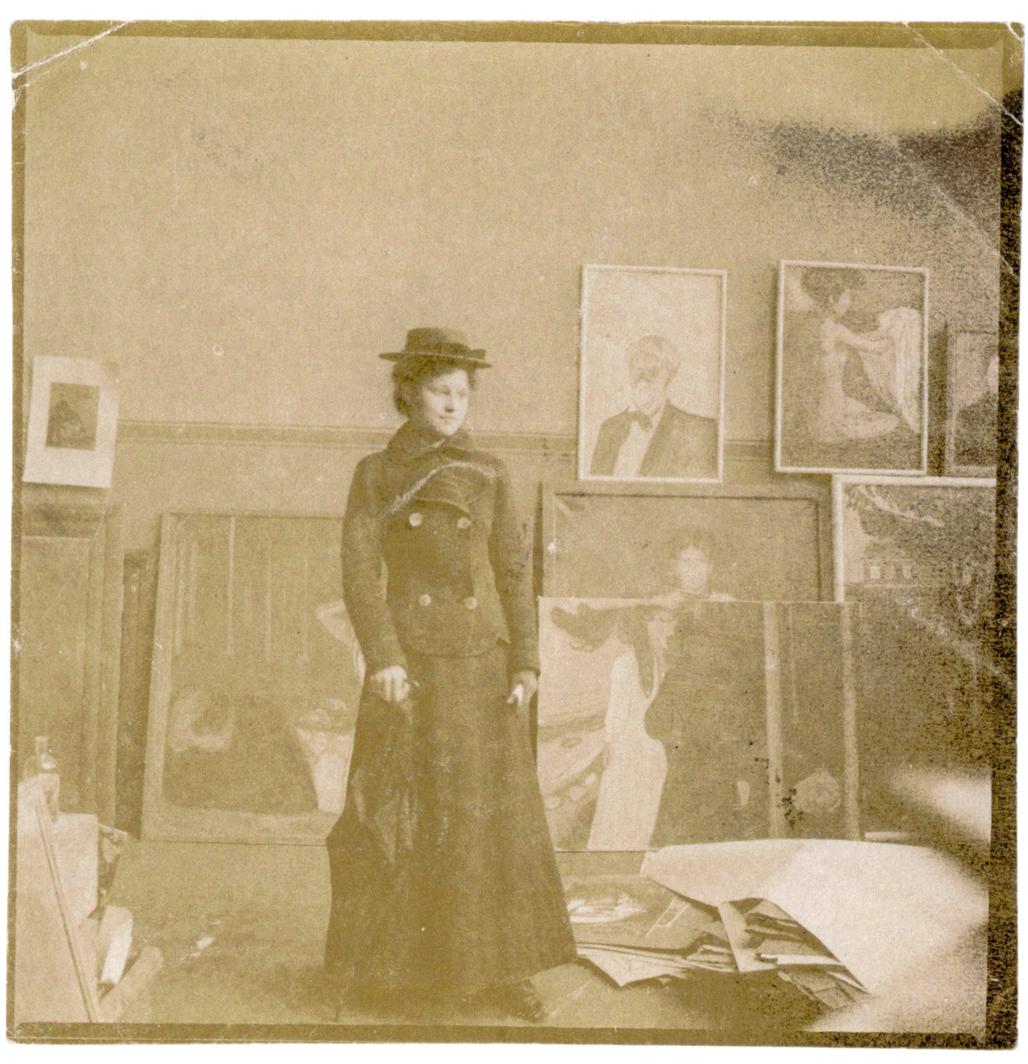

(A)
Edvard Munch
Marta Sandal in Munch's
Studio, Lützowstrasse 82
Berlin — 1902
Munchmuseet — Oslo

(B)
Edvard Munch
The Wieck Brothers in Munch's
Studio, Lützowstrasse 82
Berlin — 1902
Munchmuseet — Oslo

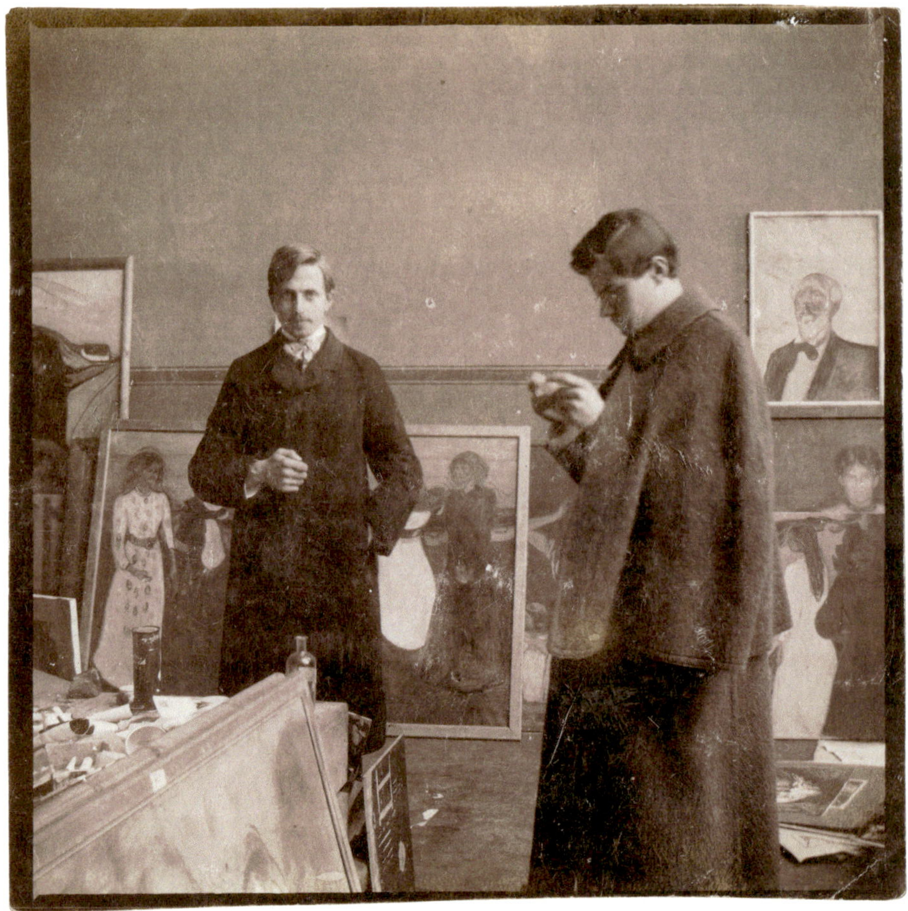

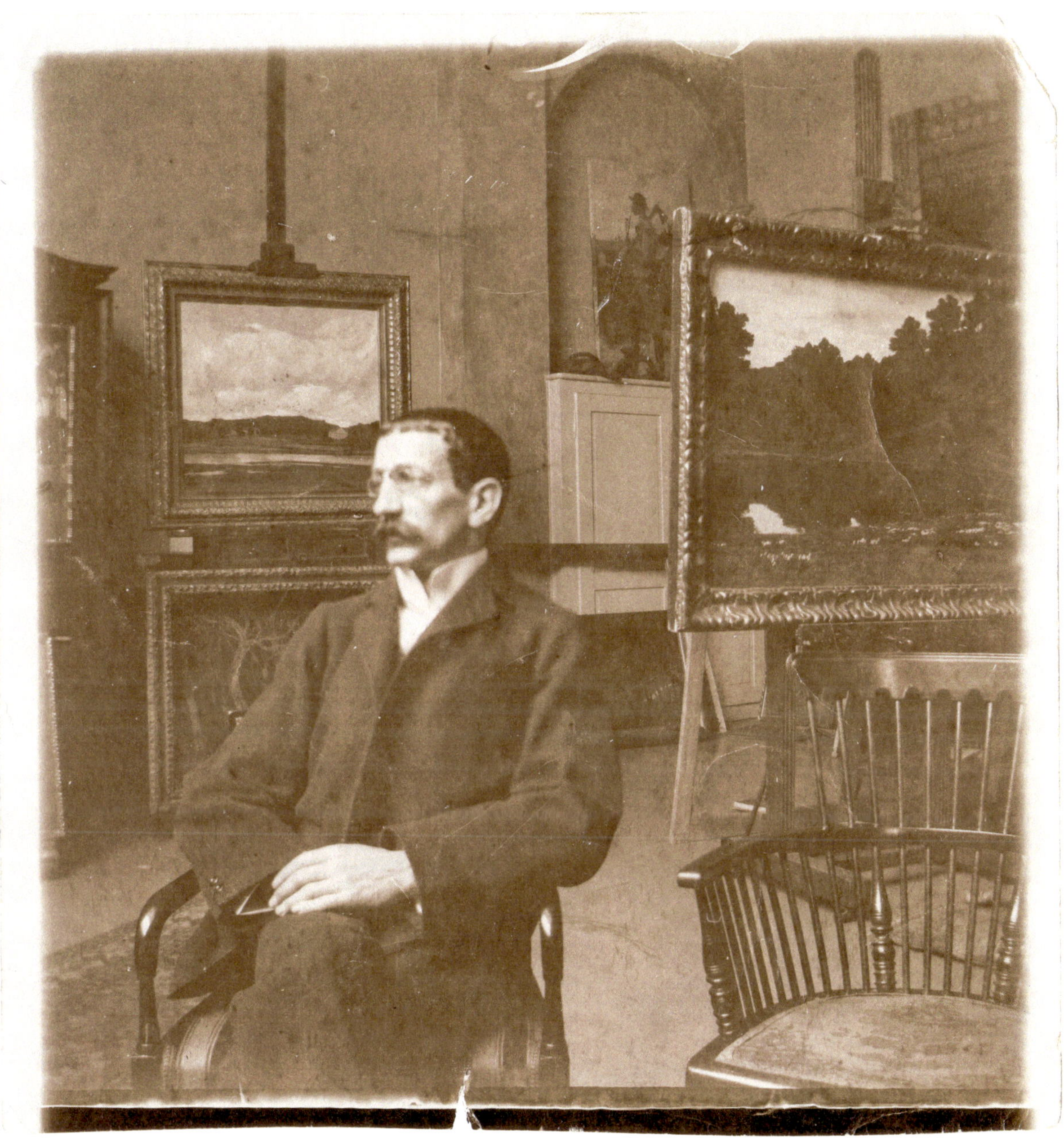

Edvard Munch
Walter Leistikow in His Studio — 1902
Munchmuseet — Oslo

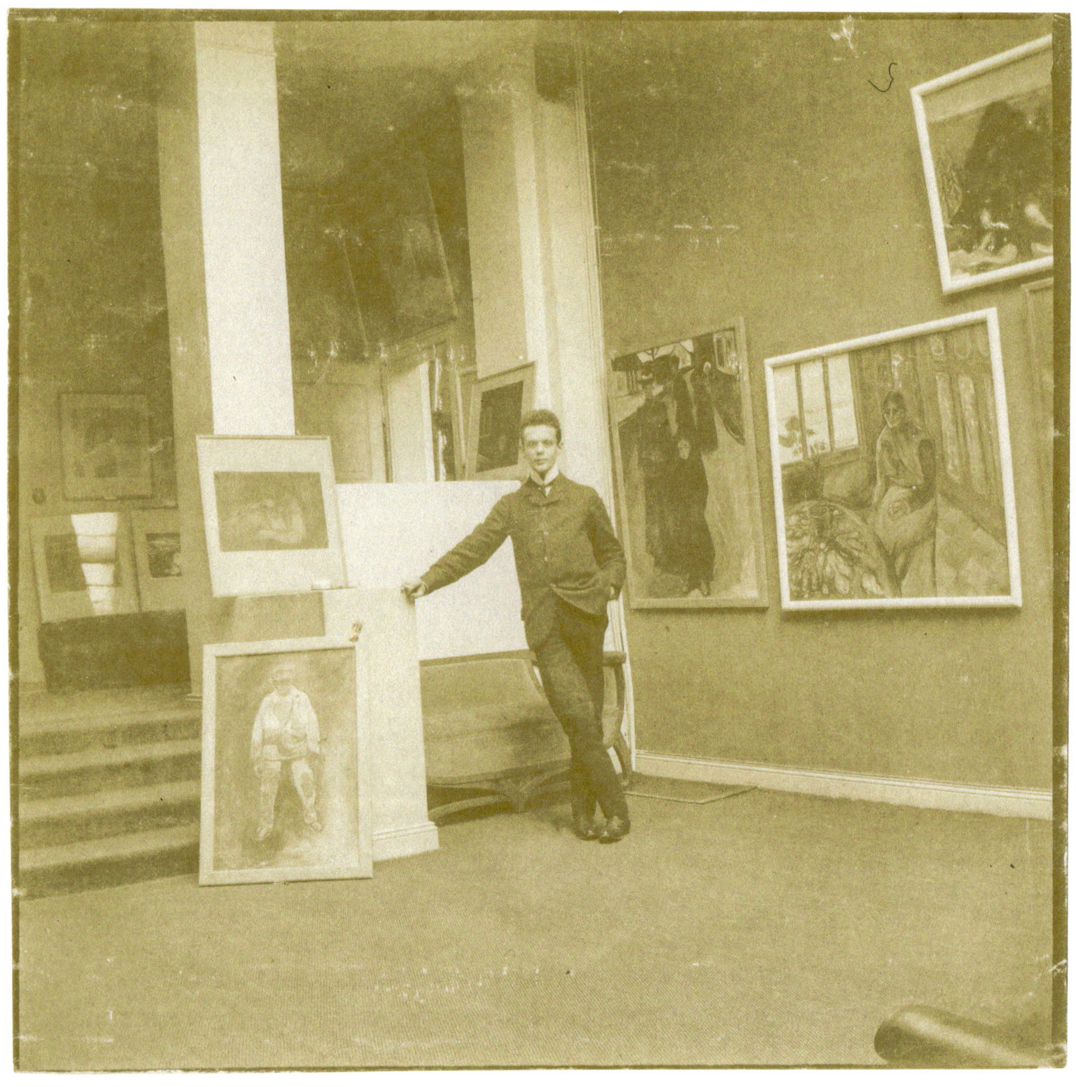

Edvard Munch
Paul Cassirer's Exhibition Premises, Berlin — 1903
Munchmuseet — Oslo

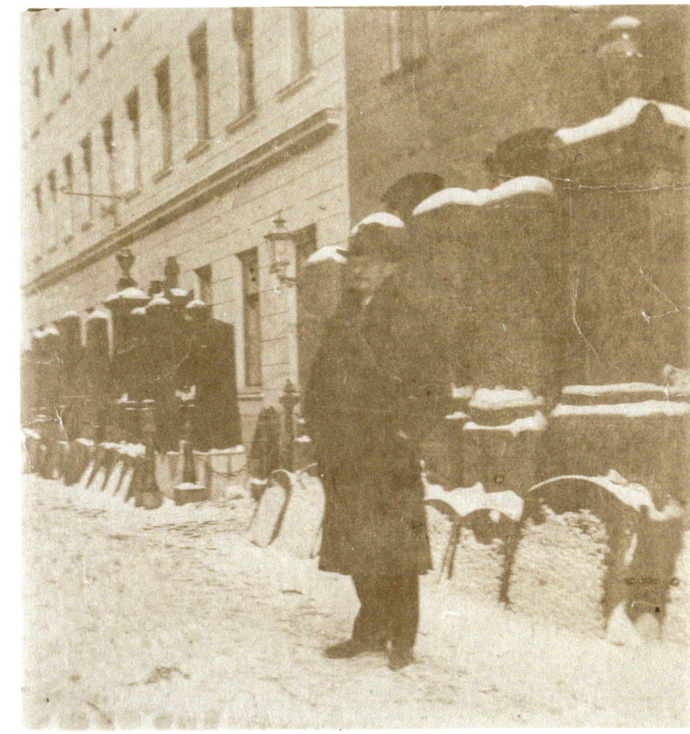

(A)
Albert Kollmann
in Front of Gravestones, Berlin — 1902
Munchmuseet — Oslo

(B)
Edvard Munch
in Front of Gravestones, Berlin — 1902
Munchmuseet — Oslo

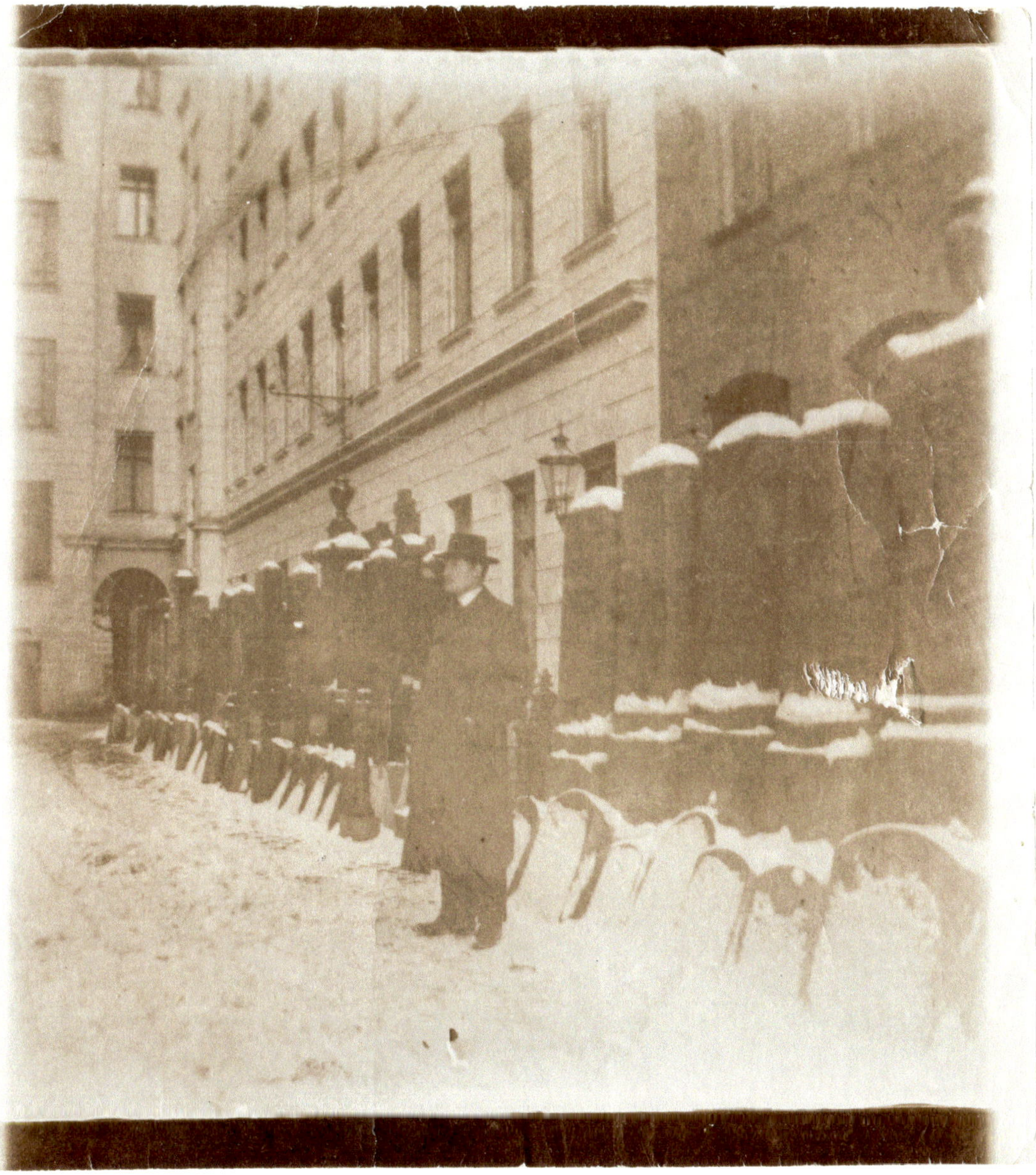

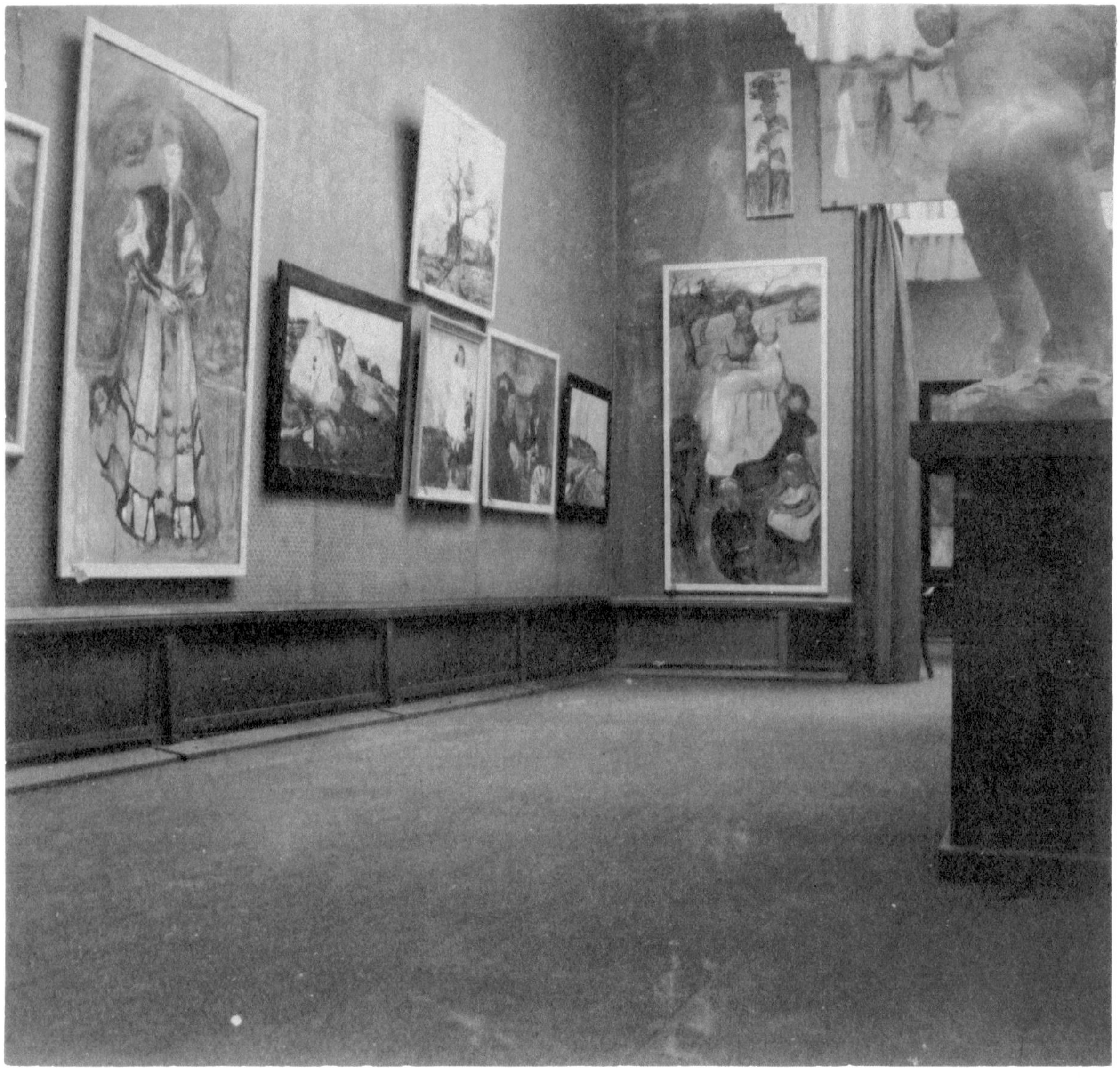

Edvard Munch
Munch's Exhibition
at Paul Cassirer, Berlin — 1907
Munchmuseet — Oslo

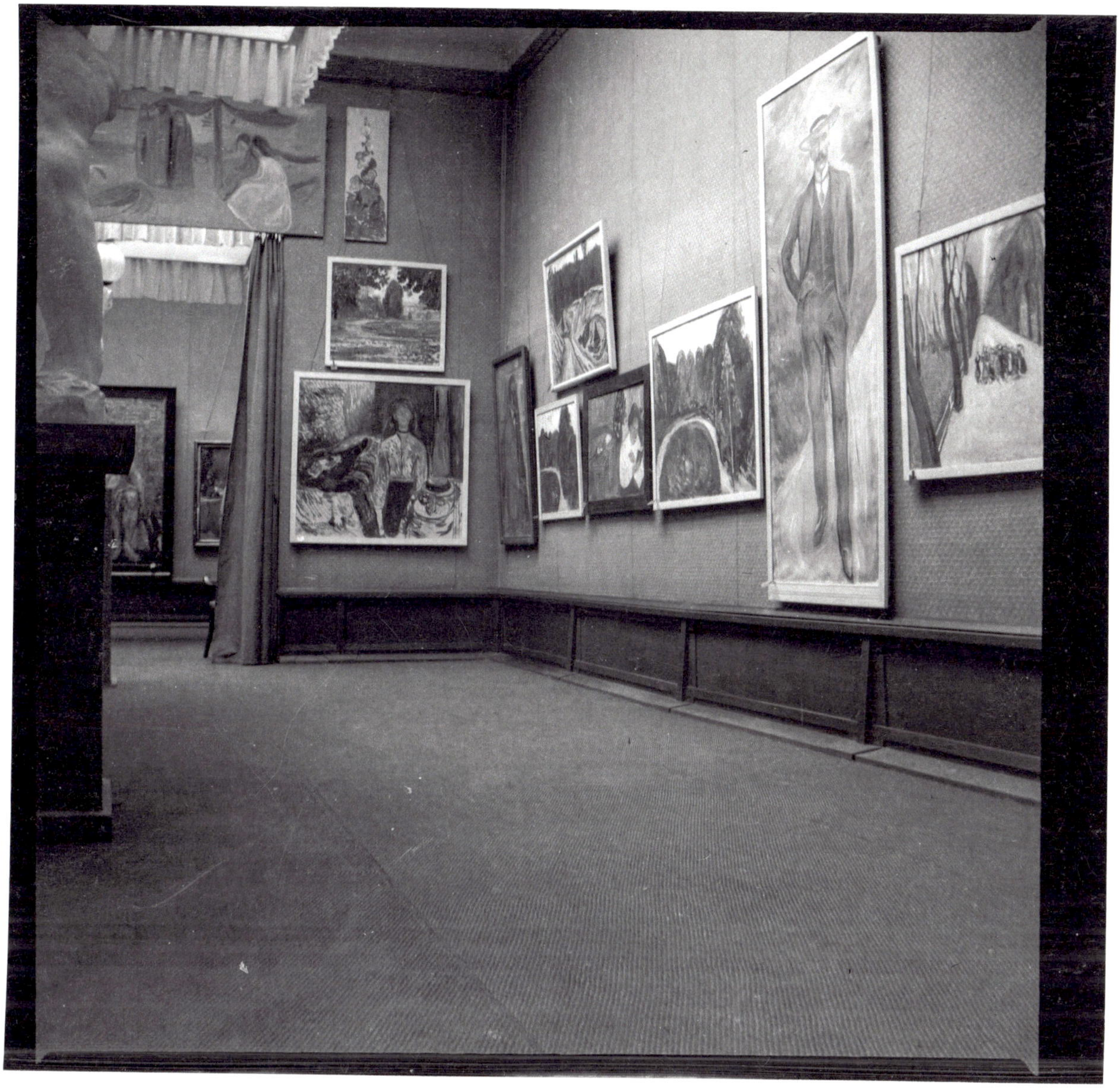

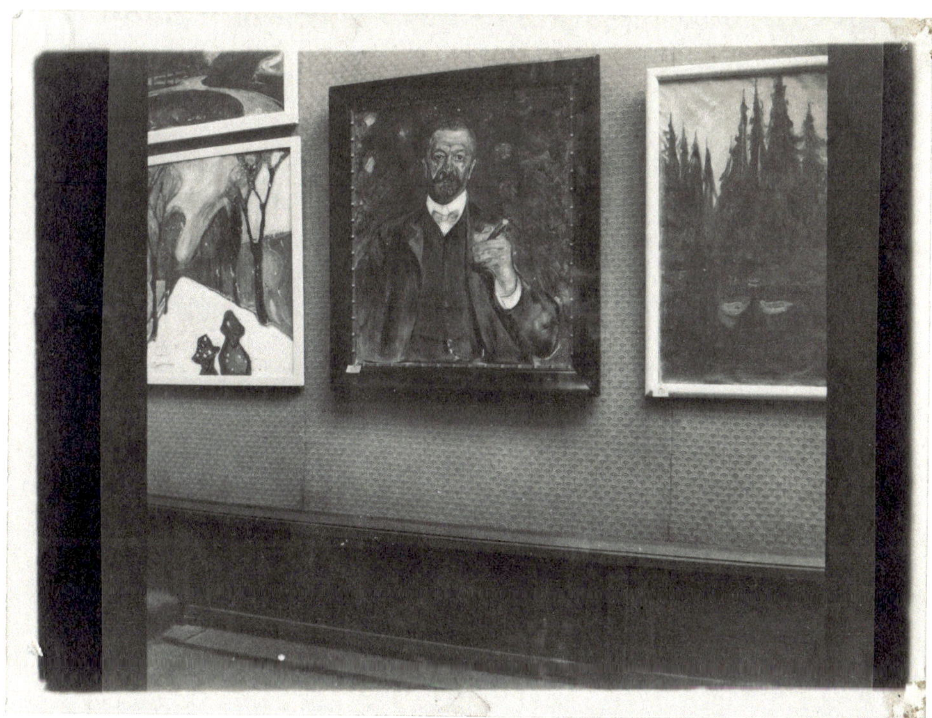

(A + B)
Edvard Munch
Munch's Exhibition
at Paul Cassirer, Berlin — 1907
Munchmuseet — Oslo

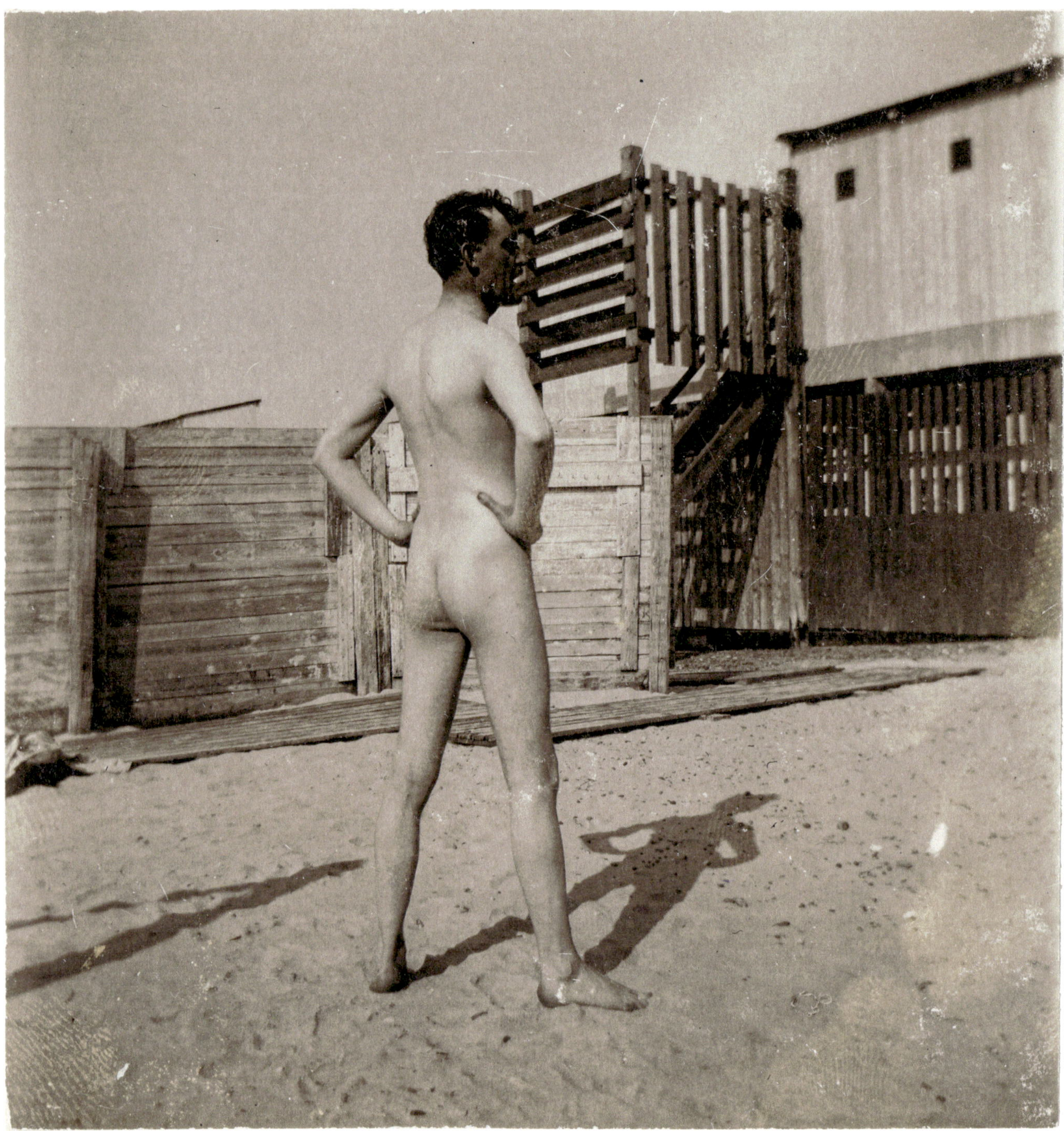

Edvard Munch
Nude Self-Portrait
Warnemünde — 1907
Munchmuseet — Oslo

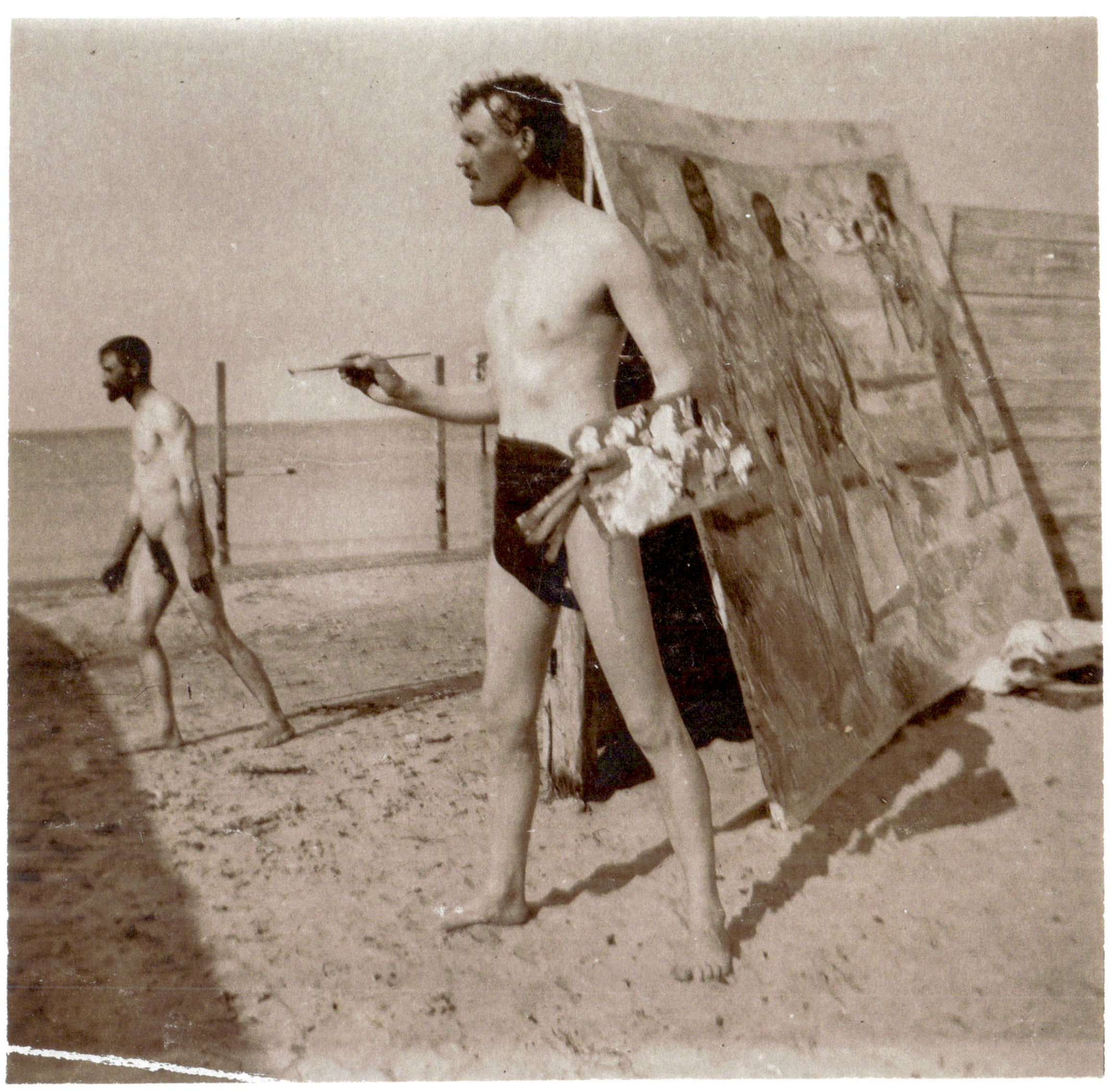

Edvard Munch
Self-Portrait with a Model on the Beach
Warnemünde — 1907
Munchmuseet — Oslo

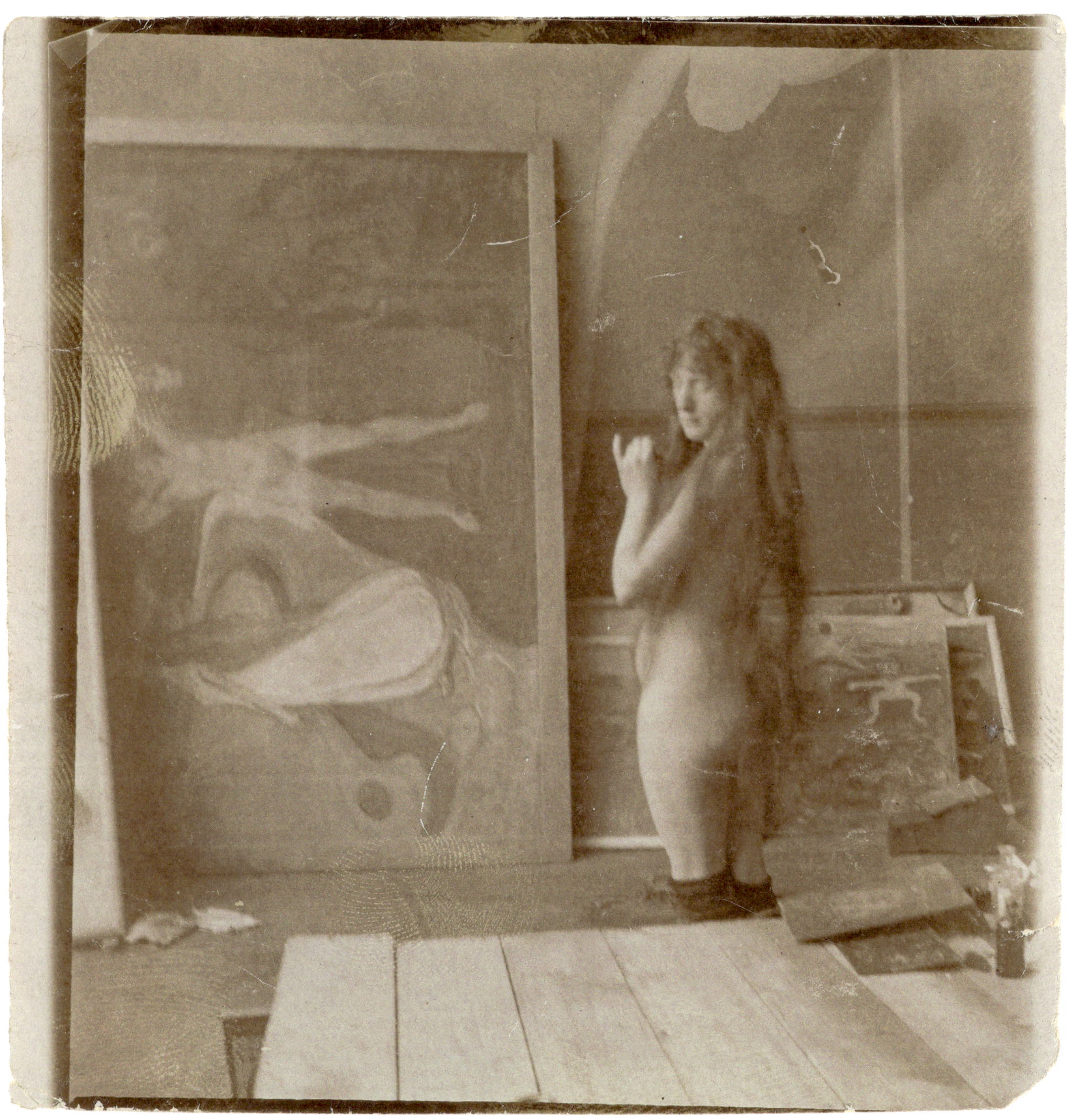

Edvard Munch
Model in Munch's Studio
Lützowstrasse 82, Berlin — 1902
Munchmuseet — Oslo

(A)
Edvard Munch
Woman with Red Hair and Green Eyes
(The Sin) — 1902
Staatliche Museen zu Berlin
Kupferstichkabinett

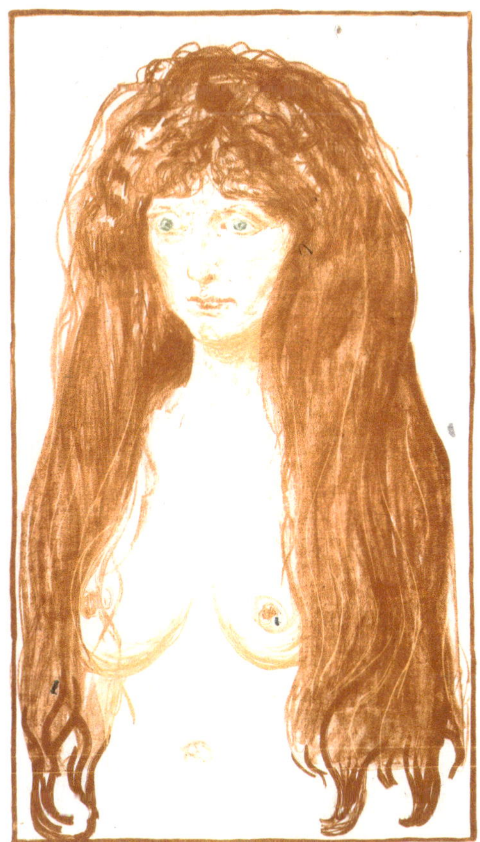

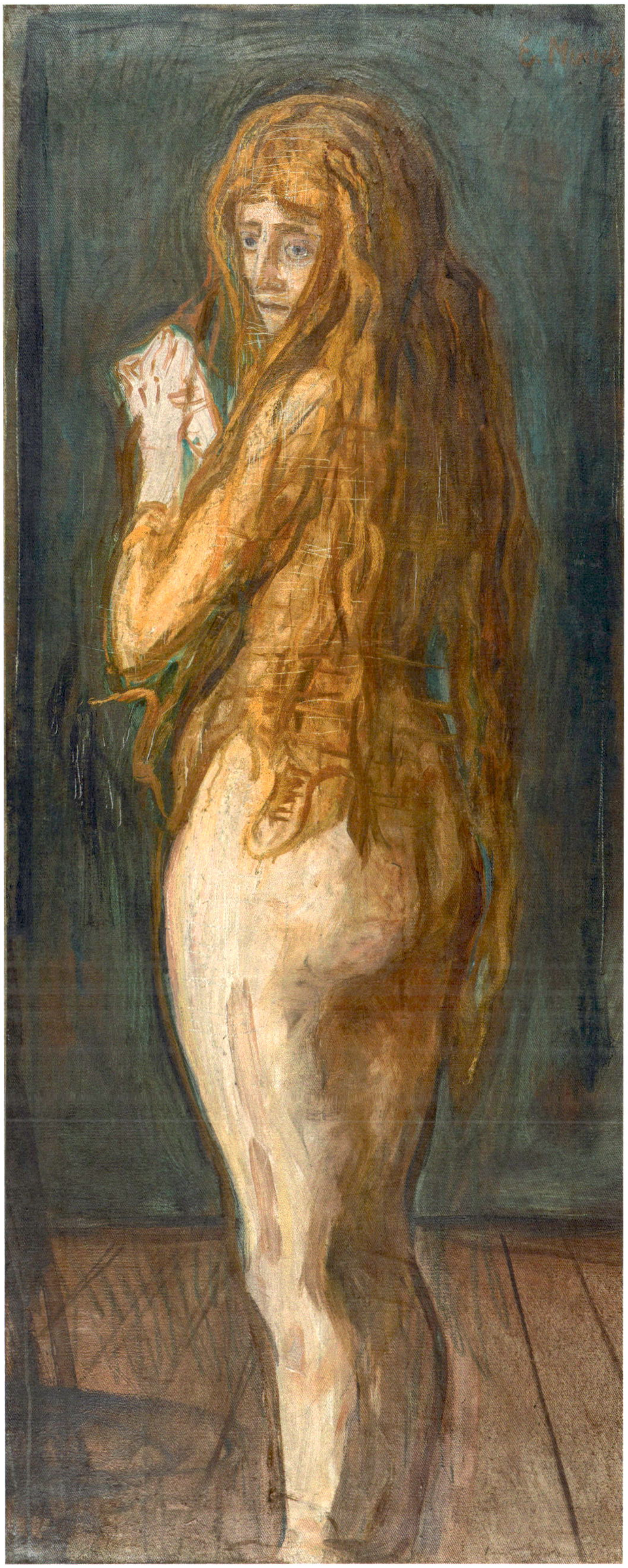

(B)
Edvard Munch
Nude with Long Red Hair — 1902
Munchmuseet — Oslo

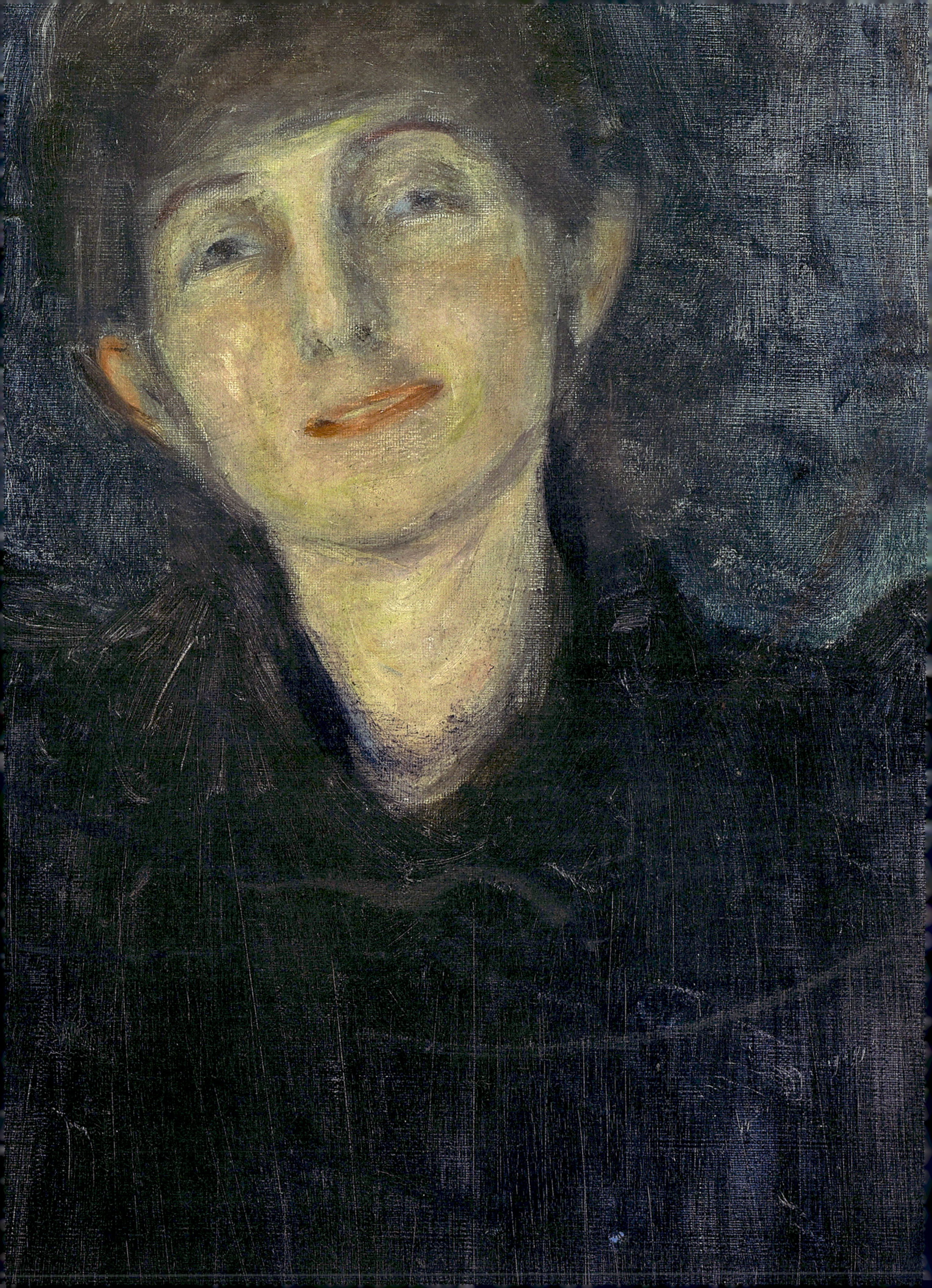

“I am absolutely not a portrait painter”

Portraits played an important role in Edvard Munch’s creative work and in his painting gaining acceptance in Berlin. Although he was convinced that he had painted psychologically interesting portraits, he said of himself: “I am absolutely not a portrait painter.” Munch saw his strengths in other areas, such as in his motifs on love and death or in his emotionally charged landscapes. His contemporaries already noticed that the one was inconceivable without the other. One critic wrote: “A painter like Munch whose every fiber is rooted in the psychological, and who cannot even render a landscape except by making its soul his own, must necessarily be a subtle portraitist.” The artist only rarely used personal attributes or details of the surroundings to characterize people. Color tones and a general spatial effect were more important to him than social aspects.

In his early years in Berlin, Munch depicted its legendary bohemia, which at the beginning of the 1890s met at the wine bar Zum schwarzen Ferkel (The Black Piglet). The sitters included the Polish writer Stanisław Przybyszewski and his future wife, the Norwegian author Dagny Juel, as well as the Swedish playwright August Strindberg. Art enthusiasts in Berlin such as Walther Rathenau and Harry Graf Kessler, who acquired the artist’s works early on, also had Munch portray them.

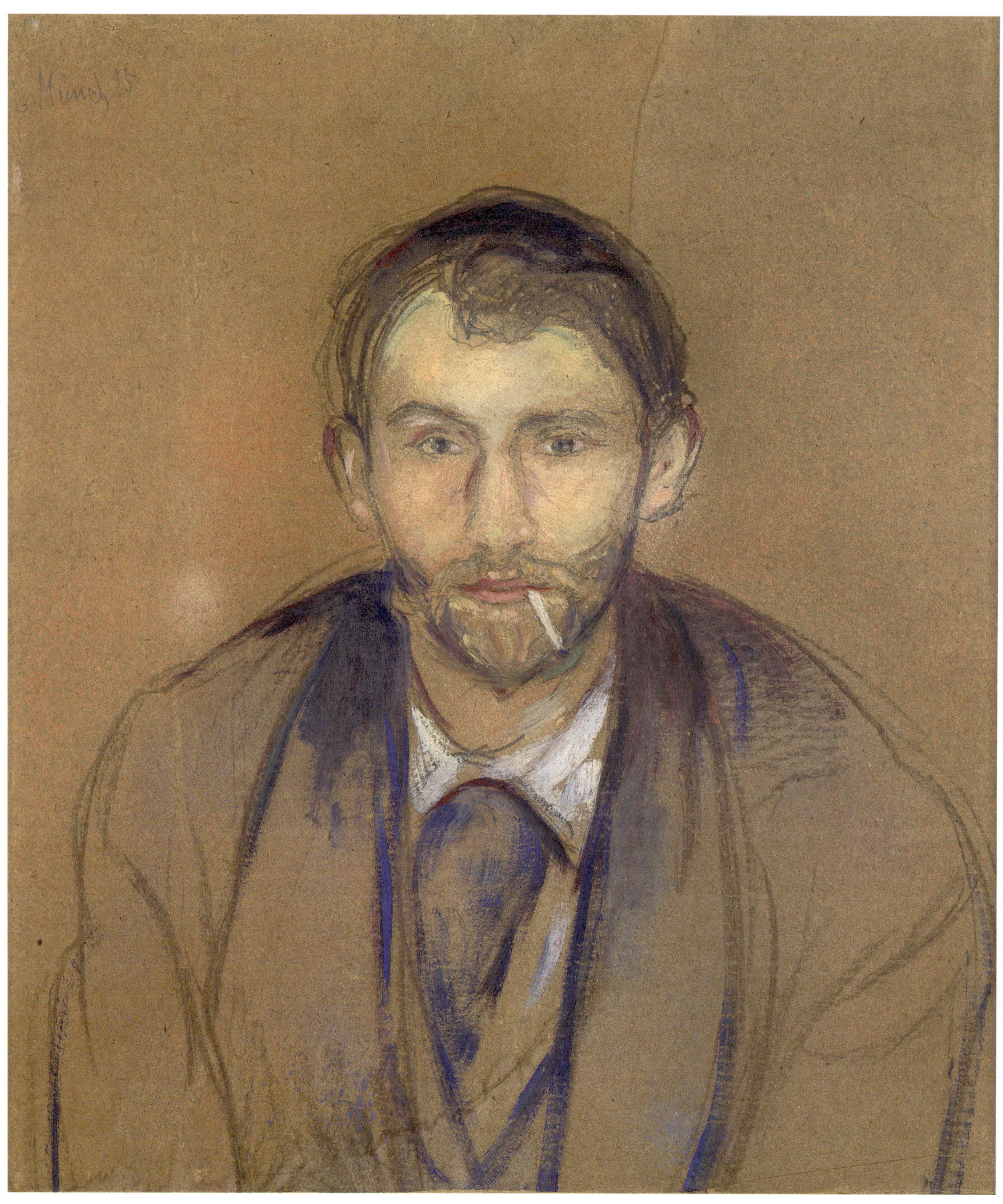

Edvard Munch
Stanisław Przybyszewski — 1895
Munchmuseet — Oslo

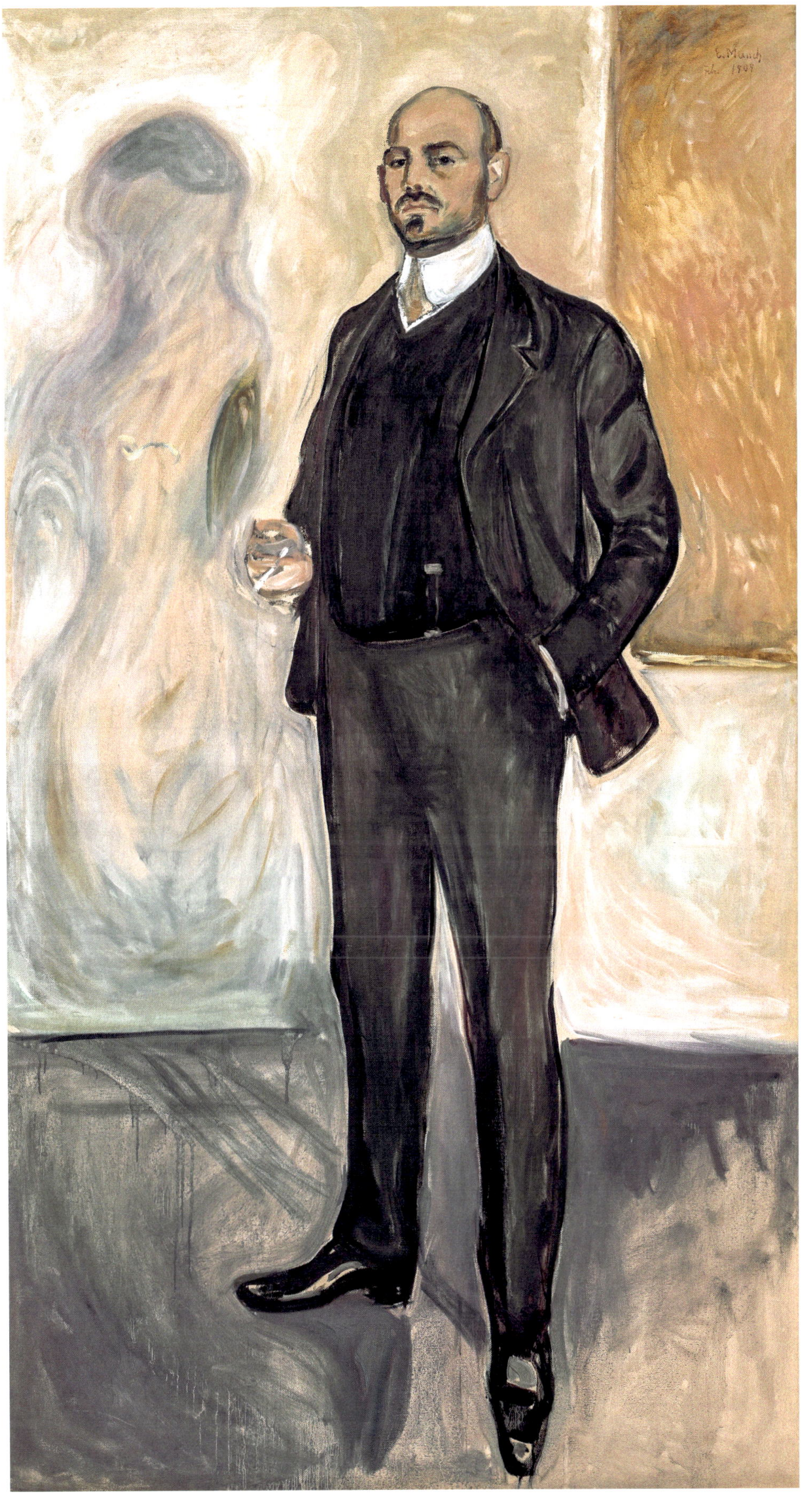

Edvard Munch
Portrait of Walther Rathenau — 1907
Stiftung Stadtmuseum — Berlin

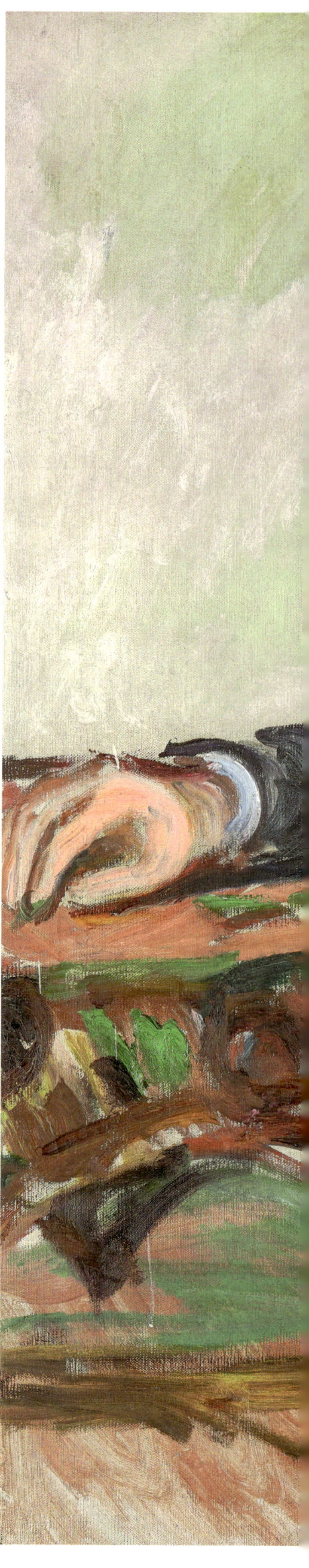

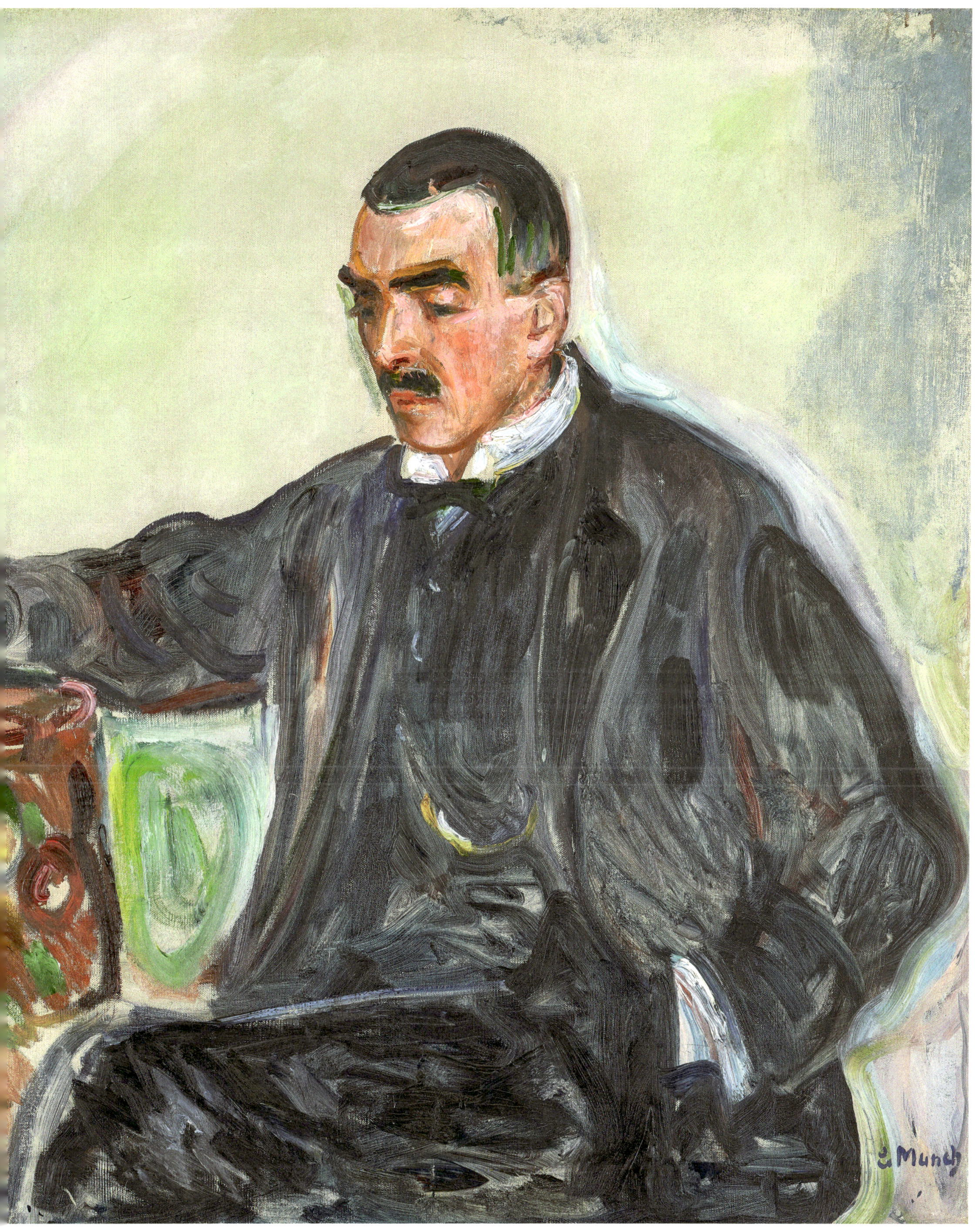

Edvard Munch
Jappe Nilssen — 1909
Munchmuseet — Oslo

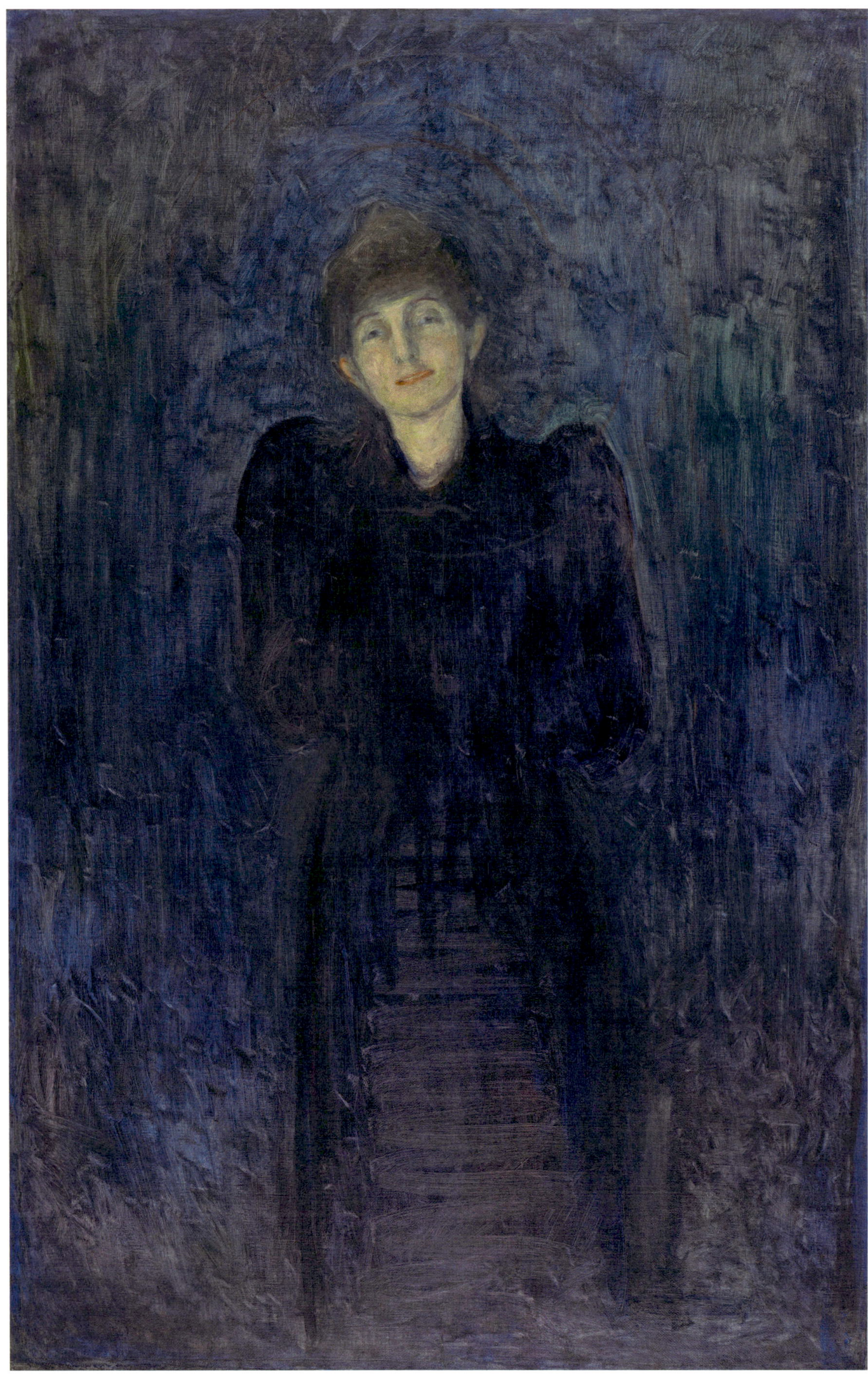

Edvard Munch
Dagny Juel Przybyszewska — 1893
Munchmuseet — Oslo

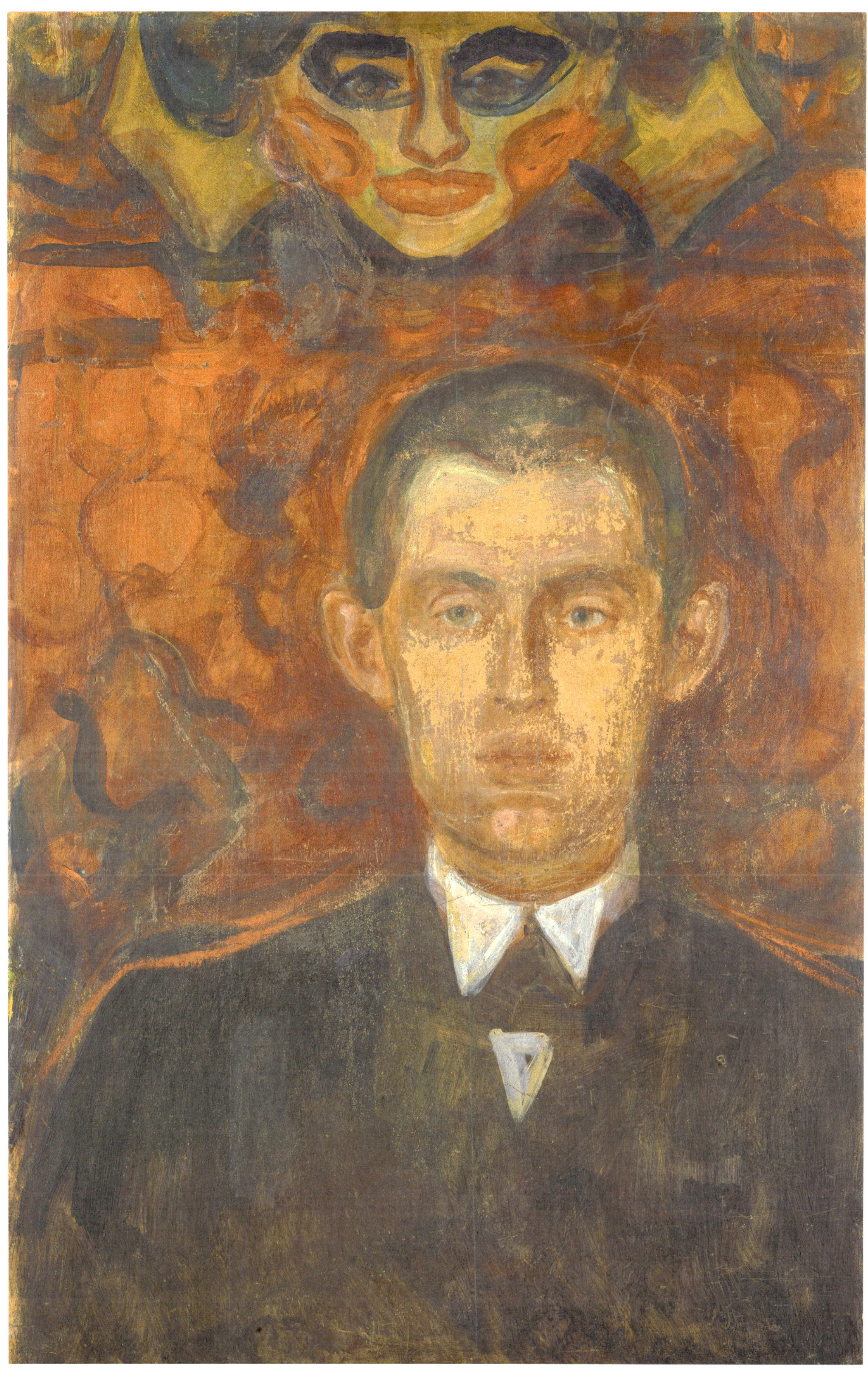

Edvard Munch
Self-Portrait under the Mask of a Woman — 1893
Munchmuseet — Oslo

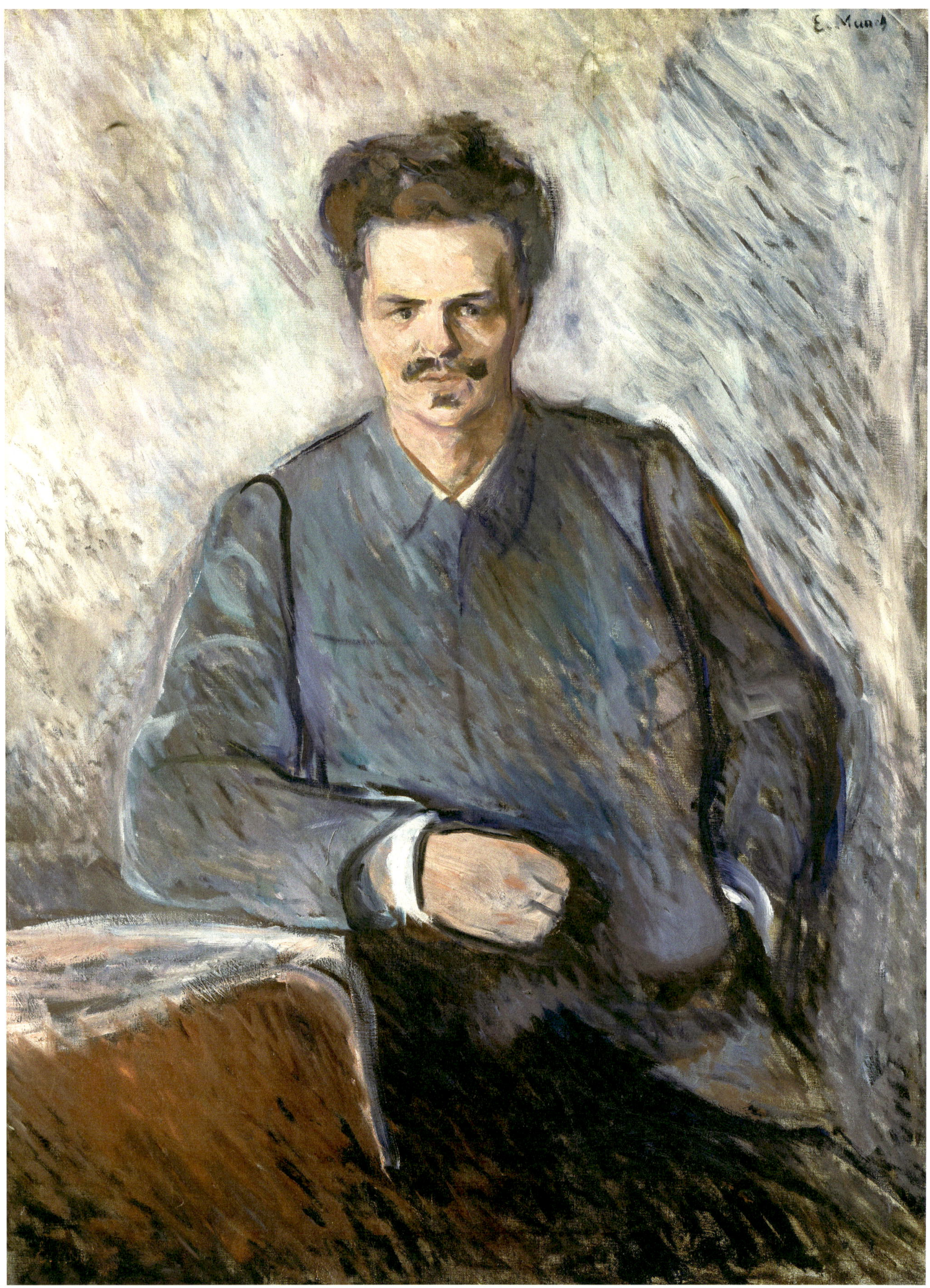

Edvard Munch
August Strindberg — 1892
Moderna Museet — Stockholm

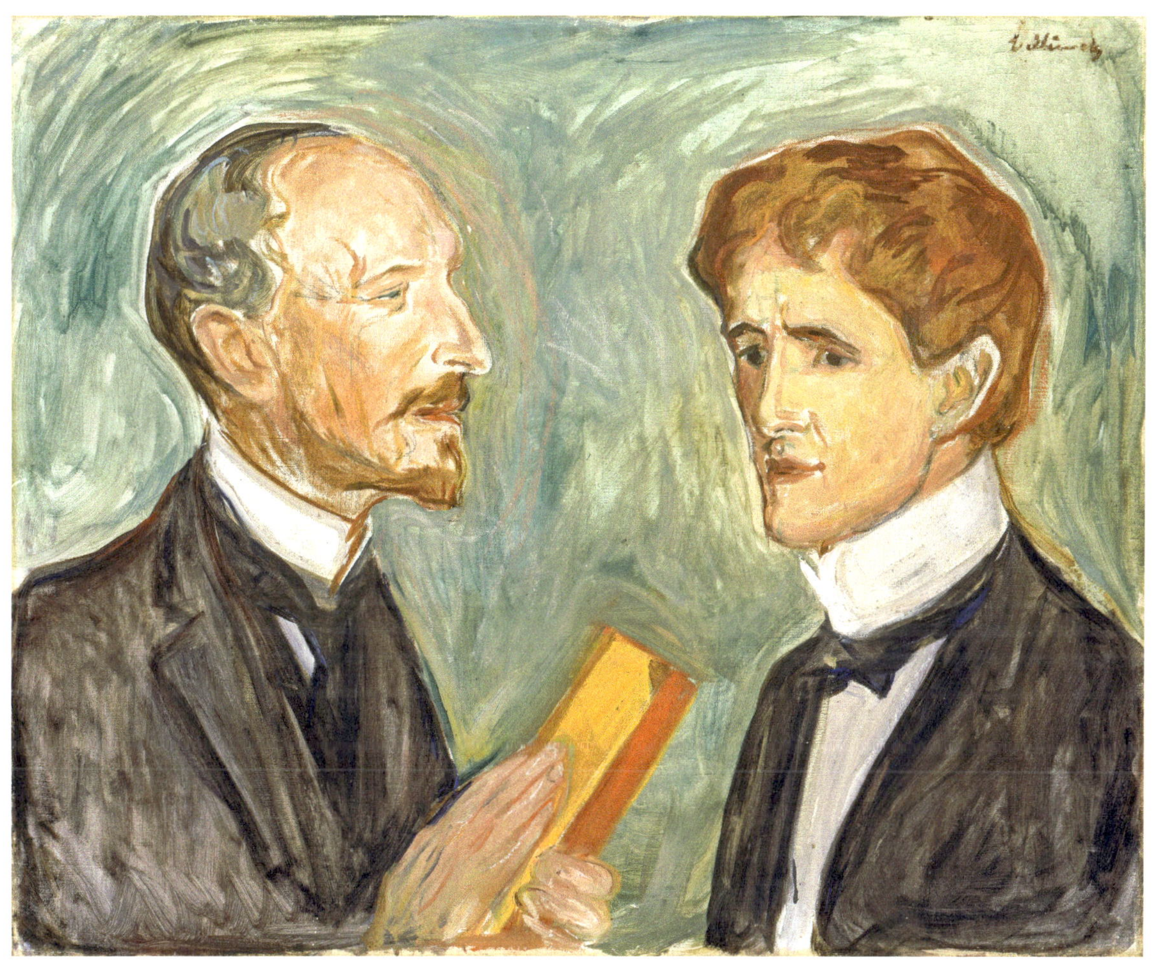

Edvard Munch
Albert Kollmann and Sten Drewsen — 1902
Hamburger Kunsthalle — Hamburg

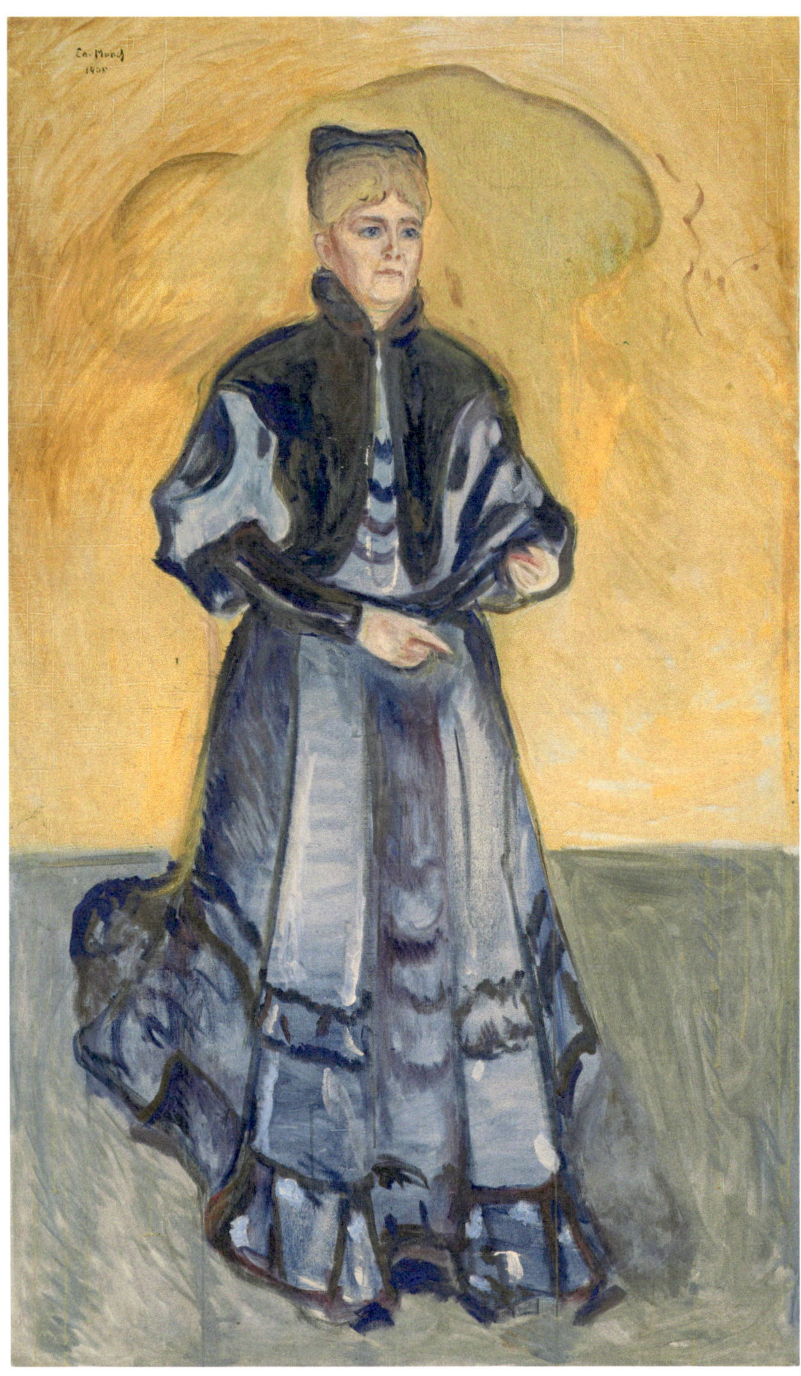

Edvard Munch
Elisabeth Förster-Nietzsche — 1906
Munchmuseet — Oslo

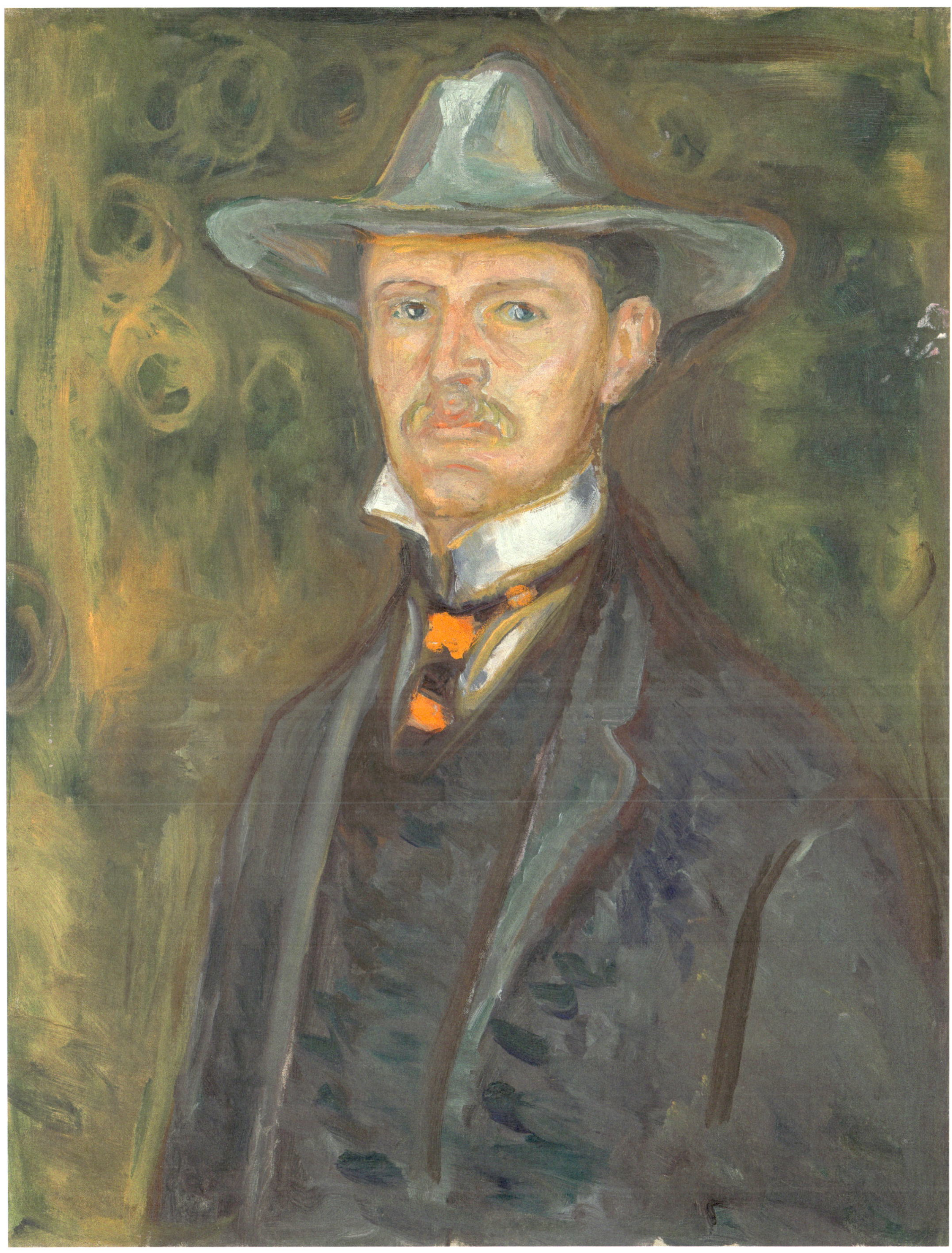

Edvard Munch
Self-Portrait in Broad-Brimmed Hat — 1905–6
Munchmuseet — Oslo

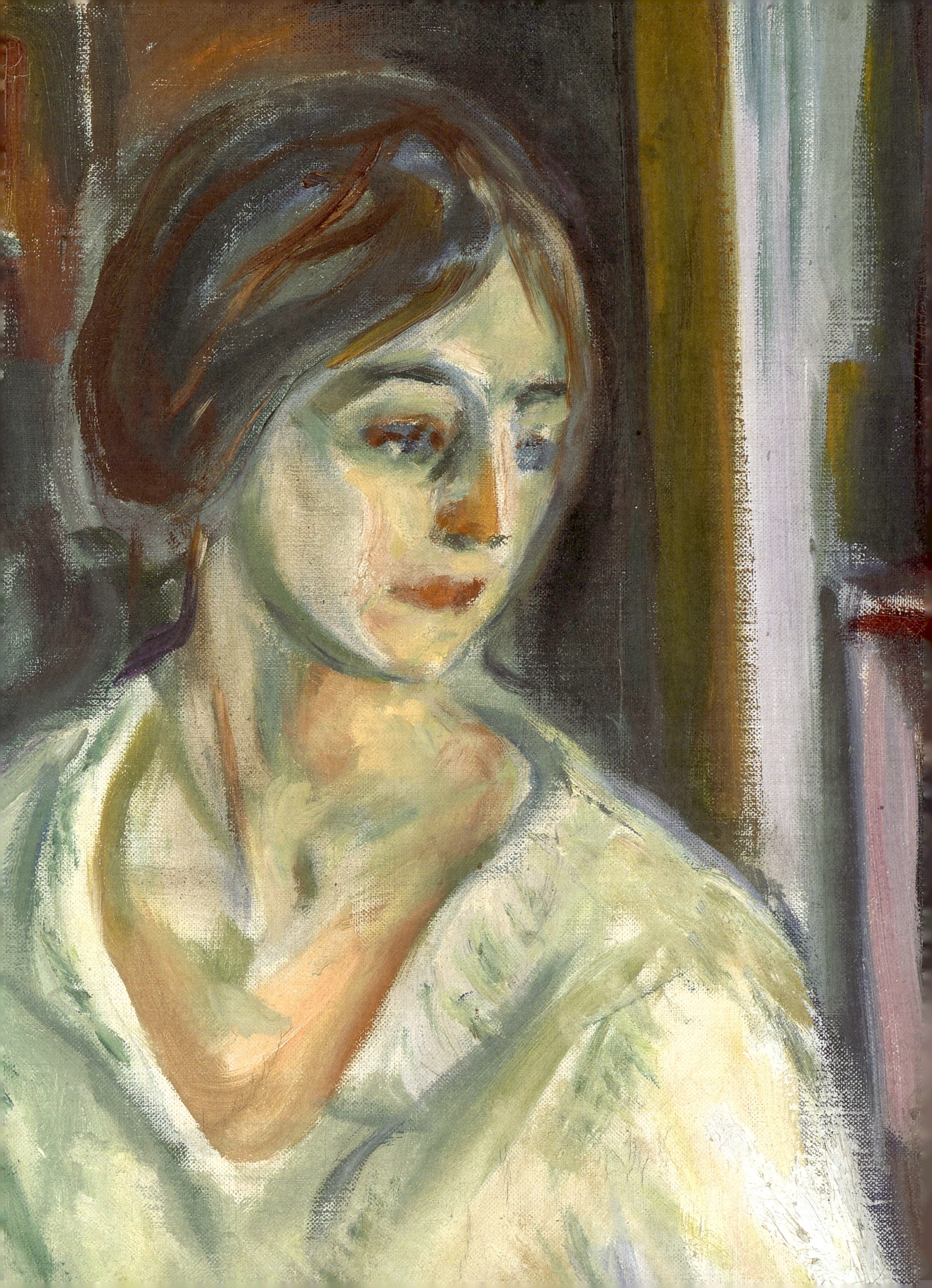

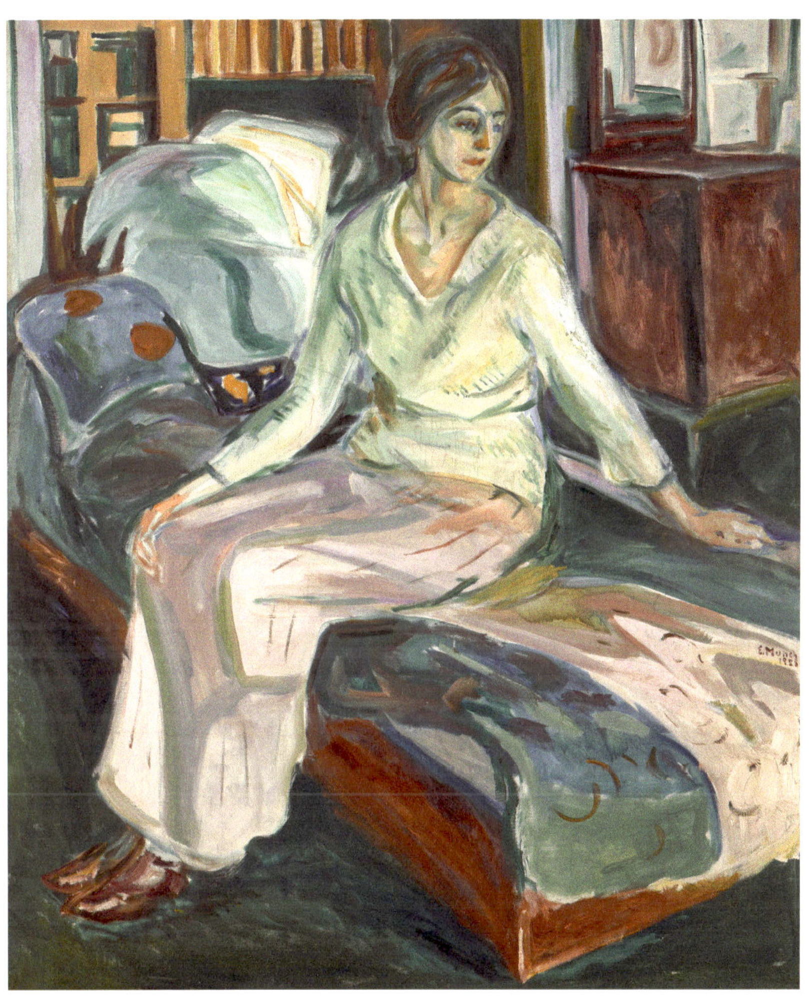

Edvard Munch
Seated Model on the Couch — 1924–26
Munchmuseet — Oslo

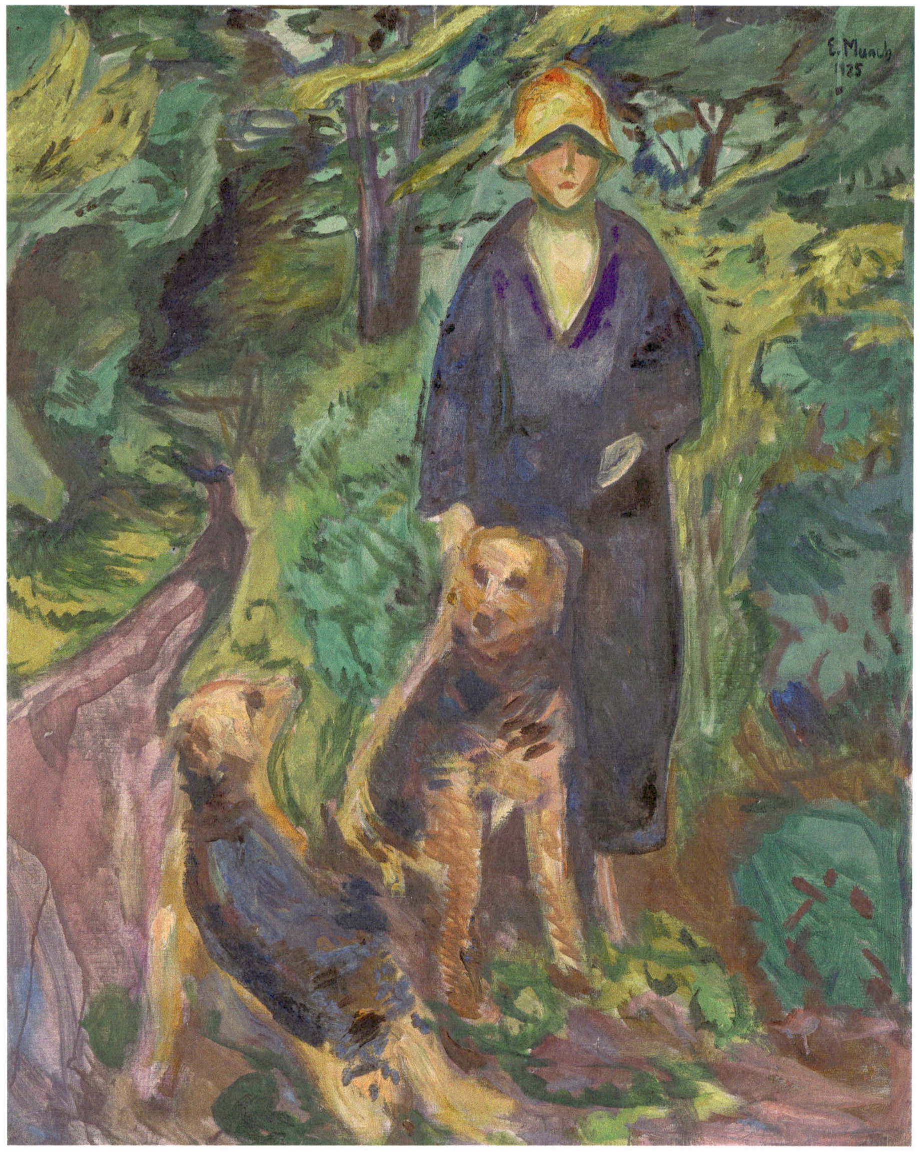

Edvard Munch
Woman with Airedale Terriers — 1925–26
Munchmuseet — Oslo

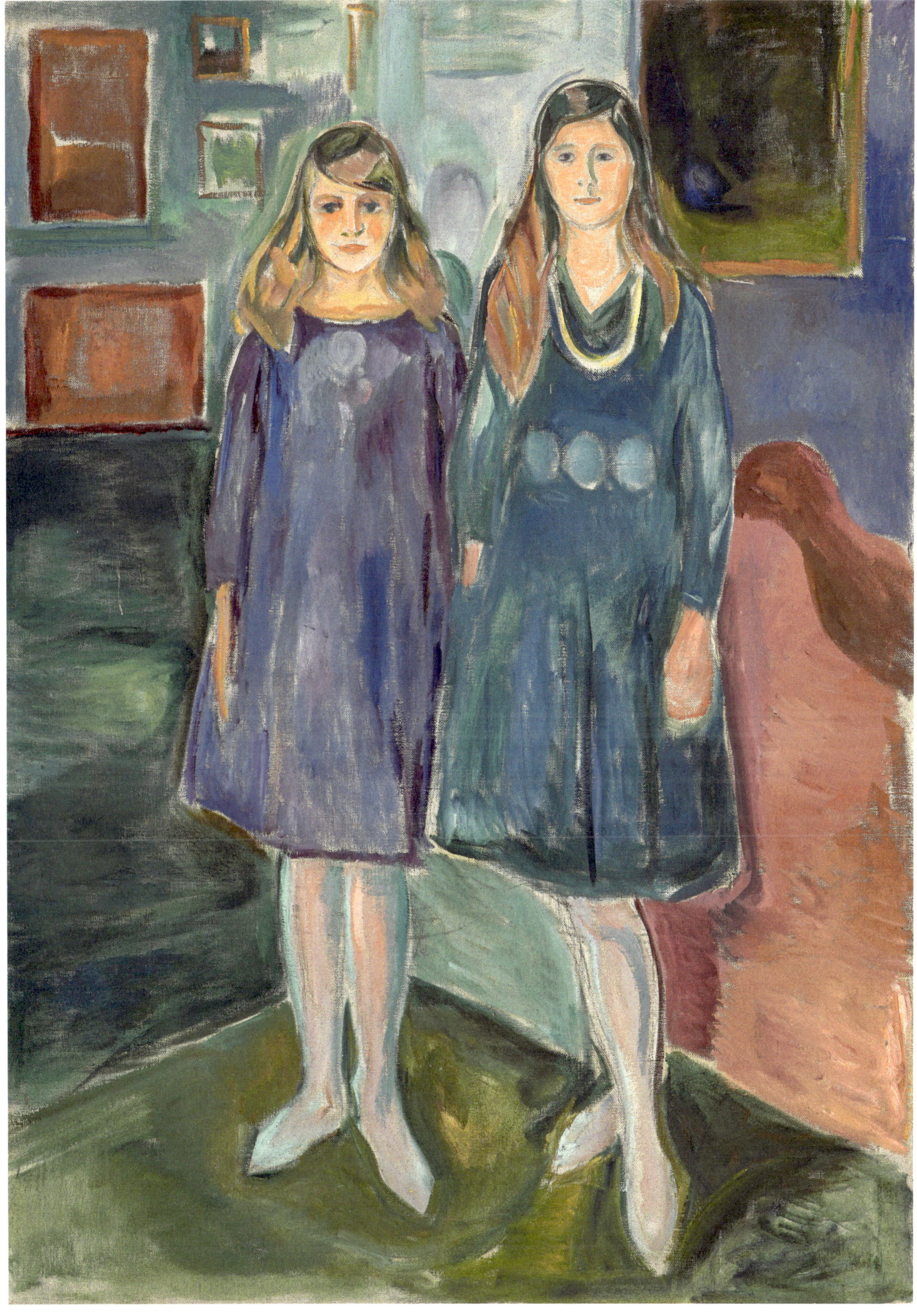

Edvard Munch
Two Teenagers — 1919
Munchmuseet — Oslo

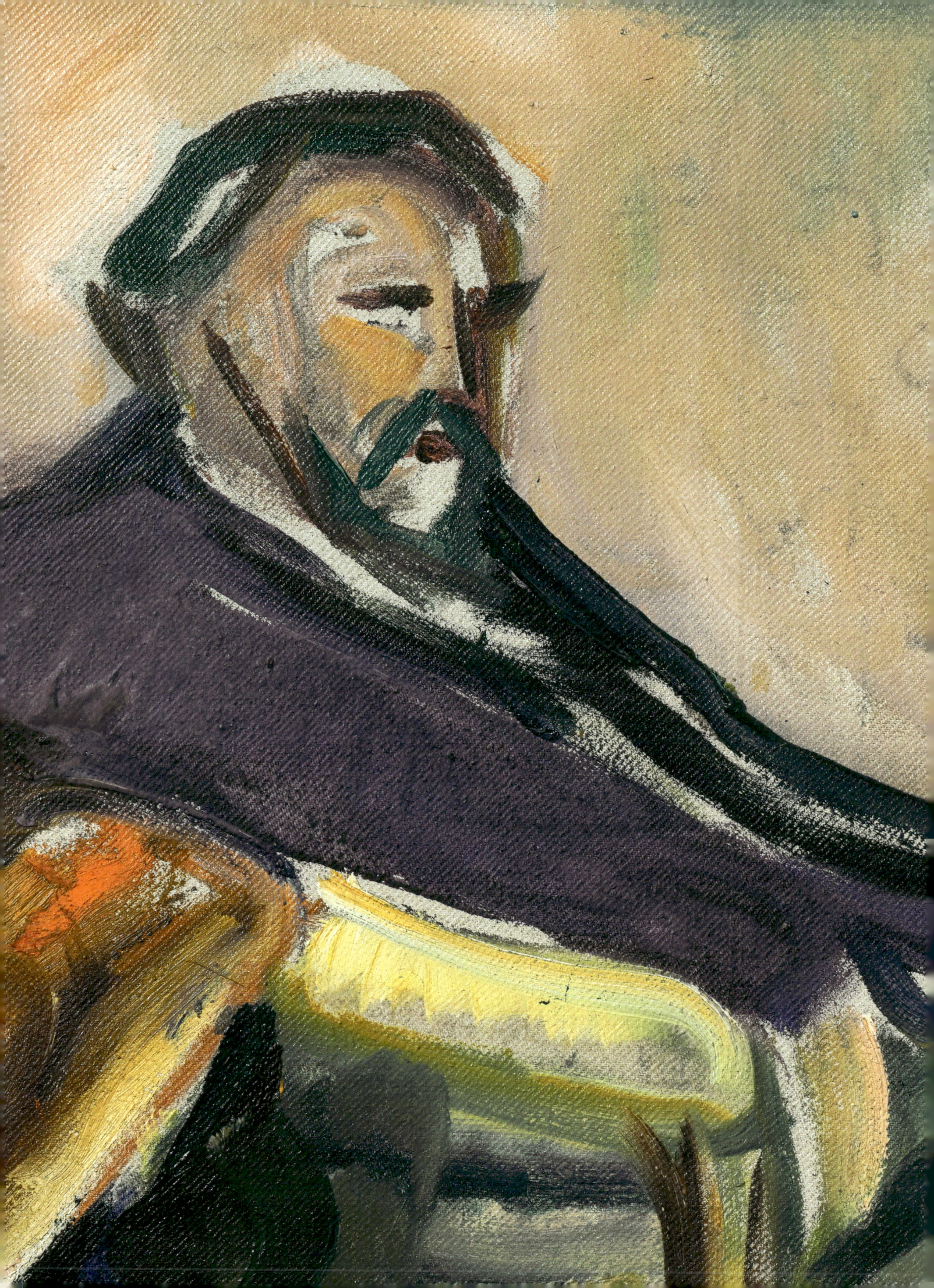

Triumph and Tragedy

"Nordic-Germanic" or "Degenerate"

In 1927, the Nationalgalerie (National Gallery) in Berlin hosted Edvard Munch's then largest retrospective, with 244 works. It was also the most extensive solo presentation that the Nationalgalerie's modern department, known as the "Gallery of the Living," had yet exhibited. Critics celebrated Munch and appropriated him for the history of German art. His name was said to stand for "the specifically Nordic sense of the world that emerged in revolt already in the 1890s." Around thirty-five years after his scandalous exhibition at the Verein Berliner Künstler, no one disputed any longer his importance for the evolution of modern art, with Munch having been celebrated since the 1910s as a precursor to Expressionism.

After the National Socialists took power in 1933, Munch's position was, on the one hand, instrumentalized in Germany as "Nordic-Germanic" but also, on the other hand, defamed as "degenerate" from early on. Ten years after his triumph at the Nationalgalerie, eighty-three of his works were confiscated from public collections as part of the action "Entartete Kunst" (Degenerate Art) in 1937, including *Snow Shovelers* from the Nationalgalerie in Berlin and *Self-Portrait after Influenza* from the Behnhaus in Lübeck. In both cases, the museums were able to get the paintings returned, thanks to this ambivalent assessment of Munch. Whereas the work in Lübeck is still in the museum's collections, along with other paintings that were successfully reclaimed at the time, the Berlin painting was destroyed during World War II.

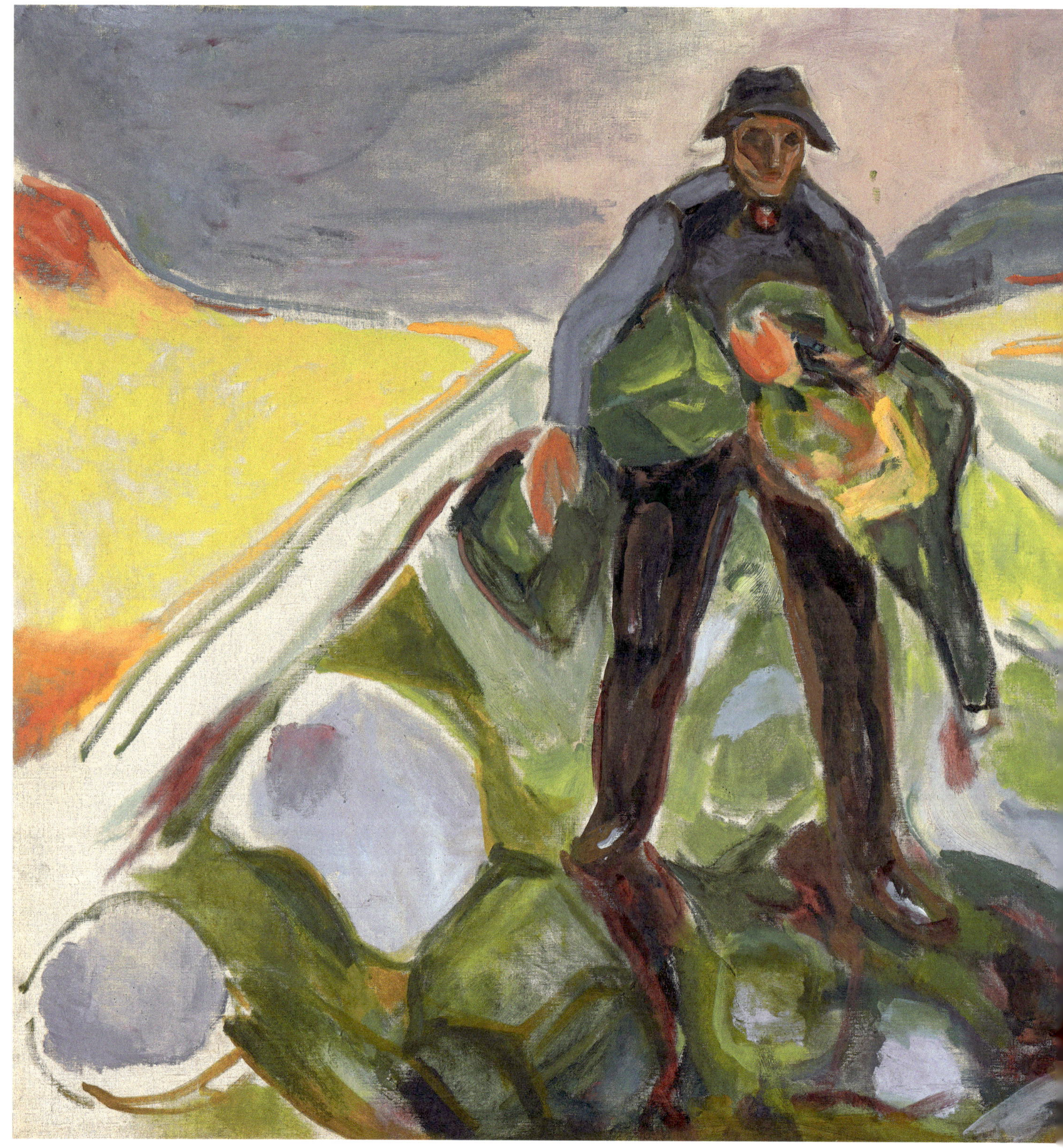

Edvard Munch
The Man in the Cabbage Field — 1943
Munchmuseet — Oslo

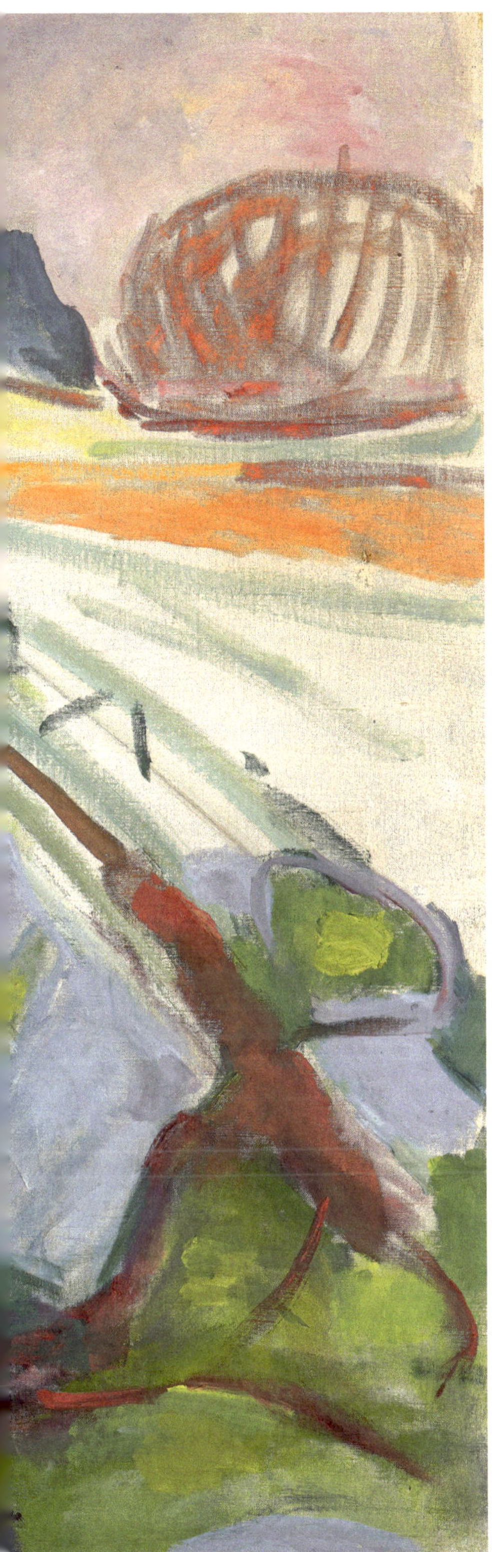

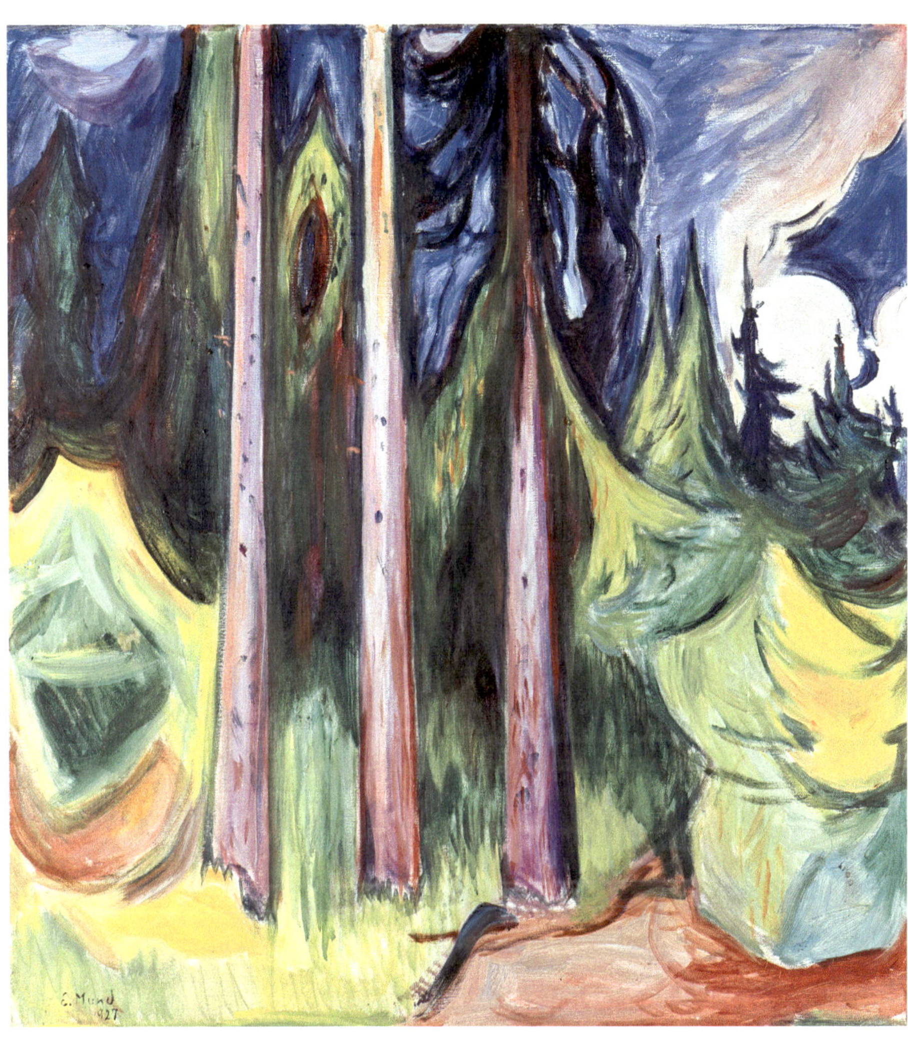

Edvard Munch
Forest — 1927
Staatliche Museen zu Berlin
Nationalgalerie

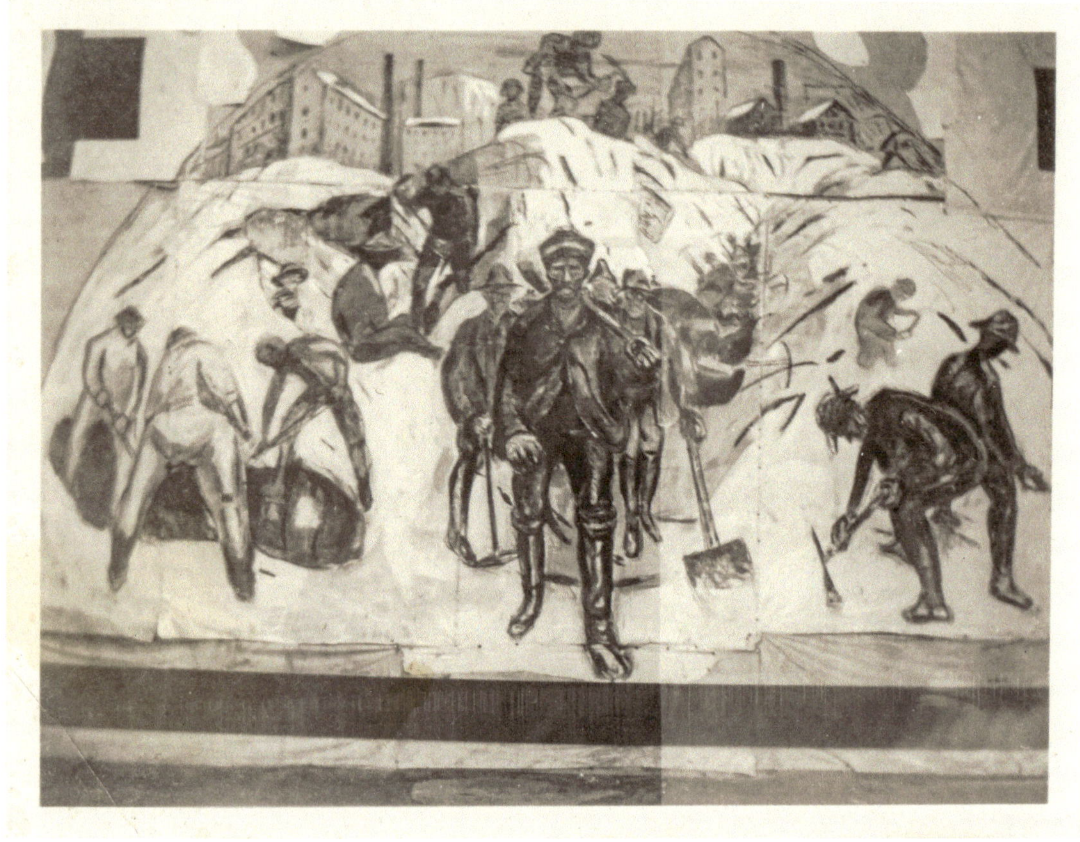

(A)
Edvard Munch
Design for a Decoration in Oslo City Hall — ca. 1930
Munchmuseet — Oslo

(B)
Edvard Munch
Snow Shovelers — 1913–14
Formerly Nationalgalerie, Berlin — destroyed

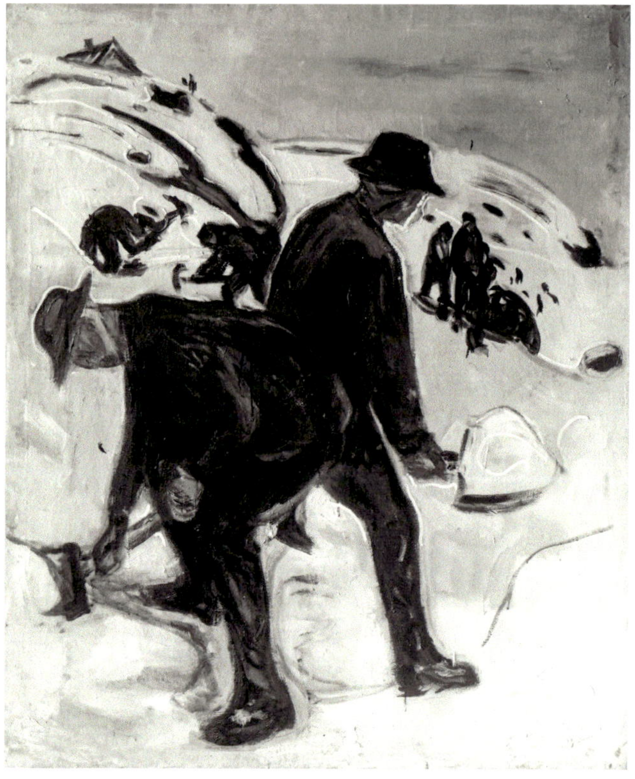

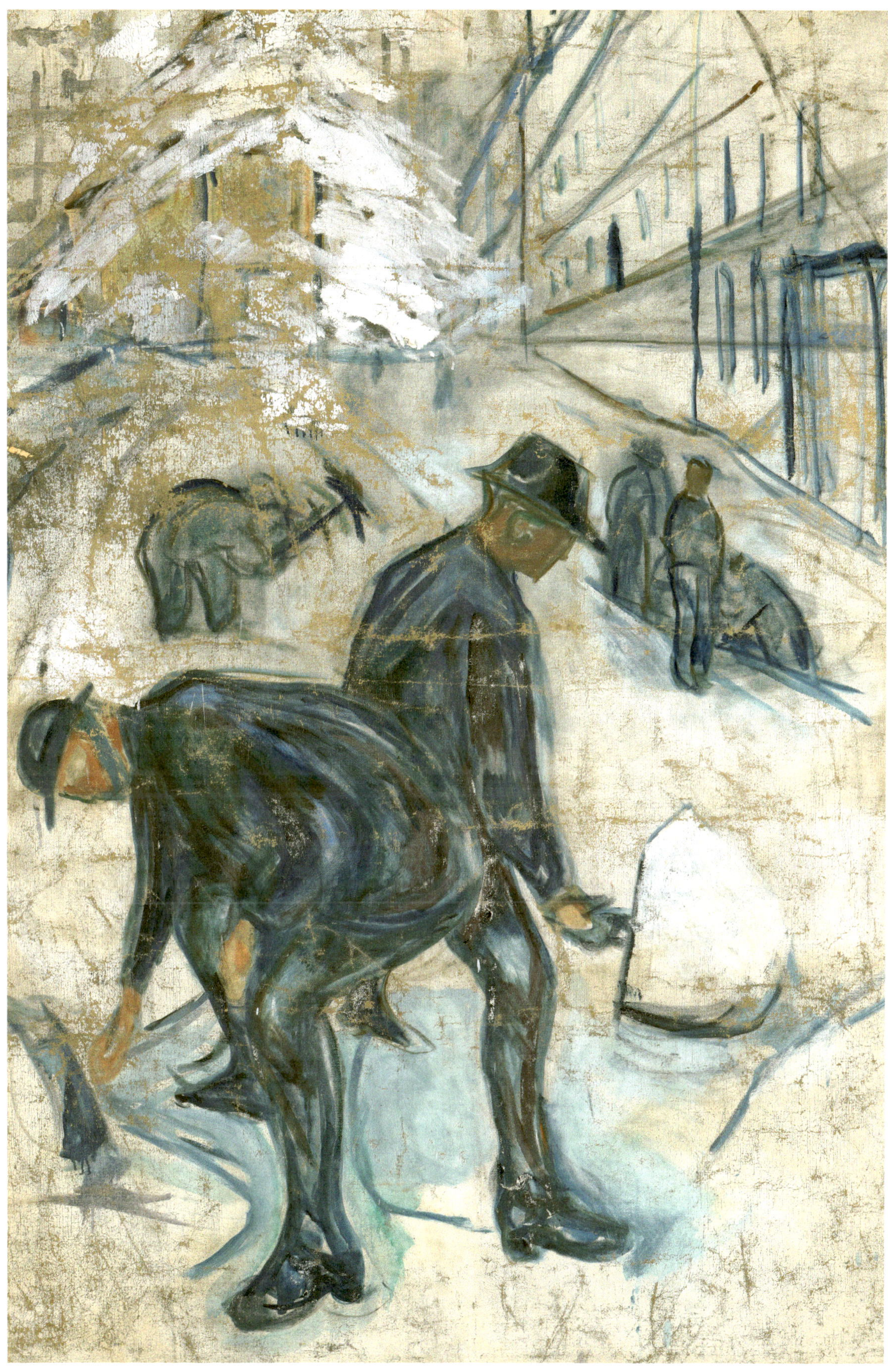

Edvard Munch
Snow Shovelers on the Building Site — 1931–33
Munchmuseet — Oslo

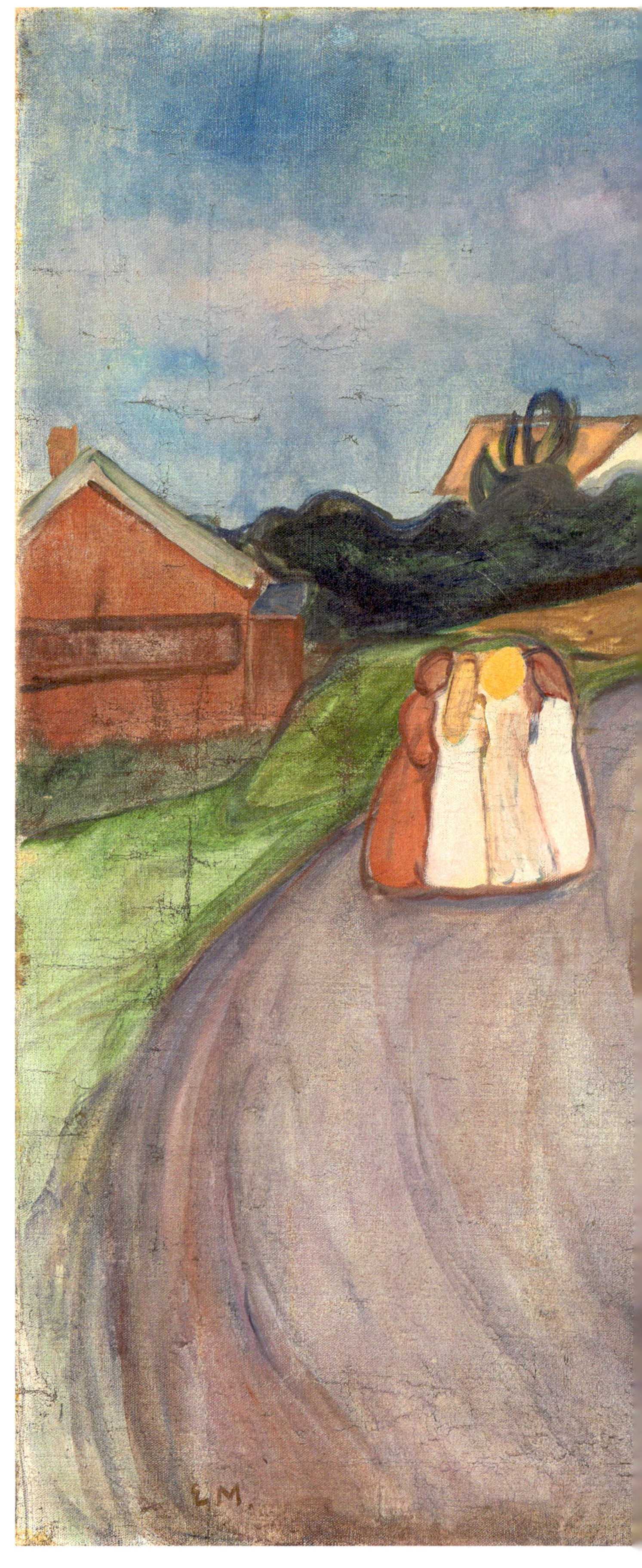
E.M.

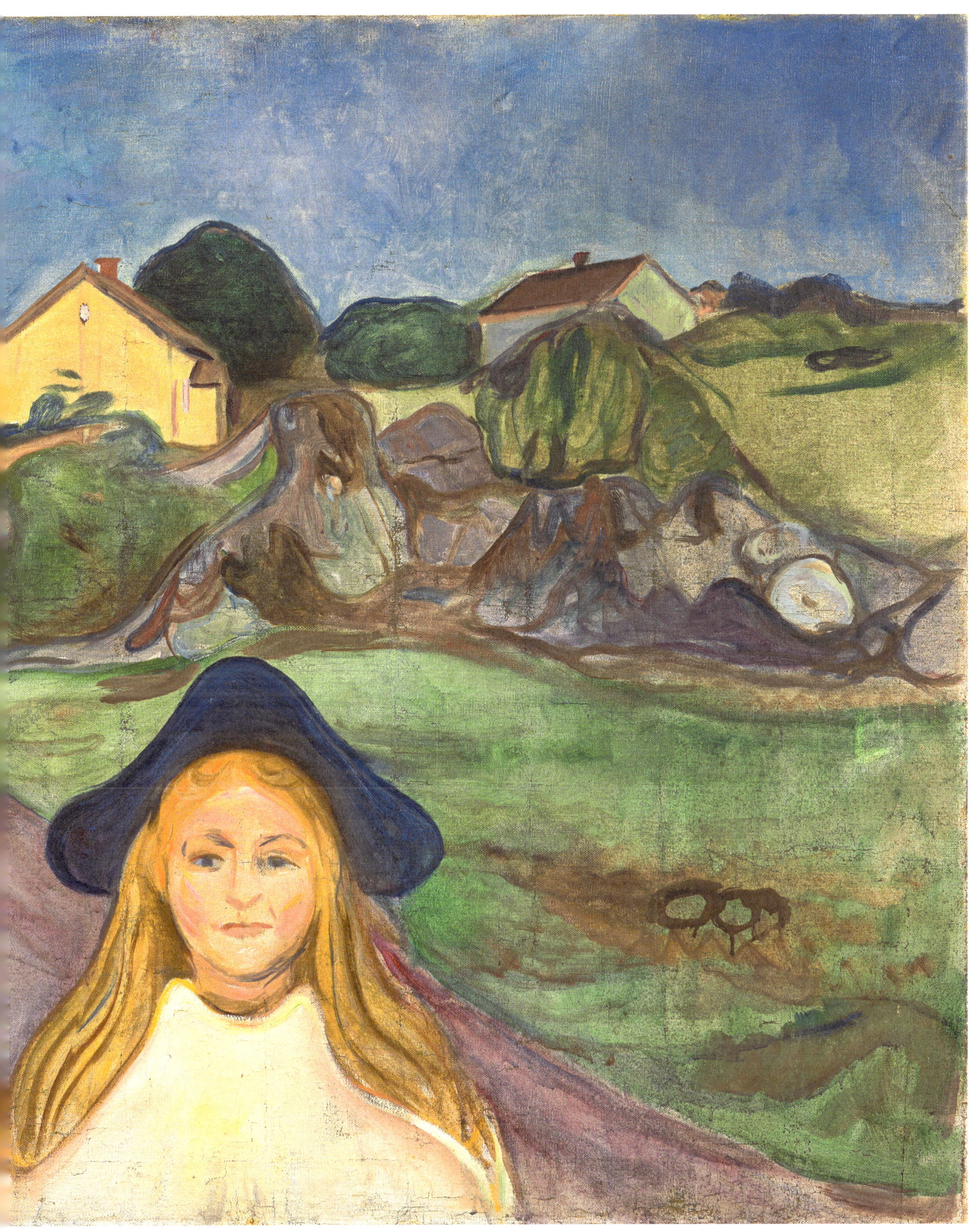

Edvard Munch
Road in Åsgårdstrand — 1901
Kunstmuseum Basel

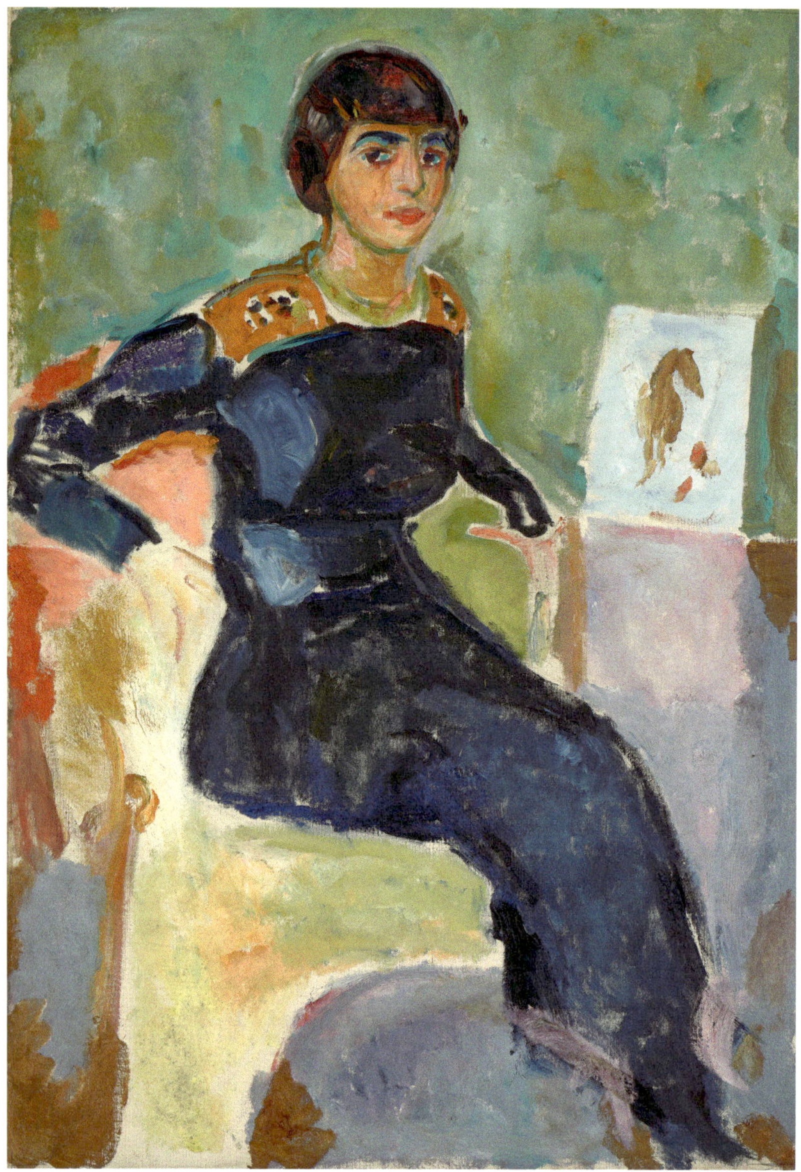

Edvard Munch
Elsa Glaser — 1913
Munchmuseet — Oslo

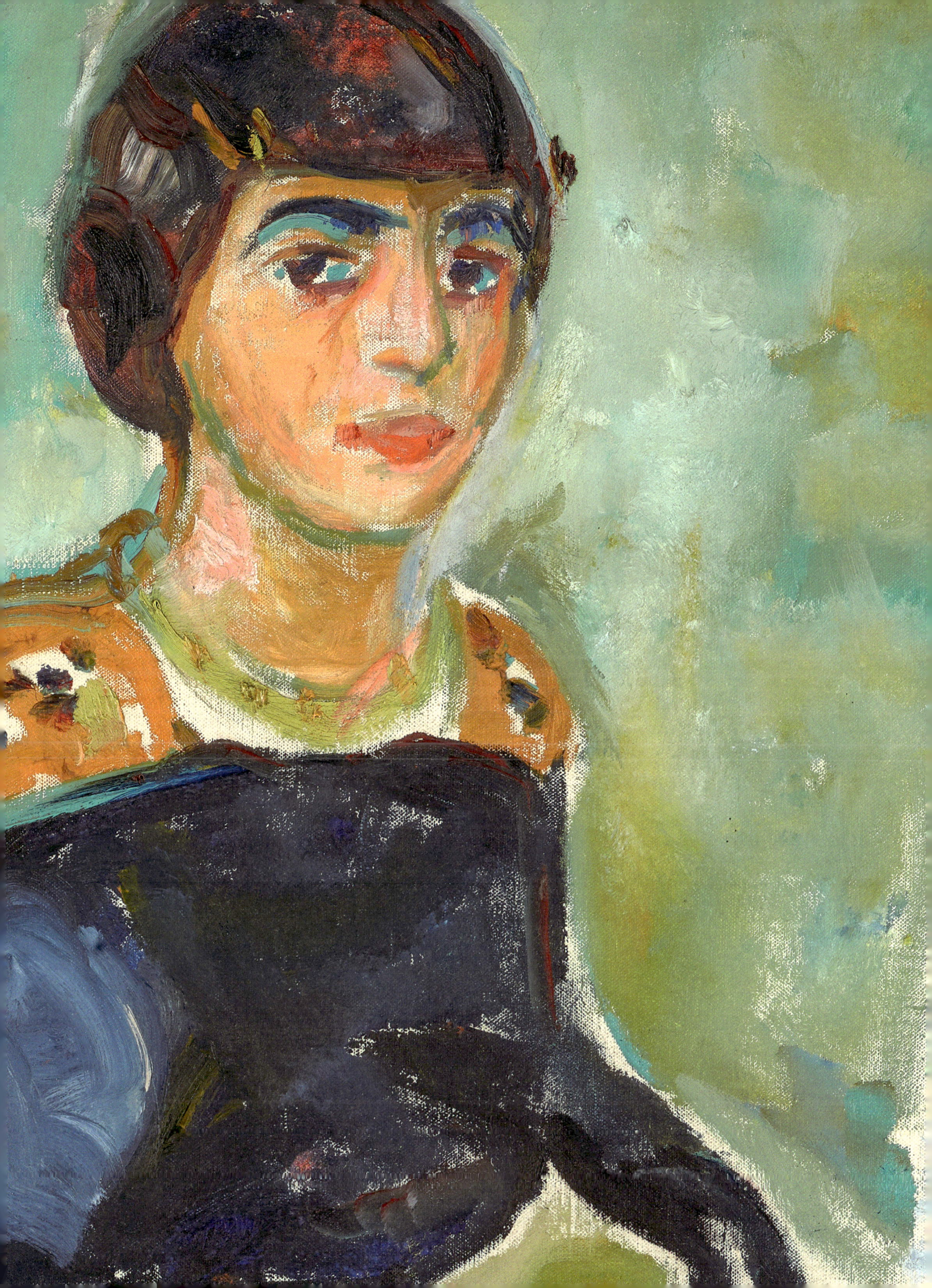

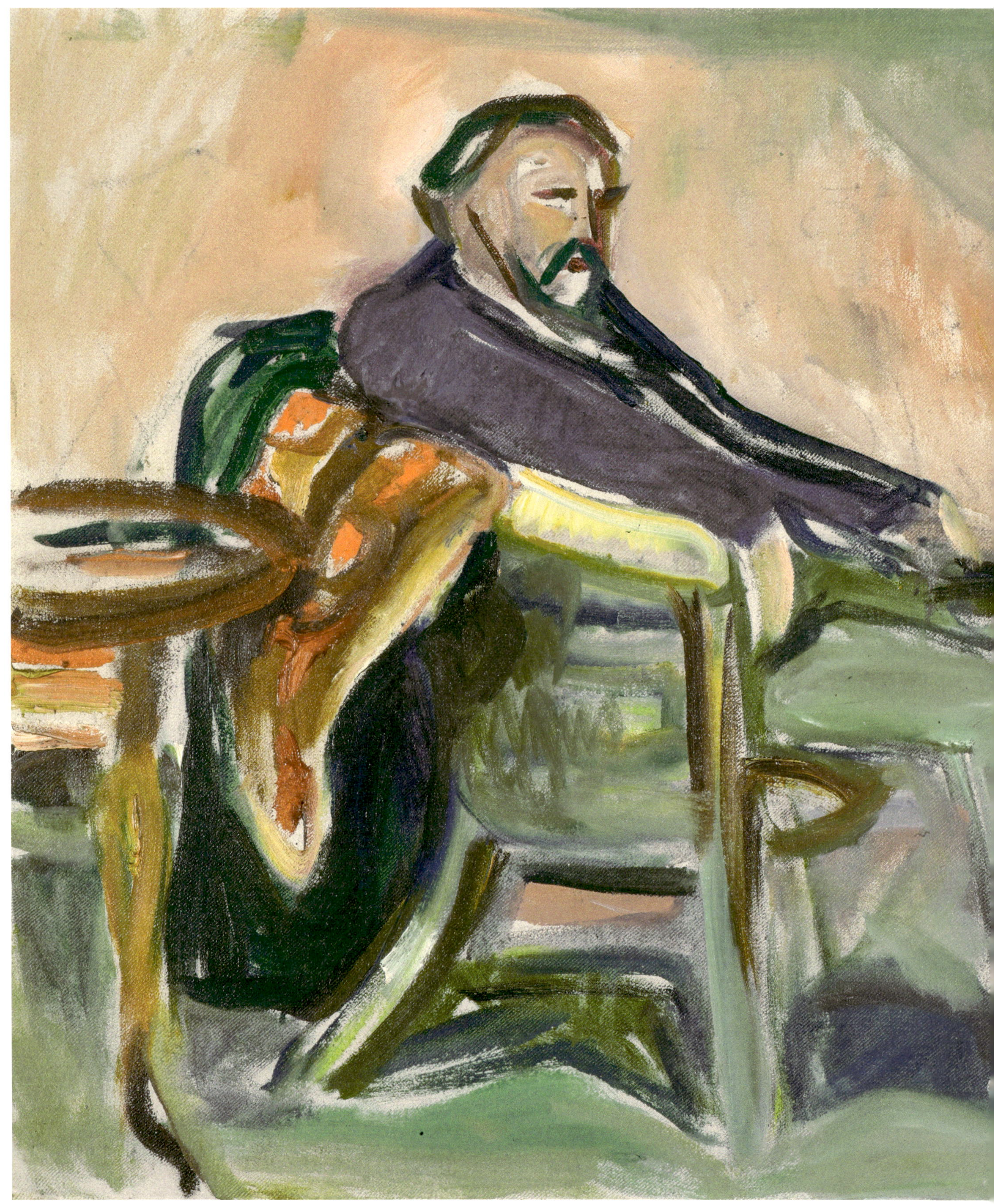

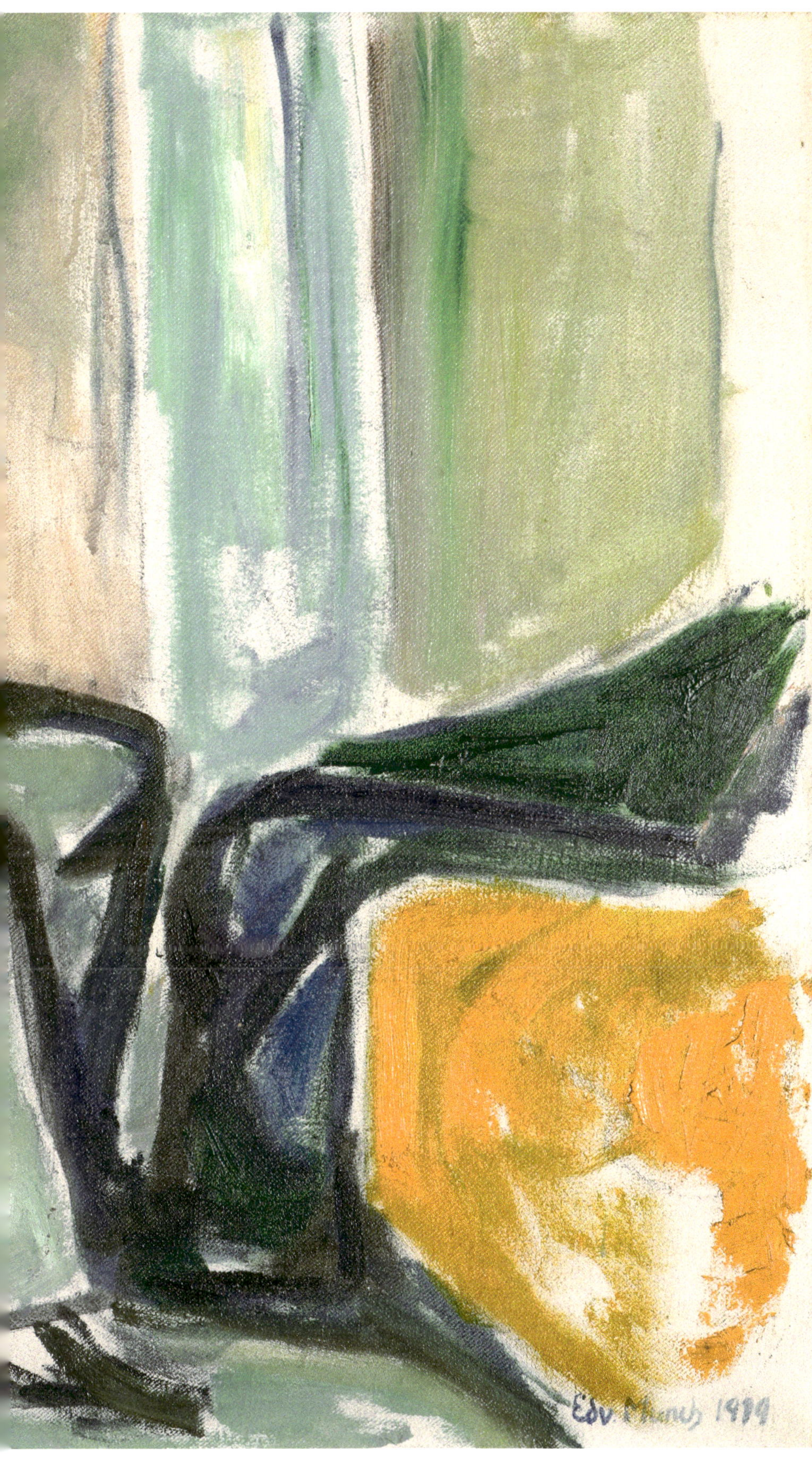

Edvard Munch
Self-Portrait after Influenza — 1919
Die Lübecker Museen,
Museum Behnhaus Drägerhaus — Lübeck

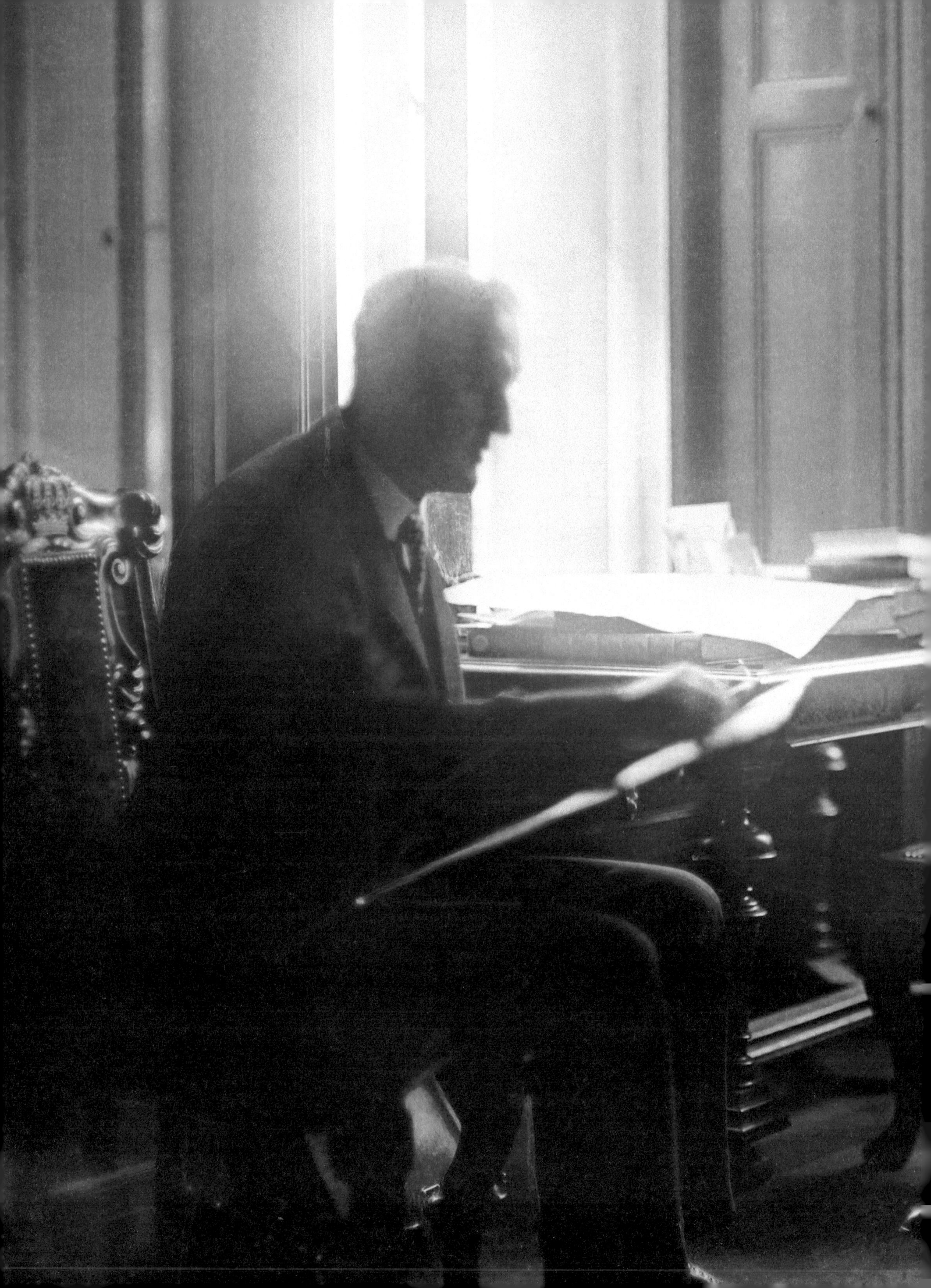

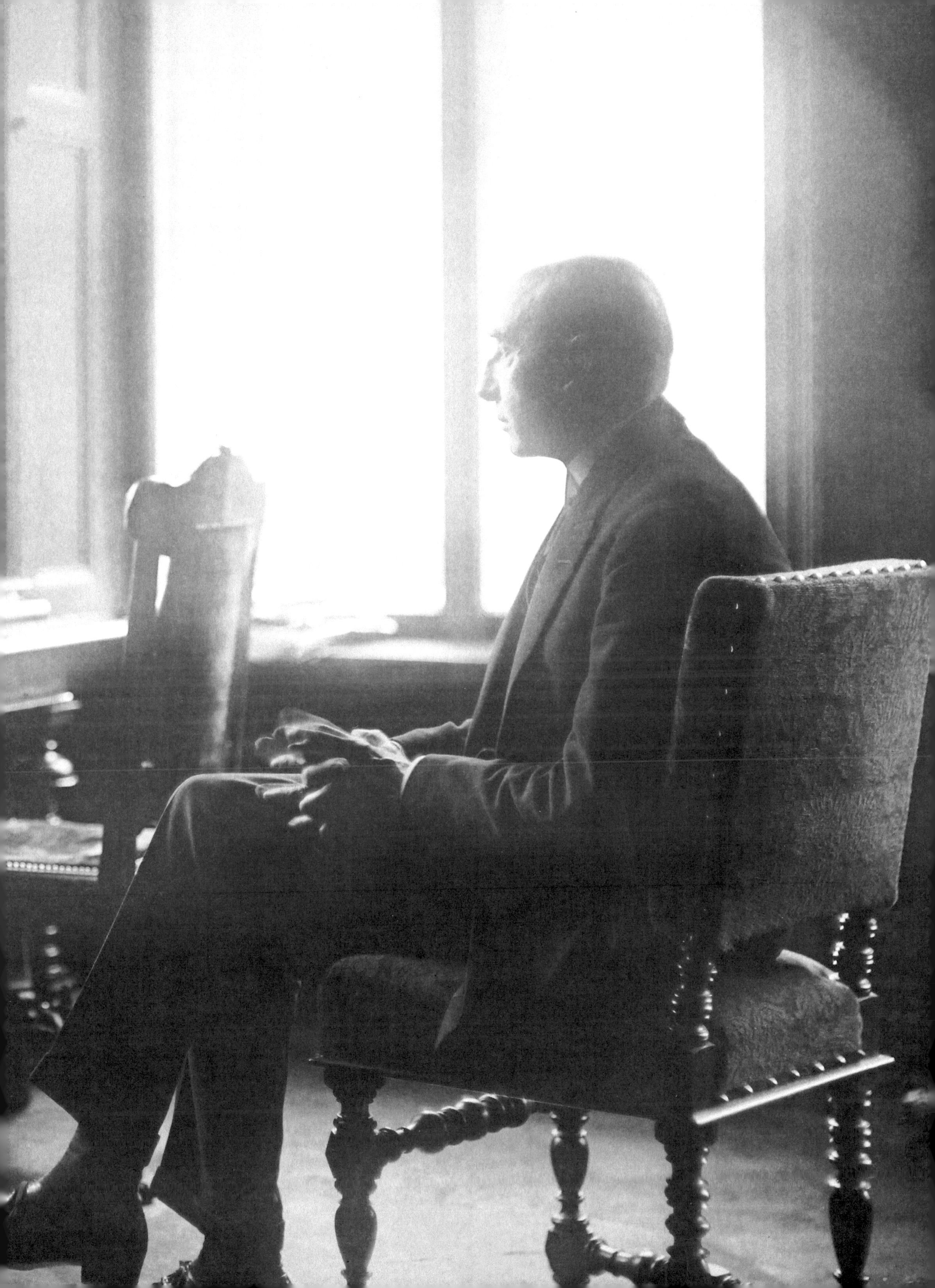

Affair, Scandal, Fiasco?

Munch's Debut in Berlin A Backstage View

Sabine Meister

In 1892, Edvard Munch's first German exhibition in Berlin led to a conflict among artists that grew into a scandal with serious consequences. It not only met with a widespread response in the press but also made it into the files of the Ministry of Education, now preserved in the Geheimes Preussisches Staatsarchiv (Prussian Secret State Archives). This scandal around Munch is one of the most famous in the history of art in Germany. It is no coincidence that it occurred in the early 1890s or that Berlin was its stage.

Munch was twenty-eight and at the beginning of his career. The painters of Kristiania's bohemia, such as Christian Krohg and Frits Thaulow, had introduced him to naturalism around 1885. Figure p.163 He showed his first solo exhibition in Kristiania (now Oslo) in 1889, which despite his young age was conceived as an exhibition presenting his development as an artist. New impressions from his study trips to France were forming his artistic identity. He knew Berlin only superficially at the time. Munch remained in the capital of the German Reich, with brief interruptions, until the mid-1890s, and by the late 1920s he had returned a number of times to the site of his international breakthrough.

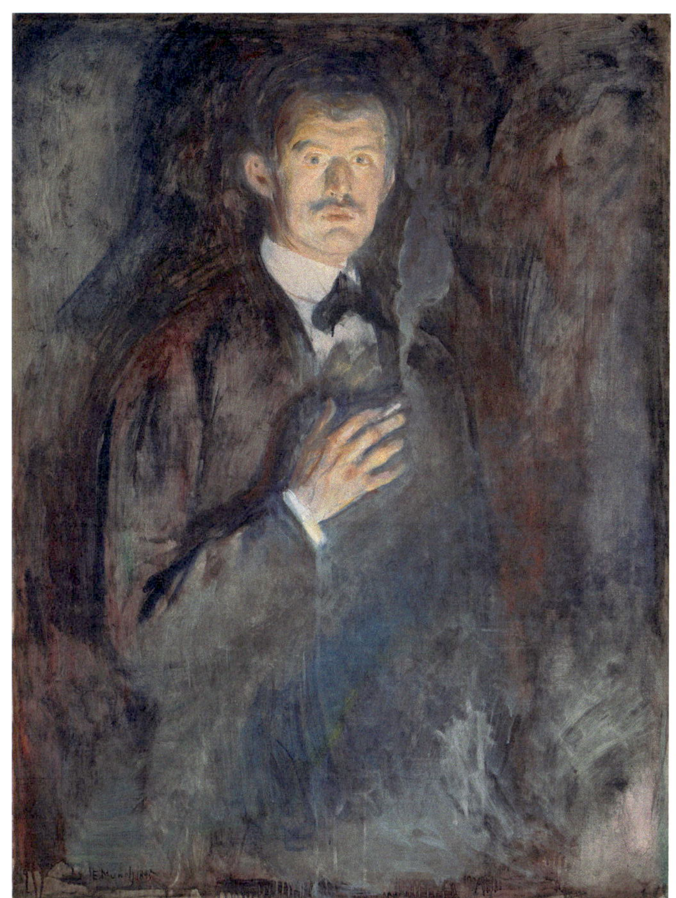

Edvard Munch
Self-Portrait with Cigarette — 1895
Nasjonalmuseet — Oslo

The new capital was undergoing a great transformation in the 1890s; it evolved from humble provincialism to a metropolis with international prestige. Its economy was prospering after victory in the war against France; the city was experiencing a construction boom fueled by reparation payments. It was dominated by an atmosphere of "national prosperity, entrepreneurial boldness, and looming catastrophes," as the journalist Karl Scheffler wrote of these "years of abundance." "Something uncanny, still undefinable, was looming everywhere, heralded by an unstoppable drive to self-destruction. All of this was reflected in the genius loci of Berlin more clearly than anywhere else. Anyone who did not experience this Berlin of unrestrained high capitalism will not easily be able to imagine it. [Around 1890] came the era of building. ... Within twenty-five years the whole new western section was built; the houses came together in rows everywhere, and streets and squares formed ... . Entire street rows took on the character of entertainment districts; colorful electric light lit up everywhere, there was movement, pleasure, and noise ... . Life in the big city was terrifying and fascinating at once."[1] The city was expanding in all directions. In 1877, Berlin had around a million residents; in 1895 it was just under 1.7 million, including nearly 27,000 foreigners.

Artists from abroad were fascinated by Berlin. Since the late 1880s, in turn, a center of enthusiasm for Nordic lands formed in Berlin, which was accelerated by Emperor William II's interest in Scandinavia and Nordic mythology—interpreted as Germanic.[2] Every year he spent several weeks of the summer on board his yacht *Hohenzollern*, mainly in Norwegian waters. The Danish writer Georg Brandes, who was one of the first literary mediators, had three extended stays in Berlin between 1868 and 1883 and described the city to Danish and German audiences from an intense and unsparing insider's perspective.[3]

The circle of artists in Friedrichshagen around Wilhelm Bölsche and Bruno Wille which included Richard Dehmel, Gerhart Hauptmann, Knut Hamsun, Dagny Juel, Stanisław Przybyszewski, and Lou Andreas-Salomé—

celebrated the Scandinavians. Walter Leistikow, who met his Danish wife in this milieu, had studied with the Norwegian painter Hans Gude, a professor at the Preussische Akademie der Künste (Prussian Academy of Arts). The Danish artist Jens Birkholm came to Berlin in the same year as Munch. They met at the wine bar Zum schwarzen Ferkel (The Black Piglet): Dehmel, August Strindberg, Gunnar Heiberg, Ola Hansson, Laura Marholm, Erich Hartleben, Adolf Paul—and Edvard Munch, a "tall, gaunt, slightly bent figure, in a brownish-yellow ulster with a pelerine. Under his black top hat, a pale, sharp-edged face with energetic chin and womanishly soft lips beneath a reddish moustache. Bright, gray, veiled eyes that always seemed to be gazing into another world. ... But then there were moments in which his shy eyes suddenly grew intense and leapt on it: the artist had 'made a big haul.'"[4] They discussed, drank, celebrated, and quarreled well into the night.[5] Gatherings in artists' bars and studios were part of the daily life of the new generation. Figure p.165B Lovis Corinth described the parties in the studio of Walter Leistikow, a painter, critic, and champion of modernism. Figure p.165A "Here the premier minds of Berlin were united: in addition to [Hugo von] Tschudi, there were [Max] Liebermann and [Franz] Skarbina, the Scandinavians [Anders] Zorn, Munch, and the writer [Gustaf af] Geijerstam; as well as Ibsen's friends Dr. Julius Elias and the theater director [Otto] Brahm."[6] These get-togethers, in particular when they led to the formation of longer-term organizations such as art societies or artists' groups, were not a matter of course. In 1878, the anti-Socialist law that Chancellor Otto von Bismarck had initiated was passed. The state was taking rigorous action against all socialist and social democratic parties and associations if it feared they posed a risk to public peace and "the harmony of the social classes."[7] The law required groups to register with the police. In 1890, it was repealed, and assemblies of several people or even the forming groups were no longer illegal—an important step for artistic freedom.

When Munch settled in Berlin in the autumn of 1892, everything was being put to the test: the annual art exhibition at the academy, which was subsidized by the state, and the associated jury and awarding of medals; the Verein Berliner Künstler (Association of Berlin Artists); the Berlin galleries; art critics; the public; and not least the standard of Berlin art itself. The art scene consisted of just two galleries worth mentioning: Fritz Gurlitt and Eduard Schulte, both of which were cautiously opening up to a new view of art.

The most important forum of exhibition in Berlin in the nineteenth century was the *Akademische Kunstausstellung* (Academic Art Exhibition), which was organized first by the Königliche Akademie der Künste (Royal Academy of Arts) in Berlin and then, from 1893 onward, together with the Verein Berliner Künstler (from then on: *Grosse Berliner Kunstausstellung* [Great Berlin Art Exhibition]), as a rule annually, as a large event from the spring to the autumn with a beer garden, artists' parades, and brass bands. In the 1880s, mediocrity reigned: history paintings, religious themes, and always the same saccharine genre paintings, which was constantly lamented by the press and the artists.[8] In a report from the capital for the journal *Die Gegenwart*, Alfred Lichtwark described the depressing situation by saying that if German painters and sculptors were to cease working for a year, no one would take note, that "it would only be noticed when they began to work again."[9] Nevertheless, between two and four thousand works of art could be seen, and the large shows were social events that earned a profit but were not an artistic success. A new generation of critics took it as an occasion to focus the protest that had been pent up in recent years. Like many of his colleagues, Emil Heilbut complained that the walls were filled to the ceiling "with the products of all directions, all styles, all formats" but "that which is good shrinks when seen with

(A)
Lovis Corinth
Dance Break at the Leistikows — 1894
Kunsthalle zu Kiel

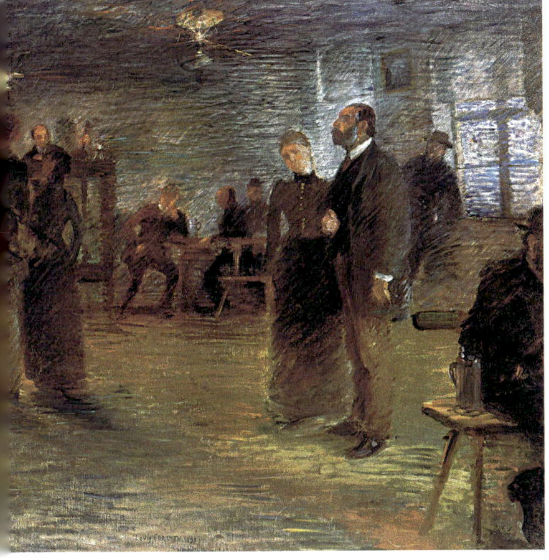

(B)
Edvard Munch
Artists around a Table
(Zum schwarzen Ferkel) — 1893
Munchmuseet — Oslo

mediocrity, swallowed up by it, just as the fat cows of the Bible were swallowed by the lean ones. Tortured, unnerved, and unsatisfied, the eye passes from gold frame to gold frame; the colors glitter and gleam; the colorfully thrown-together pictures hurry us from room to room."[10]

A new generation of artists was taking the stage; many younger painters were moving to Berlin and bringing new ideas with them. Naturalism was just getting established; Impressionism in the form of *Hellmalerei* (bright painting) was still derived predominantly from Scottish painting, not French, and was not infrequently mocked as the "purple rash" or as "green painting." A great restlessness reigned in artists' circles; it was "simmering" everywhere.[11] This dynamic development produced a creative climate for competition and experiments. Many artists even found themselves attracted by the stiff competition, because this was the place in Germany where works by the new movements were exhibited and passionately discussed.

In that ambiguous atmosphere, Munch was invited on September 24, 1892, by his compatriot Adelsteen Normann to participate in the exhibition of the Verein Berliner Künstler from November 5 to 19 in the Architektenhaus (Architects' House) at Wilhelmstrasse 92/93.[12] Figure p.166A Since the beginning of the year, Normann, who had been living in Germany for some time, had been a member of the new exhibition committee of the Verein, which had voted unanimously for the invitation. Munch had no reason to doubt its seriousness, since Normann referred to works by the artist he had recently seen in Kristiania.[13] Munch now showed fifty-five paintings, including *The Sick Child* (1885–86), *Night in Saint-Cloud* (1890), *The Kiss* (1892), and *Despair* (1892) in the rotunda on the ground floor.[14] Figures pp.166B + 26B Immediately after the opening, the exhibition caused a sensation. Even the works by the controversial Glasgow Boys—a circle of modern painters and designers in Glasgow—that were shown in parallel were barely mentioned in the press. On

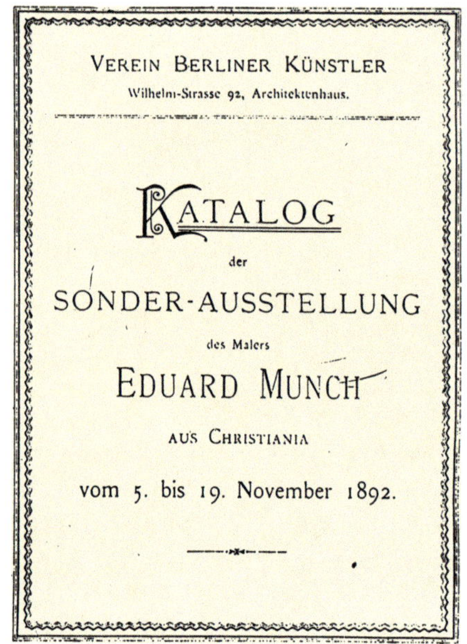

VEREIN BERLINER KÜNSTLER
Wilhelm-Strasse 92, Architektenhaus.

KATALOG
der
SONDER-AUSSTELLUNG
des Malers
EDUARD MUNCH
AUS CHRISTIANIA
vom 5. bis 19. November 1892.

(A)
Catalogue of the Edvard Munch exhibition at the Verein Berliner Künstler — 1892
Munchmuseet — Oslo

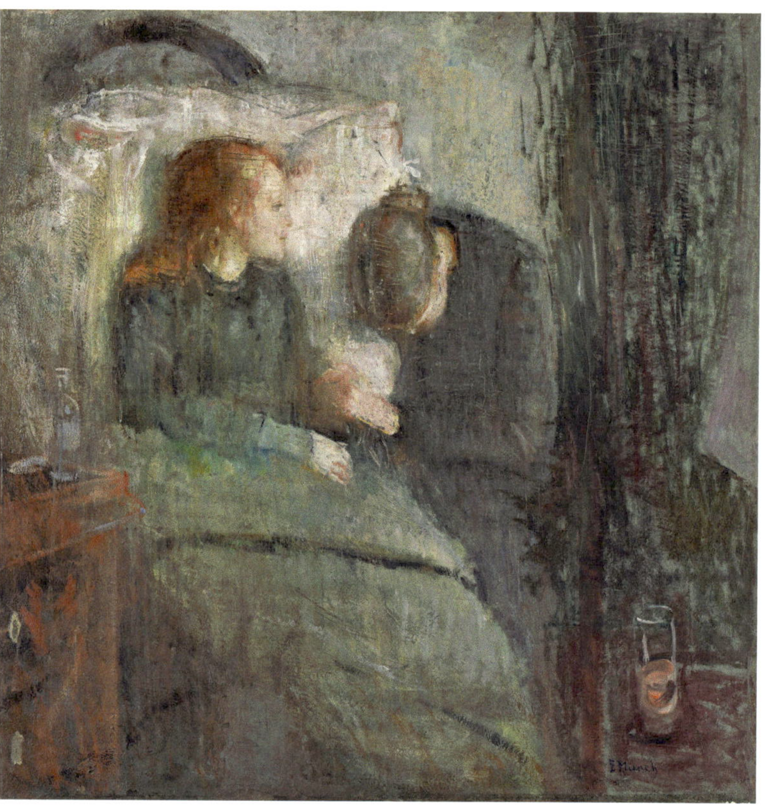

(B)
Edvard Munch
The Sick Child — 1885–86
Nasjonalmuseet — Oslo

November 12, there was a general assembly, and after a dramatic meeting a slight majority voted to have the works taken down, which was done promptly the following day.[15] Munch recognized quite correctly that he could not have had better advertisement. The gallerist Hermann Schulte organized a traveling exhibition with Munch's works and was showing it in November in the main gallery of Eduard Schulte in Düsseldorf and then in its branch in Cologne. Munch himself presented his works (with a few additions) in Berlin again in December. That was a wise decision, because he was offering those who had missed the brief scandalous exhibition an opportunity to form their own opinions and thus remained an active part of the discourse.

In the press, the affair became the Munch Case—the battleground of ideologies and cultural politics. Munch called it a "fiasco,"[16] and in a commentary on this "famous battle in the artists' society," his young colleague Leistikow called it the "Affaire Munch" (Munch Affair)—and it has entered the history books under that name.[17] He parodied the conservative artist as a "man with a long, flowing, white beard, forgotten or even dead."[18]

Leistikow's unsparing criticism was aimed at Germany's oldest artists' association, founded in 1841, in the run-up to the German revolution of March 1848, as a symbol of freedom and self-determination. In 1867, it had been granted by royal order the characteristics and rights of a legal person. The association thus gained recognition and support in the City of Berlin's budget for art policy, but lost its independence. The Verein offered prominent professional representation: there were social security provisions, excursions

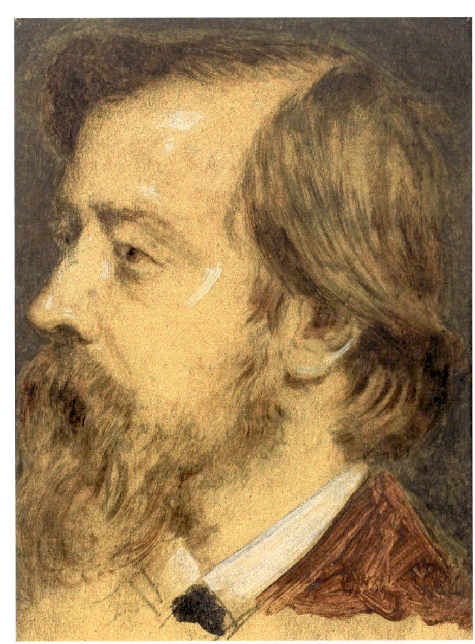

Carl Saltzmann
Portrait of Anton von Werner
ca. 1885/1890
Stiftung Stadtmuseum — Berlin

and artists' festivals, events, and its annual exhibition, but by the end of the century it was covered only in the marginal columns. It was nevertheless both highly respected by society and economically well off. The association's annual exhibitions were held in changing locations until 1898, when it opened its large Künstlerhaus (Artists' House) on Bellevuestrasse in the heart of Berlin, with large exhibition spaces, a banquet hall, a library, and rooms for displays of clothing and armor.

The painter Anton von Werner held the chair three times, initially from 1887 to 1895. Figure p.167 He wanted to lead the association into a new future, increasing the participation of Berlin artists in the city's only large exhibition. A great deal of hope was therefore invested in the exhibition of the Verein Berliner Künstler for its fiftieth anniversary in 1891. On that occasion, the Ministry of Culture and the Königliche Akademie der Künste transferred to him the responsibility for conceiving and directing the annual show as an international art exhibition, which was ordinarily in the hands of the academy.

After that success, however, Anton von Werner had to accept two serious defeats during the planning. For different reasons, Norway and France withdrew their participation in the large event. An unfortunate intervention on the part of Empress Frederick during a trip to Paris in the spring of 1891 and a lack of consultation with Anton von Werner led to a serious political crisis between Germany and France, and for a time there was a risk of war. The French called off their participation in the exhibition.[19] The withdrawal of Norway, by contrast, was based on a conflict of interest in power politics.[20] We know exactly what happened between the German and Norwegian exhibition leaders thanks to Leistikow's anonymously published essay "Epilog zur Berliner Kunst-Ausstellung" (Epilogue to the Berlin Art Exhibition).[21] Anton von Werner ignored the decision of the Norwegian committee to involve Otto Sinding as a mediator, who was accused by Hans Dahl of not being capable of performing the duties of his office objectively and according to artistic standards. Acting on his own and without transparency, von Werner then invited twenty-two other Norwegian artists of his own choice to the exhibition, clearly shifting the overall picture in the direction of traditional painting, in keeping with his and Dahl's preferences. This ignored the demand to establish an especially strict jury. The consequence was Norway's withdrawal from official participation, including Edvard Munch.[22] Leistikow commented on this event: "Like the involvement of the French, the involvement of the Norwegians had thus also fallen through, and this time at least there was no way to conceal domestic ineptitude behind patriotic outrage."[23]

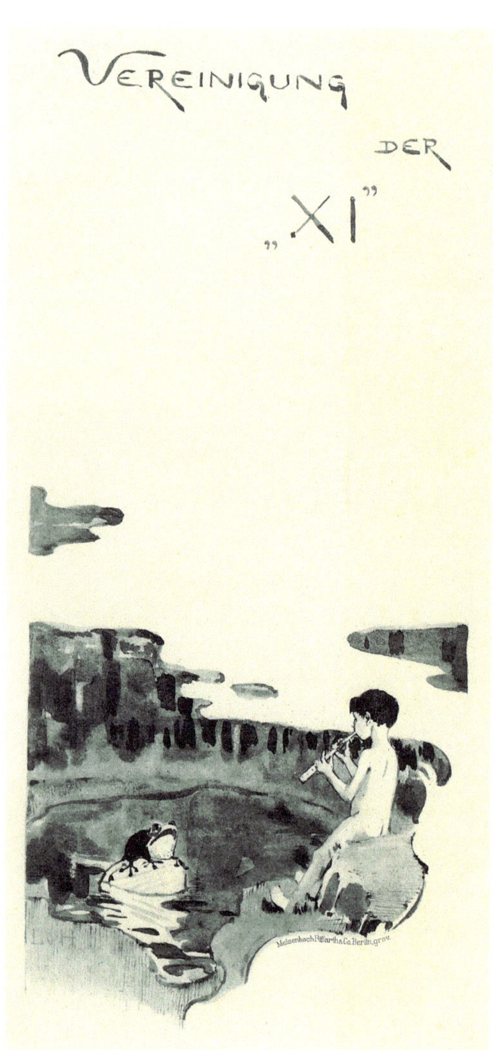

Ludwig von Hofmann
Invitation to the second exhibition of the Vereinigung der XI — March 1893
Akademie der Künste — Berlin

This conflict, which led to an entire nation officially backing out of an international project, shows how unstable the whole exhibition situation was in the early 1890s.[24] The Norwegian section resigned for reasons of self-determination, artistic quality, and fair play. The salon in Munich was happy to take it over.[25] The art historian and critic Cornelius Gurlitt commented on the absence of the Norwegians: "A quarrel between the exhibitors and the management has prevented the appearance of the younger Norwegian school. Anyone who wanted the exhibition to succeed emphatically missed them. Because, in literature as well as painting, the Norwegians are among the most progressive realists, who are turning to the new with swift determination."[26]

The academy was prepared to relinquish its monopoly, but the artists leapt out of the frying pan and into the fire, because the "artistic freedom and impartiality" that Leistikow demanded from and for Berlin artists clearly could not be guaranteed by Anton von Werner as the chairman of the Verein Berliner Künstler and of the exhibition committee, nor could it be expected by artists in the future. At the end of the century, Liebermann wrote in a letter to Wilhelm Bode: "I am of the opinion that if Anton von Werner were to be replaced by a suitable man, Berlin would soon be the leading art city not only of Germany but of the world."[27] The situation could be improved only by searching for an alternative, independent exhibition venue.

A few months later, the first modern artists' group in Germany was founded, calling itself the Vereinigung der XI (Association of the Eleven). Figure p.168 All eleven founding members—who included Max Liebermann, Franz Skarbina, Hans Herrmann, Walter Leistikow, and Ludwig von Hofmann[28]—had been involved in the exhibition in 1891, either in official posts or by participating in the exhibition, so they knew the events and constraints behind the curtains and could learn from the mistakes. From 1892 onward, always in the first quarter of the year, the group presented its works in the commercial art trade in Berlin. From 1892 to 1898, it exhibited at the gallery Kunstsalon Eduard Schulte, and in 1899 a single time at the newly opened Kunsthandlung Keller & Reiner art dealership, with an interior designed by Henry van de Velde, before dissolving and merging into the Berlin Secession.[29] Their group exhibitions were organized independently in a democratic way and in cooperation with the gallerists.

With no dogmatic insistence on any style or movement, the artists of the Vereinigung der XI wanted to present small, select, uncensored exhibitions that distinguished them both from the crowd of mediocre talents and an aesthetically outdated presentation of art. Its import was not recognized initially in broad circles of the art scene. Critics and guests who found it too much discredited the exponents of this new phenomenon as a crowd of "anarchists or semifools."[30] A few years later, however, the XI had become well established, and their concept of an annual show by a group of artists was often copied. Many exhibitions were now curated by artists in the exhibition spaces of commercial galleries, which charged admission fees like museums. Exhibitions adopted "ever more diverse forms and distinctions between private interest and public institution."[31] These early group shows served as models for the later emancipation of the art exhibition. But the reaction of the conservative majority in the early years was relentless. A storm of outrage broke out in response to the group; every year, there were loud calls to close the exhibitions. But that would have been for the gallerists to decide as owners. However, not only did they have no interest in doing so; they also saw the outrage as cold cash. *Tout Berlin* was now getting together with the new trendsetters.

The protests against Munch shortly thereafter were just as vehement. That can be explained not only by his disturbing painting but also by the fact that his exhibition activated the public's collective memory. The "Munch Affair" had a causal relationship to the first exhibition of the Vereinigung der XI. The reactions to the two events—the presentation of Munch in the rotunda as a solo exhibition and the first exhibition of an artist collective in a private gallery—shed light on each other. The excitement about the Munch exhibition functioned to some degree as a stand-in for the repressed XI Affair, which, because its exhibition could not be closed, did not cause a scandal suited to the press. The exhibition of the Vereinigung der XI that took place half a year earlier may have been part of the reason for closing the Munch exhibition. The outrage at Munch was, albeit not entirely, an outlet for mounting a defense against the modern clique.

An incident that occurred at the third XI exhibition, and which, as a rare occurrence, was precisely documented by a letter to the editor, can illustrate this well. A painter who attended the exhibition in 1894 spoke of a "softening of the brain" and of "locking up with water and bread"; the professors Paul Meyerheim, who painted animals, and Reinhold Begas, a sculptor, and a third, unidentified visitor got so loudly worked up about the paintings exhibited that the journal *Das Atelier* further heated up the discussion with a critical contribution from a reader headlined "Noblesse oblige!"[32] Meyerheim and Begas had only their bad behavior to weaponize against the exhibition because they lacked the ability to close it and thus discipline the artists. Since the works were presented in a purely commercial gallery, not a public institution, there was no possibility of an intervention from the official side.

The first XI exhibition had produced a defensive attitude that could be vented on the occasion of the Munch exhibition. The reporting on the two events was vehement and polarizing. Critical voices remarked about

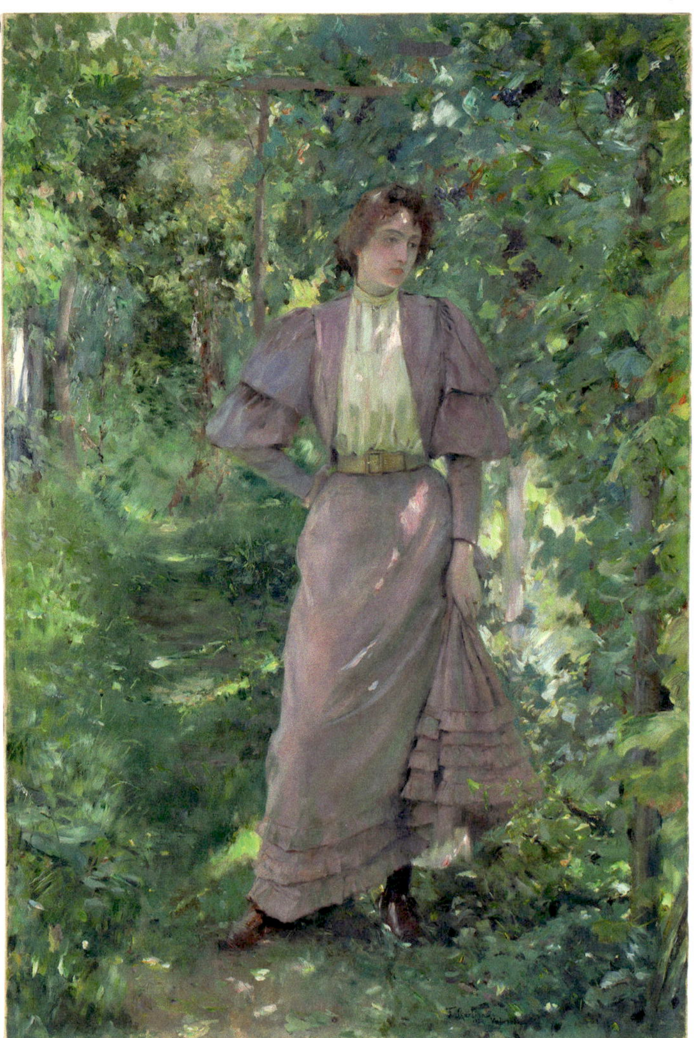

Franz Skarbina
In the Sunshine — 1893
Private collection

the Munch debate that the tumult was difficult to understand, since similar "works ... have already been exhibited everywhere."[33] The scandal around Munch reaffirmed the Vereinigung der XI's concept of small, curated group exhibitions. The commercial gallery proved to be a protective space from sanctions, a place of freedom. The modern movement could be seen here. The division among artists was in the air. In 1892, Munch had come to Berlin at the right time to foster that process. He certainly noticed himself that it was only in part about his new visual language and new look at humanity. Munch commented bluntly on the reactions to his art in 1892: "I did not hear an assessment that truly understood it"[34]—and he did so even though he had not only been savaged in Berlin but also highly praised (as he himself recognized), and even though he had been written about and debated to an extent whose equivalent could be found today only in social media. "They're writing for and against me in all the papers every day."[35]

In his commentary—which was supposedly defending Munch—Leistikow showed only a hint of understanding and did so without really discussing Munch's work. "It was a personality speaking here, loud, audibly, with a resonating voice; it had something individual, compelling." Further down, it reads: "But this is not about Munch and his exhibition here [but] about something bigger, further."[36] Leistikow used the scandal to amplify it and to criticize the situation in Berlin.

Max Liebermann, who was a good fifteen years older, remained silent on the subject. The eloquent artist wrote to Maximilian Harden: "I will gladly share with you my ideas about the case of Munch, but in person, because the pen is too unfamiliar and therefore too heavy for me."[37] That is the only

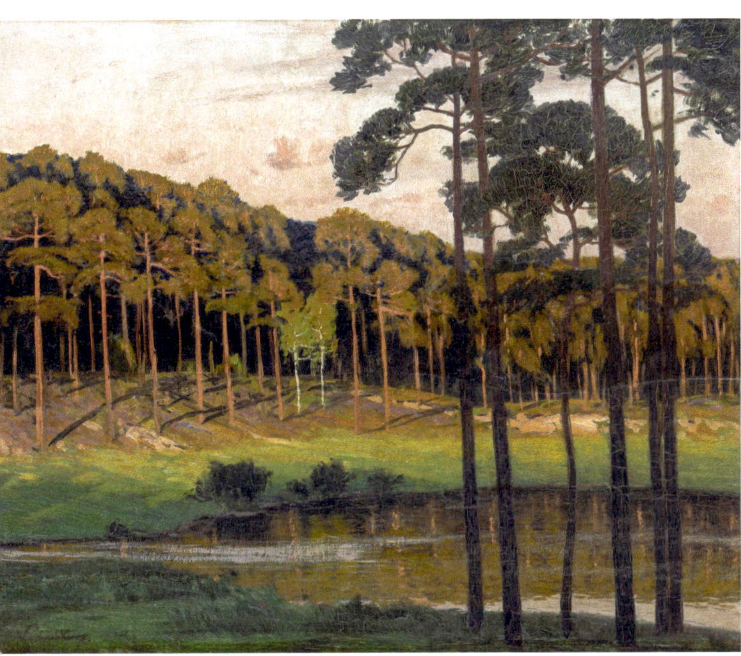

Walter Leistikow
Schlachtensee — ca. 1900
Bröhan-Museum — Berlin

surviving letter by Liebermann that refers to the scandal. Like Leistikow, he used the crisis to his advantage: strategically. Przybyszewski wrote in his memoirs: "Liebermann had long been searching for a pretext to strike a decisive blow against the old ways and to bring some fresh air into the stuffy meeting room of the jury, which stank of the decay of disgusting Byzantinism. ... Liebermann's tactical ... protest caused several stormy meetings at the Kunstverein, and the end result was the complete split of the association."[38]

Most of those involved did not suspect that the painter whom the Berlin art scene was arguing about, and whose exhibition was used for a triumph or at least partial victory on the battleground of modernism, would later become world famous. The more famous Munch became over the years and decades, the more the story about the failure of the Verein Berliner Künstler and the victory of the modern movement took shape. On one side, the conservatives, the old men with long, white beards (Leistikow very deliberately contributed to this narrative); and on the morally correct side, the young and innovative. Figure p.171 Between these alleged, oft-evoked two camps, though in fact a sharp division never existed, the writers' guild dug the trench ever deeper: by means of ignorance and a lack of sources, by means of omission, skilled abridgement, mythmaking, and heroization. This narrative is found first in contemporaneous accounts, and then art historians intensified it. The affair had long since become a "scandal." In the age of the Internet, the flawed accounts of the Munch scandal and the beginnings of modernism that have been published digitally have exploded, and the old familiar mistakes and new ones have taken on grotesque qualities.

Curt Glaser, who had supported and advised Munch for many years, began his monograph on the artist in 1922 by reflecting on what the scandal had done with the artist and his art: "The name Edvard Munch represents a program. It is this artist's fate that his art was not evaluated purely and for its own sake but was rather a battleground when it first appeared before a large audience."[39] Munch, he claims, did not have an easy fate, since "it is difficult to say which side poses the greater risk: the false admirer or the true enemy." What we now regard as obvious about his work, for all its continuing fascination — namely, that his art is precisely what it is — is what Glaser emphasizes as Edvard Munch's unique quality and great achievement: "that he did not lower himself to get closer to the applause of the crowd."

(1) Karl Scheffler, *Die fetten und die mageren Jahre: Ein Arbeits- und Lebensbericht* (Wädenswil, 2011), pp. 325–27.

(2) Berlin 1997–98; Ingeborg Becker, "The Wilderness and the City of Lights: Northern Polarities, or Finland's Artists between National Romanticism and the International Scene," in *Now the Light Comes from the North: Art Nouveau in Finland*, ed. Ingeborg Becker, trans. Michael Loughridge et al., exh. cat. Bröhan-Museum (Berlin, 2002), pp. 14–21. There was also a *vague scandinave* in Paris, which Max Liebermann experienced during his stay there. On this, see Cecilia Lengefeld, *Anders Zorn: Eine Künstlerkarriere in Deutschland* (Berlin, 2004), pp. 105–6.

(3) Brandes 1885, esp. "Berlin som Verdensstad," pp. 410–19.

(4) This description is that of Adolf Paul, reprinted in Rave 1965, p. 177.

(5) Carl Ludwig Schleich, *Besonnte Vergangenheit: Lebenserinnerungen, 1859–1919* (Berlin, 1920), esp. pp. 340–41.

(6) Corinth 1910, p. 62.

(7) "Gesetz gegen die gemeingefährlichen Bestrebungen der Sozialdemokratie" (October 21, 1878), sec. 1, https://library.fes.de/pdf-files/netzquelle/sozialistengesetz.pdf.

(8) When traveling through Hamburg in 1891, Munch wrote in his sketchbook of "repulsive German art—languishing women—battle scenes ... you're just disgusted." MM T 128, Munchmuseet, Oslo (this document and all of the archival materials in Munchmuseet that follow are accessible at emunch.no).

(9) Alfred Lichtwark, "Aus der Hauptstadt: Bildende Künste," *Die Gegenwart* 27, no. 5 (1885): p. 78.

(10) Hermann Helferich [pseudonym of Emil Heilbut], *Neue Kunst* (Berlin, 1887), p. 14.

(11) Philipp Franck, *Vom Taunus zum Wannsee: Erinnerungen* (Berlin, 1920), p. 126.

(12) Adelsteen Normann to Munch, September 24, 1892, Munchmuseet, Oslo, MM K 789.

(13) Munch's exhibition in the Tostrupgård there in September 1892 was nearly identical to the exhibition in Berlin.

(14) *Katalog der Sonder-Ausstellung des Malers Eduard* [*sic*] *Munch aus Christiania, vom 5. bis 19. November 1892* (Berlin, 1892). On the exhibits, see Krisch 1997, pp. 23–25.

(15) For a detailed account of this, see Dominik Bartmann, *Anton von Werner: Zur Kunst und Kulturpolitik im Deutschen Kaiserreich* (Berlin, 1985); Heller 1993; Kneher 1994; Krisch 1997.

(16) Edvard Munch to Karen Bjølstad on November 26, 1892, Munchmuseet, Oslo, MM N 787.

(17) Walter Leistikow (under the pseudonym Walter Selber), in Leistikow 1892, p. 1296; reprinted in Meister 2006, pp. 386–91, www.freidok.uni-freiburg.de/volltexte/2769.

(18) Leistikow 1892, p. 1296.

(19) Dominik Bartmann, *Anton von Werner: Zur Kunst und Kulturpolitik im Deutschen Kaiserreich* (Berlin, 1985), pp. 179–87, and Françoise Forster-Hahn, "'La Confraternité de l'art': Deutsch-französische Ausstellungspolitik von 1871 bis 1914," *Zeitschrift für Kunstgeschichte* 48, no. 4 (1985): pp. 506–37.

(20) Heller 1993, esp. p. 103.

(21) [Walter Leistikow], "Epilog zur Berliner Kunst-Ausstellung," *Freie Bühne* 2 (1891): pp. 963–66; on the attribution to Leistikow, see Meister 2006; reprinted in Meister 2006, pp. 382–85.

(22) The artists represented unofficially were Adelsteen Normann, Hans Dahl, Johannes Grimelund, Nielsen Sörensen, Gerhard Munthe, and Gunnar Berg. See Dr. van Eyck, "Die Malerei auf der internationalen Ausstellung des Vereins Berliner Künstler, 1891: II.: Dänemark und Skandinavien," *Das Atelier* 1, no. 15 (1890–91): pp. 1–6, see p. 6.

(23) Leistikow 1891 (see note 21), p. 965.

(24) Anton von Werner's decision not to intervene in Munch's invitation was connected to this crisis, but his motive was presumably not—as is sometimes assumed—to make amends. Rather, it was based on his instinct to preserve his power. Von Werner was afraid of losing his chair. In January 1892, he was reelected chairman of the Verein Berliner Künstler with a majority of a single vote. "There was a storm of opposition against A. von Werner. I contribute to it, of course, to the best of my ability, as do almost all the younger artists … . A single vote saved him from ruin this time." Walter Leistikow to his parents, January 7, 1892, in *Walter Leistikow: Briefe von 1889 bis 1908*, ed. Margrit Bröhan, comp. and annot. Sabine Meister, Veröffentlichung des Bröhan-Museums 33 (Berlin, 2018), letter no. 7, p. 28.

(25) *Illustrierter Katalog der Münchener Jahresausstellung von Kunstwerken aller Nationen im kgl. Glaspalaste 1891* (Munich, 1891); Munch exhibited three works: *Summer Night, Night, Portrait* (cat. nos. 1082–84), p. 74.

(26) Quoted in Werner Doede, *Berlin: Kunst und Künstler seit 1870; Anfänge und Entwicklungen* (Recklinghausen, 1961), pp. 52–53. No source for the quotation is indicated there.

(27) Max Liebermann to Wilhelm Bode, February 18, 1899, in *Max Liebermann: Jahrhundertwende*, ed. Angelika Wesenberg, exh. cat. Alte Nationalgalerie, Berlin (Berlin, 1997), p. 309, n. 42.

(28) The others were Jacob Alberts, George Mosson, Konrad Müller-Kurzwelly, Hugo Schnars-Alquist, Friedrich Stahl, and Hugo Vogel. In a change of members later, Max Klinger, Dora Hitz, and Martin Brandenburg replaced Müller-Kurzwelly, Herrmann, and Vogel. In 1897, Arnold Böcklin was named an honorary member.

(29) The Berlin Secession was officially founded on January 9–10, 1899. See *Kölnische Zeitung*, January 11, 1899, no. 29, p. 2. Munch was a member from 1904 until it split in 1913. He left on the advice of Curt Glaser; Curt Glaser to Edvard Munch, June 14, 1913, Munchmuseet, Oslo, MM K 2266.

(30) His colleague Paul Schultze-Naumburg thus paraphrased the fuss in the media retrospectively in a review of an exhibition by Ludwig von Hofmann; Paul Schultze-Naumburg, "Ludwig von Hofmann," *Die Kunst für Alle* 14, no. 14 (April 15, 1899): pp. 212–15, esp. p. 213.

(31) Ekkehard Mai, *Expositionen: Geschichte und Kritik des Ausstellungswesens* (Munich, 1986), p. 19.

(32) Letter to the editor, "Noblesse oblige!," *Das Atelier* 4, no. 5 (1894): pp. 4–5.

(33) *Kreuz-Zeitung*, November 12, 1892.

(34) Edvard Munch to Johan Rohde, February 3, 1893, quoted from Munich, Hamburg, Berlin 1994–95, p. 63.

(35) Edvard Munch to Karen Bjølstad, November 12, 1892, Munchmuseet, Oslo MM 785.

(36) Leistikow 1892, pp. 1297–98.

(37) Max Liebermann to Maximilian Harden, December 24, 1892, in Braun 2011–21, no. 1, letter no. 206, p. 260.

(38) Przybyszewski 1985, p. 201 (by "Kunstverein" he meant "Künstlerverein"); Max Liebermann to colleagues and members of the Verein Berliner Künstler, November 14, 1892, to obtain more votes against the closing; an enclosed, preprinted postcard was intended to make it easier for other members to take the step of publicly announcing their disapproval of the closing of the exhibition and to thus shift the power relationships; Geheimes Staatsarchiv Berlin, Rep. 76 Ve Sect. 4 Part IV, no. 2, vol. 2, fol. 251.

(39) Curt Glaser, *Edvard Munch*, 3rd ed. (1917; repr., Berlin, 1922), pp. 9 and 10. I am grateful to Dominik Bartmann and Jens Ketels for their kind support and for providing me with materials, notes, and books.

Explaining Life

Edvard Munch's *Frieze of Life* at the Berlin Secession in 1902

Janina Nentwig

In the winter of 1901–2, Edvard Munch was having financial difficulties. He knew neither how he would be able to extend the rental contract for his Berlin studio, nor how to get his hands on important works that he was storing in Kristiania, present-day Oslo, as security for various loans. A shipping accident unexpectedly helped him out of this tight spot. On December 9, 1901, the steamer *Kong Alf* encountered a heavy storm on its way from Hamburg to Kristiania. It had works by Norwegian artists on board that had been shown in an exhibition in Munich—as well as several containers of acid and gunpowder. There was an explosion that destroyed a painting by Munch as well. The painting *Two Human Beings* belonged to the industrialist Olaf Schou and was insured for the considerable sum of 2,000 crowns. The injured party immediately acquired a new work by the artist. This assured that Munch could remain in Berlin for the time being, and he was able to retrieve his paintings in Kristiania.[1] Nothing more stood in the way of a prestigious presentation in the German capital. If not for the damage on the *Kong Alf*, one of the most important stages in Munch's career might never have occurred: his participation in the fifth exhibition of the Berlin Secession, which was held from April 26 to October 5, 1902. In the sculpture hall of the exhibition building on Kantstrasse, he presented, for the first time in full, a project he would later call *The Frieze of Life*. Munch regarded it as one of his most important works, "if not the most important."[2]

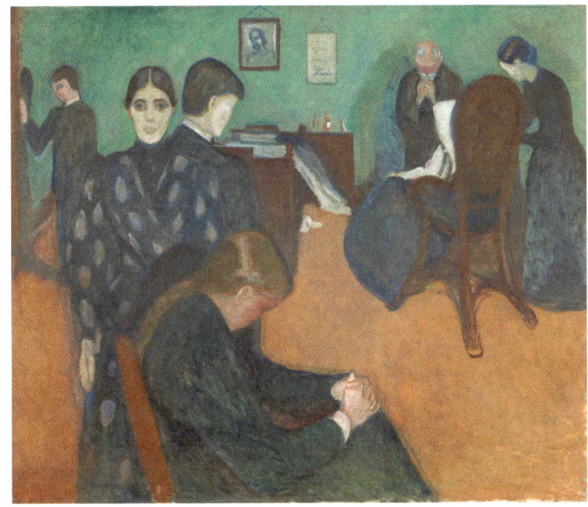

(A)
Edvard Munch
Death in the Sickroom — 1893
Munchmuseet — Oslo

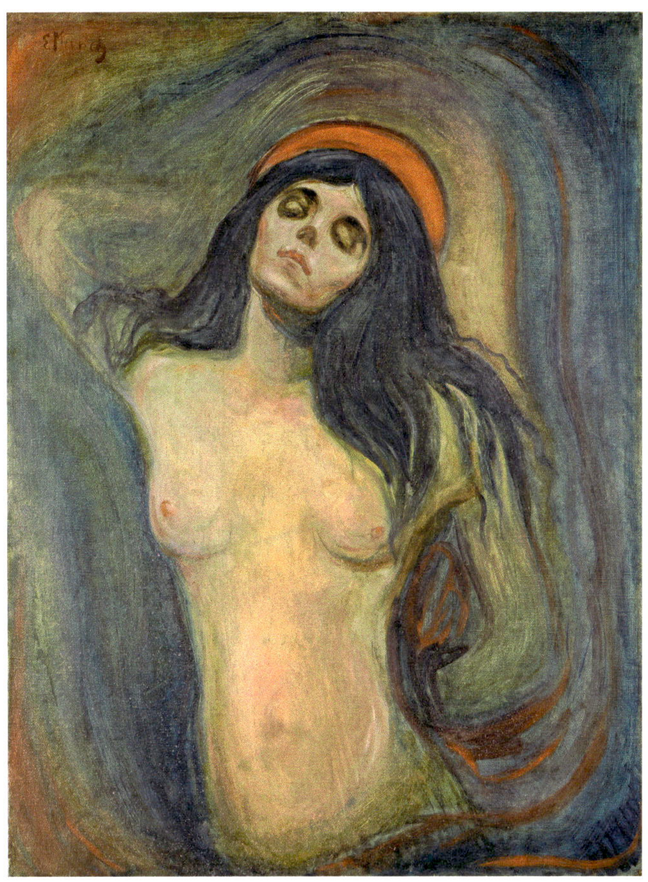

(B)
Edvard Munch
Madonna — 1894
Munchmuseet — Oslo

The Frieze of Life Begins in Berlin

Series, group, cycle—Munch and his contemporaries used many terms for the "work and exhibition concept" that occupied the artist for nearly his entire life.[3] It is a group of changing paintings that revolve around Munch's major themes: love, anxiety, and death. In 1918, on the occasion of an exhibition at the Blomqvist art dealership in Kristiania, the artist introduced the name *The Frieze of Life*, which has since gained acceptance.[4] His series of variations repeatedly included different versions of iconic motifs such as *The Kiss*, *Madonna*, *The Scream*, and *Death in the Sickroom*, which the artist connected to personal experiences in numerous texts and notes. Figures pp. 57, 175A + B, 225B In many of his paintings, Munch worked through the early deaths of his mother and older sister and also his love affairs that ended tragically: first with Milly Thaulow, who was married, and then from 1898 with his fiancée, Tulla Larsen. These works were far more than autobiographical documents, however, not least in their combination: "In my art I have endeavoured to explain life to myself and sought to gain clarity about my fate. I have also thought that it might contribute to others attaining clarity about their fates," he declared in retrospect.[5] From the outset, the artist presented his *Frieze of Life* with a great sense of mission. From the 1890s onward, he showed the associated works in different numbers and with changing titles, in various arrangements and spaces, in numerous places in Europe: in solo exhibitions he organized himself, in art galleries, in group exhibitions of renowned artists' associations, and not least in his own studio in Ekely, Norway, to which the reclusive Munch withdrew in 1916.[6] His stated goal was to find a permanent place for *The Frieze of Life*, perhaps even having a building erected especially for it and repainting the frieze completely as a work that relates to its architecture. Munch drew several designs for such a "chapel of art,"[7] but it was never realized.[8] Uwe M. Schneede rightly calls *The Frieze of Life* a "work in progress" and sees it as one of the central projects of modernity because of its "open view of the unfinishable."[9]

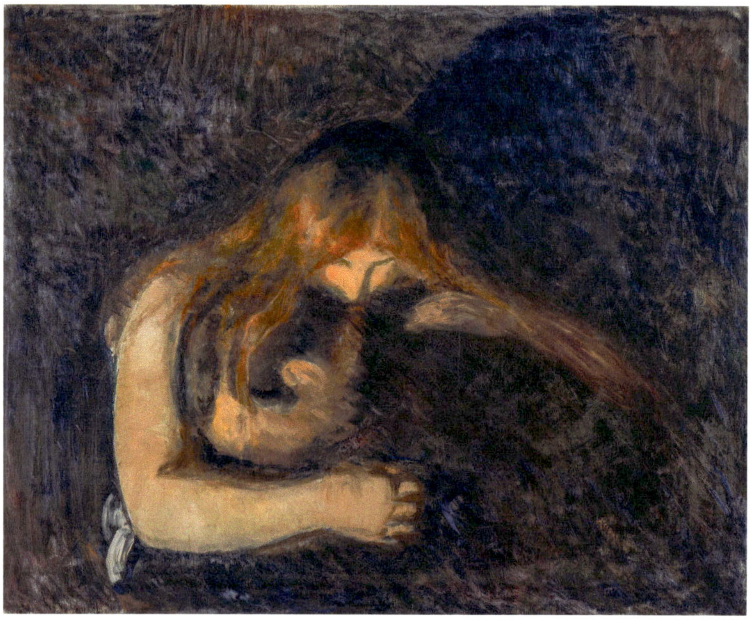

Edvard Munch
Vampire — 1893
Gothenburg Museum of Art

Munch worked on his *Frieze of Life* for a good four decades—with interruptions. He made crucial steps in its development during his stays in Berlin. The young Norwegian not only belonged to the heavy-drinking bohemia at the wine bar Zum schwarzen Ferkel (The Black Piglet), as August Strindberg had christened it, but was also working on his first "studies for a series of paintings" in 1893. To his friend Johan Rohde in Copenhagen, Munch wrote: "Well—what I am doing now will be different—I must strive for more uniformity." The paintings that "were now rather difficult to understand—will be, I believe, more easily understood when they all come together—it will be about love and death."[10] Munch was reacting to the broad rejection of his art, not least on the occasion of the premature closing of the scandalous exhibition at the Verein Berliner Künstler (Association of Berlin Artists) in 1892, which had been shown thereafter at the Düsseldorf and Cologne branches of the Galerie Eduard Schulte and finally at the Equitable-Palast (Equitable-Palace) in Berlin. Buyers of his art continued to be rare, but people were curious about the paintings that had been condemned as enigmatic and unfinished and caused so much controversy. Admission fees alone earned him 1,800 marks for the tour,[11] which at the time was more than twice the average annual income in Germany.[12] Now Munch needed to keep public attention from fading and to better communicate his art. He showed his first *Study for a Series "Love"* in an exhibition for which he had rented two rooms in a commercial building on the boulevard Unter den Linden in the winter of 1893–94. The six-part series included brand-new works such as *Despair* (now *The Scream*) and *Love and Pain* (now *Vampire*), the latter of which Munch had painted in his room in a Berlin boarding house.[13] Figure p.176 He achieved the "uniformity" he was striving for not only in the thematic arrangement but also in terms of style. The associated pictures were painted in an expressive, solidified style that he had refined over the summer in Norway.[14] But the strategy that the works would explain one another did not succeed with the public or the press. The series was ignored by critics, and Munch's paintings continued to be considered "bizarre ideas hurriedly tossed off in a bilious mood."[15] Undeterred, the artist expanded the series the following autumn for his exhibition at the Konstförening (Arts Society) in Stockholm without changing the arc of tension conceived in Berlin. Although the fifteen paintings did not describe a strict plot with recurring protagonists, they traced the path of two lovers in an open, psychologically condensed way:[16] from their first encounter by way of passionate but also tortuous desire to separation and unfathomable hopelessness, represented by—how could it be otherwise?—*The Scream*. The series could then be seen, with few changes, at the Galerie Ugo Barroccio in Berlin in 1895, where Munch was exhibited with the Finnish artist Axel Gallén. The relativizing word “study” was now dropped in the catalogue. Munch had found a valid form. After moving to Paris, he showed the series again in 1896 with ten paintings at the Maison de l’Art Nouveau of Siegfried Bing, with, among other works, fourteen etchings and lithographs, which he also combined under the title *L’amour.*[17] Munch did not lose sight of the plan he had formulated three years earlier to combine love and death in a series. He realized it first in prints. The artist had discovered this medium in Berlin in late 1894 and initially used it primarily for motifs he had developed in his paintings.[18] He was, however, never able to realize a planned portfolio titled *The Mirror* that would show life as a whole and connect these two sets of motifs.[19] Not until 1902, at the Berlin Secession, did Munch have an opportunity to show a large series of paintings on love and death.[20] His *Darstellung einer Reihe von Lebensbildern* (Depiction of a Series of Images of Life) consisted of twenty-two works presented as a continuous frieze just under the ceiling of the sculpture hall.[21] This installation was extraordinary in several respects and is considered the first formulation of the classic *Frieze of Life*, which Munch would vary over the following decades, including for his large retrospective at the Nationalgalerie (National Gallery) in Berlin in 1927, where the project was represented by eleven paintings.[22]

Despite the close connection of *The Frieze of Life* to Berlin, Munch publicly downplayed the importance of his time in Germany on the occasion of the aforementioned exhibition in his native city in October 1918. He said that the “first, loose” designs had already been made in Kristiania in 1888, and others during a stay in Paris that followed. Munch strongly protested “that the ideas for the subject matter of this frieze were influenced by German thought and my contact with Strindberg.”[23] Near the end of World War I, which the German Reich had begun together with Austria-Hungary, such distancing was understandable. Munch wanted to be perceived as a Norwegian artist and not to have the roots of his projects located in the intellectual milieu in which he had moved in Berlin from 1892 onward.[24] In Germany, in turn, the appropriation of his work as “Germanic” had already become part of the canon by this time.[25] Reinhold Heller sums up the influence that Kristiania, Paris, and Berlin had on Munch: “Kristiania ... gave birth to Munch’s imagery and Paris provided the stylistic vocabulary to manifest it, but Berlin transformed isolated pictorial utterings into a bold, coherent cycle of paintings as *The Frieze of Life* gestated and began to emerge.”[26] But how exactly did that transformation occur? To answer this question, it pays to look more closely at the exhibition of the Berlin Secession. What led to this comprehensive presentation that first united the paintings on love and death in a frieze? Was Munch free in his artistic decisions, or did the Secession influence them? What was the association hoping for by offering the still-misunderstood Norwegian artist such a large presentation—especially given that it was his first time exhibiting in its spaces, and considering that he would not become a full member until 1904?

Win-Win Situation: The Fifth Exhibition of the Berlin Secession

The main reason why Munch moved back to Berlin in late 1901 was not the Berlin Secession but rather its managing director, the art dealer Paul Cassirer.[27] Presumably in the autumn of that year Cassirer had expressed interest in having an exhibition in his Kunstsalon. It was being discussed for the coming February or March.[28] Munch rented a space in a large studio building at Lützowstrasse 82. He was already familiar with the place through his friend Walter Leistikow, who had worked there himself several years earlier. Munch was enthusiastic: "An ideal studio—with gas for light and cooking."[29] Figure p.120 After the insurance money from Schou made it possible for him to bring his paintings to Berlin, Cassirer accepted their delivery.[30] It is not known why the plan to work with the gallery failed at first. Perhaps the economic risk of such an undertaking seemed too high after all to the businessman,[31] and he sent the paintings to the Berlin Secession and waited to see how Munch would be received this time. Or perhaps he declined for other, tactical reasons, since the avant-garde association was extremely turbulent at the time.[32] Whereas Chairman Max Liebermann, Cassirer, and members such as Leistikow and Ludwig von Hofmann wanted to emphasize current foreign art in the exhibitions, there was bitter resistance to that orientation from more conservative members. It seemed only logical that progressive Secessionists would be interested in Munch, who ten years earlier had been like a match to the powder keg of the Berlin art scene and thus prepared the way to the founding of the Secession. Even before Cassirer confirmed receipt of Munch's crates of paintings on January 27, 1902, he had received a visit from Leistikow. Liebermann, too, announced himself.[33]

Already on February 7, Munch proudly wrote home to say he had been invited to show around a dozen paintings at the upcoming annual exhibition of the Secession.[34] Just a week later, on February 14, newspapers reported that the group was splitting up.[35] Sixteen artists, including Otto Heinrich Engel and Oskar Frenzel, two members of the board who are barely remembered today, and the painter Julie Wolfthorn all left the association. Those departing members criticized above all Cassirer's influence, saying that he was bringing his own personal commercial interests into the Secession, as well as the increasing dominance of non-German, too modern positions, of the sort Munch also represented.[36] Further emphasis of progressiveness and internationality after the exodus of the opposition was all but demanded of the new board that had been quickly reformed and immediately took over the directing of the exhibition. Figure p.179C Although Liebermann's statements about Munch had until then been rather dismissive, and Cassier was not completely persuaded by his art either,[37] the number of exhibits granted him increased sharply. On March 18, the artist wrote his to friend Andreas Aubert: "Liebermann proposed exhibiting at the Secession not only the nine paintings but also the whole cycle of paintings on love and death that has been so scorned—it is not at all certain that will be tolerated."[38] Munch was speaking of a cycle on love and death here as a given, even though he had thus far produced only one as a series of prints. Plans to do so with his paintings had, however, presumably ripened considerably earlier.[39]

In addition to Cassirer, Liebermann, and Leistikow, a fourth name comes up in the letters that document further preparations. Albert Kollmann, an acquaintance of Liebermann's, a person of private means, and a *marchand amateur*, had become a close confidant and enterprising agent of the

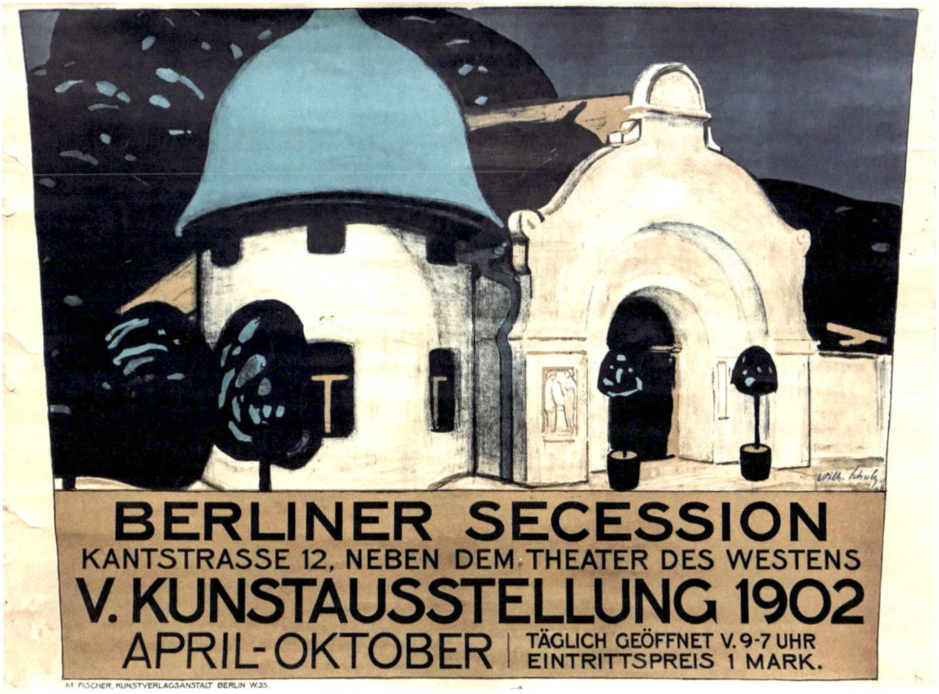

(A)
Wilhelm Schulz
Poster for the fifth exhibition of the Berlin Secession — 1902
Museumsberg — Flensburg

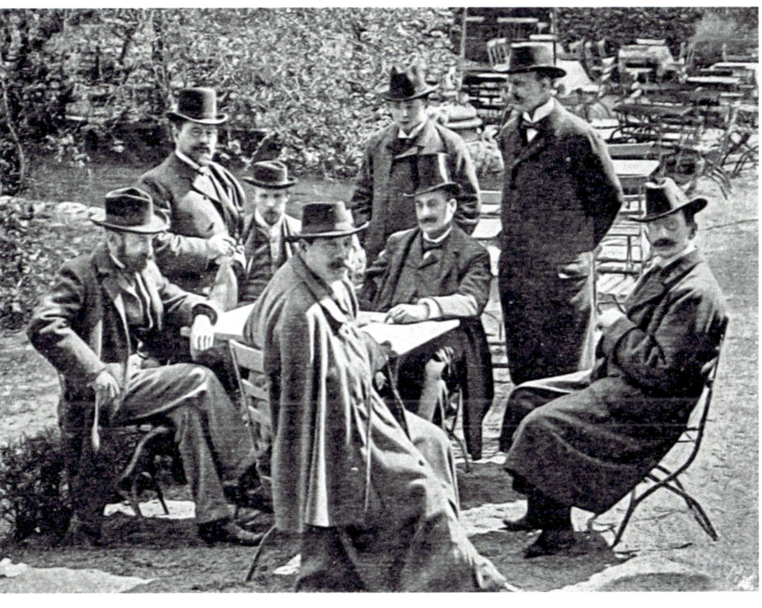

(B)
Floor plan of the exhibition building of the Berlin Secession, Kantstrasse 12 — 1902

(C)
Board of the Berlin Secession, from left to right, front row: August Gaul, Lovis Corinth, Walter Leistikow, back row: Max Slevogt, Fritz Klimsch, Paul Cassirer, Max Liebermann, Ludwig von Hofmann — 1902

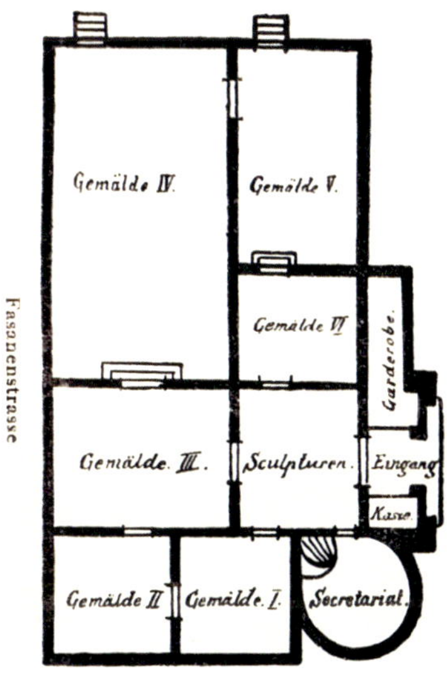

Norwegian artist in the winter of 1901–2.[40] On March 21, 1902, Kollmann was able to report to the collector Max Linde in Lübeck: "Liebermann, in the name of the Secession, has asked Munch to install his entire cycle of Symbolist paintings (ca. twenty-five) as a frieze in the foyer of the exhibition building. I was just out there with M. to take measurement, and these days he is working on color sketches … ."[41] Around thirty-five paintings were unloaded on Kantstrasse on March 26, Kollmann informed Linde in another letter." So this season is entirely under Munch's sign. And now we get straight to work. …"[42] If one can trust the arithmetic of this trained businessman, Munch brought considerably more exhibits than the twenty-eight listed in the exhibition catalogue. In the end, six landscapes and portraits were selected along with twenty-two works as a *Darstellung einer Reihe von Lebensbildern* (Depiction of a Series of Paintings of Life)—the aforementioned frieze—including many paintings that had already been a part of the series on love.[43] On April 8, three weeks before the exhibition began, the *Berliner Tageblatt* announced Munch's participation as one of the high points, though not without mentioning the scandal of 1892: "The sculpture hall was decorated this time with a frieze by the Norwegian artist Munch, who had caused a real storm around a decade ago with his painterly experiments and application to join the Verein Berliner Künstler. The frieze is a depiction of human passions and life forces, connected by an idea and color chords; the individual parts are framed with white fabric."[44] The foreign participation was not extensive this time, as was further explained in the brief news item. Munch was functioning as a prominent showpiece for the exhibition and stood for the Berlin Secession's catching up with the international avant-garde.

Showing All of Life: The Series Becomes a Frieze

Given that emphatic position, the site for Munch's installation was very probably a compromise. The sculpture hall was indeed the very first room of a tour of the exhibition, through which viewers also exited again. But it lacked large, continuous wall surfaces because of its five doorways. Figure p.179B Munch had never exhibited his works publicly in the form of a frieze—which is by definition a strip or band with ornaments or figurative depictions to articulate and decorate a wall. Over the course of the nineteenth century, the frieze had experienced a revival, especially in painting.[45] Munch, too, had for a time a "desire for very large decorations," which he wanted to create in close connection with the architecture.[46] He found inspiration for this, among other places, in the monumental paintings of his compatriot Adolph Tidemand in the Villa Oscarshall in Oslo[47] and in Symbolist murals and friezes by the Nabis, Pierre Puvis de Chavannes, Hans von Marées, and Max Klinger, for example.[48] The decision to hang the cycle as a frieze was presumably not least due to practical reasons, alongside artistic considerations. In order to incorporate a sufficient number of paintings, they had to be placed above the passageways and hence right under the ceiling. Even so, with a room measuring 9.3 by 7.5 meters, as Munch noted in his sketchbook,[49] the selected paintings were nevertheless hung close together, and the reduction from the planned twenty-five works to twenty-two was unavoidable. The existing architecture necessarily turned what had been series and cycles into a frieze divided into four chapters according to the available walls. The cycle of love and death that had previously been thought of as dualistic therefore had to be subdivided further. In the catalogue, Munch titled the sections "Keimen der Liebe" (Sprouting

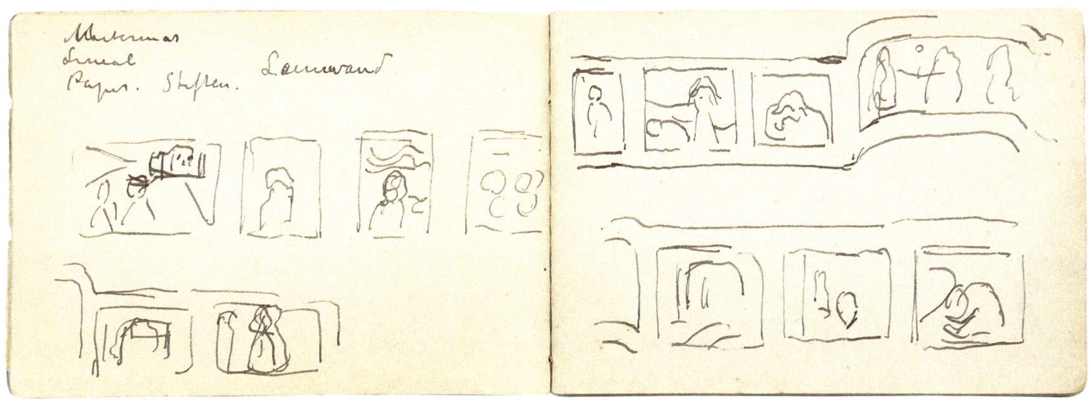

Edvard Munch
Sketches for the Berlin Secession exhibition — 1902
Munchmuseet — Oslo

of Love), "Blühen und Vergehen der Liebe" (Blossoming and Fading of Love), "Lebensangst" (Anxiety of Life), and "Tod" (Death). With regard to the difficult problem of reconstructing the frieze, the majority of scholars agree that the sequence of paintings in the exhibition space corresponded to that in the catalogue.[50] If that is the case, a long process of clarification must have preceded the final hanging: in a sketchbook Munch recorded several different possible combinations including a surrounding framing.[51] Figure p.181 None of these summary designs precisely reflect the sequence of works in the catalogue, so that the drawings would have to be thought of as preliminary stages.[52] Regardless of their actual sequence, the innovative organization brought the works closer together than in the series and made the "poem about life, love, and death"[53] even more compelling. Nevertheless, the frieze still presented an open narrative whose "meaning arises in the viewing, in a dialogue with an intersubjective framework of understanding and concepts," as Mai Britt Guleng observes. That describes a characteristic of *The Frieze of Life* that is as central as it is timeless: "the narrative is hidden in the individual viewer."[54]

The four chapters of the frieze provided the basic structure for this individual process of interpretation in 1902; according to the catalogue, the frieze began on the wall to the left of the entrance with "Keimen der Liebe." Six paintings here thematize the beginning of a love affair and of erotic or sexual experiences, including *Eye in Eye* and *Madonna*, followed by the more neutral, secular title *Love*. Figures pp.56 + 175B The adjoining longitudinal wall, which one approached directly upon entering the hall, was equally closely hung and dedicated to "Blühen und Vergehen der Liebe." There were two striking horizontal formats in this section: *Midsummer Night's Eve* (now *The Dance of Life*), according to Munch's memory,[55] which, in keeping with the sketchbook, was prominently placed above the door, and *Sphinx* (now also *Woman*). Figures pp.28 + 182 Both pictures illustrated the opposed aspects of love united in this section: intimate connection and consuming jealousy. Five paintings on "Lebensangst" followed, including *The Scream*. Finally, five paintings on death were hanging on the exit wall; according to the catalogue, the final works in the series were *Life and Death* (now *Metabolism*) and *Death and the Child*. Figures pp.183 + 185A These two works closed the series to make a true cycle: in 1902, *Metabolism*, a paraphrase of the traditional religious pictorial formula of the Fall that was later reworked, still depicted a plant with an unborn child growing out of it between the man and the woman, where there is a tree trunk today.[56] This fetus stands not for the end but for the new beginning of the tale. Likewise, the child in the second painting, who is looking out at the viewer, paralyzed by the horror of her mother's death, will have to go through such existential experiences herself over the course of her life. Not least because of its presentation and explicit identification in the catalogue as a frieze — a "conveyor of sacred meaning"[57] with a long tradition — the cycle of paintings acquired a quasi-religious charge. According

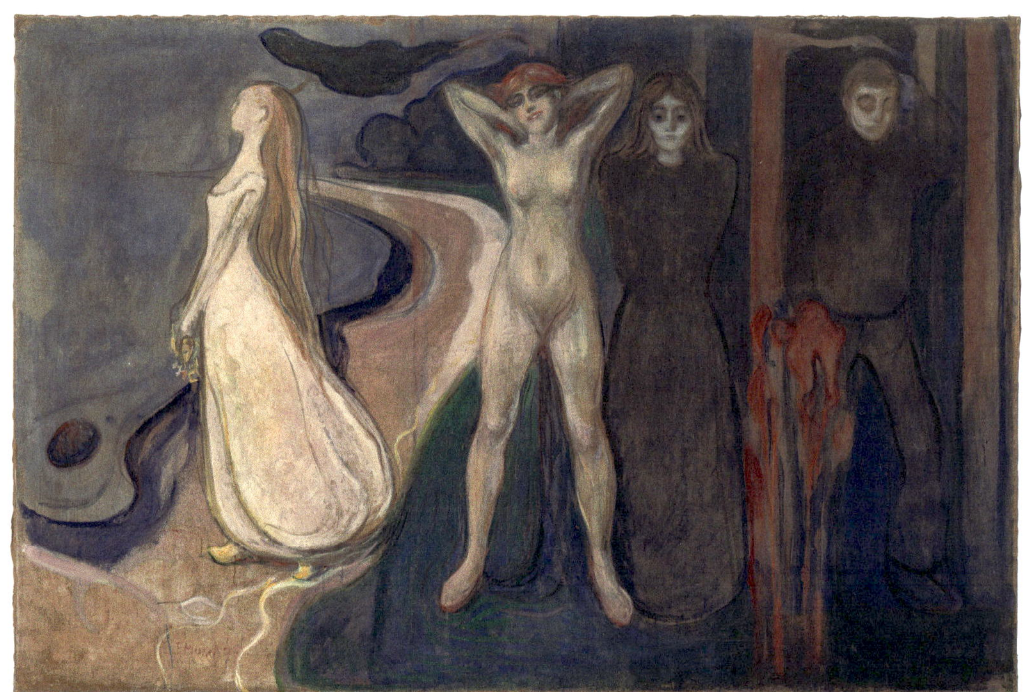

Edvard Munch
Woman — 1894
Kode — Bergen

to Robert Rosenblum, it became "a pictorial equivalent of a philosophical commentary on modern man and his fate, presented with a symbolic starkness that was to usurp the role of earlier religious imagery."[58] Many other artists of the nineteenth century pursued similar ends, including painters Munch admired such as Vincent van Gogh and Paul Gauguin, as well as Ferdinand Hodler.[59] But Munch found in Berlin a concept that was very much his own, as complex as it was open. Whereas the individual works of *The Frieze of Life* capture the alienation of modern human beings, "the individual's break with the world,"[60] the frieze as a whole turns the loneliness and isolation into a circle in which life, with its hopes, disappointments, and tragedies, is always beginning anew.[61]

Although the idea of the frieze, and the heightening of meaning he associated with it, continued to be central for Munch—which is presumably why after 1918 he used the term "frieze" even for his earlier series[62]—in retrospect the artist criticized the hanging of the paintings in the sculpture hall of the Berlin Secession as too high, "for at too great a height, the paintings lose their intimacy."[63] The artist cannot have been satisfied with the lighting of the plainly decorated room either. It was the only exhibition space without a skylight.[64] Emil Heilbut's review confirms that it was relatively dark there. Two years later, the critic recalled that in 1902 Ferdinand Hodler's painting *Wilhelm Tell* could also be seen in the foyer, "which receives only half-light."[65] If Heilbut can be believed, not only sculptures but also paintings by other artists could be seen below the frieze, perhaps together with the landscapes and portraits that Munch also showed. In the middle of the hall stood the polychromed plaster study for Klinger's monument to Beethoven, which drew considerable attention but also received a lot of criticism.[66] The continuous white frame was an effective way to guide eyes up toward Munch's paintings in the dark sculpture hall with heterogeneous pieces. It created brighter surroundings for the paintings, which not only made it easier to view them but also heightened their colors.[67] The canvas strip visually brought together works of different sizes and turned them into part of the wall, which was also covered with fabric in a matte blue.[68] Unfortunately, there are no known photographs of Munch's presentation—despite the fact that other rooms in the fifth Secession exhibition were documented.[69] The poor lighting may have made it difficult to photograph the paintings that had been installed so high. One year later, Munch framed his *Frieze of Life* paintings again for their presentation in Leipzig at the

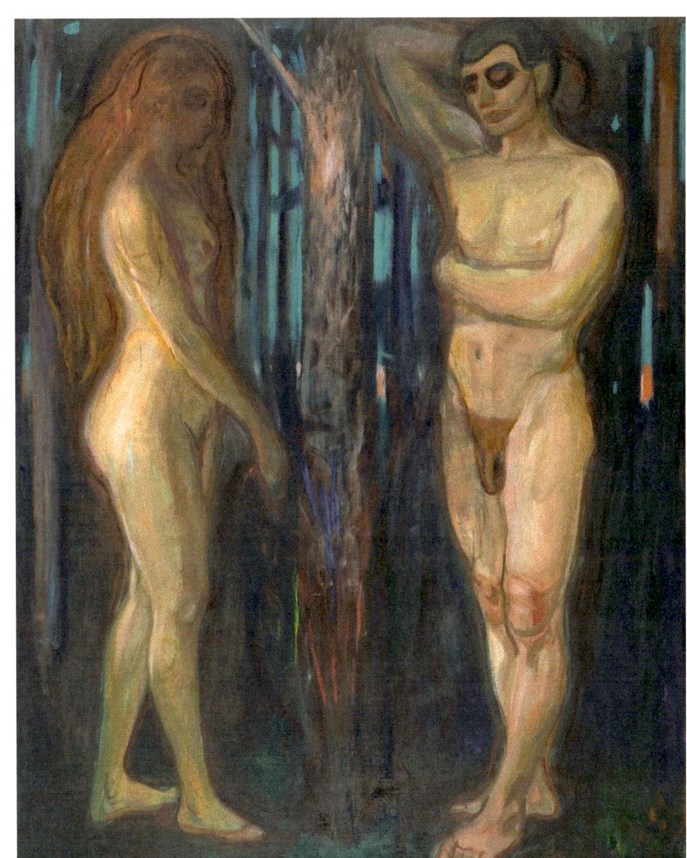

Edvard Munch
Metabolism—1898–99
Munchmuseet—Oslo

Galerie P. H. Beyer & Sohn. Three surviving photographs of that exhibition convey at least an approximate impression of the effect of the white frame when it was first used in Berlin. Figure p.186 The room in Leipzig was, however, brighter and at 10 by 15 meters considerably larger than the room in the Secession. Munch also showed only nineteen paintings at Beyer & Sohn.[70] The distances between the paintings of the frieze must therefore have been very much narrower in Berlin. In an associative text the artist later described the overall effect of the works in the Secession, which despite having been painted at different times formed a rhythmical unity both with one another and with the architecture: "The paintings came into their own thanks to their similarity and difference—differing in color and format and yet connected by certain colors and lines (and by the framing)—horizontal and vertical lines—vertical lines of the trees and walls—on the grounds—the earth—and the roofs and treetops—and the more horizontal lines—in the lines of the sea—sway lullaby [?]. There were sad, grayish-green shades in the colors of the room of the dying woman—there were cries of fire—in the blood-red sky and the sound of red, bright red—yellow—and green colors—There was a symphonic effect—Which caused quite a commotion—lots of resistance—and lots of recognition."[71]

The Reception: Commotion, Resistance, and Recognition

The great attention that Munch recalled is reflected only to a limited extent in the reporting in 1902. With his twenty-eight works, the artist held the undisputed top position of the artists exhibiting. He was followed at a great distance by Isaac Israëls, Leopold von Kalckreuth, and Wilhelm Trübner with seven works each, the recently deceased Édouard Manet with five paintings, and the Berlin sculptor Louis Tuaillon with five sculptures. Apart from Munch, Israëls, and Manet, foreign countries were not especially well represented in the number of artists—Claude Monet, James Abbott McNeill Whistler, Anders Zorn, and a few others—or the number of their works. Moreover, these artists were predominantly associated with Impressionism, which Munch had left far behind with the powerful colors and emotions of his paintings. In most articles, Munch was nevertheless discussed rather briefly; the frieze as such was scarcely mentioned, much less understood.[72] One reviewer complained that the "primitive compositions of the Norwegian artist Munch that mar the front hall of the Secession" were painted years earlier, and nearly all of them were known in Berlin, without evaluating the innovative arrangement and presentation.[73] Many journalists repeated the arguments from previous years: Munch was a neuropathological case and defender of a "subjective mysticism to which the suitability of natural vision is unreflectively sacrificed," lamented, for example, the traditional art journal *Zeitschrift für Bildende Kunst*.[74] The *Kunst-Halle: Zeitschrift für Kunst und Kunstgewerbe*, which tended to be critical of the avant-garde, was once again incensed at the raw, unfinished painting style. The best thing about the "cycle of twenty-two sheerly indescribable paintings" was, in any case, said to be the titles.[75] The majority of the visitors did not know what to make of Munch's paintings, as Hans Rosenhagen noted in the journal *Die Kunst für Alle*. The critic deftly combined the public's lack of understanding with a concise explanation of Munch's art: "They [the visitors] see his life's work, united into a frieze in the first room of the exhibition, more as a mockery of the traditional than as a revelation of new beauty. They have no feeling for the coloristic talent it takes to work with the brightest colors without looking motley and even to produce a certain tonality. They do not understand that dispensing with the depiction of details is a necessary consequence of Munch's decorative intentions. ... Munch, whatever one can say against him, remains an eminent artist who has taken something new from reality but also put something new back into it."[76]

Munch continued to bring new things into the world, and the rapid succession of his exhibitions did not abate. Among other shows, Cassirer held the artist's first exhibition in his gallery in January 1903. The fact that the "weltanschauung paintings"[77]—that is, *The Frieze of Life*—were not included was considered a plus by Rosenhagen and other reviewers, who praised the more optimistic mood and brilliant colors of the more recent paintings exhibited. *The Frieze of Life*, which Munch would never again show in public presentations with as many works as he had at the Berlin Secession, was varied by the artist not only in Leipzig but also in Kristiania in 1904 as *Frieze: Motifs from the Modern Life of the Soul* and in Prague in 1905 under the title *From the Cycle "Life."*[78] He searched unsuccessfully for patrons who would acquire the group as a whole. Munch had to separate and sell individual works, which made him very unhappy.[79] After that, the project was not exhibited again for a long time.

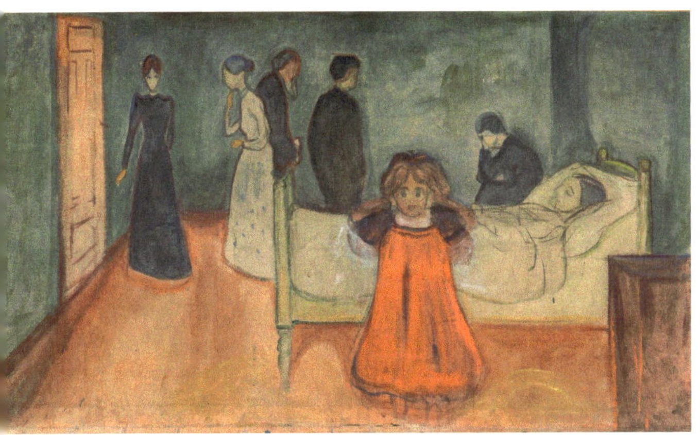

(A)
Edvard Munch
Death and the Child — 1899
Munchmuseet — Oslo

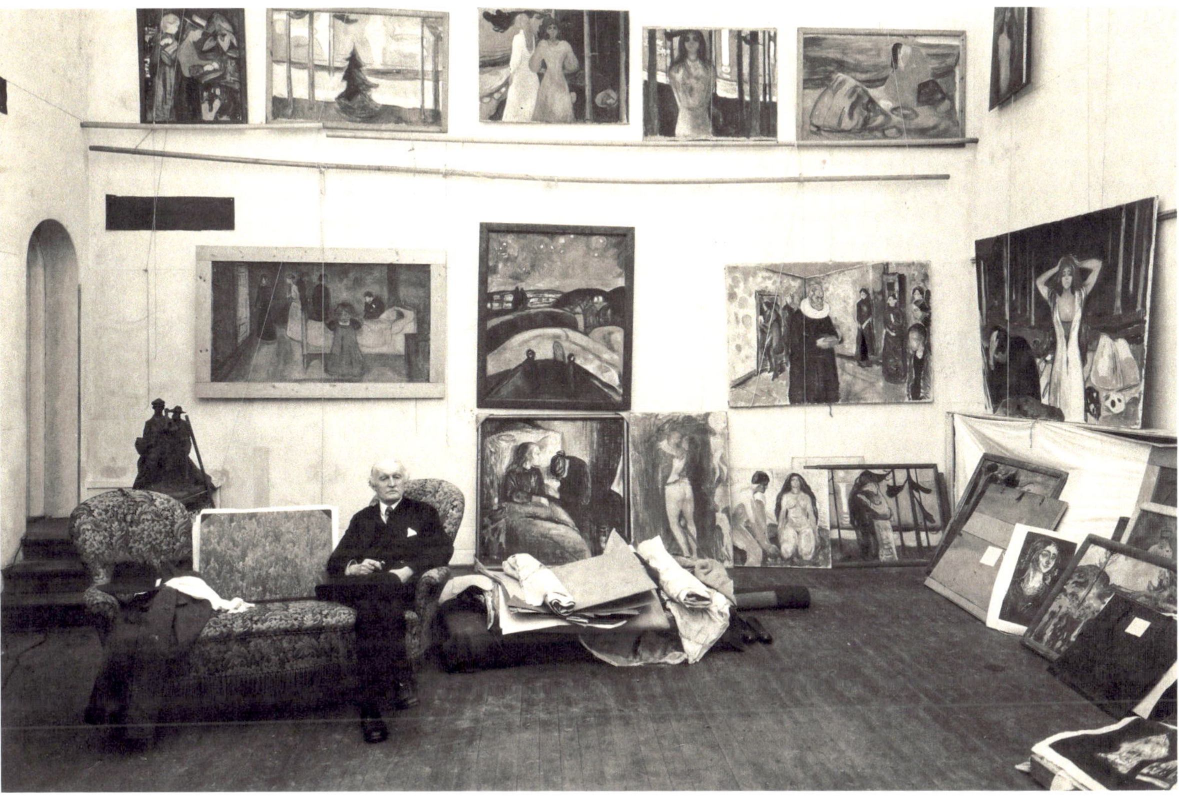

(B)
Ragnvald Væring
Edvard Munch in his winter studio in Ekely, on the occasion of his seventy-fifth birthday — 1938
Munchmuseet — Oslo

Munch dedicated himself instead to specific commissions for interior decoration, for which he emphasized the decorative qualities of his painting and paraphrased isolated motifs from *The Frieze of Life*. For Max Linde, Munch produced a colorful, multipart frieze in 1904 that was intended to decorate the nursery of his sons, but it was not accepted by the client, in part because it depicted a couple kissing.[80] Figures pp. 74–85 + 235 His frieze for a banquet hall in Max Reinhardt's Kammerspiele in Berlin was installed in 1907 but was removed just five years later during a renovation.[81] Figures pp. 86–99 + 238 After Munch had returned to Norway for good in 1909, the large commission for decoration he had yearned for finally arrived: he created a monumental cycle for the auditorium of the university in Kristiania, which he regarded as a continuation of *The Frieze of Life*.[82] He began again to work more intensely on this project that had been lying idle. At the Blomqvist art dealership in 1918, he supplemented works from the 1890s with new paintings, adding pictures from the rejected *Linde Frieze* and paraphrases of earlier motifs.[83] Munch thus remained faithful to the principle that he had developed essentially in Berlin: he repeatedly rearranged his paintings into a supraindividual and timeless depiction of love, anxiety, and death. At the same time, he documented his life's work and its stylistic development

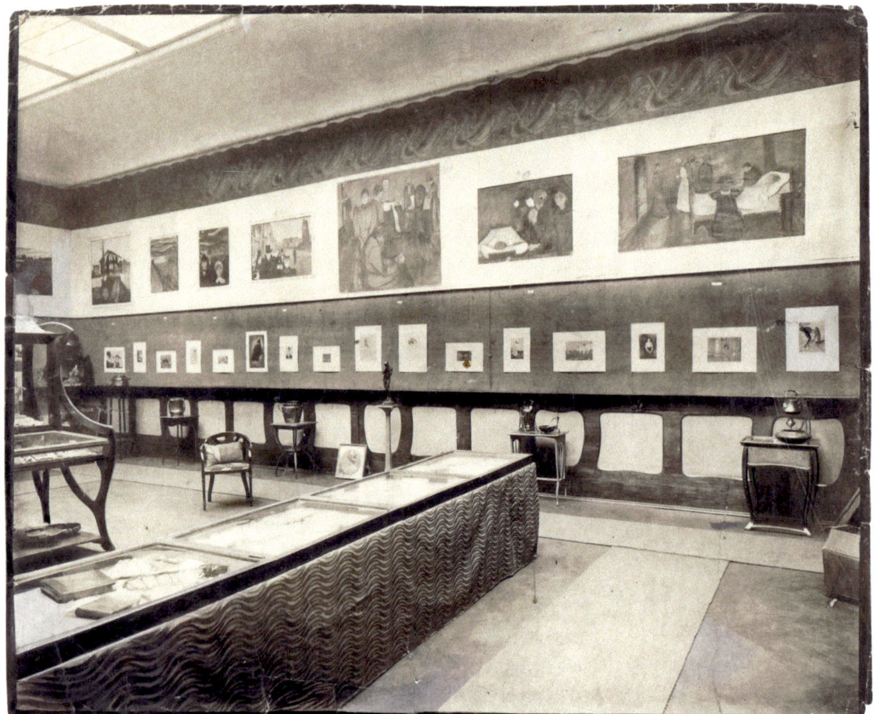

Edvard Munch's exhibition at the Galerie P.H. Beyer & Sohn, Leipzig — 1903 Munchmuseet — Oslo

in the continuously updated *Frieze of Life*. Even at an advanced age, Munch kept up this approach to his works, as demonstrated by photographs taken on the occasion of his seventy-fifth birthday.[84] Figure p.185B The artist is sitting in his studio amid his paintings, which have been arranged into another version of *The Frieze of Life*. In an undated note he remarked: "I have always worked best when I have my pictures nearby / — I felt the pictures were related to each other in content — / When I arranged them together they immediately resonated in a way that they lacked individually — they somehow could not be exhibited with others — / — So I placed them together as friezes."[85]

(1) Eggum 1982, p. 5; Kneher 1994, p. 147; and the corresponding entries in the catalogue raisonné of Munch's paintings (Woll 2009): Woll 283 and Woll 483.

(2) Edvard Munch, undated note, 1904–18, Munchmuseet, Oslo, MM N 34 (this document and all of the archival materials in Munchmuseet that follow are accessible at emunch.no). As Munch's magnum opus, *The Frieze of Life* has been broadly thematized by scholars. Accordingly, the existing literature is extensive. The insights published by Arne Eggum, Reinhold Heller, Carla Lathe, and Gerd Woll in numerous essays are fundamental (e.g., in London 1992–93). Jan Kneher (1994) and Uwe M. Schneede (1994b) provided important inspiration for my discussion. Erik Mørstad (2004) covers a critical overview of research up to 2004 and of Munch's own, largely undated statements on *The Frieze of Life*: most of the texts in which the artist commented on the making, development, and structure of *The Frieze of Life* are from around 1918 or later. Several were published by Munch in his book *Livsfrisens tilblivelse* (Munchmuseet, Oslo, MM UT 13). The information they offer must therefore be evaluated critically, especially as these texts are often of an associative, literary nature. Of the more recent secondary literature, essays by Guleng (2013) and Volle (2013 and 2014) deserve particular emphasis for shedding light on new aspects on the narration of *The Frieze of Life* and the artist's exhibition practice.

(3) Mørstad 2004, p. 125.

(4) On this exhibition, see Oslo 2002–3.

(5) Edvard Munch, undated note, 1933–49, Munchmuseet, Oslo, MM N 62. English translation by Francesca M. Nichols.

(6) On the difficulty of defining *The Frieze of Life* and reconstructing individual presentations, see, among others, Mørstad 2004, esp. pp. 123–25 and 130–44.

(7) Edvard Munch to Rasmus Meyer, undated draft letter, Munchmuseet, Oslo, MM N 1894.

(8) See, among others, Schneede 1994b, pp. 26–28; Kvech-Hoppe 2001, pp. 114–15.

(9) Schneede 1994b, p. 20.

(10) Edvard Munch to Johan Rohde, undated [March 1893], published by Henning Gran, "To brev fra Edvard Munch til en dansk maler," *Verdens Gang*, August 26, 1950, quoted in excerpts in Mørstad 2004, p. 132.

(11) Kneher 1994, p. 24.

(12) https://de.statista.com/statistik/daten/studie/1100185/umfrage/durchschnittseinkommen-im-deutschen-kaiserreich/.

(13) Paul 1927.

(14) See, among others, Kneher 1994, p. 35.

(15) Dr. R. [Jaro Springer], [Personal and studio news], *Die Kunst für Alle* 9, no. 8 (January 15, 1894): p. 123.

(16) On the narrative structure in Munch, see Guleng 2013.

(17) On the exhibitions mentioned and their reception, see, among others, Kneher 1994, pp. 32–47, 55–62, 65–76, and 92–97. Kneher argues convincingly that the series was not also shown in 1895 in Munch's exhibition at Blomqvist in Kristiania as well, as is often claimed in the related literature; see Kneher 1994, p. 83.

(18) See the essay by Andreas Schalhorn in the present catalogue.

(19) On the preparation for *The Frieze of Life* in graphic works, see Woll 1992 and Bartrum 2019a. In his exhibition on Unter den Linden in Berlin in 1893–94, Munch had presented a series titled *Ein Menschenleben* (A Human Life) that presumably consisted of drawings and watercolors; see Kneher 1994, p. 35.

(20) Although in previous exhibitions with his series on love Munch had always also shown paintings on the theme of death, he had not arranged them with the works on love in groups that were in turn expressly identified in the catalogue as a unity. In the Salon des Indépendants of 1897 in Paris, Munch showed eight or nine works on love and death, which, he recalled, were hanging together on one wall, as a small excerpt from the later *Frieze of Life*. See Arne Eggum, "Edvard Munchs Versuch, Paris zu erobern," in *Munch in Frankreich*, ed. Sabine Schulze, exh. cat. Paris, Oslo, and Frankfurt am Main (Frankfurt am Main, 1992), pp. 193–229, esp. p. 218; Kneher 1994, p. 104. In his solo exhibition at the Diorama in Kristiania that same year, Munch also showed several paintings that are included in *The Frieze of Life* but without explicitly organizing them into a cycle. See Kneher 1994, p. 114.

(21) Berlin 1902, cat. nos. 187–208.

(22) Berlin 1927, cat. nos. 49–59. On this successful exhibition, see the essay by Dieter Scholz in the present catalogue.

(23) Edvard Munch, "Livsfrisen," *Tidens Tegn*, October 15, 1918. The text published in the newspaper was the foreword to an exhibition catalogue (Munchmuseet, Oslo, MM UT 22). The artist published another article in *Tidens Tegn* on October 29, 1918, in which he reacted to criticism of his *Frieze of Life*. The two texts formed the basis for a small book that Munch published, also to accompany the exhibition, under the title *Livs-Frisen* (Munchmuseet, Oslo, MM UT 23).
(24) Mørstad 2004, pp. 140–42.
(25) März 1994, pp. 131–32.
(26) Heller 2016, pp. 36–37. See also Eggum 2000, pp. 17–21, especially on the significance of Munch's literary work for *The Frieze of Life*.
(27) On Munch and Cassirer, see the essay by Christina Feilchenfeldt in the present catalogue.
(28) Kneher 1994, p. 147.
(29) Edvard Munch to Aase Nørregard, draft letter, dated 1902, Munchmuseet, Oslo, MM N 1914.
(30) Paul Cassirer to Edvard Munch, January 27, 1902, Munchmuseet, Oslo, MM K 3485.
(31) Eggum 1982, p. 5.
(32) An entry in Gustav Schiefler's diary on November 7, 1903, also argues for Cassirer having played a central role. He reports on a meeting with the gallerist in which the latter emphasized that *he himself* had hung Munch's paintings in the front hall of the Secession; Munch and Schiefler 1987 and 1990, vol. 1, no. 53, pp. 66–67. Schneede (1994b, p. 22), by contrast, suspects that Kollmann was the driving force behind Munch's invitation. On the significance of the association's internal conflicts for Munch's exhibition, see also Kneher 1994, pp. 149–50.
(33) Edvard Munch to Albert Kollmann, January 24, 1902, Munchmuseet, MM N 3213.
(34) Edvard Munch to Andreas Aubert, February 7, 1902, Nasjonalbiblioteket, Oslo, Brevs. 32, PN 186.
(35) *Berliner Börsenzeitung*, February 14, 1902, no. 75, p. 11; *Kölnische Zeitung*, February 14, 1902, no. 124, p. 1.
(36) Munch's name was not mentioned explicitly in the explanations and critical accounts published. See, among others, the reports in *Die Kunst-Halle* 7, no. 10 (February 20, 1902): pp. 148–49; *Die Kunst für Alle* 17, no. 12 (March 15, 1902): pp. 281–82.
(37) On Liebermann's assessment, see, among others, Harry Kessler's diary entry on December 9, 1894, in Harry Graf Kessler, *Das Tagebuch, 1880–1937*, ed. Roland S. Kamzelak (Marbach am Necker, 2019), www.dla-marbach.de/edview/?project= HGKTA&document=3241. On Cassirer's skeptical attitude, see Munch and Schiefler 1987 and 1990, vol. 1, no. 53, pp. 66–67.
(38) Edvard Munch to Andreas Aubert, March 18, 1902, Nasjonalbiblioteket, Oslo, Brevs. 32, PN 187.
(39) See note 20.
(40) Pucks 1992.
(41) Albert Kollmann to Max Linde, March 21, 1902, private collection, quoted in Schneede 1994b, pp. 22–23, esp. p. 23.
(42) Albert Kollmann to Max Linde, March 27, 1902, private collection, quoted in Schneede 1994b, p. 23.
(43) Berlin 1902, cat. nos. 181–208. In a letter to his aunt, Munch writes of twenty-seven works; Edvard Munch to Karen Bjølstad, April 29, 1902, Munchmuseet, MM N 847.
(44) "Von der Ausstellung der Secession," *Berliner Tageblatt*, April 8, 1902, no. 176, n.p.
(45) Kvech-Hoppe 2001.
(46) [Julius Meier-Graefe], "E. Munch," *Dekorative Kunst* 4, no. 10 (1899): p. 133. For an introduction to Munch as a monumental painter, see Berman 2013.
(47) Mørstad 2004, pp. 148–50.
(48) Krieger 1978, pp. 30–31; Schneede 1994b, pp. 27–28.
(49) Edvard Munch, sketchbook, [1902–3], Munchmuseet, Oslo, MM T 133, inside jacket.
(50) See, among others, the reconstructions in Guleng 2013, p. 132; Munich, Hamburg, and Berlin 1994–95, pp. 265–69. On the related problems, see also Mørstad 2004, p. 134.
(51) Munch, sketchbook, [1902–3] (see note 49).
(52) Schneede, by contrast, suspects the opposite, based on the drawings, namely, that Munch changed the concept presented in the catalogue during the hanging; Schneede 1994b, p. 23.
(53) Munch 1918 (see note 23).
(54) Guleng 2013, p. 138.
(55) Schneede 1994b, pp. 23–24.
(56) This state is also documented in a photograph; see fig. in London 1992–93, p. 90. Already in Stockholm and Berlin in 1894–95, the painting probably completed the works from the series on love (see Kneher 1994, pp. 57 and 65). Munch later called it "just as necessary for the frieze as a whole as the clasp is for a belt"; Munch 1918 (see note 23), p. 2.
(57) Kvech-Hoppe 2001, p. 113.
(58) Rosenblum 1978, p. 3.
(59) Kvech-Hoppe 2001, pp. 105–9.
(60) Schneede 1994b, p. 28.
(61) Several authors (such as Schneede 1994b, p. 28, and Kvech-Hoppe 2001, pp. 113–14) interpret *The Frieze of Life* as overcoming the individual's break with the world and attribute a cathartic function that is redemptive in the religious sense. At least for the version of 1902, this interpretation seems too pointed given its cyclical structure. On the ideas of the cycle and of the unfinished in Munch's work, see also Wat 2022.
(62) See, among others, Munch 1918 (see note 23); Eggum 1992 (see note 20), p. 218.
(63) Edvard Munch to Sigurd Høst, undated draft letter, Munchmuseet, Oslo, MM N 1734. For a detailed account of Munch's conflicting desires for an intense experience of the individual paintings and a monumental frieze, see Mørstad 2004, p. 143.

(64) As the floor plan and external views of the Secession building show, the sculpture hall was directly behind the foyer and was covered by the same roof without skylights, whereas all of the other rooms had a roof with skylights. See the illustrations in Matelowski 2017, pp. 48 and 585. I am grateful to Anke Matelowski for collegial exchange on the lighting situation.

(65) [Emil] H[eilbut], "Aus der neunten Ausstellung der Berliner Secession," *Kunst und Künstler* 2 (1904): pp. 391–411, esp. p. 410.

(66) Kneher 1994, p. 158. The version of Klinger's monument to Beethoven that was executed could be seen at this same time in the Vienna Secession, where it was at the center of the association's fourteenth exhibition, which had been conceived as a *Gesamtkunstwerk* around this sculpture. That included Gustav Klimt's *Beethoven Frieze*, to which Munch's frieze in Berlin formed a kind of improvised pendant—whether planned or by chance—because of the joint presentation with Klinger; see Schneede 1994b, p. 28.

(67) I am grateful to Axel Eichhorst for sharing his ideas on these aspects.

(68) Adolf Rosenberg, "Die Ausstellung der Berliner Secession," *Kunstchronik*, n.s. 10, no. 27 (1898–99): cols. 417–22, esp. cols. 417–18.

(69) See the photographs of the picture halls in Rosenhagen 1902, pp. 433, 442, and 443.

(70) On this exhibition, see Volle 2014. It is unclear whether Munch followed the plan suggested in the Berlin sketchbook to place the paintings above the doors higher in order to emphasize them or whether he placed all the paintings at the same height as in Leipzig. A later draft letter has a sketch of the hanging of 1902 that Munch drew from memory. It suggests the latter solution. See Munch, sketchbook, [1902–3] (see note 49); and Edvard Munch to Sigurd Høst, undated draft letter (see note 63).

(71) Edvard Munch to Sigurd Høst, undated draft letter (see note 63).

(72) For a detailed account, see Kneher 1994, pp. 154–58.

(73) H. Vollmar, "Die Ausstellung der Sezession," *Norddeutsche Allgemeine Zeitung*, April 29, 1902, no. 99, supplement, p. 1.

(74) Ludwig Kaemmerer, "Eindrücke von der fünften Ausstellung der Berliner Secession 1902," *Zeitschrift für bildende Kunst*, n.s. 13, no. 8 (1902): pp. 191–99, esp. p. 194.

(75) G[eorg] G[alland], "V. Ausstellung der Berliner 'Sezession,'" *Die Kunst-Halle* 7, no. 15 (May 5, 1902): pp. 228–29, esp. p. 229.

(76) Rosenhagen 1902, p. 458.

(77) Hans Rosenhagen, "Ausstellung im Salon Cassirer," *Der Tag* (Berlin), January 31, 1903, no. 51, quoted in Echte and Feilchenfeldt 2011–16, pp. 5:241–44, esp. p. 241. On this exhibition, in which works by Philipp Klein and August Gaul were also shown, see ibid., pp. 231–54, and the essay by Christina Feilchenfeldt in the present catalogue.

(78) On these exhibitions, see, among others, Kneher 1994, pp. 199–202 and 210–15.

(79) Mørstad 2004, p. 139.

(80) Eggum 1982, pp. 33–37.

(81) See the essay by Pauline Behrmann in the present catalogue.

(82) See, among others, Berman 2022, pp. 93–94. On other decoration projects in Oslo, such as for the town hall and the Freia chocolate factory, see Berman 2013.

(83) Pettersen 2002.

(84) Heller 1992, p. 26.

(85) Munch, undated note (see note 5). English translation by Francesca M. Nichols.

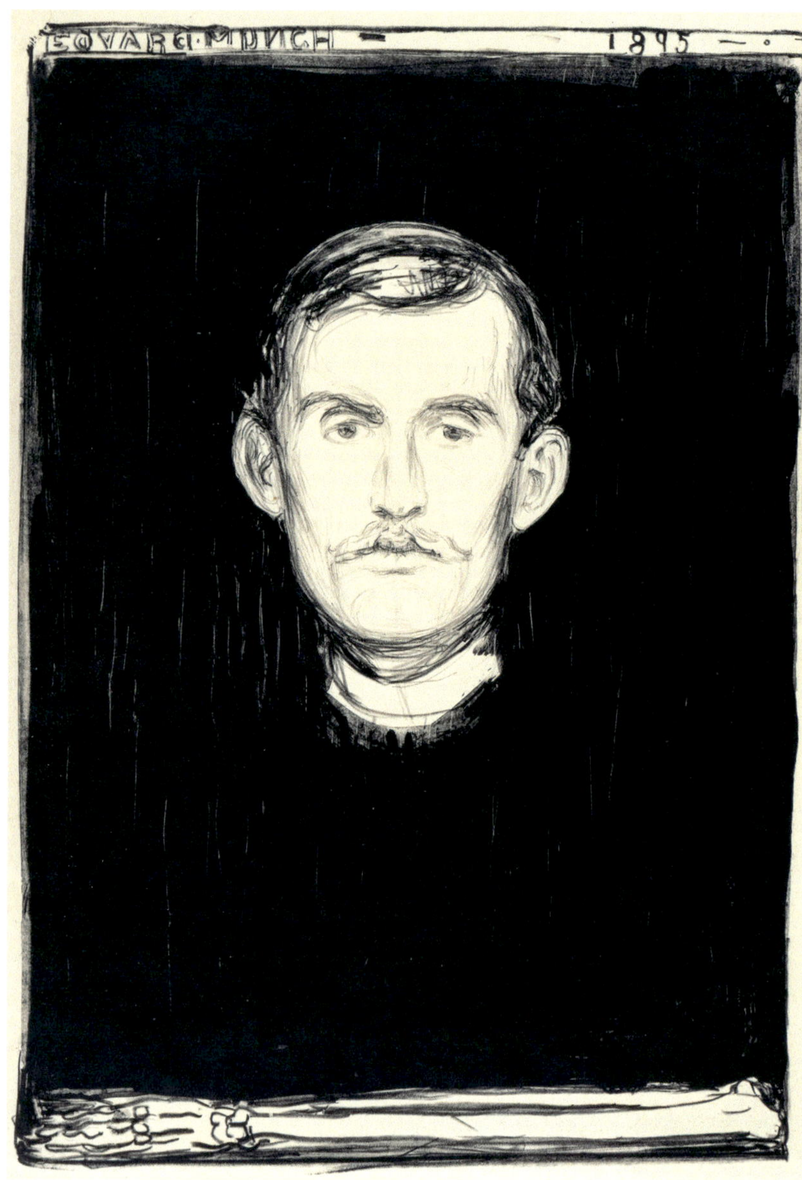

(A)
Edvard Munch
Self-Portrait (with Skeleton Arm) — 1895
Staatliche Museen zu Berlin
Kupferstichkabinett

(C)
Letter from the Otto Felsing printing house to Edvard Munch — 1906
Munchmuseet — Oslo

K3524

O. FELSING
Inh. Wilh. Felsing
Grossherzogl. Badischer Hoflieferant; Sächs. Weimarischer Hofkunstkupferdrucker
Goldene Medaillen etc.
Gegründet im Jahre 1797
Aetzerei für Photogravure · Galvanoplastische Anstalt
Photogr. Atelier für Innen- u. Aussenaufnahmen, Gemälde etc.

Fernsprecher Amt VI, 1867
Masch. M.

Berlin S. W. 11, den 16. August 1906.
8 Schönebergerstrasse

Herrn Ed. Munch, Malerradirer,
z. Zt. Weimar.

Sehr geehrter Herr Munch!

Bei Ihrem letzten Hiersein ersuchten Sie mich um Kontoauszug und versprachen mir den Restbetrag meines Guthabens umgehend einzusenden. Nachdem Sie solchen bereits am 21. Juli zugesendet erhielten, welcher mit einem Saldo von M 137,45 zu meinen Gunsten abschliesst, darf ich nunmehr wohl auf Erfüllung Ihrer Zusage umsomehr rechnen, als ich grossen eigenen Verpflichtungen nachzukommen habe.

Mit vorzüglicher Hochachtung
ergebener

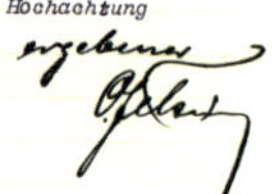

(B)
Max Klinger
Lonesome
(no. 5 of the series *Opus VIII, A Life*) — 1884
Staatliche Museen zu Berlin
Kupferstichkabinett

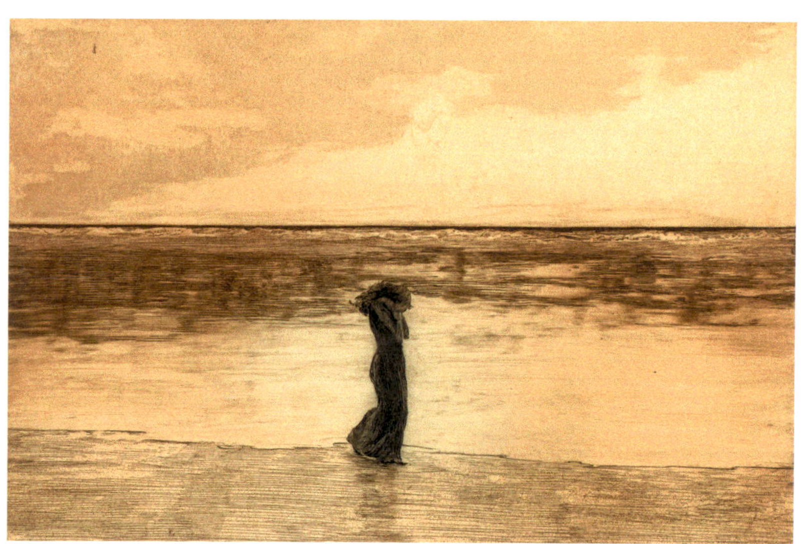

“New content creates a new vessel for itself”

Munch’s Prints of the Berlin Years and Their Path to the Kupferstichkabinett

Andreas Schalhorn

Painter-engraver—this was the title that the Berlin printing house Otto Felsing used in a collection letter of August 16, 1906, to Edvard Munch, who was staying in Weimar at the time, where he had just completed the portrait *Elisabeth Förster-Nietzsche*.[1] Figures pp.190C + 142 The term aptly marks the productive alliance of painting and printing that distinguishes Munch’s art from 1894 to 1908. During this creative phase he made around 300 prints. Many of them, often of iconic presence, have been regarded as “master prints” even before our day.[2] They were the results of the “*tempo furioso* of the first period.”[3] For even if the artist continued to produce prints until the year he died, his printmaking was different. Its point of reference was now usually drawing and no longer painting.[4]

The term *peintre-graveur*, coined at the beginning of the nineteenth century, referred to artists who produce graphic works based on their own pictorial ideas.[5] The artistically ambitious engraving gained new vitality in the second half of the nineteenth century—starting from Paris.[6] One of the German protagonists was Max Klinger, whom Munch also admired for his Symbolism. Figure p.190B At the time, such original graphic work was distinguished from then still common reproductive engraving, in which works of art by third parties—for example, paintings by Rembrandt—were translated into prints. This work was done by specialized artists such as the Berlin etcher Karl Köpping.[7]

With his printmaking, which soon included not only the intaglio techniques of drypoint and etching but also the lithograph as a planographic technique and the woodcut as a relief technique,[8] Munch represented a special case of the *peintre-graveur*: his prints of those years are most decidedly related to his own painting. Although their motifs are not new inventions, they were the equals of his paintings both artistically and in terms of their reception.

Jens Thiis, who from 1908 was the director of the Statens Kunstmuseum (State Art Museum), the future Nasjonalgalleriet (National Gallery), in Kristiania, now Oslo,[9] formulated it aptly in 1934: "One is tempted to say that even if the painter Munch had never existed, the graphic artist would always have been considered great. But we do not say it, and we are not allowed to say it, because Munch's graphic work is so closely tied to his painted work that the two cannot be separated from each other."[10] For example, a motif with important content such as *Two Human Beings (The Lonely Ones)* wandered from painting by way of etching to woodcut and decades later back to painting. Figures pp.103B, 193A + 63

Berlin, 1894–95
The Entry into Printmaking

Who precisely introduced the artist to printmaking techniques toward the end of 1894, when he was already thirty, is not known. In addition to Klinger and Köpping, the proven etchers Hermann Struck and Käthe Kollwitz have been suggested as possible teachers.[11] It is, however, more plausible to assume that he learned quickly in Berlin workshops, which had a rich tradition and were versed in a wide range of printing techniques; Munch met other artists there and saw their works.[12] One motivation for his entry into printmaking could have been a request for illustrations from the Berlin art journal *PAN* in late summer 1894, which reached the artist when he was still in Norway.[13] *PAN* would first be published in April of the following year and serve as a platform for many European *peintres-graveurs* between Symbolism and Jugendstil, including the aforementioned Klinger.

Soon after moving to Berlin, Munch took up the subject of printmaking. On November 14, 1894, he wrote to his aunt Karen Bjølstad in Kristiania: "I am in a very good mood for working—have begun etching and want to publish later a small collection of etchings."[14] The end of that year he sent his first print to Eberhard von Bodenhausen,[15] one of the founders of *PAN*, who would not be alone in his enthusiasm: Julius Meier-Graefe, one of the publishers of the journal and a member of the circle that met at the wine bar Zum schwarzen Ferkel (The Black Piglet), attended to the matter.[16] In June 1895, he published a portfolio of eight drypoints by Munch.[17] The works with motifs that refer back to paintings included the prints *The Day After*, *Two Human Beings (The Lonely Ones)*, and *The Sick Child I*, some of which were made as early as 1894.[18] Figures pp.102, 103A + B As far as the portfolio is concerned, several years later Munch was no longer certain whether all of the sheets had been printed by Carl Sabo or Ludwig Angerer.[19]

Although this high-quality production largely dispensed with provocative motifs, the success for which the artist and publisher had hoped failed to materialize. Nevertheless, Munch strengthened his efforts focused on printmaking, though he changed his technique and now began to produce lithographs as well. His first self-portrait print, *Self-Portrait (with Skeleton Arm)*, printed by the Graphische Kunstanstalt M.W. Lassally in Berlin, already made a confident statement.[20] Figures pp.190A + 113 The large print, with the artist's name and date on the upper edge, was preceded by a first version in which the figure's shoulders and arms could still be made out sketchily. In the later version, the head and neck, worked out by drawing directly on the stone, stand out separated from the otherwise uniformly black plane. The artist's face stands before us, captured frontally with great concision. As a framing element on the lower edge, corresponding to the zone of text above, a skeletal arm is

(A)
Edvard Munch
Two Human Beings (The Lonely Ones) — 1899
Staatliche Museen zu Berlin
Kupferstichkabinett

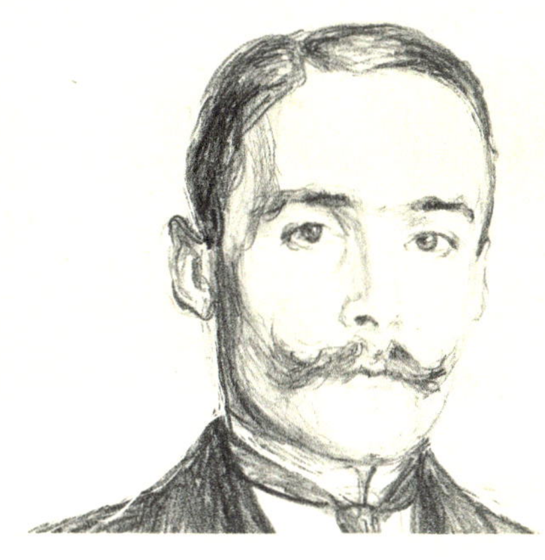

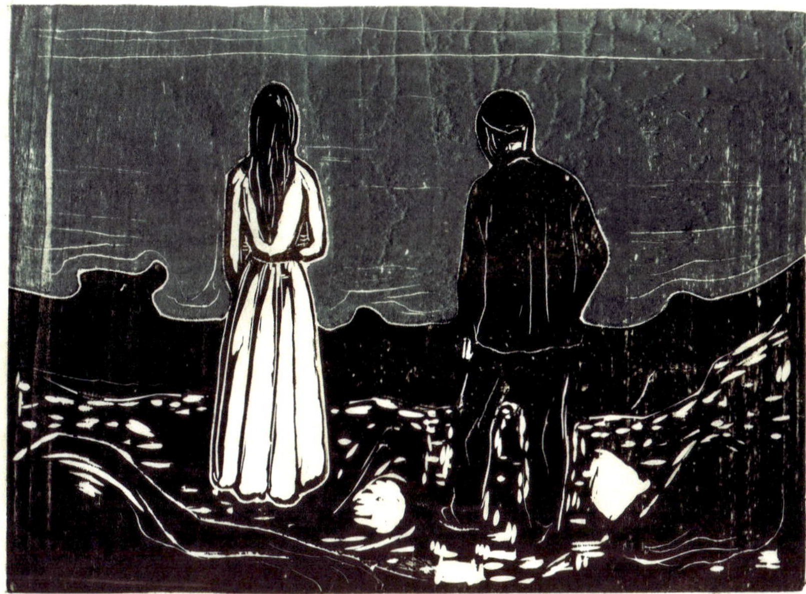

(B)
Edvard Munch
Harry Graf Kessler I — 1895
Staatliche Museen zu Berlin
Kupferstichkabinett

stretched out to the left. For all its almost religious-seeming look, in which artistic self-confidence is combined with knowledge of one's own mortality, a painted portrait of his friend the writer Stanisław Przybyszewski from 1894 was the inspiration here.[21]

In 1895, Munch received his first commission for a portrait print from Harry Graf Kessler, a founding member of *PAN* and also on its supervisory board, after Bodenhausen had called Munch to his attention. The result was two delicate yet rather objective chalk lithographs with a different focus on the sitter's head caught slightly from the side. Figures pp.193B + 114 The three sittings for the portrait found their way into Count Kessler's diary entries. On April 11, he wrote: "Artist tour … . Sat at Munch's for a lithograph. He is now living in the hotel on Mittelstrasse, two rooms; his belongings and paintings have all been seized as security, he tells me. While drawing he told me stories constantly or let me speak."[22] Two days later, it continued in the morning: "During the sitting an energetic young storeowner came with a porter and took the easel because he owed her twenty-five marks. The whole thing was executed in two minutes and seemed to go without saying."[23] After losing the easel, the artist simply placed the lithographic stone on a cane chair. Finally, on May 10, 1895, Count Kessler noted: "At noon in Berlin at Munch's and sat for two hours for my lithograph; he complains that I never look the same way twice—specifically, my eyes. Whereas he drew the two lithographs of me directly on the stone, for his *Love* cycle he now accepted the advice that Sattler[24] recently gave him at the Vier Jahreszeiten, to work on paper & then transfer the drawing to the stone. … Afterward, purchased various papers at Hess's to try for the lithograph & sent them to Munch."[25] That Munch thought in groups of works with prints—as well as with paintings—is demonstrated by this mention of a "*Love* cycle" project, which no more found final form as a multipart portfolio than an expanded version did two years later under the title *The Mirror*—he could not find publishers and patrons.[26] In choosing Alexander Liebmann, Munch was working with a Berlin printer to produce the two small lithographs who

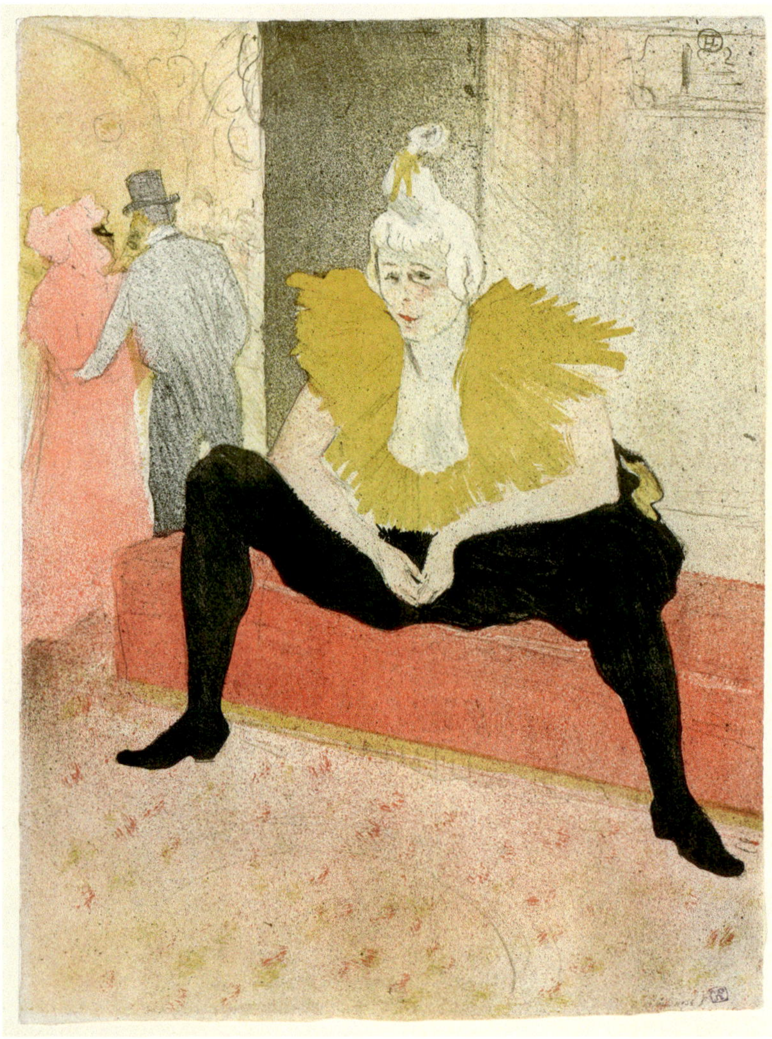

Henri de Toulouse-Lautrec
Seated Clown
(Mademoiselle Cha-U-Kao) — 1896
Staatliche Museen zu Berlin
Kupferstichkabinett

is not known to have collaborated with other artists. Liebmann, born 1871 in Berlin, had studied art in Munich and Paris. He produced landscape etchings of his own,[27] but he earned his living with printing services of various kinds. In 1896, on a business postcard sent to Munch on April 18, who was living in Paris at the time, Liebmann described himself as "Königl. Hoflieferant Buch- u. Steindruckerei Graviranstalt" (Purveyor to the Royal Court, Book Printing, Lithography, and Engraving).[28] Liebmann presumably already had his primary residence in Munich at this time, where his life would end tragically. In order to escape the deportation of people of Jewish origin, his wife, Johanna, and he took their lives on April 2, 1942.[29]

Liebmann's collaboration with Munch led to the work of the latter artist that is most famous today being turned into a print in 1895. Figure p.225B Following the painted versions from 1893, the lithograph of *The Scream* was reduced to lines printed in black. One print was colored by the artist and thus (once again) given a painterly design. The purely black-and-white version was published in December of that year in the Paris art journal *La Revue Blanche* with an explanatory text by the artist.[30] It was the perfect calling card for the French metropolis, to which Munch moved in February of the following year.

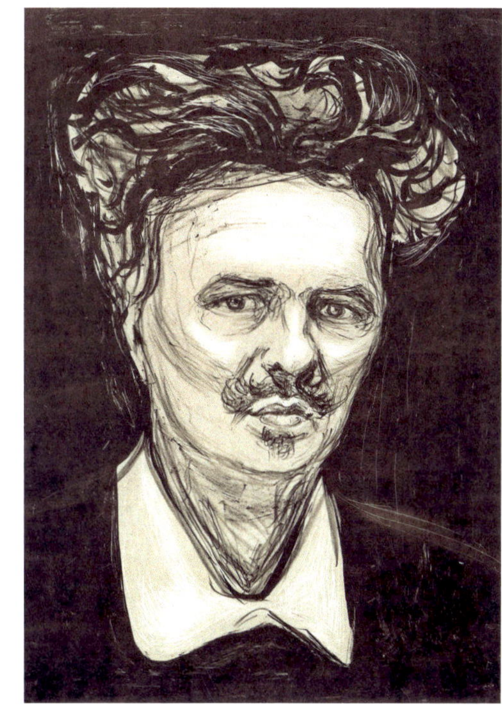

Edvard Munch
August Strindberg — 1896
Staatliche Museen zu Berlin
Kupferstichkabinett

Paris, 1896–97
The Extension of Graphic Means

Paris, which was the European center for contemporary art at the time, provided Munch with important new inspiration for his printmaking that would bear fruit in Berlin years later. In addition to Alfred Léon Lemercier, it was above all Auguste Clot, a leader in color art lithography, whom Munch chose as a printer in Paris. Clot was producing prints for numerous French artists at the time—such as Auguste Renoir, Paul Cézanne, and Odilon Redon. He ultimately convinced Munch to work more with transfer paper and thus save himself the trouble of transporting heavy lithographic stones from his studio to the printer's workshop.[31] In Paris the following year, at the suggestion of Julius Meier-Graefe, Munch acquired the recently published portfolio *Elles* by Henri de Toulouse-Lautrec,[32] which presumably inspired him to create the aforementioned portfolio of prints titled *The Mirror*—a project that would leave traces on his exhibition activity of the coming years.[33] Figure p.194

Still all in black and white, *Death in the Sickroom* was produced in 1896—a sui generis arrangement of a family as if on a stage, taking advantage of the depth of the room, in which Munch evoked the hour of the death of his sister Sophie, who had died young of tuberculosis in 1877. Unlike in *The Sick Child I*, here his sister is sitting on a chair turned away from the viewers, half covered by the tall chair back. Figures pp.110–11 + 103A The artist is standing in the center of the group of siblings in the foreground on the left. Gazing forward out of the painting is his youngest sister, Inger.

Already in his painting, Munch liked to work with a figure or group pushed into the foreground. This form of psychologizing visual narrative is also found in the lithograph *Jealousy*, in which the motif is reversed compared to the eponymous painting of 1895.[34] Figure p.109 The face that shines frontally out of a black plane has some of the features of the writer Przybyszewski and recalls Munch's face in *Self-Portrait (with Skeleton Arm)*, where the upper body of the writer has contour lines scratched out in white. Figures pp.190A + 113

In the background to the right of the strictly frontal head, a couple is standing in front of a tree, a reference to the Biblical scene of Paradise. A naked woman surrounds with her long hair—as a kind of symbol of seduction—a man in modern dress who is turning toward her, thus provoking the jealousy of the male figure in the foreground, who all but epitomizes that state. The painful experiences of the artist's complicated love relationships have left their traces here.[35] Munch began working in Paris on several portraits of writers. The first was dedicated to the writer August Strindberg, who was also living there at the time and had reviewed Munch's exhibition at the Salon de l'Art Nouveau in poetic form in the June edition of *La revue blanche*.[36] In this lithograph printed in black, Munch presents the striking head of the Swedish writer inserted into a frame of Symbolist design, of the sort he had used for his own self-portrait. Figure p.117 A naked woman is seen on the right edge. Her figure transitions above and below into lines that initially form waves and then a zigzag pattern on the left half of the frame. Munch saw them as embodying male and female principles, while the woman was also a reference to Strindberg's feminine characteristics. However, Strindberg interpreted the lines as reflecting Munch and Przybyszewski's evil intention to kill him with electric rays—a fashionable topic at the time. Moreover, Munch had left an "r" out of the writer's name: "Stindberg."[37] Munch reacted to the anger of the portrayed writer with a revision printed in two colors that concentrates entirely on the head. Figure p.195

Color thus entered Munch's lithographs in Paris. One outstanding example of this is *The Sick Child I* of 1896. Figure p.104 Two years previously, in his eponymous drypoint, the artist had depicted the girl close to death together with a woman collapsed in despair—as in his early painted version—and added a landscape embodying hope as a kind of pedestal. Figure p.103A In the new version, Munch focused on the child's head, now turned in profile to the right and propped steeply by the pillow. In the print in the Kupferstichkabinett (Museum of Prints and Drawings) in Berlin, the head is immersed in a pale, yellowish light. The German artist Paul Herrmann experienced Munch's experimental spirit while working on lithography: "I wanted to print at Clot, but was told: Not possible, Mr. Munch is booked. The lithographic stones with the large head were already lying lined up next to one another in rank and file, ready for printing. Munch arrives, stands before the row, *closes his eyes tightly* and conducts blindly by waving a finger through the air: 'Print ... gray, green, blue, brown.' He opens his eyes and says to me: 'Come, let's drink a schnaps ... .' The printer printed until Munch returned and again ordered *blindly*: 'Yellow, pink, red ... .' And so on, a couple of times ... ."[38]

In parallel with lithography, the artist was working intensely with the woodcut, for which a number of inspirations could be found in Paris: from Japanese color prints to Paul Gauguin's sheets.[39] Munch arrived at a formal idiom very much his own, which went hand in hand with an archaic-looking and yet expressive handling of the technique. Already in the woodcut *Angst (Feeling of Anxiety)*, initially printed all in black, the materiality of the—often simple—wood is visible from the vertical grain pattern.[40] Figure p.108B The working out of dazzling white faces and figures that Munch also practiced in his lithographs, using the color of the exposed paper, standing out from the nocturnal, psychologically laden black surrounding them, can be experienced here in all its radicalness. Some lines, produced by sharp cuts, run like thin threads vertically through the pictorial space and thus heighten the ghostly, oppressive atmosphere of the scene. The woodcut *Evening. Melancholy I (By the Shore)* also demonstrates, in contrast with the earlier painting and the late version in the *Reinhardt Frieze*, the dramaturgical thrust produced by the dominance of the parts printed black. Figures pp.108A, 66–67 + 98–99

Both woodcuts confirm what Gustav Schiefler, the director of Hamburg's state court and a connoisseur of graphic art, wrote of the advantages of the artist's "abstracting" graphic art: "The necessity to fill the entire plane with color, and therefore place brushstroke next to brushstroke and have to

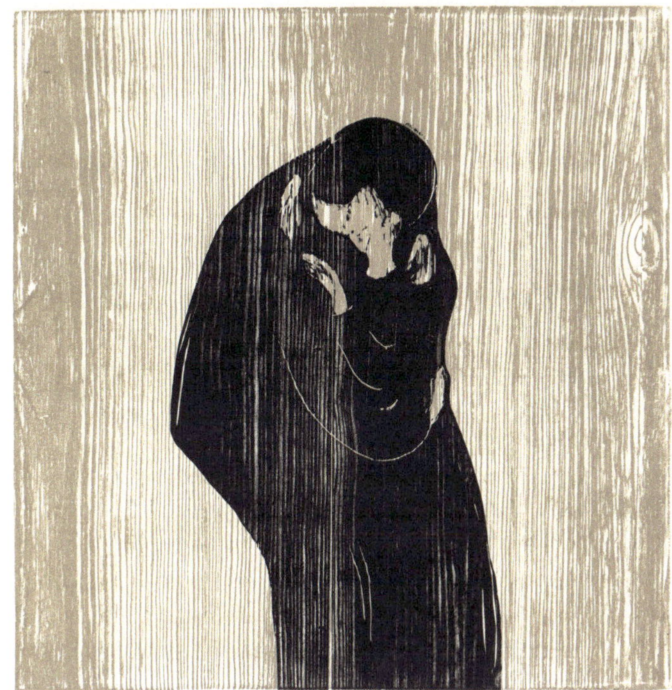

(B)
Edvard Munch
The Kiss IV — 1902
Staatliche Museen zu Berlin
Kupferstichkabinett

(A)
Edvard Munch
Vampire II — 1895
Staatliche Museen zu Berlin
Kupferstichkabinett

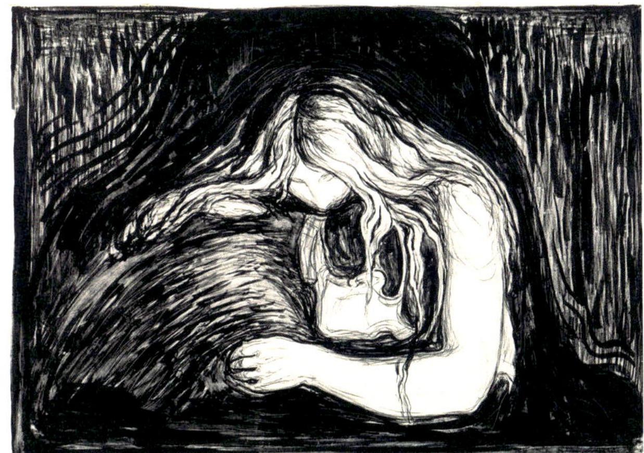

bring them into harmony with one another, can stand in the way of the power of the depiction. The graphic artist is able to liberate outwardly every line and every spot from its surroundings and therefore produce a profounder design. The crucial aspect can be emphasized more strongly, the inessential passed over more ruthlessly."[41]

Berlin, 1902–8
Successes with Printmaking

Munch left Paris in May 1897 and in the years that followed lived primarily in Norway, where he worked in Åsgårdstrand with a small printing press. He also used printer's workshops in Kristiania and Copenhagen. In late 1901, however, he returned to Berlin and started another phase as a *peintre-graveur*, in which new supporters helped him. Albert Kollmann deserves particular mention;[42] until his death in 1915, he functioned as the artist's agent. Figures pp.125A + 141 As early as 1902, he put him in contact with the ophthalmologist Max Linde from Lübeck, who was soon actively collecting and commissioning paintings and graphic art. Figure p.29B Moreover, at the end of the year Munch met the aforementioned Gustav Schiefler for the first time, who had first seen the artist's works at Linde's.[43] In the years that followed, Schiefler compiled the first catalogue raisonné of the prints, which would be published in 1907 by Bruno Cassirer in Berlin, an important publishing house for art books and the art of the book.[44]

Munch had printing plates transferred to Berlin from Norway and Paris, where many were still being stored. Munch found a new printing workshop, probably at the recommendation of Linde, in the renowned printing house of Otto Felsing, which since 1892 had been run by Wilhelm Felsing.[45]

Based on the eponymous painting from the same year, he printed *The Hearse. Potsdamer Platz.* Figures pp.70–71+119 Like the colorful painting, this unusual etching, based on the use of stencils employed in modular fashion, draws on a distressing disparateness that recalls works by James Ensor. This sheet has the brown tone so typical of Felsing prints, as it is also found, for example, in works by Max Klinger and Käthe Kollwitz, who regularly printed with him. Figure p.190B This tone met with a divided response in Munch's milieu.[46]

In Berlin, he produced woodcuts in collaboration with the W. M. Lassally printing house, which also (re)printed all of the artist's lithographs. The print *The Kiss IV* owes its existence to the fact that Munch believed that the printing blocks for an earlier work with the same thematic focus had been lost en route from Norway to Berlin. Figure p.112 The work is based on producing individual forms to which different colors were applied for printing. The artist Erich Büttner later recalled: "I went to master printer Dannenberger at Lassally and saw how Munch's graphic work was being printed. I was not a little astonished when I saw the woodcut printing plates, pieces sawed apart, some rolled with red, some with green, whereupon the square, assembled like a child's toy, went through the press and suddenly there was a multicolored print with continuous wood grain."[47] The color combinations could change, as one copy of the woodcut in the Kupferstichkabinett in Berlin proves. Figure p.197B

The use of color he had discovered in Paris continued to have an effect and led to a reworking of two lithographs that had been printed in all black in 1895. The artistic consequences are especially clear with *Vampire II*, the first version of which was printed on partially colored paper. Figures pp.107+197 As with *The Sick Child I*, Munch pushed the boundaries of the possibilities of the medium in order to find a solution comparable to painting or even a new one. In choosing the title *Vampire*, he was following a suggestion from his friend Przybyszewski, even though the print really only shows a (once again) red-haired woman kissing the neck of a man while wrapping her hair around him.[48]

In the case of the motif of *Madonna (Woman Making Love)*, an important one for Munch's concept of *The Frieze of Life*, the artist again worked with a Symbolist frame as part of the image. Figure p.105 The frame has depictions of an embryo and several sperm that express the theme of procreation. Munch placed a crescent-moon-shaped hairband in the woman's hair that is reminiscent of a halo. The artist saw his work as the "expression of a sacred emotion."[49] It is notable that the modeling of the upper body and face was drawn directly on the stone with chalk and scraper. The explicit, erotic content of the depiction was perceived by contemporaries as provocative. To turn the reading of the motif into a supposedly more neutral, religious direction, Schiefler chose the title *Annunziata* for a presentation in the Hamburger Kunsthalle in 1903, alluding to the Christian subject of the Annunciation: Munch's figure was to be identified with the Virgin Mary, who learns about her immaculate conception from the archangel Gabriel.[50] It should be borne in mind, however, that the titles *Madonna* and *Loving Woman* were presumably also suggested by Munch's circle.[51]

Another auratic portrait was created in the very productive first year of Munch's return to Berlin: *Woman with Red Hair and Green Eyes (The Sin)*. Figures p.131A After Munch purchased a Kodak No. 2 Bull's-Eye camera in February 1902,[52] he used it to photograph himself, his friends and supporters, his studio, and one of his nude models in Berlin. Figures pp.120–25+130 The young woman, who has yet to be identified, modeled for several paintings in his studio at Lützowstrasse 82. This large lithograph printed in three colors on thin Japan paper can be traced back to studies with her, too. Yet the figure here looks clearly less symbolistic, despite her nakedness and opulent red hair, than the one in

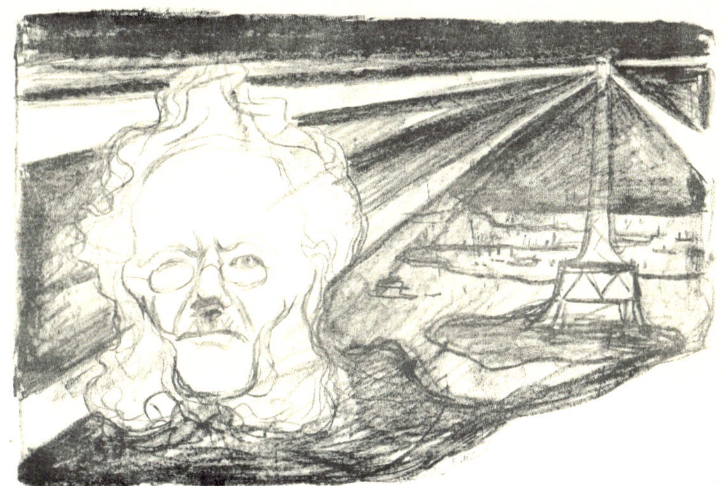

Edvard Munch
Illustration for the program for Henrik Ibsen's *John Gabriel Borkman* — 1897
Staatliche Museen zu Berlin
Kupferstichkabinett

Madonna (Woman Making Love). Rather than by a figurative frame, *The Sin* is bordered solely by a simple line in the same color as the woman's hair. The watery green of her eyes seems natural for all its incisiveness, as does her demeanor in general, which cannot, despite what the title might suggest, be associated with a femme fatale.[53]

Munch continued the series of portraits of writers he had begun in Paris with the all-black lithograph *Henrik Ibsen at the Grand Café* of 1902. Figure pp.118–19 For its composition, he returned to the illustration he had produced five years earlier for the program for Aurélien Lugné-Poë's production of Ibsen's *John Gabriel Borkman* in the Théâtre de l'Œuvre in Paris. Figure p.199 He also based his lithograph of 1902, which shows the face of the admired writer flowing like a flame, on a photograph.[54] The backdrop of the portrait is a dark curtain that opens to the right, revealing a view of a street. Unlike the compositionally comparable *Jealousy*, this scene in the background is not symbolic. Figure p.109 It shows, rather, the daily bustle on Karl Johan Street in Kristiania, home to the Grand Hotel and its café, where Munch had once met the writer.

In 1904, Munch signed a three-year exclusive contract for the distribution of his graphic work with the Berlin publisher and art dealer Bruno Cassirer. This work was now selling very well: at an exhibition of the Kunstfreunde (Friends of Art) in Hamburg alone, Munch was able to sell 800 works to private collectors that year.[55] Nevertheless, the artist, who was still suffering from financial difficulties at the time, was disappointed by Cassirer's representation. He even had to pay 1,000 marks to end the contract in 1907.[56]

In the years that followed, Munch took the sales of his graphic art into his own hands again, though he could continue to rely on the support of his agent, Albert Kollmann. Artistically productive vacations in Warnemünde in 1907 and 1908, which the artist also used to take photographs of himself, could not prevent psychological collapse. Figures pp.128 + 129 In October 1908, he sought clinical treatment in Copenhagen. From May 1909 onward, Munch resided in Norway. In Berlin, the Graphisches Kabinett J. B. Neumann in particular saw to the sale of his graphic art with numerous exhibitions from 1912 onward.[57]

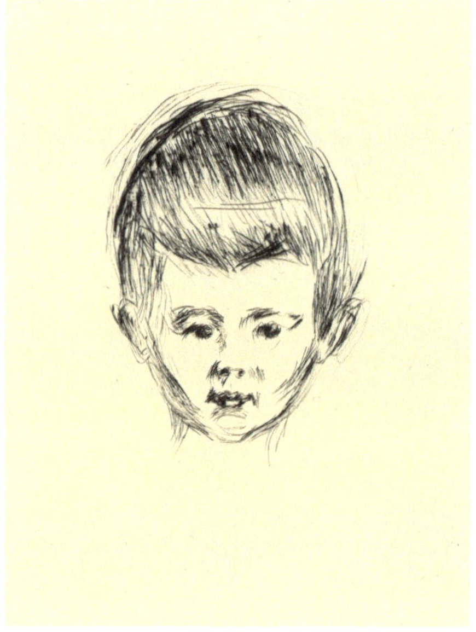

(A)
Edvard Munch
Andreas Schwarz — 1906 [1907?]
Staatliche Museen zu Berlin
Kupferstichkabinett

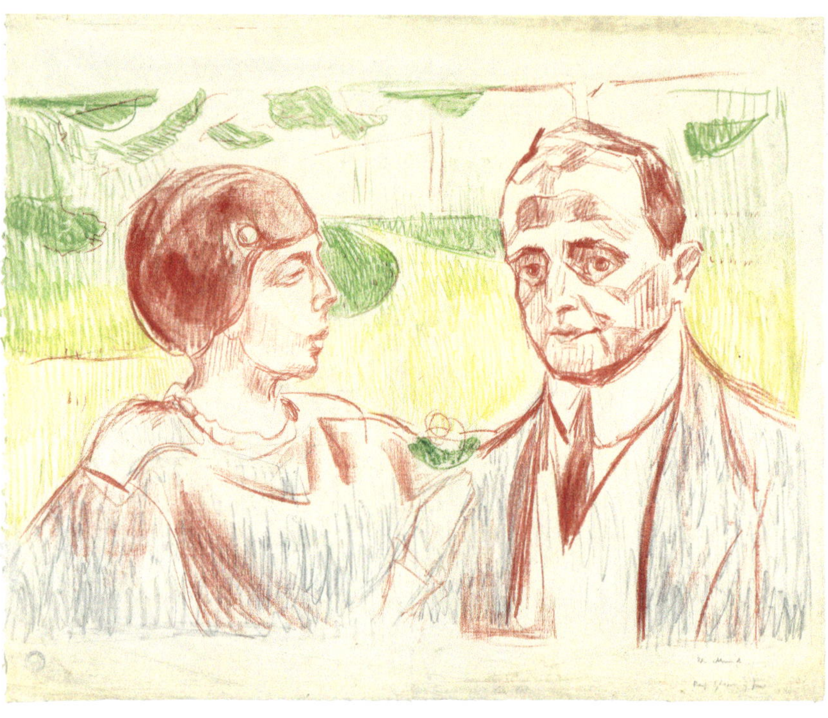

(B)
Edvard Munch
Elsa and Curt Glaser — 1913
Munchmuseet — Oslo

Munch's Graphic Work in the Kupferstichkabinett in Berlin

A few years after leaving Berlin, Munch's museum career actually began at the Kupferstichkabinett in Berlin. It was responsible for collecting contemporaneous prints for the Königliche Museen (Royal Museums), whereas the Nationalgalerie (National Gallery) was responsible for acquiring contemporary works for its collection of drawings.[58]

The Kupferstichkabinett, founded in 1831, was located on the third floor of the Neues Museum (New Museum). The Neue Abteilung (Modern Department), founded in 1897 by the director, Friedrich Lippmann, which collected prints from the early nineteenth century to the present, was given its own study hall and presentation room in the same building ten years later, where regular exhibition activity was established.[59] As early as 1903, the museum acquired four Munch prints directly from the artist, including *Self-Portrait (with Skeleton Arm)* and the second version of the Strindberg portrait.[60] Figure p.195 That made the Kupferstichkabinett the third museum collection to include Munch prints, after the Kupferstich-Kabinett in Dresden and Nasjonalmuseet in Kristiania.[61] Under the directorship of Max Lehrs, from 1904 to 1908, there were no Munch acquisitions.[62] That changed under Max J. Friedländer, the director from 1908 to 1933, whose staff member Curt Glaser would now make crucial contributions with the approval of his superior. Glaser attended to the Neue Abteilung from 1909, initially in a subordinate position, and then as a curator with the status of a civil servant from 1920 onward. Curt Glaser and his wife, Elsa, née Kolker, were themselves committed collectors of art. In 1911, on a trip together with the art dealer Hugo Perls and his wife, Käthe, one of Elsa's cousins, they acquired from Alfred Strölin in Paris several copies of the color lithograph *The Sick Child I*, one of which entered the Kupferstichkabinett the same year as an "anonymous gift." Figure p.104 Its Munch collection now grew significantly, as Glaser emphasized in a letter to Munch on December 17, 1912: "I have bought a great deal of your graphic work for the Kupferstichkabinett since I have been running the modern department."[63]

Graphic works by Munch, whom the Glasers and Perlses visited in Kristiania in the summer of 1913, were now included in the museum's exhibitions. Figure p.200B As early as December 1912, recent works by the artist were shown in the exhibition *Das Tier in der neueren Graphik* (The Animal in Recent Graphic Art); three years later, Munch was the central figure in the *Skandinavische Graphikausstellung* (Exhibition of Scandinavian Graphic Art).[64] During World War I, the number of acquisitions decreased for a time, but donations continued to be made to the museum. In 1916, they included the etched and lithographic portrait *Andreas Schwarz*. Figures pp.200A + 115 The donor was Georg Schwarz, the father of the child, born in February 1906. As a patron of the arts and former business partner of Paul Cassirer, he had been concentrating on collecting portraits in the years before this.[65]

In 1917, Bruno Cassirer published the first edition of Curt Glaser's Munch monograph;[66] five years later, the same house published Glaser's large survey *Graphik der Neuzeit* (Graphic Art of the Modern Era). It declared Munch to be the most important Nordic artist, before renowned graphic artists such as Carl Larsson, Anders Zorn, and Munch's compatriot Erik Werenskiold, because unlike them he "would enter the circle of European art not … only as a recipient but also as a contributor."[67] Moreover, Munch represented, for Glaser, "in the most recent history of graphic art the central personality to a much greater degree than any artist of the earlier nineteenth century in his era. All of the threads come together in his hand. All graphic techniques—not just the woodcut—gain through him previously unsuspected expressive possibilities. New content creates a new vessel for itself."[68]

In 1924, Curt Glaser moved to the Staatliche Kunstbibliothek (State Art Library) to serve as director. As a Jew, he was forced to resign this office in April 1933. That summer he emigrated while traveling in Switzerland; in 1941, he moved to the United States, where he died two years later.[69] At the Kupferstichkabinett, Willy Kurth, who had already been working there as a scholar for some time, continued to collect Munch works from 1924 on.[70] Glaser maintained a connection to the artist, as proven by his commitment to the large exhibition at the Nationalgalerie and probably also to the one at the Kupferstichkabinett in 1927, which showed 150 prints in parallel with the exhibition in the Kronprinzenpalais (Crown Prince's Palace).[71] In July of that year, in which the second volume of Gustav Schiefler's catalogue raisonné of Munch's graphic oeuvre was also published,[72] Glaser sold fourteen of the artist's works in his collection to the museum and thus supplemented its holdings, which he knew extremely well.[73]

From Glaser's collection of art, which he was forced to sell in two auctions in Berlin in 1933, seven Munch prints entered the museum (in addition to works by Ernst Ludwig Kirchner), three of which were returned to Curt Glaser's heirs in 2012.[74] Among other works, the woodcut *Two Human Beings (The Lonely Ones)* remained in the Kupferstichkabinett. Figure p.193A Works by Munch were acquired as late as 1936, including, from the former collection of the Cologne industrialist Heinrich Stinnes, *Portrait of August Strindberg*.[75] Figure p.117

On the occasion of Edvard Munch's seventieth birthday, on December 12, 1933, Willy Kurth wrote the artist a letter outlining with considerable pathos his role as the guiding star for the collection in politically bleak times: "The modern department of the Kupferstichkabinett in Berlin is remembering your art today with the greatest reverence and gratitude. In the rooms of our modern department, your work is still patrimonial heritage, having been a guide to German youth once around 1905, in its inner departure to new realms. Our department of modern graphic art in particular ... has doubled its holdings and can now count 230 sheets by Munch among its proudest possessions. Even in the difficult daily struggles in which recent German art is entangled, may your art exert its patronal powers on everything true and genuine. With your name on our banner, we are fighting today as we did twenty-five years ago ... . We of the modern department of the Kupferstichkabinett will not cease to cultivate the work of the man to whom all our hope turns from our profound inner plight."[76] Four years later, it was no longer possible for museums in National Socialist Germany to collect or exhibit Edvard Munch's art, whose "Nordic character" had still been emphasized as a positive after 1933[77]—Willy Kurth's words point in that direction. Only eight Munch works, however, were confiscated from the Kupferstichkabinett in the "Entartete Kunst" (Degenerate Art) action in 1937, a small number compared to other public collections.[78] Willy Kurth's protective hand will have been one essential reason for that.[79] Losses during World War II were also minimal. Today, the Kupferstichkabinett possesses 258 Munch works, making it the second-largest collection of his graphic art in the world, at some distance behind Munchmuseet in Oslo.[80]

(1) Druckerei Otto Felsing to Edvard Munch, August 16, 1906, Munchmuseet, Oslo, MM K 3524 (this document and all of the archival materials in Munchmuseet that follow are accessible at emunch.no). Felsing was still using the term in correspondence with the artist in the 1920s. Such business correspondence, which has been preserved from other Berlin printers as well, represents, in addition to several letters by the artist, some of the few documents of Munch's collaboration with printing houses. On the sources, see Woll 2003, p. 42.

(2) Ingelheim 2022.

(3) Schiefler 1927, p. 3.

(4) For the lithographs that dominated at this point, Munch primarily drew on transfer paper that was then transferred to the printing plate. Roettig 2006, pp. 25–26.

(5) The term was coined in the early nineteenth century: the Viennese artist and art scholar Johann Adam Bernhard Ritter von Bartsch gave his twenty-one-volume work dedicated to the original prints of the old masters the title *Le Peintre Graveur* (1803–21).

(6) On the art print of Munch's era, see, for example, Berlin 2000 and Buschhoff 2011.

(7) Until the 1910s, reproductive engravings were still being collected on a large scale at the Kupferstichkabinett in Berlin, for example.

(8) In Paris, he also produced several mezzotints from 1896 to 1898. See Roettig 2006, pp. 22–23.

(9) https://emunch.no/person.xhtml?id=pe458.

(10) Thiis 1934, p. 35.

(11) On this, see Woll 2001, pp. 10–11 and 25, n. 15.

(12) Woll 2003, pp. 41–42.

(13) Gilman 2006, p. 227.

(14) Edvard Munch to Karen Bjølstad, November 14, 1894, Munchmuseet, Oslo, MM N 807.

(15) Woll 2001, pp. 10 and 25, n. 16.

(16) See the essay by Stefanie Heckmann in the present catalogue.

(17) Julius Meier-Graefe, ed., *Edvard Munch: Acht Radierungen* (Berlin, 1895). Ten copies of the portfolio were printed on Japan paper as a deluxe version and fifty-five copies from the steel-coated plate were offered on thick, beige wove paper. Meier-Graefe wrote the afterword.

(18) The Kupferstichkabinett in Berlin also has a rare proof of *The Sick Child I* (inv. no. 802-1912).

(19) Carl Sabo was located at Wilhelmstrasse 10 and (in 1902) Wilhelmstrasse 133. Ludwig Angerer's workshop was at Wassertorstrasse 59 in present-day Kreuzberg.

(20) The printing house, founded in 1823 and located at Ritterstrasse 26, established itself in 1902 as the most important workshop in Berlin for printing the artist's lithographs.

(21) Woll 2009, Woll 354. See Groth 2011b.

(22) Kamzelak and Ott 2004–18, vol. 2, p. 346 (April 11, 1895). See Woll 2001, p. 25, n. 20, and p. 26, n. 21.

(23) Kamzelak and Ott 2004–18, vol. 2, p. 347 (April 13, 1895).

(24) The Jugendstil artist Joseph Sattler (1867–1931) worked as a designer for *PAN*, among other things.

(25) Kamzelak and Ott 2004–18, vol. 2, pp. 353–54 (May 10, 1895).

(26) Woll 2001, p. 17.

(27) The Kupferstichkabinett in Berlin received four prints (including one lithograph) as gifts from the artist between 1905 and 1916.

(28) Alexander Liebmann to Edvard Munch, April 18, 1896, Munchmuseet, Oslo, MM K 3668. According to the telephone books of the time, his workshop was at Friedrichstrasse 74 (ground floor). Liebmann also printed ex libris, book ornaments, and designs for deluxe papers.

(29) See the entry on Alexander Liebmann in the online memorial book on the website of the City of Munich: https://gedenkbuch.muenchen.de/index.php?id=gedenkbuch_link&gid=414.

(30) *La Revue Blanche*, no. 60 (December 1895): p. 528. Ill. in Gilman 2006, p. 227. The text reads: "M'arrêtant, je m'appuyai à la balustrade, presque mort de fatigue. Au-dessus du fjord bleu noir pendaient des nuages, rouges comme du sang et comme des langues de feu. Mes amis s'éloignaient, et, seul, tremblant d'angoisse, je pris conscience du grand cri infini de la nature." This lithograph was published in the United States in January 1896 as a copy by the author Vance Thompson in the magazine *M'lle New York*, with reference to the Norwegian's art being unsuitable for young girls: "spermatozoidal and spiritual." See Gilman 2006, p. 228.

(31) Woll 2003, p. 49.

(32) Woll 2001, p. 15.

(33) On this, see the essay by Janina Nentwig in the present catalogue.

(34) The work could still have been printed by Lassally in Berlin. See Woll 2009, Woll 379.

(35) Nierhoff-Wielk 2011a.

(36) Gilman 2006, p. 228.

(37) Katharina Groth (2011a, pp. 104 and 168, n. 8) remarks that "Stindberg" is Swedish for "bloated, fat mountain" or "mountain with hot air," but this is dubious. In Norwegian, *stint* means "full."

(38) Büttner 1934, p. 92; Roettig 2006, p. 22.

(39) On Gauguin in particular, see Bartrum 2019b, p. 84, and Buschhoff 2011, p. 224. The woodcuts he made in Paris were printed by Clot or Lemercier.

(40) Munch had already done a lithograph of *Anxiety* that year. The Parisian gallerist and publisher Ambroise Vollard integrated it into the first volume of his *Album des peintres-graveurs*.

(41) Schiefler 1907, pp. 19–20.

(42) *The Sick Girl I* came from Kollmann's collection to the Kupferstichkabinett in Berlin in 1912.

(43) On Schiefler and Munch, see Woesthoff 2006.

(44) Schiefler 1907. On Munch's relationship to Bruno Cassirer and his cousin Paul, see the essay by Christina Feilchenfeldt in the present catalogue.

(45) Woll 2001, p. 17.

(46) Woll 2003, p. 47.

(47) Büttner 1934, p. 100. See also Woll 2003, pp. 41–42.

(48) Roettig 2006, p. 25.

(49) According to Gustav Schiefler, Munch found "it understandable that we did not want to exhibit the *Madonna*. He believes that this sort of thing could indeed be dangerous for young girls. Same with *The Kiss*. But he himself sees in these depictions the expression of a sacred emotion." Munch and Schiefler 1987 and 1990, vol. 1, p. 71.

(50) Berlin 2003–4, pp. 57–58, no. 42.

(51) Buchhart 2003, p. 137.

(52) Chéroux 2012, p. 56.

(53) Berlin 2003–4, pp. 64–65, no. 60.

(54) Berlin 2003–4, pp. 163–64, no. 147.

(55) Gilman 2006, p. 232.

(56) Woll 2013, p. 23.

(57) An overview of the exhibitions can be found in Woll 2001, pp. 470–74.

(58) The Nationalgalerie did indeed acquire its first paintings by the artist in 1930 but no drawings.

(59) See Schalhorn 2022, p. 50.

(60) The two other works were a print of the etching *The Sick Child I* (1894, inv. no. 113-1902) and the top half (!) of *Madonna (Woman Making Love)* (1895/1902, inv. no. 112-1903).

61 Whereas a print was donated by Woldemar von Seidlitz to the museum in Dresden in 1896 and another in 1900 (information kindly provided by Olaf Simon, Kupferstich-Kabinett Dresden), the national museum in Kristiania acquired a set of thirty-one etchings and lithographs in 1898. See Woll 2001, p. 17. Not until 1918 would the Kunsthalle Bremen become the first German museum to acquire a painting by the artist: *The Child and Death* (1899, Woll 447).

(62) Lehrs relied instead on Max Liebermann and Käthe Kollwitz when building up the Neue Abteilung. See Schalhorn 2022, p. 51.

(63) Curt Glaser to Edvard Munch, December 17, 1912, Munchmuseet, Oslo, MM K 2257. On Glaser's engagement for Munch, see, for example, Achenbach 2003, pp. 10–11.

(64) Between 1913 and 1928 the Kupferstichkabinett showed Munch in five regular, rather small presentations; in 1927, there was a large exhibition in parallel with the one of the Nationalgalerie in the Kronprinzenpalais. See Achenbach 2003, p. 13, n. 2.

(65) Ustvedt 2013, pp. 222–23. A year later, Leo Blumenreich, co-owner and director of the Galerie Paul Cassirer, donated *The Hearse on Potsdamer Platz* to the museum.

(66) Glaser 1917.

(67) Glaser 1922, p. 422.

(68) Glaser 1922, pp. 517–18. See Achenbach 2003, p. 11.

(69) For an extensive account of Curt Glaser, see Strobl 2006 and Basel 2022 (as an introduction: Haldemann and Scherrer 2022).

(70) For a detailed account of Willy Kurth and his significance, see Anita Beloubek-Hammer, *Die Aktion "Entartete Kunst" 1937 im Berliner Kupferstichkabinett: Kustos Willy Kurth rettet Meisterblätter der Moderne* (Berlin, 2023).

(71) On this, see the essay by Dieter Scholz in the present catalogue.

(72) Schiefler 1927. Unlike the first volume, this one was published by the Euphorion-Verlag, Berlin.

(73) Inv. nos. 272- to 285-1927. Among these works were *The Day After, Death in the Sick Room, Evening (Melancholy I)*, *Anxiety*, and the Ibsen portrait.

(74) Schalhorn 2022, p. 49.

(75) Achenbach 2003, p. 128, cat. no. 109. Stinnes had assembled a collection of 200,000 prints and drawings in the 1920s. See Woll 2013, p. 39, and note 58 above.

(76) Willy Kurth to Edvard Munch, December 12, 1933, Munchmuseet, Oslo, MM K 3645. I am grateful to Judith Rauser, Basel, for pointing me to this source.

(77) März 1994, pp. 133–34. On the change in the meaning of the term *Nordisch* (Nordic), see the essay by Stefanie Heckmann in the present catalogue.

(78) Achenbach 2003, pp. 247–48, cat. nos. 1–6 and 9. They include the lithographs *The Scream* and *Anna and Walter Leistikow*, which are missing from the collection today. The woodcut *Man's Head in Woman's Hair* (1896), by contrast, could be bought back from the British art trade in 1999.

(79) Kind reference by Anita Beloubek-Hammer in an email to the author, March 14, 2023.

(80) The Kupferstichkabinett's most recent acquisition from a private collection was that of *The Sin*. In 2022, a third version of the lithograph *The Sick Child I* was bequeathed to the museum from a private collection.

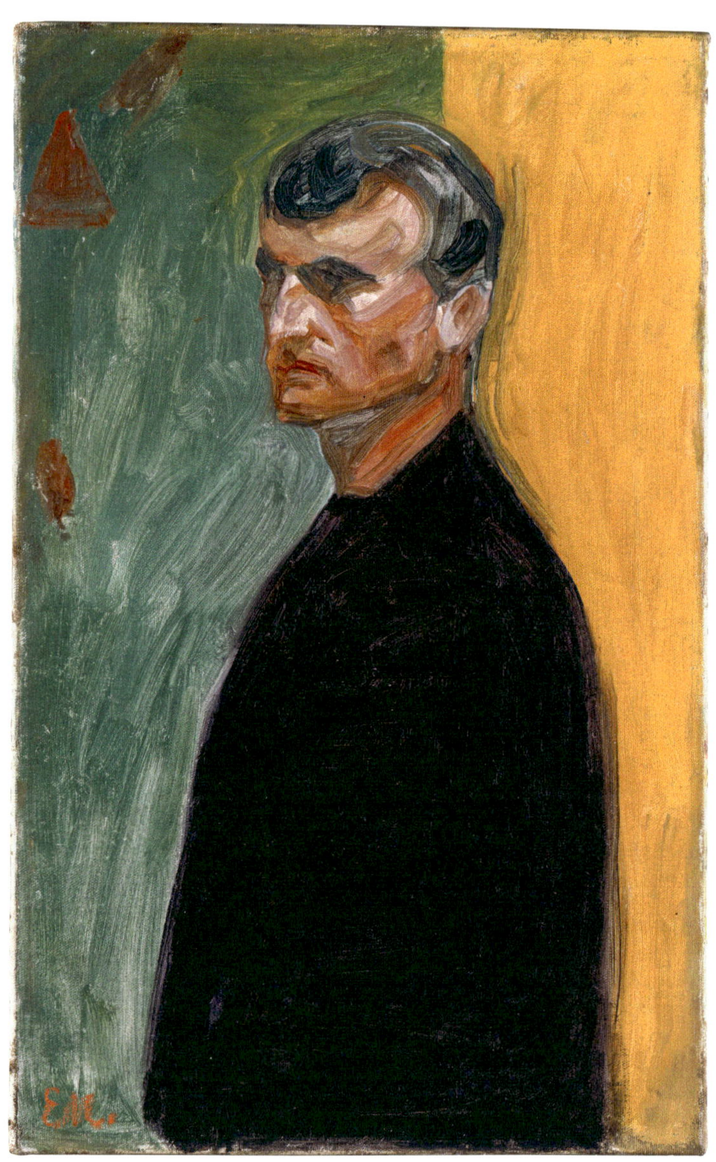

Edvard Munch
Self-Portrait (Against Two-Colored Background) — [ca. 1903]
Heidi Horten Collection — Vienna

No Simple Relationship

Edvard Munch and the Kunsthandlung Paul Cassirer

Christina Feilchenfeldt

The first exhibition in Germany in which Edvard Munch was represented was held in Munich at the Königlicher Glaspalast (Royal Glass Palace) in 1891. Three of his works were shown there along with works by other Norwegian artists who were not welcome in Berlin because of "anarchistic" tendencies.[1] In November 1892, Munch's solo exhibition at the Verein Berliner Künstler (Association of Berlin Artists) followed, with fifty-five paintings in the Rotunda of the Architektenhaus (Architects' House) at Wilhelmstrasse 92/93, which was, famously, closed after seven days and entered the annals of history as the "Affaire Munch" (Munch Affair). The controversy ultimately led to the founding of the Berlin Secession and thus helped modernism gain acceptance—first in the capital of the Reich and later in the rest of Germany.[2]

Munch lived in Berlin until early 1908, but also in later years he visited the city repeatedly. That enabled him to have a substantial influence on the art market there and to win over several influential supporters. The Berlin art dealer Eduard Schulte was the first to offer to exhibit Munch's works in 1892, immediately after the uproar. However, he wanted to show them in his branches in Düsseldorf and Cologne, not in Berlin. The artist agreed to that proposal, but later regretted the decision, as he wrote in a letter to his aunt, because he could have earned "many thousand crowns" in Berlin during that time.[3] After the fuss over the exhibition at the Verein Berliner Künstler, everyone was talking about his painting, and Munch was "suddenly the most famous man in the entire German Reich."[4] He therefore decided in December 1892 to repeat the scandalous exhibition at the Equitable-Palast on Friedrichstrasse for one and a half months, supplemented by the portrait of August Strindberg he had just finished and several additional drawings.[5] After an exhibition in 1893 in rooms on the boulevard Unter den Linden that Munch had rented for that express purpose, the Galerie Ugo Barroccio presented twenty-nine of his paintings in 1895.[6] It was his participation in the fifth exhibition of the Berlin Secession in 1902 that was, however, a milestone for Munch's breakthrough as an artist.

The Exhibition Policy of the Berlin Secession and the Kunsthandlung Paul Cassirer

The year 1898 was crucial for the evolution of the landscape of art in Berlin: on May 2, the process of founding the Berlin Secession was begun, and on November 1 the cousins Bruno and Paul Cassirer opened their gallery at Viktoriastrasse 35 in Berlin-Tiergarten. The opening exhibition included fifty-five works by Max Liebermann, twenty-six sculptures by the Belgian artist Constantin Meunier, and twenty-seven works by Edgar Degas. Liebermann, the chairman of the Berlin Secession, who contributed substantially to the success of the Cassirers' gallery not only as an artist but also as a collector, was thus represented in its exhibition program from the outset. Walter Leistikow, who was a friend of Paul Cassirer's and whose works would also be seen frequently in the gallery in the coming years, was the first clerk of the Secession, and Paul and Bruno Cassirer were appointed secretaries. The Cassirers shared a non-voting seat on the board; initially, they were entrusted with the planning and execution of the exhibition building at Kantstrasse 12 designed by Hans Grisebach. The building opened on May 19, 1899, with a premiere exhibition of 330 paintings and graphic works as well as fifty sculptures. Sixty-five artists were founding members of the association.[7]

In the second Secession exhibition, more than 10 percent of the 414 exhibits were by foreign artists, thus doing justice to an international ambition intended from the beginning. Munch was first represented in the fifth exhibition in 1902, which opened festively on April 26 with, among other things, twenty-eight of his works. Paul Cassirer was responsible for printing the catalogue, being clearly identified as its publisher by his name on the first page. In a three-page foreword, the directors of the exhibition tried to explain their choice of art to the public: they sought "to select the works of art not according to a traditional academic pattern but rather according to the individuality expressed in them ... . And not only can taste, famously, not be discussed, but it is also subject to perpetual fluctuations." Édouard Manet and Arnold Böcklin are cited as examples of such changes in taste, since both painters "were derided and laughed at for an entire generation, until now, when they are praised above all—and imitated." And, finally, as if the public had to be prepared specifically for Munch's art: "Every newly emerging genius alters taste: the artist imposes his ideal of beauty on us, and, whether we want to or not—and usually we do not want to, because the new makes it necessary to relearn—we have to obey him."[8]

The subject of this text from Liebermann's pen is in keeping with the task that Paul Cassirer had set himself when founding his gallery, namely, introducing and establishing French Impressionism in Germany. In the beginning, he was still pursuing this goal together with his cousin Bruno. Serious differences between them led to the business being divided up between the two in 1901, with Bruno taking over as director of the publishing house and Paul continuing to run the art dealership. The exhibitions in Paul Cassirer's spaces in Berlin, and until 1906 in Hamburg, reflect his efforts in a variety of ways. He received support in this from Hugo von Tschudi, the director of the Nationalgalerie (National Gallery) in Berlin at the time, who, like Cassirer and Max Liebermann, opposed the antiquated art doctrine of Emperor William II and made numerous purchases in the gallery on Viktoriastrasse. Tschudi's successor, Ludwig Justi, explicitly regretted in his *Führer zu den Gemälden der sogenannten Expressionisten in der National-Galerie* (Guide to the Paintings by the So-Called Expressionists in the National Gallery), published in 1921, that there was no work by Edvard Munch in the collection. He says that his art was formative for modernism, but unfortunately the museum's funds were no longer sufficient for an acquisition.[9]

Like Cassirer, who wanted to present to the Berlin public in his gallery not only works by dead artists but also a selection of contemporaries, the Berlin Secession had a stated goal of revealing to visitors the modernity and cosmopolitanism of Berlin, which was redefining itself as a city for art. The fifth Secession exhibition, ten years after the "Munch Affair," thus represented a special honor for the Norwegian artist and was widely reported in the daily press. Munch himself emphasized the influence of the Secession president Liebermann, who had spoken out in favor of his art and suggested the presentation of *The Frieze of Life*. Munch was given a place of honor in the exhibition in the face of resistance from conservative members.[10]

Despite this booming beginning, Munch was not able to achieve a real breakthrough or, apart from a few exceptions, persuade either the specialist press or the public.[11] And even Liebermann expressed himself rather critically behind closed doors. He lamented several times the sketchiness of Munch's painting, but he praised without reservation the quality of his graphic works.[12] In the years that followed, Munch was repeatedly invited to participate in the Secession exhibitions and on January 12, 1904, was elected a regular member of the Berlin Secession.[13]

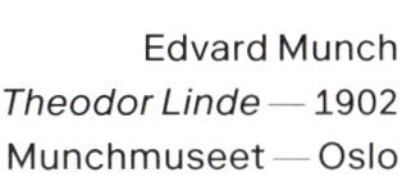

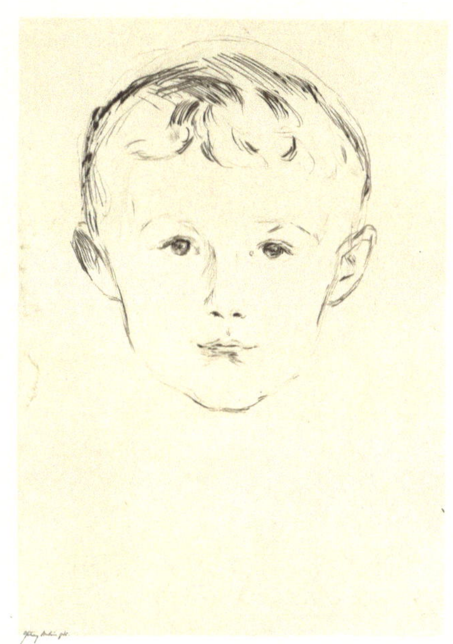

Edvard Munch
Theodor Linde — 1902
Munchmuseet — Oslo

1903 First Exhibitions with Works by Edvard Munch at the Kunsthandlung Paul Cassirer in Berlin and Hamburg

In the years from 1903 to 1921, Munch was represented in ten exhibitions at Paul Cassirer's spaces in Berlin and three times in Hamburg. In addition, numerous works, above all graphic works, are recorded in the gallery's account books. Unfortunately, these entries can only be identified with difficulty because Munch frequently gave several variations on a theme the same title, so that the details in the account books in the Paul Cassirer & Walter Feilchenfeldt Archiv in Zurich often cannot be clearly connected to a specific piece—especially when the chain of provenance has not been completely accounted for. In addition, it is not always clear from the entries whether they refer to a painting or a graphic work.[14] Because no correspondence from the gallery is held by the Paul Cassirer Archiv, the letters in the archives of Munchmuseet in Oslo represent an important contribution to understanding the business relationship between Munch and the Kunsthandlung Cassirer.

Only half of the roughly sixty works entered in Paul Cassirer's account books were actually sold, and those were primarily of graphic nature. Munch was involved from the outset in choosing prices for his works and had a small number of enthusiastic supporters in Germany who contributed to the spread of his art and assured him commissions. Albert Kollmann, *marchand amateur* and passionate collector of Munch's work, who had met him at Max Liebermann's, was particularly active as his patron. The ophthalmologist Max Linde of Lübeck and the textile industrialist Herbert Esche of Chemnitz, who commissioned numerous pieces from Munch, did not buy from the Galerie Cassirer but rather directly from the artist. Linde had, however, purchased from Cassirer two works by Paul Cezanne[15] as well as one each by Édouard Manet and Paul Gauguin in 1904, and Esche acquired a painting by Vincent van Gogh there in

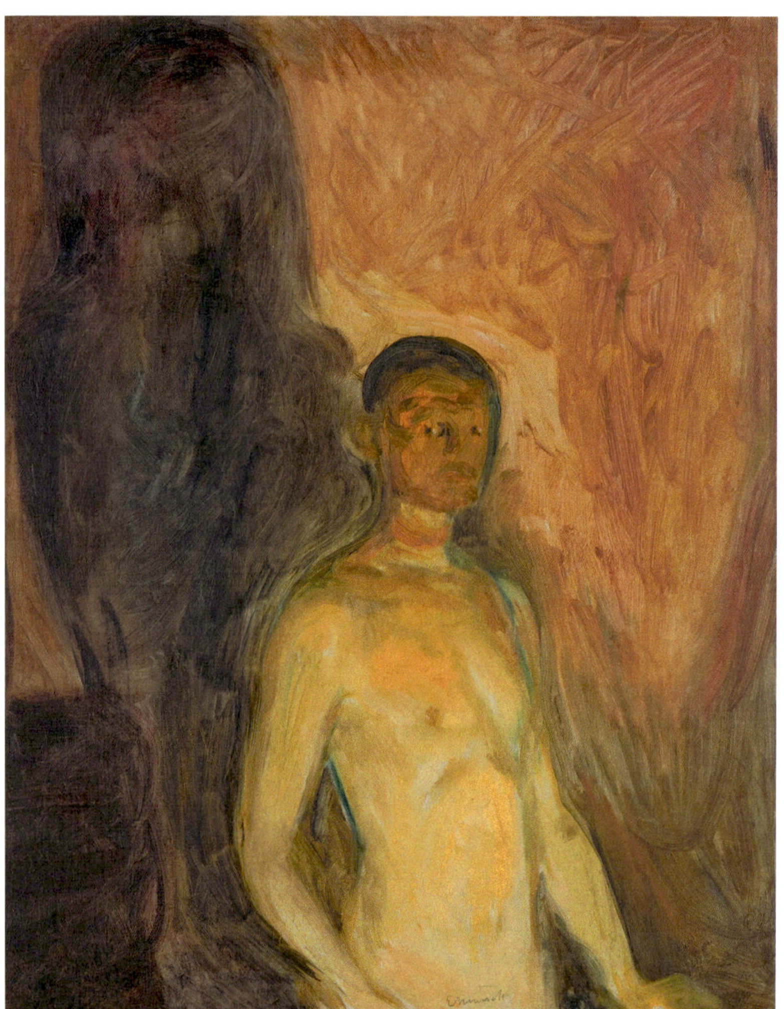

Edvard Munch
Self-Portrait in Hell — 1903
Munchmuseet — Oslo

1905.[16] The collector Curt Glaser purchased two Munch paintings at Cassirer in January and April 1910, before getting to know the artist personally two years later.[17] In 1917, he published the first German-language monograph on Munch with Bruno Cassirer.[18]

The first exhibition in the rooms on Viktoriastrasse in which Munch participated was held from January 17 to February 1, 1903, and showed his works with exhibits by Philipp Klein and August Gaul. With twenty-seven paintings and his entire graphic oeuvre, however, Munch had by far the most exhibits. Klein, who was born in Mannheim and is largely forgotten today, had been exhibiting regularly in the rooms of the Berlin Secession since its founding. He exemplarily illustrates Cassirer's concept of presenting to the Berlin public completely different artists together in around ten exhibitions annually. The sculptor August Gaul was also a founding member of the Secession and his works were repeatedly seen at Cassirer's gallery. In an essay on the exhibitions in Berlin art salons, the critic Hans Rosenhagen commented that a painter like Klein, "for all his welcome gift," had a difficult time next to an artist like Munch: "in any case, the exhibition proves that Munch is one of the strongest and most notable talents in all of modern art."[19]

Munch showed two self-portraits in this exhibition: a very recent, rather sketchily executed portrait in oil from around 1903 and a lithograph from 1895.[20] Figures pp. 204 + 113 The depiction of the vague background in yellow and green explains perfectly why the majority of the public and of critics rejected his painting. Curt Glaser, who was well disposed to the artist from the outset, tried to explain the seemingly unfinished quality of his works, as expressed in this self-portrait, as follows: "Munch has no specific technique, just as the purely painterly seems to be a matter of indifference to him in general. ... But all of the superficial things of painting can only be a hindrance to him when he follows the impulses of the moment to capture the fleeting visions of his soul on the planar surface."[21] Experts and critics assessed the artist's graphic works differently. His etchings in particular were always praised in the press but also in artists' circles, for example, the "delicately contoured child's head" of Theodor Linde in the first exhibition at Cassirer.[22] Figure p.207 Gustav Schiefler, patron of the arts in Hamburg and the author of the first catalogue raisonné of Munch's graphic oeuvre, commented on February 3, 1903, in his notes on Max Liebermann that the latter had spoken with admiration about Munch's etching technique during a visit to Cassirer, with his German spelling reflecting Liebermann's Berlin accent: "his [Liebermann's] etchings were nothing next to them."[23]

It cannot be proven that there were sales during or after the exhibition at Cassirer, because no books of sales or purchases have been preserved from this first phase of his activities as an art dealer. The presentation of Munch's graphic works in such large numbers may have served to give the public a more comprehensive overview of the controversial artist's work; moreover, Cassirer may also have seen lower prices as a way to win over new collectors.[24] In fact, the dealer seems to have expected to benefit commercially from a larger offering of Munch's prints, because shortly after the Berlin exhibition he showed an extensive selection again, this time in his branch on the Jungfernstieg in Hamburg.[25] Unfortunately, no sales are known here either; according to Linde, this was due in part to Paul Cassirer's stance. Linde remarked to Munch: "It is Cassirer's fault that you have not sold anything yet; he said to me that you are incredibly expensive .... I would not reduce your prices too much."[26] Presumably there were some sales, since on March 27, 1903, Cassirer arranged for a payment of 1,674.85 francs to the artist, who was staying in Paris.[27]

The gallerist was unfazed by the bad press and organized a second show with Munch's participation from November 5 to December 1 of the same year. The dealer was perhaps trying to establish a stronger tie to this unusual artist and for that reason made it possible for him to present his artwork again in the gallery's newly opened skylight room. Munch was, in any case, enthusiastic and found that at Cassirer his "paintings ... work exceptionally well in a separate room."[28] This time works by Francisco de Goya and Ulrich Hübner were shown along with seventeen Munch paintings. Once again, the reviews were devastating for the most part; the skylight room with Munch's works was said to be a "chamber of horrors" with the "sad monstrosities of an incurably sick brain."[29]

Cassirer was indeed expecting a great deal from exhibition visitors by placing Goya's fine and "cleanly painted"[30] portraits next to Munch's *Self-Portrait in Hell.* Figure p.208 Paintings such as *Sanatorium* and *Corridor into the Sanatorium* must also have been disturbing for a majority of the public.[31] The account books in the Paul Cassirer & Walter Feilchenfeldt Archiv in Zurich do not document any sales for this period. For the year 1903, there are only two transactions listed, without prices: on December 14, an etching titled *Death and Life* was sent to the Berlin Secession and a piece titled *Vampires*, but not more closely described, was sold on December 16 to a buyer named Dr. Herz. The reviews in the Berlin press of both exhibitions were completely negative, with the exception of the reviews by Julius Elias and Curt Glaser.[32] Nevertheless, already in December 1904 there was another exhibition at Cassirer, which presented nineteen works by the artist, seventeen of which were portraits.[33] Albert Kollmann had given Paul Cassirer and Max Linde a tour of Munch's studio in the artist's absence in June of that year. As Kollmann later reported to Munch, Cassirer then definitely wanted to present an exhibition of portraits.[34]

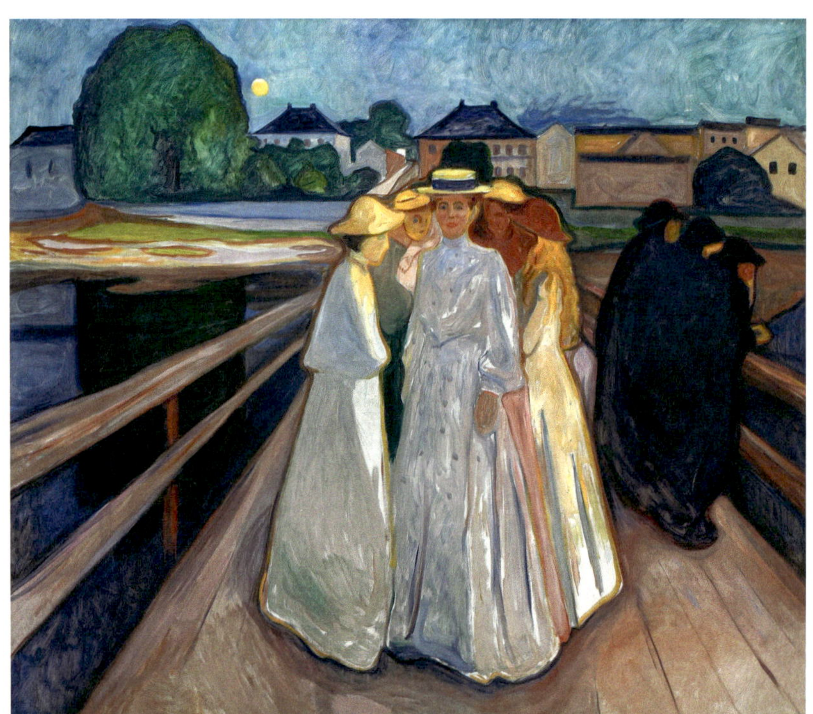

Edvard Munch
On the Bridge — 1903
Thielska Galleriet — Stockholm

1904–5 and 1907
Portraits by Edvard Munch at Paul Cassirer and Increasing Commercial Success

"Munch is a born portraitist, not only because he is a phenomenal born draftsman but because his seeing is intuiting, because he grasps instinctively ... the only side from which the person being portrayed can be depicted characteristically." Max Liebermann wrote these lines on the occasion of the artist's seventieth birthday on December 12, 1933.[35] Cassirer was indeed trying to convince his audience of Munch's abilities as a portraitist with an extensive presentation as early as 1904–5. Munch had shortly before signed an exclusive contract for the sale of his graphic works with Bruno Cassirer, and he had contracted with Wilhelm Suhr of the Galerie Commeter in Hamburg for the sale of his paintings.[36] Paul Cassirer must have been all the more eager to have a successful exhibition in his gallery of Munch's work. In 1907, however, both contracts were canceled, and Cassirer, after founding the Pan-Presse in 1908, undertook producing prints himself, including graphic works by Munch.[37]

After Cassirer had presented portraits by Vincent van Gogh to Berliners from November 22 to December 17, 1904, the gallery opened an exhibition with Munch's works on December 19. For Berlin art critics, these painters were certainly comparable, and perhaps Cassirer was also picturing a comparative show of the two modernists when he exhibited Munch's latest portraits at his gallery. As they had with the Van Gogh show, critical and dismissive voices in the press mixed with euphoric ones.[38] Only after a break of two years did Cassirer decide to present exhibits by Munch in a collective show, and again he showed primarily portraits. From February 18 to 24, 1907, the "collections of Paul Baum, Lovis Corinth, Georg Kolbe, Adolphe Monticelli, Edvard Munch, works by Joseph Oppenheimer and Hermann Pleuer" could be viewed at Viktoriastrasse 35. The exhibits by Munch included the full-length portrait of Harry Graf Kessler and his portrait of Friedrich Nietzsche.[39] Figures pp. 126, 127 + 264B The reviews were mixed, but Gustav Schiefler paid explicit tribute to Cassirer's efforts on behalf of the artist: "The exhibition is quite magnificent. ... Perhaps it is necessary to understand that it does not entirely conform to a man like Paul Cassirer, who developed his taste from the serene colorism ... of Impressionism that

(A)
Entry in Cassirer's account book — 1907
Paul Cassirer & Walter
Feilchenfeldt Archiv — Zurich

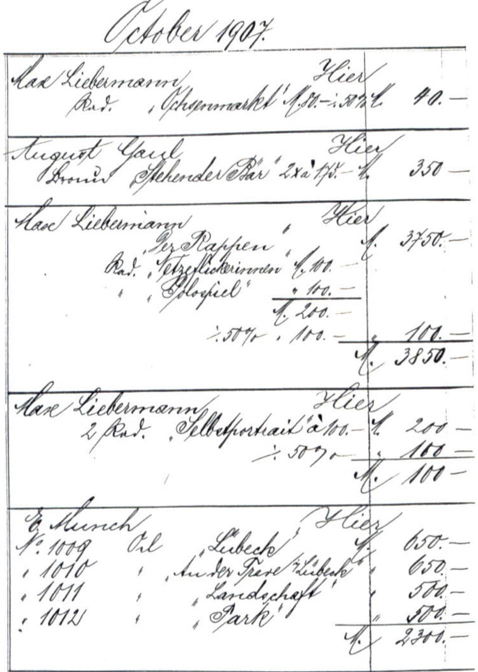

October 1907.

Max Liebermann Hier
Rad. „Ochsenmarkt" M. 80.– ÷ 50% M. 40.–

August Gaul Hier
Bronze „Stehender Bär" 2 x à 175.– M. 350.–

Max Liebermann Hier
„Der Rappen" M. 3750.–
Rad. „Netzflickerinnen" M. 100.–
" „Polospiel" " 100.–
M. 200.–
÷ 50% " 100.– " 100.–
M. 3850.–

Max Liebermann Hier
2 Rad. „Selbstportrait" à 100.– M. 200.–
÷ 50% " 100.–
M. 100.–

E. Munch Hier
No. 1009 Öl „Lübeck" M. 650.–
" 1010 " „An der Trave Lübeck" " 650.–
" 1011 " „Landschaft" " 500.–
" 1012 " „Park" " 500.–
M. 2300.–

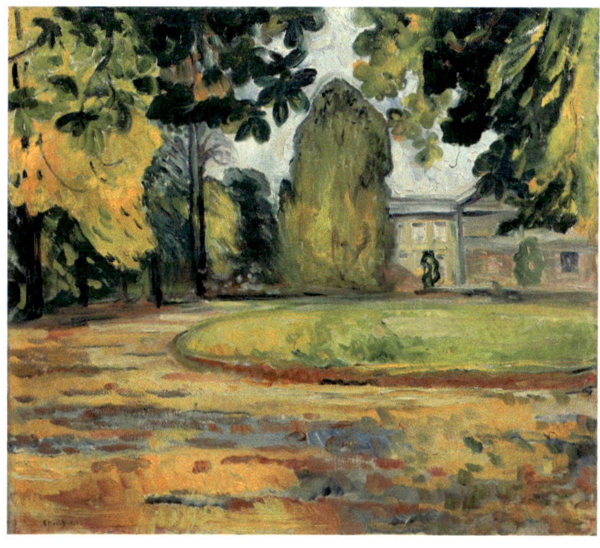

(B)
Edvard Munch
Park in Kösen — 1906
Österreichische Galerie Belvedere — Vienna

has now grown old, and that he does not really want it to come out against Impressionism. Nevertheless, it is admirable that he has made such room for it in his salon."[40]

Schiefler's assessment is surely true, since introducing Impressionism to Germany was Paul Cassirer's declared mission, and his special admiration for the art of Manet, Cezanne, and Van Gogh was the driving force of his activity. Barely a year after Cezanne's death on October 22, 1906, Cassirer decided to present sixty-nine watercolors by the French artist with twenty-four works by Munch.[41] Cezanne's apparently unfinished watercolors seemed just as strange to the public as Munch's compositions. The painting *Norwegian Summer Night* of 1903 from Max Linde's collection is now called *On the Bridge*: only the figure turned toward the viewer has facial features that are worked out, whereas the people in the background look sketchier. Figure p.210 The group of three young women in bright clothes contrasts with the merely suggested dark figures on the right edge. A Scandinavian midnight sun visible in the background lights the scene, giving it a dreamlike, diffuse character.

Cassirer's repeated decision to present Munch's works extensively was surely based on his own close connection to the art direction of the Berlin Secession, which also showed his art regularly. The sale of Munch's works still did not produce significant receipts. According to his account books, in 1907 Cassirer had taken over eight works directly from the artist, including three oil paintings, but sold only four graphic works that year. Figure p.211A Their vague titles usually make it impossible to identify them with certainty from the account books. The entry in Paul Cassirer's account book numbered 1011/1012 can, however, be identified without any doubt: it corresponds to *Park*, number 89 in the first exhibition catalogue of 1907.[42] Figure p.211B According to Paul Cassirer's account book, the painting was purchased from the artist for 500 marks on October 18, 1907, and sold to the collector Hugo Perls on February 18, 1910, for 600 marks.

1912–14 The Sonderbund Exhibition in Cologne and Edvard Munch's Artistic Breakthrough in Germany

The year 1912 brought Munch's artistic breakthrough in Germany. It began with Heinrich Thannhauser exhibiting more than a hundred works at his Moderne Galerie in Munich. Cassirer would have liked to show that exhibition in Berlin as well and wrote the artist on February 22, 1912: "Please consider once again whether you can't make it possible for the collection to go from Munich to me. You know, after all, that I have always had the greatest interest in your works."[43]

Munch's influence on the new generation of artists was now openly discussed; he was described as a kind of father figure for Expressionism.[44] The "Germanic" quality of his art was emphasized, and at the same time it was proclaimed that Impressionism had been overcome. In an article in the journal *Kunst und Künstler* on the final exhibition of the Berlin Secession, Karl Scheffler described Munch as a revolutionary who was becoming a model for young talents. A year earlier, in an extensive letter to the artist, Gustav Schiefler had observed "that something new is in the offing: that which you quite rightly call the Germanic spirit. ... The 'Germanic element' per se is not at all inherently hostile to Impressionism; on the contrary, the way it expresses itself is very much based on it, if it also overcomes it."[45]

Two years earlier, the Berlin Secession had split up, which also led to Cassirer temporarily resigning from his posts. The Neue Secession (New Secession) was founded under the leadership of the young generation of artists, most of whom were Expressionists. In 1912, Paul Cassirer took over as director again, against the resistance of numerous members, and collaborated closely with Max Slevogt as chair of the jury.[46] Munch was also represented in the group's exhibition that year. The organizers of the famous Sonderbund (Special League) exhibition in Cologne, which promised a comprehensive overview of current art in Europe from May 5 to September 30, had invited Munch as a guest of honor and paid tribute to him with an exhibition space of his own.[47] His thirty-two exhibits were shown at a great distance from Munch's Norwegian colleagues, on a par with the works of Van Gogh, Cezanne, Gauguin, Pablo Picasso, and the now largely forgotten August Deusser, each of whom also had a dedicated room. The owner is indicated for several of Munch's works; for example, next to catalogue number 526, the *Double Portrait* of 1897, Dr. Walter [*sic*] Rathenau of Berlin is named. Catalogue number 535, *Kinderbild* (Painting of Children) of 1905, now known as *Esche's Children*, is identified as being the property of Herbert Esche.[48] Figure p.213

Paul Cassirer did not end up taking the Thannhauser exhibition in 1912, but the Berlin art dealer did have a "gallery exhibition" from October 24 to December 2 after adding a large skylight room, which included a Munch painting titled *Strasse* (Street) under the catalogue number 101a.[49] Figure pp.154–55 This was the only exhibition catalogue for which Cassirer wrote a foreword, because this anniversary exhibition was an attempt to offer a survey of his activity of the past fifteen years by showing "German and French artists, alive and already dead, young and old, side by side."[50] Immediately after this anniversary show,

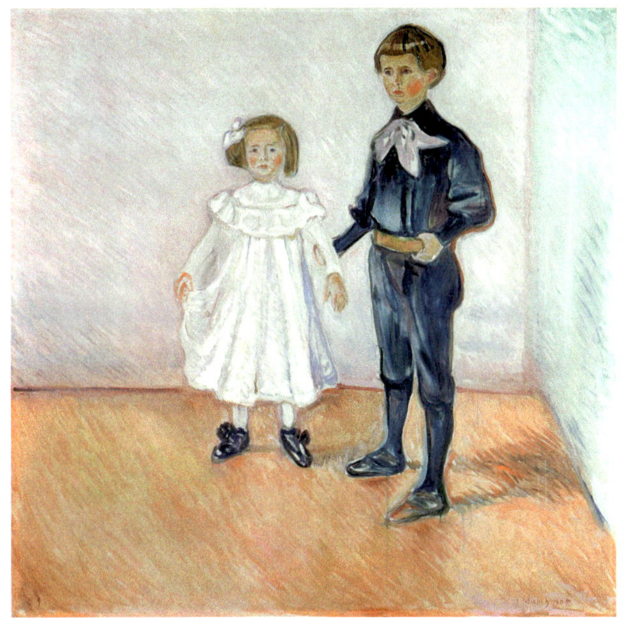

Edvard Munch
Portrait of Children (Erdmute and Hans-Herbert Esche) — 1905
Kunsthaus Zürich

Munch was represented in a Cassirer exhibition again with seven paintings and twelve graphic works. Their effect, according to Albert Kollmann, was wonderful and after the conversion the light for Munch was "fabulous: Cassirer himself extraordinarily pleased, admired your paintings."[51]

Although the account books for 1912 list no sales at all, Munch seems to have been very satisfied with the prices he was able to get for his works in the meantime, as is clear from a number of letters. Cassirer is said to have planned an exhibition for the following year as well, as Albert Kollmann wrote to Munch in Kristiania on September 12,[52] but for unknown reasons it never took place.

1914–22
Exhibitions and Auctions with Works by Edvard Munch and the Involvement of the Kunsthandlung Paul Cassirer

In February 1914, there was a retrospective of Munch's works at the Galerie Fritz Gurlitt in Berlin, which was followed by a show at Alfred Flechtheim in Düsseldorf. This appears to have motivated Paul Cassirer as well to continue working on Munch's behalf. It may also have played a role that since his success in the Sonderbund exhibition Munch had been mentioned in the same breath as Cezanne, Van Gogh, and Gauguin and was thus numbered among the classics.[53]

On January 2, 1914, Cassirer took over twelve Munch works from Gurlitt, seven of which they owned jointly. If they were later sold, their sale must have been handled by Gurlitt, because no sales from this group are listed in Cassirer's account books. Alfred Flechtheim showed a large number of Munch paintings from March 28 to April 17, 1914, together with several drawings and lithographs. Financial failure, however, forced him to close his gallery already in 1917 and to have his inventory auctioned by Cassirer in Berlin. That included two works by Munch: lot number 190, *Landschaft* (Landscape), was acquired by the Nationalmuseum in Kristiania, and lot 191, *Schneelandschaft* (Snowy Landscape), was bought by Fritz Gurlitt.[54]

From 1916 to 1932, the Kunsthandlung Paul Cassirer was in charge of eighty-two auctions in cooperation with the Munich auctioneer Hugo Helbing. Some of the auctions were held at Cassirer, some in the ballroom of the

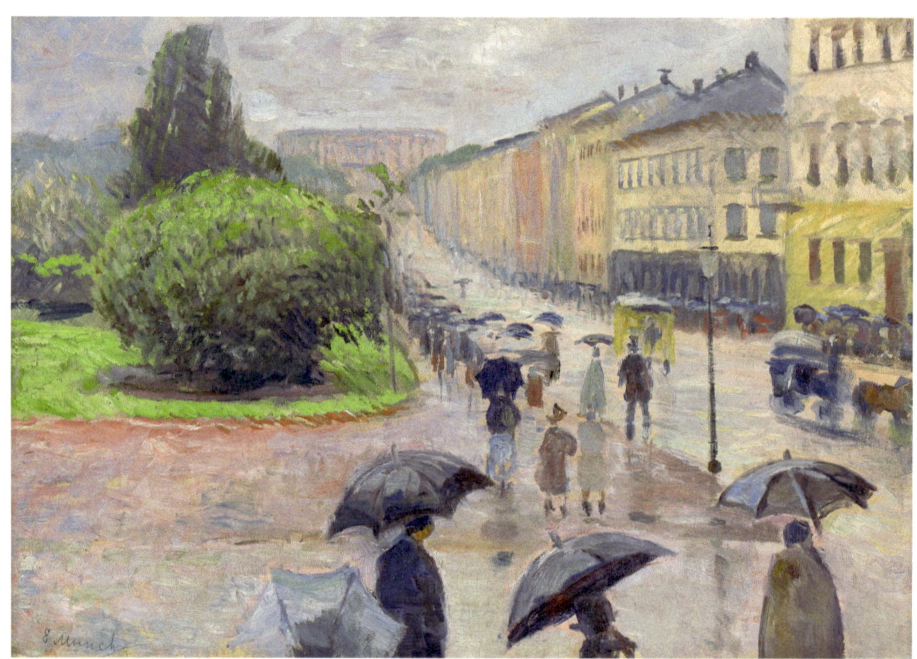

(A)
Edvard Munch
Karl Johan in the Rain — 1891
Munchmuseet — Oslo

(B)
Edvard Munch
Gamblers in Monte Carlo — 1892
Munchmuseet — Oslo

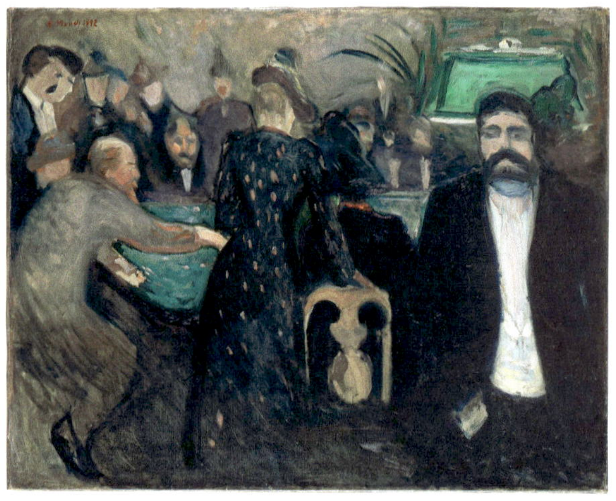

Grandhotel Esplanade in Berlin or at other locations. Works by Munch were auctioned in four of these: the collection of Leo Lewin in Breslau was auctioned on April 12, 1927, and lot number 21, *Grosse Küstenlandschaft* (Large Coastal Landscape) by Munch, was knocked down to the Galerie Thannhauser in Munich. Lewin had purchased the landscape from Cassirer on April 30, 1921.[55]

The painting collection of the Berlin businessman Fritz Hess, which had been previewed in Berlin and Lucerne, went under the hammer on September 1, 1931, with the Auktionshaus Theodor Fischer in Lucerne in cooperation with Paul Cassirer at the Hotel National in Lucerne. The painting with the lot number 26, *Karl-Johann-Strasse in Oslo* (Karl Johan in Oslo), now *Karl Johan in the Rain*, which had been in the collection of Walther Rathenau, was not sold, whereas the lot numbered 27, *Mondschein* (Moonlight), was also purchased by the Galerie Thannhauser.[56] Figure p.214A Carl Sachs, too, who had donated his considerable collection of German graphic art to the Schlesisches Museum (Silesian Museum) in his native city of Breslau, auctioned his graphic works from other countries at Cassirer. The auction was held in cooperation with the Kunsthandlung C.G. Boerner in Leipzig and included forty graphic works by Munch. All but five were sold.

For the eighty-first and hence penultimate auction in which the Kunsthandlung Paul Cassirer was involved, again held in Berlin on October 20, 1932, the actress Tilla Durieux submitted the painting *Spielsalon in Monte Carlo*, now *Spieler in Monte Carlo* (Gamblers in Monte Carlo), with the lot number 67, according to the gallery's protocol catalogue. Figure p.214B Her second marriage had been to Paul Cassirer, and she wedded the factory owner Ludwig Katzenellenbogen in 1930. He and his first wife, Estella, had also assembled an art collection, which was divided up after their divorce, and still today confusion arises about questions of the provenance of the pieces from the two collections.[57]

Finally, two exhibitions that contributed crucially to Munch's international success should not go unmentioned. No correspondence at all between Cassirer and Munch during the war years is known, but on February 21, 1919, the gallerist wrote the artist that he still owed him 7,189.15 marks for the sale of etchings. Shortly thereafter, Cassirer asked Munch for a new opportunity to present an exhibition of his works in Berlin. He wrote that he was still a great admirer of his art, and Berlin would show him a very different "spiritual gratitude" than it had in the past.[58] In April 1921, the final, comprehensive presentation of Munch's works at Paul Cassirer took place. The foreword of the corresponding exhibition catalogue is the text that Walter Leistikow published under the pseudonym Walter Selber in the journal *Freie Bühne* on the occasion of the scandalous exhibition in Berlin in 1892. The show included twenty-four paintings from 1905 to 1917. In addition, ninety graphic exhibits worth 7,289.05 marks were offered for sale.[59] Cassirer wrote to the artist on April 12, 1921, that he had "enthusiastically interested" buyers for the paintings and hoped that the artist would permit him to sell several works and would tell him new prices.[60]

In May of that year, the director of the Kunsthaus Zürich, Wilhelm Wartmann, contacted Paul Cassirer. Ever since the large presentation at Thannhauser in 1912, he had been wanting to have a similar show in Zurich, and now the time for "a very large exhibition" seemed to have arrived finally: "It should not be fewer than around forty paintings; there would be room for more than a hundred."[61] Munch himself made a preliminary selection in the Berlin exhibition, and the following year, on May 18, 1922, the artist's largest show thus far opened, with seventy-five paintings and around 300 etchings, lithographs, and woodcuts at the Kunsthaus Zürich. Wartmann wrote an extensive foreword for the Zurich catalogue in which he described the artist's career to museum visitors and referred to past exhibitions and publications on Munch and listed his collectors. The event was a success with the public, and with the artist's agreement it was even extended and then shown in Bern and Basel.

The final letter to Munch with "Paul Cassirer" on its letterhead was sent by Grete Ring, who had been a partner in the gallery since 1924 and ran the business with Walter Feilchenfeldt after the death of Paul Cassirer on January 7, 1926. On November 27, 1926, she wrote to Munch that she would like to take over the exhibits then being presented at the Kunsthalle Mannheim for a show in Berlin.[62] Munch turned her down, explaining that some of the works in question were not yet finished; moreover, Berlin had "had three large exhibitions in the past six years—while Oslo none—I am thus not ignoring Berlin as Miss Ring writes."[63]

Purchases and sales of Munch's works are also documented in the account books during World War I and up to 1927. The letters in Munchmuseet in Oslo supplement that information and provide a picture of a fruitful, not always simple relationship between artist and art dealer, which Gustav Schiefler summed up in a letter to his wife on October 17, 1931: "As a rule, the art dealer lacks the sensitivity he needs in dealing with artists; in that respect Paul Cassirer was an exception—to a degree!"[64]

(1) Schneede 1994a, p. 14.
(2) See the essay by Sabine Meister in the present catalogue.
(3) Edvard Munch to Karen Bjølstad, November 17, 1892, Munchmuseet, Oslo, MM N 786 (this document and all of the archival materials in Munchmuseet that follow are accessible at emunch.no).
(4) Corinth 1910, p. 48.
(5) Kneher 1994, p. 23.
(6) Kneher 1994, p. 65.
(7) See Matelowski 2017, p. 60: "The Secessionists were supported and promoted by a dense network of art dealers, journalists, and patrons."
(8) Berlin 1902, p. 12.
(9) Ludwig Justi, *Neue Kunst: Ein Führer zu den Gemälden der sogenannten Expressionisten in der Nationalgalerie* (Berlin, 1921), pp. 16–17.
(10) Kneher 1994, p. 151. See also the essay by Janina Nentwig in the present catalogue.
(11) Kneher 1994, p. 154.
(12) Gustav Schiefler, "Tagebuch-Aufzeichnungen bis 1906 über Max Liebermann," entry on July 2, 1906, in Braun 2011–21, vol. 3, "Anhänge," p. 520.
(13) Max Liebermann and Walter Leistikow to Edvard Munch, January 14, 1904, in Braun 2011–21, vol. 9/I, "Nachträge," letter 355, p. 349.
(14) The catalogue raisonné of the paintings by Gerd Woll (Woll 2009) by no means gives the detailed provenance of every work, so it is not always possible to identify each one.
(15) The spelling of the name Cezanne in this essay follows the guidelines of the online catalogue raisonné of the artist's work. It was verified in the notary's office in Aix-en-Provence. The Cezanne family was originally from Italy, see www.cezannecatalogue.com.
(16) Entry in the account books in the Paul Cassirer & Walter Feilchenfeldt Archiv, Zurich.
(17) Entry in the account books in the Paul Cassirer & Walter Feilchenfeldt Archiv, Zurich: *An der Trave in Lübeck* (By the Trave in Lübeck) (purchased from Munch on October 18, 1907, and sold to Glaser on April 20, 1910); *Landschaft* (Landscape) (purchased from Munch on October 18, 1907, and sold to Glaser on January 9, 1910).
(18) Glaser 1917.
(19) Hans Rosenhagen, "Aus den Berliner Kunstsalons," *Die Kunst: Monatshefte für freie und angewandte Kunst* 7, no. 18 (1902–3): p. 265.
(20) Echte and Feilchenfeldt 2011–16 (Quellenstudien zur Kunst 5), pp. 233–56 (p. 232: Edvard Munch, *Self-Portrait*, 1895, Woll 37; p. 235: *Self-Portrait* [ca. 1903], Woll 620, dated 1904).
(21) Curt Glaser, "Munch Ausstellung im Salon Cassirer, Berlin," *Hamburgischer Correspondent,* January 30, 1903, no. 49. Quoted in Echte and Feilchenfeldt 2011–16 (Quellenstudien zur Kunst 5), p. 238.
(22) Oscar Bie, "Hier und dort," *Berliner Börsen-Courier*, no. 41, January 25, 1903, quoted in Echte and Feilchenfeldt 2011–16 (Quellenstudien zur Kunst 5), p. 234: *Portrait of Theodor Linde*, 1902, Woll 214.
(23) Gustav Schiefler, "Tagebuch-Aufzeichnungen bis 1906 über Max Liebermann," entry on February 3, 1903, in Braun 2011–21, vol. 3, "Anhänge," p. 504.
(24) Clarke 2000. Munch's graphic work also varied the motifs of the painting and therefore offered its own perspective on one and the same theme. On the commercial aspect, see pp. 51–52.

(25) Kneher (1994, p. 168) suspects that there were around ninety-two works, of which Bernd Echte was able to identify several based on mentions of specific works in the daily press (Echte and Feilchenfeldt 2011–16 [Quellenstudien zur Kunst 5], p. 256). Unfortunately, the documents of the Hamburg branch of Paul Cassirer are no longer extant.

(26) Max Linde to Edvard Munch, undated letter (early February 1903), Munchmuseet, Oslo, MM K 2762.

(27) Kneher 1994, pp. 170 and 434, n. 61.

(28) Edvard Munch to Ludwig Ravensburg, November 13, 1903, Munchmuseet, Oslo, MM N 2802.

(29) Quoted in Echte and Feilchenfeldt 2011–16 (Quellenstudien zur Kunst 5), pp. 377 and 386.

(30) Quoted in Echte and Feilchenfeldt 2011–16 (Quellenstudien zur Kunst 5), p. 376.

(31) Woll 2009, Woll 556: *Self-Portrait in Hell*, 1903, Woll 522: *Sanatorium*, 1902–3; Woll 552: *Landowner in the Park*, 1903 (the painting's title was apparently changed later).

(32) Echte and Feilchenfeldt 2011–16 (Quellenstudien zur Kunst 5), pp. 237–38.

(33) Works by Edvard Munch, Jacob Alberts, Hans R. Lichtenberger, Oskar Moll, Heinrich Zille, Auguste Renoir, and Albert Lebourg, December 19, 1904, to January 19, 1905. See Echte and Feilchenfeldt 2011–16 (Quellenstudien zur Kunst 5), pp. 601–22.

(34) Albert Kollmann to Edvard Munch, June 11, 1904, Munchmuseet, Oslo, MM K 2648.

(35) Max Liebermann, *Er hat sein Leben für die Kunst geopfert*, quoted in Braun 2011–21, vol. 9/I. 1933, pp. 023–24.

(36) Wilhelm Suhr to Edvard Munch, June 11, 1904, Munchmuseet, Oslo, MM K 3863: "Moreover, I have committed to sell … in the two years (April 1, 1905–1907) paintings for 6,000 marks." Wilhelm Suhr to Edvard Munch, June 11, 1904, Munchmuseet, Oslo, MM K 3863: "According to our contract, a settlement or payment of paintings purchased shall occur only between you and me and not via a third person." See also Munchmuseet, Oslo, MM K 2790. The signature MM K 2790 includes various letters between Linde, Schiefler, and Harry Graf Kessler, as well as a draft contract with Bruno Cassirer.

(37) Following the seven-year waiting period after dividing the business with Bruno Cassirer, Paul Cassirer founded a publishing house and associated printer: the Pan-Presse.

(38) For a summary of various reviews of the exhibition, see Echte and Feilchenfeldt 2011–16 (Quellenstudien zur Kunst 5), pp. 601–22.

(39) Woll 2009, Woll 696: *Harry Graf Kessler*, 1906; Woll 691: *Friedrich Nietzsche*, 1906.

(40) Gustav Schiefler, diary entry, February 15–16, 1907, quoted in Munch and Schiefler 1987 and 1990, no. 290, pp. 225–26, esp. p. 226.

(41) "Kollektionen Paul Cézanne, Curt Herrmann, Henri Matisse, Edvard Munch. 30. September bis 18. Oktober 1907"; see Echte and Feilchenfeldt 2011–16 (Quellenstudien zur Kunst 7), pp. 493–524.

(42) Woll 2009, Woll 684: *Park in Kösen*, 1906.

(43) Paul Cassirer to Edvard Munch, February 22, 1912, Munchmuseet, Oslo, MM K 3403.

(44) Emil Waldmann, *Beiträge zur Kunst des XIX. Jahrhunderts und unserer Zeit* (Düsseldorf, 1913), p. 107: "Impressionism, it is said, has been flogged to death, now it is Expressionism's turn. … The secret, not always recognized father of this movement is Edvard Munch."

(45) Karl Scheffler, "Die letzte Ausstellung der Berliner Sezession," *Kunst und Künstler* 10, no. 12 (1912): p. 205. Gustav Schiefler to Edvard Munch, January 28, 1911, Munchmuseet, Oslo, MM K 3188.

(46) Matelowski 2017, pp. 70–73.

(47) Dr. Richard Reiche to Edvard Munch, January 30, 1912, Munchmuseet, Oslo, MM K 3472. See Cologne 1912, p. 65.

(48) Woll 2009, Woll 399: *Paul Herrmann and Paul Contard*, 1897; Woll 651: *Esche's Children*, 1905, p. 663.

(49) The painting was Curt Glaser's *Street in Åsgårdstrand* (Woll 2009, Woll 486).

(50) Quoted in Echte and Feilchenfeldt 2011–16 (Quellenstudien zur Kunst 10), p. 92.

(51) Albert Kollmann to Edvard Munch, December 4, 1912, Munchmuseet, Oslo, MM K 2709.

(52) Albert Kollmann to Edvard Munch, September 12, 1912, Munchmuseet, Oslo, MM K 2702.

(53) *Edvard Munch, Ernst Barlach: Galerie Alfred Flechtheim, 28. März bis 17. April 1914*, exh. cat. (Düsseldorf, 1914), pp. 3–4.

(54) "Protokoll-Katalog," Paul Cassirer & Walter Feilchenfeldt Archiv, Zurich. In 1919 and in 1921, Alfred Flechtheim again opened galleries in Düsseldorf and Berlin. In 1933, the National Socialist seizure of power forced him into exile, where he died impoverished in 1937.

(55) According to the Cassirer account books, *Small Coastal Landscape* by Munch was acquired by Lewin on June 9, 1931, and not auctioned.

(56) Woll 2009, Woll 240: *Karl Johan in the Rain*, 1891; Woll 302: *Night in Saint Cloud*, 1893.

(57) Woll 2009, Woll 262: *Gamblers in Monte Carlo*, 1892. In the catalogue raisonné, Estella Katzenellenbogen is wrongly listed in the provenance as the painting's owner.

(58) Paul Cassirer to Edvard Munch, August 6, 1919, Munchmuseet, Oslo, MM K 3496.

(59) A copy of the contract is in the Paul Cassirer & Walter Feilchenfeldt Archiv, Zurich.

(60) Paul Cassirer to Edvard Munch, April 12, 1921, Munchmuseet, Oslo, MM K 3502.

(61) Iris Bruderer-Oswald, *Der innere Klang der Kunst: Wilhelm Wartmann und das Kunsthaus Zürich* (Basel, 2023), p. 116.

(62) Grete Ring to Edvard Munch, November 27, 1926, Munchmuseet, Oslo, MM K 3505.

(63) Edvard Munch to Curt Glaser, dated November 1926, Munchmuseet, Oslo, MM K 3434.

(64) Gustav Schiefler to Luise Schiefler, October 17, 1931, Munchmuseet, Oslo, MM K 3434.

Genius of the North

Making the Image of Munch

Lars Toft-Eriksen

In his 1904 overview of modern art, the influential German art critic Julius Meier-Graefe argued that Edvard Munch's artistic temperament attested to a particular Nordic or Northern imagination.[1] Figure p.219 His art was said to lack the refined hallmarks of culture,[2] eschew the dogmas of realistic depiction, and fail to conform to academic conventions. On the contrary, according to Meier-Graefe, his artworks, like those of Paul Gauguin, appeared savage, in the sense that they seemed instinctive and from a world not confined by outer reality. Moreover, at its best, his art could be regarded as hallucinations, as far-seeing symbols of a new world order. It served to reveal psychological states of being, freeing the human mind from rigid rationalism and moralism. Furthermore, Meier-Graefe argued that the artist's work had to be understood as the product of his people and his *Heimat*.[3] In other words, Munch's art was to be seen in the light of a particular Nordic psychological sensibility, as if the twilight of the North had made its people more sensitive to the inner workings of the mind.

As the exhibition at the Berlinische Galerie demonstrates, the German reception of Munch at the turn of the twentieth century marked a change in the notion of the "magic of the North," as Stefan Zweig put it in 1925.[4] The magic was no longer to be found in romantic or realistic depictions of wild

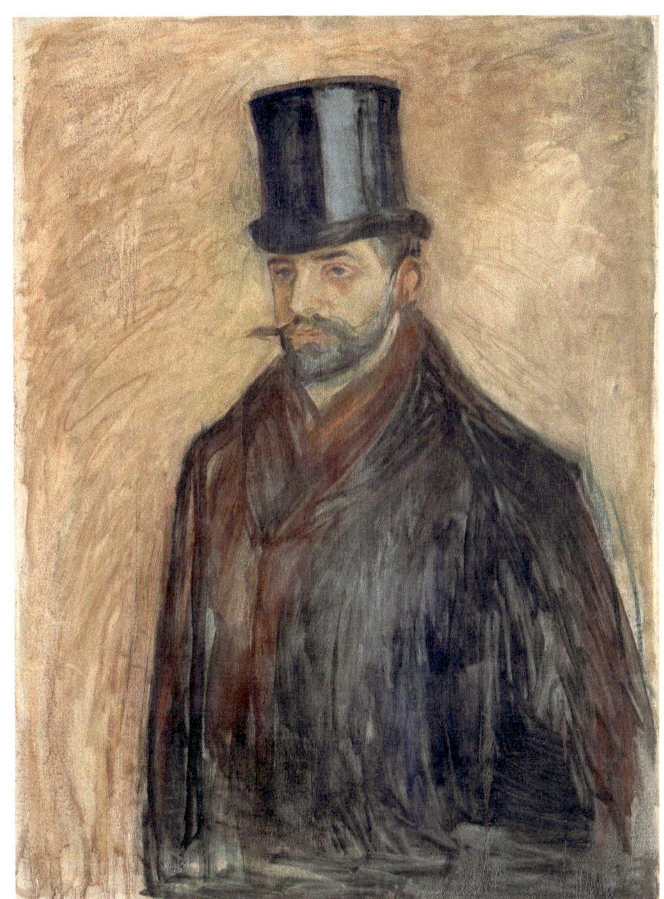

Edvard Munch
Julius Meier-Graefe — ca. 1894
Nasjonalmuseet — Oslo

and untamed nature, but in the psychologically dense work of writers such as Henrik Ibsen, August Strindberg, Georg Brandes, and Knut Hamsun. According to Zweig, these authors were perceived as leading the way into new territories of the soul, and their literary work was seen as primal sources of hitherto unknown psychological problems. Even though Zweig's account addressed authors, it bears significance to the German reception of Edvard Munch, as exemplified by Meier-Graefe above. Going further back, to Meier-Graefe's essay "Edvard Munch," included in his 1895 publication of a portfolio of Munch's prints, it becomes clear that the critic's later characterization of the artist relates to a post-Romantic conception of the artist genius.[5] In this essay Meier-Graefe argues that the artist genius, like an apostle, protests the social conventions of his time; and, like an anarchist, seeks to turn the masses against their oppressor. The critic is, in other words, advocating an avant-garde notion of art, where the artist seeks a new world order through provocation and revolt, although oftentimes being misunderstood by the public he is to lead.

It may be reasonable to understand Meier-Graefe's essay against the backdrop of the public reception of Munch's 1892 exhibition at the Verein Berliner Künstler (Association of Berlin Artists). The exhibition caused a controversy in the German press and consequently provoked a public scandal.[6] Conservative critics perceived Munch's work as ugly, formless, and brutal. The critic of Berlin's newspaper *Freisinnige Zeitung*, however, viewed the criticism of Munch's work in the light of Max Nordau's recently published book *Degeneration* (1892), in which the author condemned modern art as decadent, morally degenerate, and ugly. This critique noted smugly and ironically that: "He [Nordau] fashions his view of a healthy normal artist according to the heart of good philistinism and its much-vaunted, healthy common sense; anything above and beyond that is degeneracy, hysteria, madness."[7] In line with Nordau's reasoning, the Verein Berliner Künstler denounced Munch's art and prematurely closed the exhibition after just a week. Likewise, the critic of the daily

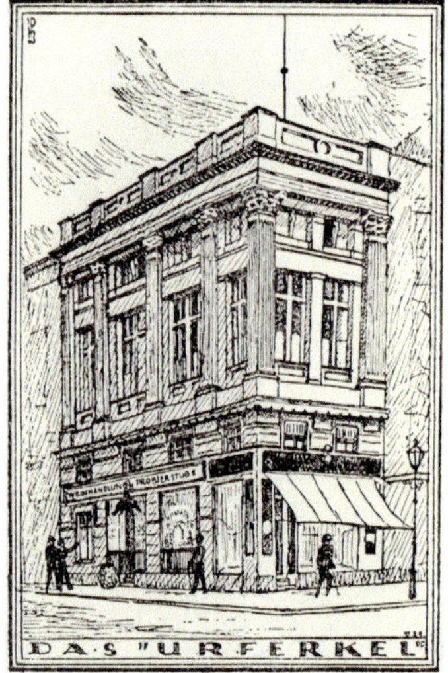

(A)
Adolf Paul
The "Urferkel" and Strindberg's Round Table — 1920
Munchmuseet — Oslo

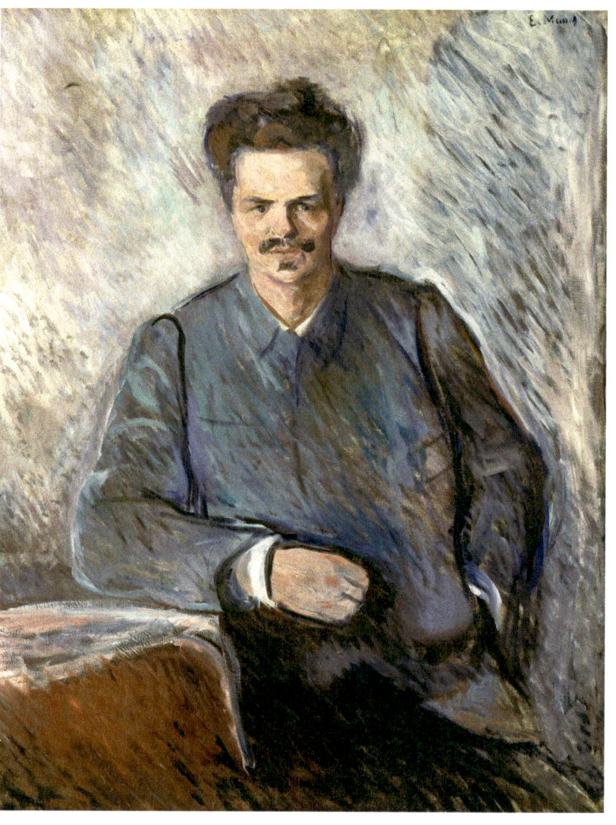

(B)
Edvard Munch
August Strindberg — 1892
Moderna Museet — Stockholm

newspaper *Berliner Börsen-Courier*, on the occasion of Munch's self-planned 1893 show on the boulevard Unter den Linden in Berlin, wondered: "Is that art or is it madness?"[8] Notably, the critics not only applied their rhetoric to the technique and form of Munch's paintings, but also saw this as a consequence of his subject matter and his personality.

Munch himself understood how to capitalize on the ordeal as a *succès de scandale* and how to thereby promote a mythic image of himself as an artist. Art historian Jay Clarke has noted how Munch managed to take advantage of the "Affaire Munch" (Munch Affair) in terms of recognizing the value of provocation and controversy, and also how this could be incorporated into the image of himself as a misunderstood outsider.[9] There is little doubt that Munch blatantly speculated on the effect of provocation. At the height of the controversy, just prior to the closing of his 1892 Berlin show at the Verein Berliner Künstler, Munch noted in a letter to his aunt that nothing could be better in terms of publicity than the show being closed.[10] Munch went on to promptly organize six exhibitions at various locations throughout Germany. With the exhibition and its scandal, a fundamental topos in the legend of Munch became entrenched. The image of Munch as a misunderstood, visionary, and deeply original artist was secured by the juxtaposition of his radical art, the negative critique, and his subsequent success. In other words, the figure or the notion of the artist genius was of essence in the early promotion of Munch in Germany.

Munch as Artist Genius

The notion of the visionary artist genius finds its roots in German Romanticist thinkers like Wilhelm Heinrich Wackenroder and Johann Georg Sulzer. The latter argued that the artist, rather than depicting outer reality, should seek to envision the world of ideas through his imagination in a Platonic sense. However, with the writings of the French Post-Romanticist poet Charles Baudelaire, the notion of the visionary artist genius finds a more distinct modern iteration, preparing the ground for the public perception of artists such as Vincent van Gogh, Paul Gauguin, and Edvard Munch. In *The Painter of Modern Life* (1863), Baudelaire upheld that artistic genius was a matter of unrestrained seeing; that it, in an animalistic and ecstatic mode, illuminated new realties.[11] In an essay on Eugène Delacroix (1861), Baudelaire was more specific in terms of arguing that this extraordinary ability to see related to dreams, understood as visions coming from deep meditation.[12] According to Baudelaire, the artist "... should only paint in accordance with what he sees and what he feels."[13] By "seeing" he was referring not to an objective act of recording nature, but to the subjectivity of the gaze and a certain sense of introspection.

In juxtaposition to a positivist stance, he asserted a doctrine of imagination, claiming that "the 'imaginists' say, 'I want to illuminate things with my mind, and to project their reflection upon other minds.'"[14] For Baudelaire, the source of artistic genius was to be found in creative imagination and the representation of the artist's soul. The imagination of the artist genius was a visionary mental faculty of metaphysical consequence, letting the artist perceive hidden dimensions of the world, compensating for the paucities of positivism. Drawing on Emanuel Swedenborg's mystic theories of universal correspondence between the spiritual and the natural, Baudelaire developed an aesthetic theory of correspondence, where the artist through imagination and introspection would overcome the gap of subject and object. The artist was, by means of his skills, to decipher the visions of his soul through the rearrangement of nature's source material, and thus make the hidden order of nature visible to others.

Prophet of the Soul

Baudelaire's notion of the visionary artist marked a shift from a mimetic and objective representation of reality, but it also signified a new role for the artist as a cultural figure. In *The Vocation of the Artist*, Deborah J. Haynes examines how the notion of the visionary artist was fundamental to the vocational image prescribed to the artist in the nineteenth and twentieth centuries, and how it was closely related to the image of the artist as a prophet or *seer*. With the notion of the avant-garde, epitomized in the poetry of Arthur Rimbaud, the image of the artist as a prophet was to take on a more distinct character. As Haynes argues, with the ideals of inner visions and creative imagination, art became "the language of the lonely man," alienated from society, envisioning new revolutionary realities.[15] This alienated avant-garde figure assumed the role of the creator genius, "... characterized by an emotional hypersensitivity

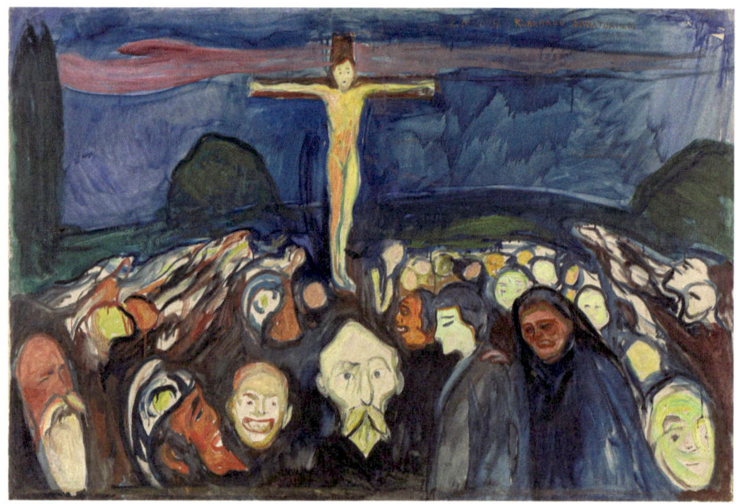

(A)
Edvard Munch
Golgotha — 1900
Munchmuseet — Oslo

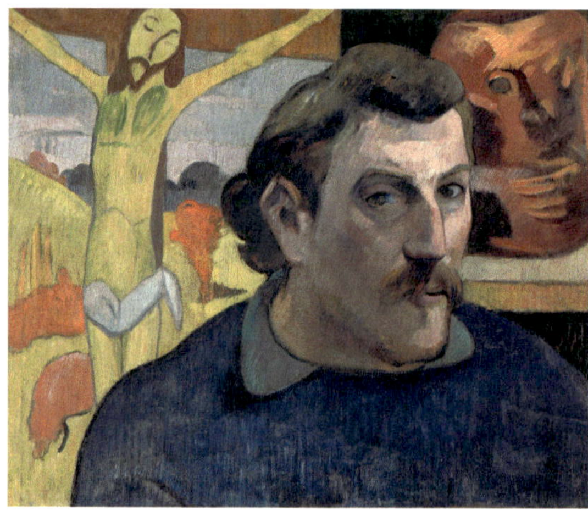

(B)
Paul Gauguin
Self-Portrait with the Yellow Christ — 1890–91
Musée d'Orsay — Paris

that made 'him' superior to others; by a need for withdrawal from society, by a conviction that an artist was destined to suffer ...; and by a special genius that allowed the artist to express all this through creative forms."[16] With the rise of the Symbolist movement in the late 1880s and its visionary credo of changing the world through a disclosure of the inner life of man, the artist was—in line with Baudelaire—to be imagined as an Orphic prophet.[17]

Charles Baudelaire's notion of the visionary artist genius was of importance to an avant-garde and Symbolist circle of writers, poets, artists, and intellectuals in Berlin during the 1890s, oftentimes referred to as a group by the name of Zum schwarzen Ferkel (The Black Piglet). Figure p.220A The Swedish dramatist August Strindberg was a key figure within this circle, to which Edvard Munch belonged. Figures pp.220B + 140 Strindberg moved to Friedrichshagen, on the outskirts of Berlin, in 1890, where he became acquainted with members of the radical group of poets and intellectuals called the Friedrichshagener Dichterkreis (Friedrichshagen Poetry Circle), which included members such as Richard Dehmel, Felix Holländer, Ola Hansson, Dagny Juel, Knut Hamsun, and Stanisław Przybyszewski, but also notabilities such as Rudolf Steiner and Magnus Hirschfeld. After a short while, Strindberg moved to the city and gathered several of his acquaintances from Friedrichshagen at the Zum schwarzen Ferkel wine bar on Unter den Linden. Within these circles, Strindberg took on the task of disseminating new French poetry and aesthetic theory, including the writings of Baudelaire. The Swede had spent considerable time in Paris with its avant-garde circle of artists, where he befriended Paul Gauguin, among others. Baudelaire's notion of the artist as a prophet of the soul was key to the French Symbolist group the Nabis (The Prophets), which were close to Gauguin.

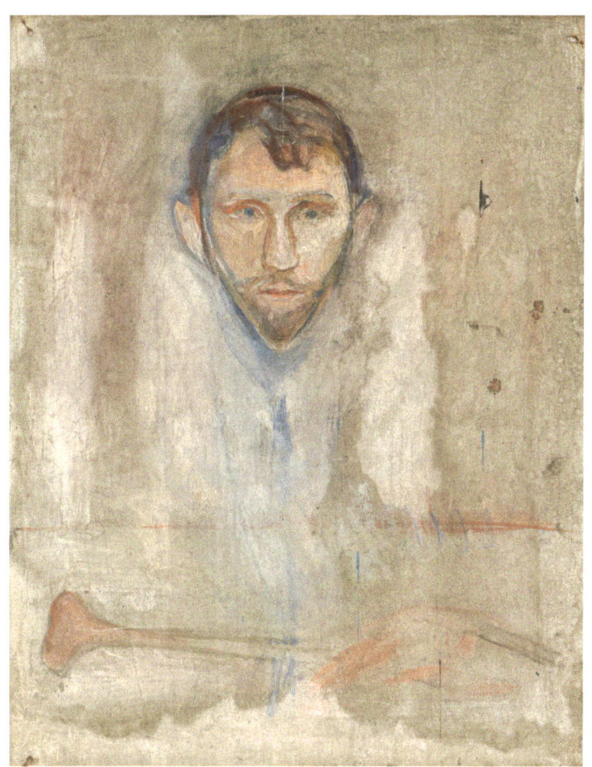

Edvard Munch
Stanisław Przybyszewski — 1894
Munchmuseet — Oslo

The name of the group refers to the Hebrew word *nabhï*. Finding its etymological root in the Greek *prophetes*, the word denotes a "seer" or "one who announces divine messages." In line with the name of the group, the visionary faculties of, for instance, Gauguin were at the heart of the matter when the critic Gabriel-Albert Aurier, in his essay "Symbolism in Painting" ⟨1891⟩, characterized the artist as a creator of life in its essence, thereby alluding to an image of the artist as a divine creator genius.[18] Aurier highlighted Gauguin's visionary faculties as being key to his creativity, characterizing him as an "inspired seer," who by means of his "inner eye" created an absolute ideist art, giving symbolic insight into divinity and the world of ideas.[19] The notion of the artist as a visionary prophet is evident in a number of works by Gauguin, for instance in *Self-Portrait with the Yellow Christ* ⟨1890–91⟩, in which the artist not only juxtaposes himself with Christ, but also paints his own self-portrait as the image of the prophet. Figure p.222B A similar representation of the artist is present in Munch's painting *Golgotha* ⟨1900⟩, where the facial characteristics of Munch are clearly discernible in the face of Christ. Figure p.222A

Aurier's Baudelairean notion of the artist as a visionary of the inner world futhermore finds resonance in Munch's written piece known by the name of the "Saint Cloud Manifesto," which was penned in Paris in 1889–90 and presents his artistic credo: "People would understand the sanctity and power of it and take off their hats as in a church.—I would create a number of such pictures. One shall no longer paint interiors, people reading and women knitting. They will all be people who are alive, who breathe and feel, and suffer and love."[20]

In this passage Munch advocated the depiction of the invisible drama of the psyche, rather than the representation of outer reality. Later on, Munch juxtaposed his credo with an aphorism from his notebooks, dated 1909–11: "The photographic camera cannot compete with the brush and palette—as long as it cannot be used in heaven or hell."[21] The aphorism resonates with the Symbolist image of the artist as a visionary of the soul. Furthermore, the statement may very well be understood in the light of Baudelaire's 1859 essay on photography, in which he claimed that the new technology was of no use to the artist and his quest for introspection.

Psychic Naturalism

Edvard Munch was instrumental in the shaping and promotion of his own public persona.[22] Already by the 1890s he had recognized the significance of his self-image as an artist, and, as noted above, with the precipitate closing of his 1892 exhibition in Berlin he demonstrated an understanding of how to play the media attention of controversy in favor of his artistic project and career. It is evident that Munch worked intensively on his own persona, laying the groundwork for his image. In a survey article on the literature on Munch, the art historian Arne Eggum argues that Munch's self-staging was instrumental to the reception of his work.[23]

The image of Munch promoted by Julius Meier-Graefe may thus be understood against the background of Munch's self-staging within Berlin's artistic scene of the 1890s. Moreover, Meier-Graefe was affiliated with the group Zum schwarzen Ferkel, and one may sense Baudelaire's ideas in his characterization of Munch as an artist. However, the influence of the French poet is far more distinct in the writings of the Polish writer Stanisław Przybyszewski, who befriended Munch in 1892 in Berlin.[24] Figure p.223 In his *Auf den Wegen der Seele* (On the Paths of the Soul, 1897), which among others addresses Munch, Przybyszewski noted how the true artist, as a prophet, had to rise up against the injudicious "plebs [who have] always hated the soul."[25] Lamenting the lack of genius and the pitiful state of culture and arts under the reign of rationalism and naturalism, Przybyszewski claimed that only a few artists—Munch among them—gave promise of a true art envisioning the inner life of the soul: "Once art used to be practised only by God's darlings, by prophets who hid themselves in caves, seeking visions of a liberated soul; by anchorites who led lonely lives in the wilderness. …[T]hose few ones in whom the old tradition of the sacredness of thought and art is alive more than ever before; those few ones who create only at the moments of the most intense flight of the soul, its most painful explosion; new prophets who proclaim the soul's eternal return; mystics endowed with grace who encompass the world not only with their eye or ear, but with a sacred organ of the soul … ."[26] In line with Baudelaire's declaration of a semidivine faculty of imagination, Symbolist writers like Przybyszewski conferred a special status on the artist. By means of his visionary ability to reveal the hidden nature of the world and thus lay the ground for new realities and human redemption, the artist was here too conceptualized as an inspired and creative genius comparable to a prophet.

In the essay "Psychischer Naturalismus" (Psychic Naturalism), Przybyszewski gave a more thorough art-theoretical account of Munch's art. The essay was first published in the Berlin journal *Neue deutsche Rundschau* in 1894, and later that same year it appeared, in a modified version, in a small booklet published under the title *Das Werk des Edvard Munch* (The Work of Edvard Munch).[27] Figure p.225A In the essay, much reminiscent of an avant-garde manifesto, Przybyszewski sought to lay the ground for a new kind of realism, uncovering, so to speak, the unconscious life of man. Recounting a dream literally coming true, Przybyszewski described the revelatory experience of sensing the unconscious, which according to the author was to be equated with seeing one of Munch's artworks: "These impressions of sight and sound lay somewhere deep in another consciousness; they lay there catching hold of other, related impressions, ordering them and combining them into logical sequences until

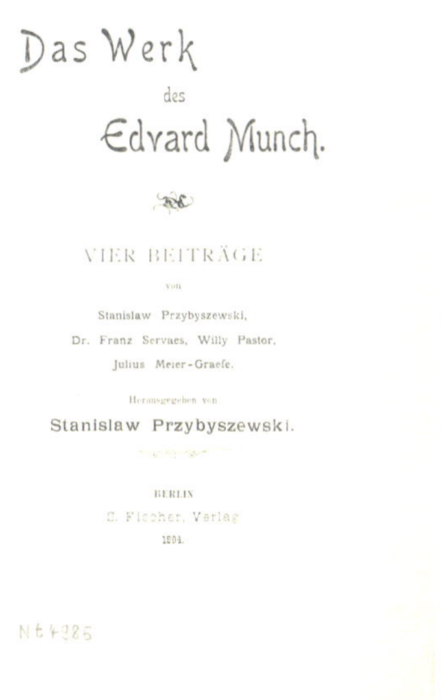

Das Werk
des
Edvard Munch.

VIER BEITRÄGE
von
Stanislaw Przybyszewski,
Dr. Franz Servaes, Willy Pastor,
Julius Meier-Graefe.

Herausgegeben von
Stanislaw Przybyszewski.

BERLIN
S. Fischer, Verlag
1894.

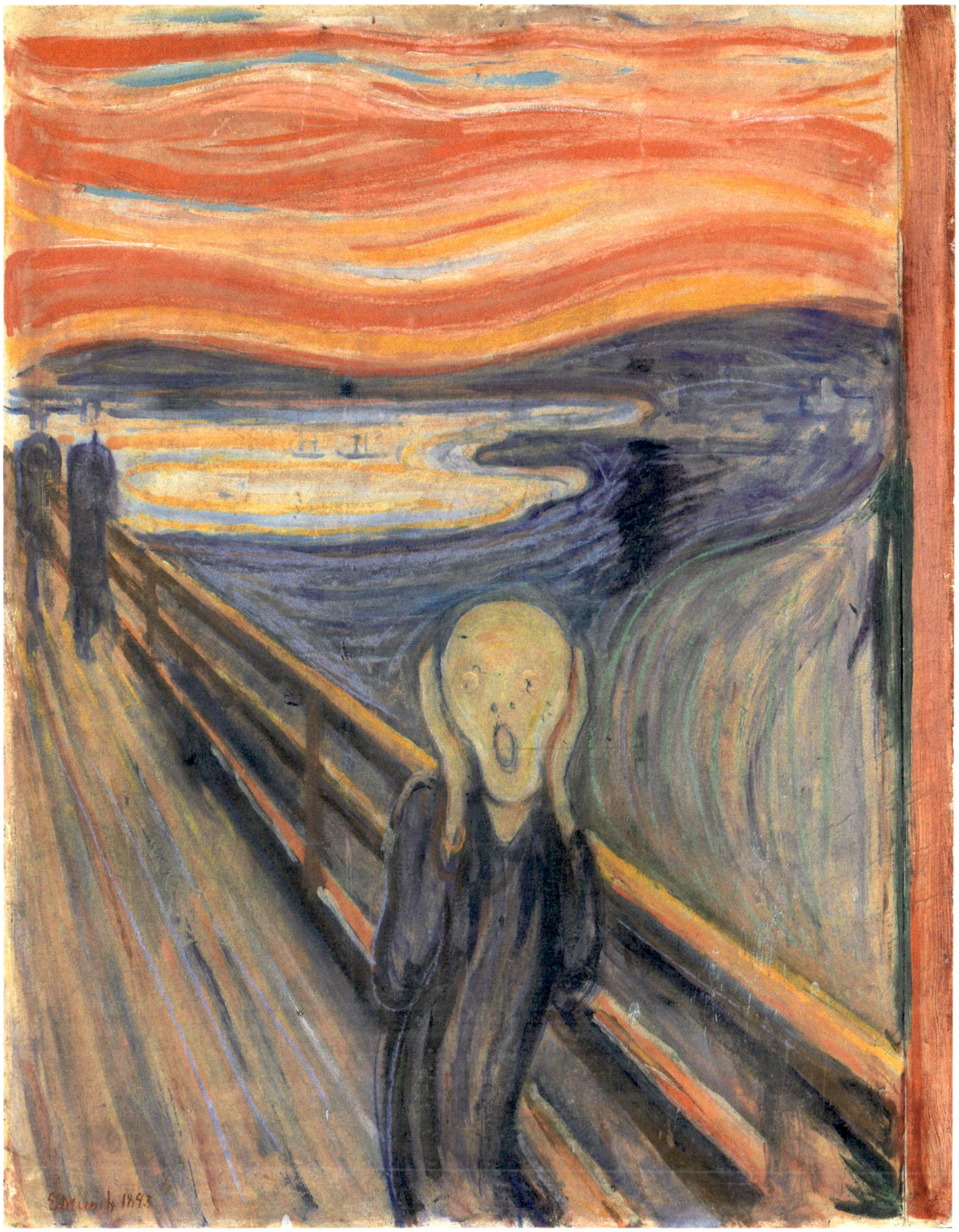

(A)
Stanisław Przybyszewski
The Work of Edvard Munch
1894
Staatsbibliothek zu Berlin,
Preussischer Kulturbesitz

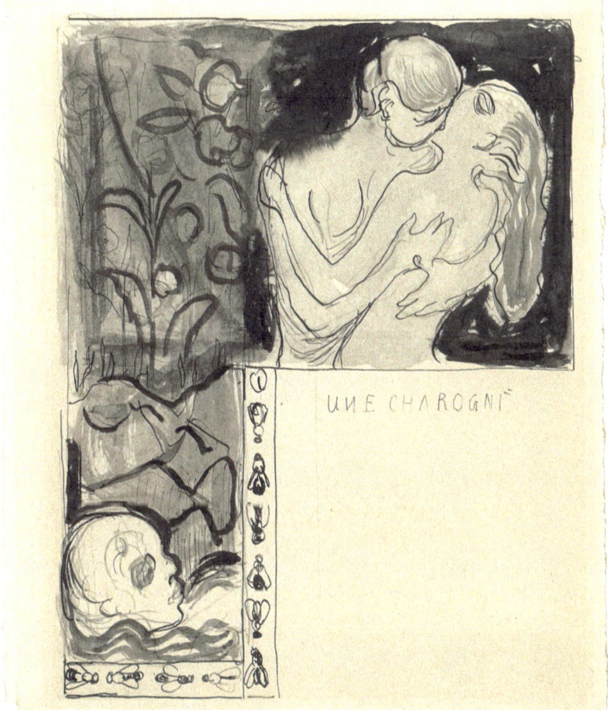

(B)
Edvard Munch
The Scream — 1893
Nasjonalmuseet — Oslo

(C)
Edvard Munch
Une charogne (illustration for
Charles Baudelaire's *Les fleurs du mal*) — 1896
Munchmuseet — Oslo

they suddenly appeared in my personality's consciousness. This manifestation of my individuality, with its ability to see and hear that which my personality cannot perceive, this revelation of a Something within me that is living a life other than the one of which I am aware and that has finer senses than those at my command, this Other within me—it was this that filled me with disquiet."[28]

In these couple of paragraphs, Przybyszewski claimed that the mental experience of a dream coming true in real life afforded him a sudden revelation of the unconscious, of the secrets it holds, and—most importantly—of another dimension within oneself. In a synesthetic line of reasoning, Przybyszewski argued that this experience facilitated a correspondence between the conscious and the unconscious, enabling him to become aware of his own unconscious self. He claimed that this "something" within himself that led a life of its own made him realize that his self held forces and dimensions of which he was not aware. Przybyszewski explicitly stated that he used the terms "individuality" and "personality" to denote the unconscious and the conscious respectively. By doing so, he wanted to avoid the notion of the unconscious being inferior to the conscious, as "the lowest, 'scarcely perceptible,' rung of consciousness."[29] On the contrary, he wished to accentuate the unconscious as an individualizing concept, opening up hitherto unknown dimensions of the mind with the potential to change the self.

Przybyszewski then went on to argue that Munch was the first artist who had ever truly tapped into this realm of the unconscious: "Edvard Munch is the first to have attempted to depict the finest and most subtle movements of the soul exactly as they appear—spontaneously and completely independent of any mental process—in the unalloyed consciousness of the individuality."[30] Analyzing a number of works by Munch, including *The Scream*, Przybyszewski concluded that Munch had broken with all artistic traditions by seeking to depict the unconscious state of humanity in its purest form; that is to say, by means of his extraordinary sensory faculties and his creative powers Munch was able to see and reveal "the innermost depths of the soul."[31] Figure p.225B Przybyszewski thus argued that Munch had laid the ground for a new mode of artistic expression conceptualized under the notion of psychic naturalism. Munch finished *The Scream* in the fall of 1893 and exhibited it, under the title *Verzweiflung*, for the first time in December of the same year in a rented space on Unter den Linden in Berlin.

As Lidia Głuchowska argues in an essay on Munch and Przybyszewski, the latter's concept of psychic naturalism rested on theories developed in his 1892 treatise *Zur Psychologie des Individuums* (On the Psychology of the Individual).[32] In this work, Przybyszewski introduced his theory of the "naked soul," by which he asserted that artistic cognition should take place in an uncontrollable state of irrationality and unconsciousness. By doing so, the artist could reach the realm of the unconscious and reveal this through his art. In his essay on Munch, the author suggests such a reading of the artist's work: "… Munch offers us the pure naked emotions of the individuality. His landscape is the absolute correlate of naked feeling; every quiver of the nerves exposed as the ecstasy of pain reaches its climax [and] is translated into a corresponding colour-sensation."[33] As opposed to earlier artists who had aimed to express emotions, Przybyszewski claimed that Munch, through the correspondence of the unconscious and the conscious, managed to impart the former in a direct and immediate manner. While others resorted to indirect means of expression, Munch was able to convey psychological phenomena immediately: "He paints things as only a naked individuality can see them whose gaze has turned from the world of external phenomena to the life within."[34] In other words, Munch was, in Przybyszewski's eyes, an artist with an extraordinary ability to sense

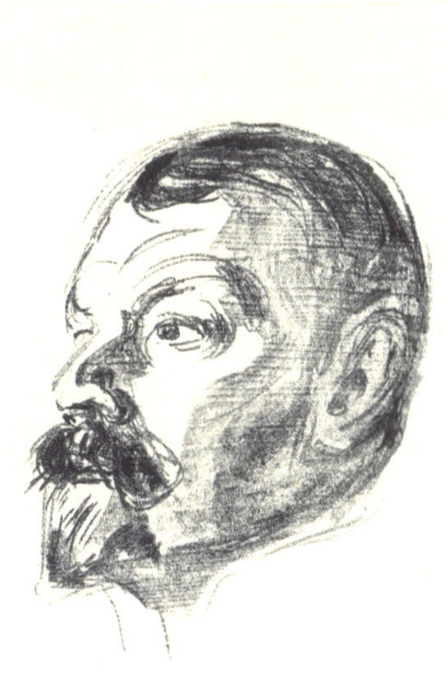

Edvard Munch
Jens Thiis — 1913
Munchmuseet — Oslo

the emotional impulses of the unconscious, lend them expression, and thus bring them to universal significance. According to Przybyszewski, Munch's artworks were to be equated with the revelatory effect of dreams, visions, and clairvoyance.[35] With reference to Baudelaire's 1869 poem "Le Confiteor de l'artiste" (Artist's Confiteor), Przybyszewski then upheld that the "mystical emotional process" of Munch's work was exactly the same as that of Baudelaire's poem: "All these things think through me, or I think through them .... When I say they think, I mean musically, and pictorially, with no quibbles, no 'if thens,' no 'therefores.'"[36] As the quote from Baudelaire's poem suggests, Munch was to be regarded as a prophet of dreams and intoxicated states of mind.

To briefly summarize, by the mid-1890s the image of Munch as a visionary and avant-garde genius paving the royal road to the unconscious, to paraphrase Sigmund Freud, was well established within the avant-garde circles of Berlin. Other than Munch himself, a number of writers belonging to the group Zum schwarzen Ferkel, such as Meier-Graefe and Przybyszewski, contributed substantially to the dissemination of this image. However, as noted at the beginning of this essay, the image of Munch as a visionary and avant-garde artist genius was soon to be assonated with his Nordic background. Meier-Graefe was among the first to make this association, when arguing that Munch's ability to explore the hitherto hidden realms of the mind related to his ethnic background.

Munch: A Nordic Genius?

The Norwegian art historian and director of the National Gallery in Oslo, Jens Thiis, would later expound on Meier-Graefe's promotion of Munch as a Nordic genius. Figure p.227 Munch was, according to Thiis, to be regarded as a visionary artist of great, misunderstood originality, leading the way into the future. Moreover, his art was to be viewed in light of his personality and his life experience, which bore the tokens of genius in terms of agony, alienation, reclusiveness, emotive irrationality, madness, and disease. In the final chapter of Thiis's monumental 1933 monograph on Munch, specifically addressing the artist's genius, he is hailed for his prophetic and redemptive greatness. The author described Munch as a "flickering" and "alien light," leading the way through a world of uncontrollable desires, angst, and annihilation.[37] The rhetoric of national and ethnic superiority features prominently in Thiis's praise of Munch's genius; the source of this was to be found in his pure Norwegian heritage of intellectual and spiritual superiority, which for many generations had managed to stay "... surprisingly free of the infusion of foreign blood."[38] The racially purebred origin of Munch's genius was addressed already in 1908, when Thiis in an essay published in the German journal *Zeitschrift für bildende Kunst* proclaimed that Munch had descended from "a pure blooded Norwegian aristocratic family."[39] Thiis underlined that this purebred lineage of genius had found its cradle in a mountainous region of Norway centuries ago, thereby suggesting a correlation between Munch's genius, his pedigree, and the land. With Thiis's appraisal of Munch's so-called Nordic genius, the image of the visionary artist attained a more ideologically dire hue.

As is well known, the notion of the genius as a prophetic and visionary redeemer with an original capacity to recreate the world was, a few decades later, in 1925, to be evoked when Adolf Hitler in *Mein Kampf* (My Struggle) upheld creative genius to be a fundamentally defining characteristic of the so-called Aryan race. By 1918, the Austrian cultural critic Edgar Zilsel had already cautioned against what, by the early twentieth century, had become a widespread European cult—or religion, as he called it—of genius, fueled by nationalism and modern mass media.[40] Zilsel argued that the notion of genius entailed a personality ideal that in its hero worship could be abused for political purposes. Art historian Patricia Berman has studied how Meier-Graefe and others—in order to introduce a broad scope of international artists to the conservative public of Wilhelmine Germany—strategically applied a rhetoric of Germanic or Nordic national identity in the construction of genealogies of genius.[41] The idea of genius was now paired with ideas of ethnicity and race. This was also the case with Munch's image, in which narratives of national, ethnic, and racial superiority played a key role, as evident in Thiis's 1908 essay. Even though Munch's art in the 1930s was deemed degenerate by the National Socialist government of Germany, the notion of him as a genius of the North remained important to the Nazis' reception of the artist. In line with the Norwegian author Knut Hamsun, Munch was hailed for his Aryan genius. On the occasion of Munch's seventieth birthday, Joseph Goebbels demonstrated this admiration by sending the artist a telegram,[42] praising him as counting among the greatest of all Germanic artists.

Author's Note
This paper is to a large extent founded on: Lars Toft-Eriksen, "Based on a True Story: Rereading Rolf Stenersen's Image of Edvard Munch and the Myth of Genius" (PhD diss., University of Oslo, 2020).

(1) Julius Meier-Graefe, *Entwicklungsgeschichte der modernen Kunst*, vol. 1 (Stuttgart, 1904), pp. 392–94.

(2) Meier-Graefe 1904 (see note 1), p. 393.

(3) Meier-Graefe 1904 (see note 1), p. 394.

(4) Zweig 1925, p. 256.

(5) Julius Meier-Graefe, *Edvard Munch: Acht Radierungen* (Berlin, 1895).

(6) See the essay by Sabine Meister in the present catalogue.

(7) [Leopold Schönhoff], "Kunst und Wissenschaft: Der Bruch innerhalb der Künstlerschaft Berlins," *Freisinnige Zeitung*, no. 268, insert, November 15, 1892, n.p. Quoted in Clarke 2005, p. 188.

(8) Ln [probably Isidor Landau], "Neue Bilder," *Berliner Börsen-Courier*, December 10, 1893; on Landau, see Krisch 1997, p. 40, n. 163.

(9) Clarke 2005, pp. 185–204.

(10) Edvard Munch to Karen Bjølstad, November 12, 1892, Munchmuseet, Oslo, MM N 785 (this document and all of the archival materials in Munchmuseet that follow are accessible at emunch.no).

(11) Charles Baudelaire, "The Painter of Modern Life," in Charles Baudelaire, *The Painter of Modern Life*, trans. P. E. Charvet (London, 2010), p. 11.

(12) Charles Baudelaire, "The Life and Work of Eugène Delacroix," in Baudelaire 2010 (see note 11), p. 63.

(13) Charles Baudelaire, "The Queen of the Faculties," in Baudelaire, *Art in Paris 1845–1862: Salons and Other Exhibitions*, ed. and trans. Jonathan Mayne (Oxford, 1965), p. 155.

(14) Charles Baudelaire, "The Governance of the Imagination," in Baudelaire 1965 (see note 13), p. 162.

(15) Deborah J. Haynes, *The Vocation of the Artist* (Cambridge, 1997), p. 109.

(16) Haynes 1997 (see note 15), p. 110.

(17) For a general discussion of the figure of the visionary artist within Symbolism, see Michelle Facos, *Symbolist Art in Context* (Berkeley, 2009), pp. 30–62. Iris Müller-Westermann has suggested that a number of Munch's self-portraits from the 1890s may be seen in light of the Symbolist idea of the visionary artist. See Müller-Westermann 1996, pp. 79–87.

(18) Gabriel-Albert Aurier, "Le Symbolisme en peinture—Paul Gauguin," *Mercure de France* (March 1891): pp. 155–65, published in English as "Symbolism in Painting: Paul Gauguin," in *Symbolist Art Theories: A Critical Anthology*, ed. Henri Dorra (Berkeley, 1994), pp. 192–203, esp. p. 202.

(19) Aurier 1994 (see note 18), pp. 197–98.

(20) Edvard Munch, *Livsfrisens tilblivelse* (Oslo, 1928), pp. 4–7; Munchmuseet, Oslo, MM UT 13, 1928(?).

(21) Munch 1928 (see note 20), p. 1. "Fotografiapparatet kan ikke konkurrere med pensel og palet—saalenge det ikke kan brukes I helvete og himmelen."

(22) See, among others, Müller-Westermann 2005; Guleng and Ydstie 2008; Clarke 2009.

(23) Arne Eggum, "Litteraturen om Munch gjennom nitti år," *Kunst og Kultur* 4, no. 65 (1982): pp. 270–79.

(24) For discussions of Munch's association with Stanisław Przybyszewski, see Jaworska 1995; Głuchowska 2013, pp. 182–93.

(25) Przybyszewski 1897, p. 13, published in English as Stanisław Przybyszewski, "On the Paths of the Soul" (1897), in Nielsen 2015, p. 59.

(26) Przybyszewski 1897, pp. 16–17, quoted in English from Przybyszewski 1897/2015 (see note 25), pp. 60–61.

(27) Przybyszewski 1894c; Przybyszewski 1894b. For a discussion of Przybyszewski's concept of "psychic naturalism" in relation to Munch's art, see Lathe 1979, pp. 135–46.

(28) Przybyszewski 1894b, p. 12, published in English as Stanisław Przybyszewski, "The Work of Edvard Munch" (1894), in Nielsen 2015, p. 83.

(29) Przybyszewski 1894b, p. 12, quoted in English from Przybyszewski 1894/2015 (see note 28), p. 83.

(30) Przybyszewski 1894b, p. 16, quoted in English from Przybyszewski 1894/2015 (see note 28), p. 85.

(31) Przybyszewski 1894b, p. 16, quoted in English from Przybyszewski 1894/2015 (see note 28), p. 85.

(32) Głuchowska 2013, pp. 182–93.

(33) Przybyszewski 1894b, p. 24, quoted in English from Przybyszewski 1894/2015 (see note 28), p. 89.

(34) Przybyszewski 1894b, p. 25, quoted in English from Przybyszewski 1894/2015 (see note 28), p. 89.

(35) For a discussion of Przybyszewski's notion of the visionary in light of esotericism, see Faxneld 2015, pp. 92–105.

(36) Przybyszewski 2015 (see note 28), pp. 87 and 91, n. 24. See also Przybyszewski 1894b, p. 23. In Przybyszewski's original 1894 German text, Baudelaire is quoted in French. For this English translation of the same passage, see Charles Baudelaire, "Artist's Confiteor," in Charles Baudelaire, *Paris Spleen*, trans. Louise Varèse (New York, 1970), p. 3.

(37) Thiis 1933, p. 323. "… et flakkende … fremmed lys …."

(38) Thiis 1933, p. 3. "… merkelig fri for innblanding av fremmed blod."

(39) Jens Thiis, "Edvard Munch," *Zeitschrift für bildende Kunst,* n.s. 19, no. 6 (1908): pp. 133–43, esp. p. 133. "Edvard Munch, Norwegens größte malerische Begabung, enstammt einem reinblütigen norwegischen Aristokrat geschlecht."

(40) Edgar Zilsel, *Die Geniereligion: Ein kritischer Versuch über das moderne Persönlichkeitsideal, mit einer historischen Begründung*, 2nd ed. (Frankfurt am Main, 2016), orig. pub. Vienna, 1918. For contextual discussions of Zilsel's cultural critique, see Julia Barbara Köhne, "The Cult of Genius in Germany and Austria at the Dawn of the Twentieth Century," in *Genealogies of Genius*, ed. Joyce E. Chaplin and Darrin M. McMahon (New York, 2016), pp. 115–36.

(41) Patricia G. Berman, "The Invention of History: Julius Meier-Graefe, German Modernism and the Genealogy of Genius," in *Imagining Modern German Culture: 1889–1910*, ed. Françoise Forster-Hahn, exh. cat. National Gallery of Art (Washington, DC, 1996), pp. 91–105.

(42) See the essay by Stefanie Heckmann in the present catalogue.

A Norwegian Summer Night

Munch's Frieze for the Kammerspiele of the Deutsches Theater in Berlin

Pauline Behrmann

Chamber Theater of the Deutsches Theater, Berlin, view from the south — 1942
Architekturmuseum, Technische Universität Berlin

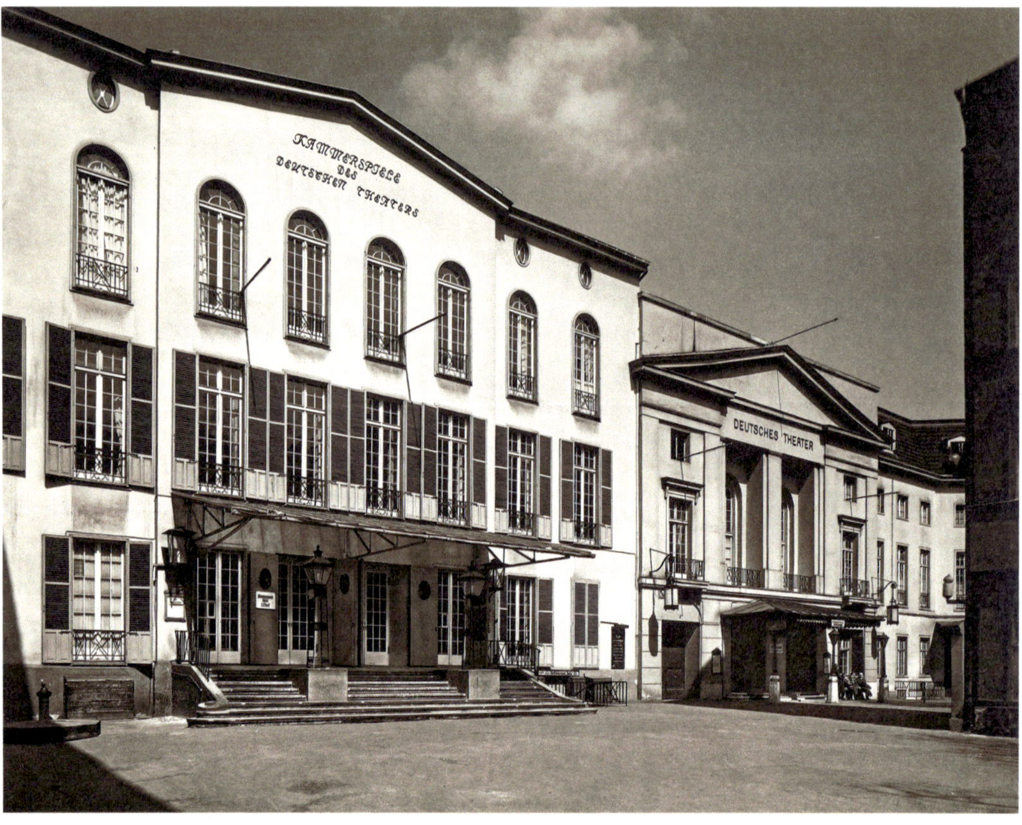

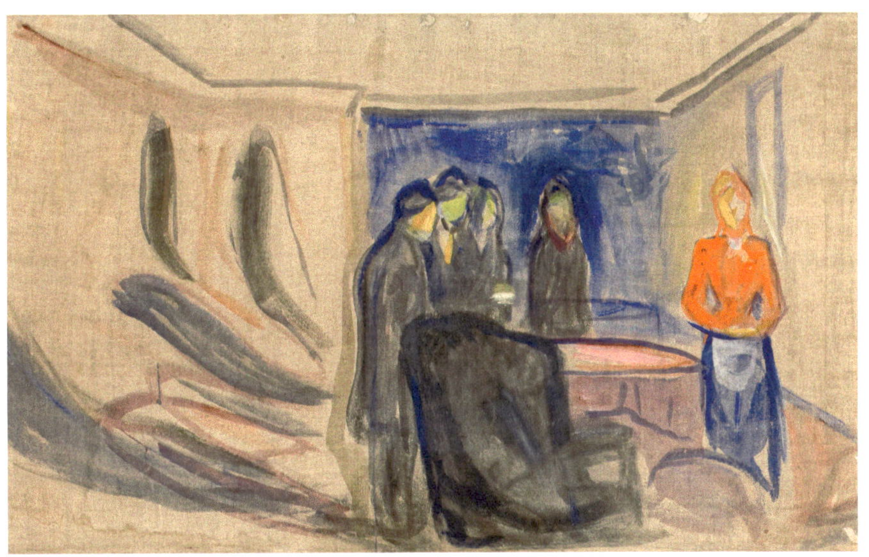

Edvard Munch
Set design for Henrik Ibsen's *Ghosts* — 1906
Munchmuseet — Oslo

"I often think of our work together. Those ... were interesting times, although I was, unfortunately, so very sick," Edvard Munch wrote from Kragerø, Norway, in November 1909 to the theater man Max Reinhardt in Berlin. "I ask you to be so kind as to write me ... about how the frieze is doing. How is it? Have there been changes? Or is everything just as it was?"[1] A few months earlier, the artist had returned to his homeland for the long term, after undergoing a detoxification program in Copenhagen for alcoholism and psychological problems. Now he was asking about the frieze, completed in 1907, for the Kammerspiele of the Deutsches Theater (German Theater), of which Reinhardt was the owner and managing director. Figures pp.86–99 + 238 Munch had always seen designing decorative works for public spaces as a special opportunity.[2] In 1934 he noted: "But can't all new murals be shown as in Renaissance times. The art then becomes the property of the people again—we all own the work of art. A painter's work does not have to disappear like a rag in a home where only a few people see it."[3] Seen against that backdrop, Munch's letter to Reinhardt raises questions: Why did the collaboration between the two end after just two years? And why did the artist worry about the state of the cycle?

An Unusual Cooperation

Munch and Reinhardt probably first met in Berlin around 1900 through a shared contact such as Walther Rathenau or Harry Graf Kessler.[4] When they met again at a reception at the Nietzsche-Archiv in Weimar on February 11, 1906,[5] Reinhardt was in the process of renovating a canteen next to the Deutsches Theater at Schumannstrasse 13a in Berlin. Figure p.230 The opening of the new Kammerspiele (Chamber Theater) was planned for November 8, 1906, with the play *Ghosts: A Family Drama in Three Acts* by Henrik Ibsen, who had died recently. Around the turn of the century, the Norwegian author was celebrated as an important exponent of progressive Scandinavian literature and naturalist theater. Reinhardt had seen *Ghosts* as a young actor, in Vienna, among other places, and had been enthusiastic about Ibsen's work ever since. He had many opportunities to perform onstage himself in this play from 1881, including at the Deutsches Theater, to which he had switched in 1894.[6]

With *Ghosts*, Reinhardt was choosing a play for the dedication of his new venue that had already made history in Berlin theater:[7] Otto Brahm had presented it for the opening of the legendary Freie Bühne, which would

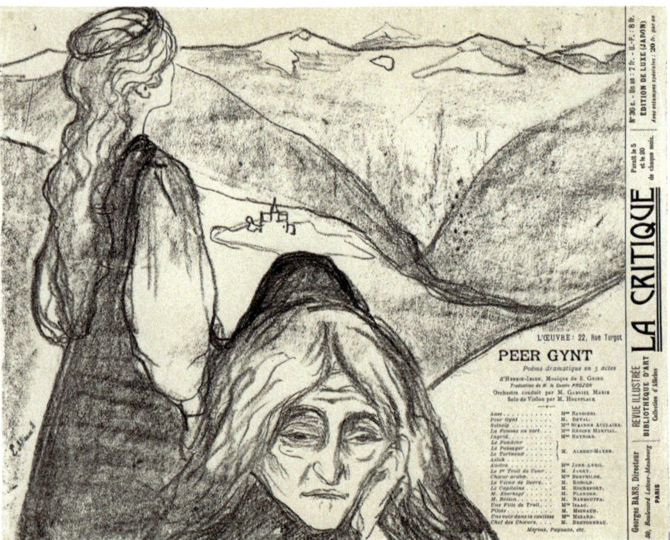

(A)
Edvard Munch
Theater program for Henrik Ibsen's
Peer Gynt — 1896
Munchmuseet — Oslo

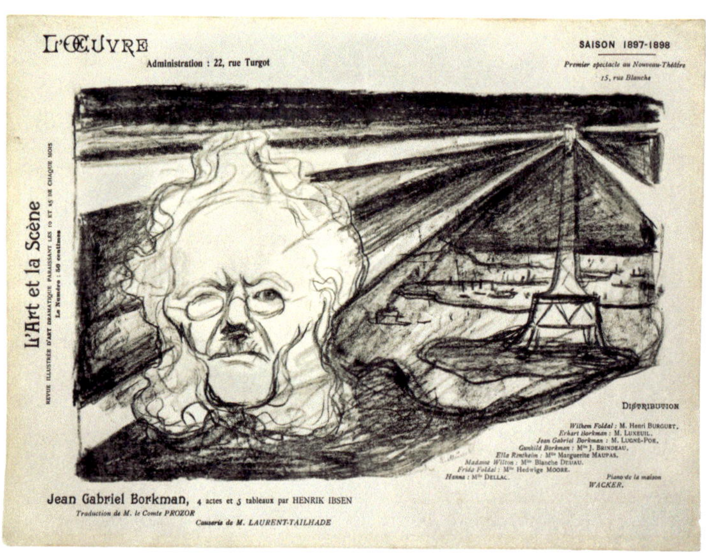

(B)
Edvard Munch
Theater program for Henrik Ibsen's
John Gabriel Borkman — 1897
Munchmuseet — Oslo

be pioneering for modern theater in Germany, and five years later he had introduced his directorship at the Deutsches Theater with it.[8] Reinhardt followed Brahm as managing director and set new directions with his production of *Ghosts*. He was searching for an artist who could convincingly develop the stage set and the atmosphere in the room. He chose Ibsen's compatriot Munch, who not only shared Ibsen's cultural background but was also familiar with his work. The dramatist and the artist thirty-five years his junior had first met in Oslo in 1891, and from that time onward Munch grappled with Ibsen's work again and again. Among other things, he designed the programs for performances of *Peer Gynt* and *John Gabriel Borkman* at the Théâtre de l'Œuvre in Paris in 1896 and 1897.[9] Figures p.232A+B But Munch will have had a particular connection to *Ghost*, since "in no other drama by Ibsen did Munch find his own family's fate of sickness, madness, and death as closely mirrored."[10]

Reinhardt's dramaturge and director Felix Hollaender first asked in person in a meeting in Weimar whether Munch could make sketches of stage sets for *Ghosts*.[11] He repeated the request in a letter he sent to Munch in the early summer of 1906, and at the same time provided details about the task for the Berlin project: "It would now please us greatly if you would decide to draw a sketch for the decoration. ... what we wish is merely to receive a sketch from you that can be transferred to the stage from which we ... could derive inspiration. We believe that no other painter can capture the character of Ibsen's family tragedy than you."[12] It is not known when exactly Munch agreed to create the desired drawings for Reinhardt.[13] Arthur Kahane, Reinhardt's dramaturge, recalled a good twenty years later: "It was difficult to win over the headstrong man; it ultimately succeeded because of an opportunity no artist could resist: letting him decorate a room in the Kammerspiele—the banquet hall on the second floor—however he wished. The result, a magnificent by-product of this *Ghosts* commission, was a series of paintings that later became famous under the name *Reinhardt Frieze*."[14] With his new performance space, Reinhardt was implementing the idea of a small theater with a private character in which the auditorium and stage were pushed close together. It was intended to enable viewers to experience more directly the psychology of the figures on the stage. Reinhardt was taking up the threads of discussion of a so-called intimate theater, which had been widely talked about in the world of theater beginning with pioneers such as August Strindberg.[15] Not least in the Berlin bohemian circle around the wine bar Zum schwarzen Ferkel, to which not only Strindberg but also Munch and the writer Max Dauthendey belonged in the 1890s, the "art of the intimate" was an important theme.[16] *Ghosts* not only initiated the chamber play as a new form of theater, but its premiere was also the beginning of a special form of collaboration: until that time, fine artists had been active at the theater as designers of programs and stage sets. Engaging an artist to provide design ideas and atmospheric impulses was a novelty, as Angela Lampe emphasizes in her essay "Munch and Max Reinhardt's Modern Stage." In the modern dramas of Ibsen and others, interiors were no longer just the "external framework for a person's life" but reflected "the inner life of the modern individual."[17] Reinhardt recognized this connection and emphasized in his instructions to Munch: "The interior in Ibsen has been indescribably neglected and mishandled. I am of the opinion that it accounts for an essential part of the *much* which stands between and behind the words in Ibsen and not only frames but also symbolizes the plot."[18] The director's goal was "to set the mood in the space by means of colour, which he regarded as a fundamental feature of stage design."[19] This was based on Munch's atmospheric "mood sketches,"[20] which were then turned into stage sets by Ernst Stern. Figure p.231

With his new approach, Reinhardt had his finger on the pulse of the time. Whereas the sociocritical art of the naturalists still dominated the art and theater world of Berlin, grappling with the human psyche was becoming increasingly significant. Society had "grown tired of the drabness of naturalism" and of the sociocritical, moralistic repertoires and yearned for an "art of beautiful dreams, of delicate psychological sensations, and of splendid colors."[21] Reinhardt is regarded today as an important innovator of Berlin's theater. With the Kammerspiele he created an innovative performance venue committed to presenting psychologically empathetic plays; he chose above all classics such as *Ghosts* to present on stage the multilayered world of human emotion. In doing so he was seeking a closer interplay of theater, fine art, and literature. His set designer Stern observed of the collaboration with Munch: "In order to live freely, the mimic needs space modulated by form, light, and above all color."[22]

This staging of *Ghosts*, in which Reinhardt once again took on a role himself, was celebrated as a success, as was the stage set based on Munch's sketches.[23] It was only natural that the cooperation should continue. In 1907, Munch created set designs for another Ibsen play: *Hedda Gabler*.[24] In parallel with that, the artist was working on a multipart decorative cycle for the Kammerspiele for which Reinhardt had commissioned him. Because the construction work on the upper story of the Kammerspiele had not been completed, even though the theater was already in operation, a large part of the frieze was painted without Munch really having become familiar with the space for which it was intended, as Roland März points out in his account of the work's genesis.[25]

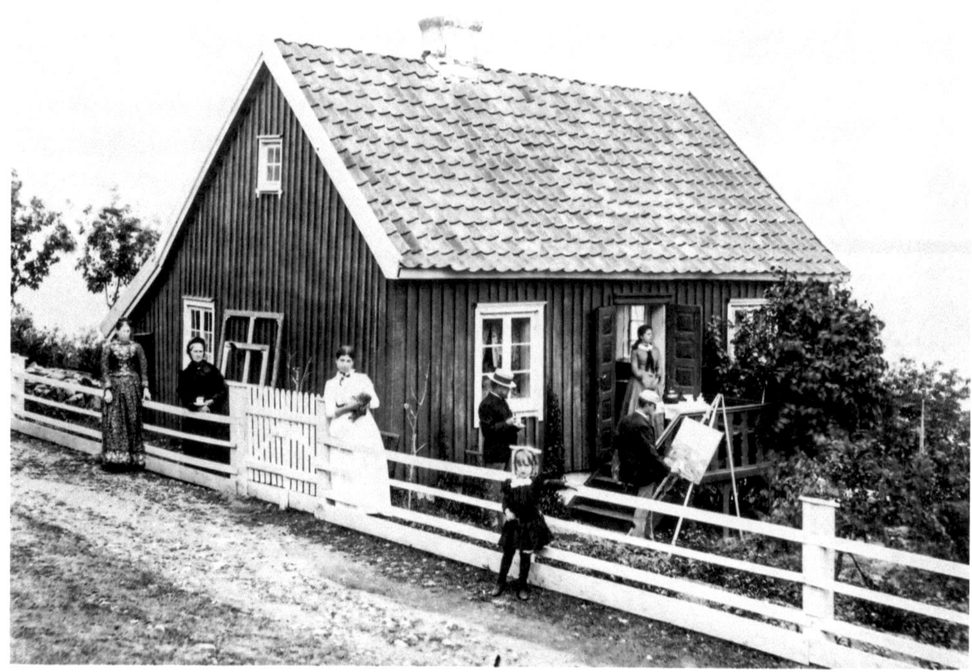

Edvard Munch painting in Åsgårdstrand — 1889
Munchmuseet — Oslo

The Frieze for the Kammerspiele

The *Reinhardt Frieze* was the second large mural decoration that Munch painted for a specific space. After he had created individual works for private premises as a young artist, his patron Max Linde commissioned him in 1904 to paint a series for the children's room in his villa in Lübeck.[26] Designing an entire cycle for a specified place represented a new challenge for the artist. The *Linde Frieze* includes ten oil paintings that were not only identical in height but also connected to one another by the common theme of the seasons and by the "style of decorative lines and planes."[27] Figures pp.74–85 The client wanted above all landscapes, so that the series consists primarily of park and beach scenes. Although Munch tried to conform to Linde's ideas, the commission ended in disappointment for the artist. Linde rejected the frieze, not least because he felt that works such as *Kissing Couples in the Park* were inappropriate for a children's room. Figure p.235 Moreover, Munch was certainly self-critical enough to recognize that his expressive paintings of powerful colors looked like a "bomb" in the Empire-style room, and thus expressed the dissonance between the series and the architecture.[28]

Two years later, while he was working on the designs for *Ghosts*, Munch was given another opportunity to decorate an entire room with a cycle of paintings in the Kammerspiele in Berlin. This project was mentioned for the first time in a letter from Reinhardt's close collaborator Arthur Kahane to Munch in July 1906: "In addition, Director Reinhardt repeats his request that you paint the frieze discussed with him for our new small theater. Would it be possible for you to come to Berlin toward the end of August?"[29] Kahane's phrasing suggests that Munch took his time before agreeing on the frieze. The disappointment and uncertainty about the rejection of the *Linde Frieze* presumably still weighed on him, but he began work already in the summer, even before he had an official contract in his hands.[30] Munch's friend the collector Gustav Schiefler described in his diary in September 1906 a brief visit to Munch in Bad Kösen, Thuringia, where the artist, whose health was suffering, was taking the cure: "He showed me a frieze he had painted for a room in Reinhardt's Kammerspiele in Berlin—an assembly room or foyer. They were scenes from a

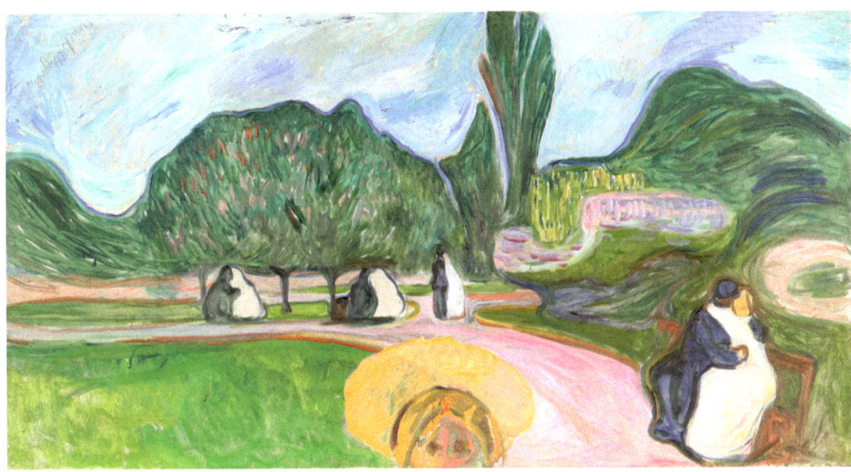

Edvard Munch
Kissing Couples in the Park (The Linde Frieze) — 1904
Munchmuseet — Oslo

kind of summer festival that young girls and men are celebrating together: the girls are standing in groups on the beach; the young men are arriving in boats; they dance and play together, and then the youths depart, and in the last painting a melancholic girl ... is sitting on the seashore, sad."[31] The individual parts of the frieze, which Munch did not bring to Berlin until a year later, were apparently already far along at this point, a few months after Kahane's letter.[32]

Scholars assume that the *Reinhardt Frieze* consisted of twelve canvases in all, nine of which are now in the Neue Nationalgalerie (New National Gallery) in Berlin.[33] Figures pp.86–99 It is not known in which sequence they were hung in the Kammerspiele. Much as he had in Linde's villa, Munch placed the works beneath the ceiling but above the doors, which is in keeping with the traditional position of a frieze—an arrangement that Munch had already tried out at the Berlin Secession in 1902, when he presented his *Frieze of Life* in the sculpture hall there.[34] *The Frieze of Life* is a series of changing pictures revolving around love, anxiety, and death. In the individual scenes of the frieze for the theater in Berlin, which vary between pure landscape motifs and pictorial spaces defined by groups of figures, Munch took up elements of *The Frieze of Life*, including *Dance of Life*, *Summer Night*, *The Kiss*, *The Lonely Ones*, and *Melancholy*. In the *Reinhardt Frieze*, as previously in the series for Linde, Munch concentrated on the motifs of love and left out anxiety and death as themes. Both works are closely connected to *The Frieze of Life*. In retrospect, he also used the title *Frieze of Life* for the wall decoration he created for the Kammerspiele.[35]

In comparison to the two previous cycles, in the *Reinhardt Frieze* Munch emphasized the compositional and narrative context as well as the decorative character of the paintings, which are no longer perceived as individual works but as "sections of a frieze."[36] The twelve canvases are, with three exceptions, horizontal formats of slightly different dimensions. As with the *Linde Frieze*, the pictures have a uniform height of 90 centimeters. In all of the works, the beach represents a kind of stage for the actions that Schiefler outlined in his diary entry and alludes to the area around the spa town Åsgårdstrand, where Munch spent the summer for the first time in 1889 and acquired a small house in 1897.[37] Figure p.234 The shore, the sea, and the horizon are "the three constant compositional levels in all these works."[38] The artist creates a close connection between the scenes by means of the consistent location and the corresponding composition. This impression is reinforced not least by the horizon line that runs through all of the works as a contour of the shore. Rhythmic vertical elements also recur frequently: trees, figures, and reflections of the moon in the water are indicated only summarily and conceived to show their effect when seen from a distance. The figures are made anonymous by their reduced appearance and are more like ciphers than individual characters.[39] They convey emotional expression, but because they are stylized and appear repeatedly, they also lend a decorative impression.[40] As if in a play, they adopt certain roles and present an encounter between young women and men over the course of the series that concludes with the isolated girl on the shore.

The painting technique also contributes to the impression of a self-contained, coherent cycle. Whereas Munch preferred painting in oils on principle, he chose a lime casein tempera for the *Reinhardt Frieze*. Perhaps he had been inspired by works of the artists' group the Nabis in Paris, whose decorative art of the mid-1890s was often executed in tempera paints.[41] The use of thinned tempera paint on unprimed canvas of a coarse structure enabled the artist to produce a uniform, watercolor-like timbre in the individual scenes, while at the same time drawing parallels to mural painting. This impression results from the interplay of raw canvas and the paint, which is absorbed by the support and thus resembles a fresco, in which the pigments bond with the still wet plaster. Using the tempera technique, Munch achieves a muted coloration and fluid forms that support the uniform overall tones of the cycle.

The Location of the *Reinhardt Frieze:* A Salon on the Upper Floor

As previously with the *Linde Frieze*, which did not harmonize with the intended room, Munch was also initially dissatisfied with the existing architecture for his Kammerspiele cycle. In the winter of 1906 he wrote to his friend the art historian Jens Thiis, who was the director of the museum in Trondheim at the time: "I have taken on a project right now that is making me despair.—I am painting a frieze for the Kammerspiele; decorating a certain place with something is unusual and difficult for me—and almost impossible when the theater is as small as it is here—and decorated in a fine Biedermeier style. Biedermeier and me!!"[42] Not only the "Biedermeier style" presented a challenge; so did the fact that Munch only received more detailed information about the location planned for his painting in the first half of 1907. In late February, the theater invited the artist to meet with the architect William Müller, who was responsible for the conversion, in order to "express his view about the room where the frieze was to be installed."[43] In May 1907, Munch finally received an elevation of the wall for the relevant "Salon on the upper floor" with the announcement that he could soon begin with the "frieze works" there.[44] But not until November did Munch inform his patron Schiefler with relief: "My frieze is finished and, I believe, successful."[45]

No photographs of the hall or its frieze in its original form exist. Many of the construction files were destroyed or lost during World War II, including the elevation of the wall mentioned in the correspondence. Scholars have long assumed that the frieze was hanging in a bean-shaped hall on the upper floor of the Kammerspiele. This conclusion is based on a plan of the ground floor published in 1912, which shows what is still today called the Bohnensaal (Bean Room).[46] Figure p.237B It has, however, not been proven that the upper floor had the same floor plan. The assumption that the frieze was also in an oval hall must therefore be questioned critically, as Nikolaus Bernau convincingly demonstrated in 2005.[47] Munch left behind no clues in his notes and letters that could offer information about the room's layout. There is a watercolor drawing from 1906–7 that illustrates a possible sequence of the frieze and hence is connected to the integration of the cycle in the theater. Figure p.237A However, because not all scenes in the sketch can be ascribed to the *Reinhardt Frieze*, the study

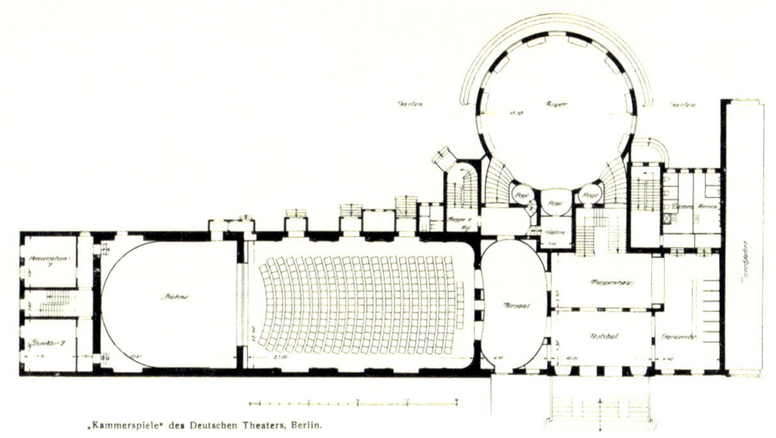

(A)
Edvard Munch
Designs for a frieze — 1906–7
Munchmuseet — Oslo

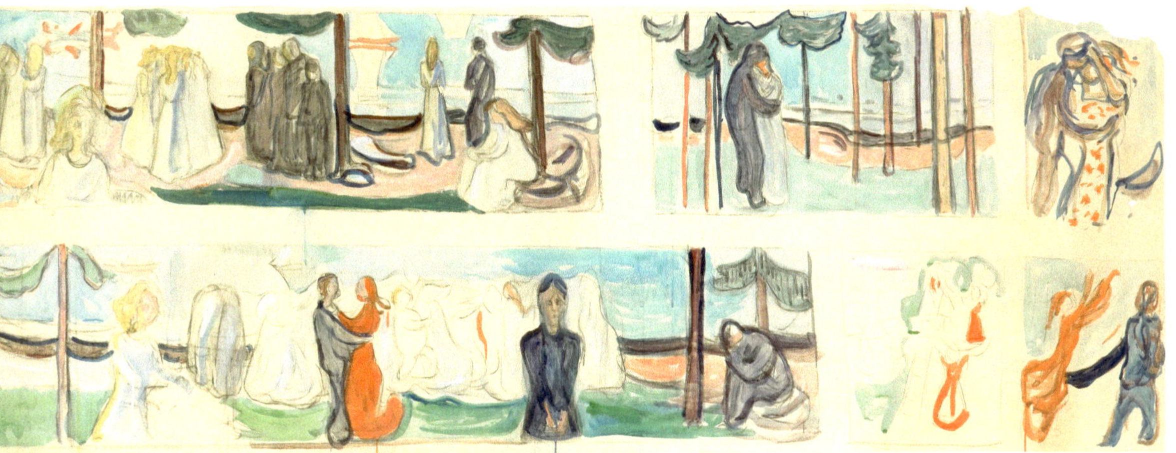

(B)
William Müller
Chamber Theater of the Deutsches Theater, Berlin, plan of the ground floor
[1906]

is not so much proof of a specific sequence for the frieze but rather evidence of how Munch assembled and arranged series of paintings.[48] Moreover, the drawing provides no hints about the interior architecture intended to surround the cycle. All we have today that can provide reference points are descriptions from Munch's milieu. The lack of interest in the architecture of the room in the known reports by his contemporaries suggests, according to Bernau, that it must have been a rather simply designed room without elaborate decor.[49]

Nikolaus Bernau also points to an undated plan that shows the state of the Kammerspiele prior to the conversion of 1912.[50] Because it is labeled a "floor plan ... for a heating project," scholars did not initially identify it as a plan of the upper story.[51] It shows a room on the upper floor, with a rectangular plan and two windows, that provides access to the loges in the back. Bernau suspects this is where Munch's frieze was presented. This thesis is in keeping with a description by the artist, who wrote to his aunt Karen Bjølstad in December 1907 that he had painted the frieze for a "main hall" and the paintings led "around all four walls."[52] This description does not suggest a bean-shaped floor plan. Bernau cites as another argument a statement by Curt Glaser in which, if the room had had a special form, he presumably would have mentioned it. Glaser wrote in his Munch monograph of 1917: "Max Reinhardt ... provided the artist with a hall in the newly opened Kammerspiele building. And here Munch created a new and final variation on his great work. The hall had originally been intended as a foyer. For practical reasons, however, it proved to be unsuited to that purpose. So it remained closed off and inaccessible. The work ... was condemned to a hidden existence."[53] The room was indeed rarely used, usually "only once a year when the large carnival celebration took place in the Kammerspiele."[54] A relative of

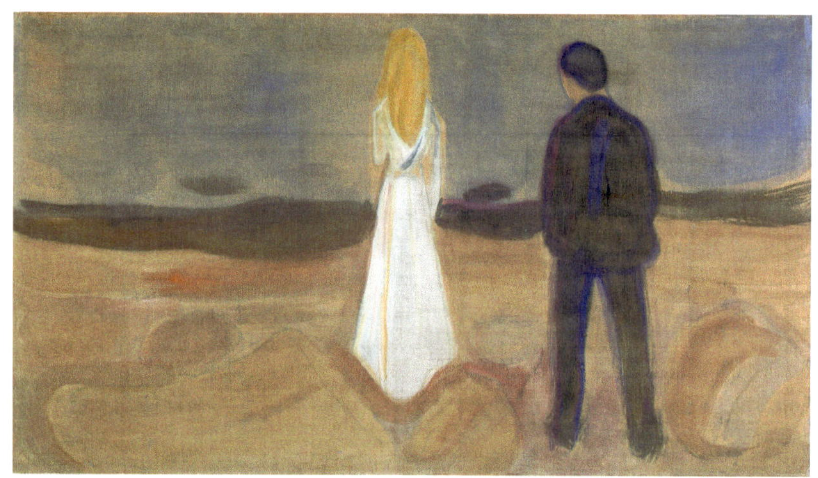

(A)
Edvard Munch
Two Human Beings. The Lonely Ones (The Reinhardt Frieze) — 1906–7
Museum Folkwang — Essen

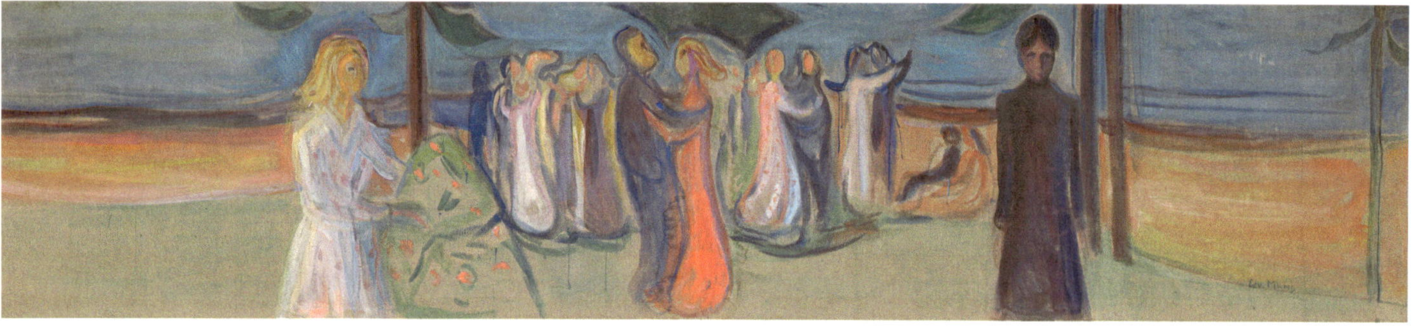

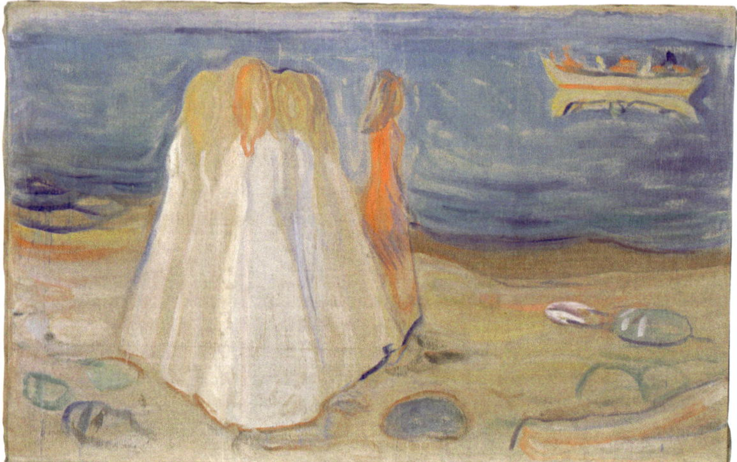

(B)
Edvard Munch
Dance on the Beach (The Reinhardt Frieze) — 1906–7
Private collection

(C)
Edvard Munch
Young Women on the Beach (The Reinhardt Frieze) — 1906–7
Hamburger Kunsthalle — Hamburg

Glaser, the art dealer Hugo Perls confirms that the frieze was only rarely visible to a larger audience: "But the hall was open only once a year, and that was during carnival. The dancing couples could have seen the paintings, perhaps, if they had not been directly under the five-meter-high ceiling."[55] Since the cycle was scarcely seen in the Kammerspiele, it is unsurprising that Munch expressed concern about the state of the frieze in the letter to Reinhardt in 1909 cited at the beginning of this essay, and only a few contemporaneous sources are known that document the work and its effect.[56]

Between Wall Decoration and Series

For Munch, the opportunity to decorate a room with his frieze had been a decisive reason for accepting Reinhardt's commission for *Ghosts* in 1906. Although Munch first used the title *Frieze of Life* publicly in 1918, he had been working with the idea of the cycle for several decades. This engagement was so profound that the concept of the frieze can be seen as the guiding idea behind Munch's entire oeuvre.[57] Munch was part of a movement dedicated to the "reinvention of decorative painting for both public and private commissioners."[58] Not least the Nabis, whose circle Munch met personally in Paris, worked with decorative art and emphasized instead of the isolated work the larger ensemble of paintings: "panneaux décoratifs."[59] They understood "decorative" to mean a "structure that was supposed to connect not only the elements to one another but also beyond the frame to the surrounding space."[60] This was achieved above all by means of a clearly articulated composition, repeating motifs, and connecting lines, of the sort Munch also used in his frieze. By commissioning works, Reinhardt offered artists the opportunity to unfold their visions in public spaces and at the same time drew inspiration from the artistic movements of his time.[61] Munch and Reinhardt had in common that they understood the idea of the "art of the soul"[62] as a rejection of the conservatism of their time. They were open to European influences and strove for an art focusing on the psyche of the individual. The "purely human," revealed in a "profound and refined art of the soul," was an important aspect for this generation of progressive artists.[63]

Connecting to his concept of *The Frieze of Life*, which he interpreted "as an architectural element as well as a painting series,"[64] Munch was trying to find a form for the *Reinhardt Frieze* in which painting and architecture forge a close connection.[65] What Munch called the "Biedermeier style" of the theater and the fact that he worked on the frieze for more than a year without knowing the specific room in detail both suggest, however, that he conceived the cycle more as a self-contained, freestanding series and less as a wall decoration for a very specific location. To connect the individual paintings, he employed artistic means that the Nabis had already used for their murals, but he was able to integrate his concept for the design into the room in the Kammerspiele only to a limited extent. Nor was his wish to have his frieze accessible to the public over the long term satisfied: after being largely hidden for five years, the cycle was removed during a renovation in the Kammerspiele in 1912 and broken up. After all the paintings were seen together once more at the Galerie Gurlitt in Berlin in 1914, they were sold to various collectors, including Glaser.[66] The frieze's original coherent form seems irretrievably lost today. In addition to the nine works in the Neue Nationalgalerie in Berlin, there is one painting each in the Hamburger Kunsthalle in Hamburg and the Museum Folkwang in Essen. Figures p.238C + A A final part of the frieze, which had been in Glaser's possession until 1933, when he auctioned it under pressure from persecution by the National Socialists for his Jewish origins, was long held in a private collection in Oslo. It was auctioned on March 1, 2023, at Sotheby's in London.[67] Figure p.238B

The completion of the *Reinhardt Frieze* was also the end of Munch's work in the theater. When Schiefler asked him in 1914 whether he could produce decorations for a Strindberg play at the Thalia-Schauspielhaus in Hamburg, he rejected the offer.[68] The "work for the Kammerspiele was both the highpoint and the endpoint of his involvement with stage dramas,"[69] but the artist continued to make uncommissioned graphic works on plays by Ibsen, and did so well into his late work.[70] At the Deutsches Theater, Munch was remembered as a progressive artist because of his frieze. Anna Elisabeth Weirauch, a member of Reinhardt's ensemble, observed nearly six decades later: "We actors ... grew up with Munch's frieze, ... and learned to understand—and love—it. And so we were opened not only to Edvard Munch but to art then modern in general."[71]

Author's Note
This essay was written as part of the author's research internship and was heavily revised during the process of editing the German original.

(1) Edvard Munch to Max Reinhardt, November 16, 1909, Munchmuseet, Oslo, MM N 3454 (this document and all of the archival materials in Munchmuseet that follow are accessible at emunch.no).

(2) On Munch's commissions for decorations and their reception, see Berman 2013.

(3) Edvard Munch, note, 1934, Munchmuseet, Oslo, MM N 79, p. 3.

(4) März 1998, p. 9.

(5) Volker Wahl, *Jena als Kunststadt: Begegnungen mit der modernen Kunst in der thüringischen Universitätsstadt zwischen 1900 und 1933* (Leipzig, 1988), p. 93.

(6) Wolgast 2011, pp. 12–13.

(7) On the importance of the play *Ghosts* in Berlin around the turn of the century, see Norbert Jaron, Renate Möhrmann, and Hedwig Müller, eds., *Berlin: Theater der Jahrhundertwende; Bühnengeschichte der Reichshauptstadt im Spiegel der Kritik, 1889–1914* (Tübingen, 1986), pp. 5–6, 44, 67–68, and 75–83; on the history of the Deutsches Theater, see Alexander Weigel, *Das Deutsche Theater: Eine Geschichte in Bildern* (Berlin, 1999), and Michael Kuschnia, ed., *100 Jahre Deutsches Theater Berlin, 1883–1983* (Berlin, 1983).

(8) Wolgast 2011, p. 12.

(9) Lathe 1983, pp. 192–95; on Munch and Ibsen, see also Zurich 1976.

(10) März 1998, p. 10. For a detailed account of the commission for *Ghosts*, see Wolgast 2011; on the parallels between Munch's own biography and the play, see Wolgast 2011, pp. 25–26.

(11) The chronology of the collaboration of Munch and Reinhardt can only be sketched approximately because most of the sources are undated. The meeting between Munch and Hollaender must have taken place during the first half of 1906. Hollaender refers to it in an undated letter, which Wolgast persuasively dates to the early summer of 1906, after Ibsen's death on May 23. See Felix Hollaender to Edvard Munch, undated letter, Munchmuseet, Oslo, MM K 5157, and Wolgast 2011, p. 22, n. 20.

(12) Felix Hollaender to Edvard Munch, undated letter (see note 11).

(13) Wolgast 2011, p. 23. Munch declared his readiness to make sketches for the set design of *Ghosts* by early July at the latest, as is clear from Arthur Kahane to Edvard Munch, July 11, 1906 (Munchmuseet, Oslo, MM K 5150).

(14) Arthur Kahane, "Edvard Munch," *Berliner Tageblatt*, no. 509, October 28, 1926, first supplement, p. [5].

(15) See, in detail, Marianne Streisand, *Intimität: Begriffsgeschichte und Entdeckung der Intimität auf dem Theater um 1900* (Munich, 2001), esp. on Reinhardt, pp. 300–28. The first "intimate theater" in Germany that was expressly called such was organized by Max Halbe in 1895 in a private apartment in Munich; see ibid., pp. 271–88.

(16) Max Dauthendey published his book *Die Kunst des Intimen* in 1893, in which he cites Munch's work as an example of an intimate, modern "art of the soul"; see Lampe 2012, p. 113.

(17) Lampe 2012, p. 116.

(18) Max Reinhardt to Edvard Munch, notes for the interior of *Ghosts*, undated, Munchmuseet, Oslo, MM K 5159.

(19) Lampe 2012, p. 115.

(20) The term *Stimmungsskizzen* (mood sketches) was used by Reinhardt and his team for the designs they solicited from Munch, for example, in Reinhardt's notes on the play (see note 18). They were not to be too detailed, in order to leave some room for the director's own ideas and those of all involved. It was a working method intended to encourage a creative dialogue between the arts. See Wolgast 2011, pp. 23–25.

(21) Jaron, Möhrmann, and Müller 1986 (see note 7), pp. 611 and 66.

(22) Ernst Stern, *Bühnenbildner bei Max Reinhardt* (Berlin [GDR], 1955), p. 39. See also Jaron, Möhrmann, and Müller 1986 (see note 7), p. 68.

(23) Jaron, Möhrmann, and Müller 1986 (see note 7), pp. 609–18; Lampe 2012, p. 110.

(24) Munch received the official commission for this in January 1907; see Arthur Kahane to Edvard Munch, January 28, 1907, Munchmuseet, Oslo, MM K 5152.

(25) März 1998, pp. 14–16. März outlines the complicated contract negotiations for the frieze, which dragged on until the turn of the year 1906–7.

(26) For details, see Eggum 1982.

(27) Kvech-Hoppe 2001, p. 102.

(28) Edvard Munch to Ludvig Ravensberg, December 9, 1904, Munchmuseet, Oslo, MM N 2819, p. 3. See also Eggum 1982, p. 34.

(29) Arthur Kahane to Edvard Munch, July 11, 1906, Munchmuseet, Oslo, MM K 5150.

(30) März 1998, pp. 14–16.

(31) Gustav Schiefler, diary entry of September 7, 1906, quoted in Munch and Schiefler 1987 and 1990, p. 1:192, no. 235.

(32) Edvard Munch to Helge and Ragnhild Bäckström, August 16, 1907, Munchmuseet, Oslo, MM N 3327. The artist had apparently originally assumed that he would be hanging the works in the theater in October 1906; see Edvard Munch, draft letter to an unknown recipient, September 27, 1906, Munchmuseet, Oslo, MM N 2573.

(33) See the catalogue raisonné of Munch's paintings: Woll 2009, Woll 725–36. There are numerous paintings now regarded as studies, for example, Woll 712–24. Munch himself reported to Schiefler in September 1907 that he had painted the freeze "twice"; Munch and Schiefler 1987 and 1990, p. 1:255, no. 344. The first attempt to reconstruct the *Reinhardt Frieze* was for the exhibition *Edvard Munch: Der Lebensfries*, presented at the Nationalgalerie in Berlin from February 24 to April 16, 1978. See Krieger 1978, pp. 32–63, but it was based on the wrong floor plan of its location (see note 46).

(34) Kvech-Hoppe 2001, p. 103. On Munch's *Frieze of Life* in the Berlin Secession in 1902, see the essay by Janina Nentwig in the present catalogue.

(35) Edvard Munch, Notebook, 1931–32, Munchmuseet, Oslo, MM T 2703, p. [12].

(36) For a detailed account, see Kvech-Hoppe 2001, p. 103.

(37) Krieger 1978, p. 54.

(38) Kvech-Hoppe 2001, p. 103.

(39) Munch depicted figures in block-like groups already in his sketches for *Ghosts* and took up this form again in the frieze. The abstract depiction of figures was also due to the frieze's position under the ceiling.

(40) Kvech-Hoppe 2001, p. 103.

(41) Krieger 1978, p. 32; Kvech-Hoppe 2001, p. 103.

(42) Edvard Munch to Jens Thiis, undated letter, 1906, Munchmuseet, Oslo, MM N 2054.

(43) Efraim Frisch to Edvard Munch, February 28, 1907, Munchmuseet, Oslo, MM K 5149.

(44) Fritz Sohm to Edvard Munch, May 13, 1907, Munchmuseet, Oslo, MM K 5151.

(45) Edvard Munch to Gustav Schiefler, November 8, 1907, quoted in Munch and Schiefler 1987 and 1990 , p. 1:262, no. 357.

(46) See Krieger 1978, p. 42, which is cited by many authors as the source for this assumption. The plan of the ground floor is from Emil Högg, "William Müller und sein Werk," *Der Baumeister* 5, no. 2 (1912): pp. 121–32, esp. p. 128. According to Krieger's caption, the room on the upper floor, where the *Reinhardt Frieze* was hung, was "identical in form and size" to the bean-shaped room on the ground floor; Krieger 1978, p. 33.

(47) Bernau 2005, pp. 72–74.

(48) Krieger 1978, p. 63.

(49) Bernau 2005, p. 74.

(50) Bernau 2005, p. 72.

(51) Bernau 2005, p. 72.

(52) Edvard Munch to Karen Bjølstad, December 26, 1907, Munchmuseet, Oslo, MM N 932. Krieger mistakenly identifies Jens Thiis as the recipient of this letter. This incorrect attribution has been frequently adopted in later scholarship by, among others, März (1998, p. 17).

(53) Glaser 1917, p. 8.

(54) Glaser 1917, p. 8.

(55) Hugo Perls, *Warum ist Kamilla schön? Von Kunst, Künstlern und Kunsthandel* (Munich, 1962), p. 18.

(56) Kneher 1994, p. 259.

(57) Krieger 1978, p. 32.

(58) Berman 2013, p. 163.

(59) Krieger 1978, p. 31; Kvech-Hoppe 2001, pp. 95–102.

(60) Krieger 1978, p. 31.

(61) Berman 2013, p. 165.

(62) "What I am imagining is a kind of chamber music of the theater. ... One really needs two stages next to each other: a large one for the classics and a smaller, intimate one for the chamber art of the modern writer. ... because in many cases it will be necessary to perform modern writers as classics and certain classic works with the whole intimacy of the modern art of the soul." Max Reinhardt in conversation with Arthur Kahane, 1901, quoted in Arthur Kahane, "Begegnungen: Max Reinhardt," in Kahane, *Tagebuch des Dramaturgen* (Berlin, 1927), https://www.projekt-gutenberg.org/kahane/dramatur/chap014.html.

(63) Max Reinhardt in conversation with Arthur Kahane, 1901 (see note 62).

(64) Berman 2013, p. 163.

(65) Berman 2013, p. 164.

(66) On the provenance and exhibition history of the individual paintings, see Woll 2009, Woll 725–36. Glaser owned three parts of the *Reinhardt Frieze* (Woll 730, 735, 736). He donated two of the paintings to the Nationalgalerie. See the essay by Dieter Scholz in the present catalogue.

(67) See https://www.sothebys.com/en/buy/auction/2023/modern-contemporary-evening-auction/dans-paa-stranden-reinhardt-frisen- dance-on-the-2. The profit of 16.9 million pounds sterling from the auction was divided between the previous owners and the heirs of the Glaser family; see https://www.dailymail.co.uk/news/article-11811525/Edvard-Munch-painting-hidden-Nazis-barn-Scream-sells-auction-nearly-17m.html.

(68) Lampe 2012, p. 110.

(69) Lampe 2012, p. 110.

(70) The catalogue raisonné of Munch's graphic oeuvre lists for 1930 works for *John Gabriel Borkman* (Woll 714) and the play *The Pretenders* from 1864 (Woll 721–22), among others. The collection of Munchmuseet also has several late drawings connected to Ibsen's works, for example, MM.T.02056 and MM.T.01625.

(71) Anna Elisabeth Weirauch to Horst Behrend, October 3, 1966, quoted in Krieger 1978, p. 42. Weirauch recalled that the actors saw the frieze almost daily. Perhaps the room was used for rehearsals. It was, however, accessible to the public only during carnival festivities.

Exceeding All Expectations

The Large Munch Retrospective at the Nationalgalerie in Berlin in 1927

Dieter Scholz

The press celebrated as a sensation the large Edvard Munch retrospective shown at the Kronprinzenpalais, the former palace of the crown prince, of the Nationalgalerie (National Gallery) in Berlin from March 12 to May 15, 1927.[1] Thirty-five years after his controversial first appearance in the German capital, when his paintings had triggered a storm of outrage in 1892 while shown at the Verein Berliner Künstler (Association of Berlin Artists), the Norwegian painter had reached the status of a classic of modern art. He was now believed to have paved the way for Expressionism, and his work was praised to the skies.

The Choice of Berlin

Ludwig Justi, the director of the Nationalgalerie on Berlin's Museumsinsel (Museum Island), had encountered Munch's painting in 1896, when he was still a student, and had appreciated it ever since.[2] When he took over as head of the Nationalgalerie in 1909, however, Justi's freedom was decidedly limited for a long time, because the German Emperor William II had the final word on acquisitions for the collection. Only after the emperor abdicated in late 1918 could Justi acquire and exhibit modern works of art. That also freed up the

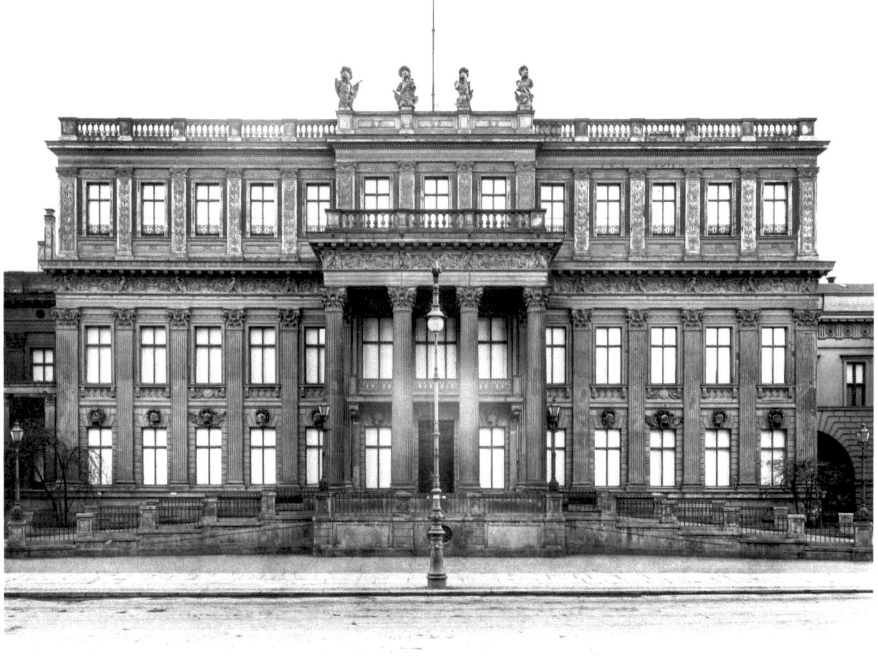

Kronprinzenpalais, Berlin — 1927
Staatliche Museen zu Berlin
Zentralarchiv

Kronprinzenpalais on the stately boulevard Unter den Linden, which was used from August 1919 as the "Modern Department of the Nationalgalerie" to supplement the Nationalgalerie's original building on the Museumsinsel. Figure p.243 It was expressly dedicated to contemporary art as a "Gallery of the Living," as Justi expressed it.[3] In his *Führer zu den Gemälden der sogenannten Expressionisten in der National-Galerie* (Guide to the Paintings by the So-Called Expressionists in the National Gallery), published in 1921, Justi discussed Edvard Munch alongside Vincent van Gogh and Ferdinand Hodler as the most important inspiration for the new stylistic movement. However, at the same time he confessed: "The National-Galerie does not own a single painting by Munch, Hodler, Van Gogh; previously, acquisitions and even gifts [of their works] were not permitted; today, our funds are no longer adequate. Nevertheless, there will at least be temporary and changing exhibitions of their art thanks to loans."[4]

When Justi wrote this, two Munch paintings on loan could be seen in the Kronprinzenpalais together with works by Erich Heckel, Ernst Ludwig Kirchner, and Wilhelm Lehmbruck.[5] The situation was entirely different in the Kupferstichkabinett (Museum of Prints and Drawings), which was located on the third floor of the Neues Museum (New Museum) on the Museumsinsel. Because it had been less the focus of the emperor's attention, graphic works by Munch had been acquired for the first time already in 1903. Its holdings grew enormously when Curt Glaser was in charge of the modern department of the Kupferstichkabinett from 1909 to 1924. Glaser had then become the director of the Staatliche Kunstbibliothek (State Art Library), which collected architectural and ornamental prints, fashion illustrations, photography, posters, and commercial graphic art. Together with his wife, Elsa, the daughter of a wealthy factory owner, he also assembled an important private collection.

In late 1912, Glaser came into direct contact with Munch, who portrayed the couple the following year when they were visiting Norway.[6] Figure p.244A In 1917, Glaser published the first German-language monograph on the artist's work.[7] It was therefore only logical that Justi should turn to Glaser when he wished to organize an exhibition in Berlin, after the Städtische Kunsthalle Mannheim had presented the largest Munch exhibition in years in late 1926, including loans from the Glaser collection. Justi's desire was communicated to the artist by Glaser on December 28, 1926: "Dear Mr. Munch! Justi was in

(A)
Edvard Munch
Curt and Elsa Glaser — 1913
National Gallery of Art,
Epstein Family Collection — Washington, DC

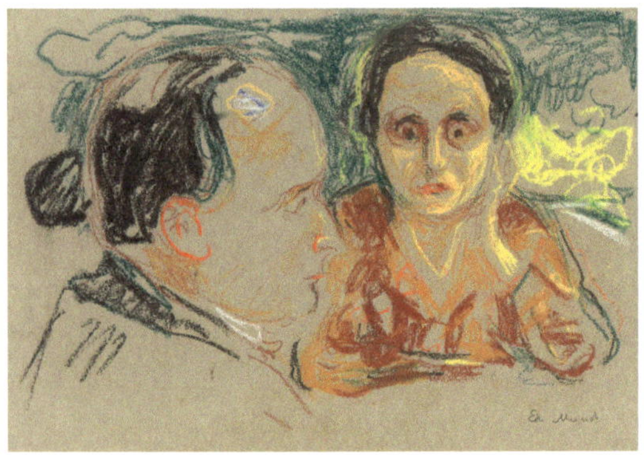

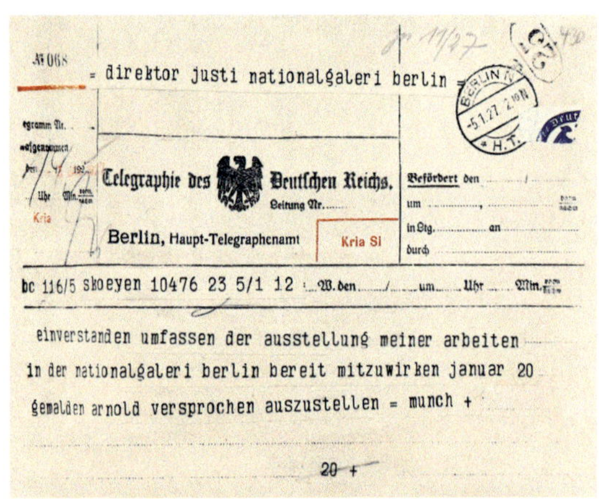
direktor justi nationalgaleri berlin

Telegraphie des Deutschen Reichs.
Berlin, Haupt-Telegraphenamt

bc 116/5 skoeyen 10476 23 5/1 12

einverstanden umfassen der ausstellung meiner arbeiten in der nationalgaleri berlin bereit mitzuwirken januar 20 gemalden arnold versprochen auszustellen = munch +

20 +

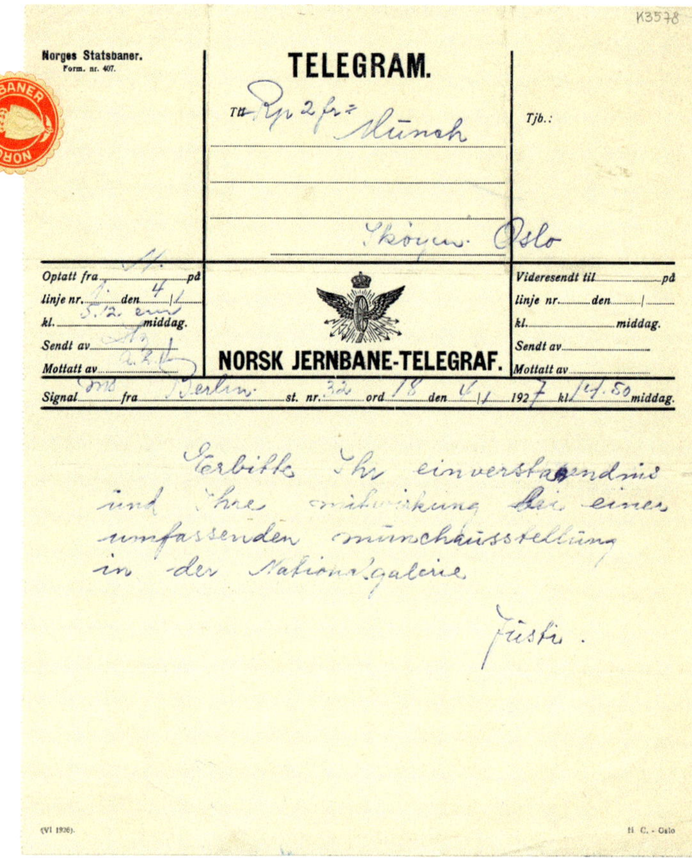
Norges Statsbaner.
Form. nr. 407.

TELEGRAM.

Prof. Munch
Skøyen Oslo

NORSK JERNBANE-TELEGRAF.

Signal ... fra Berlin ... 1927 kl 14.50 middag.

Erbitte Ihr einverständnis und Ihre mitwirkung bei einer umfassenden munchausstellung in der Nationalgalerie

Justi.

(B)
Telegram from Ludwig Justi
to Edvard Munch — January 4, 1927
Munchmuseet — Oslo

(C)
Telegram from Edvard Munch
to Ludwig Justi — January 5, 1927
Staatliche Museen zu Berlin, Zentralarchiv

Mannheim and wrote me from there to say he would very much like to do an exhibition at the Kronprinzenpalais. But he would like a larger exhibition, the works in Mannheim from private collections and also more from you and perhaps also from museums, Oslo, Bergen etc. Ideally already in the second half of January. Gutbier would then have to wait. I am writing this to you only briefly at first in order to hear what you have to say about the plan. If you consider it feasible, the necessary work would have to be begun immediately. Sincerely yours, with best wishes for the new year, C. Glaser."[8]

One month earlier, it had still appeared that Munch's more recent works would travel from Mannheim to the Kunsthandlung Paul Cassirer in Berlin, as his partner Grete Ring had campaigned for that and found an advocate in Glaser.[9] Munch, however, had wanted to give priority to the Galerie Ernst Arnold in Dresden, run by the art dealer Ludwig Wilhelm Gutbier. But the prospect of having a museum presentation in the German capital, rather than an exhibition in a gallery in Saxony, was so tempting that the artist postponed the show in Dresden without hesitation.[10] Justi telegraphed him his official request on January 4, 1927.[11] The reply came two days later, also by telegram. Figures p.244B+C Munch agreed to an extensive exhibition of his works at the Nationalgalerie in Berlin, indicating that he was prepared to assist, even though he had promised to exhibit twenty paintings at the Galerie Arnold in January.[12] The Berliners immediately got in contact with Dresden, and two days later Glaser was already able to report that the problem had been solved and to announce that he would visit the artist together with Justi.[13]

The Preparation for the Exhibition

The two colleagues from the Staatliche Museen zu Berlin (National Museums in Berlin) arrived in Oslo on January 12, 1927, where they had Munch show them current and older works; and they also discussed the concept and selection for the retrospective in Berlin. Shortly before it opened, Glaser published an atmospherically dense text about that visit to Munch in the journal *Kunst und Künstler* in early March 1927: "I was in Oslo for a few days, and Munch said that he would bring out for me a number of his best recent works from the various dungeons in which they were being held. He spoke of an outdoor exhibition. When I came back out to meet him, a magnificent surprise awaited me. The day was bright with snow, and on the exterior walls of the buildings in the large garden stood, next to and above one another, highly colorful paintings that looked like they could not drink up enough light, unfolding their full magic for the first time here outdoors, in the full, radiant brightness. Warm colors of the richness of summer in the middle of the cold winter snow! It was an unforgettable impression. As we walked slowly from one painting to the other, snow began to fall, and gradually the colorful splendor vanished beneath the white blanket that clung to the surface in a thick layer. Munch trudged around with a straw broom, sweeping off now one painting then another, so it could be seen. I was a little concerned that the snow could damage the pictures. But Munch said: 'No, no, they are used to it.' Then they were stored away again, one after the other, in the buildings, and the most beautiful Munch exhibition I have ever seen was over."[14]

Glaser's report suggests that his encounter with the artist had been just the two of them, but there is also a text by Justi that describes the same event, also in the first person: "Munch then showed me paintings, all painted by him, but outside of his home. He lent me tall rubber boots that reached above the knee. For the viewing we stomped through deep snow to several buildings at various distances from his residence, not comfortably heated glasshouses but enormous roofless wooden sheds, under high snow; the paintings were standing in them, some had fallen over and were lying facing downward in the snow. Munch said: 'That's fine because this way I can see how much my paints can withstand.' The paintings were not stacked in front of one another in order to display them singly but each one was standing alone so that one could see all of them by looking around."[15]

Both texts convey the impression of an exclusive meeting with the respective author, although Glaser and Justi had visited Munch together. That had its reason: even if they maintained the outward appearance of professionalism, the relationship between the two colleagues was rather tense. While working as a director, Glaser also published as an art critic, and when, in this capacity, he had mockingly described Justi's Nationalgalerie as an "old ladies' gallery" in late 1918[16]—which later led to the withdrawal of a private collection of Biedermeier portraits—he had lastingly disgruntled Justi.[17] In his view, Glaser and Karl Scheffler, the editor of *Kunst und Künstler*, belonged to the "Liebermann clique hostile to me," to whom the Ministry of Culture listened more than to him.[18] As the president of the Preussische Akademie der Künste (Prussian Academy of Arts), Max Liebermann did indeed have a strong influence on cultural policy and rejected Expressionism.[19] In his book *Berliner Museumskrieg* (Berlin Museum War), Scheffler had in turn explicitly called for

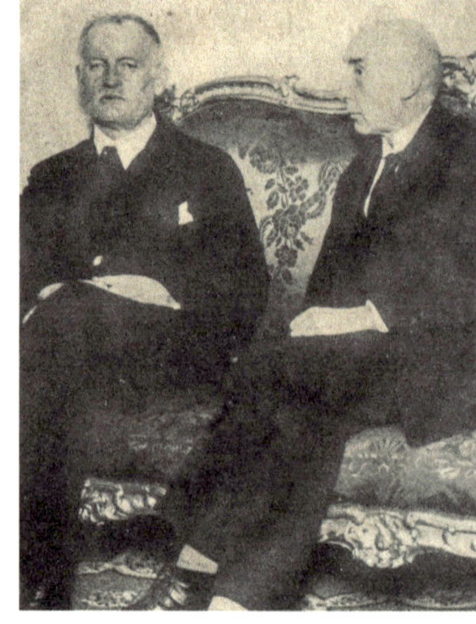

Edvard Munch and Ludwig Justi in Oslo — 1927
Staatsbibliothek zu Berlin, Preussischer Kulturbesitz

Justi to be removed from his post.[20] Glaser and Justi were, however, allied in their enthusiasm for Munch's work and continued to cooperate. A photograph was taken during their visit to the artist's home that shows Munch and Justi together.[21] Figure p.246 On their return journey, the two German museum people stopped in Copenhagen on January 15 to ask the museum there for a loan as well, and Glaser sent a postcard to Munch thanking him for "the beautiful exhibition in the snow."[22]

In order to organize transportation and arrange additional loans, Justi's research associate Ludwig Thormaehlen left Berlin for Oslo on January 28. He also stopped in Copenhagen, where he noticed the photograph of Munch and Justi in the *Bilder-Courier*, the magazine supplement to the daily newspaper *Berliner Börsen-Courier*, as he wrote in one of his messages to the library manager of the Kronprinzenpalais, Clara Schneider: "Director Justi's presence here was in the newspaper."[23] Thormaehlen stayed in Oslo from January 31 to February 17, living with his friend the art historian Henrik Grevenor and his wife, the ballet dancer and choreographer Inga Jacobi. His local activities were not without complications,[24] and the artist also created difficulties for him, for example, concerning permission to reproduce specific motifs for selected art journals: "He is terribly capricious, calling me up an hour after I had squeezed a telegram out of him granting permission, in order to then rescind it. In general, he calls every three hours, day and night. The Grävenors [*sic*] now refer to the telephone as Munch. But he is in a great mood. I can't talk him out of coming to Berlin; I can only postpone the date and claim we needed ten days to test the hanging. ... Emphasized that he would not, of course, meddle with the exhibition. He speaks enthusiastically every day about the splendid way that Corinth was shown off in his day (in contrast to Munich and Dresden) and hopes that we will do the same with his things. Consequently, he would prefer the Nationalgalerie. But I persuade him that the K.P. [Kronprinzenpalais] gets three times as many visitors and has much better light, and he believes me."[25]

Lovis Corinth had been honored in 1923, on the occasion of his sixty-fifth birthday, with an anniversary exhibition at the Kronprinzenpalais, the "Gallery of the Living," but after he died in 1925, Justi programmatically organized a memorial exhibition in the Nationalgalerie on the Museumsinsel opposite it.[26] While the Impressionism of the deceased artist had now found its place in the museum, Justi's concept was to show Munch in the Kronprinzenpalais as a forerunner of Expressionism. On February 24, 1927, the Berlin press reported that preparations for the Munch exhibition had begun,[27] and a week later an opening date was communicated for the first time.[28] The artist came to Berlin during the installation, and Justi reported in retrospect: "Munch was

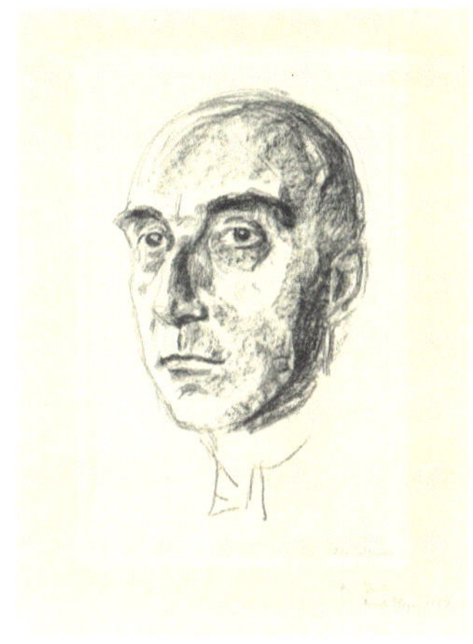

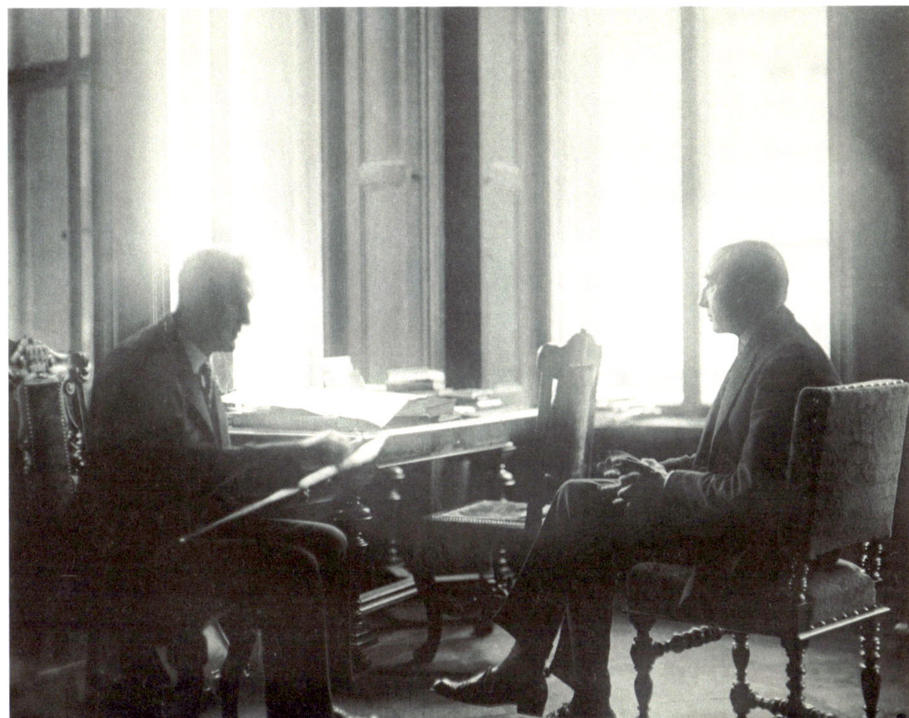

(A)
Edvard Munch
Dr. Ludwig Justi — 1927
Staatliche Museen zu Berlin
Kupferstichkabinett

(B)
Edvard Munch drawing Ludwig Justi
in the Kronprinzenpalais, Berlin — 1927
Munchmuseet — Oslo

very pleased and said it was the best exhibition of his paintings ever. He came every morning, very talkative. Then he also wanted to do a portrait of me, a lithograph. He now sat opposite me in the crown prince's former salon, silently and strangely changed. His eyes, wide-open and fixed, were sharply focused on me as if he wanted to devour me. He was drawing directly on the lithographic stone. ... Suddenly Munch had departed, no one knew where."[29] The portrait sitting is documented in a photograph; there are two surviving drawings[30] and the lithograph.[31] Figures p.247A+B

The Opening of the Exhibition

On March 12, 1927, the Munch exhibition at the Kronprinzenpalais opened, having been arranged in the briefest span of time. Figure p.248 It had 244 catalogue entries; for the first time, all three floors of the building had been cleared for a special exhibition. A separate exhibition was shown in parallel at the Kupferstichkabinett in the Neues Museum with around 150 etchings, woodcuts, and lithographs by the artist. Thormaehlen had reported from Oslo that Munch had "repeatedly suggested" that Jens Thiis "be allowed to give the opening speech"; he was the director of Norway's Nasjonalgalleriet (National Gallery) and wanted to bring Justi's retrospective there.[32] But Justi did not go along with the painter's idea. In his autobiography he described the practices in his own institution in contrast to Liebermann's speeches at the Preussische Akademie der Künste: "In general, my exhibitions opened without any speech at all, in contrast to those at the academy, where, every time, Liebermann gave a long speech from the throne in the presence of the minister, with citations from Goethe and Kant, which was then published in the *Tageblatt*. If anyone

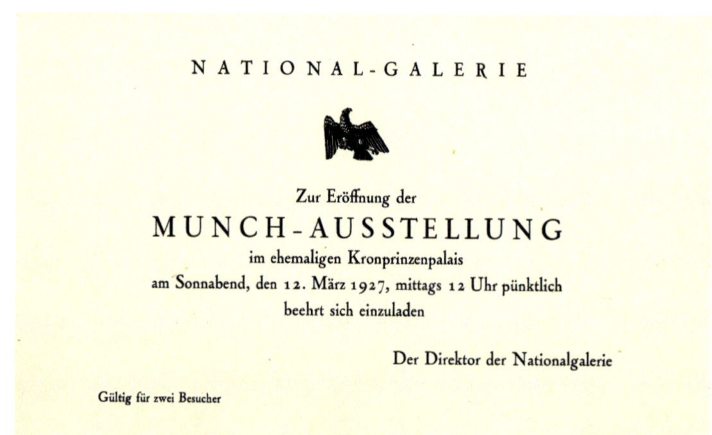
NATIONAL-GALERIE

Zur Eröffnung der

MUNCH-AUSSTELLUNG

im ehemaligen Kronprinzenpalais

am Sonnabend, den 12. März 1927, mittags 12 Uhr pünktlich

beehrt sich einzuladen

Der Direktor der Nationalgalerie

Gültig für zwei Besucher

Invitation to the Munch exhibition, Nationalgalerie, Kronprinzenpalais, Berlin — March 1927
Staatliche Museen zu Berlin Zentralarchiv

spoke at all, I let others do it, a writer or friend of the arts who was especially close to the artist exhibited. ... With the Munch exhibition, the ministry wanted Glaser to give the opening speech. I rejected that. I was threatened that then the minister would not speak either. I replied that a speech from the minister was not necessary. The Glaser speech was not given; I no longer recall whether [Carl Heinrich] Becker did in fact speak."[33]

The newspaper *Berliner Tageblatt* reported in detail, however: "The large Munch exhibition in the modern department of the Nationalgalerie was opened by the Minister of Science, Art, and Popular Education, Professor Dr. *Becker*. The black, red, and gold flag and the Prussian flag flew above the former crown prince's palace. The crowd arriving at the exhibition is extraordinary. Shortly after noon, greeted by Privy Councilor Dr. Ludwig Justi, the director of the Nationalgalerie, the minister arrives in the company of State Secretary *Lammers* and Privy Councilor Professor Dr. Wilhelm *Waetzold[t]*, as well as the Italian ambassador, *Aldrovandi-Marescotti*, the Norwegian envoy *Scheel*, the Swedish envoy *v. Wirsen*, the Danish envoy *Zahle*, and the envoy from Finland, *Holma*. The Foreign Office is represented by Count *Bassewitz*. In addition, one sees the director general of the Staatliche Museen, Privy Councilor Dr. Otto *v. Falke*; Privy Councilor Dr. *Wiegand* of the antiquities collections; Privy Councilor Dr. Max J. *Friedländer* of the Kupferstichkabinett Berlin; and numerous other Berlin museum directors. The museums of the Reich, such as Darmstadt, Chemnitz, and others, have also sent their directors to Berlin. At a quarter past twelve, Minister Becker and the guests enter the Liebermann-Saal, whose [walls] are now decorated with works by Edvard Munch, like all of the other rooms of the former Kronprinzenpalais. The minister steps up to the podium in front of Munch's portrait of Walt[h]er Rathenau, which the Norwegian artist painted in 1907. Thirty-five years ago, he said, the Berlin exhibition of Munch arranged by the Kunstverein had to be closed shortly after its opening because the 'outrage' of the older artists back then at the young guest was so great. Today, the Nationalgalerie has made the entire former Kronprinzenpalais available to present a comprehensive exhibition of the Nordic master's works. That shows how much those alive today revere the most important painter of the North. That also shows, said the minister, how much judgments about art change, and we are experiencing once again the spectacle of yesterday's revolutionary becoming today's classic. I believe, said the minister, that I am not saying too much by calling this Munch exhibition of the Nationalgalerie Berlin an *event of European rank*. Minister Becker also emphasized that Munch, as much as he is a Norwegian, sees Berlin as his adoptive city. It is a case of a national achievement becoming an achievement of supranational rank. In conclusion, the minister thanked the museums and private collectors of the North as well as Munch's biographer, Professor Kurt *Glaser*, the director of the Staatliche Kunstbibliothek in Berlin, who mediated between the artist and the Nationalgalerie. Minister Becker then declared the exhibition open. Edvard *Munch* himself did not participate in the opening festivities; a few days earlier, however, he had visited Privy Councilor *Justi* in *Berlin* and saw his exhibition in the making."[34]

Munch, who always avoided the opening of his own exhibitions, had already continued from Berlin to Rome for recreation. In his thank-you for the catalogue and newspaper reports, he noted: "It annoyed me to see that the Norwegian envoy did not speak at the opening. I thought that had been agreed on."[35] Justi agreed with him: "I was also sorry that the Norwegian envoy did not speak. I guided him through the exhibition a few days before the opening and asked him to say a few words ahead of our minister of culture. But he strictly refused, because, he said, he spoke German too badly. I told him he spoke excellently and, moreover, that he could read his speech. But he remained firm."[36]

The Response in the Press

The reviews were enthusiastic and in some cases full of pathos: "Kind words of enthusiastic agreement seem small compared to this work of a very great man, which we are now permitted to view reverently like an enormous natural event."[37] They praised the comprehensive, survey-like character "of an exhibition consisting of a quarter thousand pictures"[38] as well as "the exemplary hanging of the pictures."[39] "The way Privy Councilor Justi divided up the abundance of paintings, creating individual, self-contained spaces, establishing a special room for the large designs for the university murals in Oslo down in the vestibule on the ground floor as an introduction to the whole, placing a few more giant sketches upstairs in the stairwell—that really deserves to be treated in the same detail. This arrangement represented not only an immense task but also an exemplary approach to the essence and context of the individual works; in a room like the one on the second floor in which the large male portraits—Rathenau, Schlittgen, Count Kessler—and the various landscapes are combined with the girls on a bridge; in the small room with a balcony showing the self-portraits next to early and late starry nights, the experience of Munch becomes so strong, in a way that has scarcely ever been felt before."[40]

Another review reads: "Justi's Munch exhibition was highly anticipated but it exceeded all expectations that had been harbored. The entire Kronprinzenpalais has been transformed into a Munch museum. ... On entering the exhibition, one is standing opposite the three great studies for his famous magnum opus, the paintings for the auditorium of Oslo University. ... Munch is still working on these cartoons—as Kurt Glaser, who visited him with Justi on the occasion of this exhibition, tells us."[41] One of the three large-format studies "shows the sun rising and shining over a rocky landscape. And its light continues—admittedly, one cannot easily see this here, but one believes Dr. Tormählen [*sic*], who deserves great credit with this exhibition—across all of the paintings, summing up the entire room in this way."[42] Another review mentions "the enormous sun, of which Professor Kossinna observed that it is exactly like the bronze sun disks of Munch's Scandinavian forefathers."[43] Figures p.250A+B

This makes it clear that it was not just the art historians Justi, Glaser, and Thormaehlen who spoke to the press; the Gustaf Kossinna quoted here was a prehistorian at the Universität Berlin who saw himself as a representative

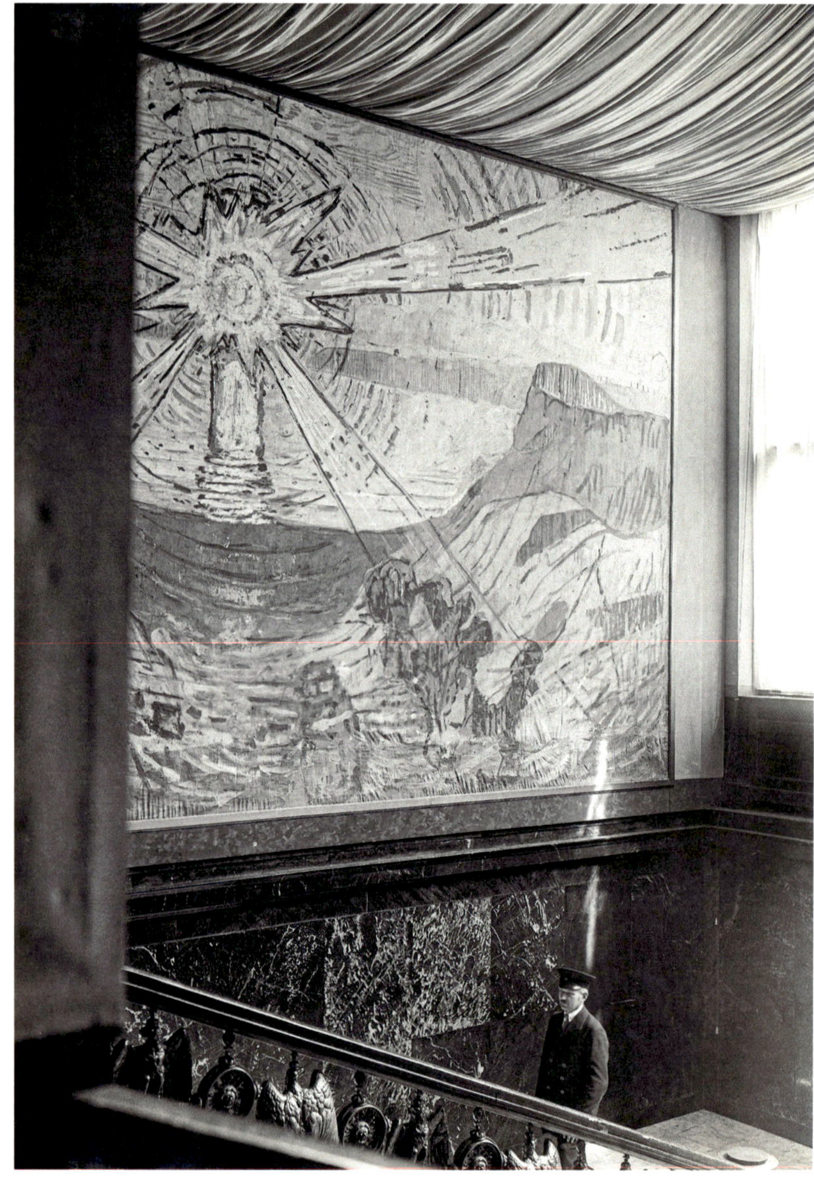

(A)

View of the stairwell in the Kronprinzenpalais, during the Munch exhibition (with a detail of the painting *The Sun*, 1910–11) — 1927
Staatliche Museen zu Berlin, Zentralarchiv

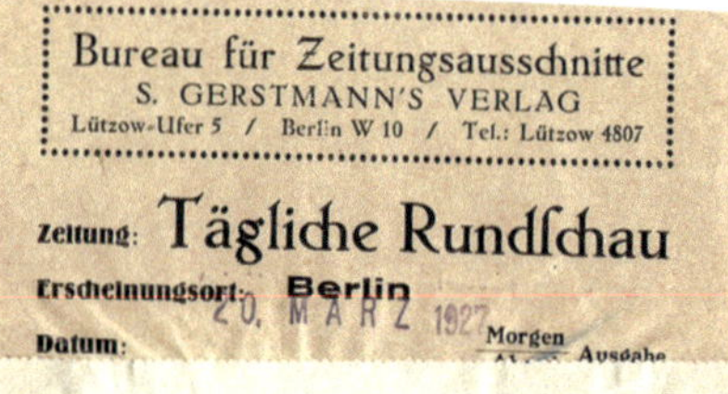

Bureau für Zeitungsausschnitte
S. GERSTMANN'S VERLAG
Lützow-Ufer 5 / Berlin W 10 / Tel.: Lützow 4807

Zeitung: Tägliche Rundschau
Erscheinungsort: Berlin
Datum: 20. MÄRZ 1927
Morgen Ausgabe

14

Eine Edvard-Munch-Ausstellung in Berlin
In der Nationalgalerie in Berlin wurde eine Ausstellung von 244 Gemälden und Zeichnungen des berühmten norwegischen Malers Edvard Munch eröffnet. Blick in den Saal, in dem u. a. die bekannten Bilder Munchs „Die Schneeschipper" und „Bauer im Kohlfeld" hängen Sennecke

(B)

View of one room in the Munch exhibition, Kronprinzenpalais (with the paintings *Corn Field*, 1917, *Snow Shovelers*, 1913–14, *Corn Harvest*, 1917, and *The Man in the Cabbage Field*, 1916) — 1927
Staatliche Museen zu Berlin, Zentralarchiv

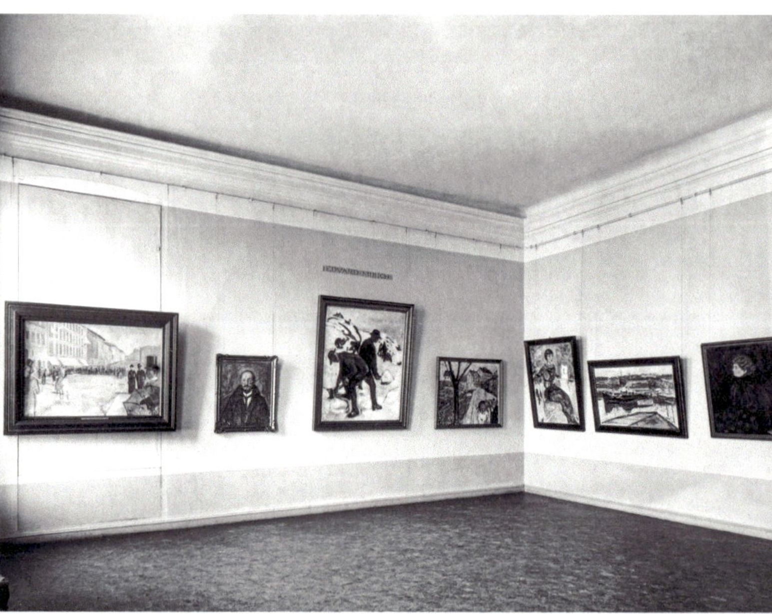

(C)

View of the Munch room in the Kronprinzenpalais, Berlin, 1933 (with the paintings *Music on Karl Johan*, 1889, *Albert Kollmann*, 1901–2, *Snow Shovelers*, 1913–14, *Street in Kragerø*, 1910–11, *Elsa Glaser*, 1913, *The Harbor in Lübeck*, 1907, and *Selma Fontheim*, 1894) — 1933
Staatliche Museen zu Berlin, Zentralarchiv

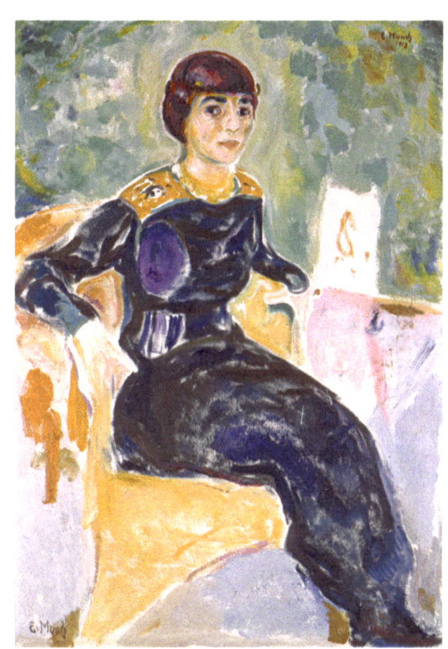

Edvard Munch
Portrait of Elsa Glaser — 1913
Kunsthaus Zürich

of a *völkisch* (racist nationalist) archaeology and cofounded the Nationalsozialistische Gesellschaft für deutsche Kultur (National Socialist Society for German Culture) in 1928. Such tones could also be heard in some of the reviews themselves, for example, when Munch is called "the true progenitor of Germanic expressive art" or when the same article states: "The homeland of the Nordic people is, today more than ever, the soul; as it was for Rembrandt, the painter of the soul, so it is for Munch, the Magus of the North."[44] In another article Munch is called "our Norwegian friend" but the quintessence of his painting is described as "Germanic world, Germanic people, Germanic landscape."[45] In the catalogue of the earlier exhibition in Mannheim, too, the director, Gustav F. Hartlaub, had called Munch's art "nationalist-Germanic"; for him, the painter was "a deeply *Germanic* artist."[46]

After the Exhibition

Ludwig Justi's foreword for the Berlin catalogue, by contrast, was decidedly objective and free of nationalistic interpretations.[47] He recommended Glaser's book, expressed special thanks to his colleague, and included a full-page illustration of a portrait of Glaser's wife, Elsa.[48] Figure p.251 Glaser responded by helping his colleague with a permanent presence of the artist, since an acquisition had not proved possible.[49] After the exhibition in the Kronprinzenpalais, Glaser wrote to Munch: "To help Justi achieve his goal and make a worthy representation of your art here in the Galerie possible, I have decided to make something from my collection available as a loan."[50] Three important Munch paintings of Glaser's—*Embrace* (1903) from the *Linde Frieze* and *Mourning* (now called *Melancholy*) and *Persecution* (now titled *Two Human Beings: The Lonely Ones*) from the *Reinhardt Frieze* (both 1906–7)—did indeed enter the museum, first as loans but then as acquisitions in 1930–31. Together with an oil sketch for the stage set for Henrik Ibsen's drama *Ghosts* in Berlin (1906), which was acquired by the Verein der Freunde der Nationalgalerie (Association of Friends of the National Gallery), founded in 1929, and the painting *Snow Shovelers* (1913–14), which Munch had donated during the exhibition in 1927, the museum ultimately had a respectable collection of the painter's work. Justi assessed these paintings in detail in his guide to the artworks in the

Kronprinzenpalais in 1931.[51] In October 1932, Glaser donated Munch's painting *Music on Karl Johan* (1889) and made additional loans as well.[52] Figure p.250C

The Berlin exhibition, which was reported on continuously in the German-language press until it closed on May 15, 1927,[53] was the best-attended show yet in the Kronprinzenpalais, with 30,325 admission tickets sold[54] (in Mannheim it had been 5,203[55]). Its success led to the collection's holdings being expanded and hence to a fundamental gain for the museum. But Glaser and Justi could enjoy the fruits of their efforts only for a limited time. Immediately after National Socialist rule began, Glaser was suspended from duty in April 1933 because of his Jewish origins and then dismissed from state service in September 1933, having already left Germany by that time. Justi was suspended on July 1, 1933, and in May 1934 transferred to a curator's position in the Staatliche Kunstbibliothek, Glaser's previous place of employment. Munch's paintings also remained only briefly. In 1937, the loans from private collections were returned; the museum's own works were confiscated at the Kronprinzenpalais in the "Entartete Kunst" (Degenerate Art) action and thus removed from the Nationalgalerie.

(1) Oscar Bie wrote of a "sensation for the art-loving public"; Oscar Bie, "Munch-Ausstellung in Berlin," *Dresdner Neueste Nachrichten*, March 17, 1927.

(2) "I had seen Munch's art when just twenty." Justi 2000, vol. 1, p. 442.

(3) Ludwig Justi to Ernst Ludwig Kirchner, June 20, 1919, Staatliche Museen zu Berlin—Preussischer Kulturbesitz, Zentralarchiv (hereafter SMB-PK, ZA), I/NG 0467, fol. 211. On the history and importance of the Kronprinzenpalais, see Jana Baumann, *Museum als Avantgarde: Museen moderner Kunst in Deutschland, 1918–1933* (Berlin, 2016), pp. 23–85.

(4) Ludwig Justi, *Neue Kunst: Ein Führer zu den Gemälden der sogenannten Expressionisten in der National-Galerie* (Berlin, 1921), p. 17.

(5) National-Galerie, *Verzeichnis der im ehemaligen Kronprinzen-Palais ausgestellten Kunstwerke* (Berlin, 1920), p. 12. The two Munch paintings are identified, *See* (Lake) and *Dorf* (Village), but in the loan correspondence they are called *Landschaft* (Landscape) and *Dorfstrasse, Sommernacht* (Village Street, Summer Night) (SMB-PK, ZA, I/NG 854, fols. 353 and 355) and are now called *Spring Landscape* and *Street in Åsgårdstrand*; see the catalogue raisonné of the paintings: Woll 2009, Woll 627, and Woll 487. They came from Maria Newman, who after the death of her husband lived in Berlin from 1917 to 1920, but the works loaned in March 1920 were returned to her already in September 1920 when she moved to Hamburg.

(6) On the proposal for a later date, see Rother and Koss 2022, pp. 43 and 46, n. 22.

(7) Glaser 1917. The book was so successful that there was a revised and expanded third edition in 1923.

(8) Curt Glaser to Edvard Munch, December 28, 1926, Munchmuseet, Oslo, MM K 2358 (this document and all of the archival materials in Munchmuseet that follow are accessible at emunch.no).

(9) Curt Glaser to Edvard Munch, November 18, 1926, Munchmuseet, Oslo, MM K 2357; on this, see Dorn 1988, p. 269.

(10) Edvard Munch to Ludwig Wilhelm Gutbier, January 2, 1927, Munchmuseet, Oslo, MM N 3347.

(21) *Bilder-Courier*, magazine supplement, *Berliner Börsen-Courier*, January 30, 1927.

(22) Curt Glaser to Edvard Munch, January 15, 1927, Munchmuseet, Oslo, MM K 2360.

(23) Ludwig Thormaehlen to Clara Schneider, January 30, 1927, SMB-PK, ZA, I/NG 0678, fol. 513.

(24) Brauner 1994, p. 128.

(25) Ludwig Thormaehlen to Clara Schneider, February 17, 1927, SMB-ZA I/NG 0678, fol. 517. The misspelling of Grevenor's name results from Thormaehlen having dictated his last two messages from Oslo at the German embassy.

(26) The Corinth memorial exhibition in Berlin, which Munch had apparently seen, ran from January 20 to the end of April 1926; see *Lovis Corinth*, exh. cat. Haus der Kunst, Munich, and Nationalgalerie, Staatliche Museen zu Berlin (Munich, 1996), pp. 23–24.

(27) *Berliner Börsen-Courier*, February 24, 1927, morning edition.

(28) *Berliner Tageblatt*, March 4, 1927, evening edition.

(29) Justi 1958, p. 8.

(30) Munchmuseet, Oslo, MM T 2877 and 2878.

(31) Woll 2001, Woll 679.

(32) Ludwig Thormaehlen to Clara Schneider, February 14, 1927, SMB-PK, ZA, I/NG 0678, fol. 516.

(33) Justi 2000, vol. 1, pp. 473–74.

(34) Fritz Stahl, "Edvard Munch: In der Neuen Nationalgalerie," *Berliner Tageblatt*, March 12, 1927, evening edition.

(35) Edvard Munch to Ludwig Justi, April 1, 1927, Archiv der Berlin-Brandenburgischen Akademie der Wissenschaften, Nachlass Ludwig Justi, Korrespondenz; see also Werner Heiland-Justi, *Von Beckmann bis Zschokke: Künstlerbriefe an Ludwig Justi* (Lindenberg im Allgäu, 2017), p. 78.

(36) Ludwig Justi to Edvard Munch, April 6, 1927, Munchmuseet, Oslo, MM K 3580.

(37) Ernst Collin, "Das Werk Edvard Munchs: Die Ausstellung im Kronprinzenpalais," *Berliner Volkszeitung*, March 12, 1927, evening edition.

(11) Ludwig Justi to Edvard Munch, January 4, 1927, Munchmuseet, Oslo, MM K 3578.

(12) Edvard Munch to Ludwig Justi, January 5, 1927, SMB-PK, ZA, I/NG 0678, fol. 430.

(13) Curt Glaser to Edvard Munch, January 7, 1927, Munchmuseet, Oslo, MM K 2359.

(14) Glaser 1927, pp. 206–7; excerpts of Glaser's discussions were reprinted in many daily newspapers, for example, the *Berliner Börsen-Zeitung*, March 11, 1927, morning edition.

(15) Justi 1958, p. 7.

(16) Curt Glaser, "Deutsche Malerei im neunzehnten Jahrhundert," *Kunst und Künstler* 17, no. 3 (1918): pp. 104–13, esp. p. 108.

(17) The position of the Nationalgalerie was represented by Justi's research associate L[udwig] Thormaehlen, "Eine Schädigung unseres Kunstbesitzes," *Vorwärts*, no. 365, August 5, 1921, morning edition, p. 2; on this, see Strobl 2006, pp. 148–50.

(18) Justi 2000, vol. 1, p. 401, see also p. 163.

(19) Martin Faass, "Max Liebermann und Ludwig Justi," *Jahrbuch der Berliner Museen*, n.s., vol. 52 (2010), supplement, "Ludwig Justi: Kunst und Öffentlichkeit," pp. 67–71.

(20) Karl Scheffler, *Berliner Museumskrieg* (Berlin, 1921), p. 104; on this, see Dieter Scholz, "Karl Scheffler und die Nationalgalerie," in *"... das Wort, dem alle Mühe galt: Die Kunst": Karl Scheffler, 1869–1951*, comp. and ed. Michael Krejsa and Anke Matelowski, Akademie der Künste, Archiv-Blätter 15 (Berlin, 2006), pp. 15–24.

(38) "Edvard Munch-Ausstellung im Kronprinzenpalais," *Berliner Morgenzeitung*, March 13, 1927.

(39) Anton Mayer, "Edvard Munch: Ausstellung im Kronprinzenpalais," *8 Uhr-Abendblatt*, March 12, 1927.

(40) [Paul] Fechter, "Munch im Kronprinzenpalais: Zur heutigen Eröffnung," *Deutsche Allgemeine Zeitung*, March 12, 1927, evening edition.

(41) Franz Markl, "Die grosse Munchausstellung in der Nationalgalerie: Zur heutigen Eröffnung," *Steglitzer Anzeiger*, March 12, 1927.

(42) Stahl 1927 (see note 34).

(43) Willy Ganske, "Edvard Munch: Ausstellung im Kronprinzenpalais," *Berliner Lokal-Anzeiger*, March 12, 1927, evening edition.

(44) Oscar Gehrig, "Eduard [*sic*] Munch: Zur Ausstellung im Kronprinzenpalais," *Germania*, March 16, 1927, morning edition.

(45) Franz Servaes, "Die Edvard-Munch-Ausstellung der Nationalgalerie," *Der Tag*, March 13, 1927; on this, see Clarke 2013, p. 175.

(46) G. F. Hartlaub, "Edvard Munch," in *Edvard Munch: Gemälde und Graphik*, exh. cat. Städtische Kunsthalle Mannheim (Mannheim, 1926), pp. 3–12, esp. pp. 11–12.

(47) On Justi's later, quite different statements, see Eugen Blume, "Ludwig Justi und der Nationalsozialismus," *Jahrbuch der Berliner Museen*, supplement (see note 19), pp. 41–44, and Peter Betthausen, *Schule des Sehens: Ludwig Justi und die Nationalgalerie* (Berlin, 2010), p. 185.

(48) Ludwig Justi, in Berlin 1927, pp. 3–9, esp. pp. 8–9, and pp. 36–37, no. 155. The painting is now in the Kunsthaus Zürich. See also the second version of this portrait in the present catalogue, fig. pp. 156–57.

(49) Justi had already tried unsuccessfully in 1923 to acquire a Munch painting from the Berlin-based gallerist Friedrich Adolf Lutz; see F. A. Lutz to Edvard Munch, October 31, 1923, Munchmuseet, Oslo, MM K 3573.

(50) Curt Glaser to Edvard Munch, July 3, 1927, Munchmuseet, Oslo, MM K 2368.

(51) Ludwig Justi, *Von Corinth zu Klee* (Berlin, 1931), pp. 109–16.

(52) Strobl 2006, p. 32; Sieber 2022, pp. 138–40.

(53) There are sixty-nine reviews as newspaper clippings in the exhibition files in the Zentralarchiv der Staatlichen Museen zu Berlin (Central Archive of the National Museums in Berlin). Only rarely do they mention that the Kupferstichkabinett on the upper floor of the Altes Museum (Old Museum) was presenting its collections of prints by Munch to accompany the show.

(54) [Otto] Linke, "Statistik zum Besuch der Munch-Ausstellung, Berlin," May 16, 1927, SMB-PK, ZA, I/NG 0678, fol. 518.

(55) Dorn 1988, p. 270.

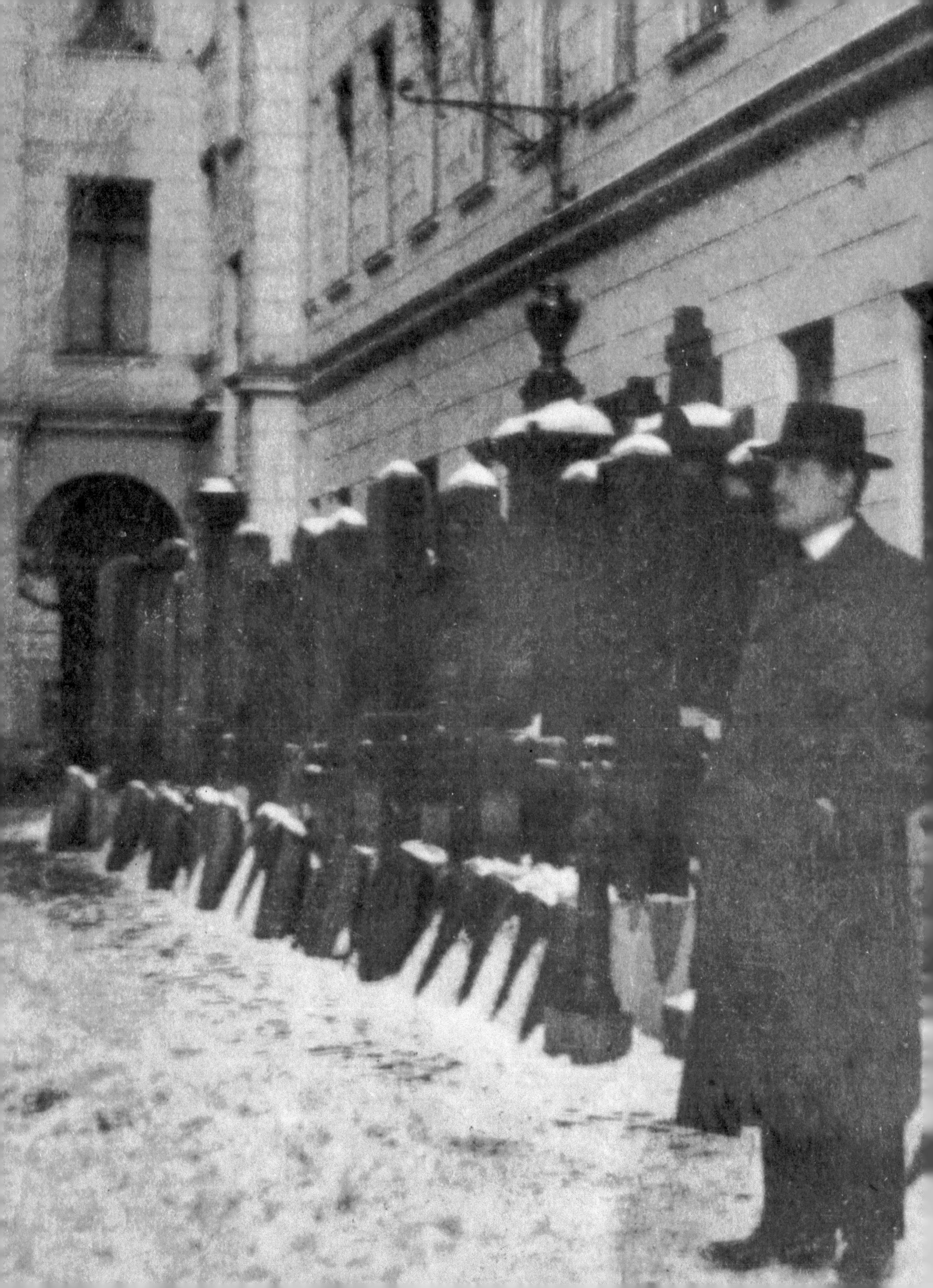

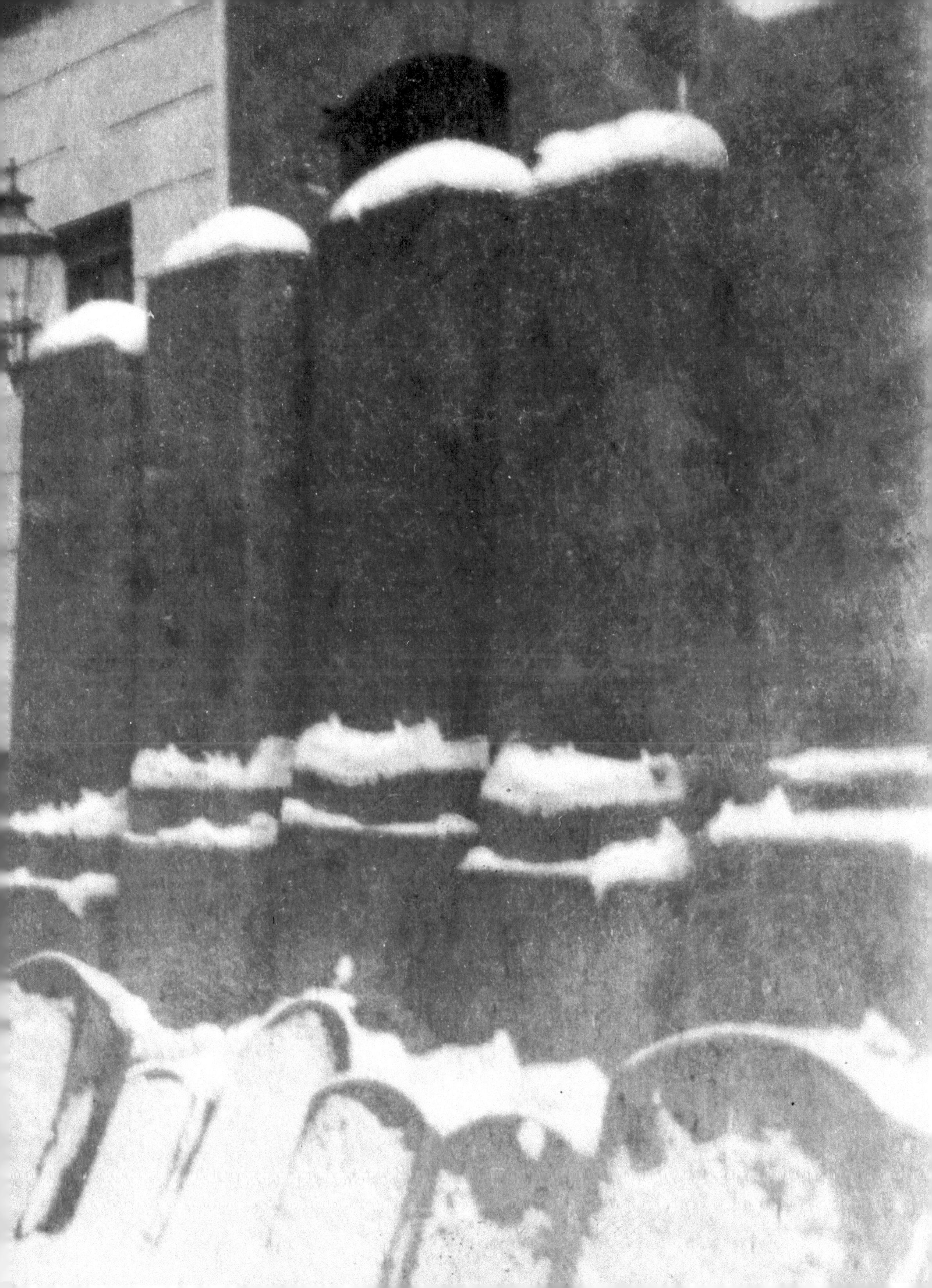

Edvard Munch and Berlin

1863

Edvard Munch is born on December 12 in the Norwegian municipality of Løten.

Shortly after Edvard's birth, the family moves to the capital, Kristiania (now Oslo). Edvard is the second of five siblings. His father, Dr. Christian Munch, is a military physician.

His mother, Laura Cathrine Munch, dies of tuberculosis when Munch is five. His older sister, Sophie, also dies of the same illness when just fifteen.

After the death of his mother, her sister, Karen Bjølstad, takes care of the Munch children. Edvard's aunt encourages his artistic talent. Munch is often very sick as a child. His health continues to be frail all his life.

1881

After breaking off his study of architecture, Munch enrolls at the Kongelige Tegneskole (Royal Drawing School) in Kristiania. His goal is to become a painter. In the years that follow, he comes into contact with progressive Norwegian artists—for example, Christian Krohg, who supports him. Munch participates in his first exhibitions and belongs to the bohemian circle around the anarchist writer Hans Jæger.

1885

In the spring, Munch undertakes a three-week study trip to Paris. The avant-garde scene there profoundly impresses him. During a summer stay on the Oslofjord, he begins an affair with the married Milly Thaulow. The relationship ends traumatically for the twenty-one-year-old artist.

In the autumn exhibition in Kristiania the following year, he shows the first version of his painting *The Sick Child*, in which he comes to terms with the death of his sister. The painting is controversially debated by the public and the press.

1889

Munch organizes his first solo exhibition in Kristiania with sixty-three paintings and forty-six drawings and participates in the Exposition Universelle in Paris with one painting. He spends the summer, as he will do so often in the coming years, in Åsgårdstrand. With a state scholarship, he travels to Paris in the fall, where he attends the art school of Léon Bonnat. In November, his father dies. At the end of the year, he moves to the suburb of Saint-Cloud, where he writes his artistic credo, known as the "Saint Cloud Manifesto." Munch wants to create an art that shows existential feelings and mental states.

With two more state scholarships, Munch secures additional stays in France, above all in Paris, by 1892.

1891

Munch's first show in Germany is held in Berlin on the occasion of the international exhibition for the fiftieth anniversary of the Verein Berliner Künstler (Association of Berlin Artists). Owing to friction between its chairman, Anton von Werner, and the Norwegian selection committee, however, Norway does not participate officially. Many artists, including Munch, exhibit instead in the *Münchener Jahresausstellung von Kunstwerken aller Nationen* (Munich Annual Exhibition of Artworks of All Nations).

1892

The Berlin-based Norwegian landscape painter Adelsteen Normann invites Munch in the name of the Verein Berliner Künstler to participate in a solo exhibition. His presentation with fifty-five paintings in the Architektenhaus (Architects' House) at Wilhelmstrasse 92/93 opens on November 5 and triggers a scandal that enters the annals of art history as the "Affaire Munch" (Munch Affair). The show, which is taken down again already on November 13 because of protests from conservative members of the association, can be seen immediately thereafter in Düsseldorf and Cologne at branches of the Galerie Eduard Schulte. Munch harnesses this publicity and moves to Berlin. From December 26, he shows the exhibition again on his own initiative in the elegant Equitable-Palast (Equitable-Palace) on Friedrichstrasse.

Munch lives and works primarily in Berlin from 1892 to 1895, spending the summer months in Norway. In the city on the Spree River, he is a regular at Café Bauer on the boulevard Unter den Linden and the wine bar Zum schwarzen Ferkel (The Black Piglet).

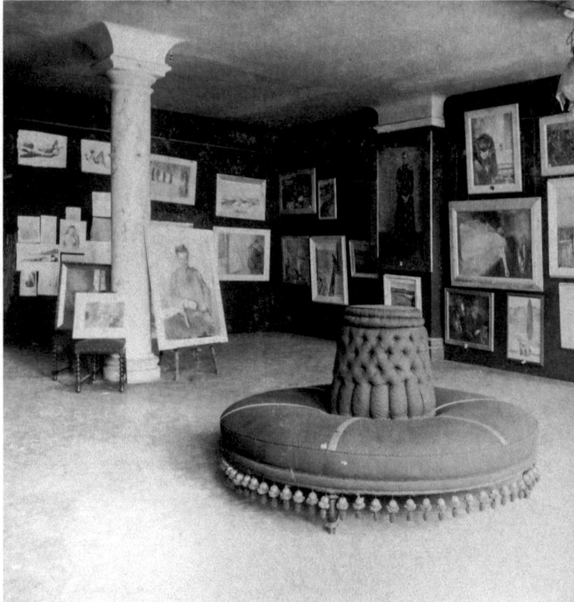

(A)
Max Marschalk
Edvard Munch's exhibition at the Equitable-Palast, Berlin — 1892–93
Munchmuseet — Oslo

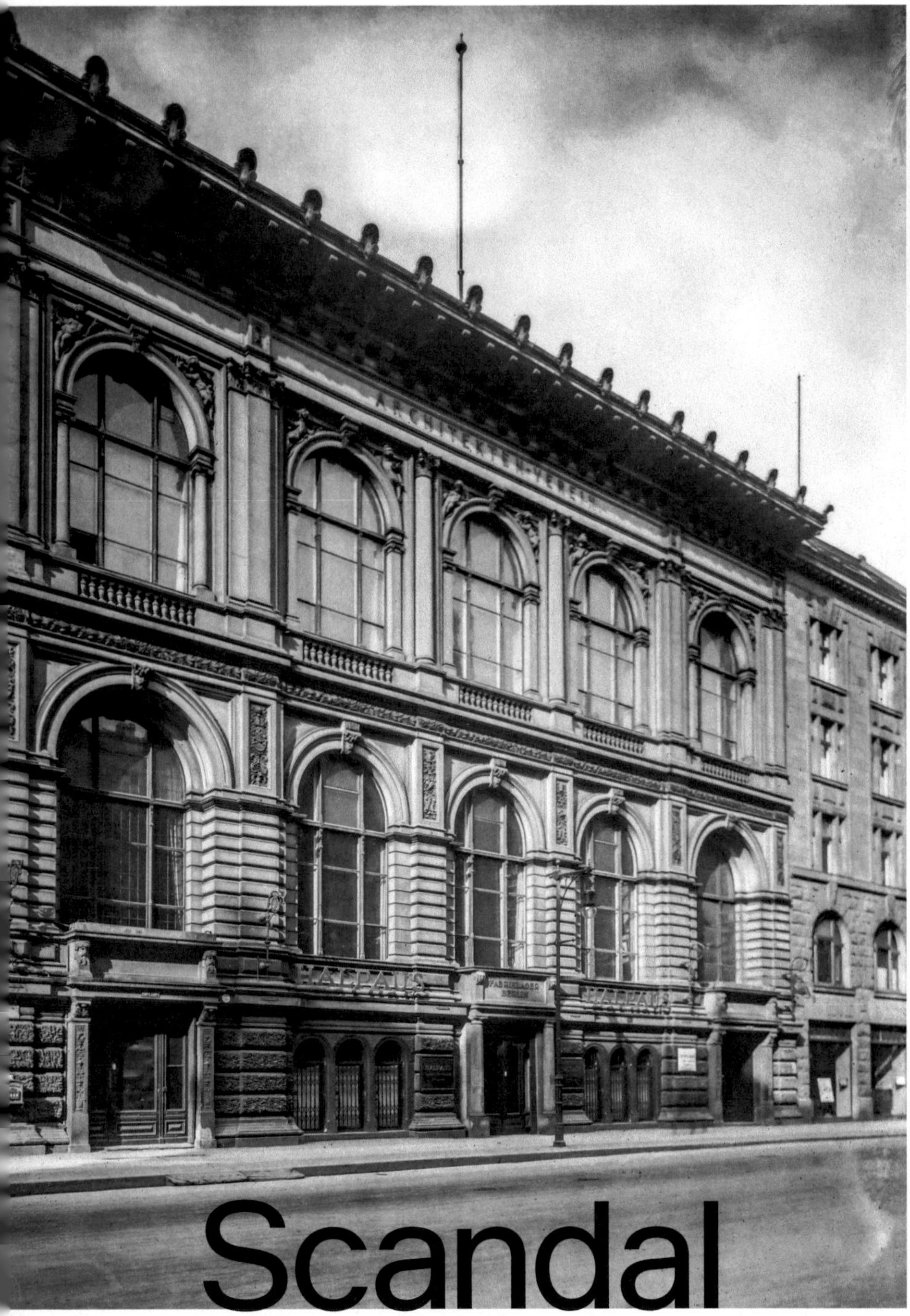

(B)
Architektenhaus
Berlin, Wilhelmstrasse 92/93 — ca. 1920–30
Bildarchiv Foto Marburg

Scandal

The modernist era in Berlin—and with it the international career of the Norwegian artist Edvard Munch—begins with a bang in 1892. It is triggered by his first exhibition in the city on the Spree, which closes soon after its opening.

Already in 1889, his compatriot Christian Krohg sees Munch as the great innovator of modern Norwegian painting, which in his view spans three generations. The Germans—the "brown ones"—who depicted nature and peasant motifs in the subdued color of the Düsseldorf school of painters were followed by the "blue" plein-air painters. For Krohg, a third generation begins with Munch, though the public in Norway—and that was also true of Berlin in 1892—had not even moved from the first to the second generation in its understanding.[1]

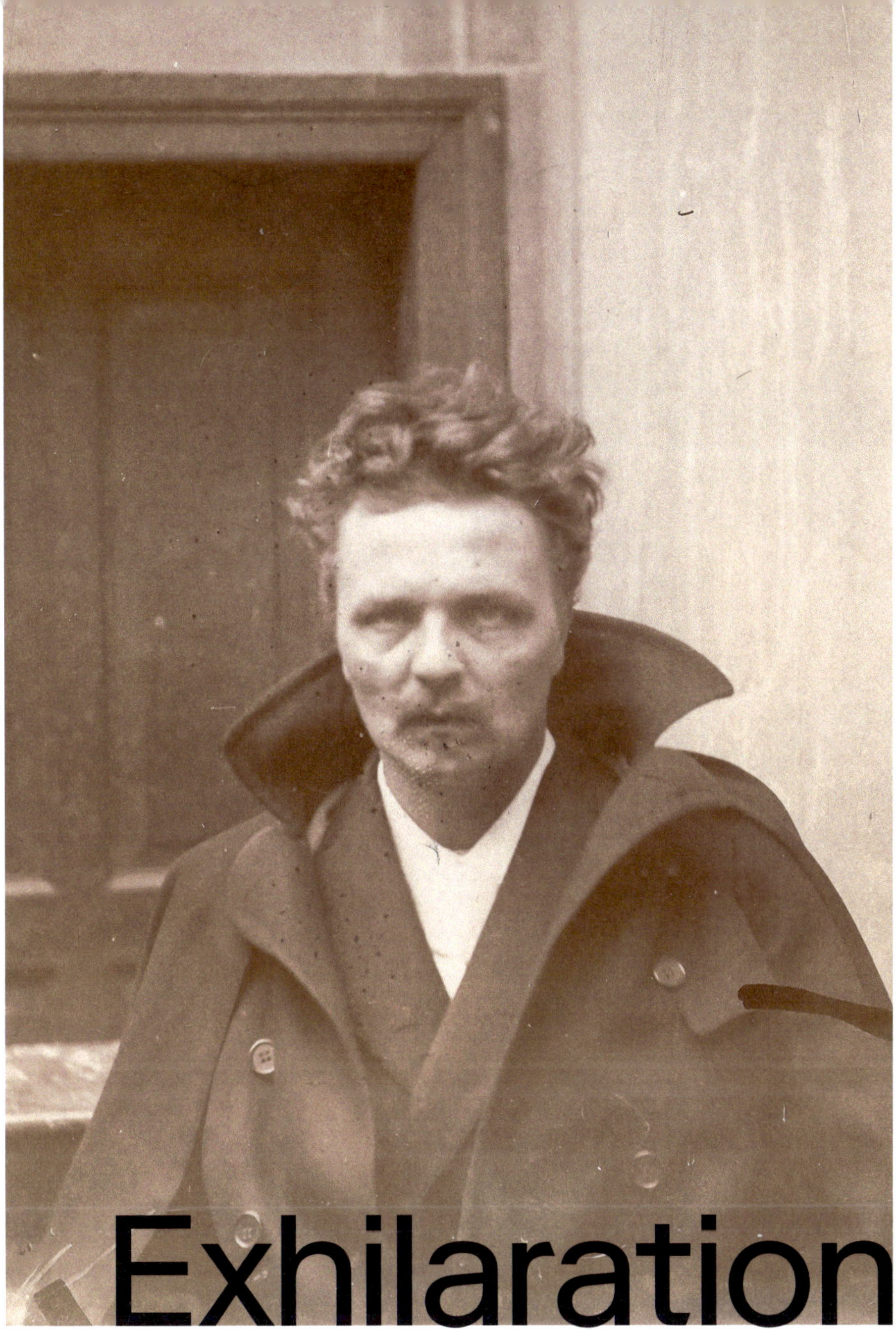

(A)
August Strindberg
Self-Portrait, Berlin — 1892–93
Kungliga Biblioteket — Stockholm

(B)
Edvard Munch and Adolf Paul — ca. 1894
Munchmuseet — Oslo

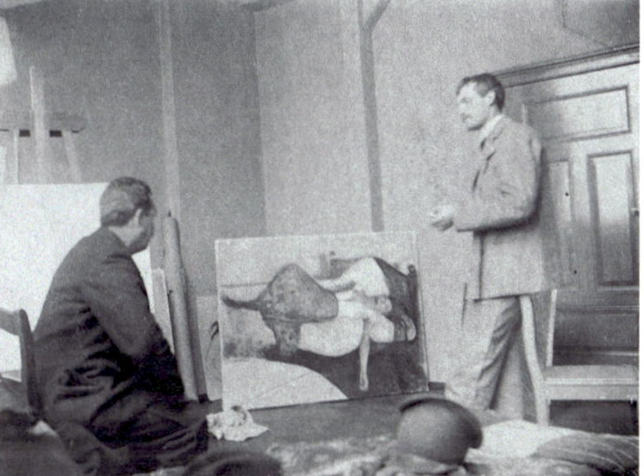

Exhilaration

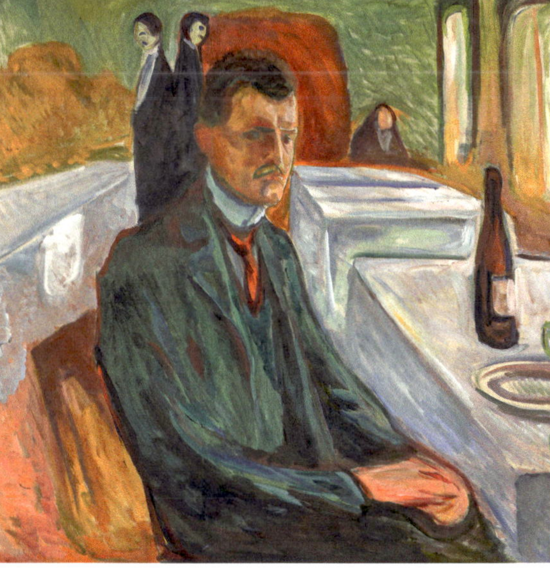

(C)
Edvard Munch
Self-Portrait with a Bottle of Wine — 1906
Munchmuseet — Oslo

"One day—the 'Ferkel' had just been founded—a young Norwegian showed up there, in a bright coat with a pelerine, a top hat on his head, and dreamy eyes in a tired, annoyed, but energetically etched face. It was Munch."[2] In the Berlin wine bar Zum schwarzen Ferkel, the bohemians meet, including many Scandinavians such as August Strindberg. Free of bourgeois constraints, they drink, philosophize, debate, and dance into the early morning hours.

Edvard Munch, who consumes large quantities of alcohol, appreciates exhilaration as a stimulant for his creativity. Over the years, however, friends react to his excesses with concern: "Just quit the damned drinking! Berlin is a dangerous place, and your honorable compatriots are all more or less friends of fluids," as the collector Max Linde admonished the artist in 1906.[3]

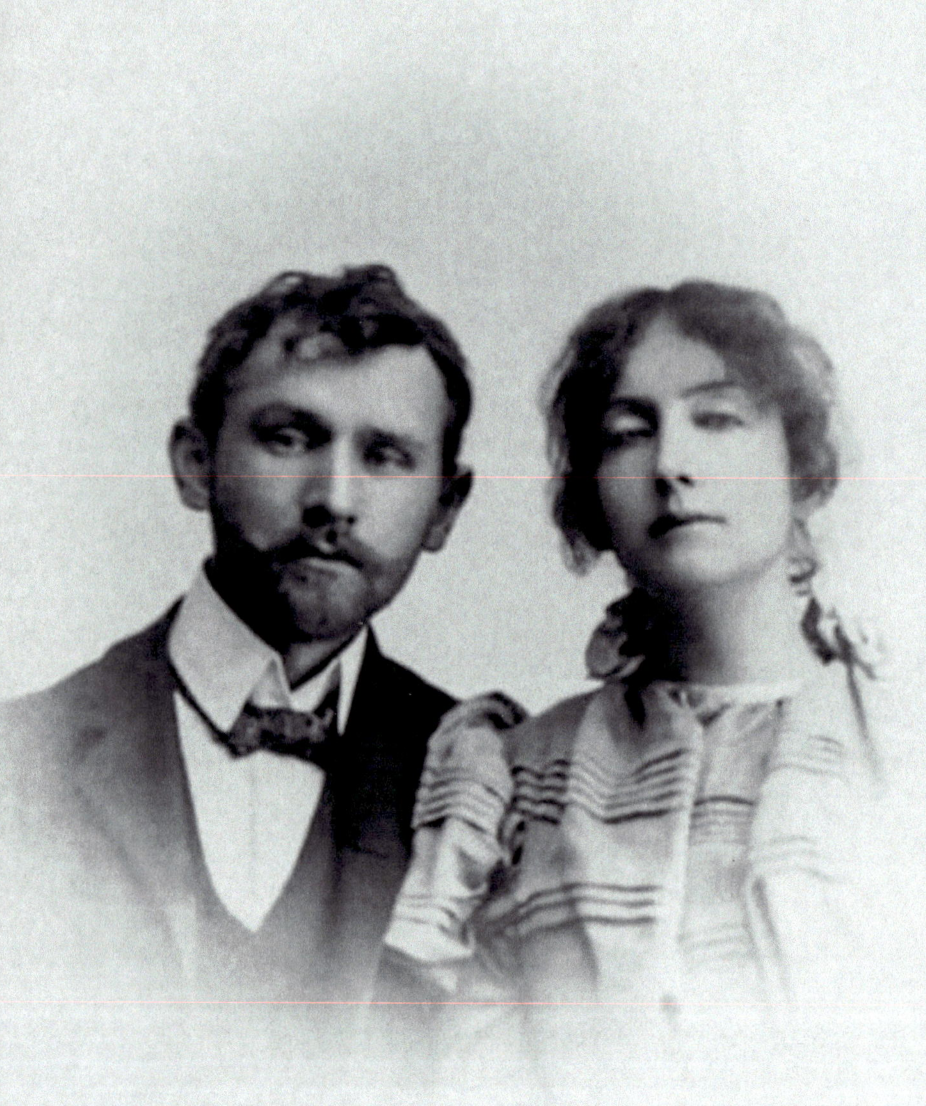

(A)
Dagny and Stanisław Przybyszewski — 1897–98

(B)
August Haraldsson
Dagny Juel — 1884
Munchmuseet — Oslo

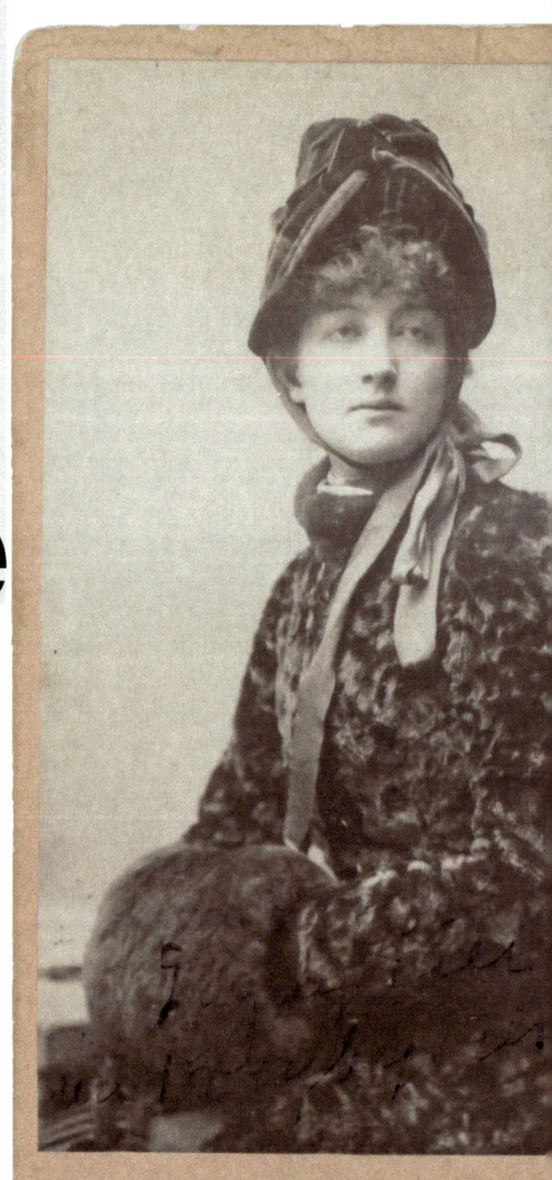

Muse

"Slender, with the forms of a Madonna of the trecento, with a smile that made men rabid," was how the art critic Julius Meier-Graefe describes the pianist and writer Dagny Juel. "She was a very delicate queen, full of high spirits, audacious cheekiness, and a boyish dignity that remained unscathed even amid chaotic frenzy."[4] For many men in the Zum schwarzen Ferkel circle, the Norwegian woman becomes a projection screen for erotic and misogynistic fantasies.

Edvard Munch was friends with Juel: "Her unbelievable beauty and electrifying nature and intelligence—and so Norwegianly feminine and personal ...! exotically aristocratic—all of this did not give the scandal mongers peace in their dark corners," he writes in retrospect.[5] He sees her as the type of modern woman that he depicts in many works.

(A)
Edvard Munch
The Scream — 1910 (?)
Munchmuseet — Oslo

(B)
Edvard Munch
Three sketches for *The Scream* — 1893–95
Munchmuseet — Oslo

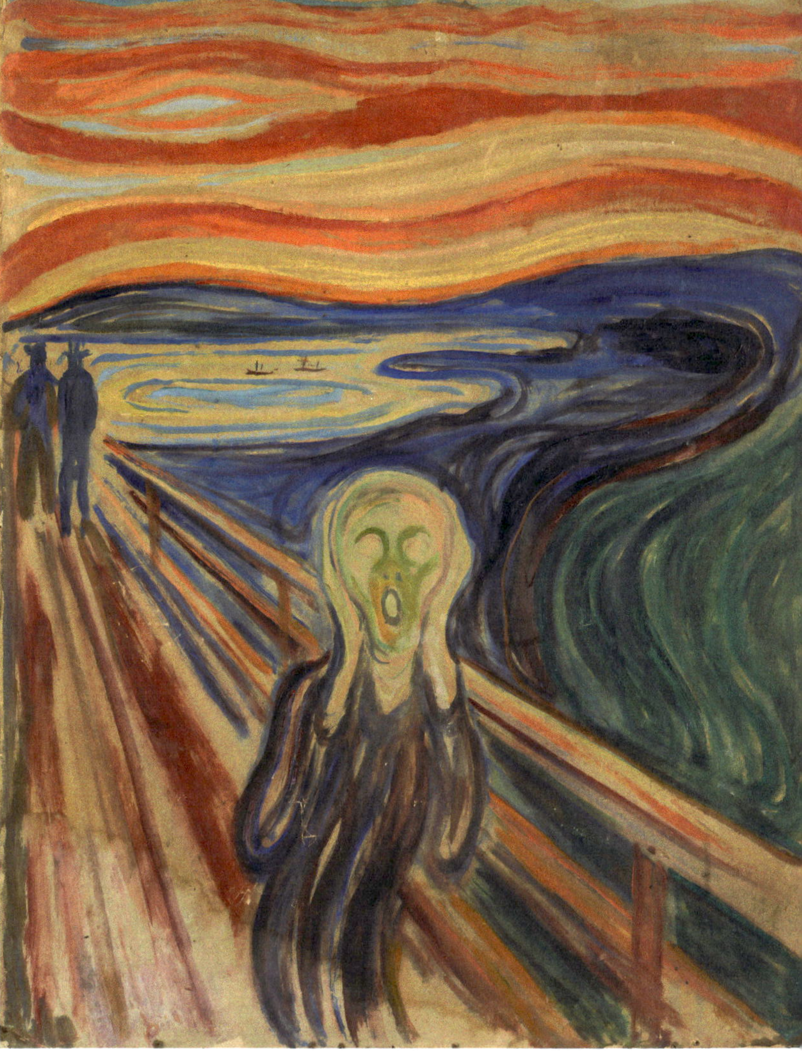

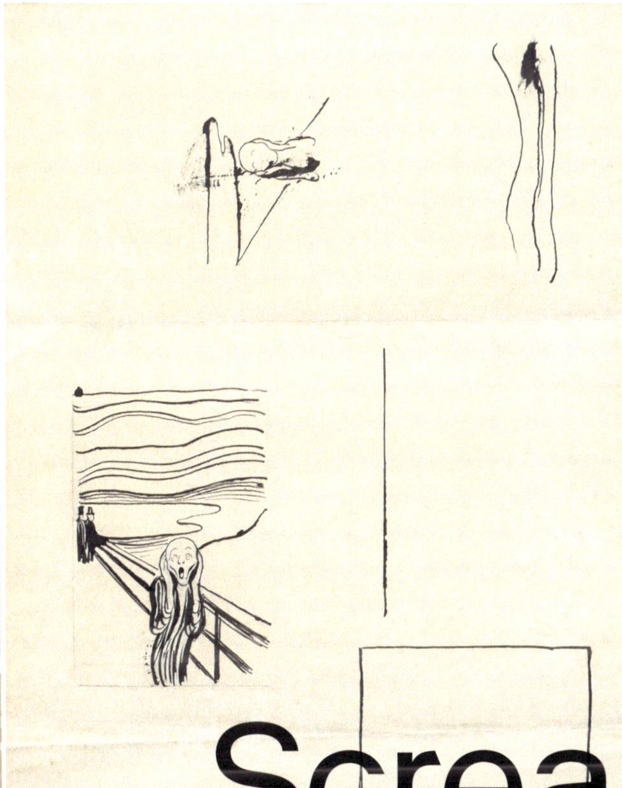

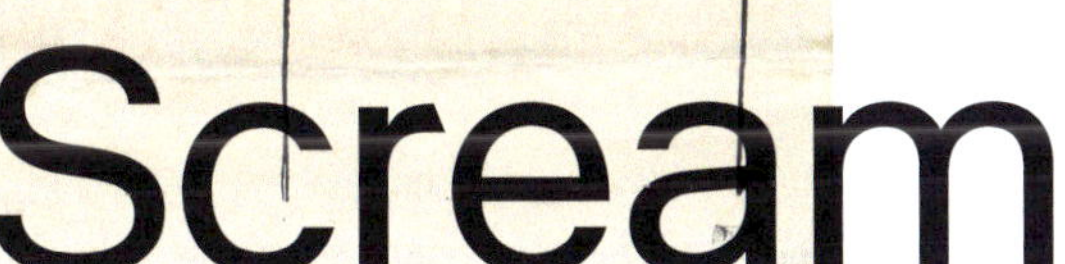

Scream

Edvard Munch's most famous painting, *The Scream*, is shown in public for the first time in Berlin. The artist gradually develops the motif and employs it several times in paintings and graphic works. He presents it under the title *Despair* in December 1893 in the rooms of a commercial space on the boulevard Unter den Linden. "If Mr. Munch was looking to snub the public forcefully, he has indeed succeeded," vents one critic.[6]

Munch writes of its making: "I was walking along the road with two friends. The sun set. I felt a tinge of melancholy. Suddenly the sky became a bloody red. … And I looked at the flaming clouds that hung like blood and a sword over the blue-black fjord and city. My friends walked on. I stood there, trembling with fright. And I felt a loud, unending scream piercing nature."[7]

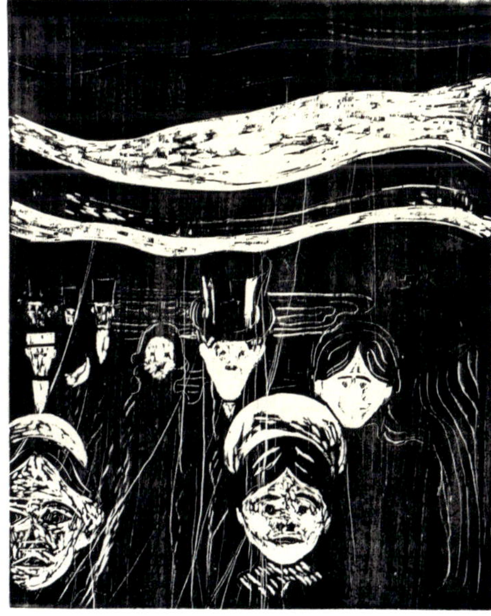

(C)
Edvard Munch
Angst (Feeling of Anxiety) — 1896
Staatliche Museen zu Berlin
Kupferstichkabinett

1893

Munch rents two rooms in a commercial building at Unter den Linden 19 and organizes an exhibition of his paintings that opens on December 3. For the first time, he arranges six paintings into a series, which he titles *Love*. He will continue deliberately grouping works into series and cycles until the end of his life. It is the beginning of his work on what he will later call *The Frieze of Life*.

Munch's closest friends in Berlin include the Polish writer Stanisław Przybyszewski and the Norwegian music student Dagny Juel. She is the lionized center of the Ferkel circle. Juel marries Przybyszewski and later turns to writing.

1894

Przybyszewski edits the first book on Munch, with an essay of his own and one each by his writer friends Julius Meier-Graefe, Franz Servaes, and Willy Pastor. Munch discovers the medium of printmaking. In addition to artistic curiosity, he is motivated by the hope of a larger customer base. He teaches himself the techniques of etching and lithography very quickly in 1894–95. Berlin printers offer him important assistance in this regard.

1895

In March, Munch exhibits with the Finnish artist Axel Gallén at the Galerie Ugo Barroccio on Unter den Linden. The series *Love* has now grown to fifteen works. As with his previous exhibitions, however, Munch finds hardly anyone interested in acquiring his works. His supporters include the intellectuals Baron Eberhard von Bodenhausen, Harry Graf Kessler, and Julius Meier-Graefe. The last named publishes a portfolio of eight etchings by Munch in June. Bodenhausen and Meier-Graefe are crucially involved in the founding of the avant-garde art journal *PAN*, which is published in Berlin.

Munch spends most of the second half of the year in Norway. In December, his brother Andreas dies of pneumonia.

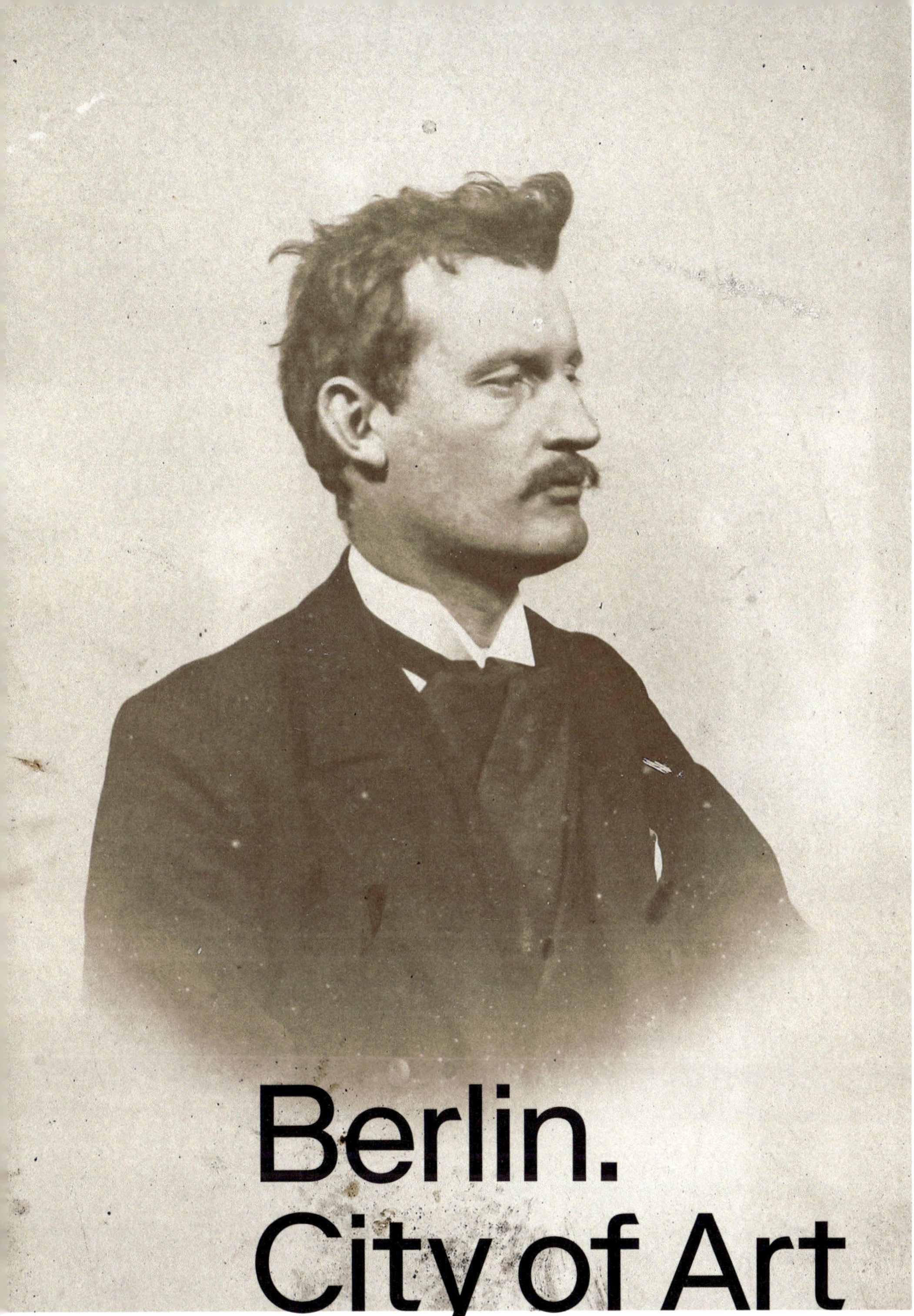

(A)
Portrait of Edvard Munch
Berlin — ca. 1905
Munchmuseet — Oslo

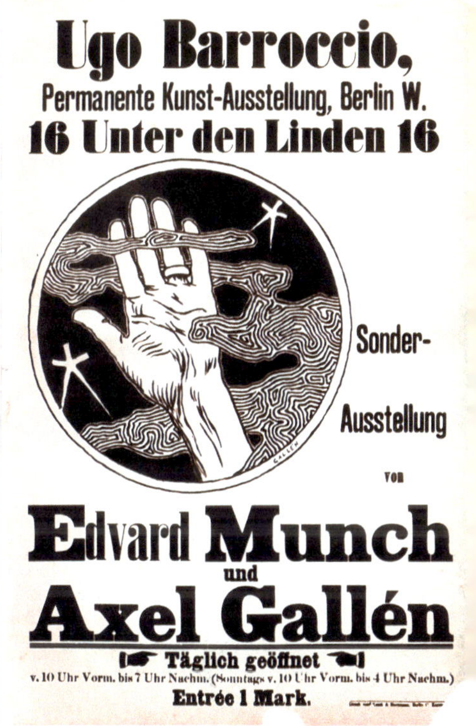

(B)
Axel Gallén
Poster for Edvard Munch and
Axel Gallén's Exhibition — 1895
Ateneum — Helsinki

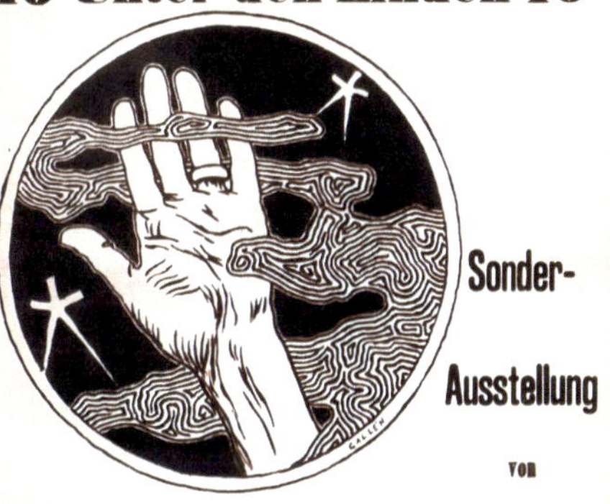

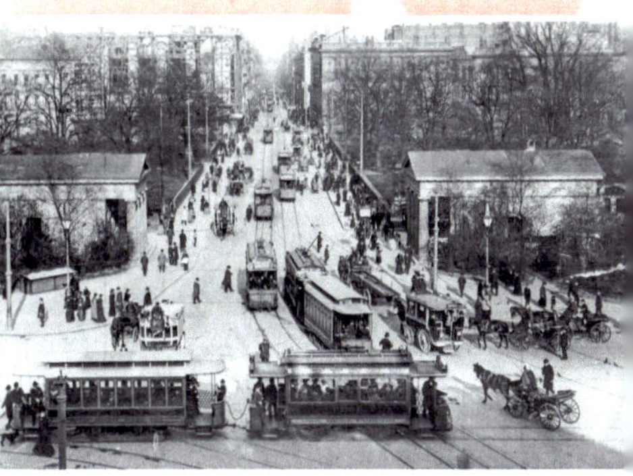

(C)
Potsdamer Platz
Berlin — before 1904
ullstein bild

Berlin. City of Art

Already during his lifetime, there was no doubt: Edvard Munch becomes Munch in Berlin. An article on the occasion of the large retrospective at the Nationalgalerie in Berlin in 1927 reads: "Artists all swear by Paris, and they may be right. But they need—their art needs—a shot of Berlin to thrive properly. ... Of Munch who learned in Paris but became in Berlin!"[8]

Munch himself is ambivalent about the city at first. Early on, he recognizes the opportunity that the budding Berlin art scene offers him. In a letter home in 1894, however, he also writes: "I do, however, have the feeling that I will soon have enough of Berlin—then I will travel either to Paris or home to Norway—Berlin will never be a city of art, or at least not for a long time."[9]

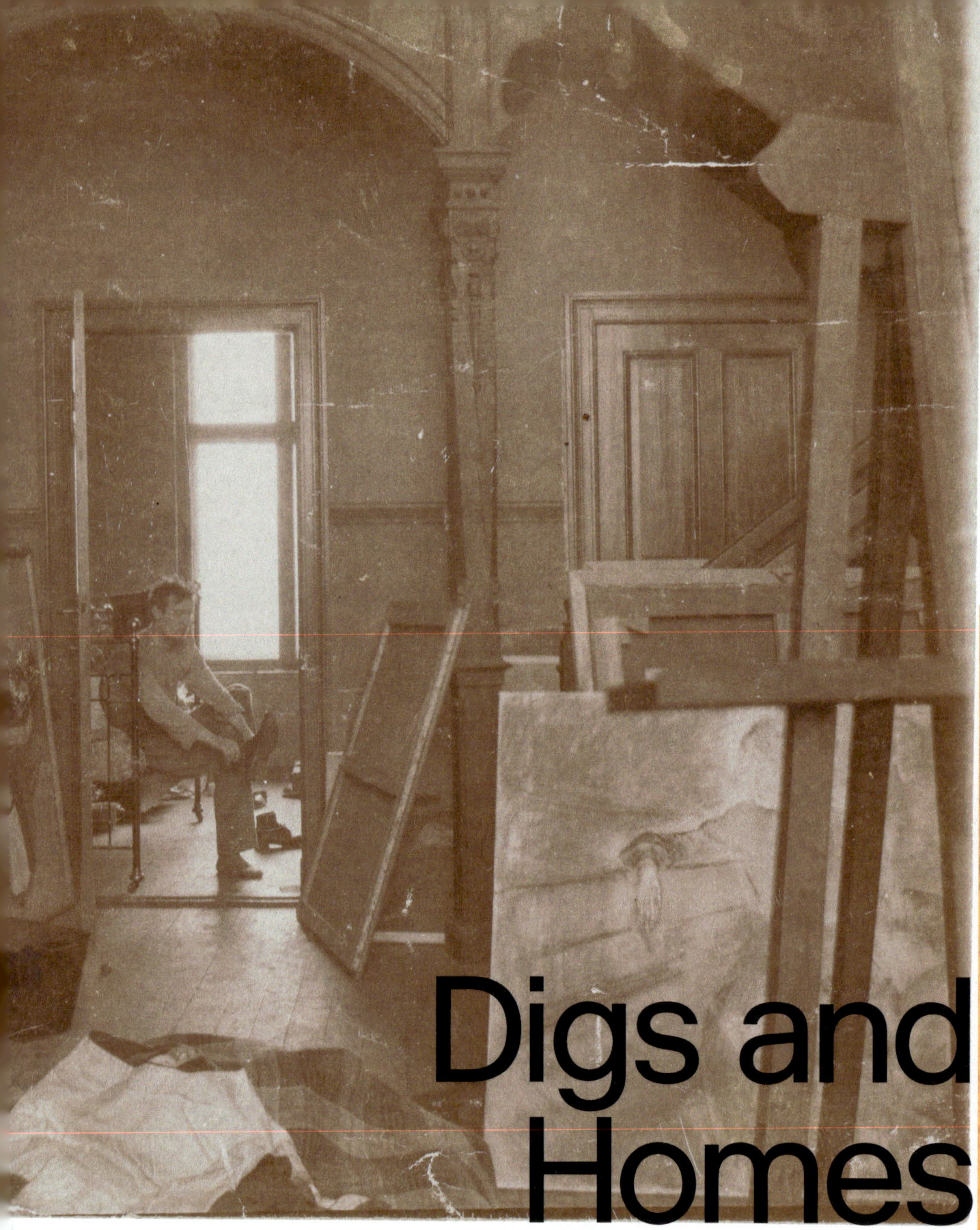

(A)
Edvard Munch
Self-Portrait in His Studio, Lützowstrasse 82, Berlin — 1902
Munchmuseet — Oslo

(B)
Edvard Munch
Harry Graf Kessler — 1906
Staatliche Museen zu Berlin
Nationalgalerie

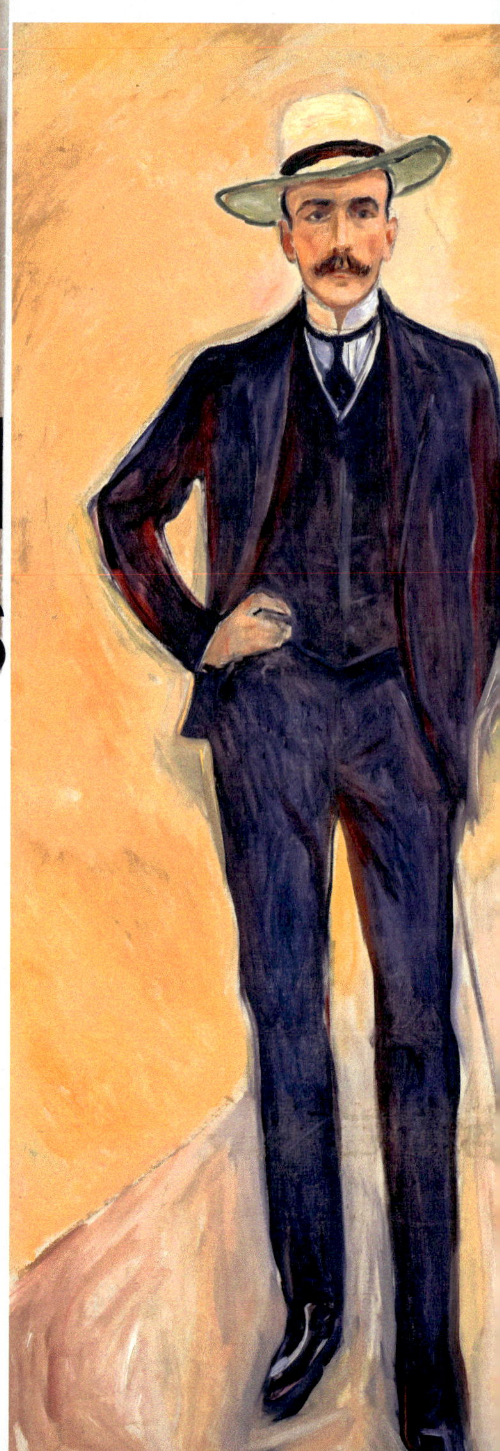

Digs and Homes

Edvard Munch often changes his modest accommodations in hotels and guesthouses in Berlin. Harry Graf Kessler describes a visit to Englische Strasse 23c in Charlottenburg in 1895: "Munch lives in a student's digs four floors up …. He has emptied the living room and uses it as his studio. Through the two curtainless windows the pale winter light falls on large, colorful, unfinished paintings, lying against the walls. A bitter mixture of turpentine thinner and cigarette smoke reaches your nostrils."[10] Munch moves into a hotel soon thereafter. He has to leave his apartment "because of certain small animals."[11]

When Munch comes to Berlin for an extended stay at the end of 1901, he rents a more comfortable space at Lützowstrasse 82. "An ideal studio — with gas for light and cooking," the artist enthuses.[12]

)
etter from Edvard Munch
Karen Bjølstad — November 14, 1894
unchmuseet — Oslo

Berlin 14/11 94 N807

Kjære tante! Det synes vel
jeg er dårlig til at skrive – Grunden
er at jeg har været så optaget – først
udstillingen i Stockholm og så her
hvor jeg har havt mange ting
at gjøre – jeg var for nogle dage
siden i Hamburg – hvor jeg gjorde et
portrætbestilling færdig og tjente på
det 200 mk. Du ser det begynder
at se lysere ud med forholdene –
I Stockholm var der i de sidste
dage trængsel på udstillingen så
jeg tilbød for kunsthandleren
vel tjener et par hundrede kroner
til ham. – Jeg er i meget godt arbeids-
humør – har begyndt at radere
for muligens senere at udgive en
liden samling – raderinger – Det er

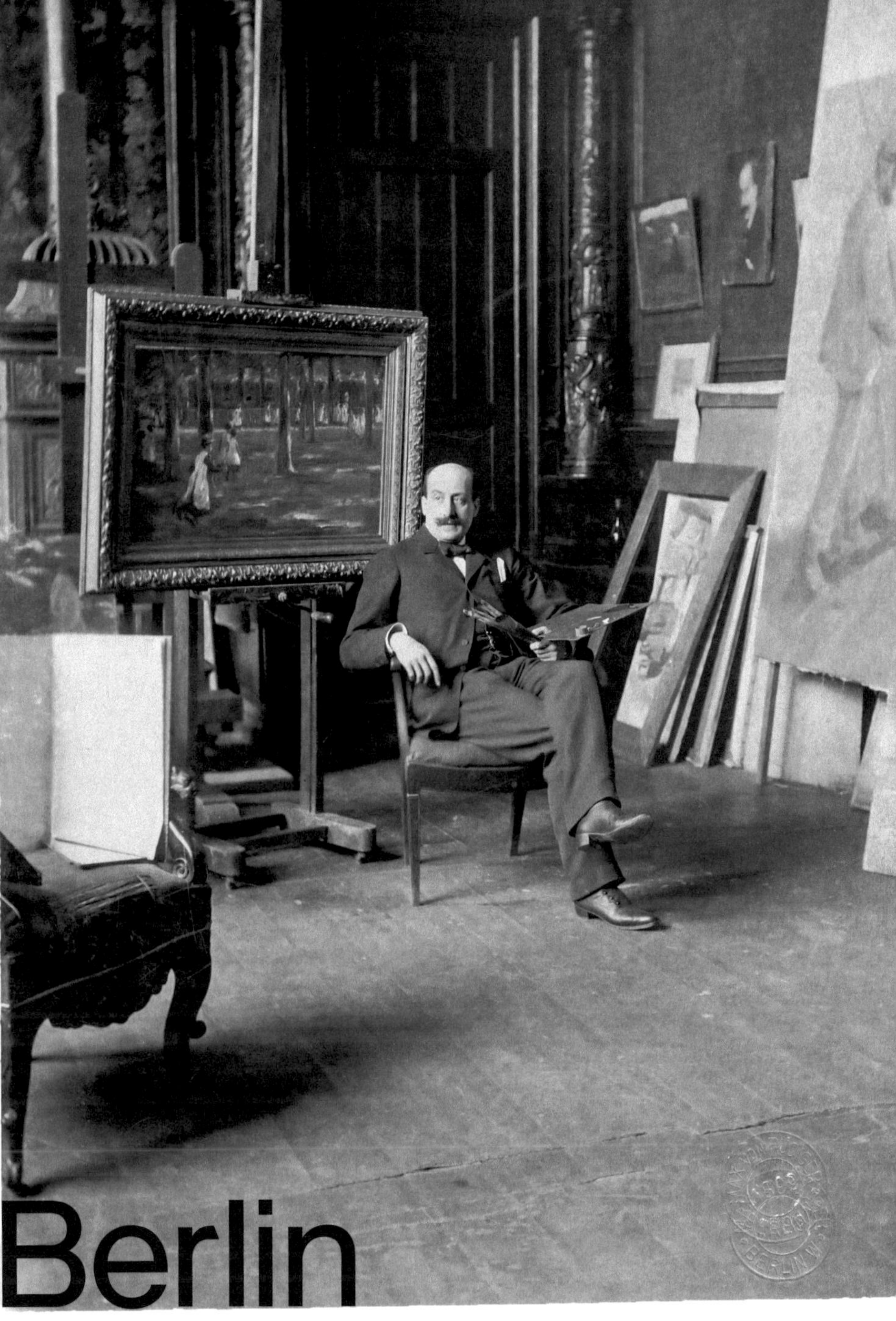

Berlin Network

(B)
Max von Rüdiger Liebermann in His Atelier — 1899
bpk Bildagentur

"I am in a very good mood for work," Edvard Munch writes to his aunt from Berlin in 1894: "have begun etching and will perhaps later publish a small collection—etchings—I have not seen a Norwegian winter in five years now and yearn for it now and then—but I am better off remaining where I have the wealthiest acquaintances."[13]

The Berlin Secessionist Max Liebermann is also part of Munch's network in Berlin. He is said to have appreciated in particular the etchings of the Norwegian artist, who was a good sixteen years younger. But Liebermann didn't want to have anything to do with Munch's painting: "He [Liebermann] once said: 'Others act as if they could do more than they really can; Munch is a clever man; he does the opposite.'"[14]

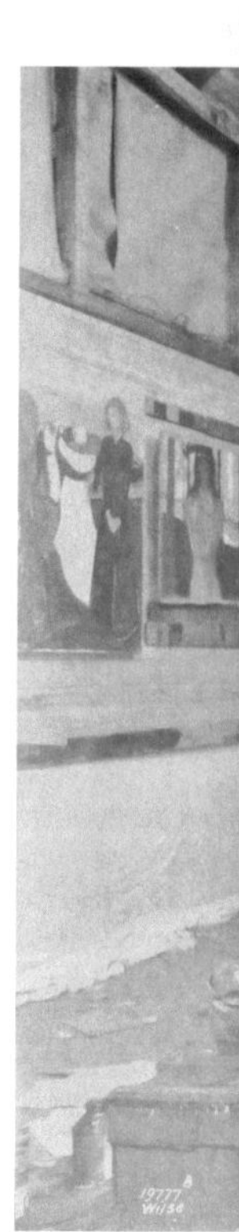

1896

Munch moves to Paris, where he meets Meier-Graefe and Strindberg again. He works intensely on his printmaking abilities and now introduces color as a means of expression. He produces his first woodcuts and lithographs.

Munch tries to establish footing in Paris the following year as well—unsuccessfully.

1898

Munch travels constantly back and forth between Norway, France, and Germany. From 1899 onward, he spends time in Italy more often as well. Among other places, Munch lives for a time in Berlin again and again.

In September 1898, he meets Tulla Larsen in Kristiania. It is the beginning of an *amour fou*. His health continues to be highly unstable. In the following years, he repeatedly receives treatment in sanatoriums.

1902

After moving back to Berlin in late 1901 and occupying a studio at Lützowstrasse 82, in the spring of 1902 Munch scores an important success at the Berlin Secession. Under the title *Depiction of a Series of Images of Life*, he presents, among other things, twenty-two paintings as a frieze in the association's sculpture hall. The Secession hopes to improve its international profile with this extensive appearance by the Norwegian artist. What will later be called *The Frieze of Life* is little appreciated by critics, but Munch is able to establish important contacts during this year, in part with the help of Albert Kollmann, who works hard to arrange commissions and sales for the artist.

In the summer in Åsgårdstrand, he has a dramatic conflict with Tulla Larsen. The two separate.

(A)
F. Lippens
Edvard Munch, Berlin — 1902–4
Munchmuseet — Oslo

(B)
Anders Beer Wilse
Munch's hanging of *The Frieze of Life* in his studio, Ekely — 1925
Munchmuseet — Oslo

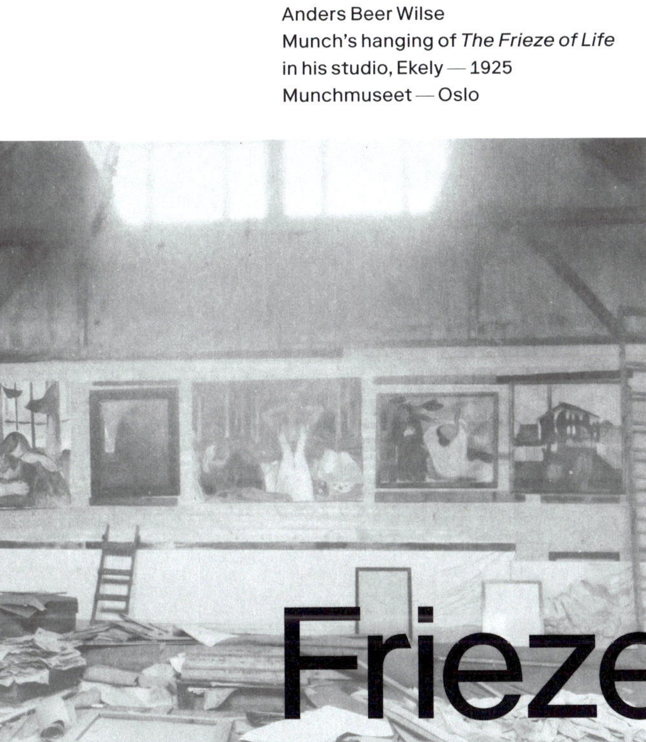

Frieze of Life

Edvard Munch's psychologically condensed works trigger alienation and rejection in the public. In Berlin, he therefore pursued the idea of presenting his paintings as a coherent story of love and death. "Currently, I am working on studies for a series of paintings," he writes to a friend from Charlottenburg in the early 1890s. "These [paintings] that were now rather difficult to understand—will be, I believe, more easily understood when they all come together—it will be about love and death."[15]

"I arranged them together and felt that some of the pictures were connected to each other in content," recalls the artist years later. "When they were positioned together there immediately arose a resonance between them and they became totally different than when [displayed] individually. It became a symphony."[16]

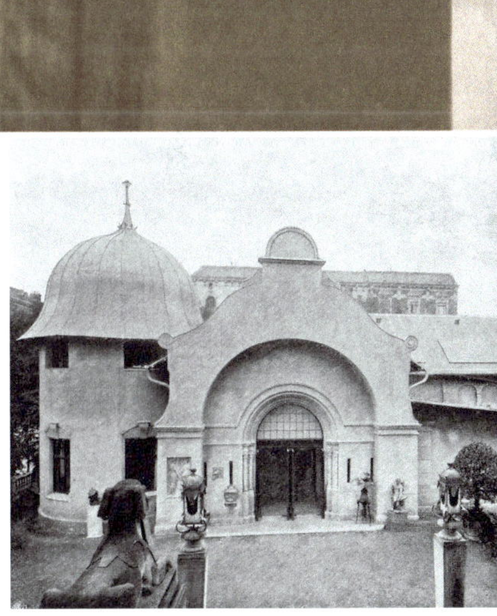

(C)
Building of the Berlin Secession, Kantstrasse 12 — 1899

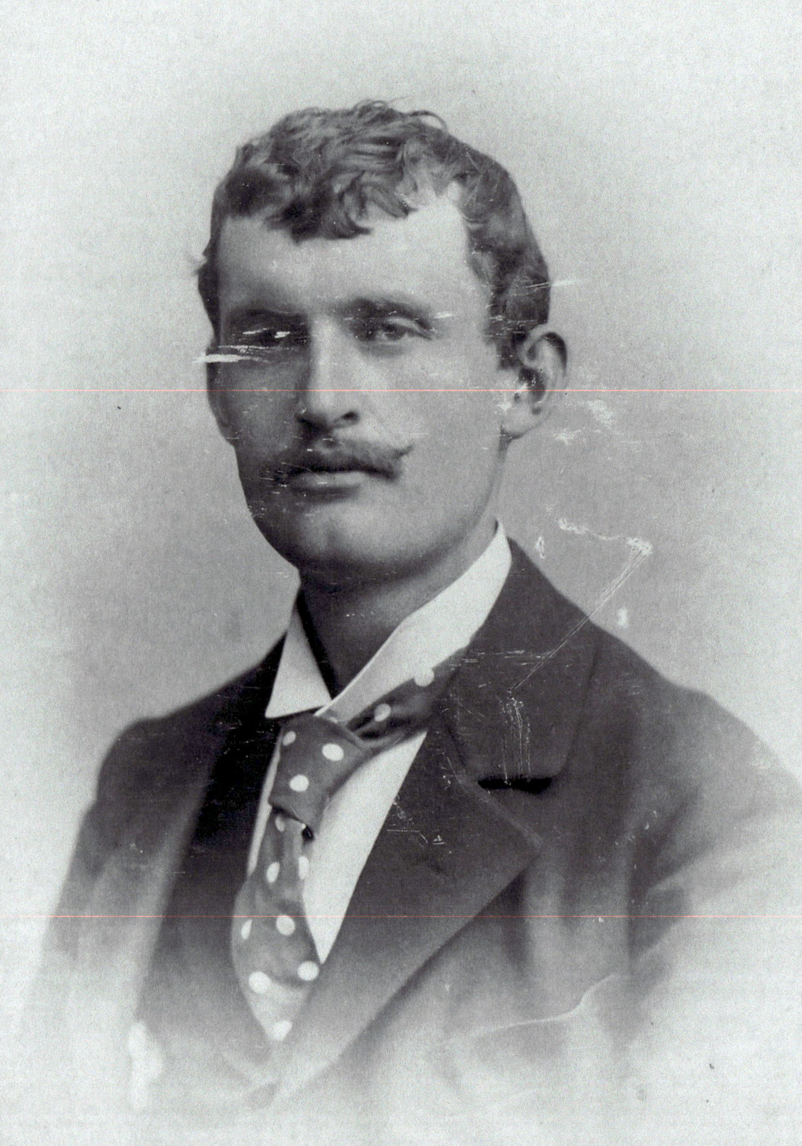

(A)
Christoffer Gade Rude
Edvard Munch — ca. 1892
Munchmuseet — Oslo

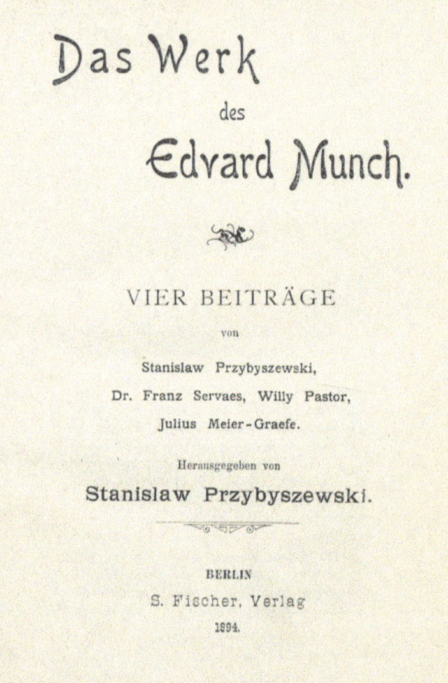

Das Werk
des
Edvard Munch.

VIER BEITRÄGE
von
Stanislaw Przybyszewski,
Dr. Franz Servaes, Willy Pastor,
Julius Meier-Graefe.

Herausgegeben von
Stanislaw Przybyszewski.

BERLIN
S. Fischer, Verlag
1894.

(B)
Stanisław Przybyszewski
The Work of Edvard Munch — 1894

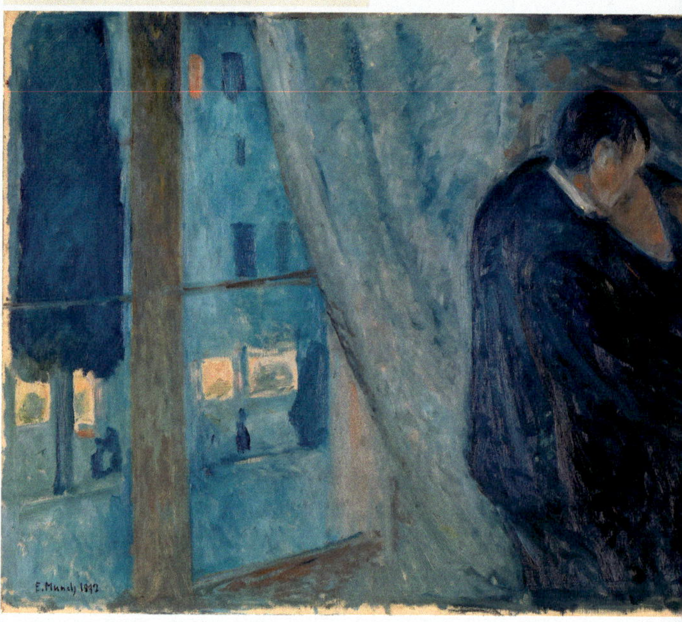

(C)
Edvard Munch
The Kiss — 1892
Nasjonalmuseet — Oslo

Unfinished

"Excesses of naturalism that have never before been exhibited in Berlin," an enraged Berlin critic writes in 1892 about an Edvard Munch exhibition.[17] He attributes to the works "formlessness, brutality of painting, rawness, and vulgarity of sensation" and characterizes them as "raw house painting works."[18] The accusation of the unfinished or sketchy is a thread running through reviews of Munch's art.

There are, however, other voices as well, even early on. The art critic Franz Servaes recognizes in 1894: "For it is not the completed, the whole, the finished, or even the overripe that stimulates Munch's painting. The unexplored, the inaccessible, and the impossible is what satisfies the dream of his nights—and days. For Munch is a dreamer in bright daylight."[19]

(A)
Tulla Larsen and Edvard Munch — ca. 1899
Munchmuseet — Oslo

(B)
X-ray image of Munch's left hand — 1902
Munchmuseet — Oslo

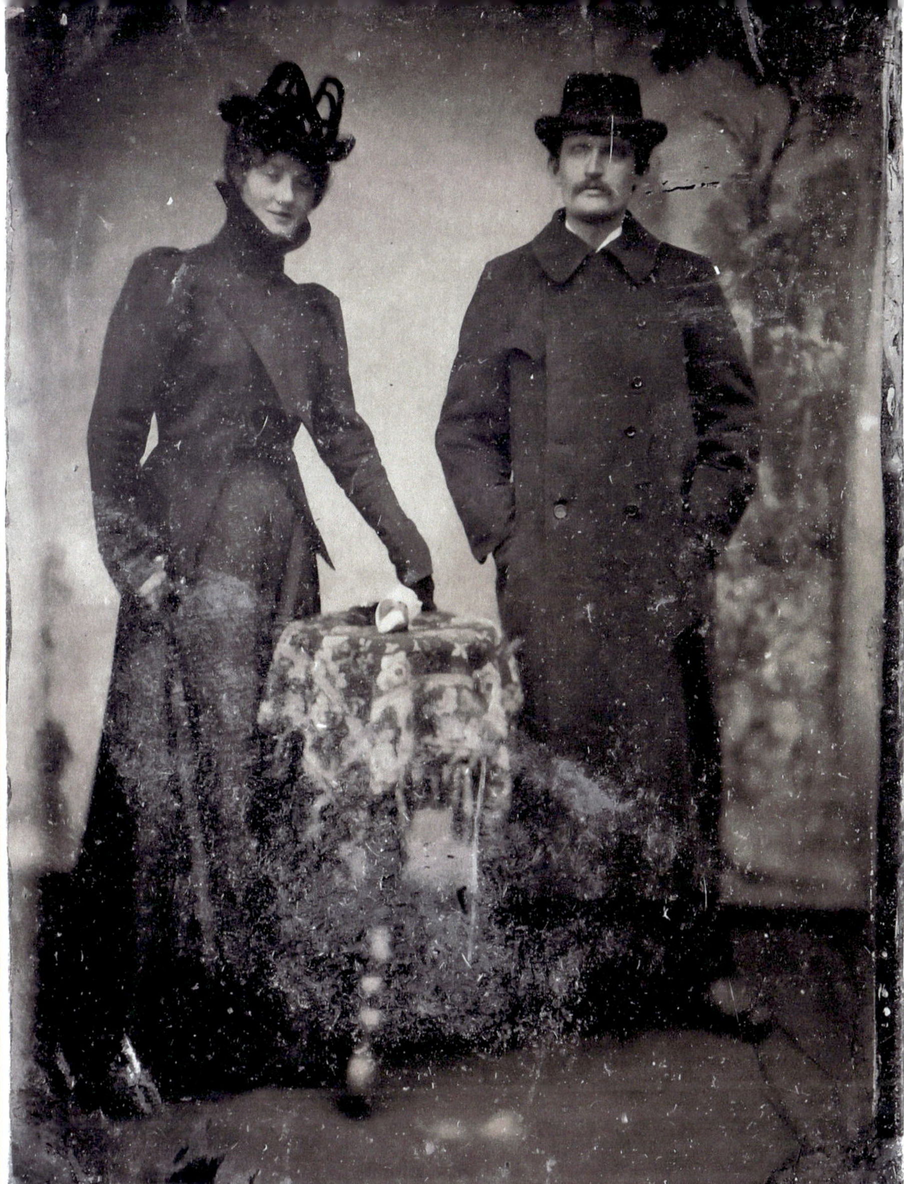

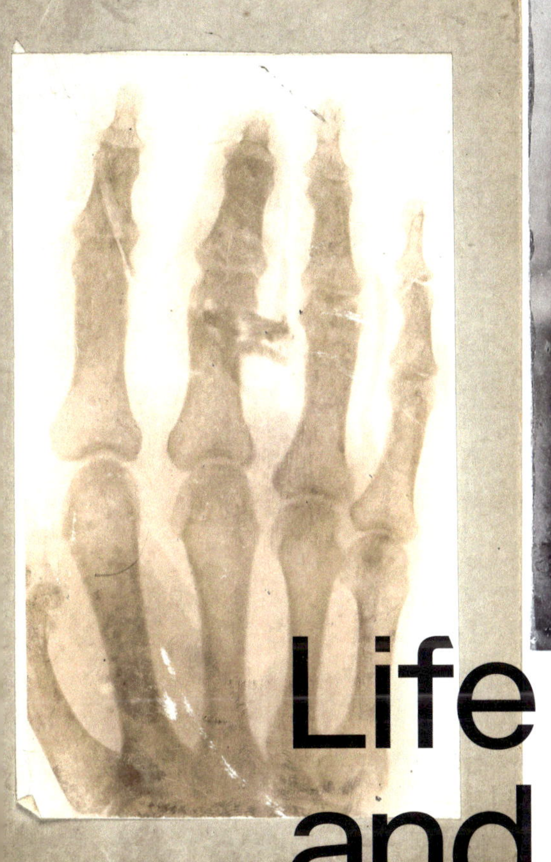

Life and Love

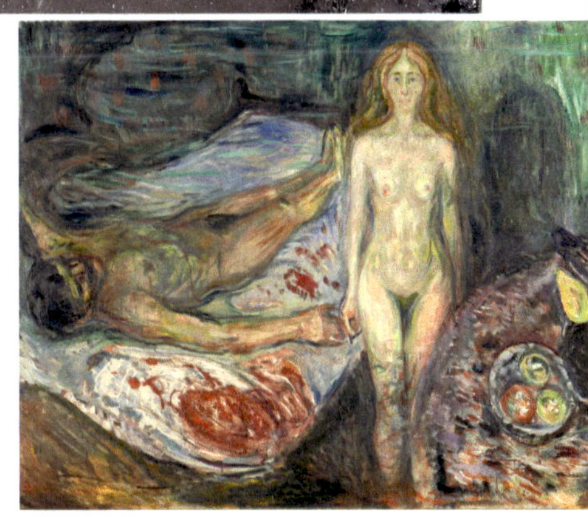

(C)
Edvard Munch
The Death of Marat I — 1907
Munchmuseet — Oslo

Mathilde "Tulla" Larsen—a wine dealer's daughter—and Edvard Munch meet in 1898 in Kristiania (now Oslo). They fall in love, take trips, get engaged, separate, reunite, and finally go their separate ways in 1902. The affair ends tragically with the artist's middle finger being shot. The exact circumstances have yet to be explained.

The emotional highs and lows of this relationship provide Munch with material for his great themes of love and death for many years. In a draft letter to his lover in 1899, which she presumably never receives, he asks her: "and do not reproach me but lament me. I who neither can nor wish to live, I who merely sit in the window with my painful longing, observing the motley, strange, terrible life around me."[20]

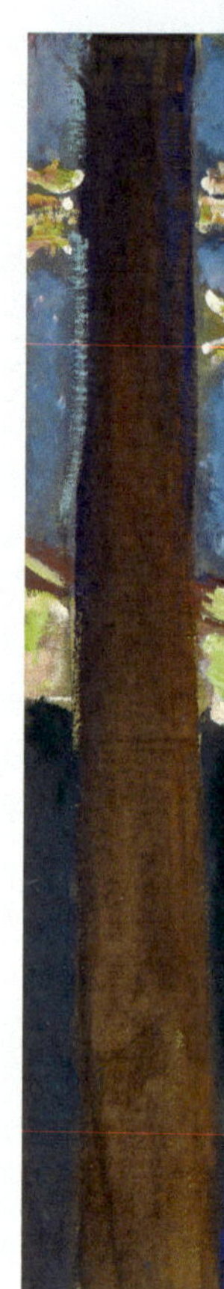

1904

Munch continues to live primarily in Berlin in the autumn and winter months while spending summers in Norway.

He becomes a member of the Berlin Secession and signs a contract with the publisher Bruno Cassirer, who now distributes his prints exclusively. Bruno is the cousin of the art dealer Paul Cassirer, who from 1903 onward regularly shows Munch in his Kunstsalon (gallery) at Viktoriastrasse 35 in the wealthy district of Tiergarten.

In 1905, Munch signs an exclusive contract with the Galerie Commeter in Hamburg for the sale of his paintings.

1906

Munch spends time in Weimar and Bad Kösen, among other places. The Berlin theater intendant and director Max Reinhardt asks Munch to contribute to the set design for Henrik Ibsen's drama *Ghosts*, for the opening of the Kammerspiele (Chamber Theater) of the Deutsches Theater in Berlin. Munch also produces "atmospheric sketches" for the production of *Hedda Gabler*, also by Ibsen, which follows *Ghosts*. Moreover, Reinhardt commissions the artist to design a decorative cycle for a reception hall of the Kammerspiele, which will later be called the *Reinhardt Frieze*.

1907

In January, Munch begins working on a portrait of the industrialist and future German foreign minister Walther Rathenau, who already owns two of his paintings and several prints. Figure p.135

The artist ends his contracts with Bruno Cassirer and the Galerie Commeter and again handles the distribution of his art himself. He spends the summer in Warnemünde on the Baltic Sea.

In the autumn and winter of 1907–8, Munch is again living in Berlin. It will be his final extended stay in the city. The *Reinhardt Frieze* is installed at the end of the year. The hall in the Kammerspiele is, however, only rarely accessible to the public. Later, in 1912, the frieze is removed during a renovation.

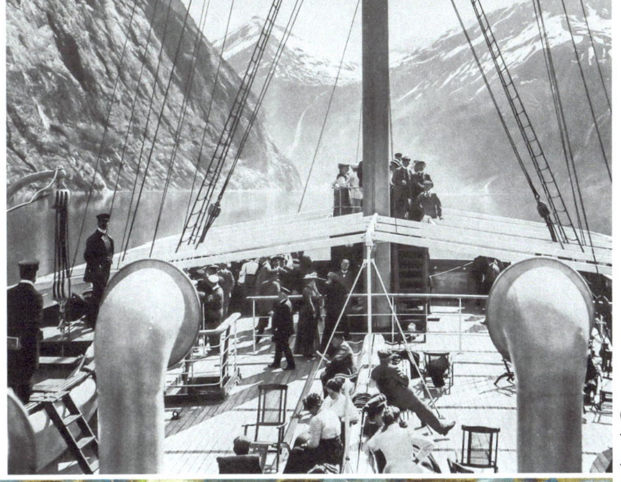

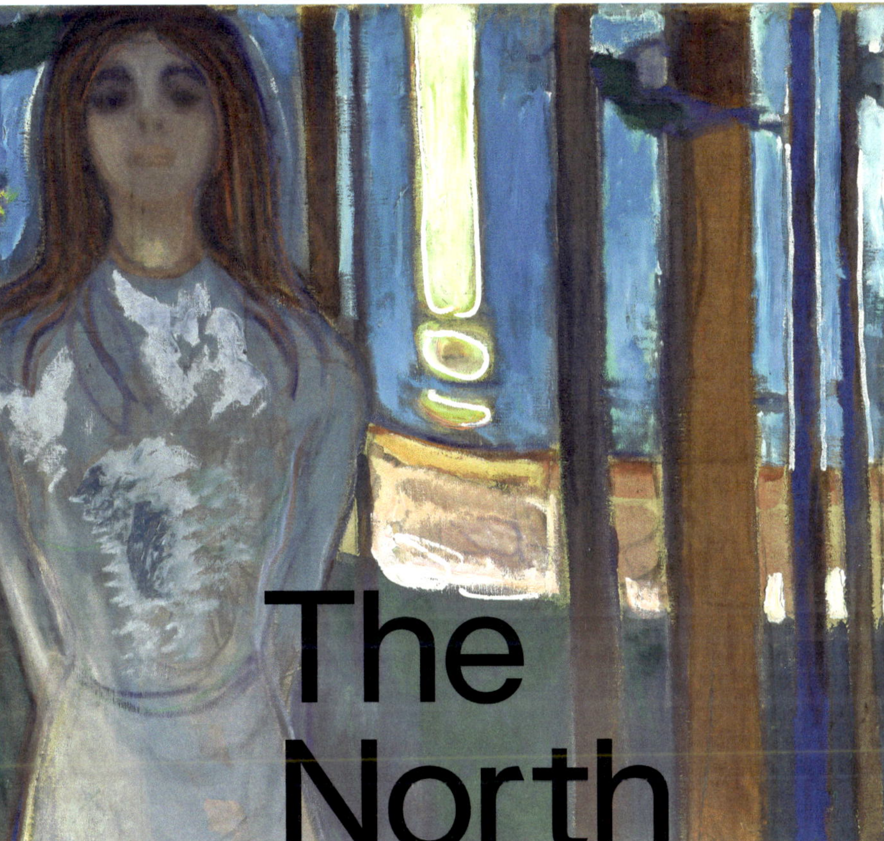

The North

(A)
The steamship *Meteor* passing through the Norwegian fjords — 1906
Kieler Stadt- und Schifffahrtsmuseum — Kiel

(B)
Edvard Munch
Summer Night (The Voice) — 1896
Munchmuseet — Oslo

(C)
Promotional poster of the Hamburg–South America Steamship Company — 1928
Deutsches Historisches Museum — Berlin

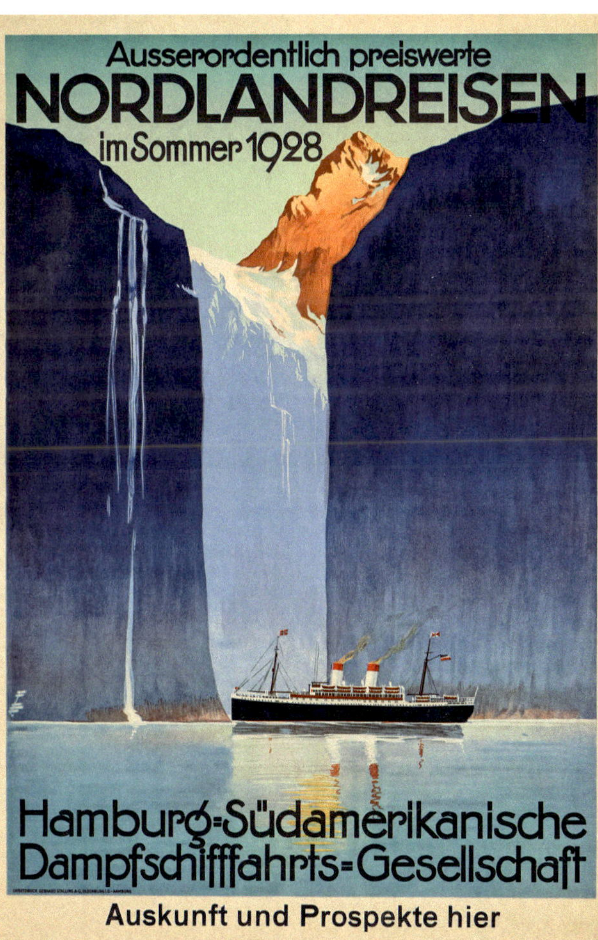

"With Edvard Munch, an entirely new art begins: the Nordic," the Expressionist writer Theodor Däubler praises the artist in a journal in 1919. At the end of that decade, Berlin matter-of-factly regards Munch "as one of our modern artists who, though full of Parisian culture, have left Impressionism behind." For Däubler, that explains why Munch was not understood for so long. Or, Däubler corrects himself: "let's say more correctly: Munch was appreciated in Berlin as an outstanding talent from early on."[21]

Däubler is alluding to the Wilhelmine era's enthusiasm for a romantic North. He gives this as one reason the Norwegian painter was invited to Berlin at the end of the nineteenth century. He does not mention the scandal around Munch's exhibition in 1892 and rejection of that time.

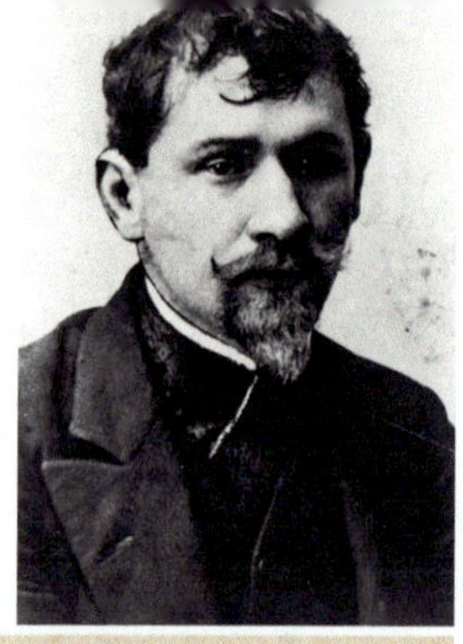

(A)
Stanisław Przybyszewski — n.d.
Narodowe Archiwum
Cyfrowe — Warsaw

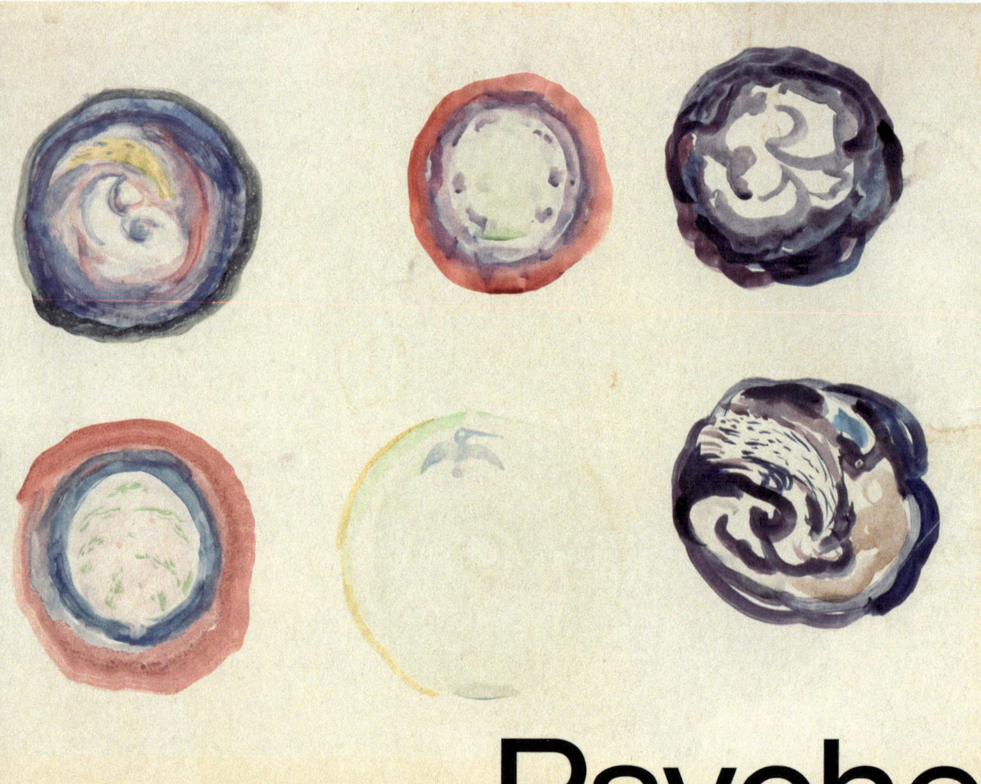

(B)
Edvard Munch
Six sketches for *The Afflicted Eye* — 1930
Munchmuseet — Oslo

(C)
Edvard Munch
Self-Portrait in Hell — 1903
Munchmuseet — Oslo

Psyche

"Edvard Munch is the first to have attempted to depict the finest and most subtle movements of the soul,"[22] the Polish writer and close friend Stanisław Przybyszewski writes in 1894. Przybyszewski first studies medicine in Berlin and then becomes an influential figure in Berlin's bohemia. Munch's image as a hypersensitive genius who reveals inner worlds and truths in his art can be traced back to Przybyszewski and the circle around Zum schwarzen Ferkel in Berlin.

Munch's concentration on the human psyche takes place against the backdrop of the pioneering psychological research of his day — especially concerning the unconscious — by Wilhelm Wundt and Sigmund Freud, among others. For Munch, the psyche has unexploited potential that should be explored in art: "Mankind, you are/great, because you have/the world within yourselves."[23]

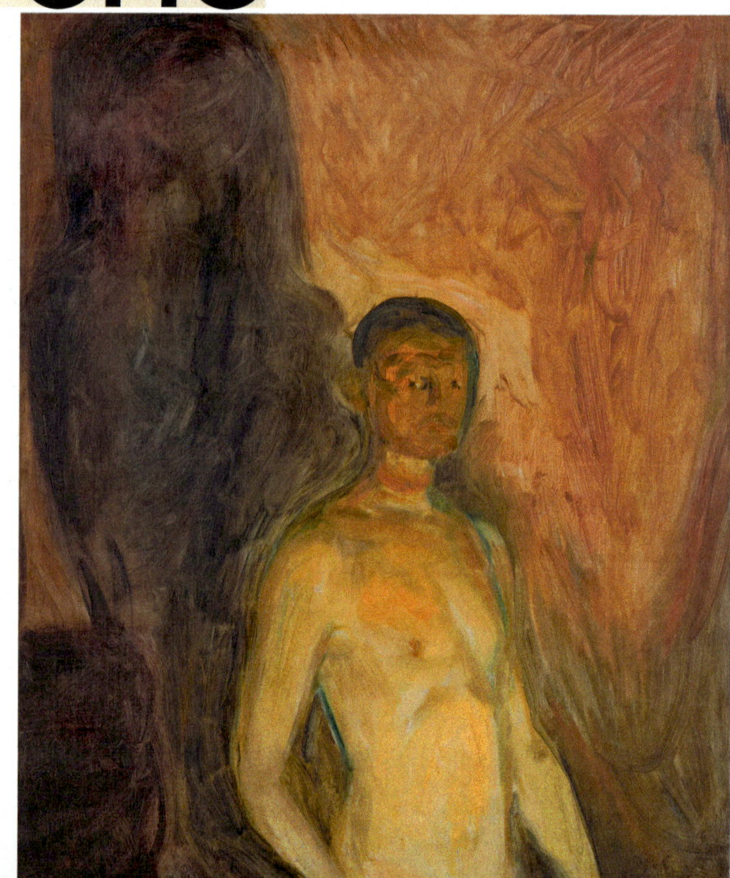

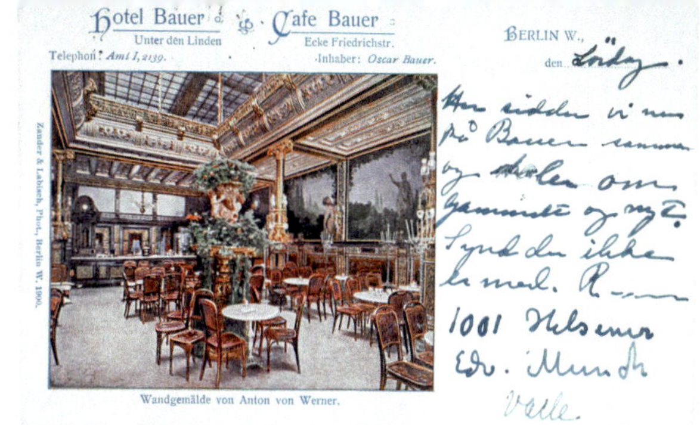

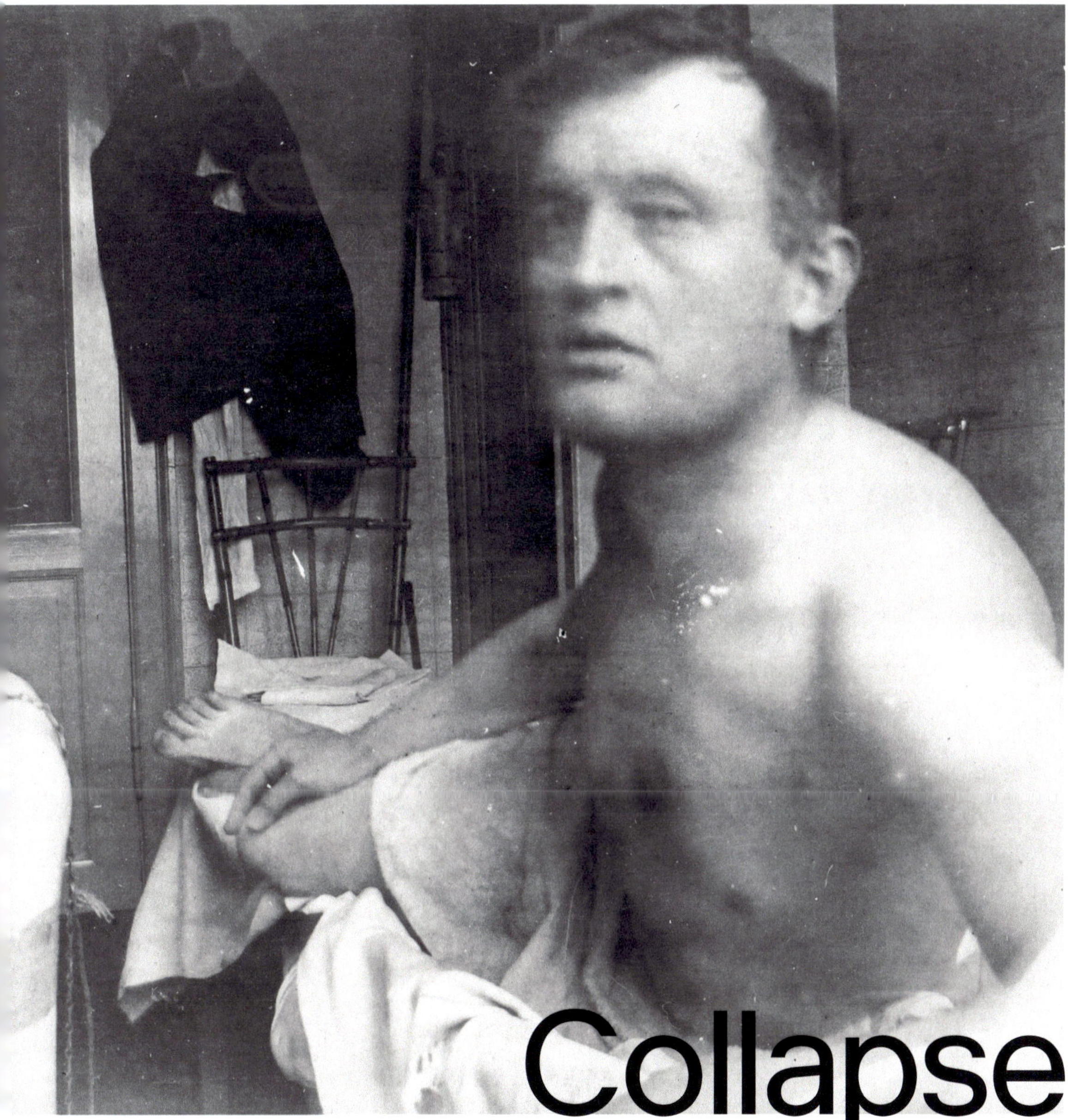

(A)
Postcard from Edvard Munch
to Helge Bäckström
Café Bauer — October 20, 1906
Munchmuseet — Oslo

(B)
Edvard Munch
Self-Portrait at the Clinic
Copenhagen — 1908–9
Munchmuseet — Oslo

Collapse

After the tragic end of his relationship with Tulla Larsen, Edvard Munch loses himself in alcoholic excesses. Especially in Berlin, with its hard-drinking artists and numerous variety theaters, cafés, and bars offering distraction. The painter increasingly suffers from mood swings, hallucinations, and paranoia. He seeks rest and relaxation at the beach in Warnemünde, among other places.

In October 1908, Munch has a nervous breakdown while drinking whisky in Copenhagen. He enters a private clinic in search of rest and detoxification, successfully: "For me, the period of alcohol, with its mixture of pain and joy, is over — a wondrous world is closed to me."[24]

1908

Munch again spends several summer months in Warnemünde. In August, he departs for Copenhagen. In the autumn, Munch suffers a nervous breakdown and is treated for several months in the clinic of Dr. Daniel Jacobson in Copenhagen.

In his Norwegian homeland, he receives official honors: the Statens Kunstmuseum (State Art Museum) in Kristiania, the future Nasjonalgalleriet (National Gallery), acquires numerous major works by the artist, and he is awarded the Kongelige Norske Sankt Olavs Orden (Royal Norwegian Order of Saint Olav).

1909

Munch is released from the clinic in the spring and moves permanently to Norway. He visits Berlin only sporadically from now on. He lives first in Kragerø and begins working on decorating the auditorium of the University of Kristiania, for which a competition is announced. The debates over the designs submitted continue until 1914.

Munch will have large exhibitions in Norway and throughout Europe in the coming years.

1912

Munch is represented by thirty-two paintings in the Sonderbund exhibition in Cologne and is celebrated as a pioneer of the avant-garde alongside Vincent van Gogh, Paul Gauguin, and Paul Cézanne.

Munch meets the art historian Curt Glaser, who is in charge of the "Modern Department" of the Kupferstichkabinett (Museum of Prints and Drawings) in Berlin. Under Glaser's aegis, the department acquires an extensive collection of Munch's prints and drawings.

1913

The Berlin Secession breaks up after long internal conflicts. A small group around Lovis Corinth continues to exist as the Secession, but the majority of the members, under the leadership of Max Liebermann and Paul Cassirer, leaves the association. The "Rump Secession" offers Munch an honorary membership, but he turns it down. The artists who leave organize an autumn exhibition, where Munch shows his designs for the decoration of the auditorium of the University of Kristiania, about which disagreement still reigns in Norway. In Berlin, the paintings are received with enthusiasm.

The university accepts Munch's paintings for the auditorium the following year.

1916

During World War I, Munch stays in touch with Germany as much as possible. He purchases the Ekely estate near Oslo, where he will live until his death. The murals for the auditorium of the University of Kristiania are handed over to the public.

1923

Munch is named a member of the Preussische Akademie der Künste (Prussian Academy of the Arts) in Berlin.

In the 1920s, many German museums make an effort to acquire works by Munch. The artist is, however, scarcely willing to sell paintings in his possession any longer.

1927

After Munch was honored by an extensive exhibition at the Kunsthalle Mannheim the previous year, Berlin's Nationalgalerie opens the largest retrospective on Edvard Munch thus far in March 1927 with 244 works. At the same time, around 150 graphic works are shown at the Kupferstichkabinett. The show is a triumph. Critics celebrate him as a classic and appropriate him as a German artist. Munch donates the painting *Snow Shovelers* to the Nationalgalerie. Figure p.152B

The Berlin exhibition travels to Nasjonalgalleriet in Oslo, where works are added.

1930

The Nationalgalerie in Berlin purchases three works by Munch in 1930–31. Supplemented by loans and donations, there are six of his paintings in the museum's collection in 1932.

An eye ailment afflicts Munch in 1930 and 1931.

1933

Munch receives the Grand Cross of the Sankt Olavs Orden in Norway.

After the National Socialists rise to power in Germany, Munch's reception as "Germanic" takes on an ideological quality. At the same time, his art stands for the modernism they defamed as "degenerate."

1937

Eighty-three works by Munch are confiscated from German collections in the "Entartete Kunst" (Degenerate Art) action. Several of these works are auctioned in Norway in 1938–39.

1940

A good seven months after World War II begins, German troops occupy Norway on April 9. The seventy-six-year-old Munch writes a will bequeathing all of his works and his literary remains to the City of Oslo. Today, they represent the core of the collection of Munchmuseet in Oslo.

1944

Edvard Munch dies at Ekely on January 23.

(1) Quoted in Næss 2015, p. 91.
(2) Paul 1927.
(3) Max Linde to Edvard Munch, April 16, 1906, Munchmuseet, Oslo, MM K 2819.
(4) Julius Meier-Graefe, "Munch" (1927), in Meier-Graefe, *Grundstoffe der Bilder: Ausgewählte Schriften*, ed. Carl Linfert (Munich, 1959), pp. 177–84, esp. p. 177.
(5) Quoted in Mary Kay Norseng, *Dagny: Dagny Juel Przybyszewska, the Woman and the Myth* (Seattle, WA, 1991), p. 26
(6) *Berliner Börsen-Courier*, December 10, 1893.
(7) Edvard Munch quoted in Heller 1984, p. 76.
(8) Paul 1927.
(9) Edvard Munch to Karen Bjølstad, October 24, 1894, Munchmuseet, Oslo, MM N 806.
(10) Harry Graf Kessler, *Journey to the Abyss: The Diaries of Count Harry Kessler, 1880–1918*, ed. and trans. Laird M. Easton (New York, 2012), pp. 126–27.
(11) Edvard Munch to Karen Bjølstad, February 3, 1895, Munchmuseet, Oslo, MM N 808.
(12) Quoted in Næss 2015, p. 234.
(13) Edvard Munch to Karen Bjølstad, November 14, 1894, Munchmuseet, Oslo, MM N 807.
(14) Gustav Schiefler, *Meine Graphik-Sammlung* (Hamburg, 1927), p. 33.
(15) Edvard Munch to Johan Rohde, undated letter, quoted in German in Munich, Hamburg, and Berlin 1994–95, p. 63.
(16) Edvard Munch, note, 1930–34, Munchmuseet, Oslo, MM N 46.
(17) Rosenberg 1892b, p. 74.
(18) Rosenberg 1892b, p. 74.
(19) Servaes 1894, pp. 55–56.
(20) Edvard Munch to Tulla Larsen, May 25, 1899 (draft letter), Munchmuseet, Oslo, MM N 1813.
(21) Theodor Däubler, "Munch," *Das Junge Deutschland: Monatsschrift für Theater und Literatur* 2, no. 8 (1919): pp. 206–7, esp. p. 207.
(22) Przybyszewski 1894b, p. 16, published in English as Stanisław Przybyszewski, "The Work of Edvard Munch" (1894), in Nielsen 2015, p. 85.
(23) Poul Erik Tøjner, *Munch in His Own Words* (Munich, 2003), p. 199.
(24) Edvard Munch to Jappe Nilssen, December 28, 1908, Nasjonalbiblioteket, Oslo. Brevs. 604, PN 712.

Berlin City Map 1902

The exhibition venues, meeting places, studios, and dwellings frequented by Edvard Munch and his contemporaries

(1) Exhibition building of the Berlin Secession, Kurfürstendamm 208/209 (1905–14, as of 1914 the exhibition building of the Freie Secession)

(2) Graphisches Kabinett J. B. Neumann, Kurfürstendamm 33 (1910/11–15)

(3) Exhibition building of the Berlin Secession, Kantstrasse 12 (1899–1905)

(4) Graphisches Kabinett J. B. Neumann, Kurfürstendamm 232 (1915–25)

(5) Studio of the painter Leonard Boldt, Münchener Strasse 50

(6) Bruno Cassirer publishers, Derfflingerstrasse 16 (1901–11)

(7) Galerie Alfred Flechtheim, Lützowufer 13 (1921–33)

(8) Edvard Munch's studio, Lützowstrasse 82 (1901–2 and 1903–4)

(9) Kunstsalon Fritz Gurlitt, Potsdamer Strasse 113, Villa II (1905–25)

(10) Kunsthandlung Keller & Reiner, Potsdamer Strasse 122 (1897–1909)

(11) Kunstsalon Paul Cassirer, Viktoriastrasse 35 (1898–1934)

(12) Harry Graf Kessler's apartment, Köthener Strasse 28/29 (as of 1898)

(13) Verein Berliner Künstler, Architektenhaus, Wilhelmstrasse 92/93

(14) Equitable-Palast, Friedrichstrasse 59–60

(15) Akademie der Künste zu Berlin, Pariser Platz 4 (1907–37)

(16) Wine bar Zum schwarzen Ferkel, Unter den Linden 76 (until 1905)

(17) Kunstsalon Eduard Schulte, Unter den Linden 75/76 (1906–34)

(18) Kunstsalon Eduard Schulte, Unter den Linden 1 (1891–1906)

(19) Galerie Ugo Barroccio, Unter den Linden 16

(20) Café Bauer, Unter den Linden 26 (today 29)

(21) Nationalgalerie, Kronprinzenpalais, Unter den Linden (1919–37)

(22) Kupferstichkabinett, Neues Museum, Museumsinsel

(23) Deutsches Theater, Kammerspiele, Schumannstrasse 13a (as of 1906)

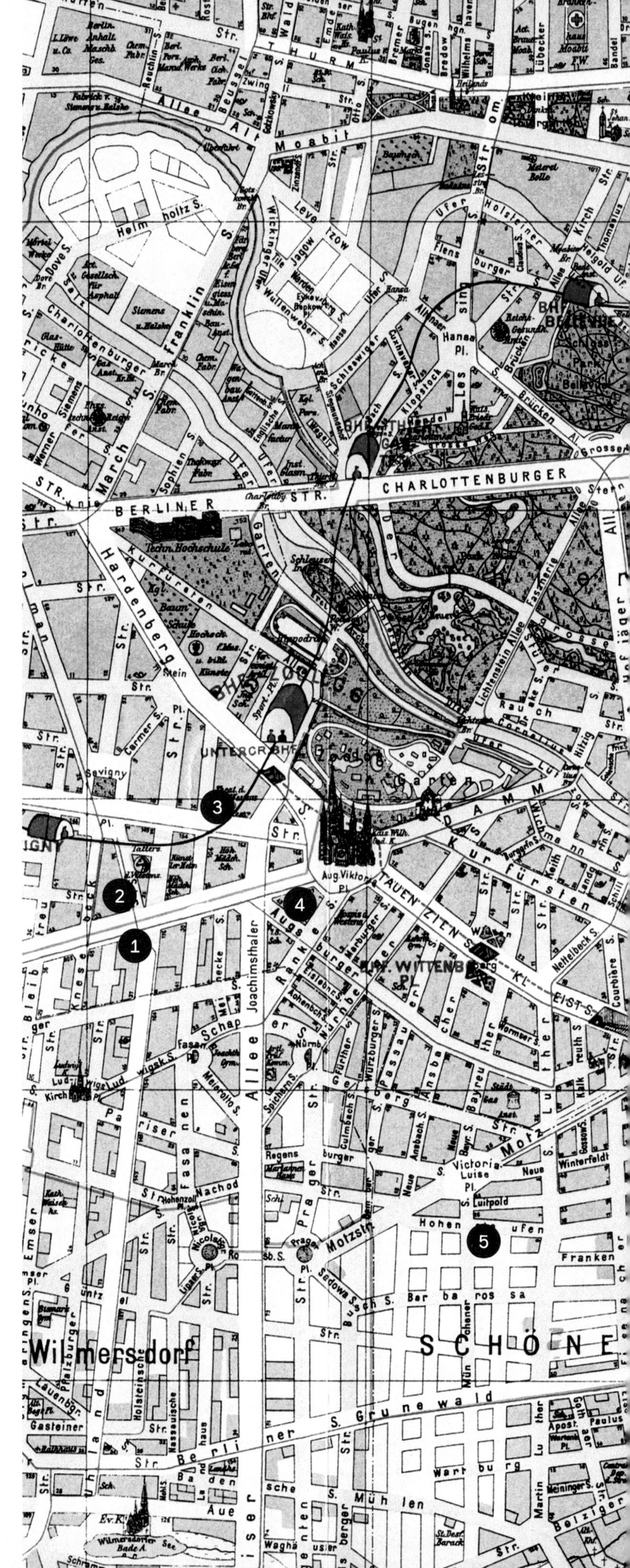

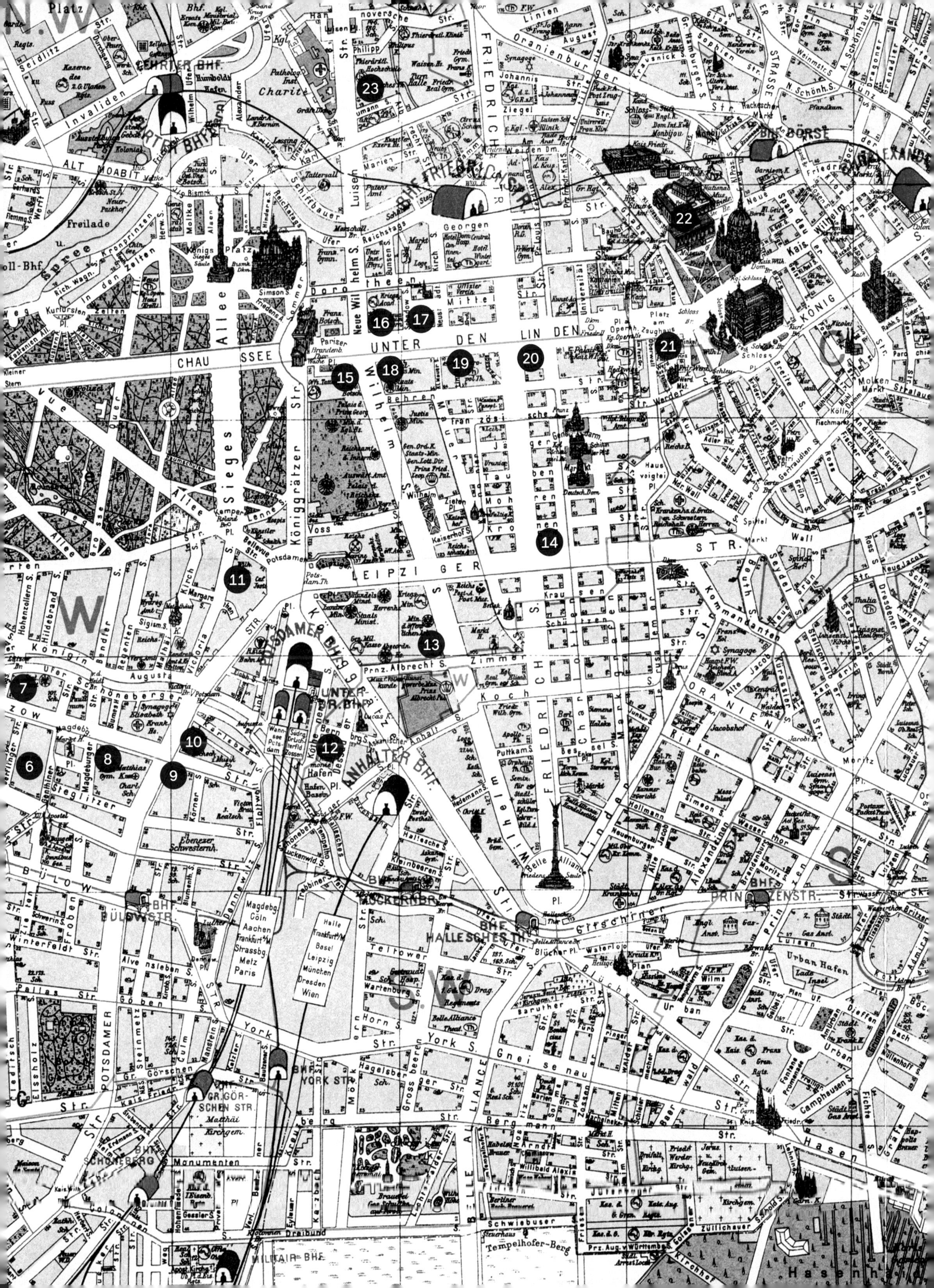

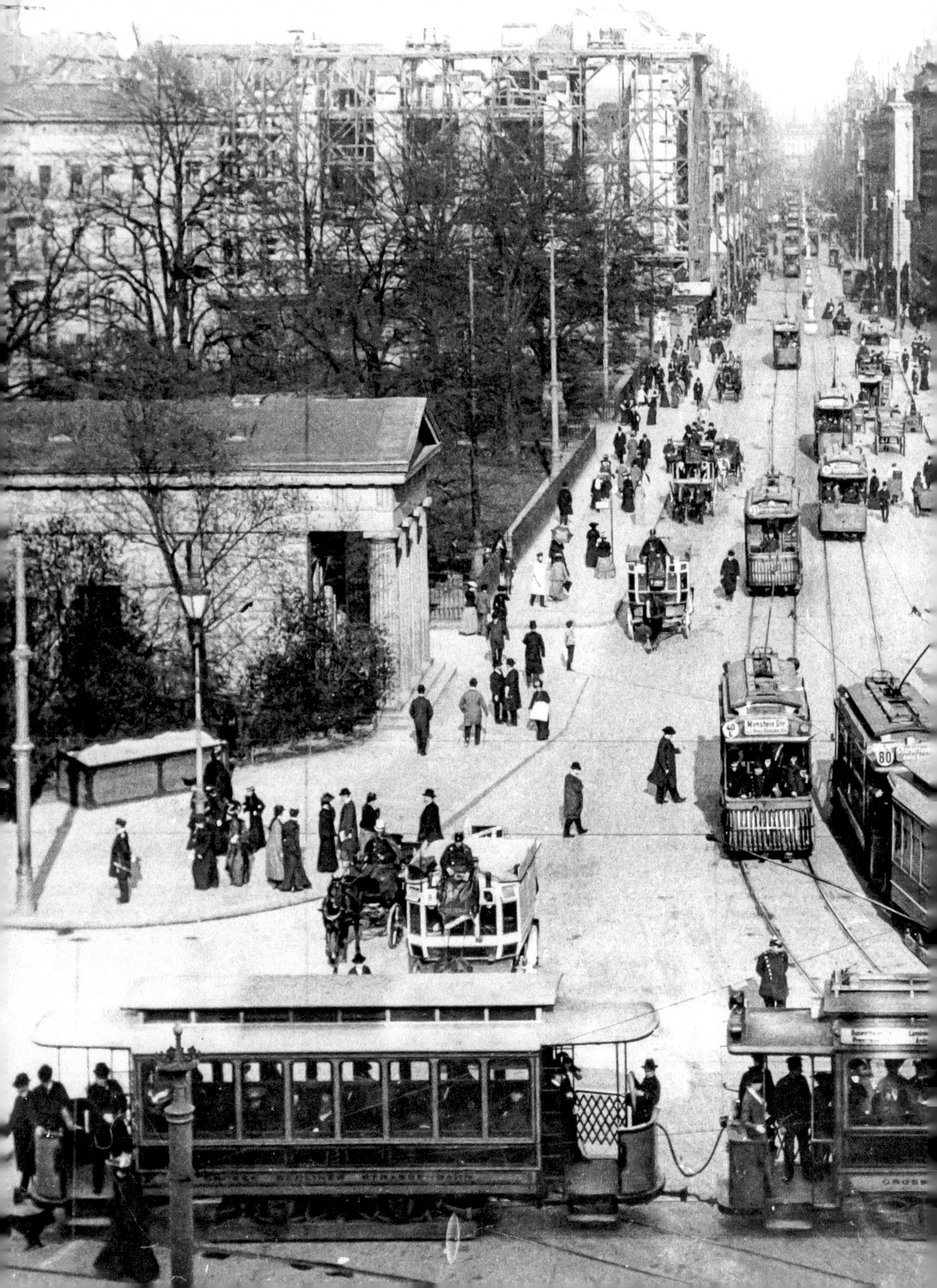
40
L
Monstein Str
80

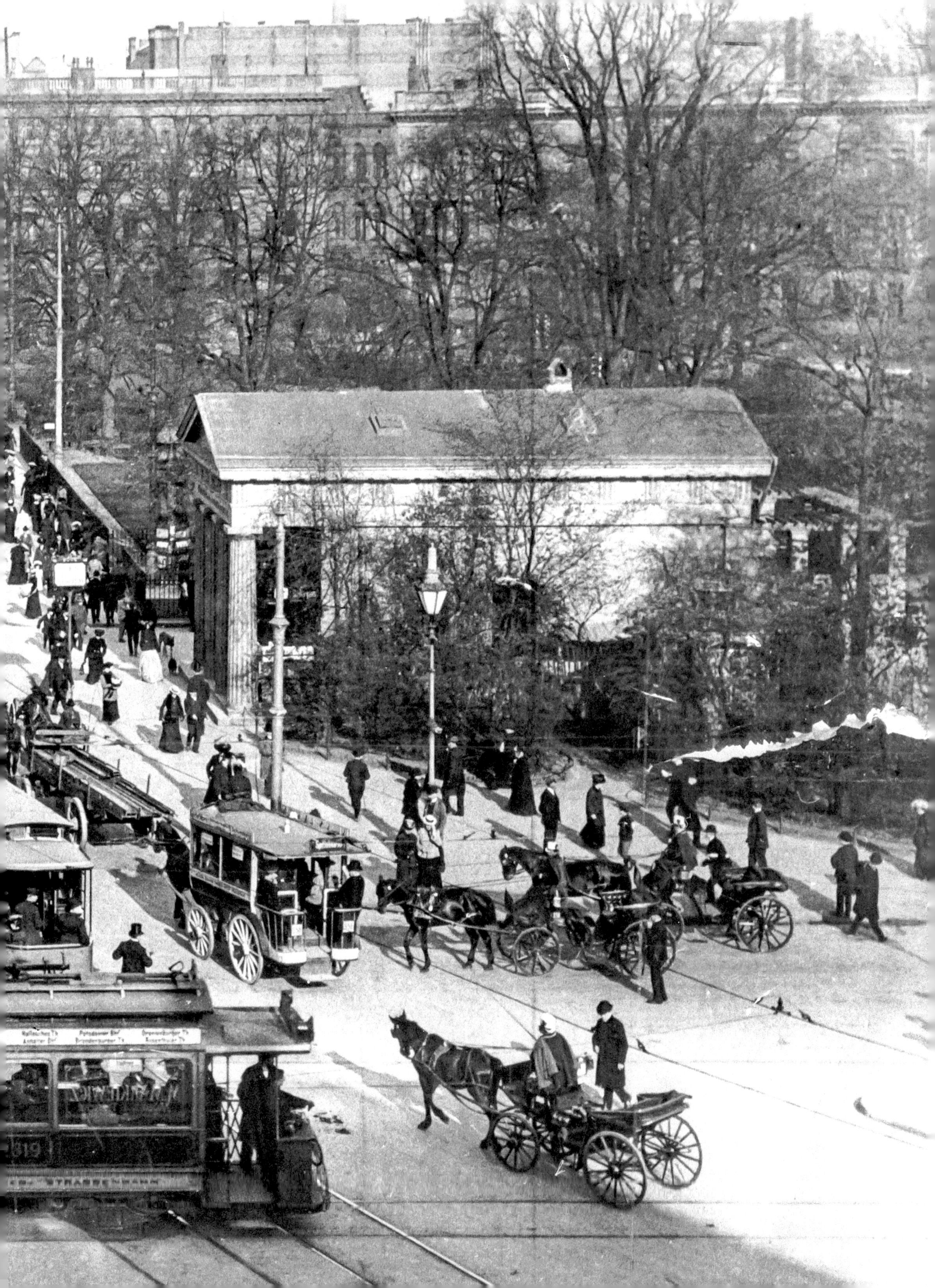

Edvard Munch Exhibitions in Berlin 1892 to 1933

1892

Verein Berliner Künstler, Architektenhaus, Wilhelmstrasse 92/93
Sonder-Ausstellung des Malers Eduard [sic] Munch aus Christiania
(Special Exhibition of the Painter Eduard [sic] Munch from Christiania)
November 5–12, 1892
55 paintings

Equitable-Palast, Friedrichstrasse 59–60
Sonderausstellung des Malers Eduard [sic] Munch aus Christiania
(Special Exhibition of the Painter Eduard [sic] Munch from Christiania)
December 26, 1892, to January 12, 1893
56 paintings, 12 drawings, sketches, and studies

1893

Hohenzollern-Panorama am Lehrter Bahnhof
Freie Berliner Kunst-Ausstellung: Salon der Zurückgewiesenen
(Free Berlin Art Exhibition: Salon of the Rejected)
June 1893, 2 pastels

[Commercial building] Unter den Linden 19
Eduard [*sic*] *Munch Gemälde-Ausstellung*
(Eduard [sic] Munch Paintings Exhibition)
December 3, 1893, to [January] 1894
25 paintings, 25 watercolors and drawings

1895

Galerie Ugo Barroccio, Unter den Linden 16
Edvard Munch und Axel Gallén
March 3–24, 1895
29 paintings, 17 prints and drawings

1896

Landesausstellungsgebäude am Lehrter Bahnhof
Internationale Kunst-Ausstellung Berlin 1896: Zur Feier des 200-jährigen Bestehens der Königlichen Akademie der Künste
(International Art Exhibition in Berlin in 1896: For the Celebration of the Bicentennial of the Royal Academy of the Arts)
May 3 to September 30, 1896
1 painting

1898

Kunstgewerbemuseum zu Berlin, Prinz-Albrecht-Strasse 8 (since 1951 Niederkirchnerstraße 8)
[International exhibition of graphic art], March to April 1898
Unknown number of works

Kunsthandlung Keller & Reiner, Potsdamer Strasse 122
[Small solo presentation as part of the gallery's program]
Opening April 8, runs through April 1898
Unknown number of paintings and prints

1902

Exhibition building of the Berlin Secession, Kantstrasse 12
Fünfte Kunstausstellung der Berliner Secession (Fifth Art Exhibition of the Berlin Secession)
April 26 to October 5, 1902
28 paintings, 22 of which are presented as *Darstellung einer Reihe von Lebensbildern* (Depiction of a Series of Images of Life), which will later be called *The Frieze of Life*

Kunstsalon Eduard Schulte, Unter den Linden 1
[Gallery exhibition with Edvard Munch participating]
November 1902
Unknown number of prints

1903

Kunstsalon Paul Cassirer, Viktoriastrasse 35
Collectionen Edvard Munch, Philipp Klein, August Gaul
Fifth year, fourth exhibition
January 17 to February 1, 1903
23 paintings, 9 prints

Kunstsalon Paul Cassirer, Viktoriastrasse 35, *Collectionen Francisco de Goya: Collectionen Ulrich Hübner und Ed. Munch*
Sixth year, second exhibition
November 5 to December 1, 1903
16 paintings, unknown number of drawings and prints

Exhibition building of the Berlin Secession, Kantstrasse 12
Achte Kunstausstellung der Berliner Secession: Zeichnende Künste (Eighth Art Exhibition of the Berlin Secession: Drawing Arts)
November 14, 1903, to early 1904
47 prints

1904

Kunstsalon Paul Cassirer, Viktoriastrasse 35
Werke von Edvard Munch, Jacob Alberts, Hans R. Lichtenberger, Oskar Moll, Heinrich Zille, Auguste Renoir, Albert Lebourg
Seventh year, third exhibition
December 19, 1904, to January 19, 1905
20 paintings

1906

Studio of the painter Leonard Boldt, Münchener Strasse 50
[Exhibition of the *Linde Frieze*]
January to February 1906
10 paintings

Exhibition building of the Berlin Secession, Kurfürstendamm 208/209
Elfte Ausstellung der Berliner Secession (Eleventh Exhibition of the Berlin Secession)
April 21 to October 7, 1906
5 paintings

Kunstsalon Eduard Schulte, Unter den Linden 75/76
[Solo presentation as part of the gallery's program]
May 13 to July 7, 1906
At least 14 paintings

1907

Kunstsalon Paul Cassirer, Viktoriastrasse 35
Kollektionen Paul Baum, Lovis Corinth, Georg Kolbe, Adolphe Monticelli, Edvard Munch: Werke von Joseph Oppenheimer und Hermann Pleuer
Ninth year, fifth exhibition
January 24 to February 18, 1907
30 paintings

Exhibition building of the Berlin Secession, Kurfürstendamm 208/209
Dreizehnte Ausstellung der Berliner Secession (Thirteenth Exhibition of the Berlin Secession)
April 20 to August 18, 1907
4 paintings

Kunstsalon Paul Cassirer, Viktoriastrasse 35
Kollektionen Paul Cézanne, Curt Herrmann, Henri Matisse, Edvard Munch, tenth year, first exhibition
September 30 to October 18, 1907
36 paintings

Kunstsalon Paul Cassirer, Viktoriastrasse 35, *Vierzehnte Ausstellung der Berliner Secession: Zeichnende Künste* (Fourteenth Exhibition of the Berlin Secession: Drawing Arts), December 6, 1907, to January 5, 1908, 15 prints

1908

Verein für deutsches Kunstgewerbe [Künstlerhaus, Bellevuestrasse 3]
[Designs for theater decorations and costume designs], from April 8, 1908, duration unknown
Unknown number of sketches

Exhibition building of the Berlin Secession, Kurfürstendamm 208/209, *Fünfzehnte Ausstellung der Berliner Secession* (Fifteenth Exhibition of the Berlin Secession)
April 14 to September 13, 1908
4 paintings

Exhibition building of the Berlin Secession, Kurfürstendamm 208/209, *Sechzehnte Ausstellung der Berliner Secession: Zeichnende Künste* (Sixteenth Exhibition of the Berlin Secession: Drawing Arts)
December 5, 1908, to January 10, 1909, 26 prints

1909

Exhibition building of the Berlin Secession, Kurfürstendamm 208/209
Neunzehnte Ausstellung der Berliner Secession: Zeichnende Künste (Nineteenth Exhibition of the Berlin Secession: Drawing Arts)
November 27, 1909, to January 9, 1910, 17 prints

1910

Exhibition building of the Berlin Secession, Kurfürstendamm 208/209
Zwanzigste Ausstellung der Berliner Secession (Twentieth Exhibition of the Berlin Secession)
April 16 to September 25, 1910
2 paintings

Exhibition building of the Berlin Secession, Kurfürstendamm 208/209
Einundzwanzigste Ausstellung der Berliner Secession: Zeichnende Künste (Twenty-First Exhibition of the Berlin Secession: Drawing Arts)
November 26, 1910, to January 15, 1911, 1 painting

1912

Graphisches Kabinett J. B. Neumann, Kurfürstendamm 33
Edvard Munch, August 1912
About 80 graphic works

Kunstsalon Fritz Gurlitt, Potsdamer Strasse 113, Villa II
[Gallery exhibition with the participation of Edvard Munch]
October 1912, unknown number of graphic works

Kunstsalon Paul Cassirer, Viktoriastrasse 35
Galerie-Ausstellung
Fifteenth year, first exhibition
October 24 to December 2, 1912
1 painting

Exhibition building of the Berlin Secession, Kurfürstendamm 208/209
Fünfundzwanzigste Ausstellung der Berliner Secession: Zeichnende Künste
(Twenty-Fifth Exhibition of the Berlin Secession: Drawing Arts)
November 2 to December 29, 1912
12 prints

Graphisches Kabinett J. B. Neumann, Kurfürstendamm 33
Edvard Munch
November 1912
Unknown number of prints
Kunstsalon Paul Cassirer, Viktoriastrasse 35
Kollektionen Leopold von Kalckreuth, Edvard Munch, Theo von Brockhusen, Walter-Kurau: Werke von Robert Breyer, Hannah de Grahl, Ulrich Hübner, Max Brenner
Fifteenth year, second exhibition
December 5, 1912, to early January 1913
7 paintings, 2 prints

1913

Kunstsalon Paul Cassirer, Viktoriastrasse 35
Max Beckmann, Walter Bondy
Fifteenth year, fourth exhibition
January 23 to mid-February 1913
Unknown number of prints
Exhibition building, Kurfürstendamm 208/209
Herbst-Ausstellung 1913
(Autumn Exhibition 1913)
[Exhibition of artists who left the Secession]
November 1 to December 20, 1913
12 paintings

Graphisches Kabinett J. B. Neumann, Kurfürstendamm 33
Edvard Munch, December 1913
Unknown number of prints

Kupferstichkabinett, Neues Museum, Museumsinsel
Das Tier in der neueren Graphik
(The Animal in Recent Graphic Art)
December 1913
Unknown number of works

1914

Kunstsalon Fritz Gurlitt, Potsdamer Strasse 113, Villa II
Kollektiv-Ausstellung Edvard Munch (Collective Exhibition of Edvard Munch)
February to March 1914
81 paintings

Kunsthandlung Amsler & Ruthardt, Behrenstrasse 29a
Edvard Munch
March 1914, 109 prints

Kunstsalon Fritz Gurlitt, Potsdamer Strasse 113, Villa II
[Exhibition of the *Reinhardt Frieze*]
October to November 1914
12 (?) paintings

1915

Kupferstichkabinett, Neues Museum, Museumsinsel
Skandinavische Graphikausstellung
(Scandinavian Graphics Exhibition)
April 1915
Unknown number of prints

Graphisches Kabinett J. B. Neumann, Kurfürstendamm 232
Edvard Munch: Sein graphisches Werk (Edvard Munch: His Graphic Work)
November to December 1915
128 prints

1917

Galerie Alfred Flechtheim, Kurfürstendamm 208/209
Moderne Gemälde
(Modern Paintings)
June 1–4, 1917, 2 paintings

1918

Kunstsalon Paul Cassirer, Viktoriastrasse 35
Sommerausstellung
(Summer Exhibition)
August 1918, 1 painting

1919

Freie Secession, Kurfürstendamm 208/209
Freie Secession: Sommerausstellung
(Free Secession: Summer Exhibition)
May 25 to July 1, 1919
1 painting

Freie Secession, [Kurfürstendamm 208/209]
Schwarz-Weiss Ausstellung
(Black-and-White Exhibition)
November to December 1919
Unknown number of prints

1921

Kupferstichkabinett, Neues Museum, Museumsinsel
Die Radierung (The Etching)
January 1921
Unknown number of works

Kunstsalon Paul Cassirer, Viktoriastrasse 35
Edvard Munch: Bildern [sic] und graphische Werke
(Edvard Munch: Paintings and Graphic Works)
April 1921, 24 paintings, 90 prints

Graphisches Kabinett J. B. Neumann, Kurfürstendamm 232
Sommer-Ausstellung
(Summer Exhibition)
July to August 1921
Unknown number of works

1923

Galerie Lutz, Unter den Linden 21
Freie Secession: Frühjahrsausstellung
(Free Secession: Spring Exhibition)
February to March 1923
3 paintings

Akademie der Künste zu Berlin, Pariser Platz 4
Frühjahrsausstellung
(Spring Exhibition)
May 1–26, 1923, about 15 paintings

1924

Akademie der Künste zu Berlin, Pariser Platz 4
Herbst-Ausstellung
(Autumn Exhibition)
October 1924, 33 prints

1927

Nationalgalerie, Kronprinzenpalais, Unter den Linden
Edvard Munch
March 12 to May 15, 1927
223 paintings, 21 watercolors and drawings

Kupferstichkabinett, Neues Museum, Museumsinsel
[Solo exhibition]
Opening on March 12, 1927
150 etchings, woodcuts, and lithographs

Galerie Thannhauser, Bellevuestrasse 13
Eröffnungsausstellung
(Opening Exhibition)
June to July 1927, 2 paintings

1929

Galerie Ferdinand Möller, Schöneberger Ufer 38 (now 78)
Edv. Munch: Ausstellung alter und neuer Graphik, Gemälde
(Edv. Munch: Exhibition of Old and New Graphic Art, Paintings)
April 20 to May 20, 1929
104 prints

1930

Galerie Alfred Flechtheim, Lützowufer 13
Renoir und andere
(Renoir and Others)
July 1930
Unknown number of works

1931

Galerie Alfred Flechtheim, Lützowufer 13, *Edvard Munch*
April 18 to May 12, 1931
17 paintings, 130 prints, 18 watercolors, pastels, and drawings

1933

Kronprinzenpalais, Unter den Linden
Norwegische Ausstellung
(Norwegian Exhibition)
May 1933, at least 7 paintings

This list of Munch's exhibitions in Berlin is based on the following secondary literature: Kneher 1994; Munich, Hamburg, and Berlin 1994–95, pp. 255–60; Woll 2001, pp. 470–74; Woll 2009, pp. 1615–34; Echte and Feilchenfeldt 2011–16; Matelowski 2017, pp. 591–606.

List of Works in the Exhibition

p. 44
Themistokles von Eckenbrecher,
The "Auguste Victoria" in the Nærøyfjord,
1900,
oil on canvas,
162 × 222 cm,
Staatliche Schlösser, Gärten und Kunstsammlungen Mecklenburg-Vorpommern, Schwerin

p. 45 A
Axel Gállen (from 1907: Akseli Gallen-Kallela),
White Roses,
1906,
oil on canvas,
62 × 58 cm,
private collection, northern Germany

p. 45 B
Walter Leistikow,
Fjord Landscape,
ca. 1897,
oil on cardboard,
46.5 × 63 cm,
Berlinische Galerie, purchased by the Senator für Kulturelle Angelegenheiten (Security Fund)

p. 46 A
Hans Hermann,
Blossoming Trees,
1894,
oil on canvas,
106.5 × 132.5 cm,
Berlinische Galerie, permanent endowment by Dr. Jörg Thiede-Stiftung

p. 46 B
Ludwig von Hofmann,
The Pink Cloud,
ca. 1903,
oil on canvas,
70 × 61 cm,
Berlinische Galerie, purchased by Berlinische Galerie

p. 47
Walter Leistikow,
Evening at Schlachtensee,
ca. 1895,
oil on canvas,
73 × 93 cm,
Stiftung Stadtmuseum Berlin

p. 42
pp. 48–49
Adelsteen Normann,
Summer Evening in the Lofoten,
before 1891,
oil on canvas,
180 × 275 cm,
Staatliche Museen zu Berlin, Nationalgalerie

pp. 50–51
Edvard Munch,
Starry Night,
1922–24,
oil on canvas,
80.5 × 65 cm,
Munchmuseet, Oslo,
Woll 1453

pp. 52–53
Edvard Munch,
Winter Night,
ca. 1900,
oil on canvas,
81 × 121 cm,
Kunsthaus Zürich, 1931,
Woll 475

p. 56
Edvard Munch,
Eye in Eye,
1899–1900,
oil on canvas,
136 × 110 cm,
Munchmuseet, Oslo,
Woll 461

p. 57
Edvard Munch,
The Kiss,
1897,
tempera and oil on canvas,
87 × 80 cm,
Munchmuseet, Oslo,
Woll 400

pp. 58–59
Edvard Munch,
Vampire,
1916–18,
oil on canvas,
83 × 104.5 cm,
Munchmuseet, Oslo,
Woll 1175

pp. 60–61
Edvard Munch,
Red and White,
1899–1900,
oil on canvas,
93.5 × 129.5 cm,
Munchmuseet, Oslo,
Woll 463

p. 4
pp. 62–63
Edvard Munch,
Two Human Beings (The Lonely Ones),
ca. 1935,
oil on canvas,
91 × 129.5 cm,
Munchmuseet, Oslo,
Woll 1719

pp. 64–65
Edvard Munch,
Woman,
1925,
oil on canvas,
152.5 × 227.5 cm,
Munchmuseet, Oslo,
Woll 1564

pp. 66–67
Edvard Munch,
Melancholy (Evening),
1891,
oil, pencil, and crayon on canvas,
73.5 × 100.5 cm,
Munchmuseet, Oslo,
Woll 241

pp. 68–69
Edvard Munch,
Sanatorium,
1902–3,
casein on canvas,
70.5 × 85 cm,
Munchmuseet, Oslo,
Woll 522

p. 69
Edvard Munch,
Jealousy,
1907,
oil on canvas,
89 × 82.5 cm,
Munchmuseet, Oslo,
Woll 783

pp. 70–71
Edvard Munch,
The Hearse on Potsdamer Platz,
1902,
oil on canvas,
68 × 98 cm,
Munchmuseet, Oslo,
Woll 519

pp. 72–73
Edvard Munch,
Death and Spring,
1893,
oil on canvas,
73 × 94.5 cm,
Munchmuseet, Oslo,
Woll 325

pp. 74–75
Edvard Munch,
Trees by the Beach (The Linde Frieze),
1904,
oil on canvas,
93 × 167.5 cm,
Munchmuseet, Oslo,
Woll 609

pp. 76–77
Edvard Munch,
Summer in the Park (The Linde Frieze),
1904,
oil on canvas,
92 × 172 cm,
Munchmuseet, Oslo,
Woll 607

pp. 78–79
Edvard Munch,
Girls Watering Flowers (The Linde Frieze),
1904,
oil on canvas,
101 × 80.5 cm,
Munchmuseet, Oslo,
Woll 612

p. 54
pp. 80–83
Edvard Munch,
Dance on the Beach (The Linde Frieze),
1904,
oil on canvas,
90 × 314.5 cm,
Munchmuseet, Oslo,
Woll 614

pp. 84–85
Edvard Munch,
Young People on the Beach (The Linde Frieze),
1904,
oil on canvas,
90.5 × 175 cm,
Munchmuseet, Oslo,
Woll 608

pp. 86–87
Edvard Munch,
Moonlight on the Sea (The Reinhardt Frieze),
1906–7,
tempera on canvas,
91 × 157.5 cm,
Staatliche Museen zu Berlin,
Nationalgalerie.
Acquired in 1966 with support from the State of Berlin,
Woll 725

pp. 88–89
Edvard Munch,
Desire (The Reinhardt Frieze),
1906–7,
tempera on canvas,
91 × 252 cm,
Staatliche Museen zu Berlin,
Nationalgalerie.
Acquired in 1966 with support from the State of Berlin,
Woll 729

pp. 90–91
Edvard Munch,
Summer Night (The Reinhardt Frieze),
1906–7,
tempera on canvas,
91 × 252 cm,
Staatliche Museen zu Berlin,
Nationalgalerie.
Acquired in 1966 with support from the State of Berlin,
Woll 728

p. 92
Edvard Munch,
Young Women Picking Fruit (The Reinhardt Frieze),
1906–7,
tempera on canvas,
89.5 × 70 cm,
Staatliche Museen zu Berlin,
Nationalgalerie.
Acquired in 1966 with support from the State of Berlin,
Woll 732

p. 93 A
Edvard Munch,
Sun Flower (The Reinhardt Frieze),
1906–7,
tempera on canvas,
89.5 × 70 cm,
Staatliche Museen zu Berlin,
Nationalgalerie.
Acquired in 1966 with support from the State of Berlin,
Woll 733

p. 93 B
Edvard Munch,
Two Young Women in Red and White (The Reinhardt Frieze),
1906–7,
tempera on canvas,
90 × 70 cm,
Staatliche Museen zu Berlin,
Nationalgalerie.
Acquired in 1966 with support from the State of Berlin,
Woll 726

pp. 94–95
Edvard Munch,
Kiss on the Beach (The Reinhardt Frieze),
1906–7,
tempera on canvas,
90 × 155 cm,
Staatliche Museen zu Berlin,
Nationalgalerie.
Acquired in 1966 with support from the State of Berlin,
Woll 731

pp. 96–97
Edvard Munch,
Trees by the Sea (The Reinhardt Frieze),
1906–7,
tempera on canvas,
91 × 157.5 cm,
Staatliche Museen zu Berlin,
Nationalgalerie.
Acquired in 1966 with support from the State of Berlin,
Woll 727

pp. 98–99
Edvard Munch,
Melancholy (The Reinhardt Frieze),
1906–7,
tempera on canvas,
87 × 156 cm,
Staatliche Museen zu Berlin,
Nationalgalerie.
Acquired in 1997 with support from the Ernst von Siemens Kunststiftung and the Kulturstiftung der Länder,
Woll 736

p. 102
Edvard Munch,
The Day After,
1894,
drypoint,
44.8/45.2 × 59.1 cm,
Staatliche Museen zu Berlin,
Kupferstichkabinett,
Woll 10

p. 103 A
Edvard Munch,
The Sick Child I,
1894,
drypoint,
58.4 × 46/46.5 cm,
Staatliche Museen zu Berlin,
Kupferstichkabinett,
Woll 7

p. 103 B
Edvard Munch,
Two Human Beings (The Lonely Ones),
1894,
drypoint,
32.1/33 × 47.4/48.2 cm,
Staatliche Museen zu Berlin,
Kupferstichkabinett,
Woll 13

p. 104
Edvard Munch,
The Sick Child I,
1896,
color lithograph,
55.5 × 68.3 cm,
Staatliche Museen zu Berlin,
Kupferstichkabinett,
Woll 72

p. 105
Edvard Munch,
Madonna (Woman Making Love),
1895/1902,
color lithograph and color woodcut,
60.5 × 50.1 cm,
Staatliche Museen zu Berlin,
Kupferstichkabinett,
Woll 39

pp. 106–7
Edvard Munch,
Vampire II,
1902,
color lithograph,
51 × 69.5 cm,
Munchmuseet, Oslo,
Woll 41

p. 108 A
Edvard Munch,
Evening. Melancholy I (By the Shore),
1896,
woodcut,
47.2 × 62.6 cm,
Staatliche Museen zu Berlin,
Kupferstichkabinett,
Woll 91

p. 108 B
Edvard Munch,
Angst (Feeling of Anxiety),
1896,
woodcut,
71.3 × 60 cm,
Staatliche Museen zu Berlin,
Kupferstichkabinett,
Woll 93

p. 109
Edvard Munch,
Jealousy II,
1896,
lithograph,
57.7 × 79.5/80.2 cm,
Staatliche Museen zu Berlin,
Kupferstichkabinett,
Woll 69

p. 100
pp. 110–11
Edvard Munch,
Death in the Sickroom,
1896,
lithograph,
45.8 × 62.3 cm,
Staatliche Museen zu Berlin,
Kupferstichkabinett,
Woll 65

p. 112
Edvard Munch,
The Kiss IV,
1902,
color woodcut,
60.0 × 79.5 cm,
Munchmuseet, Oslo,
Woll 204

p. 113
Edvard Munch,
Self-Portrait (with Skeleton Arm),
1895,
lithograph (second state),
ca. 55.1 × 40 cm (40.5 cm),
Staatliche Museen zu Berlin,
Kupferstichkabinett,
Woll 37

p. 114
Edvard Munch,
Harry Graf Kessler II,
1895,
lithograph,
57.2 × 37.8 cm,
Staatliche Museen zu Berlin,
Kupferstichkabinett,
Woll 36

p. 115
Edvard Munch,
Andreas Schwarz,
1906 [1907?],
lithograph,
58 × 41.7 cm,
Staatliche Museen zu Berlin,
Kupferstichkabinett,
Woll 281

p. 116
Edvard Munch,
Anna and Walter Leistikow,
1902,
lithograph,
64.2 × 96.7 cm,
Munchmuseet, Oslo,
Woll 196

p. 117
Edvard Munch,
August Strindberg,
1896,
lithograph,
66.8 × 50 cm,
Staatliche Museen zu Berlin,
Kupferstichkabinett,
Woll 66

pp. 118–19
Edvard Munch,
Henrik Ibsen at the Grand Café,
1902,
lithograph,
53.9/54.7 × 75.8 cm,
Staatliche Museen zu Berlin,
Kupferstichkabinett,
Woll 200

p. 119
Edvard Munch,
The Hearse. Potsdamer Platz,
1902,
line etching, drypoint,
and open bite
(third and final state),
35 × 50 cm,
Staatliche Museen zu Berlin,
Kupferstichkabinett,
Woll 178

Front endpaper
p. 120
Edvard Munch,
Self-Portrait in His Studio,
Lützowstrasse 82, Berlin,
1902,
reproduction: inkjet print;
original: collodion paper,
8.7 × 8.7 cm,
Munchmuseet, Oslo

pp. 40–41
p. 121 A
Edvard Munch,
Self-Portrait on a Valise
in His Studio,
Lützowstrasse 82,
Berlin, 1902,
reproduction: inkjet print;
original: collodion paper,
7.9 × 8 cm,
Munchmuseet, Oslo

p. 121 B
Edvard Munch,
Self-Portrait on a Valise
in His Studio,
Lützowstrasse 82,
Berlin, 1902,
reproduction: inkjet print;
original: collodion paper,
8 × 8.8 cm,
Munchmuseet, Oslo

p. 122 A
Edvard Munch,
Marta Sandal in Munch's Studio,
Lützowstrasse 82,
Berlin, 1902,
reproduction: inkjet print;
original: gelatin-silver paper,
9.1 × 9 cm,
Munchmuseet, Oslo

p. 122 B
Edvard Munch,
The Wieck Brothers
in Munch's Studio,
Lützowstrasse 82, Berlin,
1902,
reproduction: inkjet print;
original: collodion paper,
9.8 × 9 cm,
Munchmuseet, Oslo

p. 123
Edvard Munch,
Walter Leistikow in His Studio,
Berlin, 1902,
reproduction: inkjet print;
original: collodion paper,
9.2 × 9 cm,
Munchmuseet, Oslo

p. 124
Edvard Munch,
Paul Cassirer's Exhibition
Premises, Berlin, 1903,
reproduction: inkjet print;
original: gelatin-silver paper,
8.8 × 9.2 cm,
Munchmuseet, Oslo

p. 125 A
Edvard Munch,
Albert Kollmann in Front
of Gravestones,
Berlin, 1902,
reproduction: inkjet print;
original: collodion paper,
8.5 × 8.3 cm,
Munchmuseet, Oslo

p. 125 B
pp. 254–55
Edvard Munch in Front of
Gravestones, Berlin,
1902,
reproduction: inkjet print;
original: collodion paper,
9.4 × 8.8 cm,
Munchmuseet, Oslo

p. 126
Edvard Munch,
Munch's Exhibition
at Paul Cassirer,
Berlin, 1907,
reproduction: inkjet print;
original: gelatin-silver paper,
8.1 × 8.6 cm,
Munchmuseet, Oslo

p. 127 A
Edvard Munch,
Munch's Exhibition
at Paul Cassirer,
Berlin, 1907,
reproduction: inkjet print;
original: negative,
Munchmuseet, Oslo

p. 127 B
Edvard Munch,
Munch's Exhibition
at Paul Cassirer,
Berlin, 1907,
reproduction: inkjet print;
original: gelatin-silver paper,
9 × 12 cm,
Munchmuseet, Oslo

p. 128
Edvard Munch,
Nude Self-Portrait,
Warnemünde, 1907,
reproduction: inkjet print;
original: collodion paper,
8.5 × 8.3 cm,
Munchmuseet, Oslo

p. 129
Edvard Munch,
Self-Portrait with a Model
on the Beach,
Warnemünde, 1907,
reproduction: inkjet print;
original: collodion paper,
8.3 × 8.7 cm,
Munchmuseet, Oslo

p. 130
Edvard Munch,
Model in Munch's Studio,
Lützowstrasse 82,
Berlin, 1902,
reproduction: inkjet print;
original: collodion paper,
9 × 9.2 cm,
Munchmuseet, Oslo

p. 131 A
Edvard Munch,
Woman with Red Hair and Green Eyes (The Sin),
1902,
color lithograph (second state),
83.7 × 55 cm,
Staatliche Museen zu Berlin,
Kupferstichkabinett,
Woll 198

p. 131 B
Edvard Munch,
Nude with Long Red Hair,
1902,
oil on canvas,
120.5 × 50 cm,
Munchmuseet, Oslo,
Woll 503

p. 134
Edvard Munch,
Stanisław Przybyszewski,
1895,
oil and/or tempera on
unprimed cardboard,
62.5 × 56 cm,
Munchmuseet, Oslo,
Woll 383

p. 135
Edvard Munch,
Portrait of Walther Rathenau,
1907,
oil on canvas,
200 × 110 cm,
Stiftung Stadtmuseum Berlin,
Woll 744

pp. 136–37
Edvard Munch,
Jappe Nilssen,
1909,
oil on canvas,
94 × 103.5 cm,
Munchmuseet, Oslo,
Woll 833

p. 132
p. 138
Edvard Munch,
Dagny Juel Przybyszewska,
1893,
oil on canvas,
149 × 100.5 cm,
Munchmuseet, Oslo,
Woll 337

p. 12
p. 139
Edvard Munch,
Self-Portrait under the Mask of a Woman,
1893,
tempera on unprimed wooden panel,
70 × 44.5 cm,
Munchmuseet, Oslo,
Woll 310

p. 140
Edvard Munch,
August Strindberg,
1892,
oil on canvas,
122 × 91 cm,
Moderna Museet, Stockholm.
Donation from the artist in 1934,
Woll 301

p. 141
Edvard Munch,
Albert Kollmann and Sten Drewsen,
1902,
oil on canvas,
59 × 73.5 cm,
Hamburger Kunsthalle,
Hamburg, purchased in 1950,
Woll 500

p. 142
Edvard Munch,
Elisabeth Förster-Nietzsche,
1906,
oil on canvas,
165 × 100.5 cm,
Munchmuseet, Oslo,
Woll 692

p. 143
Edvard Munch,
Self-Portrait in Broad-Brimmed Hat,
1905–6,
oil on canvas,
80 × 64.5 cm,
Munchmuseet, Oslo,
Woll 650

pp. 144–45
Edvard Munch,
Seated Model on the Couch,
1924–26,
oil on canvas,
136.5 × 115.5 cm,
Munchmuseet, Oslo,
Woll 1501

p. 146
Edvard Munch,
Woman with Airedale Terriers,
1925–26,
oil on canvas,
120.5 × 99.5 cm,
Munchmuseet, Oslo,
Woll 1549

p. 147
Edvard Munch,
Two Teenagers,
1919,
oil on canvas,
179.5 × 129.5 cm,
Munchmuseet, Oslo,
Woll 1310

pp. 150–51
Edvard Munch,
The Man in the Cabbage Field,
1943,
oil on canvas,
110.5 × 150.5 cm,
Munchmuseet, Oslo,
Woll 1788

p. 7
p. 151
Edvard Munch,
Forest,
1927,
oil on canvas,
90 × 84.5 cm,
Staatliche Museen zu Berlin,
Nationalgalerie.
Acquired in 1956
by the State of Berlin,
Woll 1633

p. 152 A
Edvard Munch,
Design for a Decoration in Oslo City Hall,
ca. 1930,
reproduction: inkjet print;
original: gelatin-silver paper,
8.5 × 11.4 cm,
Munchmuseet, Oslo

p. 152 B
Edvard Munch,
Snow Shovelers,
1913–14,
oil on canvas,
151 × 128 cm,
destroyed,
formerly Nationalgalerie Berlin,
reproduction in exhibition,
Woll 1092

p. 153
Edvard Munch,
Snow Shovelers on the Building Site,
1931–33,
oil on canvas,
192.5 × 130 cm,
Munchmuseet, Oslo,
Woll 1684

pp. 154–55
Edvard Munch,
Road in Åsgårdstrand,
1901,
oil on canvas,
88.3 × 113.8 cm,
Kunstmuseum Basel,
inv. no. G 1979.8.
Gift from Sigrid Schwarz von Spreckelsen and Sigrid Katharina Schwarz, 1979,
Woll 486

pp. 156–57
Edvard Munch,
Elsa Glaser,
1913,
oil on canvas,
120 × 85 cm,
Munchmuseet, Oslo,
Woll 1064

p. 148
pp. 158–59
Edvard Munch,
Self-Portrait after Influenza,
1919,
oil on canvas,
60 × 90 cm,
Die Lübecker Museen,
Museum Behnhaus Drägerhaus, Lübeck,
Woll 1295

For works by Edvard Munch, the number of the corresponding catalogue raisonné is indicated: for the prints, Gerd Woll, ed., *Edvard Munch: The Complete Graphic Works* (New York, 2001); for the paintings, Gerd Woll, ed., *Edvard Munch: Complete Paintings: Catalogue Raisonné*, 4 vols. (New York, 2009).

References

Achenbach 2003
Achenbach, Sigrid. 2003. "Einführung." In Berlin 2003–4, pp. 9–13.

Achenbach 2022
Achenbach, Sigrid. "Schwarz-Weiss in Berlin: Die Grafik Liebermanns im Berliner Kupferstichkabinett und Max J. Friedländer." In *S/W: Max Liebermanns Druckgrafik*. Edited by Lucy Wasensteiner. Exh. cat. Liebermann-Villa am Wannsee, 2022. Berlin and Munich, 2022, pp. 98–123.

Bartrum 2019a
Bartrum, Giulia. "The Inner Soul of an Artist: Munch's Background and the Development of His Frieze of Life." In London 2019, pp. 34–57.

Bartrum 2019b
Bartrum, Giulia. "Munch and the World of Printmaking." In London 2019, pp. 58–95.

Basel 2022
Der Sammler Curt Glaser: Vom Verfechter der Moderne zum Verfolgten. Edited by Anita Haldemann and Judith Rauser. Exh. cat. Kunstmuseum Basel. Berlin and Munich, 2022.

Berlin 1902
Katalog der fünften Kunstausstellung der Berliner Secession 1902. Exh. cat. Ausstellungshaus der Berliner Secession. Berlin, 1902.

Berlin 1913
Katalog der XXVI. Ausstellung der Berliner Secession 1913. Exh. cat. Ausstellungshaus am Kurfürstendamm, 2nd ed. Berlin, 1913.

Berlin 1927
Edvard Munch: Ausstellung in der Nationalgalerie. Exh. cat. Nationalgalerie Berlin, 1927. Berlin, 1927.

Berlin 1978
Edvard Munch: Der Lebensfries für Max Reinhardts Kammerspiele. Edited by Peter Krieger. Exh. cat. Nationalgalerie Berlin, Staatliche Museen zu Berlin, 1978. Berlin, 1978.

Berlin 1993
Anton von Werner: Geschichte in Bildern. Edited by Dominik Bartmann. Exh. cat. Deutsches Historisches Museum Berlin, 1993. Munich, 1993.

Berlin 2000
Anders Zorn und die europäische Graphik um 1900. Edited by Sigrid Achenbach. Exh. cat. Kupferstichkabinett, Staatliche Museen zu Berlin, 2000. Berlin, 2000.

Berlin 2003–4
Edvard Munch: Die Graphik im Berliner Kupferstichkabinett. Edited by Sigrid Achenbach. Exh. cat. Kupferstichkabinett, Staatliche Museen zu Berlin, 2003–4.

Berlin 1997–98
Wahlverwandtschaft: Skandinavien und Deutschland 1800 bis 1914. Edited by Bernd Henningsen et al. Exh. cat. Deutsches Historisches Museum Berlin, Nationalmuseum Stockholm, and Norsk Folkemuseum Oslo, 1997–98. Berlin, 1997.

Berman 1997
Berman, Patricia G. "Edvard Munch: Women, 'Woman,' and the Genesis of an Artist's Myth." In *Munch and Women: Image and Myth*. Edited by Patricia G. Berman and Jane van Nimmen. Exh. cat. San Diego Museum of Art, Portland Art Museum, Oregon, and Yale University Art Gallery, New Haven, 1997. Alexandria, 1997, pp. 11–40.

Berman 2013
Berman, Patricia G. 2013. "The Monumental Artist in Public: The Artist as Monument." In Oslo 2013, pp. 162–73.

Berman 2022
Berman, Patricia G. "Munch's Aula and the Theatre of The Sun." In Paris 2022–23, pp. 86–99.

Bernau 2005
Bernau, Nikolaus. "Wo hing Munchs 'Lebens-Fries'? Zu dem Bau der Kammerspiele und ihrem berühmtesten Schmuck." In *Max Reinhardt und das Deutsche Theater: Texte und Bilder aus Anlass des 100-jährigen Jubiläums seiner Direktion*. Edited by Roland Koberg, Bernd Stegemann, and Henrike Thomsen. Blätter des Deutschen Theaters 2. Berlin, 2005, pp. 65–77.

Brandes 1885
Brandes, Georg. *Berlin som tysk rigshovedstad*. Copenhagen, 1885.

Brandt 2019
Brandt, Lars. "Kein Puppenheim." In *Dagny Juel: Flügel in Flammen; Gesammelte Werke*. Translated from the Norwegian and with an essay by Lars Brandt. Bonn, 2019, pp. 96–167.

Braun 2011–21
Braun, Ernst, ed. *Max Liebermann: Briefe, Gesamtausgabe*. 9 vols. Schriftenreihe der Max-Liebermann-Gesellschaft Berlin e. V. Baden-Baden, 2011–21.

Brauner 1994
Brauner, Lothar. "Die Retrospektive in Berlin, 1927." In Munich, Hamburg, and Berlin 1994–95, pp. 127–30.

Bremen 2011–12
Edvard Munch: Rätsel hinter der Leinwand. Edited by Dorothee Hansen. Exh. cat. Kunsthalle Bremen 2011–12. Cologne, 2011.

Brodal 1996
Brodal, Jan. "Stanisław Przybyszewski and Dagny Juel: A Literary Partnership." In Paszkiewicz 1996, pp. 187–200.

Bruns 1998
Bruns, Karin. "Das schwarze Ferkel (Berlin)." In *Handbuch literarisch-kultureller Vereine, Gruppen und Bünde 1825–1933*. Edited by Karin Bruns, Rolf Parr, and Wulf Wülfing. Stuttgart and Weimar, 1998, pp. 406–16.

Buchhart 2003
Buchhart, Dieter. "Art: Madonna." In Vienna 2003, pp. 137–39.

Buschhoff 2011
Buschhoff, Anne. "Liebe, Angst und Tod in Werken von Edvard Munchs Zeitgenossen: Max Klinger, Odilon Redon, Félicien Rops, Felix Vallotton und andere." In Bremen 2011–12, pp. 220–35.

Büttner 1934
Büttner, Erich. "Der leibhaftige Munch." In Thiis 1934, pp. 83–101.

Cernuschi 2001
Cernuschi, Claude. "Sex and Psyche, Nature and Nurture, the Personal and the Political: Edvard Munch and German Expressionism." In *Edvard Munch: Psyche, Symbol and Expression*. Edited by Jeffrey Howe. Exh. cat. McMullen Museum of Art, Boston College. Boston, 2001, pp. 134–67.

Chéroux 2012
Chéroux, Clément. "'Write Your Life!': Photography and Autobiography." Translated by Laura Bennett. In London 2012.

Clarke 2000
Clarke, Jay A. "Munch, Liebermann, and the Question of Etched 'Reproductions.'" *Visual Resources* 16, no. 1 (2000): pp. 27–63.

Clarke 2005
Clarke, Jay A. "Munch's Critical Reception in the 1890s and His 'Place' in History." In *Seeing and Beyond: Essays on Eighteenth- to Twenty-First-Century Art in Honor of Kermit S. Champa*. Edited by Deborah J. Johnson and David Ogawa. New York et al., 2005, pp. 185–209.

Clarke 2009
Clarke, Jay A. *Becoming Edvard Munch: Influence, Anxiety, and Myth*. New Haven, CT, and London, 2009.

Clarke 2013
Clarke, Jay A. 1927. "Munch's Changing Role in Germany." *Kunst og Kultur* 96, no. 4 (2013): pp. 170–81.

Clarke 2016
Clarke, Jay A. "Woodcut as Process and Metaphor: Munch, Heckel, and Kirchner." In New York 2016, pp. 97–111.

Cologne 1912
Internationale Kunstausstellung des Sonderbundes Westdeutscher Kunstfreunde und Künstler zu Cöln 1912. Exh. cat. Städt. Ausstellungshalle am Aachener Tor. Cologne, 1912.

Corinth 1910
Corinth, Lovis. *Das Leben Walter Leistikows: Ein Stück Berliner Kulturgeschichte*. Berlin, 1910.

Cummings 2001
Cummings, Scott T. "Strange Boulder in the Whirlpool of Theater: Edvard Munch, Max Reinhardt, and Ghosts." In *Edvard Munch: Psyche, Symbol and Expression*. Edited by Jeffrey Howe. Exh. cat. McMullen Museum of Art, Boston College. Boston 2001, pp. 111–31.

Dorn 1988
Dorn, Roland. "Edvard Munch in Mannheim." In Mannheim 1988, pp. 257–91.

Echte and Feilchenfeldt 2011–16
Echte, Bernhard, and Walter Feilchenfeldt. *Kunstsalon Cassirer: Die Ausstellungen*. 6 vols. Compiled by Petra Cordioli. Quellenstudien zur Kunst, vols. 4, 5, 7–10. Wädenswil, 2011–16.

Eggum 1982
Eggum, Arne. *Der Linde-Fries: Edvard Munch und sein erster deutscher Mäzen, Dr. Max Linde*. Translated from the Norwegian by Alken Bruns. Twentieth publication by the Senat der Hansestadt Lübeck, Amt für Kultur. Lübeck, 1982.

Eggum 1989
Eggum, Arne. *Munch and Photography*. Translated by Birgit Holm. New Haven, CT, 1989.

Eggum 1991–92a
Eggum, Arne. "Importance des deux séjours de Munch en France en 1891–1892." In Paris, Oslo, Frankfurt am Main 1991–92, pp. 106–47.

Eggum 1991–92b
Eggum, Arne. "Munch et le fauvisme." In Paris, Oslo, Frankfurt am Main 1991–92, pp. 188–221.

Eggum 1991–92c
Eggum, Arne. "Munch tente de conquérir Paris, 1896–1900." In Paris, Oslo, Frankfurt am Main 1991–92, pp. 288–316.

Eggum 1994
Eggum, Arne. "Edvard Munch und die junge deutsche Kunst nach 1905." In Munich, Hamburg, and Berlin 1994–95, pp. 104–11.

Eggum 1996
Eggum, Arne. "Literary Reflections in Munch's Frieze of Life." In Paszkiewicz 1996, pp. 65–78.

Eggum 2000
Eggum, Arne. *Edvard Munch: The Frieze of Life from Painting to Graphic Art*. Oslo, 2000.

Essen and Zurich 1987–88
Edvard Munch: 1863–1944. Exh. cat. Museum Folkwang Essen and Kunsthaus Zürich, 1987–88. Bern, 1987.

Espoo 2014
Akseli Gallen-Kallela & Berlin: Die historischen Schichten der Gemälde. Exh. cat. Gallen-Kallela Museum Espoo, 2014. Espoo, 2014.

Faxneld 2015
Faxneld, Per. "Esotericism in Modernity, and the Lure of the Occult Elite: The Seekers of the Zum schwarzen Ferkel Circle." In Nielsen 2015, pp. 92–105.

Gerner 1988
Gerner, Cornelia. "Die Beschlagnahmung der Werke Munchs im Nationalsozialismus." In Mannheim 1988, pp. 340–50.

Gilman 2006
Claire Gilman. "Chronology." In New York 2006, pp. 221–38.

Glaser 1917
Glaser, Curt. *Edvard Munch*. Berlin, 1917 (2nd ed., 1922).

Glaser 1922
Glaser, Curt. *Die Graphik der Neuzeit: Vom Anfang des XIX. Jahrhunderts bis zur Gegenwart*. Berlin, 1922.

Glaser 1927
Glaser, Curt. "Besuch bei Munch." *Kunst und Künstler* 25, no. 6 (1927): pp. 203–9.

Głuchowska 2009
Głuchowska, Lidia. "Totenmesse, Lebensfries und Die Hölle: Przybyszewski, Munch, Vigeland und die protoexpressionistische Kunsttheorie." *Deshima: revue d'histoire globale des pays du Nord* (2009–10): pp. 93–130.

Głuchowska 2013
Głuchowska, Lidia. "Munch, Przybyszewski and The Scream." *Kunst og Kultur* 4 (2013): pp. 182–93.

Groth 2011a
Groth, Katharina. "Art: August Strindberg, 1896." In Bremen 2011–12, p. 104.

Groth 2011b
Groth, Katharina. "Art: Selbstbildnis mit Knochenarm, 1895." In Bremen 2011–12, p. 102.

Guleng 2013
Guleng, Mai Britt. "Die Narrative des Lebensfrieses: Edvard Munchs Bilderserie." In Oslo 2013, pp. 128–39.

Guleng and Ydstie 2008
Guleng, Mai Britt, and Ingebjørg Ydstie. *Munch Becoming "Munch": Artistic Strategies, 1880–1892*. Oslo, 2008.

Haldemann and Scherrer 2022
Haldemann, Anita, and Noemi Scherrer. "Curt Glaser: Aus der Mitte der Berliner Kunstwelt in die Emigration." In Basel 2022, pp. 10–19.

Hamburg 2006
Edvard Munch: "... aus dem modernen Seelenleben." Exh. cat. Hamburger Kunsthalle, 2006. Hamburg, 2006.

Hansen 1994
Hansen, Dorothee. "'Wir "Jungen" heben Sie auf den Schild': Munch und die Expressionisten." In Munich, Hamburg, and Berlin 1994–95, pp. 231–32.

Heller 1984
Heller, Reinhold. *Munch: His Life and Work*. London, 1984.

Heller 1992
Heller, Reinhold. "Form and Formation of Edvard Munch's Frieze of Life." In London 1992–93, pp. 25–37.

Heller 1993
Heller, Reinhold. "Anton von Werner, der Fall Munch und die Moderne im Berlin der 1890er Jahre." In Berlin 1993, pp. 101–19.

Heller 2016
Heller, Reinhold. "Edvard Munch, Germany, and Expressionism." In New York 2016, pp. 35–53.

Helsinki, Paris, and Düsseldorf 2011–12
Akseli Gallen-Kallela: Überirdisch nordisch; Finnland im Geist der Moderne. Exh. cat. Helsinki City Art Museum, Musée d'Orsay, Paris, and Museum Kunstpalast, Düsseldorf 2011–12. Ostfildern-Ruit, 2012.

Holt 2013
Holt, Cecilie Tyri. *Edvard Munch: Fotografier*. Oslo, 2013.

Ingelheim 2022
Edvard Munch: Meisterblätter. Edited by Ulrich Luckhardt. With texts by Uwe M. Schneede. Exh. cat. Kunstforum Ingelheim, Altes Rathaus, Ingelheim, 2022. Munich, 2022.

Jaworska 1995
Jaworska, Wladyslawa. "Munch—Przybyszewski." In *Totenmesse: Munch—Weiss—Przybyszewski*. Edited by Lukasz Kossowski. Warsaw, 1995, pp. 11–34.

Justi 1958
Justi, Ludwig. "Edvard Munch." In *Staatliche Museen zu Berlin, Forschungen und Berichte*, vol. 2. Berlin, 1958, pp. 7–9.

Justi 2000
Justi, Ludwig. *Werden, Wirken, Wissen: Lebenserinnerungen aus fünf Jahrzehnten*. 2 vols. Edited by Thomas W. Gaehtgens and Kurt Winkler. Quellen zur deutschen Kunstgeschichte vom Klassizismus bis zur Gegenwart 1. Berlin, 2000.

Kamzelak and Ott 2004–18
Kamzelak, Roland S., and Ulrich Ott, eds. *Harry Graf Kessler: Das Tagebuch, 1880–1937*. 9 vols. Stuttgart, 2004–18.

Klim 1992
Klim, George. *Stanisław Przybyszewski: Leben, Werk und Weltanschauung im Rahmen der deutschen Literatur der Jahrhundertwende; Biographie*. Paderborn, 1992.

Kneher 1994
Kneher, Jan. *Edvard Munch in seinen Ausstellungen zwischen 1892 und 1912: Eine Dokumentation der Ausstellungen und Studie zur Rezeptionsgeschichte von Munchs Kunst*. PhD diss., Universität Heidelberg, 1993. Worms am Rhein, 1994.

Krieger 1978
Krieger, Peter. "Edvard Munch: Der Lebensfries für Max Reinhardts Kammerspiele." In Berlin 1978, pp. 8–128.

Krisch 1997
Krisch, Monika. *Die Munch-Affäre—Rehabilitierung der Zeitungskritik: Eine Analyse ästhetischer und kulturpolitischer Beurteilungskriterien in der Kunstberichtserstattung der Berliner Tagespresse zu Munchs Ausstellung 1892*. PhD diss., Freie Universität Berlin, 1997. Blankenfelde-Mahlow bei Berlin, 1997.

Kuhn 1927
Kuhn, Alfred. "Edvard Munch und der Geist seiner Zeit." *Der Cicerone* 19, no. 5 (1927): pp. 139–47.

Kvech-Hoppe 2001
Kvech-Hoppe, Ulrike. *Der Fries im 19. Jahrhundert: Ästhetische und gattungsspezifische Aspekte einer Kunstform*. PhD diss., Universität Düsseldorf, 2000. Weimar, 2001.

Lampe 2012
Lample. Angela. "Munch and Max Reinhardt's Modern Stage." In *Edvard Munch: The Modern Eye*. Edited by Angela Lampe and Clément Chéroux. London, 2012.

Larsson 1996
Larsson, Lars Olof. "August Strindberg und Edvard Munch in Berlin." In *Grenzgänge: Skandinavisch-deutsche Nachbarschaften* 1. Edited by Heinrich Detering. Göttingen, 1996, pp. 161–78.

Lathe 1972
Lathe, Carla Anne. "The Group *Zum schwarzen Ferkel*: A Study in Early Modernism." 2 vols. PhD diss., University of East Anglia, 1972.

Lathe 1979
Lathe, Carla. "Edvard Munch and the Concept of 'Psychic Naturalism.'" *Gazette des beaux-arts* 93 (1979): pp. 134–46.

Lathe 1983
Lathe, Carla. "Edvard Munch's Dramatic Images 1892–1909." *Journal of the Warburg and Courtauld Institutes* 46 (1983): pp. 191–206.

Leistikow 1892
Selber, Walter [Leistikow, Walter]. "Die Affäre Munch." *Freie Bühne* 3, no. 12 (1892): pp. 1296–1300.

London 1992–93
Edvard Munch: The Frieze of Life. Edited by Mara-Helen Wood. Exh. cat. National Gallery, London, 1992–93. New York, 1992.

London 2019
Edvard Munch: Love and Angst. Edited by Giulia Bartrum. Exh. cat. British Museum, London, 2019. London, 2019.

Magnaguagno 1987
Magnaguagno, Guido. "Munch als Maler." In Essen and Zurich 1987–88, pp. 63–75.

Mannheim 1988
Edvard Munch: Sommernacht am Oslofjord, um 1900. Exh. cat. Kunsthalle Mannheim 1988, Mannheim, 1988.

Marx 1988
Marx, Werner. "Berlin und die Sehnsucht nach dem Norden." In Mannheim 1988, pp. 163–85.

März 1994
März, Roland. "'Das Urbild eines nordischen Künstlers': Germanenmythos, Nationalsozialismus und Edvard Munch." In Munich, Hamburg, and Berlin 1994–95, pp. 131–38.

März 1998
März, Roland. *Edvard Munch, Melancholie: Aus dem Reinhardt-Fries 1906/07*. Schriftenreihe Kulturstiftung der Länder, Patrimonia 136. Berlin, 1998.

Matelowski 2017
Matelowski, Anke. *Die Berliner Secession 1899–1937: Chronik, Kontext, Schicksal*. Quellenstudien zur Kunst 12. Wädenswil, 2017.

Meister 2006
Meister, Sabine. "Die Vereinigung der XI: Die Künstlergruppe als Keimzelle der organisierten Moderne in Berlin." PhD diss., Universität Freiburg im Breisgau, 2006.

Moormann-Schulz 2017
Moormann-Schulz, Tanja. *Der Deutsche Künstlerbund im Spiegel seiner Ausstellungspraxis 1903–1936*. PhD diss., Universität Hamburg, 2015. Frankfurt am Main, 2017.

Mørstad 2004
Mørstad, Erik. "Edvard Munchs Livsfrise: Struktur, kontekst og kritikk." *Kunst og Kultur* 87, no. 3 (2004): pp. 122–55.

Mørstad 2007
Mørstad, Erik. "The Improvisations of Edvard Munch." *Kunst og Kultur* 90, no. 3 (2007): pp. 139–60.

Müller-Westermann 1996
Müller-Westermann, Iris. "The Head in the Hand and the Hand in His Blood: Munch's Self-Comprehension as an Artist from 1895–1905." In Paszkiewicz 1996, pp. 79–87.

Müller-Westermann 2005
Müller-Westermann, Iris. *Munch by Himself*. Published on the occasion of the eponymous exhibition at Moderna Museet, Stockholm, Munchmuseet, Oslo, and Royal Academy of Arts, London. London, 2005.

Munch and Schiefler 1987 and 1990
Munch, Edvard, and Gustav Schiefler. *Briefwechsel*. Compiled by Arne Eggum, Sibylle Baumbach, Sissel Biörnstad, and Signe Böhn. 2 vols. Hamburg, 1987 and 1990.

Munich, Hamburg, and Berlin 1994–95
Munch und Deutschland. Edited by Dorothee Hansen and Uwe M. Schneede. Exh. cat. Hypo-Kunsthalle München, Kunsthalle Hamburg, and Nationalgalerie Berlin, 1994–95. Ostfildern-Ruit, 1994.

Næss 2015
Næss, Atle. *Edvard Munch: Eine Biografie*. Wiesbaden, 2015 [Oslo, 2004].

New York 2006
Edvard Munch: The Modern Life of the Soul. Edited by Kynaston McShine. Exh. cat. The Museum of Modern Art, 2006. New York, 2006.

New York 2016
Munch and Expressionism. Edited by Jill Lloyd and Reinhold Heller. Exh. cat. Neue Galerie New York, 2016. Munich, 2016.

Nielsen 2015
Nielsen, Trine Otte Bak, ed. *Vigeland + Munch: Behind the Myths*. Exh. cat. Munchmuseet, Oslo. Oslo and Brussels, 2015.

Nierhoff-Wielk 2011a
Nierhoff-Wielk, Barbara. "Art: Eifersucht II, 1896." In Bremen 2011–12, p. 45.

Nierhoff-Wielk 2011b
Nierhoff-Wielk, Barbara. "Art: Vampir, 1895." In Bremen 2011–12, p. 52.

Norseng 1991
Norseng, Mary Kay. *Dagny: Dagny Juel Przybyszewska, the Woman and the Myth*. Seattle and London, 1991.

Ohlsen 2013
Ohlsen, Nils. "Edvard Munchs visuelle Rhetorik—eine Annäherung am Beispiel ausgewählter Interieurs." In Oslo 2013, pp. 196–207.

Oslo 2002–3
Edvard Munchs livsfrise: En Rekonstruksjon av utstillingen hos Blomqvist 1918. Exh. cat. Munchmuseet, Oslo, 2002–3. Oslo, 2002.

Oslo 2013
Edvard Munch, 1863–1944. Exh. cat. Nasjonalgalleriet Oslo and Munchmuseet Oslo, 2013. Milan, 2013 [German edition, accompanied the exhibition *Munch 150*].

Paris 2011
Akseli Gallen-Kallela: Une passion finlandaise. Exh. cat. Musée d'Orsay, Paris. Ostfildern, 2011.

Paris 2022–23
Edvard Munch: A Poem of Life, Love and Death. Exh. cat. Musée d'Orsay, Paris, 2022–23. Oslo, 2022.

Paris, Frankfurt am Main, and London 2011–12
Edvard Munch: The Modern Eye. Exh. cat. Centre Pompidou, Paris, Schirn Kunsthalle, Frankfurt am Main, and Tate Modern, London, 2011–12. London, 2011.

Paris, Oslo, and Frankfurt am Main 1991–92
Munch et la France. Edited by Rodolphe Rapetti and Arne Eggum. Exh. cat. Musée d'Orsay, Paris, Munchmuseet, Oslo, and Schirn Kunsthalle, Frankfurt am Main, 1991–92. Paris, 1991.

Paszkiewicz 1996
Paszkiewicz, Piotr, ed. *Totenmesse: Modernism in the Culture of Northern and Central Europe*. Warsaw, 1996.

Paul 1927
Paul, Adolf. "Edvard Munch und Berlin—Erinnerungen." *Berliner Tageblatt*, no. 178, April 15, 1927, supplement 1, [p. 1].

Pettersen 2002
Pettersen, Petra. "Livsfrisen 1918 i Munch-Museet 2002: En kort redegjørelse for billedutvalget." In Oslo 2002–3, pp. 137–42.

Prelinger 2006
Prelinger, Elizabeth. "Metal, Stone, and Wood: Matrices of Meaning in Munch's Graphic Work." In New York 2006, pp. 52–63.

Przybyszewski 1894a
Przybyszewski, Stanisław, ed. *Das Werk des Edvard Munch: Vier Beiträge von Stanisław Przybyszewski, Dr. Franz Servaes, Willy Pastor, Julius Meier-Graefe*. Berlin, 1894.

Przybyszewski 1894b
Przybyszewski, Stanisław. [Contribution on Edvard Munch]. In Przybyszewski 1894a, pp. 9–31.

Przybyszewski 1894c
Przybyszewski, Stanisław. "Psychischer Naturalismus." *Freie Bühne* 5, no. 2 (1894): pp. 150–56.

Przybyszewski 1897
Przybyszewski, Stanisław. *Auf den Wegen der Seele*. Berlin, 1897.

Przybyszewski 1926
Przybyszewski, Stanisław. *Moi współcześni*. Wśród obcych 1. Warsaw, 1926.

Przybyszewski 1985
Przybyszewski, Stanisław. *Ferne komm ich her … Erinnerungen an Berlin und Krakau*. Leipzig and Weimar, 1985.

Pucks 1992
Pucks, Stefan. "Albert Kollmann—ein Leben für die Kunst." In *Avantgarde und Publikum: Zur Rezeption avantgardistischer Kunst in Deutschland, 1905–1933*. Edited by Henrike Junge. Cologne, Weimar, and Vienna, 1992, pp. 199–205.

Rapetti 1991–92a
Rapetti, Rodolphe. "Munch et Paris, 1889–1891." In Paris, Oslo, and Frankfurt am Main 1991–92, pp. 64–104.

Rapetti 1991–92b
Rapetti, Rodolphe. "Munch face à la critique française, 1893–1905." In Paris, Oslo, and Frankfurt am Main 1991–92, pp. 16–31.

Rauser 2022
Rauser, Judith. "Die Sammlung von Curt und Elsa Glaser." In Basel 2022, pp. 86–93.

Rave 1965
Rave, Paul Ortwin. "Munch in Berlin." *Kunst in Berlin*. Berlin, 1965, pp. 176–85.

Roettig 2006
Roettig, Petra. "'Der Schwerpunkt Ihrer Kunst liegt in der Graphik': Zum druckgraphischen Werk Edvard Munchs." In Hamburg 2006, pp. 17–26.

Rosenberg 1892a
AR [Adolf Rosenberg]. [Theater, art, and science section] "Die Bilder des Malers Munch." *Berliner Tageblatt*, no. 571, November 9, 1892, [p. 3].

Rosenberg 1892b
A. R. [Adolf Rosenberg]. "Eine Ausstellung von Ölgemälden." *Kunstchronik NF* 4, no. 5 (November 17, 1892): pp. 74–78.

Rosenblum 1978
Rosenblum, Robert. "Introduction: Edvard Munch; Some Changing Contexts." In Washington 1978, pp. 1–9.

Rosenhagen 1902
Rosenhagen, Hans. "Die fünfte Ausstellung der Berliner Secession." *Die Kunst für Alle* 17, nos. 19–20 (1902): pp. 433–46 and 457–63.

Rother and Koss 2022
Rother, Lynn, and May Koss. "'Oh, Sie sind eine Wissenschaftlerin!': Elsa Glaser und die Kunstgeschichte." In Basel 2022, pp. 40–47.

Schalhorn 2022
Schalhorn, Andreas. "Curt Glaser und die zeitgenössische Kunst im Berliner Kupferstichkabinett." In Basel 2022, pp. 49–57.

Scheffler 1902
Scheffler, Karl. "Berliner Secession." *Die Zukunft* 39 (June 14, 1902): pp. 419–30.

Scheffler 1914
Scheffler, Karl. "Edvard Munch." *Kunst und Künstler* 12, no. 8 (1914): pp. 415–24.

Schiefler 1907
Schiefler, Gustav. *Verzeichnis des graphischen Werks Edvard Munchs bis 1906*. Berlin, 1907.

Schiefler 1927
Schiefler, Gustav. *Edvard Munch: Das graphische Werk 1906–1926*. Berlin, 1927.

Schneede 1994a
Schneede, Uwe M. "'Aus der Erinnerung und mit der Phantasie': Skandinavien in Berlin—Munchs 'zweite Heimat.'" In Munich, Hamburg, and Berlin 1994–95, pp. 12–19.

Schneede 1994b
Schneede, Uwe M. "Munchs Lebensfries, zentrales Projekt der Moderne." In Munich, Hamburg, and Berlin 1994–95, pp. 20–29.

Schneede 1994c
Schneede, Uwe M. "'Eine der Säulen moderner Malerei': Munch auf der Sonderbund-Ausstellung 1912 in Köln." In Munich, Hamburg, and Berlin 1994–95, pp. 100–101.

Schulz-Albrecht 1927
Brattskoven, Otto [August Julius Schulz-Albrecht]. [Visual arts section] "Munch." *Sozialistische Monatsschrift* 33, no. 6 (1927): p. 502.

Schütz 1987
Schütz, Barbara M. "Die Farbe bei Edvard Munch." In Essen and Zurich 1987–88, pp. 77–87.

Servaes 1894
Servaes, Franz. [Contribution on Edvard Munch]. In Przybyszewski 1894a, pp. 33–56.

Sieber 2022
Sieber, Joachim. "Curt Glaser und die Munch-Sammlung am Kunsthaus Zürich." In Basel 2022, pp. 136–41.

Springer 1893a
Relling [Jaro Springer]. "Der Fall Munch." *Die Kunst für Alle* 8, no. 7 (1892–93) [January 1, 1893]: pp. 102–3.

Springer 1893b
Dr. R. [Jaro Springer]. [Note]. *Die Kunst für Alle* 8, no. 16 (1892–93) [May 15, 1893]: p. 252.

Stern 1912
Stern, Lisbeth. "Kölner Sonderbundausstellung." *Sozialistische Monatshefte* 16, nos. 18–20 (September 1912) [September 12, 1912]: pp. 1248–51.

Strobl 2006
Strobl, Andreas. *Curt Glaser: Kunsthistoriker—Kunstkritiker—Sammler; Eine deutsch-jüdische Biographie*. Cologne, Weimar, and Vienna, 2006.

Thiis 1933
Thiis, Jens. *Edvard Munch og hans samtid: Slekten, livet og kunsten, geniet*. Oslo, 1933.

Thiis 1934
Thiis, Jens. *Edvard Munch*. With an afterword by Erich Büttner. Berlin, 1934.

Thurmann-Moe 1987
Thurmann-Moe, Jan. "Bemerkungen zu Munchs Maltechnik." In Essen and Zurich 1987–88, pp. 89–99.

Topalova-Casadiego 2009
Topalova-Casadiego, Biljana. "Technical Aspects of Edvard Munch's Paintings." In Woll 2009, vol. 2, pp. 425–57.

Ustvedt 2013
Ustvedt, Øystain. "Who Was Mrs. Schwarz? On a Portrait by Edvard Munch." *Kunst og Kultur* 4, no. 96 (2013): pp. 218–29.

Vienna 2003
Edvard Munch: Theme and Variation. Edited by Klaus A. Schröder and Antonia Hoerschelmann. Translated by Elinor Ruth Waaler and John Southard. Exh. cat. Albertina, Vienna, 2003. Ostfildern-Ruit, 2003.

Volle 2013
Volle, Wenche. "Edvard Munch's Exhibition at Kunsthandlung P.H. Beyer & Sohn in 1903." *Kunst og Kultur* 96, no. 4 (2013): pp. 194–205.

Volle 2014
Volle, Wenche. "The Architecture of Edvard Munch's 'Frieze of Life.'" In *Place and Displacement: Exhibiting Architecture*. Edited by Thordis Arrhenius et al. Zurich, 2014, pp. 141–52.

Washington 1978
Edvard Munch: Symbols & Images. Exh. cat. National Gallery of Art, Washington, DC, 1978. Washington, DC, 1978.

Wat 2022
Wat, Pierre. "The Sinuous Line of Life." In Paris 2022–23, pp. 44–57.

Woesthoff 2006
Woesthoff, Indina. "Der Magier und der Jurist: Edvard Munch und Gustav Schiefler." In Hamburg 2006, pp. 32–38.

Wolff 1892
Wolff, Theodor. "Die 'Affaire Munch.'" *Berliner Tageblatt*, no. 576, November 12, 1892, [p. 5].

Wolgast 2011
Wolgast, Karin Reinhardt. "Ibsen und Munch in Berlin 'Gespenster' an den Kammerspielen des Deutschen Theaters 1906." *Divinatio: Studia Culturologica Series* 34 (2011), pp. 7–62.

Woll 1992
Woll, Gerd. "The Frieze of Life: Graphic Works." In London 1992–93, pp. 45–50.

Woll 1994
Woll, Gerd. "Munchs Grafik in Deutschland: Vom Zustandsdruck zur Massenauflage." In Munich, Hamburg, and Berlin 1994–95, pp. 46–57.

Woll 2001
Gerd Woll, ed., *Edvard Munch: The Complete Graphic Works*. New York, 2001.

Woll 2003
Woll, Gerd. 2003. "Paper in Prints by Edvard Munch." In Vienna 2003.

Woll 2009
Woll, Gerd, ed. 2009. *Edvard Munch: Complete Paintings; Catalogue Raisonné*. 4 vols. New York.

Woll 2013
"The Kunsthaus Zürich Presents Edvard Munch in 1922 with an Almost Complete Overview of His Graphic Works." In Zurich 2013, pp. 13–45.

Zurich 1976
Munch und Ibsen. Exh. cat. Kunsthaus Zürich, 1976. Zurich, 1976.

Zurich 2013
Edvard Munch: A Genius of Printmaking. Edited by Carlotta Graedel Matthäi and Franziska Lentzsch. Translated by Francesca Nichols and Geoffrey Spearing. Exh. cat. Kunsthaus Zürich. Ostfildern, 2013.

Zuschlag 1995
Zuschlag, Christoph. *"Entartete Kunst": Ausstellungsstrategien im Nazi-Deutschland*. Worms, 1995.

Zweig 1925
Stefan, Zweig. "Nachwort." In Jens Peter Jacobsen, *Niels Lyhne*. Leipzig, 1925, pp. 255–66.

Photo Credits for the Exhibited Works

Cover
Edvard Munch, *Red and White*, 1899–1900, Munchmuseet, Oslo
© Munchmuseet / Halvor Bjørngård

p. 44
© bpk | Staatliche Schlösser, Gärten und Kunstsammlungen Mecklenburg-Vorpommern / Elke Walford

p. 45 A
© Private collection, northern Germany

p. 45 B
© Berlinische Galerie / Kai-Annett Becker

p. 46 A + B
© Berlinische Galerie / Kai-Annett Becker

p. 47
© Stiftung Stadtmuseum Berlin / Hans-Joachim Bartsch, Berlin

p. 42
pp. 48–49
© Staatliche Museen zu Berlin, Nationalgalerie / Andres Kilger

pp. 50–51
© Munchmuseet / Juri Kobayashi

pp. 52–53
© Kunsthaus Zürich

p. 56
© Munchmuseet / Ove Kvavik

p. 57
© Munchmuseet / Halvor Bjørngård

pp. 58–59
© Munchmuseet / Rena Li

pp. 60–61
© Munchmuseet / Halvor Bjørngård

pp. 62–65
© Munchmuseet / Ove Kvavik

pp. 66–67
© Munchmuseet / Halvor Bjørngård

pp. 68–69
© Munchmuseet / Ove Kvavik

pp. 70–71
© Munchmuseet / Sidsel de Jong

pp. 72–73
© Munchmuseet / Juri Kobayashi

pp. 74–75
© Munchmuseet / Ove Kvavik

pp. 76–77
© Munchmuseet / Svein Andersen / Sidsel de Jong

pp. 78–79
© Munchmuseet / Ove Kvavik

p. 54
pp. 80–83
© Munchmuseet / Halvor Bjørngård

pp. 84–85
© Munchmuseet / Juri Kobayashi

pp. 86–99
p. 301
© bpk / Nationalgalerie, SMB / Jörg P. Anders

p. 102
© Staatliche Museen zu Berlin, Kupferstichkabinett / Jörg P. Anders

p. 103 A + B
© Staatliche Museen zu Berlin, Kupferstichkabinett / Dietmar Katz

p. 104
© Staatliche Museen zu Berlin, Kupferstichkabinett / Jörg P. Anders

p. 105
© bpk / Kupferstichkabinett, SMB / Volker-H. Schneider

pp. 106–7
© Munchmuseet / Rena Li

p. 108 A + B
© Staatliche Museen zu Berlin, Kupferstichkabinett / Jörg P. Anders

p. 109
© bpk / Kupferstichkabinett, SMB / Volker-H. Schneider

p. 100
pp. 110–11
© bpk / Kupferstichkabinett, SMB / Volker-H. Schneider

p. 112
© Munchmuseet / Halvor Bjørngård

p. 113
© Staatliche Museen zu Berlin, Kupferstichkabinett / Jörg P. Anders

p. 114
© Staatliche Museen zu Berlin, Kupferstichkabinett / Dietmar Katz

p. 115
© Staatliche Museen zu Berlin, Kupferstichkabinett / Dietmar Katz

p. 116
© Munchmuseet / Halvor Bjørngård

pp. 117–19
© Staatliche Museen zu Berlin, Kupferstichkabinett / Dietmar Katz

Front endpaper
pp. 40–41
pp. 120–30
pp. 254–55
© Munchmuseet

p. 131 A
© Staatliche Museen zu Berlin, Kupferstichkabinett / Jörg P. Anders

p. 131 B
© Munchmuseet / Rena Li

p. 134
© Munchmuseet / Juri Kobayashi

p. 135
© Stiftung Stadtmuseum Berlin / Oliver Ziebe, Berlin

pp. 136–37
© Munchmuseet / Halvor Bjørngård

p. 132
p. 138
© Munchmuseet / Juri Kobayashi

p. 12
p. 139
© Munchmuseet / Rena Li

p. 140
© Moderna Museet, Stockholm

p. 141
© Hamburger Kunsthalle / bpk / Elke Walford

p. 142
© Munchmuseet / Rena Li

pp. 144–45
© Munchmuseet / Ove Kvavik

p. 146
© Munchmuseet / Halvor Bjørngård

p. 147
© Munchmuseet / Ove Kvavik

pp. 150–51
© Munchmuseet / Halvor Bjørngård

p. 151
© bpk / Nationalgalerie, SMB / Jörg P. Anders

p. 152 A
© Munchmuseet

p. 152 B
© bpk / Nationalgalerie, SMB

p. 153
© Munchmuseet / Halvor Bjørngård

pp. 154–55
© Kunstmuseum Basel / Jonas Hänggi

pp. 156–57
© Munchmuseet / Ove Kvavik

p. 148
pp. 158–59
© Die Lübecker Museen, Museum Behnhaus Drägerhaus / Michael Haydn

Photo Credits for the Illustrations in the Contributions

p. 16
Edvard Munch, *Apple Tree in the Garden*, 1932–42, oil on canvas, 100.5 × 77 cm, Munchmuseet, Oslo
© Munchmuseet/Ove Kvavik

p. 17
Edvard Munch, *The Girl at the Window*, 1894, drypoint, 47.6 × 33.3 cm, Staatliche Museen zu Berlin, Kupferstichkabinett
© Staatliche Museen zu Berlin, Kupferstichkabinett/Dietmar Katz

p. 19 A
Adelsteen Normann, *Imperial Yacht "Hohenzollern,"* 1910, oil on canvas, 68.5 × 94.5 cm, Norsk Maritimt Museum, Oslo
© Norsk Maritimt Museum

p. 19 B
Edvard Munch, *Summer Night (Inger on the Beach)*, 1889, oil on canvas, 126.5 × 161.5 cm, Kode, Bergen
© Kode/Dag Fosse

p. 20 A
Edvard Munch, 1892, photograph, 14 × 21 cm, Munchmuseet, Oslo
© Munchmuseet/Aftenposten

p. 20 B
Edvard Munch, *Hans Jæger*, 1889, oil on canvas, 109 × 84 cm, Nasjonalmuseet, Oslo
© Nasjonalmuseet

p. 22
Edvard Munch, *Dagny Juel Przybyszewska*, 1893, oil on canvas, 149 × 100.5 cm, Munchmuseet, Oslo
© Munchmuseet/Juri Kobayashi

p. 23
Edvard Munch, *Stanisław Przybyszewski*, 1895, lithograph, 59.4 × 48.7 cm, Munchmuseet, Oslo
© Munchmuseet/Ove Kvavik

p. 25
Ferdinand Hodler, *Emotion*, ca. 1909, oil on canvas, 121 × 176 cm, Stiftung für Kunst, Kultur und Geschichte, Winterthur
© SKKG 2020

p. 26 A
Edvard Munch, *Portrait of Gustaf Schiefler*, 1908, oil on canvas, 135 × 119 cm, Antell Collections, Finnish National Gallery/Ateneum Art Museum, Helsinki
© Finnish National Gallery/Jukka Romu

p. 26 B
Edvard Munch, *Night in Saint-Cloud*, 1890, oil on canvas, 64.5 × 54 cm, Nasjonalmuseet, Oslo
© Børre Høstland/Nasjonalmuseet

p. 28
Edvard Munch, *The Dance of Life*, 1899–1900, oil on canvas, 125 × 191 cm, Nasjonalmuseet, Oslo
© Børre Høstland/Nasjonalmuseet

p. 29 A
Edvard Munch, *Death and the Child*, 1899, oil on canvas, 100 × 90 cm, Kunsthalle Bremen—Der Kunstverein in Bremen
© Kunsthalle Bremen/Lars Lohrisch/ARTOTHEK

p. 29 B
Edvard Munch, *Portrait of Dr. Linde*, 1904, oil on canvas, 226.5 × 101.5 cm, KST—Sondervermögen Stiftung Moritzburg, Kulturstiftung Sachsen-Anhalt, Kunstmuseum Moritzburg, Halle an der Saale
© Kulturstiftung Sachsen-Anhalt, Kunstmuseum Moritzburg Halle (Saale)/Punctum/Bertram Kober

p. 31 A
Edvard Munch, *The Sun*, 1912–13, oil on canvas, 324 × 509.5 cm, Munchmuseet, Oslo
© Munchmuseet

p. 31 B
O. Væring, Test hanging of Munch's works in the auditorium, University of Oslo, 1911, photograph, 71 × 54.4 cm, Munchmuseet, Oslo
© Munchmuseet

p. 33 A
Edvard Munch, *The Day After*, 1894, oil on canvas, 115 × 152 cm, Nasjonalmuseet, Oslo
© Børre Høstland/Jacques Lathion/Nasjonalmuseet

p. 33 B
Max Pechstein, *Woman Resting*, 1911, oil on canvas, 75 × 101 cm, private collection
© bpk

p. 34 A
Edvard Munch, *Dr. Linde's Sons*, 1903, oil on canvas, 144 × 199.5 cm, Die Lübecker Museen, Museum Behnhaus Drägerhaus
© Die Lübecker Museen, Museum Behnhaus Drägerhaus/Michael Haydn

p. 34 B
Depot room for confiscated "degenerate art" in Schloss Schönhausen, Berlin (on the right: Edvard Munch's *Dr. Linde's Sons*), 1937, photograph, 50.4 × 44.5 cm, bpk Bildagentur
© bpk

p. 163
Edvard Munch, *Self-Portrait with Cigarette*, 1895, oil on canvas, 85.5 × 110.5 cm, Nasjonalmuseet, Oslo
© Børre Høstland/Nasjonalmuseet

p. 165 A
Lovis Corinth, *Dance Break at the Leistikows*, 1894, oil on canvas, 87 × 90.5 cm, Kunsthalle zu Kiel
© Kunsthalle zu Kiel/Foto-Renard, Kiel

p. 165 B
Edvard Munch, *Artists around a Table (Zum schwarzen Ferkel)*, 1893, crayon, blue wove paper, 20.9 × 33 cm, Munchmuseet, Oslo
© Munchmuseet/Tone Margrethe Gauden

p. 166 A
Catalogue of the Edvard Munch exhibition at the Verein Berliner Künstler, 1892, Munchmuseet, Oslo
© Munchmuseet

p. 166 B
Edvard Munch, *The Sick Child*, 1885–86, oil on canvas, 120 × 118.5 cm, Nasjonalmuseet, Oslo
© Børre Høstland/Nasjonalmuseet

p. 167
Carl Saltzmann, *Portrait of Anton von Werner*, ca. 1885/1890, oil on cardboard, 36.5 × 24.3 cm, Stiftung Stadtmuseum Berlin
© Stiftung Stadtmuseum Berlin/Hans-Joachim Bartsch, Berlin

p. 168
Ludwig von Hofmann, Invitation to the second exhibition of the Vereinigung der XI, March 1893, Akademie der Künste, Berlin, Lovis-Corinth-Archiv, no. 13
© Akademie der Künste, Berlin

p. 170
Franz Skarbina, *In the Sunshine*, 1893, oil on canvas, 99.5 × 68.5 cm, private collection
© Fotostudio Bartsch, Karen Bartsch, Berlin

p. 171
Walter Leistikow, *Schlachtensee*, ca. 1900, oil on canvas, 55.5 × 67.5 cm, Bröhan-Museum, Berlin
© bpk/Bröhan-Museum/Martin Adam

p. 175 A
Edvard Munch, *Death in the Sickroom*, 1893, oil on canvas, 134.5 × 160 cm, Munchmuseet, Oslo
© Munchmuseet/Ove Kvavik

p. 175 B
Edvard Munch, *Madonna*, 1894, oil on canvas, 90 × 68.5 cm, Munchmuseet, Oslo
© Munchmuseet/Rena Li

p. 176
Edvard Munch, *Vampire*, 1893, oil on canvas, 80.5 × 100.5 cm, Gothenburg Museum of Art
© Gothenburg Museum of Art/Hossein Sehatlou

p. 179 A
Wilhelm Schulz, Poster for the fifth exhibition of the Berlin Secession, 1902, 71.1 × 94.6 cm, Museumsberg Flensburg
© Museumsberg Flensburg/Ina Steinhusen

p. 179 B
Floor plan of the exhibition building of the Berlin Secession, Kantstrasse 12, 1902, in the catalogue of the Fifth Exhibition of the Berlin Secession, Berlin, 1902, p. 3
© Berlinische Galerie

p. 179 C
Board of the Berlin Secession 1902, *Die Kunst für Alle: Malerei, Plastik, Graphik, Architektur* 17, no. 19 (1902): p. 443
© Universitätsbibliothek Heidelberg

p. 181
Edvard Munch, Sketches for the Berlin Secession exhibition, 1902, pen on paper, 11 × 16.4 cm, Munchmuseet, Oslo
© Munchmuseet/Halvor Bjørngård

p. 182
Edvard Munch, *Woman*, 1894, oil on canvas, 164.5 × 251 cm, Kode, Bergen
© Kode/Dag Fosse

p. 183
Edvard Munch, *Metabolism*, 1898–99, oil on canvas, 172.5 × 142 cm, Munchmuseet, Oslo
© Munchmuseet/Halvor Bjørngård

p. 185 A
Edvard Munch, *Death and the Child*, 1899, oil on canvas, 104 × 179.5 cm, Munchmuseet, Oslo
© Munchmuseet/Ove Kvavik

p. 185 B
Rear endpaper
Ragnvald Væring, Edvard Munch in his winter studio at Ekely, on the occasion of his seventy-fifth birthday, 1938, photograph, 54.2 × 39.8 cm, Munchmuseet, Oslo, courtesy of Munchmuseet
© Munchmuseet

p. 186
Edvard Munch's exhibition at the Galerie P. H. Beyer & Sohn, Leipzig, 1903, photograph, 82.1 × 67.1 cm, Munchmuseet, Oslo
© Munchmuseet

p. 190 A
Edvard Munch, *Self-Portrait (with Skeleton Arm)*, 1895, lithograph (second state), ca. 55.1 × 40/40.5 cm, Staatliche Museen zu Berlin, Kupferstichkabinett
© Staatliche Museen zu Berlin, Kupferstichkabinett/Jörg P. Anders

p. 190 B
Max Klinger, *Lonesome* (no. 5 of the series *Opus VIII, A Life*), 1884, etching and aquatint, 27.5 × 42.8 cm, Staatliche Museen zu Berlin, Kupferstichkabinett
© Staatliche Museen zu Berlin, Kupferstichkabinett/Dietmar Katz

p. 190 C
Letter from the Otto Felsing printing house to Edvard Munch, August 16, 1906, Munchmuseet, Oslo
© Munchmuseet

p. 193 A
Edvard Munch, *Two Human Beings (The Lonely Ones)*, 1899, woodcut, 39.5 × 55.2 cm, Staatliche Museen zu Berlin, Kupferstichkabinett
© Staatliche Museen zu Berlin, Kupferstichkabinett/Jörg P. Anders

p. 193 B
Edvard Munch, *Harry Graf Kessler I*, 1895, lithograph, 11.6 × 12.2 cm, Staatliche Museen zu Berlin, Kupferstichkabinett
© Staatliche Museen zu Berlin, Kupferstichkabinett/Dietmar Katz

p. 194
Henri de Toulouse-Lautrec, *Seated Clown (Mademoiselle Cha-U-Kao)*, 1896, color lithograph, 52.7 × 50.2 cm, Staatliche Museen zu Berlin, Kupferstichkabinett
© Staatliche Museen zu Berlin, Kupferstichkabinett/Volker-H. Schneider

p. 195
Edvard Munch, *August Strindberg*, 1896, lithograph, 44.4 × 31.6 cm, Staatliche Museen zu Berlin, Kupferstichkabinett
© Staatliche Museen zu Berlin, Kupferstichkabinett/Jörg P. Anders

p. 197 A
Edvard Munch, *Vampire II*, 1895, lithograph, 38.8 × 56 cm, Staatliche Museen zu Berlin, Kupferstichkabinett
© Staatliche Museen zu Berlin, Kupferstichkabinett/Volker-H. Schneider

p. 197 B
Edvard Munch, *The Kiss IV*, 1902, color woodcut, 47 × 47 cm, Staatliche Museen zu Berlin, Kupferstichkabinett
© Staatliche Museen zu Berlin, Kupferstichkabinett/Volker-H. Schneider

p. 199
Edvard Munch, Illustration for the program for Henrik Ibsen's *John Gabriel Borkman* (for Aurélien Lugné-Poë's production at the Théâtre de l'Œuvre, Paris), 1897, lithograph, 20.9 × 32.5 cm, Staatliche Museen zu Berlin, Kupferstichkabinett
© Staatliche Museen zu Berlin, Kupferstichkabinett/Dietmar Katz

p. 200 A
Edvard Munch, *Andreas Schwarz*, 1906 [1907?], drypoint, 28 × 20.7 cm, Staatliche Museen zu Berlin, Kupferstichkabinett
© Staatliche Museen zu Berlin, Kupferstichkabinett/Dietmar Katz

p. 200 B
Edvard Munch, *Elsa and Curt Glaser*, 1913, lithograph, 67.6 × 84.5 cm, Munchmuseet, Oslo
© Munchmuseet/Halvor Bjørngård

p. 204
Edvard Munch, *Self-Portrait (Against Two-Colored Background)*, [ca. 1903], oil on canvas, 69.5 × 44 cm, Heidi Horten Collection, Vienna
© Heidi Horten Collection

p. 207
Edvard Munch, *Theodor Linde*, 1902, drypoint, 29.8 × 21.9 cm, Munchmuseet, Oslo
© Munchmuseet/Rena Li

p. 208
Edvard Munch, *Self-Portrait in Hell*, 1903, oil on canvas, 82 × 66 cm, Munchmuseet, Oslo
© Munchmuseet/Juri Kobayashi

p. 210
Edvard Munch, *On the Bridge*, 1903, oil on canvas, 203 × 230 cm, Thielska Galleriet, Stockholm
© Thielska Galleriet/Tord Lund

p. 211 A
Entry in Cassirer's account book, 1907, Paul Cassirer & Walter Feilchenfeldt Archiv, Zurich
© Paul Cassirer & Walter Feilchenfeldt Archiv, Zurich

p. 211 B
Edvard Munch, *Park in Kösen*, 1906, oil on canvas, 70 × 80 cm, Österreichische Galerie Belvedere, Vienna
© Belvedere, Vienna

p. 213
Edvard Munch, *Portrait of Children (Erdmute and Hans-Herbert Esche)*, 1905, oil on canvas, 148 × 162.5 cm, Kunsthaus Zürich, Zurich, loan from the Herbert Eugen Esche Foundation, 1997
© Kunsthaus Zürich

p. 214 A
Edvard Munch, *Karl Johan in the Rain*, 1891, oil on canvas, 38.1 × 55.2 cm, Munchmuseet, Oslo
© Munchmuseet/Juri Kobayashi

p. 214 B
Edvard Munch, *Gamblers in Monte Carlo*, 1892, oil on canvas, 72 × 92 cm, Munchmuseet, Oslo
© Munchmuseet/Juri Kobayashi

p. 219
Edvard Munch, *Julius Meier-Graefe*, ca. 1894, oil on canvas, 100 × 75 cm, Nasjonalmuseet, Oslo
© Børre Høstland/Nasjonalmuseet

p. 220 A
Illustration for Adolf Paul's book *Das "Urferkel" und die Tafelrunde Strindbergs* (The "Urferkel" and Strindberg's Round Table), 1920, Munchmuseet, Oslo
© Munchmuseet

p. 220 B
Edvard Munch, *August Strindberg*, 1892, oil on canvas, 122 × 90 cm, Moderna Museet, Stockholm, donation from the artist in 1934
© Moderna Museet, Stockholm

p. 222 A
Edvard Munch, *Golgotha*, 1900, oil on canvas, 80 × 120 cm, Munchmuseet, Oslo
© Munchmuseet/Juri Kobayashi

p. 222 B
Paul Gauguin, *Self-Portrait with the Yellow Christ*, 1890–91, oil on canvas, 38 × 46 cm, Musée d'Orsay, Paris
© bpk | RMN—Grand Palais | René-Gabriel Ojéda

p. 223
Edvard Munch, *Stanisław Przybyszewski*, 1894, casein and distemper on canvas, 75.5 × 60.5 cm, Munchmuseet, Oslo
© Munchmuseet/Ove Kvavik

p. 225 A
Stanisław Przybyszewski, *Das Werk des Edvard Munch* (The Work of Edvard Munch), 1894, Staatsbibliothek zu Berlin, Preussischer Kulturbesitz, signature Nt 4985
© Staatsbibliothek zu Berlin, Preußischer Kulturbesitz

p. 225 B
Edvard Munch, *The Scream*, 1893, tempera and crayon on cardboard, 91 × 73.5 cm, Nasjonalmuseet, Oslo
© Børre Høstland/Nasjonalmuseet

p. 225 C
Edvard Munch, *Une charogne* (illustration for Charles Baudelaire's *Les fleurs du mal*), 1896, pen, brush, wash, pencil on wove paper, 26 × 22.6 cm, Munchmuseet, Oslo
© Munchmuseet/Halvor Bjørngård

p. 227
Edvard Munch, *Jens Thiis*, 1913, lithograph, 41 × 26.8 cm, Munchmuseet, Oslo
© Munchmuseet/Halvor Bjørngård

p. 230
Chamber Theater of the Deutsches Theater, Berlin, view from the south, 1942, photograph, 18.7 × 24.6 cm, Architekturmuseum, Technische Universität Berlin
© Architekturmuseum, Technische Universität Berlin

p. 231
Edvard Munch, Set design for Henrik Ibsen's *Ghosts*, 1906, tempera on canvas, 60.5 × 102.5 cm, Munchmuseet, Oslo
© Munchmuseet

p. 232 A
Edvard Munch, Theater program for Henrik Ibsen's *Peer Gynt*, 1896, lithograph, 24.9 × 31.8 cm, Munchmuseet, Oslo
© Munchmuseet/Svein Andersen

p. 232 B
Edvard Munch, Theater program for Henrik Ibsen's *John Gabriel Borkman*, 1897, lithograph, 27.9 × 37.4 cm, Munchmuseet, Oslo
© Munchmuseet/Svein Andersen

p. 234
Edvard Munch painting in Åsgårdstrand, 1889, photograph, 77.1 × 56.1 cm, Munchmuseet, Oslo
© Munchmuseet

p. 235
Edvard Munch, *Kissing Couples in the Park (The Linde Frieze)*, 1904, oil on canvas, 91 × 171.5 cm, Munchmuseet, Oslo
© Munchmuseet/Halvor Bjørngård

p. 237 A
Edvard Munch, Designs for a frieze, 1906–7, watercolor, crayon, black wove paper, 90.5 × 238 cm, Munchmuseet, Oslo
© Munchmuseet

p. 237 B
William Müller, Chamber Theater of the Deutsches Theater, Berlin, plan of the ground floor, [1906], *Der Baumeister* 5, no. 11 (1912): p. 128
© Universitätsbibliothek Heidelberg

p. 238 A
Edvard Munch, *Two Human Beings. The Lonely Ones (The Reinhardt Frieze)*, 1906–7, tempera on canvas, 89.5 × 159.5 cm, Museum Folkwang, Essen
© Museum Folkwang Essen/ARTOTHEK

p. 238 B
Edvard Munch, *Dance on the Beach (The Reinhardt Frieze)*, 1906–7, tempera on canvas, 90 × 402.6 cm, private collection
© Munchmuseet/Halvor Bjørngård

p. 238 C
Edvard Munch, *Young Woman on the Beach (The Reinhardt Frieze)*, 1906–7, tempera on canvas, 90 × 148 cm, Hamburger Kunsthalle, Hamburg
© Hamburger Kunsthalle/bpk/Elke Walford

p. 243
Kronprinzenpalais, Berlin, August 18, 1927, photograph, 39.8 × 39.9 cm, Staatliche Museen zu Berlin, Zentralarchiv, SMB-ZA, V/Fotoslg. 1.11./419
© Staatliche Museen zu Berlin, Zentralarchiv

p. 244 A
Edvard Munch, *Curt and Elsa Glaser*, 1913, pastel on wove (?) paper, 23.5 × 33.7 cm, National Gallery of Art, Epstein Family Collection, Washington, DC
© National Gallery of Art, Washington, DC

p. 244 B
Telegram from Ludwig Justi to Edvard Munch, January 4, 1927, Munchmuseet Oslo
© Munchmuseet

p. 244 C
Telegram from Edvard Munch to Ludwig Justi, January 5, 1927, Staatliche Museen zu Berlin, Zentralarchiv, SMB-ZA, I/NG 678, fol. 430
© Staatliche Museen zu Berlin, Zentralarchiv

p. 246
Edvard Munch and Ludwig Justi in Oslo, January 30, 1927, photograph, *Bilder-Courier*, no. 5, January 30, 1927, Staatsbibliothek zu Berlin, Preussischer Kulturbesitz, signature 2"@Ztg 786
© Staatsbibliothek zu Berlin, Preußischer Kulturbesitz

p. 247 A
Edvard Munch, *Dr. Ludwig Justi*, 1927, lithograph, 50.3 × 37.9 cm, Staatliche Museen zu Berlin, Kupferstichkabinett
© Staatliche Museen zu Berlin, Kupferstichkabinett/Dietmar Katz

pp. 160–61
p. 247 B
Edvard Munch drawing Ludwig Justi in the Kronprinzenpalais, Berlin, February–March 1927, photograph, Munchmuseet, Oslo
© Munchmuseet

p. 248
Invitation to the Munch exhibition, Nationalgalerie, Kronprinzenpalais, Berlin, March 1927, Staatliche Museen zu Berlin, Zentralarchiv, SMB-ZA, V/Slg. Künstler, Munch, Edvard
© Staatliche Museen zu Berlin, Zentralarchiv

p. 250 A
View of the stairwell in the Kronprinzenpalais, during the Munch exhibition, 1927, photograph, Staatliche Museen zu Berlin, Zentralarchiv, SMB-ZA, V/Slg. Künstler, Munch, Edvard
© Staatliche Museen zu Berlin, Zentralarchiv

p. 250 B
View of one room in the Munch exhibition, Kronprinzenpalais, newspaper clipping from the newspaper *Tägliche Rundschau*, Berlin, March 20, 1927, Staatliche Museen zu Berlin, Zentralarchiv, SMB-ZA, V/Slg. Künstler, Munch, Edvard
© Staatliche Museen zu Berlin, Zentralarchiv

p. 250 C
View of the Munch room in the Kronprinzenpalais, Berlin, 1933, photograph, Staatliche Museen zu Berlin, Zentralarchiv, SMB-ZA, V/Fotoslg. 2.17.4/482
© Staatliche Museen zu Berlin, Zentralarchiv

p. 251
Edvard Munch, *Portrait of Elsa Glaser*, 1913, oil on canvas, 120.5 × 85 cm, Kunsthaus Zürich, Zurich, 1946
© Kunsthaus Zürich

p. 258 A
Max Marschalk, Edvard Munch's exhibition at the Equitable-Palast, Berlin, 1892–93, photograph, 43.9 × 29.7 cm, Munchmuseet, Oslo
© Munchmuseet

p. 258 B
Architektenhaus, Berlin, Wilhelmstrasse 92/93, ca. 1920–30, photograph, Bildarchiv Foto Marburg
© Bildarchiv Foto Marburg

p. 259 A
August Strindberg, Self-Portrait, Berlin, 1892–93, photograph, Kungliga Biblioteket, Stockholm
© Ann-Sofie Persson/National Library of Sweden

pp. 10–11
p. 259 B
Edvard Munch and Adolf Paul, ca. 1894, photograph, 23.8 × 17.6 cm, Munchmuseet, Oslo
© Munchmuseet

p. 259 C
Edvard Munch, *Self-Portrait with a Bottle of Wine*, 1906, oil on canvas, 110.5 × 121 cm, Munchmuseet, Oslo
© Munchmuseet/Halvor Bjørngård

p. 260 A
Dagny and Stanisław Przybyszewski, 1897–98, photograph, The Picture Art Collection/Alamy Stock Photo
© The Picture Art Collection/Alamy Stock Photo

p. 260 B
August Haraldsson, Dagny Juel, 1884, photograph, 21.2 × 33.2 cm, Munchmuseet, Oslo
© Munchmuseet

p. 261 A
Edvard Munch, *The Scream*, 1910 (?), tempera and oil on unprimed cardboard, 83.5 × 66 cm, Munchmuseet, Oslo
© Munchmuseet/Halvor Bjørngård/Rena Li

p. 261 B
Edvard Munch, Three sketches for *The Scream*, 1893–95, pen and pencil on wove paper, 49.5 × 37.5 cm, Munchmuseet, Oslo
© Munchmuseet/Ove Kvavik

p. 261 C
Edvard Munch, *Angst (Feeling of Anxiety)*, 1896, woodcut, 71.3 × 60 cm, Staatliche Museen zu Berlin, Kupferstichkabinett
© Staatliche Museen zu Berlin, Kupferstichkabinett/Jörg P. Anders

p. 263 A
Portrait of Edvard Munch, Berlin, ca. 1905, photograph, 36.6 × 55.7 cm, Munchmuseet, Oslo
© Munchmuseet

p. 263 B
Axel Gallén (from 1907: Akseli Gallen-Kallela), Poster for Edvard Munch and Axel Gallén's exhibition, 1895, lithograph, 70.7 × 47.3 cm, Finnish National Gallery/Ateneum Art Museum, Helsinki
© Finnish National Gallery/Pirje Mykkänen

p. 263 C
pp. 280–81
Potsdamer Platz, Berlin, before 1904, 33.1 × 24.2 cm, ullstein bild, Berlin
© ullstein bild

p. 264 A
Edvard Munch, Self-Portrait in His Studio, Lützowstrasse 82, Berlin, 1902, collodion paper, 8.7 × 8.7 cm, Munchmuseet, Oslo
© Munchmuseet

p. 264 B
Edvard Munch, *Harry Graf Kessler*, 1906, oil on canvas, 200 × 84 cm, Staatliche Museen zu Berlin, Nationalgalerie, acquired in 1950 by the State of Berlin
© bpk/Nationalgalerie, SMB/Jörg P. Anders

p. 265 A
Letter from Edvard Munch to Karen Bjølstad, November 14, 1894, Munchmuseet, Oslo
© Munchmuseet

p. 265 B
Max von Rüdiger, Liebermann in His Atelier, 1899, photograph, 19.7 × 20.6 cm, bpk Bildagentur
© bpk/Max von Rüdiger

p. 267 A
F. Lippens, Edvard Munch, Berlin, 1902–4, photograph, 46.1 × 27.8 cm, Munchmuseet, Oslo
© Munchmuseet

p. 267 B
Anders Beer Wilse, Munch's hanging of *The Frieze of Life* in his studio, Ekely, 1925, photograph, 57 × 43 cm, Munchmuseet, Oslo
© Munchmuseet

p. 267 C
Building of the Berlin Secession, Kantstrasse 12, 1899, from *Die Kunst für Alle* 14, no. 20 (1899): p. 314
© Universitätsbibliothek Heidelberg

p. 268 A
Christoffer Gade Rude, Edvard Munch, ca. 1892, photograph, 20.5 × 33.1 cm, Munchmuseet, Oslo
© Munchmuseet

p. 268 B
Stanisław Przybyszewski, *Das Werk des Edvard Munch* (The Work of Edvard Munch), 1894, Staatsbibliothek zu Berlin, Preussischer Kulturbesitz, signature Nt 4985
© Staatsbibliothek zu Berlin, Preußischer Kulturbesitz

p. 268 C
Edvard Munch, *The Kiss*, 1892, oil on canvas, 73 × 92 cm, Nasjonalmuseet, Oslo
© Børre Høstland/Nasjonalmuseet

p. 269 A
Tulla Larsen and Edvard Munch, ca. 1899, photograph, Munchmuseet, Oslo
© Munchmuseet

p. 269 B
X-ray image of Munch's left hand, 1902, Munchmuseet, Oslo
© Munchmuseet/Halvor Bjørngård

p. 269 C
Edvard Munch, *The Death of Marat I*, 1907, oil on canvas, 150.5 × 199.5 cm, Munchmuseet, Oslo
© Munchmuseet/Halvor Bjørngård

p. 271 A
The steamship *Meteor* passing through the Norwegian fjords, photograph from the album *Nordlandfahrten Hamburg-Amerika Linie*, 1906, Kieler Stadt- und Schifffahrtsmuseum
© Kieler Stadt-und Schifffahrtsmuseum

p. 271 B
Edvard Munch, *Summer Night (The Voice)*, 1896, oil on unprimed canvas, 90.5 × 120 cm, Munchmuseet, Oslo
© Munchmuseet/Juri Kobayashi

p. 271 C
Promotional poster of the Hamburg-Südamerikanische Dampfschifffahrts-Gesellschaft (Hamburg–South America Steamship Company), 1928, offset print, 72.3 × 49.8 cm, Deutsches Historisches Museum, Berlin
© bpk/Deutsches Historisches Museum/Arne Psille

p. 272 A
Stanisław Przybyszewski, n.d., photograph, Narodowe Archiwum Cyfrowe, Warsaw
© Narodowe Archiwum Cyfrowe

p. 272 B
Edvard Munch, Six sketches for *The Afflicted Eye*, 1930, watercolor on wove paper, 50 × 64.6 cm, Munchmuseet, Oslo
© Munchmuseet/Tone Margrethe Gauden

p. 272 C
Edvard Munch, *Self-Portrait in Hell*, 1903, oil on canvas, 82 × 66 cm, Munchmuseet, Oslo
© Munchmuseet/Juri Kobayashi

p. 273 A
Postcard from Edvard Munch to Helge Bäckström, Café Bauer, October 20, 1906, Munchmuseet, Oslo
© Munchmuseet

p. 273 B
Edvard Munch, Self-Portrait at the Clinic, Copenhagen, 1908–9, gelatin-silver paper, 8.2 × 9.3 cm, Munchmuseet, Oslo
© Munchmuseet

pp. 278–79
Pharus Map of Berlin, 1902 (detail)
© Berlinische Galerie

© for the works by Max Pechstein:
© 2023 Pechstein Hamburg/Berlin

Lenders and Acknowledgments

Lenders

The Berlinische Galerie sincerely thanks all of the museums and private collectors who made loans available to the exhibition:

- Munchmuseet, Oslo
- Staatliche Museen zu Berlin, Nationalgalerie
- Staatliche Museen zu Berlin, Kupferstichkabinett
- Kunstmuseum Basel
- Stiftung Stadtmuseum Berlin
- Hamburger Kunsthalle
- Die Lübecker Museen, Museum Behnhaus Drägerhaus
- Private collection, northern Germany
- Staatliche Schlösser, Gärten und Kunstsammlungen Mecklenburg-Vorpommern—Schwerin
- Moderna Museet, Stockholm
- Kunsthaus Zürich

Acknowledgments

We also thank sincerely:

- Tone Hansen, Dr. Lars Toft-Eriksen, Kasper Teglgaard Koch, Munchmuseet, Oslo
- Dr. Joachim Jäger, Dr. Dieter Scholz, Staatliche Museen zu Berlin, Nationalgalerie
- Dr. Dagmar Korbacher, Dr. Andreas Schalhorn, Staatliche Museen zu Berlin, Kupferstichkabinett
- Dr. Ralph Gleis, Staatliche Museen zu Berlin, Nationalgalerie
- Else Kveinen, Clemens Bomsdorf, Norwegian Embassy, Berlin
- Dr. Karin Schick, Hamburger Kunsthalle, Hamburg
- Petra Schmidt-Dreyblatt, Berlin
- Iris Schönfelder, Schönfelder Restaurierung Berlin
- Paul Spies, Annette Bossmann, Stiftung Stadtmuseum Berlin
- Johanna Thierse, Berlin
- Dr. Ortrud Westheider, Museum Barberini, Potsdam

For their inspiring, collegial exchange we thank the authors of the catalogue; the translator Steven Lindberg; the copyeditors, Dawn Michelle d'Atri and Amy Klement; the designer Gregor Schreiter; and our colleagues at the Berlinische Galerie.

For generous financial support we thank:

- Hauptstadtkulturfonds
- Ernst von Siemens Kunststiftung
- International Music and Art Foundation, Vaduz
- Norwegian Embassy, Berlin

We thank sincerely all of the donors who contributed to the exhibition:

- Anne Binkley
- Ulrike Benz-Sandvoss
- Waldtraut Braun
- Gabriele Brönner-Garben
- Rotraut Engelbrecht
- Karin Hänel and Bernd Bilitewski
- Hahn Bestattung GmbH & Co. KG
- Dr. Arnulf and Ursula Jagenlauf
- Gisela Knobloch
- Marlis Meergans
- MOCK Rechtsanwälte & Notare
- Renate Seipke-Dobler
- Prof. Dr. Annegret Thieken
- Edeltraud Traugott-Minski and Thomas Minski

We are also grateful to the donors who prefer to remain anonymous.

Colophon

This publication is appearing in conjunction with the exhibition *Edvard Munch: Magic of the North* 15.9.23 – 22.1.24

This exhibition enjoys the joint patronage of Frank-Walter Steinmeier, President of the Federal Republic of Germany, and His Majesty King Harald V of Norway

A cooperation with Munchmuseet, Oslo, with crucial support from the Kupferstichkabinett and the Neue Nationalgalerie, Staatliche Museen zu Berlin.

Berlinische Galerie
Berlin's Museum of Modern Art, Photography, and Architecture
Foundation under Public Law

Alte Jakobstrasse 124–128
10969 Berlin
Tel +49 (0)30 78 902 600
Fax +49 (0)30 78 902 700

bg@berlinischegalerie.de
berlinischegalerie.de

Exhibition

Curator
Dr. Stefanie Heckmann

Research Assistance
Dr. Janina Nentwig

Trainee Curators
Pauline Behrmann
Rebecca Kruppert
Anna Bauer
Juschka Marie von Rüden
Luise Budde

Conservation Assistance
Andreas Piel
Maria Bortfeldt
Corinna Nisse

Registrar
Sabine Pinkert

Technical Director
Wolfgang Heigl

Installation
RT Ausstellungstechnik, Berlin

Exhibition Architecture
Color Scheme
david saik studio

Wall Design in Stairwell
Gregor Schreiter — GS AD D

Education
Christine van Haaren
Katrin-Marie Kaptain

Communication
Ulrike Andres
Julia Lennemann
Linus Lütcke

Consulting on
Communication Strategy
WE DO communication

PR and Marketing
Bureau N

Catalogue

Editors
Dr. Thomas Köhler
Dr. Stefanie Heckmann
Dr. Janina Nentwig

Conception
Dr. Stefanie Heckmann
Dr. Janina Nentwig

Editorial Team
Dr. Janina Nentwig
Dr. Stefanie Heckmann
Christian Tagger

Photo Editor
Pauline Behrmann

Project Director
at Hirmer Verlag
Kerstin Ludolph

Project Management
at Hirmer Verlag
Jutta Allekotte
Katja Durchholz

Translation
Steven Lindberg

Copyediting
Dawn Michelle d'Atri

Final Proofreading
Amy Klement

Design
Gregor Schreiter — GS AD D

Lithography
max-color Berlin

Production
Katja Durchholz

Typeface
LL Riforma

Paper
Magno volume, 135 g/m^2
Peydur Lissé, 135 g/m^2

Printing and Binding
Grafisches Centrum Cuno
GmbH & Co. KG, Calbe

Printed in Germany

The Deutsche Nationalbibliothek lists this publication in the Deutsche Nationalbibliografie; detailed bibliographic data are available at http://dnb.de.

Museum Edition
ISBN 978-3-940208-78-1 German
ISBN 978-3-940208-79-8 English

Trade Edition
ISBN 978-3-7774-4217-4 German
ISBN 978-3-7774-4218-1 English

hirmerpublishers.com
hirmerpublishers.co.uk

Media Partners

Wall
arte
Dussmann das KulturKaufhaus
radioeins rbb
WELTKUNST

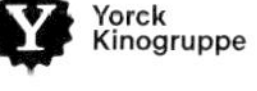

Employees Berlinische Galerie

Director
Dr. Thomas Köhler

Director of Administration
Birgitta Müller-Brandeck

Director's Office
Simona Doletzki

Curatorial Assistant to the Director
Anne Bitterwolf

Assistants to the Director of Administration
Daniela Siegel
Leyla Dibowski

Manager of Security and Sustainability
Haisam Karim

Collection Fine Arts
Dr. Stefanie Heckmann Head
Guido Faßbender
Dr. Janina Nentwig
Sabine Pinkert
Christian Tagger
Anja Elisabeth Witte

Collection Photography
Katia Reich Head
Kerstin Diether
Tanja Keppler

Collection Prints and Drawings
Dr. Ilka Voermann Head
Katharina Hoffmann
Josefine Kretschel

Collection Architecture
Ursula Müller Head
Annette Schryen
Frank Schütz

Collection Artists' Archives
Dr. Ralf Burmeister Head
Julia Bärnighausen
Denise Handte
Philip Gorki
Christiane Necker
Dr. Wolfgang Schöddert

Library
Jan-Tillmann Rierl Head
Helen Kim
Marion Molnos

Conservation
Andreas Piel Head
Maria Bortfeldt
Corinna Nisse
Katharina Siedler

Trainee Curators
Sophie Angelov
Luise Budde
Nils Philippi
Lena Schott

Communication + Education
Ulrike Andres Head
Christine van Haaren Head of Education + Outreach
Tabea Hartig
Katrin-Marie Kaptain
Atefeh Kheirabadi
Andreas Krüger
Julia Lennemann
Linus Lütcke
Paula Rosenboom
Zoe Spehr

Communication Trainees
Sarah Marcinkowski
Rosa Marie Wesle
Lina-Golly Wyrwa

Friends of the Museum
Carolin Wagner Head of Branch
Stephanie Krumbholz

Young Friends
Clara Vogel

Organization + IT
Christiane Friedrich Head
Christin Griesheim
Susana Sáez
Jan Salzberger

Finance + Controlling:
Susanne Teuber Head
Laila Ayyache
Kerstin Böhme
Dagmar Petzold

Human Resources
Christian Monschke Head
Angela Göring
Cindy Jacob

Visitor Services
Martin von Piechowski Acting Head
Reza Soltani Organization

Museum Shop
Wojciech Barlasch
Friederike von Born-Fallois
Carsten Fedderke
Dr. Eva-Maria Kaufmann
Dirk Schäfer

Visitor Support
Christiane Boese
Brigitte Heilmann
Gerhard Jende
Daniela Lamprecht
Vilma Mosteikiene
Katarina Roters
Olaf Schümann

Technical Department
Wolfgang Heigl Head
Robert Frank
Ralf Geelhaar
Andreas Kamprath
Ron Knape
Frank Rohrbeck

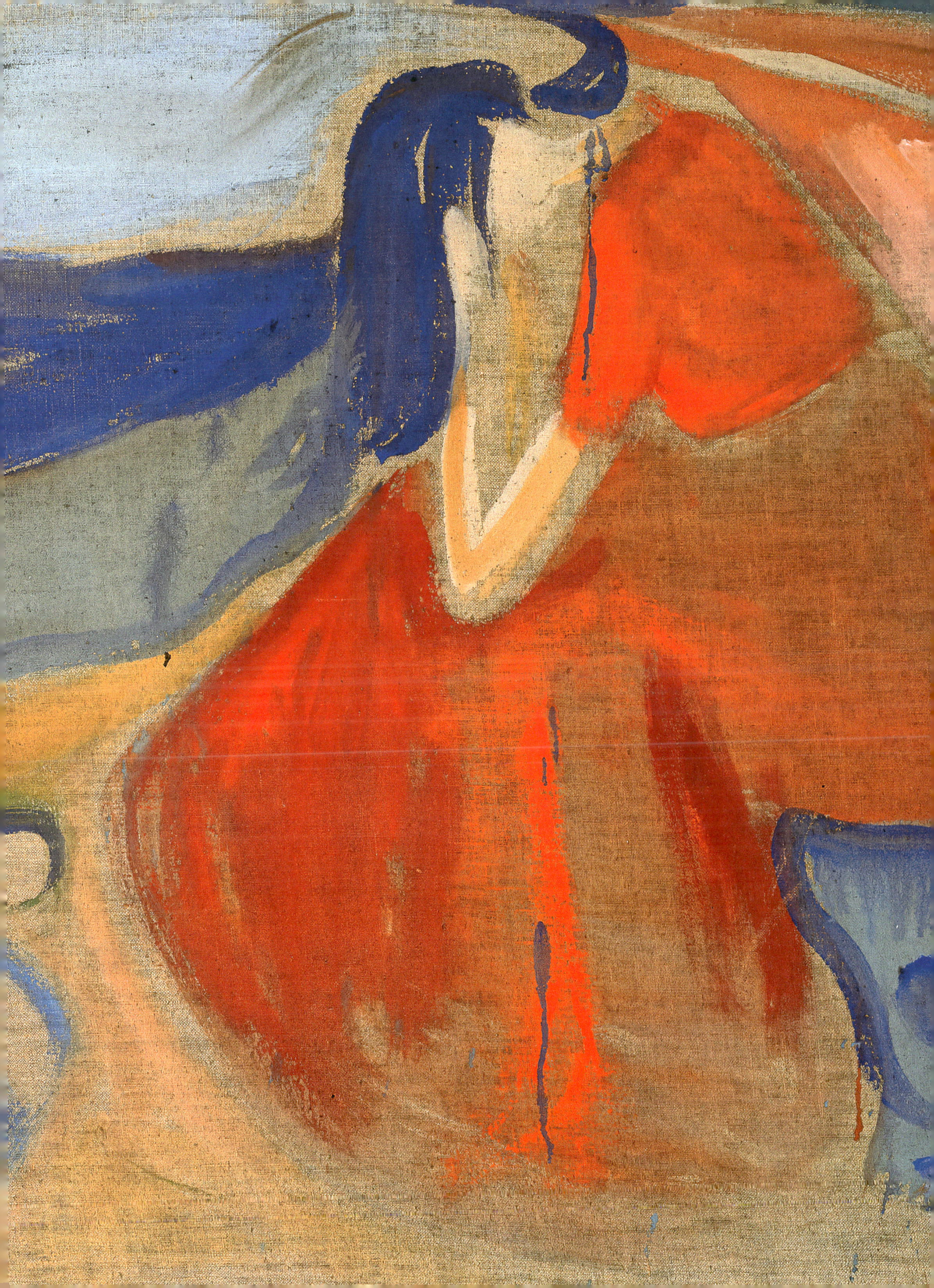

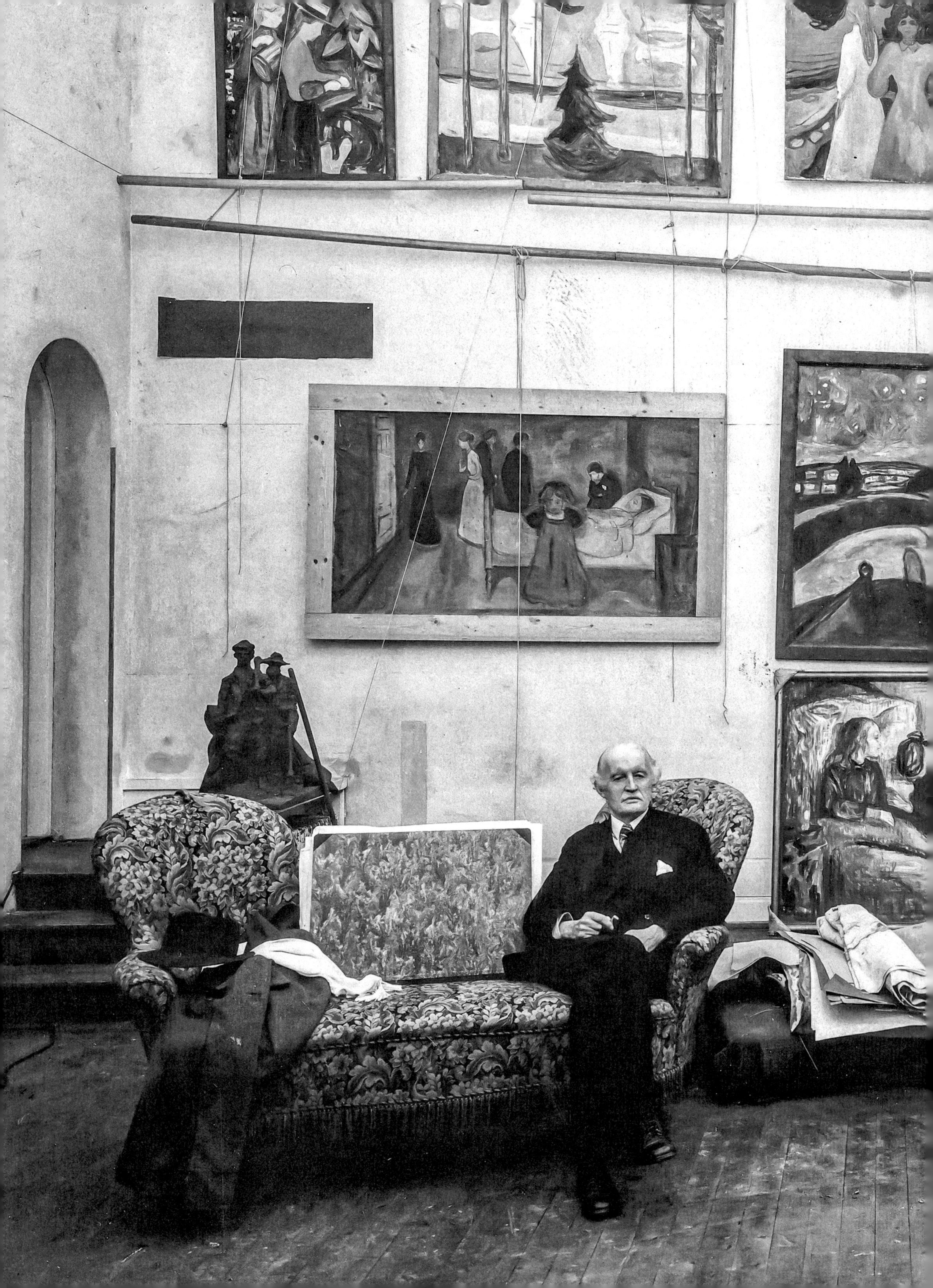